Europe and the Modern World 1870-1983

SECOND EDITION

John and Gwenneth Stokes

Longman

LONGMAN GROUP LIMITED
Longman House, Burnt Mill,
Harlow, Essex CM20 2JE, England
and Associated Companies throughout the World.

First published 1973
Second edition 1984
Second impression 1985

ISBN 0 582 33083 1 (paper)
ISBN 0 582 33195 1 (cased)

Set in 10/12 Ehrhardt, Monophoto

Produced by Longman Group (F.E.) Ltd
Printed in Hong Kong

FOR LUCY, ALEXANDRA AND VICTORIA

Authors' note

We are grateful to all those who read and commented on the manuscript, to our publishers for their help and meticulous care, and to Graham Hardy of Trinity College, Oxford, for his suggestions.

John and Gwenneth Stokes, 1983

Acknowledgements

We are grateful to the following for permission to reproduce copyright material:
Carcanet Press Ltd, Manchester for eight lines only from the poem 'To the wife of a non-interventionist statesman (March 1938)' by Edgell Rickword *Behind the Eyes: Collected Poems and Translations*; Melbourne University Press for an extract from the poem by Vance Palmer from p. 146 *Modern Australian Poetry* ed. H.M. Green, 1946; Punch Publications Ltd for a verse from *Punch* Magazine 1905; George Sassoon & Viking Penguin Inc for an extract from the poem 'Good morning . . .' by Siegfried Sassoon from *Collected Poems*; author's agents & Macmillan Inc for an extract from the poem 'An Irish Airman Foresees his Death' by W.B. Yeats from *Collected Poems* pub. Macmillan London Ltd, copyright 1919 by Macmillan Publishing Co. Inc., renewed 1947 by Bertha Georgie Yeats; The Bodley Head Ltd for Putnam & Co. for an extract from a poem from *Letters To Malaya* by Martyn Skinner.

We are grateful to the following for permission to reproduce photographs: Associated Press, cover and pages 227, 313; Associated Newspaper Group p.l.c., page 227; Barnarby's Picture Library, page 314; BBC Hulton Picture Library, pages 6, 18, 19, 26, 36, 46, 49, 87, 107 (Bettmann Archive), 125, 131, 140, 144, 146, 148, 159 (Bettmann Archive), 160, 210, 213, 228, 271; Bildarchiv d. Oesterreichischen Nationalbibliothek, Wien, page 13; Julian Bohdanowicz, page 293; British Library, page 66, 83; Buenos Aires Herald, page 263; Camera Press, page 325; City Museum and Art Gallery, Hong Kong, page 305; DACS, page 74; FAO/WFP photo: F. Mattioli, page 326; John Hillelson Agency Ltd, page 194 (photo: Robert Capa/Magnum); Michael Houser, page 307; Illustrated London News Picture Library, pages 16, 28, 32, 38, 53, 112, 151, 168, 181; Imperial War Museum, London, pages 100, 103, 104, 110, 134, 224, 226; Institute of Contemporary History and the Wiener Library, London, page 227; Jet Joint Undertaking, page 286; Keystone Press Agency, pages 139 (Central Press), 185, 188 (Central Press), 230, 236, 248, 264, 266, 275, 300, 304; David King Collection, page 128; Kladderadatsch, page 102; Courtesy Krupp, page 80; cartoons by David Low by permission of *The Standard*, pages 202, 241; Mainichi Shimbun, page 171; Mansell Collection, pages 4, 17, 20, 22, 95, 192; Museum of the City of New York, page 70; National Library of Ireland, page 59; National Maritime Museum, London, page 88; Navy Department Photo no. 80-Y-32891 in the National Archives, page 218; Nebraska State Historical Society, page 68; Peter Newark's Western Americana, page 260; Novosti Press Agency, pages 43, 122, 127, 129, 216, 252; Pacemaker Press International Ltd, page 277; Popperfoto, pages 245 (UPI), 289 (UPI), 320, 332 (Europic), 335, 336; Post Office, page 302; Press Association, page 90; Punch, pages 11, 121, 203, 284; Rhodesian Department of Information, Salisbury, page 24; Peter Roberts Collection, page 142; Dr. R. Scollard, page 170; J. & G. Stokes, pages 154, 250, 301, 302, 316, 334; Trades Union Congress, page 50; Topham, page 309; United Nations, pages 232, 321; USIS, pages 257, 294; Universal Pictorial Press, page 279; Victoria & Albert Museum, London, page 153; H. Roger Viollet, page 72, 166, 175.

We would be grateful for any information concerning the identity of copyright holders for photographs on pages 178, 207.

We are grateful to Edith Marchant and J.A.G. Stokes for the drawing on page 85.

Cover: the view from the tower of Dresden City Hall onto the ruins of some of the several thousand buildings demolished by Anglo-American air raids of 13–14 February 1945.

Contents

1 The Franco-Prussian War, 1870–71

France: the Second Empire, 1852–70

'I tell you, the empire means peace.' So said Louis Napoleon, president of the Second French Republic, in 1852. A few weeks later he was proclaimed the Emperor Napoleon III. But the Second Empire did not mean peace. Between 1854 and 1870 Napoleon III embarked on four wars and several minor expeditions. The last years of his reign were marked by a contest with Prince Otto von Bismarck, the unyielding chancellor of Prussia. The outcome was a brief but momentous war against Prussia (1870–71), the collapse of the Second Empire and the emergence of the empire of Germany.

Prussia under Bismarck

In 1815, after the Napoleonic Wars, the Germanic Confederation was set up – a loose association of thirty-nine states. The most powerful of these were Austria and Prussia. Rivalry between Austria and Prussia for dominance within Germany became acute. In 1862 Otto von Bismarck became chancellor of Prussia. Bismarck, who belonged to the traditionally conservative class of Prussian landowners, the *junkers*, had as his first task the raising of money for the reorganisation of the Prussian army. In doing this, he ignored the Prussian Landtag (parliament) and simply collected the funds required without its authorisation. His name meant, said a German liberal, 'government without a budget and rule of the sword at home and war abroad'.

Set above all on increasing Prussia's power, Bismarck aimed to exclude Austria from German affairs and to bring all the other German states under the domination of Prussia. While he was chancellor Prussia fought three successful wars, culminating in 1870–71 in the war with France. Each of these wars was preceded by careful diplomatic manoeuvring on Bismarck's part. In the second war, fought in 1866, Prussia in seven weeks overwhelmed Austria and other German states which had come to her support. By the peace treaty that followed Prussia acquired the territory of Hanover, Schleswig-Holstein and several minor German states. She then occupied two-thirds of the territory of Germany. The Germanic Confederation was dissolved

and a North German Confederation, under Prussian domination, was set up. The south German states, of which Bavaria and Württemberg were the largest, were for the time being left independent. Austria was excluded from German affairs.

After Austria's influence in German affairs was destroyed two problems confronted Bismarck on his way to achieving a Germany united under Prussian control. First, how were the south German states to be brought into a Prussian-dominated Germany? These states, though they had been in military alliance with Prussia since 1866, were suspicious of Prussian ambitions. Bavaria in particular, an old and once powerful kingdom, was not inclined to surrender her independence. Second, how could France be made to accept a union of the south German states with the North German Confederation? Already Prussia's defeat of Austria had seriously disturbed the European balance of power. France could hardly be expected to welcome any arrangement that would further upset the balance. The Franco-Prussian War solved both problems. But whether, as Bismarck later claimed, he had 'manufactured' the war with France, as he had engineered the 1866 war with Austria, is debatable. Rather, it seems, France, bent on winning prestige, rushed headlong into a war that resulted in the emergence of a Prussian-dominated German empire. For during that war, while France was powerless, the south German states surrendered their independence to Prussia (see p. 7).

Events leading to the Franco-Prussian War

For some years Spain had been in a state of turmoil. In 1868 the queen fled and was then deposed. In June 1870 news that the Spanish throne had been offered to a Prussian, Leopold of Hohenzollern-Sigmaringen, reached Paris. If a Hohenzollern were to become ruler of Spain, he might well establish Prussian influence on France's Pyrenees frontier. Public opinion in France was soon feverishly excited. Prussia was

Western Europe, 1871

informed that the establishment of Hohenzollern connections in Spain would be followed by a declaration of war against Prussia. It seems unlikely that Napoleon III was seriously contemplating war with Prussia at this stage; his aim was probably only a diplomatic victory.

Prince Leopold's father, on his son's behalf, declined the Spanish offer. But Napoleon's advisers and the Empress Eugénie's circle were not satisfied. Napoleon, elderly and suffering from kidneystone, was inclined to listen to the often unwise advice of the empress. Count Benedetti, French ambassador to Prussia, was directed to request King William of Prussia to guarantee that no Hohenzollern would ever accept the Spanish throne. Benedetti met the king at Ems, a health resort. King William, though he refused to give the 'guarantee', behaved with courtesy and gave no cause for offence to the French ambassador. However, a telegram reporting the Ems meeting to the press was so worded by Bismarck as to give offence to France.

When Bismarck's misleading account of the Ems meeting was published in France, crowds gathered on city boulevards and in village squares; everywhere there was wild talk of national honour and angry threats of revenge. France was in no position to engage in another war, let alone for trivial reasons. But Napoleon, whatever he himself thought, would by then have found it virtually impossible to resist public opinion.

The Franco-Prussian War, 1870-71

On 15 July 1870 Napoleon decided to declare war on Prussia. 'This is my war', said Eugénie. The declaration of war and the wild outburst of national feeling in France seemed proof to many people in Europe of French aggressiveness. And Bismarck at this juncture made public a proposal made earlier by Napoleon III for the French annexation of Belgium. Bavaria, Württemberg and Baden, angered and alarmed at the thought of a French advance to the Rhine, turned to Prussia. As soon as war was declared, honouring the alliance made in 1866, they joined forces with Prussia.

'To Berlin' was the cry throughout France. But French soldiers were only to set foot on German soil as prisoners of war. The Prussian army moved at speed and with precision. Effective use of railways aided its commanders in taking the offensive. Meanwhile in France there was confusion; thus, men called up for duty had to travel long distances to their mobilisation points. Equipment was inferior to that of the Prussians.

The Prussians speedily occupied Alsace and Lorraine, frontier provinces where France fades away into Germany (see map opposite). A French army of some 200,000 men was bottled up in the fortress city of Metz, in western Lorraine. Napoleon, so ill that he was hardly able to sit in the saddle, set out to relieve Metz. Accompanied by his young son, the Prince Imperial, and by Marshal MacMahon, Napoleon was cut off by Prussian forces. On 1 September 1870, six weeks after the declaration of war, the emperor surrendered in the dreary town of Sedan, near the Belgian border. The Prussians took 100,000 French prisoners at Sedan.

The Second Empire may be said to have ended on 4 September 1870, when after receiving news of Napoleon's surrender the people of Paris proclaimed the establishment of a republic.

The ex-emperor was for a time a prisoner of war. Later, he joined the empress in England. There, in 1873, he died. The Prince Imperial, whose birth in 1856 had brought high hopes, died fighting for Britain in 1879, a volunteer in a Zulu war. Bonapartism, by then a spent force, more or less died with him. Eugénie lived on until 1920 and in her old age interested herself in cars and aeroplanes instead of politics.

With the collapse of the Second Empire, a Government of National Defence was set up. Jules Favre, appointed foreign minister, met Bismarck to discuss peace terms. As Bismarck insisted that France should cede territory, the war went on. The day after the interview the Prussians encircled Paris, cutting it off from supplies. Adolphe Thiers, the veteran statesman of France, who had strongly opposed the declaration of war, visited the capitals of Europe in an effort to obtain support for France; 'a pilgrim in defeat' he was unsuccessful in each case. 'Europe was abandoning France to her unhappy fate.'

On 7 October 1870 Léon Gambetta, an ardent young republican, dreaming of raising the whole countryside in a grand war of resistance, made a dramatic departure from Paris. Sitting in an open basket below a huge balloon, his face grey with fear, he unrolled the tricolour, the flag of France. 'Long life to the republic!' he shouted as he rose over the besieged city. A number of people left Paris in balloons during the Prussian siege. None had any idea where they would land; one was carried to Norway. Gambetta, after a narrow escape when crossing the Prussian encampment, landed 100 kilometres from Paris and went on to Tours on the River Loire.

Gambetta raised a large resistance army, the army of

The morning after Sedan: Napoleon III and Bismarck. Napoleon's Second Empire was about to end. Bismarck was soon to be chancellor of a new empire, the German Empire. For years to come Franco-German fears and hostility were to complicate European affairs. An engraving after the painting by W. Camphausen, 1878

the Loire, which fought with great courage and won some initial victories against the Prussians. Among those who fought with the French was the Italian patriot Garibaldi. In November French soldiers, after advancing up the Loire, occupied Orleans. For a time it seemed that Gambetta's forces might prevail over the enemy. They did not do that. But their brave resistance did much to restore the morale of the people of France.

On 27 October 1870 Metz had surrendered, releasing for action elsewhere the forces which had been besieging the city. The defeat of various French forces and the failure of attempts to break out of Paris seemed to indicate that final defeat was inevitable. Some, among them Thiers, thought the sooner negotiations were begun the better. But Paris struggled on. Winter came. Men froze to death at their posts. Girls offered to sell themselves for a morsel of bread. In January the Prussians tried to break the nerve of the citizens by bombardment. The people of Paris took refuge in their cellars. On 28 January 1871 lack of food forced Paris to surrender and Favre signed an armistice.

The Treaty of Frankfurt, *1871*

The Government of National Defence was not nationally elected. Bismarck insisted that peace terms should be submitted to properly elected representatives of the people. Elections were therefore held in February 1871. The Assembly (parliament) elected in 1871, which met first at Bordeaux, but later at Versailles, is usually known as the Versailles government. It chose Thiers as its head.

Peace terms agreed upon by Bismarck and Thiers were accepted by the Assembly and set out in the Treaty of Frankfurt signed in May 1871. The treaty required France to pay an indemnity of five billion francs, a very large sum of money then. An army of occupation was to be stationed in the eastern departments of France until the indemnity had been paid in full. And Alsace and most of northern Lorraine, including valuable mining and industrial areas, were to be ceded to Germany. Some 1,500,000 French citizens were thus to be made German subjects. Though both provinces were racially largely Germanic, both were generally French in sentiment.

The cession of Alsace-Lorraine caused great bitterness – and a determination to undo the terms of the Frankfurt treaty. 'France is mutilated', was the general cry. 'This separation will not be for always', wrote a group of Lorraine peasants on their church door. 'Two nations', said Victor Hugo, 'will henceforth be a threat to peace; one because she is defeated and one because she is victorious.'

On 11 May 1871 at a college in Metz a young man was working on a mathematical problem. A master entered the room and addressed the class. 'I have come', he said, 'to announce to you a most terrible thing; yesterday at Frankfurt our town of Metz was ceded to Germany....' He broke off, choked by tears. The young student went back to his problem – 'he plunged into his duty', said his neighbour. The young man's name was Ferdinand Foch. Nearly fifty years later, a marshal of France, commander in chief of the Allied armies, he was to return in triumph to Metz.

The Paris Commune, 1871

On 1 March 1871 the people of Paris watched the triumphal entry of German soldiers into their city. Long-existing divisions among the people of France had been deepened by defeat. Now there was a further subject of dispute – whether the government should have continued the war. A good many people in Paris thought it should have. Discontent was increased by, for example, the Versailles government's decision to end a moratorium (legal period of delay) on rents unpaid during the war.

Early in March, following a rumour that artillery used in the defence of Paris was going to be handed over to the Germans, a crowd of people seized the guns. Thiers ordered troops to remove the weapons but the crowds refused to hand them over. Then an uprising that was to bring suffering more terrible than the Prussian siege broke out in Paris.

Violent fighting began on 18 March. The regular troops were forced to withdraw to Versailles. Radical leaders proclaimed a commune, an independent city government that defied the national government. (The word 'commune' has no intrinsic connection with communism.) The Communards (the supporters of the commune) held a variety of beliefs. All were radicals. Some were anarchists, who opposed any form of

government. Others were socialists of varying opinions. Some of the Communards were foreigners – 'red foam of a century of revolutions in Europe'. The Communards hoped that other cities would follow them in defying the Versailles government. But support from the provincial cities was half-hearted.

On 2 April 1871 the Versailles government ordered its troops to besiege Paris – the second siege of the city within a few months. Thiers had refused an offer to suppress the rebels by using German troops. Instead, French prisoners of war were brought back from Germany to compel Paris to submit. In May the city was bombarded. On 21 May, a warm Sunday late in spring, the Versailles troops managed to enter the city. There followed seven days of cruel street fighting, as the regular troops forced their way, street by street, quarter by quarter, to overcome the fierce resistance of the Communards. On the third day the city seemed like a great furnace. The last real 'battle' was fought among the graves in the cemetery of Père Lachaise. By noon on 28 May the guns of Paris were silenced. The tricolour of France replaced the red flag of the Communards. By then some 30,000 people had been killed. The heaviest casualties were among the Communards. However, both sides had shown great cruelty.

On 28 May 1871 *The Times* reported:

'The fighting ... was most desperate. The women fought savagely. No quarter was given to any man, woman or child found in arms.... Numerous arrests are being made in the streets of Paris. ... Executions are inflicted now at three fixed points. ... Batches of as many as fifty and a hundred at a time are shot. ... The markets are completely empty today.'

On 30 May *The Times* said: 'Paris ... pitted itself against France and rather than be beaten has destroyed itself. ... Dust and ashes, tottering walls, twisted or molten ironwork, smoulder and stench, are all that remain.'

The Paris Commune achieved nothing constructive. Rather, it brought fresh bitterness to political life. Radicals long remembered with hatred the savage crushing of the Communards. More conservative people remembered the terrifying disregard of authority shown by the extremists who had set up the commune.

For over a hundred years the Paris Commune has been of symbolic importance to communists the world over; it was, they claim, the first time the proletariat actually held political power. Karl Marx (see p. 40) praised the Communards for trying to break the government, but criticised them for not being ruthless enough.

After the overthrow of the Paris Commune in 1871 : two Communards face a firing squad

Formal establishment of the Third Republic, 1875

At the elections in February 1871 the electorate was only considering whether peace should be made. Only after order was established in Paris could the National Assembly consider what form of government was to replace the Second Empire. Four hundred of the 650 deputies elected in 1871 were monarchists. Of these, about half were Legitimists (supporters of the Bourbon claimant to the throne, a descendant of Louis XVI). About half were Orleanists (supporters of the Orleanist branch of the Bourbon line). There were also a few Imperialists or Bonapartists. The Assembly, though strongly monarchist, had chosen a republican, Thiers, as its head. However, Thiers was a republican rather from necessity than from choice. Republicanism, he once said, 'is the form of government that divides us least'.

As the Legitimist claimant was childless there were hopes that the two monarchist parties might unite but this proved impossible. The monarchists thus remained divided and weak. Meanwhile, by-elections increased the strength of the republicans in the Assembly. In May 1873 the Assembly, which still had a monarchist majority, replaced Thiers by Marshal MacMahon, a monarchist.

Under Thiers's leadership the indemnity imposed by the Treaty of Frankfurt had been paid off much sooner than anyone had expected. So the occupation forces were withdrawn from France. Verdun's garrison was the last to leave. At 8 a.m. on the day the Germans left all the shops were shut; the whole town seemed to be asleep. But inside their houses people were waiting for a signal. Soon there was a 'dull sound' – the Prussians were leaving. As the last columns of soldiers were still crossing the drawbridge, the tricolour of France was run up to the top of one of the cathedral towers. The great bell of the cathedral rang out the hour of deliverance; all the bells of Verdun echoed its sound. Then suddenly all the doors opened. A crowd surged into the streets. People embraced with tears.

In 1875 the National Assembly passed a law declaring: 'The president of the republic shall be elected by an absolute majority of votes . . . in the National Assembly. The president shall hold office for seven years and shall be eligible for re-election.' By making this law concerning the election of a president the National Assembly was in fact declaring that France was a republic. Thus, the Third Republic formally came into being. The law by which the republic was thus accepted was passed by a majority of one. This was a shaky foundation on which to base a government. There was indeed no great enthusiasm for republican government at that time. France was still a divided country. But republicanism probably 'divided France least'.

The election of the president was entrusted to the National Assembly so as to protect France from adventurers who might win the support of the unthinking masses, as Napoleon III had done. In due course various constitutional laws were passed. Ministers were made responsible to the lower house, the Chamber of Deputies, whilst the upper house, the Senate, was so constituted as to keep radicals under control. In 1879 the government returned from Versailles to Paris.

An amnesty (1880) to Communard prisoners was in part aimed at securing support for the government. However, the appearance of the ex-prisoners was so pathetic that the sight of them stirred up fresh hatred of authority among radicals.

The German empire, 1871

After the overwhelming victory at Sedan the south German states of their own accord asked for union with Prussia. A powerful German empire in central Europe thus came into being. On 18 January 1871, ten days before Paris surrendered, the king of Prussia accepted the imperial crown of Germany in the Hall of Mirrors at Versailles. William I of Prussia was now kaiser or German emperor. But many Germans remained outside the new Germany, for example in the Habsburg Austrian empire. Again, the imperial crown was offered to the king of Prussia by the king of Bavaria on behalf of the rulers of the German states, not on behalf of their people. The rulers of the various states kept their titles and were, in theory at least, the kaiser's allies, not his subjects.

The new Germany was a federal state but within the federation one state, Prussia, held a special position. This accorded with Bismarck's goal of a Prussian-dominated Germany. Prussian rather than German in ties and feelings, he once said: 'Prussians we are, and Prussians we shall remain.' Under the constitution each of the twenty-five German states was responsible for such matters as education and public health. The larger states had privileges: for instance, Bavaria kept control of her post and telegraph system and Prussia had special powers in matters concerning the army and navy.

The imperial parliament, which met in Berlin, had two houses. The upper house, the Bundesrat, was composed of delegates appointed by the rulers of the states. Prussia had seventeen delegates; the next largest state, Bavaria, had six. Prussia was therefore in a predominant position. The lower house, the Reichstag, was elected by universal manhood suffrage. As Prussia had a majority of the population she also had a predominant position in this house. Secret voting and universal franchise gave an appearance of democracy and so won popular support. In fact the Reichstag's powers were limited. Thus its consent was not required for the collection of existing taxes. If it refused approval of the budget the allocations of the previous year were to remain in force. Whilst the upper house of the German parliament was designed to prevent change, the lower house could at most hinder the government by refusing to pass laws.

Real power in the new Germany lay in the hands of the emperor – and his chancellor if, like Bismarck, he was sufficiently forceful. For it was the kaiser who appointed the chancellor, whilst the ministers were subject to the chancellor. The chancellor and ministers were thus not responsible to parliament – they did not have to resign if they were outvoted in the Reichstag. The emperor was also commander in chief of the army and navy and had the power to declare war and make treaties. In these circumstances the leaders of the German armed forces were inclined to ignore the civilian authorities. The constitution, with its grant of universal manhood suffrage, had popular appeal. But it also gave the emperor 'divine rights' – and the divine rights were in control.

In the excitement of success liberals who had objected to Bismarck's autocratic policies, his 'government without a budget', were reconciled. His policy had 'paid'. People seemed willing to abandon their principles in return for military victories and visible success. They accepted 'the rule of the sword at home and war abroad' as right and normal. But the rule of the sword is only part of Germany's story. There is another side to her people – the side seen in the music of Beethoven, the writings of Thomas Mann, the inventive skill of von Siemens and the scientific discoveries of Helmholtz.

2 The Eastern Question

The empire of the Ottoman Turks

Some thirteen centuries ago, in the Arabian desert, the Prophet Muhammad proclaimed that there is one God, Allah (The God). Thus was born Islam, a militant faith whose followers, the Muslims, founded a mighty empire. Some centuries later the Turks succeeded to much of the Arabs' power and were converted to Islam. In 1453 Constantinople (Istanbul) fell to the Ottoman Turks.

The Turks conquered south-eastern Europe and North Africa. They ruled Cyprus and other Mediterranean islands. They conquered Hungary and twice reached the gates of Vienna. In time, they were driven back south of the Danube. But at the beginning of the nineteenth century the Turks still ruled the Balkans, the area south of the rivers Danube and Pruth. They also ruled Asia Minor, Cyprus, Syria, Palestine and much of Arabia. They loosely controlled the coast of North Africa from Egypt as far as Morocco.

The Balkans in 1870

A hotchpotch of peoples inhabited the Balkans (see map). Serbs lived along the eastern Adriatic and around Belgrade. Farther south there were the Albanians. The Aegean area was inhabited by the Greeks. Along the west coast of the Black Sea there were the Romanians and the Bulgars. Most of these people belonged to the Slav group. Most of them belonged to the Orthodox Church but some were Roman Catholics. Others, for instance the Albanians, were Muslims. The Turks lived chiefly around Constantinople and Adrianople (Edirne).

The Balkans under Turkish rule had been little developed. Officials were corrupt, torture was legal. Sometimes the rayas (the non-Muslim subjects of the Turks) found life relatively easy; sometimes they suffered terrible atrocities. As elsewhere in the Ottoman empire, the rayas alone paid taxes. Apart from this, generally there was religious freedom.

By 1870 large parts of the Balkans enjoyed some independence. Serbia had had home rule under Turkey since 1829. Her right to home rule was later guaranteed by the powers. National feeling was strong among her hotblooded peasants. Strife between the Karageorgevitch and Obrenovitch dynasties complicated affairs – only one nineteenth-century Serbian ruler, and he was insane, died at home in his bed. As national feeling grew strong Serbia looked beyond her own boundaries to the many Serbs living under foreign rule, some in Turkish Bosnia and Herzegovina, some in Habsburg territories. Montenegro, peopled by fierce mountaineers, was also virtually independent and usually acted with Serbia.

Romania, the former principalities of Moldavia and Wallachia, had in 1866 come under the rule of a Prussian prince, Carol. As with Serbia, the right to self-government under Turkish overlordship was guaranteed by the powers.

Bulgaria, as the areas inhabited chiefly by Bulgars later became, was even more backward than other Balkan lands. But its Black Sea coast and nearness to Constantinople made it of strategic interest. By 1870 national feeling was strong among the Bulgars.

Greece, fully independent since 1832, was smaller than now. Her constant aim was to enlarge her territory.

Nationalism

Nationalism caused great problems in the Balkans. At its best nationalism is the desire of a nation – of people linked by historic ties, or ties of race, language or religion, or by occupation of a particular territory, or by opposition to a common foe – to be united under its own government. So nationalists seek freedom from foreign rule, and may want to unite in one state a divided nation (as, for example, the Germans before 1871).

Nationalism can be a force for both good and evil, constructive and destructive. In the twentieth century unbridled nationalism has provoked bitter hostility and wars – as well as winning independence and a new dignity for many former subject peoples. At its worst nationalism can descend to a primitive tribalism. It can be jealous, suspicious, proud and revengeful. It can be aggressive and cruel. Nationalist propaganda can hoodwink people into believing that wrong is right.

The Balkans and the Congress of Berlin, 1878

The Eastern Question: what was it?

Turkey in the nineteenth century was 'the sick man' of Europe, whose decay gave rise to a series of problems and crises known as the Eastern Question. The basic issues of the Eastern Question were: what was to happen to the European territories of the Ottoman empire? Who would benefit when Turkey collapsed? If Turkey's subject peoples in the Balkans gained independence, who would be able to control or use them?

From about the mid-nineteenth century nationalism became increasingly strong among the peoples of the Balkans. But the story is not a simple tale of subject peoples rising against foreign rule. It was complicated by the ambitions and fears of Russia, Britain, Austria, France and later Germany and Italy – and by the rivalries of the Balkan peoples themselves. So the Eastern Question led not only to revolts against the Turks but to conflicts in which the great powers took part and to wars between the Balkan peoples.

The great powers and the Eastern Question

Austria-Hungary was in general quick to take fright at any extension of Russian power in the Balkans. Fears that Balkan nationalism might spread to Habsburg territories, also inhabited by a hotchpotch of peoples (see p. 80), many of whom were Slavs, inclined Austria to prop up Turkey. Her interest in the Balkans increased when Prussia displaced her as leader of the German states (see p. 1). While the western powers were busily occupying Africa (see Chapter 4) Austria looked for opportunities to expand in the Balkans.

Britain in general supported Turkey and opposed any extension of Russian power in the Balkans, or anywhere in the Near East. For the Russian bear, if allowed to become too powerful, might strike at Persia (Iran) and Afghanistan and thence at British India. To satisfy Britain the Black Sea had been neutralised by a treaty made in 1856 – a move directed against Russia. During the Franco-Prussian War Russia, with Bismarck's connivance, repudiated her treaty obligations and began fortifying Black Sea bases and building a Black Sea fleet. Control of Constantinople would give Russian ships entry into the Mediterranean – a prospect particularly alarming after the opening of the Suez Canal, the gateway to India, in 1869.

In general the Russian tsars looked forward to the death of 'the sick man' – provided that any new states that emerged would be subject to their influence. There were obvious reasons and possible excuses for the tsars' attitude. The majority of people in Russia belonged to the Orthodox Church, of whose Russian branch the tsar was head. And the majority of the tsars' subjects were Slavs. It is hard to know to what extent a genuine desire to help fellow Slavs and Orthodox Christians affected policy. Other powers tended to suspect Russia of trying to extend her influence when she claimed to be protecting the rights of downtrodden rayas. More important, Constantinople guarded the passage between the Mediterranean and the Black Sea – and controlled Russia's only exit from the latter. The tsars certainly hoped to extend their power in the direction of Constantinople and the strategic Straits (the Bosphorus, on which at the north-eastern end of the Sea of Marmora Constantinople stands, and the Dardanelles, at the south-western end of the Sea of Marmora, leading directly into the Mediterranean (see map p. 9)). However, Russia had to move cautiously in the Balkans, lest she should unduly antagonise the other powers.

In the later nineteenth century Pan-Slavism complicated tsarist policy. Pan-Slavism was a movement which aimed to unite all Slavs, to make them conscious of their 'power' as members of a widespread family of people. As early as 1824 a Slovak poet had urged: 'Scattered Slavs, unite into one whole.' The completion of Italian unification (see p. 77) and the emergence of the new Germany (see p. 7) gave impetus to Pan-Slavism. In time Pan-Slavism attracted followers in Russia. However, Russian Pan-Slavism often had an oppressive quality. Indeed, the tsars ruled over a large part of Poland, another Slav-inhabited country.

Trouble in the Balkans, 1874–76

In 1874 there were poor harvests in the Balkans. Yet in the areas still under Turkish rule officials insisted that peasants should pay every penny of their taxes. In 1875 rebellions broke out in the Turkish provinces of Bosnia and Herzegovina. Serbia and Montenegro also rose against the Turks. Then the Bulgars, aflame with national spirit, rebelled.

For a time Russia contented herself with joining Germany and Austria in an attempt to settle the crisis by forcing reforms upon the Turks. In May 1876 these three powers presented the sultan with the Berlin Memorandum, which listed reforms and threatened action if the Turks did not comply with these. The British prime minister, Benjamin Disraeli, opposed to this intervention, moved warships to Besika Bay, just outside the Dardanelles.

In September 1876 wily Abdul Hamid II, Abdul the Damned and Unreformed, succeeded to the rule of the Ottoman empire. Meanwhile, between April and August 1876 the Turks butchered thousands of Bulgars. On 20 September 1876 *The Times* printed a report from a British official sent to investigate atrocities among the Bulgars. He described how, after a Turkish official had forced the people of a certain village to give up first their arms and then their money, the Turks

'set upon the people and slaughtered them like sheep. A large number of people, probably about 1,000 or 1,200, took refuge in the church. ... [The Turks] fired in through the windows, and, getting upon the roof, tore off the tiles and threw burning pieces of wood and rags dipped in petroleum among the masses of unhappy human beings inside. At last the door was forced in, the massacre completed, and the inside of the church burnt.'

This Punch *cartoon, published shortly before Serbia declared war on Turkey, expresses Britain's 'Turk preserving' policy and her suspicion of Russia. All four dogs are now part of Yugoslavia*

PUNCH, OR THE LONDON CHARIVARI.—JUNE 17, 1876.

THE DOGS OF WAR.

BULL A L. "TAKE CARE, MY MAN! IT MIGHT BE AWKWARD IF YOU WAS TO LET 'EM LOOSE!"

Slav feeling throughout the Balkans became uncontrollable. In June–July 1876 Serbia and Montenegro had formally declared war on Turkey. The Bulgars joined them but their armies were defeated and the Turks invaded Serbia. In Russia public opinion was strongly in favour of war against Turkey. But for the time being the tsar followed a cautious policy.

In Britain Disraeli was following the old 'Turk-preserving' policy. In 1875 he had purchased for Britain shares in the Suez Canal (see p. 28). So Disraeli regarded any extension of Russian power towards the Suez Canal with more than the usual British horror. Stories of the Bulgarian massacres were just 'coffee house gossip' he said, scornfully and inaccurately. W.E. Gladstone, leader of the Liberals, wrote a booklet: *The Bulgarian Horrors and the Question of the East.* 'Gladstone', said Disraeli, 'is himself worse than any Bulgarian horror.' But for a time there was an outcry in Britain against the Turks.

In December 1876 a conference of the powers met in Constantinople to discuss the Balkan crisis. Lord Salisbury, the British delegate, agreed that reforms must be forced upon the Turks. But when Abdul Hamid announced that a liberal constitution safeguarding the rights of rayas as well as Muslims had been prepared the conference broke up. Abdul Hamid then withdrew the magic constitution. The peoples of the Balkans determined to continue their struggle against Turkey.

The Russo-Turkish War, 1877–78

Early in 1877 Austria promised to remain neutral if Russia went to war against Turkey. Russia in return agreed not to allow any large Slav state to be formed out of Turkish territory. Britain seemed unlikely to intervene unless Egypt and the canal communications with India were disturbed or unless Russia attacked Constantinople.

In April 1877 Tsar Alexander II declared war upon Turkey. Romania gave safe passage to the tsarist troops, who advanced into Bulgaria. There, at Plevna, the Russians were checked by the Turks. Four months later, in December 1877, the Turkish garrison, reduced by starvation, surrendered. But the siege had cost the Russians heavy casualties.

Then the Russians swept down towards Constantinople and the strategic Straits. In Britain public opinion swung back in support of the government's pro-Turk policy. Newspapers revived the old threat of the Russian bear. In music halls people shouted excitedly:

> We don't want to fight, but by Jingo if we do,
> We've got the men, we've got the ships,
>   we've got the money too.

In January 1878 Adrianople fell. However, the Russians did not go on to attack Constantinople. By then they were close to exhaustion – and aware that British warships lay at anchor in the Sea of Marmora.

The Treaty of San Stefano, 1878

Russia and Turkey agreed to an armistice and in March 1878 the Treaty of San Stefano was signed. This gave Russia a little Asian territory – Kars in Armenia – and in Europe part of Bessarabia. In compensation for the loss of this fertile territory north of the Danube mouth, Romania was given the relatively barren Dobruja farther south. Serbia and Montenegro had their frontiers extended.

But the chief feature of the peace treaty was the creation from Turkish territory of a new state, Bulgaria, stretching from the Danube to the Aegean Sea (see map p. 9). 'Big' Bulgaria was more extensive than the area inhabited by Bulgars; it also split Turkey's remaining European territory into four sections. Austria and Britain in particular were angered by this arrangement. Russia had promised Austria that no large Slav state would be formed in the Balkans without her consent. To Britain it seemed that the new Bulgaria could only be a Russian satellite.

The Congress of Berlin, 1878

When Disraeli threatened war and moved Indian troops to Malta, Russia, isolated and exhausted, submitted the San Stefano treaty to a congress of the powers. The congress met in June 1878 in Berlin. Its chairman was Bismarck. Little interested in the Balkans themselves, Bismarck would not permit changes that might upset the European balance of power to occur there.

The representatives of the great powers made the decisions at Berlin in 1878. 'We are considering the peace of Europe, not the happiness of the Bulgars', said Bismarck amid feasting and merrymaking. Serbia, Montenegro and Romania became fully independent. Serbia gained the strategic trading town of Nish (Niš)

and the surrounding district; with this she was quite dissatisfied, particularly as she had done better at San Stefano. Montenegro was given access to the Adriatic coast. Greece was to get fertile Thessaly. Russia kept Kars and the often disputed portion of Bessarabia. Romania still had to content herself with the Dobruja. 'Big' Bulgaria's brief existence was ended. Macedonia, the southerly portion, returned to Turkish rule and its mixed population of Bulgars, Serbs and Greeks continued to suffer the terrors of misrule. The middle section, Eastern Rumelia, remained a Turkish province but was to have home rule under a Christian governor. The area north of Eastern Rumelia, between the Balkan Mountains and the Danube, became Bulgaria with home rule under the overlordship of Turkey. As the statesmen at Berlin regarded this new 'Little' Bulgaria as Russia's satellite, the Balkan Mountains were regarded as in effect separating 'Russia' from Turkey. The revision of the San Stefano treaty ensured that the Aegean coastline, facing the Straits, did not fall into the hands of a state that might prove a Russian ally.

Meanwhile Disraeli revealed that the sultan had given Britain Cyprus as a base from which she could protect Turkey's Asian territories. By another agreement made before the congress met Austria was to administer the Turkish provinces of Bosnia and Herzegovina. As these provinces were largely inhabited by Serbs, Serbia and Montenegro were angered by Austria's interference. Austria was also to garrison the sanjak (district) of Novibazar, lying between Serbia and Montenegro.

After the Congress of Berlin

The Congress of Berlin, the tsar said, was 'a coalition of Europe against Russia under the chairmanship of Prince Bismarck'. Checked in the Balkans, Russia again turned east – on the road that was to lead to war against Japan in 1904 (see p. 20).

Disraeli claimed to have won 'peace with honour'. But Lord Salisbury, who went with him to Berlin, said later that Britain had 'backed the wrong horse' at the congress. In 1879 and 1880, during the Midlothian election campaign (see p. 47), Gladstone denounced Disraeli's whole approach to the Eastern Question. Gladstone's view was that the 'breasts of free men' (independent national states) would be the best obstacle against Russian expansion into south-eastern Europe. Disraeli would in fact seem to have underestimated the strength of national feeling in the Balkans. The Balkan

November 1878: a deputation from Herzegovina swears obedience to the Austrian emperor, Francis Joseph. Note the priests of the Orthodox Church. From a drawing by V. Katzler

states, when freed from Turkey, showed no special love for Russia, or indeed for any power.

Turkish power remained shaky. Nor did the condition of the rayas improve. In the 1890s hosts of Christians in Armenia were savagely murdered by order of the sultan.

Alexander of Battenberg, the first ruler of the new Bulgaria, though a nephew of the tsar, followed an anti-Russian policy. In 1885, following a rebellion against the Turks in Eastern Rumelia, Bulgaria annexed that province. Russia, who in 1878 had wanted a 'Big' Bulgaria, now wanted to maintain the status quo, for it was clear that Bulgaria had no intention of being a Russian puppet. In these circumstances Britain no longer opposed Bulgaria's enlargement. In 1886 Russian agents kidnapped Alexander. Ferdinand of Saxe-

Coburg, the Long Nosed Fox of the Balkans, later succeeded him.

Serbia demanded territorial compensation when Bulgaria annexed Eastern Rumelia. Later in 1885, when Bulgaria refused her demand, the Serbs attacked Bulgaria. The war was over within a month. After a Serbian defeat at Slivnitza Bulgaria received an ultimatum from Austria and did not follow up her victory. So neither side benefited.

Before the Congress of Berlin Russia, Germany and Austria-Hungary had, in general, been on good terms. This suited Bismarck (see p. 86). But from 1878 it became increasingly difficult for Germany to keep the friendship of both Russia and Austria – though for a time Bismarck, like a skilful circus rider mounted on two horses at once, managed to keep a hold on both of them.

3 The Far East: from isolation to world war

The opening of China to the West

By 1870 China and Japan, for long almost totally isolated from the world outside, were entangled with various western powers.

From 1644 China was under the rule of the Ch'ing[1] (Qing) dynasty from Manchuria (Dongbei). In 1800 the empire included (see map opposite) China itself, Manchuria to the watershed north of the Amur River (Heilongjiang), Mongolia, Sinkiang (Xinjiang), Tibet (Xizang) and Formosa (Taiwan). The Ryukyu Islands, Korea, Annam and Tonkin (now Vietnam), Nepal, Sikkim and Burma paid tribute and kowtowed to their overlord, the emperor of China, Son of Heaven. But by 1870 China was a paper tiger.

From 1557 the Portuguese occupied the peninsula of Macao. A few Russians had long traded in Peking (Beijing). A number of westerners, the most prominent of whom were the British, traded at Canton (Guangzhou), the only port open to foreigners until 1842. The westerners at Canton were subject to many tiresome restrictions. In general, though regarded as barbarians, they were kindly treated. But there was increasing annoyance at the restrictions on trade.

In 1839 the First Anglo-Chinese War, the so-called Opium War, broke out. After Britain had made a show of force along the China coast the Treaty of Nanking (Nanjing) (1842) ceded the 'desert' island of Hong Kong to Britain and opened five ports to British traders. Treaties with the USA and other European powers followed. To the Chinese these were the 'unequal treaties'. They gave the treaty powers extra-territorial rights (under which foreigners in China were subject to their own, not to Chinese, law). They imposed upon China a conventional tariff on imports, a tariff fixed by a convention or formal 'agreement' which the Chinese had had to accept. And by 'most favoured nation' clauses any right given to one treaty power was extended to all the treaty powers. Among these rights was the right for

[1] Chinese names in this book appear in a romanised form which in most cases differs from pinyin, the form of romanisation now official in China and often used elsewhere. A few names appear in anglicised form. Where necessary, the pinyin equivalent is given in brackets after the first appearance of a name.

missionaries – both Lord of Heaven Religion Men (Roman Catholics) and Jesus Religion Men (Protestants) – to enter the Middle Kingdom – the land which British merchants had said was 'as difficult to enter as heaven'. (The Chinese call their homeland the Middle Kingdom or Central Nation.)

In 1856–58 and 1859–60 Britain, assisted by France, won further victories against China. Treaties made in 1858 and 1860 opened eleven further ports, among them inland ports on the Yangtse. (Chang Jiang, meaning Long River, is the name now generally used. Yangtse correctly applies only to a lower stretch of the river.) The Kowloon peninsula, opposite the island of Hong Kong, was ceded to Britain. Foreigners were given wider rights to move about in China and provision was made for the exchange of diplomats.

In 1858 the Russo-Chinese frontier was moved south to the Amur and in 1860 Trans-Ussuri (the Maritime Province) was ceded to Russia. These territories, gained by astute diplomacy, without even a show of force, covered just over a million square kilometres. In 1871, during a Muslim rebellion in Sinkiang (New Province), tsarist troops occupied Ili to 'protect' Russians trading there. In 1881 China ceded part of Ili to Russia.

Weakness in face of western attacks and a series of vast rebellions showed that changes were necessary. For a time, in an effort to resist further concessions to the West, China half-heartedly followed a 'self-strengthening' policy. Little was achieved. For example, the Empress Dowager Tz'u Hsi (Cixi), a forceful but very corrupt woman who was the real ruler of China for most of the period 1860 to 1908, diverted funds intended for a western-style navy to building a new Summer Palace and a marble pleasure 'boat'. A hundred and twenty youths sent to the USA to study were recalled when by dating American girls they showed signs of 'undue westernisation'. China remained weak and defenceless.

The loss of tributary states was evidence of the decline of the Middle Kingdom. In 1862 the eastern half of Cochin China (the southernmost part of Vietnam) was ceded to France. In 1867 western Cochin China was ceded to France. In 1882 Annam submitted to French

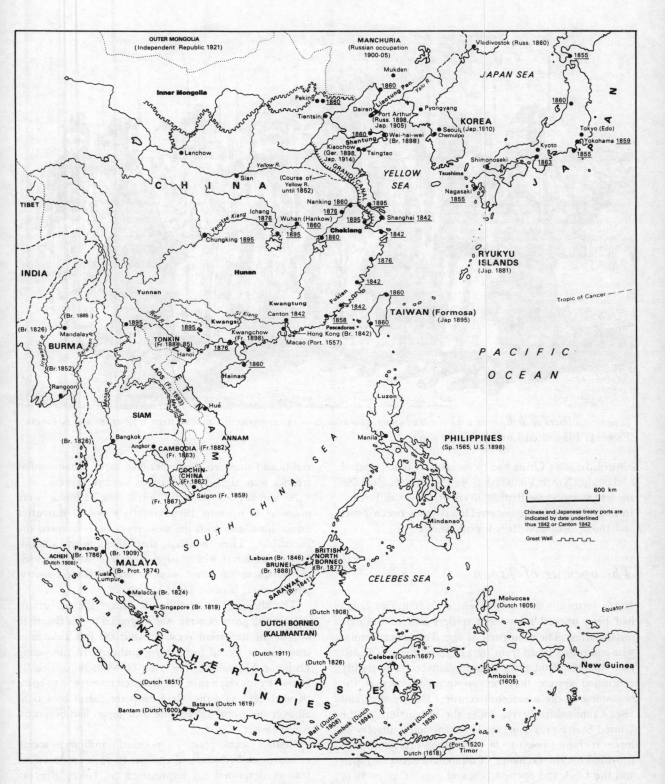

OUTER MONGOLIA
(Independent Republic 1921)

MANCHURIA
(Russian occupation
1900-05)

Vladivostok (Russ. 1860)

1855

JAPAN SEA

Inner Mongolia

Mukden

1860

1860

Peking 1860

Liaotung Pen.

Dairen

Port Arthur
(Russ. 1898)
Jap. 1905)

Pyongyang

KOREA

Tokyo (Edo)

Tientsin

Wei-hai-wei
(Br. 1898)

Seoul
(Jap. 1910)

Chemulpo

Kyoto

Yokohama 1859

1855

Lanchow

1860

Kiaochow
(Ger. 1898.
Jap. 1914)

Shantung

Tsingtao

Shimonoseki

1863

J A

Tsushima

TIBET

C H I N A

Sian

(Course of
Yellow R.
until 1852)

Yellow R.

GRAND CANAL

Nanking 1860

1876

Nagasaki
1855

YELLOW
SEA

INDIA

Yangtse Kiang

Ichang
1876

Wuhan (Hankow)
1860

1895

Chungking 1895

1895

Chekiang

1860

1895

1895

Shanghai 1842

1842

RYUKYU
ISLANDS
(Jap. 1881)

Hunan

Yunnan

1842

1876

Kwangtung

Fukien

1842

1860

TAIWAN (Formosa)
(Jap 1895)

Tropic of Cancer

(Br. 1885)

1895

Kwangsi

Si Kiang

Canton 1842

1858

1860

Pescadores

(Br. 1826)

Mandalay

Red R.

TONKIN
(Fr. 1884-85)

Kwangchow
(Fr. 1898)

Hong Kong (Br. 1842)

Macao (Port. 1557)

BURMA

Salween R.

Hanoi

1876

PACIFIC

OCEAN

(Br. 1852)

LAOS
(Fr. 1893)

1860

Rangoon

Irrawaddy R.

Mekong R.

V I E T N A M

Hainan

Hué

Luzon

SIAM

Menam R.

ANNAM

Manila

PHILIPPINES
(Sp. 1565, U.S. 1898)

Bangkok

Angkor

CAMBODIA
(Fr. 1863)

(Fr. 1882)

(Br. 1826)

COCHIN-
CHINA
(Fr. 1862)

Saigon (Fr. 1859)

(Fr. 1867)

0   600 km

Chinese and Japanese treaty ports are
indicated by date underlined
thus 1842 or Canton 1842

Mindanao

Great Wall

Penang
(Br. 1909)

ACHEH
(Dutch 1908)

MALAYA
(Br. Prot. 1874)

SOUTH CHINA SEA

Labuan (Br. 1846)

BRITISH
NORTH
BORNEO
(Br. 1877)

Moluccas
(Dutch 1605)

Equator

Kuala
Lumpur

BRUNEI
(Br. 1888)

CELEBES SEA

Malacca (Br. 1824)

SARAWAK
(Br. 1841)

Singapore (Br. 1819)

(Dutch 1908)

DUTCH BORNEO
(KALIMANTAN)

New Guinea

S U M A T R A

(Dutch 1911)

(Dutch 1826)

Celebes (Dutch 1667)

N E T H E R L A N D S   E A S T

Amboina
(1605)

(Dutch 1851)

Batavia (Dutch 1619)

I N D I E S

Bantam (Dutch 1600)

J a v a

Bali (Dutch
1908)

Lombok (Dutch
1894)

Flores (Dutch
1859)

(Port. 1520)

Dutch (1618)

Timor

Imperialism in the Far East. (For territories lost by China to Russia see p. 35)

Japanese soldiers at drill, some with the traditional two swords of the samurai, all with western style rifles and bayonets. From the Illustrated London News, *1864*

control. In 1885 China had to recognise French control of Tonkin (North Vietnam) as well as Annam. In 1886 she had to recognise British sovereignty over all Burma. In 1890 Sikkim, in the eastern Himalayas between Tibet and India, became a British protectorate.

The opening of Japan

In the sixteenth and early seventeenth centuries Japan had been opened to western traders and to Catholic missionaries. Then shoguns of the Tokugawa family, who controlled Japan from 1603 to 1867, virtually sealed their homeland off from outside contacts. The tightly controlled system they set up seemed intact at the beginning of the nineteenth century. But in 1853 and 1854 Commodore Perry, under the instructions of the United States president, made a non-violent display of force at Edo (Tokyo). In 1858 the Treaty of Edo provided for the exchange of diplomats between Japan and the USA and opened Edo and four other ports to American traders. It gave Americans extra-territorial

rights and imposed a conventional tariff. Soon similar treaties were signed with various western powers.

A number of powerful lords, the daimyo, were opposed to opening their country's doors. But after minor hostilities with the westerners they accepted the inevitable. They realised that they must submit. Determination to win revision of the unequal treaties led the Japanese to adopt western ways: 'Rich country, strong army' became Japan's slogan.

The shogun, whose full title meant the barbarian-conquering great general, was disgraced by his failure to oppose the barbarian West. In 1867 the last Tokugawa shogun was forced to 'restore' authority to the young Emperor Mutsuhito. The rule of Mutsuhito, usually known by his reign title, Meiji, lasted from 1867 to 1912. 'Knowledge', said the Meiji Emperor, 'shall be sought all over the world.' Before he died Japan had become a world power.

Change came fast – political, military, social, economic and educational change. In 1872 an American teacher described his impressions of Tokyo after an absence of a year:

'Thousands wearing hats, boots, coats; carriages numerous. ... Shops full of foreign wares. Soldiers all uniformed, armed with Chassepot rifles. New bridges span the canals. Police in uniform. Hospitals, schools, and colleges; girls' seminaries numerous. Railway nearly finished. ... German medical professors occupy [an] old monastery. ... Scientific American gentlemen are housed in the shogun's Hall of Rest. French military officers live in the [town dwelling] of Ii Kamon no kami, whose son is studying in Brooklyn.'

Meanwhile Japanese children bouncing their rubber balls recited the Civilisation Ball-bouncing Song: 'Gaslight, steam engines, carriages, cameras, telescopes, lightning-conductors, newspapers, schools, postal system, steamships' – 'the ten desirable things from the West'.

In 1889 the Meiji Emperor granted his people a constitution, providing for a Diet (parliament) with an appointed upper house and a lower house elected on a very narrow franchise. Real power was left with the emperor, to whom the cabinet was responsible.

By the end of the nineteenth century Japan was 'modern' – and strong – enough for the western powers to give up their extra-territorial rights. The conventional tariff ended in 1911.

By the beginning of the twentieth century the wholesale self-strengthening of the Meiji era seemed to have been entirely successful. Japan was the Britain of the East. And the fanatical loyalty, pride, patriotism and courage of the samurai (warrior caste) were now found throughout society, in peasant and factory worker, in cabinet minister and industrialist. All were citizens of the Land of the Gods. All believed that death in battle for the emperor was truly glorious.

The Sino-Japanese War, 1894–95

After the Meiji Restoration a Chinese statesman warned: 'Japan's power is daily expanding and her ambition is not small. ... And Japan is as near to us as a stranger in the courtyard or on the threshold is to the folk within a house.' In 1881 China had to recognise Japanese sovereignty over the Ryukyu Islands. In 1876, after a display of force by Japanese warships, Korea, another Chinese tributary, had to open three ports to Japanese traders. After that there was intense rivalry between China and Japan for control of Korea. The position was complicated by the presence of the Russians to the north. At Vladivostok, Lord of the East, they had built a fortress town.

In 1894 both Japan and China sent troops to Korea to support two opposing political parties. In July, without any declaration of war, the Japanese torpedoed a ship carrying Chinese reinforcements to Korea. On 1 August 1894 China and Japan formally declared war.

In September the Chinese fleet was defeated in a battle fought off the mouth of the Yalu, the river which, with its deep gorges, separates Korea from Manchuria. The two Chinese ironclads that took part in this battle are said to have had between them three heavy shells. In October the Japanese crossed the Yalu into Manchuria. In November Port Arthur (Lushun), with its naval base and dockyard, fell to the Japanese. Early in February 1895 China sought peace.

In April 1895 the Treaty of Shimonoseki declared Korea to be independent. China had to pay a heavy indemnity and to open further ports. She ceded to Japan Taiwan and the strategic Liaotung (Liaodong) peninsula, at the tip of which lay Port Arthur. Six days later the Dreibund – Russia, France and Germany – 'advised' Japan to return Liaotung to China. Japan, with no ally to support her, could not oppose the three powers. 'Bear the unbearable', said the Meiji Emperor to his people. But Japan gained much prestige, becoming almost overnight the first non-European great

The Empress of Japan, 1906. By then her husband, Britain's ally since 1902, had been made a Knight of the Garter. Compare this picture with that on p. 19

*China's veteran stateman, Li Hung-chang, meets
Gladstone at Hawarden (1896). Li had represented the
emperor at Tsar Nicholas II's coronation and negotiated
the treaty allowing Russia to build the Chinese Eastern
Railway. He then went on a world tour. China's
isolation seemed to have ended*

power in modern times. The militarists won favour.
From 1900 only generals and admirals on the active list
could serve as ministers for the army and navy which
thus had much influence on the government.

In Korea Japanese influence increased. At the
ancestral tombs the ruler of Korea renounced allegiance
to China, the Great Kingdom as the Koreans had
called it.

Slicing the Chinese melon and the 'open door' policy

After the Sino-Japanese War the powers scrambled for
concessions in China. To imperialists China, 'the sick
man' of the Far East, was 'the melon', soft and ripe for
slicing. Fear of the growth of Japanese and Russian
power was partly responsible for the scramble for
concessions. Above all, probably, there was this feeling:
Russia and Japan have already taken territory – and
want more; China is likely to be partitioned – we are not
going to be left out.

The scramble for concessions began in 1895 with a
successful demand by the French for mining rights in

south China. A treaty with Russia in 1896 permitted the
construction of the Chinese Eastern Railway, to go
across Manchuria to Vladivostok. In November 1897,
faced with the kaiser's gunboat policy, China gave
Germany a ninety-nine-year lease of Kiaochow Bay
(Jiaozhou Wan) in Shantung (Shandong). Tsingtao
(Qingdao) became a German naval base. Germany also
obtained railway and mining rights in Shantung. A few
months later, while Russian warships lay off Port
Arthur, China granted Russia a twenty-five-year lease of
the Liaotung peninsula – from which Japan had been
excluded three years before by the Dreibund. The tsar
gained two ice-free ports – Dalianwan and Port Arthur
(now together known as Lüda). Port Arthur, which
became a great naval base, threatened Japan. It also
looked towards Peking. And Russia was allowed to build
the South Manchurian Railway, linking Port Arthur
with the Chinese Eastern Railway.

In April 1898 France was granted a ninety-nine-year
lease of territory in Kwangtung (Guangdong). China
also promised that she would not give to any power
other than France Kwangtung, Kwangsi (Guangxi),
Yunnan or the island of Hainan (Hainan Dao). In 1898
Britain was given a ninety-nine-year lease of the New
Territories – regarded as essential to the defence of
Hong Kong. (The leased territory, which includes many
islands, covers nearly 1,000 square kilometres and
contains over nine-tenths of the area of the colony of
Hong Kong. In the New Territories are now situated
most of the water supplies, the airport and many of
the industries of Hong Kong.) Britain also received a
lease of Wei Hai Wei (Weihai) – to last as long as Russia
should occupy Port Arthur.

Various areas became 'spheres of influence'. Germany
had a sphere in Shantung, Britain in the Yangtse valley,
whilst Japan had special rights in Fukien (Fujian)
opposite Taiwan. The French sphere was Kwangtung,
Kwangsi, Yunnan and Hainan. Russia's interests were
in Manchuria. The 'rights' of the powers in these
spheres were somewhat shadowy but included mining
and railway concessions. And there was the expectation
that if China broke up each sphere would become a
colony of the particular power interested. Leopold
Amery, who in 1900 was head of *The Times* foreign
department, recalling the heyday of imperialism in
China, wrote: '[People thought that] if the feeble control
of the Manchu dynasty should break down entirely . . .
[Britain] might have to take on greater responsibilities,
particularly in the Yangtse valley. . . . No one was
clamouring to see Queen Victoria empress of China. . . .

But no one at the time of the Diamond Jubilee [1897] . . . would have dismissed the idea as inconceivable.'

The sphere-owning powers made mutual agreements defining their respective rights. Thus, Russia and Britain came to an agreement concerning the building of railways. The British building zone was to be the provinces adjoining the Yangtse, and Hunan and Chekiang (Zhejiang) whilst Russia was to be free to construct railways north of the Great Wall. When foreign powers were free to agree among themselves as to where they should construct railways, China was far from being a sovereign and independent state!

American statesmen kept a sharp watch on the scramble for concessions, for the USA was by then a Pacific power (see p. 64). In 1899 John Hay, the American secretary of state, sent notes to Britain, Germany, Russia, France and Japan. The notes recognised their spheres of influence, but each power was asked not to interfere with the rights of others in its zone. The five powers accepted Hay's proposals, though Russia's reply was vague. In 1900 Hay issued a sterner note, which the other powers at least did not reject. A consequence of this 'open door' policy was that the USA appeared to have accepted some responsibility for preserving China's territory.

During the difficult period of adjustment that followed China's opening by the West many foreigners gave her people a lifetime of service in the hope that they might achieve a new prosperity. These helpful foreigners were often mistaken in their methods, but their devotion and self-sacrifice were as much a part of the story as were the selfishness and imperialism of others.

The Boxer Uprising, 1900

In 1898 a reform movement under the young Emperor Kuang Hsu (Guangxu) was thwarted by the empress dowager, his aunt, who made him a virtual prisoner. In the same year peasant bands, known as Boxers, began attacking Christian converts and mission stations. The Boxers belonged to a secret society, the Righteous and Harmonious Boxing Order, whose members practised a kind of oriental boxing. The Boxers believed that nothing, not even foreign bullets, could harm them: 'Gunshot cannot wound nor can water drown.'

In June 1900 Boxer bands entered Peking. An international relief force sent to protect foreigners in Peking was driven back to Tientsin (Tianjin). The allied

commanders then captured the Taku (Dagu) forts not far from Tientsin. The empress dowager, in a suicidal policy of supporting the Boxers, replied with an edict which in effect declared war against the world. In Peking in the diplomatic quarter a handful of foreigners held out against the Boxers and imperial troops. In north China the Boxers had a free hand but the viceroys of the Yangtse and southern provinces ignored Tz'u Hsi's declaration of war.

In July 1900 allied forces captured Tientsin. A relief force of troops from eight nations left for Peking. News of its advance caused panic among the Boxers. 'Like snow they melted.' The empress dowager put on the coarse blue clothes of a peasant and left with the young emperor 'on an autumn tour of inspection of the western

Tz'u Hsi, photographed about the time of the Boxer Uprising, seated on a peacock throne. She wears Manchu court dress and a pearl cape, and sheaths protect her long finger nails. The characters at the top from right to left mean: 'Great Ch'ing State: Tz'u (Compassionate) Hsi (Auspicious) Empress Dowager'

Allied officers and troops and Chinese officials stand by at an execution of Boxers (1901). The execution of Boxer leaders was required by the Boxer Protocol. (Drawn after a contemporary photograph)

provinces'. Peking was occupied – and looted – by the forces of the victorious powers. The Boxer Protocol, signed in September 1901, caused deep humiliation in China. The diplomatic quarter in Peking was to be permanently guarded by foreign troops. The Taku forts were to be burnt down. And China had to pay a heavy indemnity to states whose nationals had suffered at the hands of the Boxers.

In January 1902 a train with seats upholstered in yellow silk and furnished with two thrones, a western-style bed and an elegant opium-smoker's set, brought Tz'u Hsi and the captive emperor back to Peking. The empress bowed graciously to foreign residents watching her arrival. It was time to change her ways. Already she had issued a startling decree: 'It is not foolish to put fresh strings in a musical instrument. . . . So far we have copied only the outer clothes of the West. We must go farther. We must . . . reform completely.'

Tz'u Hsi's reformation came too late. The revolutionary Sun Yat-sen and his followers were at work among Chinese immigrants overseas. They had already cut off their queues (plaits of hair or 'pigtails' worn by men as a sign of obedience to Manchu rule). They were 'preaching treason in lands across the seas', indeed in China itself.

The Russo-Japanese War, 1904–05

In January 1902 Japan entered into an alliance with Great Britain – the first alliance made by Britain with an oriental power. Britain recognised that Japan had special 'interests' in Korea. If either power went to war to maintain the Far Eastern status quo, the other promised to remain neutral. If either had to wage war against two powers, her ally was bound to join her.

The result of the Anglo-Japanese Alliance was that Japan felt free to stand up to Russia whose step by step advance she had watched with suspicion and anger. After 1900 there were two main causes of friction: the failure of the Russians to withdraw troops sent to Manchuria during the Boxer Uprising, and Russian penetration of Korea. By 1904 the Japanese felt ready to test themselves against the Russians. But to the tsar it was unthinkable that Japanese could defeat Russians. So Russia went her way, knowing that war would almost certainly come if she failed to withdraw her troops from Manchuria.

On 8 February 1904 Admiral Togo struck by night at Russian warships anchored in Port Arthur. Two swift attacks did considerable damage. Japanese troops disembarked at the Korean port of Chemulpo (Inchon) and went on by train to Seoul, which they promptly occupied. War was declared on 10 February.

The Russian Pacific fleet, attempting to force its way out of Port Arthur and Vladivostok, was destroyed, ship by ship. In May 1904 a Japanese army defeated the Russians on the banks of the Yalu River. Landings were then made in Manchuria – Chinese territory. A Japanese force surrounded Port Arthur, which held out until January 1905. From late February to mid-March 1905 a battle in which three-quarters of a million men fought raged outside Mukden (Shenyang). The Japanese were victorious and occupied Mukden – capital of Manchuria, burial place of the ancestors of the Manchu emperors of China, and a strategic railway centre.

In May 1905 the Russian Baltic fleet, after an epic voyage of eight months, was close to Vladivostok. On 27 May, at sunrise, a Japanese cruiser reported, by wireless, sighting the Russian vessels off the island of Tsushima. The great Russian warships looked impressive, but their equipment was out of date and they were short of ammunition. At Tsushima Togo won a great victory. Only two of about forty Russian ships reached Vladivostok.

But there could be no complete and final victory over vast Russia. By the late summer of 1905 the Japanese as well as the Russians were anxious for peace. Both powers therefore welcomed President Theodore Roosevelt's invitation to send representatives to the USA to discuss peace terms. In September 1905, in New Hampshire, the Treaty of Portsmouth was signed. Russia recognised Japan's 'special position' in Korea. Both powers agreed to withdraw their troops from Manchuria. But the Liaotung peninsula was to be leased to Japan if China agreed. China, unable to do otherwise, agreed. Japan thus obtained Port Arthur and Dalianwan. This area was usually referred to as the Kwantung (Guandong) Leased Territory and the Japanese forces stationed there as the Kwantung army. (Kwantung is not to be confused with Kwangtung, the southern province of China.) Russian railway and mining rights in southern Manchuria passed to the Japanese. Karafuto, the southern half of the island of Sakhalin, was ceded to Japan.

The Japanese and the Russians soon drew together to protect their interests. A series of agreements provided in effect that Japan should have the chief influence in southern Manchuria whilst Russia was to have a free hand in the north – all Chinese territory.

In Korea Japanese influence increased. Japanese was made the official language. In 1909 Marquis Ito,

Japanese resident-general in Seoul, was assassinated by a Korean nationalist. Nine months later the king of Korea was ordered to invite the emperor of Japan to annex his kingdom. This the emperor did. Thereafter the Japanese called Korea Chosen (Morning Calm).

Change in China

After the Russo-Japanese War, when two foreign powers disputed their right to control Chinese territory, China's reform movement accelerated. A reasonably effective army was built up. Banks were founded and an effort made to reform the currency. Technical schools were built and factories appeared in the treaty ports. Railway construction greatly increased. Legal reforms were made in the hope of persuading the powers to give up their extra-territorial rights. There were campaigns against opium smoking and the custom of binding the feet of young girls.

In 1905 the examinations on the basis of which China's scholar administrators (the mandarins of her civil service) had long been selected were ended. They had become a barrier to progress. Not only was their conduct often dishonest, but the classical curriculum was unsuited to the times. The demolition of the old cells in which for centuries candidates had been locked up during the examinations was a turning point in China's history.

In 1905 about 100,000 students were receiving a 'modern' education. By 1910 there were about 1,500,000 children at western-style schools. Mission schools enjoyed a new popularity. Students were sent to study abroad, particularly in Japan. But students who enjoyed a western education became increasingly critical of existing institutions in China. Many became revolutionaries. Dr Sun Yat-sen, around whom the revolutionary movement among overseas Chinese developed, was educated in Hawaii and then in Hong Kong, at Queen's College and the College of Medicine.

China becomes a republic

In 1908 the captive emperor, Kuang Hsu, and the empress dowager died – on successive days. The years 1910–11 were marked by increased taxation, poor harvests, plague and flood. An attempt by the government to increase its authority in the provinces led to unrest. In 1911, on 10 October (the Double Tenth), a

1911, a private coach brings provincial viceroys to safety in Shanghai. In times of trouble Shanghai's International Settlement and other concession areas gave refuge to many Chinese – high and low

revolt which began in Hankow (Hankou) spread until much of China was in the hands of republicans. In the words of a Chinese proverb: 'Everyone gave a shove to the tumbling wall.' In December the rebels proclaimed a republic and elected Sun Yat-sen provisional president. In February 1912 the last emperor of China, the six-year-old Manchu Hsuan T'ung (Xuantung), abdicated and China became Asia's first republic.

There followed years of extreme confusion. In an effort to preserve unity Sun resigned in favour of Yuan Shih-k'ai (Yuan Shikai), the organiser of the new army. In 1913 Yuan declared Sun Yat-sen's party, the Kuomintang (National People's Party), illegal and Sun had to flee to Japan. In 1915 Yuan unsuccessfully tried to have himself made emperor and a few months later died. The confusion in China deepened. The government in Peking was divided and lacked authority. In the provinces military governors, warlords who were little better than large-scale brigands, held control. In the south Sun Yat-sen attempted to set up an alternative Canton government.

In August 1914, shortly after the outbreak of the First World War, Japan declared war on Germany and seized Germany's leased territory at Kiaochow Bay in Shantung. In January 1915 Japan made the Twenty-one Demands on China. Her aim was to reduce China to one vast Japanese sphere of influence. 'China could not', said the British ambassador to Peking, 'argue with a highwayman well armed.' With important modifications, China accepted the Twenty-one Demands. The Chinese never regarded this acceptance as binding. Japanese businessmen and goods were boycotted.

In August 1917 China declared war on Germany in return for an Allied promise to revise the conventional tariff and to suspend the Boxer indemnity payments. In the grip of the warlords and torn by intermittent civil war, China could give little help to the Allies. However, some 200,000 Chinese labourers did useful work in France and in Mesopotamia. Japan reaped great benefits. Her industry, merchant marine and commerce were much stimulated by the war.

Imperialism in South-east Asia and the Pacific

South-east Asia, divided by mountains, mighty rivers and seas, is the home of peoples of various races, of many languages and of several religions. Britain, France and Holland for long had interests there. In the nineteenth century they came to control almost the whole region.

The reasons for imperialist activity were much the same as in Africa (see pp. 24–5) – national rivalry, desire for trade, strategic interests, missionary interests and so on. The acquisition of one territory often pushed the occupying power into further acquisitions to defend it. And the weakness of local rulers seemed almost to invite occupation.

By 1885 the whole of Burma was under British rule. By 1870 the Straits Settlements (Penang, Malacca and Singapore) were a British crown colony. Disorder in the Malay states, under the rule of weak and corrupt sultans and torn by quarrels between immigrant Chinese tin miners belonging to rival secret societies, threatened the Straits Settlements. After 1874 four Malay states agreed to accept British residents. The sultans kept their titles and courts but the British were in real control. In 1896 these states came together as the Federated Malay States. In 1909 five other states – the Unfederated Malay States – came under British influence, but kept greater control of their internal affairs.

In Borneo in 1841 the sultan of Brunei's agent granted to James Brooke, an English adventurer, territory in what is now the Malaysian state of Sarawak. In time the Brookes, the White Rajahs, ruled all the area that is now Sarawak. (One area they took left Brunei's shrunken sultanate divided in two.) In 1846 the sultan of Brunei ceded the island of Labuan to Britain. Later the British North Borneo Company won control from Brunei over what is now the Malaysian state of Sabah. The granting of trading and administrative rights to this company was a strange reversion to the days of the East India Company – and foreshadowed the grant of similar powers to chartered companies in Africa. In 1888 Sarawak, North Borneo and Brunei (from which the name Borneo derives) became British protectorates. The rest of Borneo was part of the Netherlands (Dutch) East Indies. Dutch Borneo (Kalimantan) was larger by far than British Borneo.

The French established their rule over all Indo-China, the area east of Siam and bordering south China. By 1885 Vietnam and most of Cambodia (Kampuchea) were under French control. These territories became the Indo-Chinese Union. This was later enlarged by the addition of Laos and western Cambodia, the area containing the great Khmer temples of Angkor.

The Netherlands East Indies (now Indonesia) had its beginnings early in the seventeenth century. In 1619 the Dutch made Batavia (Jakarta) their headquarters. Gradually Dutch influence was extended over many of the islands of South-east Asia. Holland's empire was completed with the defeat by 1908 of the Achinese of northern Sumatra and of the Balinese, after bitter guerilla wars. In 1906 a Balinese rajah and 400 of his subjects, all wearing their finest clothes and jewellery, committed *puputan* (mass suicide) rather than submit. The eastern half of the island of Timor remained Portuguese.

Siam (Thailand) was strong enough not to invite occupation, strong enough to occupy parts of Cambodia and Laos. Moreover, the British did all they could to keep Siam as a buffer state against the westward expansion of the French from Vietnam. And limited concessions to the West by two wise and progressive rulers, Rama IV (Mongkut) and Rama V (Chulalong-korn), also helped Siam, alone of South-east Asian states, to retain its independence. Both rulers made attempts to modernise Siam. It was King Mongkut who employed 'Anna' (Mrs Leonowens) – immortalised in the musical *Anna and the King of Siam* – to tutor his children.

In the second half of the nineteenth century there was a small-scale scramble for the islands of the Pacific Ocean. In some islands traders were active. Others were acquired as coaling stations or as links in a trans-Pacific cable system. Sometimes occupation was based on historical grounds of first discovery. Sometimes occupation was simply to prevent occupation by another power. By 1914 every tiny dot on the map of the Pacific had the name of some western power beside it.

4 Foreign flags fly over Africa

Imperialism in Africa

Until well into the nineteenth century Europeans knew little about the interior of Africa. For centuries it remained the Dark Continent, pictured by mapmakers with strange beasts and strange people. Yet Egypt had been one of civilisation's earliest centres. In Ethiopia (Abyssinia) the Christian Coptic Church had long been established. Civilisation in the Negro kingdom of Ghana had reached a high level. The culture of the Muslim Arabs flourished along the north African coast. Timbuktu in Mali was once a centre of Muslim learning. And the stone ruins found in Zimbabwe and elsewhere in southern Africa are the work of people with an advanced culture.

A scramble for Africa in the last quarter of the nineteenth century left by 1900 only two territories independent: Liberia, set up as a home for freed slaves, which was an independent republic, and the kingdom of Ethiopia. Elsewhere foreign flags flew over all the continent.

There were a number of reasons for Europe's growing interest in Africa. The old hope of converting the Africans to Christianity was one. Humanitarians,

Extensive ruins in Zimbabwe are evidence of an ancient culture. The dzimbahwe *(stone houses) were the burial places of chieftains*

appalled by the ignorance and savage cruelty revealed by explorers in some parts of the continent, were eager to set things right. The trade in slaves between West Africa and the West Indies and America had been more or less ended early in the nineteenth century, but Livingstone's explorations showed that an equally hideous slave trade was still conducted between East Africa and Arabia. However, most of the Europeans who went to Africa went to trade. Missionaries and humanitarians for their part hoped that trade would open a road for Christianity and more civilised ways. 'If English merchants would come up the Zambezi ... the slave trader would very soon be driven out of the market', wrote Livingstone, a missionary himself.

Ivory, gold and slaves had earlier lured traders to Africa's coasts. In the nineteenth century traders sought less interesting goods – cotton, rubber, and palm oil for the manufacture of tinplate and soap. They sought markets too. The Africans, it seemed, could use vast quantities of cheap cotton cloth and ironware. As opportunities for investment of capital in Europe were decreasing, investors sought openings in Africa. The flow of capital to Africa was not in the long run vast, but this does not mean that economic motives were not important – only that there was overmuch optimism. Trade proved profitable, but less so than had been expected.

Parts of Africa were of strategic value. Colonies and spheres of influence were status symbols. Lastly, sheer momentum in part explains European expansion into Africa. Against their will at times, the intruders moved farther on, one advance seeming to make further advances almost inevitable.

African national feeling or at least fierce tribal pride was sometimes evident. But effective resistance against the Europeans, with their efficient arms and organisation, was in the long run impossible. However, Africa had 'weapons' of another kind and because of these relatively little of the continent was colonised in the strict sense. Some parts were so unhealthy that only a handful of administrators and traders ever went there. The death rate of British soldiers serving in West Africa was at one time 75 per cent – men under sentence of death could get a reprieve by volunteering for service there. However, in Kenya and the Rhodesias and Cape Colony Europeans did settle. French and Italian colonists made homes on the north coast. Many Portuguese later settled in Angola and Mozambique.

The degree of control exercised by westerners varied considerably, European 'rule' being in some cases of a limited nature. Again, Europeans had varying ideas about their relations with the Africans. The French prided themselves on following a policy of assimilation of native subjects. Belgium, while showing some concern for the material well-being of Africans, thought them quite unfit to have any civil rights. The British, manfully shouldering the White Man's Burden, tried to do 'the right thing' by their subjects. Their approach was paternal and dutiful.

Europe's dominance over Africa proved relatively brief:

> And all our pomp of yesterday
> Is one with Nineveh and Tyre.

Now that the fires of imperialism have burnt out it should be remembered that this brief-lived expansion was a creative as well as a disruptive force.

South Africa

The British and the Boers

Certain European powers had established themselves in Africa long before the scramble for territory began.

Cape Colony was taken by the British from the Dutch during the Napoleonic Wars. Until the Suez Canal was cut in 1869 Cape Town was a port of call for all vessels en route to India and the Far East.

Boers (farmers of Dutch descent) outnumbered the British settlers in Cape Colony. Deeply attached to their stern Calvinist faith, the Boers regarded themselves as a chosen people to whom other races – especially the Kaffirs or Bantu of South Africa whom they used as slaves – were inferior. But the British, wrote the sister of a Boer leader, put their Kaffirs 'on an equal footing with Christians, contrary to the laws of God, and the natural distinctions of race and religion'. And the Boers regarded South Africa as theirs by right of long occupation. The Kaffirs, like the British, were relative latecomers.

In 1833 slaves in all British territories were emancipated. Between 1835 and 1843 some 12,000 discontented Boers left Cape Colony. Some trekked to Natal. Natal, which was on the route to India, became a British colony. Other Boers trekked beyond the Orange and Vaal rivers and set up what became the Orange Free State and the Transvaal or South African Republic (see map p. 27).

As the Boers who settled beyond the Orange and Vaal

In 1888, two years after the discovery of gold at the Rand, Uitlanders oversee Africans working at a mine belonging to the Republic Gold Mining Company

rivers were British subjects they were regarded as more or less under British sovereignty. But in 1852 Britain recognised the independence of the Transvaal, and in 1854 that of the Orange Free State. Trouble with neighbouring Zulu tribes later led to British protection of the two Boer states. In 1877, following a Zulu victory, Britain annexed the Transvaal. A British force later invaded Zululand. The Zulus ambushed part of this force at Isandhlwana (1879) and disembowelled their captives. Reinforcements were sent and Cetewayo, the Zulu warrior king, was captured after a British victory at Ulundi, the site of the royal kraal (village).

Once the power of Cetewayo was broken the Boers of the Transvaal saw no reason for remaining under British rule. In December 1880 they invaded Natal and the First Boer War began. In 1881, some months after a British defeat at Majuba Hill, the Convention of Pretoria gave home rule to the Transvaal – but the Boers remained hostile.

The discovery in 1886 of goldfields at the Rand, near Johannesburg, brought great changes to the Transvaal. Soon the Boer farmers were outnumbered by the

Uitlanders, foreigners who came to work in the mines. Most of the Uitlanders were British. Meanwhile, Paul Kruger, Calvinist, nationalist and anti-British, had become president of the Transvaal. As a boy he had trekked with other discontented Boers from Cape Colony. Blindly determined not to make any concessions, Kruger opposed giving the franchise to the Uitlanders, though most of the Transvaal's revenue came from the taxes they paid.

In 1885 the British occupied Bechuanaland (see map opposite); this cut off the Transvaal from the Germans in South-west Africa (Namibia). Cecil Rhodes, an Englishman who made a fortune from Kimberley diamonds and Rand gold, played an important part in the occupation of Bechuanaland. 'The more of the world we inhabit the better it is for the human race ... the absorption of the greater portion of the world under our rule simply means the end of all wars', he wrote. His dearest wish was that Britain should rule a great swathe of territory from the Cape to Cairo along which would run a Cape to Cairo railway.

Rhodes organised the colonisation by the British

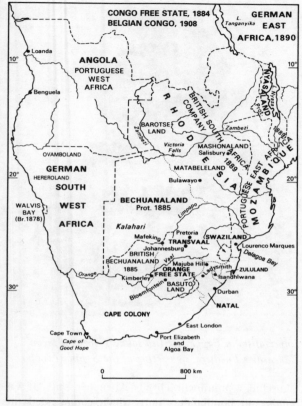

Southern Africa about 1900

South Africa Company (1889) of Rhodesia. The territory that became Southern Rhodesia (Zimbabwe) and Northern Rhodesia (Zambia) was taken over from the Matabele (Long Spears), a warlike Zulu tribe, and other tribes. Rhodes's dealings with these tribes were high-handed. On the other hand the Matabele kings were brutal tyrants who had conquered the peaceful Mashona tribesmen of Southern Rhodesia. The chartered company administered the two Rhodesias until 1923.

In 1895 the Uitlanders made plans for an uprising to take place in Johannesburg in December. Rhodes, then prime minister of Cape Colony, posted a force of mounted police, under Dr Jameson, an official of the British South Africa Company, on the eastern border of Bechuanaland. Jameson was to await news of the uprising and then sweep down on Johannesburg. The uprising did not take place but Jameson, on his own initiative, moved towards Johannesburg. On 1 January 1896 he was captured by the Boers. Rhodes had to resign as prime minister of Cape Colony. Kaiser William II greatly excited public opinion in Britain by sending a

telegram to Kruger, congratulating him on having dealt with the affair 'without appealing to friendly powers'.

The Boer War, 1899–1902

When a Boer policeman on trial for killing a British worker was acquitted and praised by the trial judge feeling ran high among the Uitlanders. In England the *Daily Mail*, which had first appeared in 1896, whipped up anti-Boer feeling. In March 1899 thousands of Uitlanders petitioned Queen Victoria listing their grievances. Jan Smuts, the young attorney general of the Transvaal, tried to negotiate with Sir Alfred Milner, British high commissioner at the Cape. Smuts and Joseph Chamberlain, colonial secretary in Salisbury's Conservative government, wanted a settlement. Milner and Kruger were uncompromising. The negotiations broke down and in October 1899 war broke out between the Transvaal and Britain.

Though Britain was regarded as bullying the Boers, Kruger could get no more than sympathy from the other European powers. Germany continued to sell munitions to the Transvaal – that was all. Canada and the Australian colonies sent troops to help the British. In Britain opinion was divided over this Second Boer War. 'Soldiers of the Queen' was the song of the day but many Liberals opposed what they saw only as interference with the Transvaal's internal affairs.

The Orange Free State allied itself with the Transvaal, giving the Boers an initial superiority in numbers. Moreover, the British troops were not trained for the open warfare of the veldt (grassland). For a time the outlook for the British, besieged at Mafeking, Kimberley and Ladysmith, was bleak. But in due course, and amid frantic excitement in Britain, the sieges were ended.

By September 1900 the British under Lord Roberts had defeated the regular Boer forces. But until April 1902 Boer men and women, and children too, fought a guerilla war. It was impossible to know who or where the enemy was. In these circumstances Lord Kitchener, who followed Roberts as commander, set up concentration camps into which Boer civilians were herded. There was an outcry in Britain following the disclosure of insanitary conditions and a high death rate in the camps. This led to some improvement but more than 20,000 Boers died in the camps.

In April 1902 the Boers surrendered. There were then over 100,000 'internees' in the camps. By the Treaty of Vereeniging (May 1902) Britain annexed the Transvaal and the Orange Free State. The Boers were given full political rights. Their language, Afrikaans, was to be used in schools and in law courts. Farmers were given grants to re-establish their properties. In 1906 the two Boer colonies were given self-government.

By the South Africa Act of 1909, Cape Colony, Natal, the Transvaal and the Orange Colony (the former Orange Free State) were joined to form the Union of South Africa. Louis Botha, a Boer who was the first prime minister of the union, aided by Smuts, established friendly relations with Britain. During the First World War Smuts was invited to be a member of the imperial war cabinet. And during the Second World War he became a trusted adviser of Winston Churchill, who as a young war correspondent had been captured by the Boers.

The Union of South Africa was from the outset composed of disparate elements. The Boers (Afrikaners) opposed the integration of the Kaffirs and of the Coloureds (people of mixed blood) with the white population. Their sense of superiority was the seed from which apartheid grew (see p. 323). The settlers of British descent, who in general were not in sympathy with such sentiments, have always been a minority.

Egypt

Both the French and British had interests in Egypt, nominally a Turkish vassal. The French had invested much capital there. Britain's interest was largely strategic, especially after the opening of the Suez Canal, the 'gate and key' to India and the East. In 1875 Disraeli bought up shares in the canal company from the bankrupt khedive of Egypt. By 1882 over 80 per cent of tonnage using the canal was British. When Khedive Ismail became heavily indebted to British and French creditors Anglo-French control was established over Egypt's finances (1878), principally to secure payment of interest on the debts.

In 1881 nationalists led by Arabi Pasha set out to free Egypt from western control and from any interference by Turkey. In June 1882 a number of Europeans were killed during riots in Alexandria. British ships then bombarded Alexandria and troops were sent to guard the canal. A few weeks later British troops defeated Arabi Pasha and occupied Cairo. Turkey, France and Italy had declined to assist the British. In England there was much criticism of Gladstone and the Liberals, who were responsible for the intervention. Lord Randolph

Imperialism in Egypt: British soldiers, some of them Lancashire Fusiliers, sightseeing at the Sphinx (1906)

Churchill, a prominent Tory backbencher, said: 'It was bonds and bondholders only which commanded the British troops.' From 1883 to 1907 Lord Cromer, 'the Pharaoh of modern Egypt', re-ordered her finances.

The British occupation of Egypt was intended to continue only until order was restored. But the British remained in Egypt, under various arrangements, until 1922 – and continued to station troops there until after the Second World War. Cromer had no doubt of the benefits of British 'rule': 'Everywhere law reigns supreme. Justice is no longer bought and sold. . . . Lastly, the schoolmaster is abroad, with results which . . . cannot fail to be important.'

The Sudan, which had been under loose Egyptian control, in 1882 rose in revolt under a religious leader, the Mahdi. His followers, the Dervishes, believed him to be the Muslim Messiah. In January 1884 General Gordon was sent to the Sudan to arrange the evacuation of Egyptian troops. In March 1884 he and his troops were attacked by Dervishes and penned up in Khartoum. In January 1885 a relief force under Sir Garnet Wolseley approached Khartoum – only to learn that the city had been captured and Gordon killed two days before. GOM, the Grand Old Man, Gladstone, the prime minister, became MOG, the Murderer of

Gordon. For thirteen years the Sudan was abandoned to the Dervishes.

Algeria and Tunisia

Between 1830 and 1847 the French conquered Algeria. Under the policy of assimilation Algeria elected representatives to the French National Assembly. However, the franchise was narrow and Muslims, the majority of the population, were in effect denied political rights. From Algeria the French tended to spread out into Tunisia. A number of Italians having settled in Tunisia, Italy was much opposed to French control. As a 'new' power, Italy especially regarded colonies as a status symbol. She also wanted colonies to help solve the problem of over-population in her backward south. But after the Franco-Prussian War Bismarck encouraged the French to penetrate Tunisia and so turn their thoughts from a possible war of revenge against Germany. In 1878, at the Congress of Berlin, Britain promised to recognise French interests in Tunisia. In 1881 the French invaded Tunisia on the ground that Tunisian tribesmen were causing disturbances in Algeria. The bey (Turkish governor) of Tunis then recognised a French protectorate over Tunisia.

The rest of the African continent to 1884

Portugal, the earliest colonial power in Africa, held Portuguese Guinea, islands in the Bight of Biafra, and the large territories of Angola and Mozambique (see map p. 27). Her ambition was to acquire the area between Angola and Mozambique. The Azores, Madeira and the Cape Verde Islands were also Portuguese.

Spain, the other early colonial power, had a protectorate over Rio de Oro, south of Morocco. The Canary Islands were also Spanish.

On the west coast the British held Sierra Leone (founded as a home for freed slaves) and trading posts on the Gold Coast (Ghana) and in Gambia. In 1874 the Ashanti tribes in the hinterland of the Gold Coast, warriors who at one time used the skull of a British governor as a goblet, were overcome by forces under Garnet Wolseley. The British also established themselves in Lagos and along the neighbouring coast of Nigeria in 1861.

The French had toeholds on the west coast – in Senegal, the Ivory Coast and Dahomey – and were in effective occupation of part of the French Congo.

In 1883 the Germans began the occupation of South-west Africa (Namibia).

The Berlin Conference on African Affairs, 1884–85

The scramble for Africa sprang partly from Germany's sudden entry into the colonial arena – and perhaps from Britain's intervention in Egypt. German industry was expanding rapidly and traders were interested in the opportunities offered by Africa. Like the British, they formed trading companies and established trading posts and the government later stepped in. Bismarck said he was 'not a colonial man' but had no objection to 'picking up' colonies in this way provided it did not involve expenditure and did not unduly antagonise Britain. The German attempt to gain colonies provoked the British to occupy areas they might otherwise have neglected. The French hastened to occupy other areas. The Italians, not wanting to be left out, eventually took possession of territories no one else wanted.

From November 1884 to February 1885 a conference met in Berlin to deal with the competing interests of the powers in Africa. Bismarck was chairman. Fourteen European states (including Turkey) and the USA sent representatives. Vague claims were then being made by Portugal to long stretches of the west coast. With typical assurance if not arrogance the powers agreed that only 'effective occupation' entitled a state to coastal holdings and consequent penetration and occupation of the hinterlands. Any state taking possession of a territory was to notify the others, thus giving them an opportunity to put forward any conflicting claims. The result was that the powers hastened to take 'effective occupation' of areas in which they had interests. The consequent scramble for territory was made without open conflict, though not without crises. By and large the powers stuck to the 'effective occupation' rule, probably because they were not in the last resort prepared to go to war over African territory – except against Africans.

The Berlin conference also dealt with the situation which had arisen in the Congo basin, where the International Association of the Congo (founded by Leopold II of Belgium) had acquired large but quite undefined territories. It was agreed to recognise the

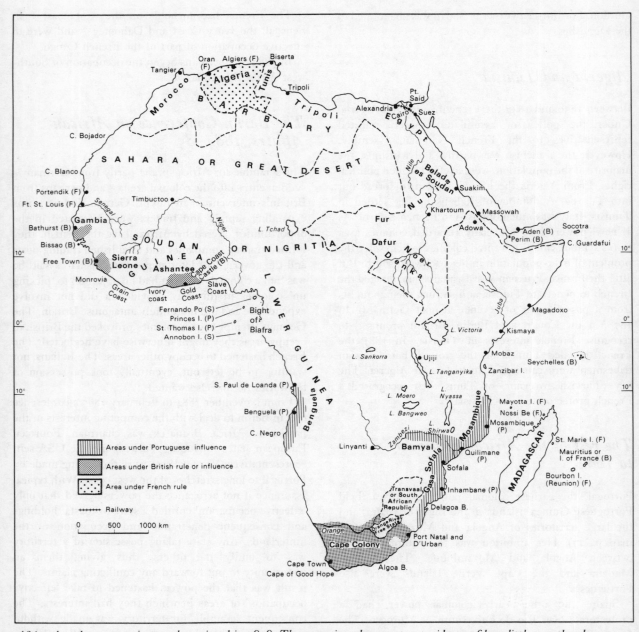

Africa, based on a map in an atlas printed in 1878. The map gives documentary evidence of how little was then known about the interior of Africa – for example the sources of the Nile were still being disputed. Note how little of Africa was subject to western influence. The only railway runs from Alexandria to Suez

territory occupied by the association as the Congo Free State on condition that all nations could trade freely there. The Belgian government entrusted the new state to the personal control of King Leopold. The Congo Free State was later enlarged – eventually its area was eighty times that of Belgium. Rich in ivory and rubber,

the Free State was ruthlessly exploited by Leopold. In 1908 the Belgian government took over the administration of the Belgian Congo (as it then became) and matters improved.

At Berlin the powers also agreed to help in suppressing the slave trade. In 1890, together with

Persia, Zanzibar and the Congo Free State, they met in Brussels to agree on measures to end the trade.

The scramble for Africa

After the Berlin conference the British, by a combination of skilful diplomacy, enlightened administration and war, extended their territories in West Africa to include the whole of Nigeria and the Gold Coast. Southern Nigeria became a British protectorate. In 1886 the British government granted a charter to the Royal Niger Company. To forestall French penetration into northern Nigeria the company made agreements with the local Muslim rulers, the emirs. By 1888 chieftains had put their marks on 168 treaties in the form below:

'We, the undersigned Chiefs of —— with a view to the bettering of the condition of our country and people, do this day cede to the Royal Niger Company for ever, the whole of our territory extending from ——. The said Royal Niger Company ... have full power to mine, farm, and build in any portion of our country. ... In consideration of the foregoing, the said Royal Niger Company ... bind themselves not to interfere with any of the native laws or customs of the country ... [and] agree to pay native owners of land a reasonable amount for any portion they may require ... [and] bind themselves to protect the said Chiefs from the attacks of any neighbouring aggressive tribes. The said Royal Niger Company ... also agree to pay the said Chiefs —— measures native value.'

In northern Nigeria the administration of justice and the collection of taxes were left to the emirs. This arrangement continued when in 1899 the British government took over northern Nigeria from the company. As in other cases of indirect rule, the native administration, though it did not bring great progress, did give stability. It also tended to create a part-westernised élite and this was apt to cause friction.

Britain's control of the Gold Coast was based on conquest. The last of four wars fought against the disciplined forces of the Ashanti kings ended in 1896.

After 1884 the Germans began the occupation of the Cameroons and of Togoland. Conflict with the British in Nigeria and the Gold Coast was avoided by frontier agreements.

After 1884 the French advanced with extraordinary speed from Dahomey, the Ivory Coast and Senegal towards the upper reaches of the Niger. In 1893 they occupied Timbuktu and a region north of the Congo. These advances made it necessary to make frontier agreements with both the Germans and the British. In due course the French occupied all the territory comprised in what was later named French West Africa (Mauritania, Senegal, French Guinea, Ivory Coast, Dahomey, Upper Volta, French Sudan and Niger) and French Equatorial Africa (the colonies of Chad, Gabon, Middle Congo and Ubangi-Shari).

In 1890, while Salisbury was prime minister, Britain made agreements with Germany, France and Portugal. The treaty with Germany provided that the British should have Kenya and Uganda (British East Africa), thus barring the Germans from the headwaters of the Nile. The Germans were to have Tanganyika (German East Africa). Germany recognised a British protectorate over Zanzibar, whilst Britain gave up Heligoland (in the North Sea).

The French in 1890 established a protectorate over Madagascar (Malagasy). Salisbury's agreement with them recognised their position in Madagascar; in return they recognised Britain's protectorate over Zanzibar.

The Salisbury treaty with Portugal recognised Nyasaland (Malawi) and Barotseland (Northern Rhodesia, now Zambia) as British; in return Angola and Mozambique were enlarged.

The crisis at Fashoda, 1898

The British had hopes of creating a belt of territory running north-south through Africa – Rhodes's 'Africa British from the Cape to Cairo'. The French aimed to control a belt running from the west to the east coast. French ambitions were bound to lead to conflict with Britain.

In 1896 British and Egyptian troops, led by Kitchener, sirdar (commander in chief) of the Egyptian army, began the reconquest of the Sudan. In the same year the French ordered Major Marchand to advance from French Middle Congo to Fashoda on the upper reaches of the White Nile in the Sudan. So Marchand, a man who had risen from the ranks, set out on an epic journey.

Kitchener made slow progress but in September 1898 he defeated the Dervishes, led by the Mahdi's successor, at Omdurman. Three days later he learned that Marchand had been in occupation of Fashoda, several hundred kilometres farther upstream, since July. With

A 'Treaty Map' of Africa from the Illustrated London News *of 24 September 1898. This gives documentary evidence of the vast changes in Africa after the Berlin conference. Some of the treaties were made with African chieftains (see p. 31), others were made amongst the western powers themselves. So the continent was carved up*

ships, guns and soldiers he advanced to Fashoda. There, when Marchand politely refused to lower the French flag, Kitchener hoisted the Egyptian standard beside it.

Soon the telegraph wires were humming and Fashoda found itself the centre of a crisis that threatened the peace of Europe. The British and the Egyptians would

not allow the French to control the headwaters of the river on which Egypt depends. For the French to withdraw at Britain's demand involved much loss of prestige. But Salisbury stood firm and France, aware that her ally, Russia (see p. 87), was unwilling to intervene on her behalf, decided to yield. After six weeks

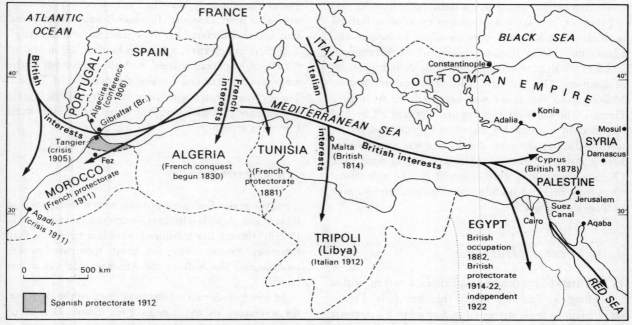

French, British and Italian occupation of Ottoman territories in North Africa, and the Moroccan crises, 1905, 1911

of tension Marchand was ordered to leave Fashoda. In 1899 an Anglo-French convention fixed the watershed of the Nile and Congo rivers as the boundary between French and British territory. The Sudan then became a condominium under joint Anglo-Egyptian control. In deference to French feelings Fashoda was renamed Kodok. The crisis there marked a low point in Anglo-French relations; after this co-operation replaced rivalry.

The Moroccan crises, 1905 and 1911

The sultanate of Morocco, occupying a strategic position facing the Strait of Gibraltar (see map above), remained as unstable as Egypt had been when Britain intervened there. In 1901 Italy, in return for a promised free hand in Tripoli (Libya), recognised French interests in Morocco. In 1904 Britain, who held Gibraltar, agreed that France had special interests in Morocco. But by this time Kaiser William II had adopted a policy of provoking France and Britain.

In March 1905 the kaiser paid a surprise visit to Tangier. In a bold speech he claimed to guarantee the independence of Morocco and demanded that its affairs be submitted to an international conference. The French had to agree, and a conference met in 1906 at

Algeçiras in Spain. Germany was trying to test the value of the new Anglo-French Entente (see p. 90), to see how far Britain would support France. At Algeçiras it became clear that British backing for France was real. Italy, Spain and Russia also upheld French interests. However, it was agreed that Morocco should remain independent, but French and Spanish police forces were to keep order there.

In May 1911, claiming that Algeria was endangered by disorder in Morocco, French troops occupied Fez, which was under attack from nomad tribes. Germany again stepped in. In July 1911 a German gunboat, the *Panther*, was sent to Agadir, a small port on the Atlantic coast of Morocco, on the ground that the interests of German nationals were in danger. Germany did have economic interests in the area but the only German subject in Agadir was one who went there so that the *Panther* could have someone to 'rescue'. For a time feelings were so high that war between France and Germany seemed possible. Fear that the Germans might seize Agadir and build a naval base there, relatively close to Gibraltar, excited British public opinion. The British fleet was prepared for action. Lloyd George, chancellor of the exchequer, hitherto regarded as anti-imperialist, said in a speech at the Mansion House in London that to preserve the peace 'only by surrender of the great and beneficent position won by centuries of British heroism and achievement' would be an unbearable humiliation.

However, this second Moroccan crisis soon burned itself out. The Russians were unwilling to support the French in a colonial dispute. Britain, whose real concern was for Gibraltar, would give France no definite promise of support. The Germans had little real interest in Morocco and the kaiser was not prepared to involve Germany in war over the dispute. Perhaps all he had intended by rattling his sword at Agadir was to get territorial concessions. He did. France was recognised as having a protectorate over Morocco but in return the German Cameroons were enlarged by two substantial slices from French Middle Congo. Spain received a zone in Tangier in 1912.

Last to come: Italy

In 1882 Italy began penetrating Eritrea, a barren strip of land along the Red Sea. About this time Italy, France and Britain were all interested in Somaliland, a strategic but forbidding area at the entrance to the Red Sea. France obtained the smallest portion of Somaliland with the port of Djibouti, opposite Aden. Britain got an in-between portion. Italy acquired by far the largest portion, from Cape Guardafui to the border of British East Africa.

West of Eritrea and Somaliland, Ethiopia occupied a strategic position on account of its nearness to the headwaters of the Nile. In 1896 an Italian army of 20,000 men that had advanced from Eritrea into Ethiopia was destroyed at Adowa. The Italians had to admit Ethiopia's independence. In 1898, when Marchand's expedition approached the Nile from the west, a French-Ethiopian expedition penetrated the

Sudan from the east. After the Fashoda crisis the French withdrew from Ethiopia. In 1906 Britain, France and Italy together declared her 'independence and integrity'.

In September 1911, a few weeks after the arrival of the *Panther* at Agadir, Italy, with the agreement of the other powers, attacked Turkey, the overlord of Tripoli. Turkey was defeated with some difficulty. By the Treaty of Lausanne (October 1912) she ceded Tripoli (renamed Libya) to Italy.

An assessment

Thus the major European powers, with the exception of Russia and Austria-Hungary, won 'places in the sun'. Britain, though her territories were less extensive than those of France, was the most fortunate in her possessions. The bulk of the African trade was in her hands.

In some cases much harm was done to the Africans, for example, in the Congo Free State. But much constructive work was done by European administrators and engineers, doctors and scientists, teachers and missionaries, and by traders too. By the early twentieth century the slave trade, from which Africans as well as Europeans and Arabs had drawn profits, was ended except in Ethiopia. The foreign flags have been lowered now. The independent African states have inherited much of value from the time when they were under western rule. But some of them are troubled by an aggressive nationalism and an interest in power politics which are also products of their colonial past.

Questions remain: could Africa have been left in isolation for much longer? If she had been left alone, would that have benefited her?

5 The empire of Russia – from autocracy towards revolution

The huge autocracy

In 1870 the tsar of Russia's rule ran from icy northern wastes and forests of conifers down through fertile cornlands to the shores of the Black Sea. It stretched from the Baltic coast, east across the great plains of Eurasia to the Pacific (see map below). During the second half of the nineteenth century the population of the empire grew from some 80 million to over 120 million. The majority of these people were Slavs. However, the Slavs of Russia differed in various ways from one another. The Little Russians (Ukrainians), for example, spoke a different language from the Great Russians, the dominant group from around Moscow. The Byelorussians (White Russians) from the area

neighbouring Poland were different again. In Finland and parts of central Asia people of Turkic stock were under Russian rule. Germans inhabited the Baltic provinces. Until 1861 the mass of the people were serfs who in general were as ignorant as the beasts they tended.

Russian Poland, which in 1815 had been placed under the personal rule of the tsars, had enjoyed certain constitutional rights, but these were soon taken away. Finland, acquired by Russia in 1809, had also been granted a constitution. In 1870 the Finns, less restless than the Poles, still had their rights.

No other subjects of the tsar had any civil or political

The empire of Russia

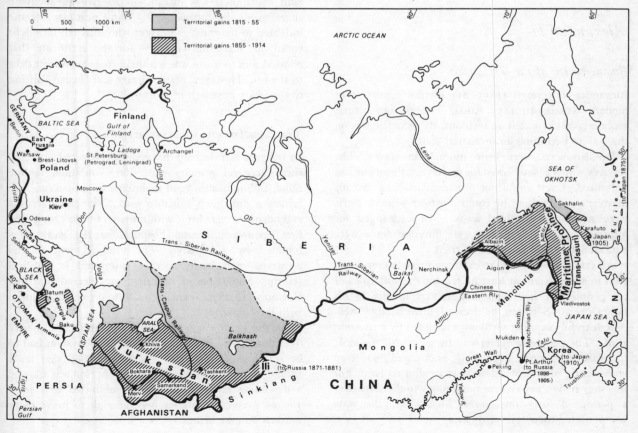

rights, though in 1864 Alexander II granted limited responsibilities to the zemstvos (see below). Except in Finland the tsar was free to rule his empire as he pleased. His royal ukase (decree) was law. For the tsar, like many others – kings, emperors, sultans – throughout history, was an absolute ruler, a ruler whose power, being unchecked by parliament or constitution, had no limit. The tsar had of course hosts of officials to carry out his orders. He had a council of state and ministers whom he himself appointed. But he was not obliged to follow their advice – or to dismiss them if their policies were unpopular. He had too his secret police. The one practical restriction upon the tsar's power was the fear that his people might rise in rebellion – or that someone might assassinate him. In fact many Russians regarded their all-powerful tsar as their Little Father. But during the nineteenth century ideas about liberal and constitutional rule penetrated to Russia. Educated people increasingly questioned the validity of autocracy, absolute rule by one individual. Some became determined to remove the 'heavy-hanging chains' of autocracy that weighed Russia down.

Alexander II

Emancipation of the serfs, 1861

Alexander II's reign (1855–81) divides feudal from modern Russia. In 1855 Russia had an agricultural economy shakily based on serfdom. By 1881 she was on the way to becoming an industrial state.

Russian serfs were little more than slaves. The services which a 'soul' owed his master were more or less unlimited. A serf could not protect himself against his master, against whom he could not bear witness. Serfs were sometimes gambled away – or exchanged for hunting dogs. Though most were illiterate, some were educated and held positions of trust.

Alexander II realised the need for a free labour force. And to some extent at least he felt for the sufferings of his people. He had seen endless serf revolts in his father's reign. Serfdom, he decided, must be abolished. After careful planning serfdom was ended by a ukase in 1861. 'The people are erect and transformed; the look, the walk, the speech, everything, is changed', wrote an enthusiastic official. Most serfs were allotted land. For this they had to pay redemption money to the state over a period of forty-nine years. Meanwhile, the state compensated their former owners.

A Russian farmer ploughing in 1880; with such primitive equipment yields were low

Ownership of the peasants' land was collective, title being held by the mirs (village councils). The mirs collected the redemption money from the peasants and distributed seed grain and farm tools. The strip system of cultivation was still practised and wooden ploughs were still in use. Some of the strips were too narrow to turn a plough on. Farm yields were low. Moreover, the land distributed was insufficient to give an adequate share to all the former serfs. Many peasants became indebted to the mirs. A peasant who thus fell into debt could not leave his village – for the certificate that allowed him to move was withheld from anyone in debt to the mir. However, many former serfs began drifting to the cities in search of work.

The zemstvos and other reforms

In 1864 the tsar decreed that zemstvos (elected councils) should control primary education, sanitation, famine relief, public health, road maintenance and so on. The zemstvos did much valuable work. Numerous schools and hospitals were built with zemstvo funds. One of the first open-door mental hospitals in the world was founded by a zemstvo. The establishment of the zemstvos made many people interested in political reform. Some began wanting an elected national assembly. In 1870 towns were allowed to elect councils with local powers.

As the landowners had exercised judicial authority over their serfs, after liberation the legal system had to be refashioned. The new system provided that trials should be held in public. An accused person was allowed a defending lawyer. Facts were submitted to a jury. Judges were paid salaries high enough to make them unlikely to take bribes.

Journalists had greater freedom. Government control over the universities was relaxed. The Jews, a substantial group among Russia's minorities, were better treated than before. On the other hand, publication of popular writings in the Ukrainian language was not allowed.

Conscription (compulsory military service) and a shorter term of service in the army were introduced. The burden of military service, which hitherto had fallen upon the peasants, was now to be shared more equally. Officers were forbidden to administer certain harsh punishments customary in the Russian army. An effort was made to teach all soldiers to read and write.

New ideas, terrorism and repression

In the years after emancipation Russia seethed with new ideas. Liberals asked for a national assembly with at least advisory powers. Alexander II replied that the common folk regarded him as their God-given ruler; their Little Father could not share his power with others. The peasants for their part were sure the tsar did not know how poor they were after emancipation. It was the officials whom they blamed for all their ills.

Groups with vague and varying revolutionary aims were increasing in numbers. One group which attracted a good deal of attention was the Narodniks or Populists. (*Narod* means people.) The Narodniks believed that a classless socialist society (see p. 40) should be established by the peasants before Russia passed through an industrial and capitalist phase. Their ideal was a state made up of innumerable independent peasant communes. In the 1870s students, women as well as men, went 'out to the people'. They lived in the villages, working as innkeepers or nurses or blacksmiths, and tried to teach their revolutionary ideas to the masses. The peasants were not very interested. Some handed the unwelcome visitors over to the police. Some Narodniks believed in terrorism. In 1874 a thousand young Narodniks were sent to prison.

Anarchists were prominent, though their 'leader' Mikhail Bakunin, an aristocrat who escaped from Siberian exile, was active in western Europe, not in Russia itself. To destroy, Bakunin said, is to construct and so the passion to destroy is noble. Anarchists, believing that the Golden Age would begin only when a stateless free society was created, were ready to kill the agents of government, officials and rulers. Yet the basis of anarchist doctrine was the belief that people are by nature good and that with the absence of all control this

goodness will assert itself. The anarchist Prince Kropotkin, who preached the necessity of violence to destroy government, was a most lovable man. Above all anarchism was unrealistic and offered nothing constructive.

Earnest young terrorists made life uneasy for many who held high office. In 1879 a terrorist society, the People's Will, passed sentence of death on 'Alexander Romanov', the tsar. The result of violence and revolutionary propaganda was repression. Political offenders and terrorists were tried by special courts, without a jury, and sentenced to death or to long exile in Siberia. Education was tightly controlled again. Many young men and women fled and studied abroad, particularly in Zurich. Censorship became strict again. The authority of the zemstvos was cut down. Yet from time to time Alexander attempted to end the unrest by fresh liberal concessions.

In 1880 an explosion in the dining room of the Winter Palace in St Petersburg reflected the troubled state of Russia. The Little Father of the Russians was attended by a heavy guard; secret police – and sickening fear – shadowed him as well as his subjects. In March 1881, in a St Petersburg street, a home-made bomb exploded beside a carriage in which the tsar was riding. Alexander stepped down and spoke to one of his bodyguard who had been injured. Then a Polish student, a member of the People's Will, threw a bomb at the tsar's feet. Alexander, fatally injured, asked to be taken 'home to the palace'. A sad procession set out for the Winter Palace; the dying tsar, held in his brother's arms, lay in a sledge; beside it rode the Cossack guards, the blood from their wounds spattering the coats of their horses and staining the snow. Alexander died an hour later

Territorial gains and foreign relations

There were considerable territorial gains in central Asia during Alexander II's reign. In 1864 the conquest of the Caucasus was completed. Turkestan, including the ancient cities of Tashkent, Bokhara and Samarkand, was added to the tsar's empire (see map p. 35). Next the khan of Khiva and Kokand submitted. In 1879 a forward policy in Afghanistan led to British intervention there (see pp. 153). In 1879 the building of the Trans-Caspian Railway was begun. The conquest of Merv in 1884, after Alexander II's death, provoked considerable 'Mervousness' in Britain, who continued to fear the extension of Russian influence towards India.

The territories gained by Russia in central Asia and

*St Petersburg: the terrorists who assassinated the tsar await execution. Sofia Perovskaya, the leader, and two others receive the last rites. The placards bear the word 'tsaricide'. (*Illustrated London News, *April 1881)*

the vast territories gained from China in 1858, 1860 and 1881 (see p. 14) were comparable in area to those gained by Britain and France in Africa and Asia. Russia's gains, contiguous with existing territories, have proved more lasting. Parts of former empires and rich civilisations, they became as much colonial areas as Africa was to other powers – useful as markets and sources of raw materials and to absorb surplus population. Subject peoples were required to use the Russian language and to accept Russian culture and institutions.

Bismarck, warning Russia to keep out of the Balkans, once said: 'Russia has nothing to do in the West; she only contracts [dangerous ideas] there; her mission is in Asia; there she stands for civilisation.' As a result of the check she received at the Congress of Berlin (see p. 12) Russia looked with renewed interest to the Far East. In the 1890s she increased her influence in northern China (see p. 18). Her ambitions extended beyond Manchuria, to Korea, Mongolia and Tibet.

After the Congress of Berlin Russia's position in

Europe was relatively isolated. Her friendship with France (see p. 87) had not yet begun. In 1879 Bismarck, driven to choose between Austria and Russia, chose Austria as Germany's ally (see p. 86). And Russia's rivalry with Britain in Persia, Afghanistan and Tibet was acute.

Alexander II's reign is notable for its literature and music. Himself little interested in such matters, he ruled the Russia of Turgenev (1818–83) and Dostoyevsky (1821–81). Dostoyevsky, after facing a tsarist firing squad, was reprieved at the last minute and sent instead to a prison camp. His novels show the intense dissatisfaction and the self-questioning typical of the Russians in their period of 'liberation'. The writings of Tolstoy (1828–1910) and Chekhov (1860–1904) show the increasing turmoil of Russian society. The composers Rimsky-Korsakov and Tchaikovsky were contemporaries of Alexander II. Tchaikovsky's 'Marche Slave' was written for a concert held in Moscow in aid of soldiers wounded during the war in Serbia (see p. 11); a Serbian folk tune is used in the work.

Alexander III: repression

Alexander III, a giant of a man who could bend a horseshoe in his hands, ruled Russia from 1881 to 1894. He relied for advice on his tutor, Konstantin Pobedonostsev. When Alexander became tsar Pobedonostsev wrote to him:

'If they begin to sing the old siren's song, that it is necessary to ... yield to so-called public opinion, for God's sake, Your Majesty, do not believe and do not listen! This will be ruin, the ruin of Russia and of you. ... It is necessary to end, at once, now, all talk about freedom of the press, about high-handed meetings, about a representative assembly.'

This arch reactionary was also the tutor of the next tsar. Always opposed to reforms, Alexander was convinced by the murder of his father that liberal policies were 'a failure'. Acts of violence strengthened his determination to oppose all change. Censorship was stricter than ever. Priests had to submit their sermons for official approval. Secondary education was limited to children from the upper classes. Student associations were forbidden. But mass arrests and exile, even whippings, did not crush the young men and women of Russia.

Minority groups were subject to disabilities. The Jews suffered most and many emigrated, some to western Europe, others to the USA. In the 1880s Zionist groups, who sought to establish a home for Jews in Palestine, began forming in Russia. The first batch of Jewish immigrants from Russia arrived in Palestine, then under Turkish rule, in 1882. German Lutherans living in the Baltic districts were not allowed to build new churches; Orthodox Christianity was the only religion officially acceptable. Muslims were ordered to become Christians.

Meanwhile, many Russians had been gaining experience in the zemstvos and liberal groups had been urging that their power should be extended. Instead, in 1889 their authority was cut down. They were allowed less control over finances and a change in the electoral laws produced a more conservative membership.

Industrial development

There was considerable industrial development during the reigns of Alexander III and his successor. In 1892 Serge de Witte became minister of finance, a post he held for eleven years. French loans (see p. 87) made

possible the building of railways, which in turn aided industrial growth. At this time Russia was building more railways, some privately owned, many state-owned, than any other country. The Trans-Siberian Railway, begun in 1891, linking Moscow with Vladivostok (see map p. 35), opened Siberia and the Maritime Province to agriculture, mining and industry. Between 1892 and 1902 Russia's production of coal doubled. Production of oil in the Caucasus increased five-fold between 1885 and 1905. Witte protected new industries by tariffs, only such imports as heavy machinery being allowed in without payment of a high duty. By about 1900 Russia had some three million factory workers.

Conditions were extremely harsh, but the workers, forbidden to form unions and fiercely competing for employment, were helpless. Despite the passing of various factory acts, children, ill-fed and unhealthy, worked for long hours in prison-like surroundings. Wages, not always paid regularly, were pitifully low. 'Cabbage soup and gruel, that's our diet', the workers said. 'Though we all look at the same sun, we don't all eat the same dinner', was a common saying among the poor. Their only pleasures were occasional drinking bouts.

The peasant population of Russia almost doubled between emancipation and 1900. On the death of a farmer his land was reallocated among his family, so as the years went by the peasants' holdings grew smaller. Yields remained low for farming methods made little advance. Between 1865 and 1905 a million and a half peasants went to Siberia, where fresh land was available.

The Socialist Revolutionaries

During the reigns of Alexander III and his successor Nicholas II revolutionary groups became more active. The largest group was the Socialist Revolutionaries who took over many of the ideas of the Populists (Narodniks). Like the Narodniks, the Socialist Revolutionaries had a terrorist section, the Combat Section. The Socialist Revolutionaries were willing to work with other groups, including moderate liberals, to achieve their aims. Their plans for what is often called Russian Socialism were vague but like the Narodniks they regarded the peasants as the basis on which to build a new society. They favoured the communal holding of land. Part of their attraction lay in their programme of immediate action by for example seizing land – the (Marxist) Social Democrats' programme (see p. 41) seemed to relate to a more distant future.

Socialism and Marxism

In the first half of the nineteenth century in France,
Germany and Britain people indignant at the evils of
society sought to end them by arousing a sense of right
and justice. Some produced vague schemes for ideal
communities. Under their influence a movement aiming
at social and economic reconstruction as well as political
reforms began. These people were aware of the
increasing prosperity enjoyed by a few as a result of the
workers' labour. As 'socialists' they wanted to make the
production and use of wealth 'social', for the good of all.
So they said society should take over control of the
means of production from greedy, competitive
individuals. These early socialists were later called
Utopian socialists. (Utopia comes from the Greek word
meaning nowhere. Their society, critics said, was
impossible of realisation, it could exist nowhere.) The
Utopian socialists dreamed of an ideal society but did
not know how to bring it into being.

Scientific socialism had its origins in January 1848
with the publication of a pamphlet of some thirty pages.
This pamphlet, *The Communist Manifesto*, was written
by Karl Marx, a German Jew living in exile, and his
friend Friedrich Engels. Marx claimed to know how the
ideal society would be brought into being. A manifesto is
not only a statement of belief; it is also a programme of
action. 'Workers of the world unite', wrote Marx. The
union of all workers was the first step in his programme:
'You have nothing to lose but your chains.' By uniting,
Marx said, the workers would be strong enough to
overthrow capitalist society; then they could establish a
society in which there would be no selfish competition.
Everyone would willingly work for the good of society.
Everyone would receive from society everything he
needed: 'From each according to his ability; to each
according to his needs.' Marx did not allow for man's
selfish nature; people seem to need incentives and are
inclined to work hardest for themselves.

Marx claimed his form of socialism was 'scientific'. It
was based, he said, not on ideals or on moral beliefs. It
was based on the 'laws of history', laws as scientific as
the 'laws of gravity'. All history, he said, has been a
struggle between classes. When one class won control,
another class emerged to resume the conflict. Every
dominant class, he said, owed its existence to its material
possessions, its wealth – in older days slaves and land,
later capital. This was the theory of dialectical
materialism, of the class struggle that arises from
material possessions, from wealth. One final class

*From a Danish collection of caricatures (1904–08), this
'socialist parable' aims to show the evils of absolute
monarchy, constitutional monarchy and middle-class
democracy – and the orderly bliss of socialist democracy*

conflict, Marx said, would occur. This conflict would bring into being the ideal communist society in which the struggle for possessions would end. Marx did not explain why no new classes with conflicting interests would arise in the future.

The two classes that would take part in the final conflict were the capitalists (often referred to as the bourgeoisie) and the proletariat, the new class that the industrial revolution had brought into being, the industrial workers of the great manufacturing cities that were springing up all over the world. In earlier times, said Marx, the peasants had land to use, tools to work with, houses of some sort to live in. The proletariat were propertyless – without tools, without homes, without any share in the means of production. Their only 'possession' was their ability to work – their labour, which they sold for wages to the capitalists. Marx did not foresee that the proletariat might in time acquire property. He did not realise that capitalism might change. Capitalism as we know it is very different from capitalism in Marx's day.

Soon after the publication of *The Communist Manifesto* Marx settled in London. He spent much of his time in the reading room of the British Museum. He wrote *Das Kapital* (Capital), 1867, in which he examined the growth and working of the capitalist system and foretold its destruction. In 1864 he founded the First International Workingmen's Association with the aim of spreading socialist ideas. The First International achieved little and was dissolved in 1876. In 1889 the Second International was founded in Paris.

The Russian Social Democrats

In 1872 *Das Kapital* was translated into Russian. The ideas of Marx spread among the skilled workers of the growing proletariat – public ownership of the means of production seemed a magic formula ensuring them a proper share in the wealth they helped to create. But the popularity of the Socialist Revolutionaries was an obstacle to the spread of Marxism – until in time the Bolsheviks (see p. 128) annihilated them.

In 1883 Georgi Plekhanov, a former Populist, founded in Geneva Russia's first Marxist organisation. In 1898, when Nicholas II was tsar, Plekhanov's followers founded the (Marxist) Russian Social Democratic (Workers') Party. Informers found their way into the conference and all present were arrested.

Towards the end of the nineteenth century the

international socialist movement was divided as to how a socialist society was to be brought into existence. Marx had said that the capitalist system would inevitably break down, probably after a war between capitalist states. Within the socialist parties formed in most industrialised states by about 1880, as later within the Second International, some argued that step by step gradual reform would eventually transform capitalist societies. Others, those socialists who became known as communists, argued that existing institutions must be overthrown by violent revolution.

In 1903 the Russian Social Democrats held their second conference in Brussels but police activity led the delegates to adjourn to London. At this conference the party split into two groups, the Mensheviks and the Bolsheviks, though it was not until 1912 that they became separate parties. The Mensheviks, or minority group, were in favour of gradual reform and were willing to co-operate with less radical socialists. The Bolsheviks, or majority group (*bolshoi* means large), insisted on the overthrow by force of the existing régime. But the Bolsheviks did not believe in individual acts of terrorism as practised by the Narodniks and the Socialist Revolutionaries. What the Bolshevik leaders believed in was the use of mass terror – the organised destruction of whole sections of society – in order to realise their aims.

Neither the Socialist Revolutionaries nor the Social Democrats were at first parties as we know them. Their leaders for much of the time were unable to show themselves in Russia, especially in St Petersburg or Moscow. They spread their ideas largely by letters and pamphlets written in Switzerland or some other place of refuge.

Lenin the Bolshevik leader

After the 1903 conference of the Russian Social Democrats Lenin, the leader of the majority Bolshevik group, became the dominant force in the Russian revolutionary movement. Vladimir Ilyich Ulyanov (Lenin was his undercover name) was born in 1870, the son of an inspector of schools. In 1887 his elder brother, a Populist, was hanged for taking part in a plot to assassinate Alexander III. In 1891 Lenin graduated in law as an external student of the University of St Petersburg. His first written work of importance was a criticism of the Populists. In 1895 he was imprisoned and was in exile in Siberia when other Marxists formed the Social Democratic Party. In 1900 Lenin went to

Geneva. There he founded the revolutionary paper *Iskra* (Spark). Printed on thin cigarette paper, *Iskra* was smuggled into Russia. Lenin was well aware that the masses needed the skilled leadership of a Marxist élite to act as a spearhead. Left to themselves, he feared, the masses would be content simply to win better wages and shorter hours – or in the case of the peasants to grab land. He demanded that his followers should accept absolute unity of leadership and dogma. Above all they had to accept the policy of seizing power by violent revolution. However, Lenin himself, always a realist and an opportunist, was willing to disregard Marxist theory when he thought it necessary. The general belief was that socialism could be achieved only in countries with a capitalist economy and a proletariat to oppose it. Russia in Lenin's day was still basically an agricultural peasant economy and so not yet destined for revolution. Nonetheless Lenin set his heart on achieving the socialist revolution.

Nicholas II

Continued unrest

Alexander III was succeeded in 1894 by his son, Nicholas II. There was little to blame in Nicholas's private life. There was nothing to praise in his conduct of public affairs. A firm believer in autocracy, but weak-willed and lacking in ideas, he simply tried to follow his father in upholding the crumbling old order.

The opening months of Nicholas's reign were clouded by a disaster that occurred at the time of his coronation. Near Moscow, while coins and scarves were being distributed to the poor, a mad rush of people caused a grandstand to collapse like a house of cards. Some 3,000 people were killed. That night the tsar and his wife, glittering with diamonds, attended a grand ball. The next day they visited the injured in hospital.

Continual strikes showed the unrest of the urban workers. Some strikes broke out without any direction, others were stirred up by Marxists. The number of strikes rose from 53 in 1895 to 152 in 1898; all supported demands for higher wages. But behind these claims was a demand for political power.

In 1902 Plehve, an extreme reactionary, became minister of the interior, responsible for police and security. In his time Russia was a land seething with revolutionary ideas, a land of fear and hatred. Revolutionaries in disguise walked the streets of towns and villages; behind them, also in disguise, came the secret police.

Under Plehve minority groups suffered again. To turn attention from the objects of discontent, organised attacks (pogroms) on Jews were provoked. The Finns had so far managed to keep their privileges. Under Nicholas II their constitution was suspended, they were forced to use the Russian language and were no longer allowed to have their own army and postal service. The Ukraine and Byelorussia were also disturbed. In Byelorussia religious persecution made matters worse. Poland, the Baltic provinces, the Caucasus and central Asia were restive.

The 1905 Revolution

In 1902 the German emperor, when a guest at a Russian naval display, greeted Nicholas as the Admiral of the Pacific. 'The Admiral of the Atlantic', the kaiser said, 'salutes the Admiral of the Pacific.' In the Russo-Japanese War of 1904–05 the 'Admiral of the Pacific' was defeated in every encounter with the enemy (see p. 21). Not for the first time the inefficiency and corruption of tsarist Russia were exposed. Plehve had said: 'We need a small victorious war to halt the tide of revolution.' But Lenin declared: 'If the forces of the tsar are defeated, that will urge on the revolutionaries.'

In July 1904 the hated Plehve was assassinated by a Socialist Revolutionary. Later that year liberals at a zemstvo congress asked for freedom of speech, of the press, of assembly, and for certain social reforms. They asked also for an elected national assembly.

On Sunday 22 January 1905, just after the fall of Port Arthur to the Japanese, a priest, Father Gapon, led a procession of factory workers towards the Winter Palace in St Petersburg. The workers intended to petition their Little Father for a minimum wage and certain political reforms. The crowds moved peaceably through the streets carrying icons and portraits of the tsar, and singing hymns and patriotic songs. But troops were ordered to disperse the workers and the thousands of people who had come to watch them. Soon all was confusion. The soldiers fired, and a troop of cavalry charged the crowds. Several hundred people, men and women and children, were killed on that Bloody Sunday. People began calling their Little Father the Murdering Tsar.

Soon strikes brought life almost to a standstill. In February the governor general of Moscow was murdered in the Kremlin. Peasants formed unions, set fire to large estates and sometimes killed their landlords. More often they marched them to the nearest railway station, told them to 'get out', and seized their land. In May 1905 came news of the naval defeat at Tsushima. In June the crew of the battleship *Potemkin* mutinied. Having thrown their officers overboard, they bombarded Odessa and terrorised tsarist officials.

In August the tsar promised to summon an elected national assembly, a Duma. However, the Duma was to have only advisory powers. Further violence followed this concession, which most people regarded as useless. A rail strike that began in Moscow in October spread over the entire country. Before long all the workers of Russia – even the stars of the Russian ballet – seemed to be on strike. On 30 October 1905, not long after the Treaty of Portsmouth ended the war with Japan, Nicholas promised to call an elected national assembly with legislative powers. This pledge is known as the October Manifesto.

Three days before the manifesto was issued revolutionaries in St Petersburg had formed a soviet of workers' deputies. (The word soviet has no intrinsic connection with communism; it means advice or council. The tsar's council of state was a soviet.) Leon Trotsky, a Menshevik, directed the St Petersburg soviet. Its members were representatives of the still illegal trade unions or of large factories. The St Petersburg soviet issued a manifesto calling all workers to unite under the red flag, the banner of the proletariat of all lands. Before long there were more than 500 such soviets in Russia.

The granting of an elected Duma seemed a revolutionary change. But the October Manifesto was signed in a time of crisis by an autocrat determined to give away as little as possible. The Duma was unlikely to be allowed any real power.

In November 1905 the Poles, not for the first time, demanded self-government. Witte, by then prime minister, imposed martial law in Poland. The Moscow soviet, in sympathy with the Poles, and dissatisfied with the October Manifesto, ordered another strike. Late in November the Black Sea fleet mutinied. In December the Moscow garrison mutinied. Strikes continued.

But by the end of the year most people seemed weary of strikes and violence. The police rounded up strike leaders and peasant agitators who were sentenced to death or exile. The workers' soviets disappeared for the time being. Most of the leaders of the St Petersburg and Moscow soviets had been arrested. Lenin, who had managed to return to St Petersburg, escaped abroad again. Disturbances dragged on until January 1906. By then the 1905 Revolution was over.

The period of the Dumas

In December 1905 Witte promised virtually universal franchise for the Duma. From 1906 trade unions,

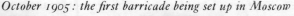

October 1905: the first barricade being set up in Moscow

though not given the right to strike, were legalised and the redemption payments due by the peasants were ended. Witte seemed too ready to yield to popular demands, so early in 1906 Nicholas dismissed him. Soon Piotr Stolypin was appointed prime minister.

In May 1906, shortly after Witte was dismissed, the Duma met for the first time. The Russians, quite unused to voting for a parliament, tended to vote for a man rather than for a 'party'. Most of those elected belonged to a newly founded party, the Constitutional Democrats, usually known as the Cadets (CDs). The Cadets were moderates who wanted parliamentary government, not revolution. Next in number were the Trudovik (Labour) men. The Trudoviks were in fact Socialist Revolutionaries calling themselves by another name because their party was illegal. The Trudoviks aimed at turning over the land to the peasants and so had strong support in the countryside. There were a few ethnic 'parties', representing national minorities, and a few Octobrists. The Octobrists were very mild liberals, who were entirely satisfied by the October Manifesto. The leaders of the Bolsheviks and the Mensheviks boycotted the elections. However, a few Mensheviks found their way into this first Duma.

The October Manifesto provided that no law could be made without the Duma's consent. However, the tsar was left in control of the armed forces, and upon their loyalty his power finally rested. Again, ministers were responsible only to the tsar. And the tsar had the right to raise loans and in a degree to control finance independently of the Duma.

The Cadets demanded a general amnesty, responsible government and other reforms but the tsar and his advisers refused to listen. When the Cadets passed a vote of censure against the ministry, after only a few weeks of life the first Duma was dissolved – its members found the doors locked against them. Some deputies then went off to Finland, where they issued the Vyborg Resolution urging the people to resist the government by refusing to pay taxes and to serve in the army. The former Duma members were deprived of their civil rights, so newly won. Some were imprisoned. The Menshevik deputies, after a secret trial, were sent to Siberia.

Despite trickery at the elections the second Duma, which met in March 1907, had an increased number of left-wing members. An extreme right-wing group also emerged. Known as the Bolsheviks of the Right, these men opposed the October Manifesto as too radical and thought there should be no Duma at all. The second Duma was dissolved in June 1907.

Changes were then made in the electoral laws with the object of keeping radicals out of the parliament. These changes increased the strength of conservatives, while the voting power of workers and peasants and minority groups such as the Poles was cut down. The third Duma, elected on this narrower franchise, sat from November 1907 to 1912. It was controlled by the Octobrists.

Stolypin: land reforms and repression

In 1906 Stolypin decreed that the mirs should no longer issue passports to enable a peasant to change his place of residence. Also in 1906 a peasant was given the right to demand his own title to the land he farmed. A peasant could increase his allotment by surrendering his common right in pasture land. A state bank gave credit for the purchase of land. Some fourteen million people acqured a stake, if only a small one, in the land. Some, the 'tight fists', or kulaks, acquired a relatively large stake, and produced a surplus of food for sale in the towns and for export to western Europe. Peasants displaced by the kulaks abandoned their villages and swelled the industrial labour force. Others succeeded in buying their own land. By 1917 some three-quarters of the land in Russia was owned by peasants.

Stolypin's aim was to build up a class of fairly substantial, conservative farmers – a class that would be a rampart against revolution. It was hoped too to increase farm yields. However, the creation of the new kulak class split Russia's peasants into two sections – the 'have-plentys' and the 'have-much-lesses'. There was further migration to Siberia in these years.

Stolypin used two weapons in his attempt to uphold tsardom – land reform and repression. Land-hungry farmers were not the only ones who arrived in Siberia; many thousands of political offenders were sent into exile there. As the October Manifesto claimed to protect citizens from arbitrary imprisonment, Stolypin arranged speedy trials for political offenders. Punishment was swift too. So many people were hanged while he was prime minister that the gallows acquired a grim nickname – Stolypin's necktie. In 1911 Stolypin was assassinated while listening to the music of Rimsky-Korsakov in the magnificent opera house at Kiev, capital of the restless Ukraine.

Like the third Duma, the fourth Duma, which sat from 1912 until the February Revolution of 1917 (see p. 122), had an Octobrist majority. For a time Stolypin's reforms and good harvests made things easier. The surplus of grain for sale within Russia and for export increased. Industry developed rapidly. By 1914 the value of exports was almost half that of the USA, though Russian production was much less per head of population. In 1908 universal primary schooling for four years had been introduced; by 1914 50,000 new schools had been built. Various factory acts improved conditions of work. Lenin, marooned in western Europe, complained that Russia was getting on too well – so well that he feared that the revolution might not come in his time.

From 1912 strikes became more frequent – as also in other parts of Europe at that time. It was in 1912 that striking workers on the Lena goldfield in Siberia were shot down by police: Bloody Sunday, it seemed, had come again.

From war to the eve of revolution

In 1914 the First World War broke out. There was for a time considerable patriotic enthusiasm in Russia. It was perhaps in an excess of zeal that a ukase forbade the production and sale of vodka. The sale of vodka had been a state monopoly; with prohibition a third of the government's income was cut off at the very time when there was need for increased revenue.

By 1915 the bulk of Germany's and Austria's forces were engaged on the eastern (Russian) battlefront (see p. 98). Russian casualties were already very high, even for a country with a large population. The Russians fought with great bravery but they were often poorly equipped. Some soldiers went into battle armed with wooden farm tools. Some fought in winter in bare feet. Transport arrangements were muddled. Officers were issued with old and inaccurate maps. The tsar once said, 'There are villages and towns here but my map shows nothing of the sort.'

In 1915 the tsar took over as commander in chief. Absent from his capital he was more than ever out of touch with his people. The Tsarina Alexandra was left in charge of affairs in Petrograd. (In 1914 the German name St Petersburg was changed to its Russian form, Petrograd.) Alexandra, who was iron-willed and had much influence over the tsar, was a narrow and foolish busybody. 'It's a sad home where the cow instructs the bull', the peasants said. Alexandra believed firmly that autocratic rule was right for Russia. 'Be more autocratic, my own sweetheart', she advised Nicholas. Her one aim was to preserve the throne for 'Baby', her delicate young

son. Tortured by fears for this child, who suffered from haemophilia, she had fallen under the spell of Rasputin, a so-called holy man but dirty, evil and a drunkard. From 1906 to 1916 Rasputin had much influence in Russia – in making appointments to high office, even in deciding military moves. He did seem to have some strange power over the prince, who on several occasions recovered after being visited by him. In December 1916 Rasputin was murdered by Prince Yusupov and his body thrown into the River Neva. But with Rasputin gone it was easier to blame the government and the Romanov dynasty for all the troubles of Russia.

In 1916 some in high office in Petrograd were urging that peace be made. But Germany's proclamation of an independent Poland, shortly before Rasputin's murder, aroused a storm of protest in Russia and the peace talks came to an abrupt end.

Meanwhile the cost of living had risen considerably but wages remained stationary. Workers in munitions factories toiled for long hours to earn the little extra that enabled them to survive. The distribution of food was inefficient. Long lines of tired and hungry people stood waiting for bread in Russian cities. The arrival of great numbers of refugees from the war-torn western provinces brought further problems. The winter of 1916 was unusually severe, and fuel was short. The number of strikes increased. War-weary soldiers began drifting back to their villages. All Russia was weary of the government's mismanagement of affairs. Frequent changes of ministers led to worse confusion.

The tsar's advisers were urging him to make changes, to appoint ministers whom the people would support. But Nicholas seemed blind to what was happening.

In 1905 the English magazine *Punch* had predicted what might happen:

> Little tsar, beware the hour
> When the people strike at power;
> Soul and body held in thrall
> They are human after all.
> Thrones that reek of blood and tears
> Fall before the avenging years.
> While you watch your sinking star,
> Tremble, tremble, little tsar.

In February 1917 the president of the Duma warned Nicholas that a revolution was coming; he urged the tsar to listen to a report he had made. 'Hurry up', said Nicholas impatiently, 'I am going to visit the Grand Duke Michael, to have tea with him.'

6 The United Kingdom: the new society emerging

A liberal state

In 1870 Britain was a 'liberal' state. To define a Liberal is easy. A Liberal is a member of the Liberal Party. But liberalism cannot be equated with the Liberal Party. Though that party has played a central part in the liberal movement liberalism has not been the monopoly of the Liberals.

Liberalism is not easy to define. The ideas of liberals have changed with the times. Liberals have always stood for freedom of the press and of speech, the right to hold meetings and to form associations. They have always demanded freedom from arbitrary arrest or imprisonment. By these standards all our political parties are liberal. Typical nineteenth-century liberals favoured parliamentary, representative and responsible government – government by an elected parliament with ministers who must resign if the majority of members disagree with them. But not all liberals a hundred years ago were in favour of all adult males having the right to vote. The franchise, many liberals then believed, should only be given to 'responsible' citizens, to men with certain property and educational qualifications. Such liberals would today be called reactionaries, reactors against reform. The nineteenth century had too its radical liberals; they sought reforms that seemed to go to the very root (*radix*) of society. A liberal who a hundred years ago favoured giving the vote to women would have been called a dangerous radical. It follows that many of the policies of the Conservative Party of our day would once have been labelled radical.

In time British liberalism had to give up its cherished policy of *laissez-faire*. *Laissez-faire* means: 'Leave things alone. Don't interfere.' In the belief that if all are free to make their own choices all will be better off, governments were to interfere as little as possible in the workings of society, especially in economic affairs. But it became increasingly clear that 'interference' was necessary if the real freedom of all was to be secured. And it is to freedom that liberalism is dedicated.

*Victorian opulence; an upper middle-class dinner party. The young girl on the left, enjoying her first London season, is disappointed at being taken in to dinner by 'a middle-aged MP'. (*Graphic, 26 April 1890*)*

A period of reform

Between 1870 and 1914 – the second half of Victoria's reign (1837–1901) with its Golden and Diamond Jubilees, the Edwardian era (1901–10) and the opening years of the more sober reign of George V (1910–36) – both the Liberals and the Conservatives (see table of ministries on p. 56) undertook numerous reforms. Following franchise extensions both parties tried to attract working-class voters. There was pressure for reform from the growing trade union movement and later from the new Labour Party. A genuine humanitarianism encouraged reform. And Britain, despite losing her lead in industry, could afford reforms. By the 1900s many workers were better off than their parents had been in 1870 – as we are materially better off than our parents.

Distribution of income in Britain, 1904

RICH 1,250,000 people share £585 million	COMFORTABLE 3,750,000 people share £245 million
POOR 38,000,000 people share £880 million	

Three classes: Britain, 1904

An English child born in 1870 might have expected to live to the age of forty-two; by 1914 a child could expect to live to fifty-three. Nonetheless the condition of workers in the 1900s was by our standards appalling, especially by contrast with the opulence of Edwardian society. In 1903, Jack London, describing the East End

of London, wrote of men who were 'caricatures' of men, 'women pale and anaemic', 'early twisted out of all shapeliness and beauty', and homeless people who were 'a welter of rags and filth'. Seebohm Rowntree described the diet of 'bread, dripping and tea; bread and butter and tea … ' and the pawnshop queues of the poor of York. Robert Tressell, in *The Ragged Trousered Philanthropists*, exposed the drabness and terrifying insecurity of the life of his fellow workers.

Parliamentary reform and party organisation

The franchise was extended three times in the nineteenth century – in 1832, 1867 and 1884. The 1832 act enfranchised only the highest stratum of the middle class. In 1867 a Conservative government passed a second Reform Act which enfranchised many town workers and virtually doubled the electorate. Most farm labourers were still excluded and the countryside remained under the domination of the landowners. But after 1867 public opinion began to count for more than the influence of such bodies as the church and the universities. Appeals direct to the people by party leaders, of which Gladstone's Midlothian campaign of 1879–80 (see p. 12) is an example, were encouraged – national rather than local issues came to dominate election campaigns.

Until the mid-nineteenth century party organisation was purely local – for nominating candidates, not for controlling them or discussing policy. In such circumstances independent members flourished, free both of patronage in their electorates and of party control in Parliament. By the early twentieth century however the parties were well organised and the practice of appointing whips to direct the votes of party members was firmly established.

In 1867 the National Union of Conservative and Constitutional Associations was formed. The National Union, accepting Conservative principles of leadership and authority, left the direction of policy very much to its parliamentary leaders, though the party conference could make suggestions. The National Liberal Federation was formed in 1877. This federation exercised some authority over the parliamentary party, impressing its ideas upon it, and so bringing about a greater degree of unity than was to be found among Conservatives. Both the Conservative National Union and the National Liberal Federation were formed by parliamentary politicians in response to the enlargement of the electorate. The Labour Party had its origins outside Parliament (see p. 51). From the outset the parliamentary Labour Party was to a large degree controlled by the movement outside Parliament.

In 1872 Gladstone's Ballot Act provided for secret voting. This act was of most effect in Ireland, where intimidation by landlords was greatest. In Gladstone's second ministry the Corrupt Practices Act (1883) regulated electoral procedure and specified the amount that could be spent by a candidate in an election campaign. In 1884 the Franchise Act gave the vote to many farm labourers. After this third Reform Act two out of three men in England had the right to vote. The Redistribution Act of 1885 divided most of the country into relatively uniform constituencies. With a few exceptions all were single member constituencies.

Trade unionism

In 1825 workers acquired the right collectively to bargain for better conditions. But their position was insecure. In 1834 six labourers from Toll Puddle (Tolpuddle) in Dorset were sentenced to seven years transportation for having administered illegal oaths while forming an agricultural workers' society. A crown witness from Half Puddle described how he was blindfolded and made to kneel down while something was read out: 'It seemed to be out of some part of the Bible.' Later, he said, the accused 'told us . . . we should have to pay a shilling then and a penny a week afterwards, to support the men when they were standing out from their work.' All six men were later pardoned. But the Tolpuddle martyrs remained a symbol of repression.

In the 1850s men from skilled trades, the upper stratum of the lower classes, began forming craft unions, exclusive organisations limited to 'the aristocracy of labour'. The founding in 1851 of the Amalgamated Society of Engineers is a landmark in union history. The craft unions, very small at first, concerned themselves with pay and hours – and standards of work too. They had little interest in politics and none in revolution. Members' subscriptions provided funeral benefits (at a time when a decent funeral, a hallmark of respectability, was an impossible dream for many people) and insured against stoppage of wages in the event of a strike and sometimes provided sickness benefits.

Soon the Amalgamated Society of Engineers had over 12,000 members and controlled relatively large funds. In 1863 the National Miners' Union was established for skilled men working at the pit face. In 1868 the Trades Union Congress (TUC) was founded and by 1871 it had formed a parliamentary committee.

The leaders of the few big unions, themselves skilled workers, had educated themselves with considerable success. The Junta, as this group of union leaders is often known, wanted legislation establishing manhood suffrage and secret ballot, shorter working hours, and schools for their children. They thought of the strike as a weapon to be used only in the last resort. The Junta had the support of a number of middle-class liberals.

In 1871, during Gladstone's first ministry, the Trade Union Act formally legalised unions and gave protection to their funds. But the Criminal Law Amendment Act of the same year made picketing illegal. Soon judges were sentencing offenders under this act – for example, women in Chipping Norton who hooted blackleg workers. In 1875, during a Conservative ministry led by Disraeli, the Conspiracy and Protection of Property Act was passed. This allowed persons acting in combination in a trade dispute to take any action which would not be punishable if taken by a person acting on his own. Peaceful picketing was thus legalised.

The 1870s were the period of 'prosperity strikes', when skilled workers struck for a nine-hour day, higher wages and similar benefits. Low rates and taxes, low rents and building costs permitted such workers to enjoy solid comforts at home, even holiday trips to the seaside. The Bank Holiday Act was passed in 1871 – the statutory holidays shone out like 'diamonds' brightening drab lives. The English weekend with the half holiday on Saturday became usual.

In the last quarter of the century England was less prosperous. The industrial revolution was proceeding apace elsewhere and there was less room for British goods in the world's markets. Importation of cheap corn from the USA and Argentina resulted in cheaper bread – but was disastrous to English agriculture. And although the overall trend of living conditions continued to be upward, slumps alternated with booms. Periodic down-swings of the economy brought unemployment and wage cuts. In 1873 the onset of a depression was marked by strikes – not for higher wages, but against wage reductions. Such reductions were often the result of sliding-scale agreements – for example, a 35 per cent fall in the price of coal was followed by wage cuts of 25 per cent.

In 1872 Joseph Arch formed the National Agricultural Labourers' Union – this was indicative of a new trend: unions of unskilled workers, organised on an industrial not on a craft basis, began to appear. In 1889 this 'New Unionism' showed its power when the ill-paid dockers, led by Ben Tillett, struck. The first manifesto of the joint strike committee stated:

'To the Trade Unionists and other workmen of the United Kingdom: The dock labourers of London . . . are on strike for an advance of a penny an hour day-work and twopence per hour overtime. The amount of work these men may obtain is only on an average three or four hours a day. . . . We, the whole of the dock workers of London, stevedores, painters, scalers, corn porters, steel porters, coal heavers . . . hydraulic crane drivers, tugmen, etc., etc., have ceased work to support these poor men. We are also calling on all the other trades of London to support us. . . . '

The dockers enjoyed widespread public sympathy, and had the guidance of leaders of the craft unions – and financial support from unionists as far away as Australia. Thus encouraged they held out for a month and won their sixpence ($2\frac{1}{2}$p) an hour – the Dockers' Tanner.

In 1897 the Amalgamated Society of Engineers struck for an eight-hour day and in protest against dilution (the employment of unskilled men). A lockout by the Employers' Federation followed. After six months the powerful engineers' union admitted defeat. When the strongest union could thus suffer defeat it is small wonder that unskilled, casual and sweated labourers were helpless. Militants had wanted the strike to continue; others said it was militancy that had brought them to their present unhappy condition.

The Labour Party and the trade unions

Towards the end of the nineteenth century some workers felt that unionism had failed to achieve social reforms. What good, they asked, had come of the wider franchise? Socialists said the ills of workers, and the slumps and booms of the trade cycle, were the inevitable accompaniments of a capitalist society.

Most of the socialist groups which began to emerge did not seek to overthrow capitalism by naked force. One formidable group, the Fabians, was set up in 1883 by Sidney Webb and his untiring wife Beatrice. Taking their name from the Roman general who by delaying

Bryant and May matchgirls on strike in 1888. These unskilled workers earned about a penny ($\frac{1}{2}$p) an hour. Many girls suffered phosphorus poisoning. They had been organised into a union by Annie Besant, then a Fabian. Their strike was successful

tactics had defeated Hannibal, the Fabians put their faith in gradualism. Capitalism, these bourgeois intellectuals said, must be eroded bit by bit, until, without any unpleasant violence, the socialist revolution had been achieved. There was inevitability, they said, in gradualism. The Fabians were great fact finders, researching with untiring enthusiasm, even, some of them, during their honeymoons. Some had contact with those in high places. At not very lavish dinner parties they cornered their contacts and made their suggestions.

Less important in the long run was the Social Democratic Federation (SDF), a Marxist group founded in 1881 by an Old Etonian, H.M. Hyndman. On Sunday 13 November 1887, the SDF, defying a police ban, held a mass meeting in Trafalgar Square. After a struggle with the police the crowd was eventually dispersed by Life Guards with their horses. So Trafalgar Square had its Bloody Sunday. Numbers of people were injured and two later died.

In 1874 two miners were elected to the House of Commons. Other workers, mostly miners, were elected

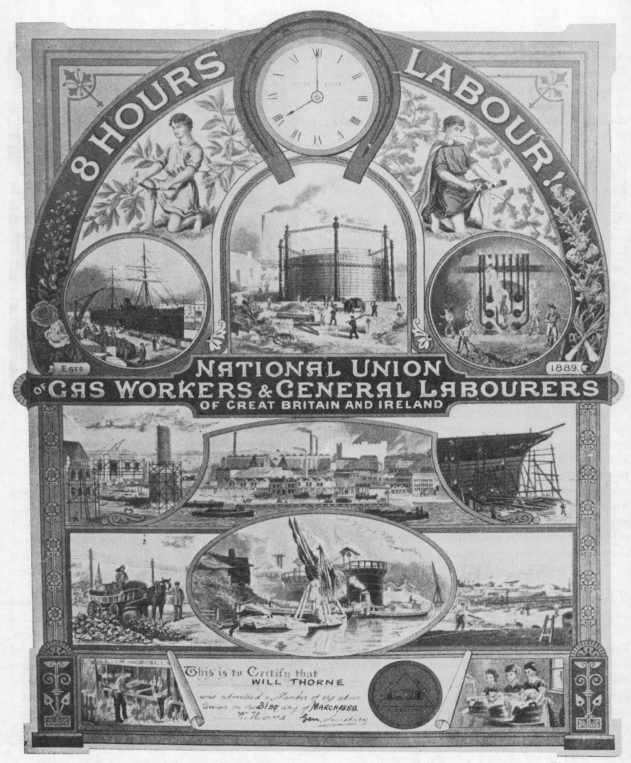

Membership certificate of Will Thorne who in 1889 organised gas and other unskilled workers in a union. Thorne was a strong supporter of the 8-hour day. In 1874 working hours had been reduced to 56 a week (10 hours a day, 6 on Saturdays)

later. These worker members, who usually voted with the Liberals, were known as Lib-Labs. In 1888 Keir Hardie, who began working in a mine when he was ten, founded the Scottish Labour Party. In 1892 Hardie was elected to the Commons – unlike other worker members he always came wearing a cloth cap, the badge of the workingman.

Regarding co-operation with the Liberals as futile Hardie in 1893 formed the Independent Labour Party (ILP). His aim was to make known the 'wants and wishes of the working classes' in parliament and for that purpose, he believed, the workers needed their own party. Trade unions were the obvious source of the financial support essential to a workers' party in days when members of parliament were unpaid. Aware that most trade unionists distrusted socialists, Hardie played down his socialist ideas in order to attract union support.

In February 1900 representatives of the Fabians, the ILP and the Social Democratic Federation, in association with the Trades Union Congress, established the Labour Representation Committee (LRC). Certain unions agreed to pay a levy to support the LRC – ten shillings (50p) per annum for every thousand members or fraction thereof. For the first time socialists and non-socialist trade unionists began working together. Though the socialists maintained the initiative the LRC continued to play down socialism for fear of frightening away moderate trade unionists.

The aim of the LRC was to build up labour representation in Parliament. Its policy was not stated beyond that; no dogma, no sacred ideology, was to clog its growth. A distinct labour group in Parliament was to co-operate with any party in legislation of direct interest to labour. That was all. Co-operation, not revolution. 'Parliament was not an enemy to be destroyed but an ally to be won.' An ILP representative, Ramsay MacDonald, the illegitimate son of a Scots farm girl, was the first secretary of the LRC. In 1903 Arthur Henderson, a foundry worker, won a by-election for the LRC against Liberal and Conservative opponents.

In 1901 the Social Democratic Federation, whose policy was near Marxist, withdrew from the LRC. The SDF's doctrinaire socialism, which did not appeal to most British workers, led to its future insignificance. In 1911 the Social Democratic Party (the former Social Democratic Federation) allied with militant ILP branches to form the British Socialist Party which in 1920 became the Communist Party of Great Britain.

In 1906 the LRC changed its name to the Labour Party. In elections earlier that year it had run 51

candidates, of whom 29 were elected. In addition to these official Labour representatives there were 24 Lib-Labs or nominees of unions not yet affiliated to the LRC. It is perhaps significant that most of the Labour members chose to appear in the Commons in respectable top hats – polished, as was the custom, by an application of stout.

England now had a tripartite party system – the Conservative and Unionist Party, the Liberals and Labour. (Since 1886 the Liberal Unionists, those Liberals who had left their party when Gladstone introduced his first home rule bill (see p. 60), had associated themselves with the Conservatives. The Conservatives and the Liberal Unionists later formed the Conservative and Unionist Party.)

In 1901, a decision of the law lords in a case between the Taff Vale Railway Company and the Amalgamated Society of Railway Servants, made it possible for a company to claim damages from union funds for losses suffered during a strike of its employees. Within a year of this threat to union funds membership of the LRC advanced from 356,000 to 861,000 – and in 1906 the LRC had its 29 members in Parliament. The Liberals in 1906 introduced a complex bill which offered partial protection to union funds. Labour then introduced their own bill protecting unions from all claims for damages. The government yielded, accepting the Labour bill as their own measure. Before the end of the year this Trade Disputes Act became law.

The 'People's Party' had arrived. No longer was it true that:

> Every boy and every gal
> That's born into this world alive
> Is either a little Lib-er-al
> Or else a little Conserv-a-tive.

Direct action

In the decade before the First World War restrictive practices were reducing the productivity of labour in Britain. Exports showed only limited growth. Meanwhile in western Europe and the USA industry, protected after the 1880s by tariffs, forged ahead. By 1900 Germany and the USA together produced more than three times as much steel as Britain. British cottons were being squeezed out of European and American markets. The export of machinery from Britain threatened to destroy her markets by enabling other states to manufacture their own goods. Nevertheless British workers remained substantially better off than their fellows in Germany and elsewhere on the continent.

In the pre-war years there were widespread strikes throughout industrialised western Europe. These strikes were connected with revolutionary syndicalism (see p. 76), which was based on the theory of a Frenchman, Georges Sorel. His *Reflections on Violence* (1908) argued that the future of democracy lay with the syndicats (the trade unions), not with parliaments. He urged that only 'direct action' could make the voices of unionists heard. He said that the class struggle must be carried forward by sabotage, by strikes, and ultimately by the general strike which would paralyse society. In Britain revolutionary syndicalism as such won little support, except on the South Wales coalfields.

Though in Britain there was a swing from parliamentary action towards direct (strike) action this was the product of circumstances rather than of theory. In 1906 W.V. Osborne, a union secretary, protested at the payment of a political levy out of union funds. In 1909 the law lords decided in favour of Osborne. So it became illegal to collect a political levy. This meant that the Labour Party could no longer rely on funds from the unions to pay Labour representatives elected to Parliament. This seemed to diminish the likelihood of Labour ever winning power. And though unemployment, which averaged 6 per cent between 1901–10, fell in 1912 to 2.3 per cent, real wages, after climbing steadily during the Victorian era, were almost stationary. Wage increases were only just keeping level with price increases.

In November 1910 there was serious rioting at the Tonypandy coalfields in South Wales. In August 1911, during riots by Liverpool dockers, two men were killed when troops opened fire. Four days later two men were killed by troops at Llanelly in Wales. A widespread strike of railwaymen ended when David Lloyd George, Liberal chancellor of the exchequer, assisted by Ramsay MacDonald, appealed to the employers to set up conciliation boards. This strike coincided with the tension following the Agadir crisis (see p. 33) and it was by appealing to their patriotism that Lloyd George won over the employers. In March 1912 over a million men took part in a national coal strike; the dispute was settled by an act setting up machinery to fix minimum wages.

The strikes of 1910–12 were accompanied by much bitterness. Ben Tillett, reporting to his union on the events of 1912, said: 'The lesson is that in future strikes the striker must ... protest against shooting, with shooting. ... The other lesson is that Parliament is a farce and a sham.... Capitalism is capitalism as a tiger is a tiger; and both are savage and pitiless towards the weak.'

By 1914 more than four million workers belonged to unions affiliated to the Trades Union Congress. Of these, the miners, the railwaymen and the transport workers (including the dockers) were the most militant. In 1914 they formed the Triple Industrial Alliance.

Meanwhile two important issues arising from the Osborne judgement had been settled. In 1911 a financial resolution in the Commons provided for members to receive a salary of £400 a year. And in 1913 a Trade Union Act allowed unions to raise a political fund provided the members had given their approval by ballot. The Labour Party thus acquired a guaranteed, regular and fairly substantial revenue, especially as union membership went on increasing. However, a union member could, if he chose, contract out of paying the political levy.

Women

Women's status and education advanced during the decades before the First World War. Florence Nightingale had shown what women can do in a public capacity. In the 1850s Frances Mary Buss and Dorothea Beale established schools for girls that were comparable with the best then provided for boys. With the spread of such schools it was natural that university education for women should follow. By 1871 there were women's colleges at the University of London, and Girton and Newnham had been founded at Cambridge. In 1882 single 'qualified' women (ratepayers) were permitted to vote for town councils, and in 1888 for the county councils then set up (see p. 55). The 1894 Local Government Act permitted qualified women, married or unmarried, to vote for and to be elected to the parish, urban and rural district councils then established. In 1907 women were permitted to sit on borough and county councils.

A National Union of Women's Suffrage Societies was formed in 1897; its members, the suffragists, were not very forceful. In 1903 Mrs Emmeline Pankhurst, strongly influenced by her two daughters, formed a body that proved more determined – the Women's Social and Political Union. From 1906 to 1914 members of this union, the suffragettes, who came mainly from the

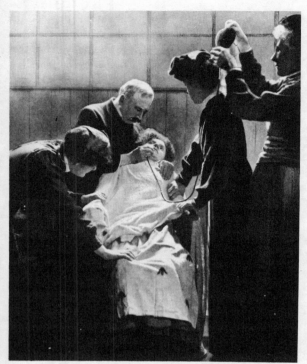

Forcible feeding through the nose of a suffragette prisoner,
1904. Note the broad arrows on her prison clothing.
(Illustrated London News, 1904)

middle classes, disturbed the peace. In 1913 Emily Davison threw herself under the king's horse during the running of the Derby, in protest at the refusal of the prime minister, Herbert Asquith, to grant the vote to women. Six thousand suffragettes paraded at her funeral. A less tragic figure was Miss Maloney, whose delight it was to pursue Winston Churchill with a muffin bell – with whose clanging she drowned his speeches. Suffragettes set out in their cars with cans of petrol and set fire to buildings in the country. Violence led to imprisonment and hunger strikes and forced feeding. In 1913 the 'Cat and Mouse Act' allowed a woman to be released from prison when hunger had made her ill; when she recovered she returned to complete her sentence. When war came in 1914 the patriotism of the militant women proved greater than their passion for the vote. With other women they played their part well, some in munitions factories, some on farms.

Reform of the House of Lords

Over the years much Liberal legislation had been frustrated by the House of Lords. In 1884, when Gladstone's Reform Act had been strongly opposed in the Lords, there was a cry of 'Mend them or end them'. In the 1890s the upper house thwarted the Grand Old Man over Irish home rule (see p. 60). In 1894 several important bills of his fourth ministry were frustrated. In six years of Conservative rule not one bill was touched.

In 1906 the Liberals had a big majority in the Commons. Yet the Lords repeatedly blocked government legislation and Arthur Balfour, Conservative leader in the Commons, approved their tactics. One after another, the Lords threw out a plural voting bill, two education bills and licensing bills. They were, said Lloyd George, 'Mr Balfour's poodle, not the watchdog of the constitution'. One would not, he said, choose a spaniel as the House of Lords was chosen – the sole qualification for membership of that body was to prove that one was 'the first of the litter'.

In 1909, Lloyd George presented his People's Budget (see p. 57). By long established convention the Lords did not interfere with financial measures. However, the Lords in November 1909 rejected the budget. Liberals attacked the House of Lords bitterly and newspapers whipped up feeling, some on one side, some on the other. Parliament was dissolved. Following the elections held in January 1910, the Liberals returned to office, but were now dependent on the support of Labour and Irish Nationalist votes (see p. 61). The People's Budget was presented again and duly passed by both houses. But the question of the Lords' powers remained unsettled.

Edward VII had agreed that if necessary enough new peers would be created to ensure the passage of a bill for reducing the powers of the House of Lords – but only if a further election showed support for such a policy. In May 1910 King Edward died. George V, who succeeded him, was also unwilling to create peers until another election had been held. In November the prime minister, Asquith, called a general election. The Liberals were returned to office (December 1910) but were still dependent on Labour and Irish Nationalist support. In May 1911 a parliament bill was passed in the Commons and was presented to the Lords. Thereupon 'the old men' 'came out of their holes' to voice their opposition. Meanwhile a list of proposed new peers, which included a number of Labour members of parliament, had been prepared and plans were made to extend the seating in the House of Lords. However, despite the fierce opposition of diehards, in August 1911 the parliament bill passed the Lords and became law. The Parliament Act provided that any money bill should become law a month after going to the Lords. The speaker of the House of Commons was authorised to rule whether a bill was a 'money bill'. All other bills passed by the Commons in three successive sessions were to become law, even if rejected by the Lords, provided two years had elapsed between the first and third passages of the bill. The maximum length of a parliament was cut from seven to five years.

Civil service, army and other reforms

The number of civil servants increased considerably from the late nineteenth century; by 1914 it was five times as large as it had been a generation before. This was inevitable with the abandonment of a *laissez-faire* policy (see p. 46) and the entry of the state into such fields as education and social insurance.

Until 1870 the higher ranks of the civil service were filled by a system of patronage or sponsorship. But sponsorship fades easily into nepotism which in addition to being 'unfair' does not always secure the greatest brains. In 1870, during Gladstone's first ministry, the administrative branch of the civil service was thrown open to all university men and a competitive examination became the basis of selection. This system, practised for centuries past in China, had been adopted in the Indian civil service in 1853.

In 1870, Edward Cardwell, Gladstone's secretary of state for war, amid bitter opposition, ended the purchase of officers' commissions in the army. Abolition of the purchase system – like the institution of examinations for entry to the civil service – was seen by some people as an attack on 'property' rights. It was in fact an attack on privilege and inefficiency. Long-term enlistment of soldiers was replaced by six years' service, followed by six years in the reserve. Cardwell also introduced the linked battalion system, whereby one battalion of an infantry regiment remained at its depot while the other served abroad. More modern equipment, breech-loading rifles for example, was provided. Flogging was abolished, first in peace time and later on active service. Cardwell's reforms did not extend to the artillery, or to the cavalry, the most conservative section of the army. Reforms by R.B. Haldane, a later Liberal secretary of state for war, included the establishment of a general staff in 1906, the building up of the territorial army, the founding of the officers training corps and arrangements for an expeditionary force.

Gladstone's first ministry saw the overhauling of the legal system. With the establishment in 1873 of the Supreme Court of Judicature, the separation of common law and equity ended. When equity (the body of law that had grown up in chancery outside the common law courts) and common law were in conflict the gentler rule of equity was to prevail.

The position of the dons, in their sheltered university precincts, also came under review. With the repeal of religious tests in 1871 fellowships at the university colleges were no longer reserved to members of the Anglican Church. Dissenters had been admitted to Oxford and Cambridge as undergraduates in the 1850s but could not proceed to a master's degree until 1871. In 1877 the rich endowments of the colleges came under supervision. More modern curricula were one result of government intervention.

The reform of local government

Local government in 1870 was 'chaotic, rudimentary and corrupt'. Sanitary and similar services were inefficient and insufficient. Following the report of a sanitary commission appointed by Disraeli, the local government board was set up in 1871. This board, which developed into the ministry of health (see p. 139), controlled locally appointed boards responsible for sanitation and health. The new boards were tied in with the boards of guardians who administered the poor law. In 1875 Disraeli's government was responsible for a Public Health Act to be administered by the local government board. In the same year an Artisans' Dwellings Act authorised local boards to conduct slum clearance schemes and there were several further such acts in the next ten years. The boards also administered the Sale of Food and Drugs Act of 1875. The local government board remained, however, singularly inactive; the country suffered in consequence – for instance there was a disastrous unconcern for town planning.

In the municipalities democratic pressures resulted in outstanding achievement. The classic example is Birmingham but Liverpool and Manchester and the cities of the north were not far behind, and in some cases ahead – Liverpool appointed a health officer nearly thirty years before Birmingham. In Birmingham it was Joseph Chamberlain, 'Radical Joe', who as lord mayor from 1873–76 'parked, paved, assized, marketed, Gas-and-Watered, and improved' the city. Later the influence of the Fabians did much the same for London.

In numerous cities the municipal authorities raised loans to provide water, gas, trams and electricity. It is hard today to realise how much such amenities meant to an earlier generation. This 'gas and water socialism' was essentially a local not a national achievement.

The County Councils Act of 1888 provided for county councils to be elected by ratepayers. These councils were to take over some of the functions of the justices of the peace and certain other authorities. Sixty-one of the larger towns became county boroughs. London (excluding the City) became a county and the London County Council was constituted. The new councils were in particular responsible for roads and bridges, and in certain cases for the police. In 1894 a Local Government Act provided for the election by ratepayers of parish councils. The same act replaced the local boards set up in 1871 by elected urban district councils and rural district councils. In 1899 twenty-eight metropolitan borough councils were set up under the London County Council to look after roads, sanitation and health.

By the end of the nineteenth century England had a system of local government capable of putting national policies into detailed operation. Better roads, cleaner and well lit, better sanitation, markets where weights and the quality of goods sold were supervised, parks, free libraries and museums began to make life more tolerable for at least some people.

State intervention

Education

The industrial revolution created a new mass society living in huge urban units. The Manchester or Birmingham way of life, once the exception, became increasingly the norm. By 1870 the most naked horrors that accompanied this revolution were a thing of the past. Gradually the unrestricted 'freedom' of a *laissez-faire* policy was being abandoned. The belief that the government should intervene by cutting down the rights of some to secure rights for the community at large was gaining support. With the acceptance of this 'philosophy of intervention' the government moved from negative prohibitions to positive action, from legislation forbidding an employer to work children in a mine to legislation providing for schools. 'You should govern', says a Chinese proverb, 'as you would cook a small fish, gently, hardly touching it.' The stage comes when such a

policy becomes unworkable. England was not a small fish; it was a pot of stew, needing constant stirring.

Until 1870 the government's contribution to education was limited to making grants to Anglican and Nonconformist schools. The Education Act of 1870 established school boards that were to set up elementary schools for children aged from five to twelve. The board schools were maintained by a local rate, supplemented by a grant from the central authority. Each board could decide whether there was to be religious instruction at its schools; however, denominational instruction, propaganda for church or chapel, was forbidden. The existing church schools were absorbed into the system.

The initial task of the new schools – well named 'elementary' – was enormous: to provide three million children with the elements of the 'three Rs', to make a largely illiterate population literate. By 1880 there were sufficient buildings and teachers to make school attendance compulsory. In 1891 elementary education became free. In 1889 county and county borough councils became responsible for technical education and were provided with substantial funds. In 1899 a board of education took over the duties of the department of education (responsible for the boards that provided elementary and higher grade elementary schools) and the department of science and art (responsible for the councils that provided technical schools).

In 1884 Victoria University, in 1893 the University of Wales, and in 1900 Birmingham University were founded.

The 1902 Education Act, which was largely the work of Robert Morant, secretary to the board of education, abolished the school boards set up in 1870. Primary and secondary as well as technical education were placed under the county and county borough councils. Voluntary (mostly Anglican) schools, which then provided education for three million children, also became subject to the councils; in return for providing their own buildings they controlled their own staff appointments. Their current expenses were to be paid for out of the rates. Nonconformists, especially in Wales, bitterly opposed Anglican schools 'taking' the ratepayers' money and many people refused to pay the proportion of their rates that went to education.

The Morant Act resulted in considerable progress in education. There was a levelling up of quality in primary schools. Teachers' salaries improved. Classes were reduced in size. By 1914 there were 200,000 children in secondary schools, many of them with free places.

Victoria University subdivided to form the

British ministries, 1870–1918

Ministry formed	Prime minister	Major acts
December 1868	W.E. Gladstone Liberal	1870: Education Act; competitive examinations for civil service; Irish Land Act. 1871: Cardwell's army reforms; Bank Holiday Act; Trade Union Act (protection for union funds); Criminal Law Amendment Act (picketing illegal); repeal of religious tests; Local government board set up. 1872: Ballot Act. 1873: Judicature Act.
February 1874	B. Disraeli Conservative	1875: Conspiracy and Protection of Property Act (peaceful picketing legalised); Public Health Act; Sale of Food and Drugs Act; Artisans Dwellings Act. 1876: Plimsoll Act (against overloading of merchant ships).
April 1880	W.E. Gladstone Liberal	1880: Compulsory school attendance. 1881: Irish Land Act. 1882: Municipal Corporations Act; Irish Coercion Act. 1883: Corrupt Practices Act. 1884: Third Reform Act. 1885: Redistribution Act; Irish Arrears Act.
June 1885	Marquis of Salisbury Conservative	Loans for Irish tenants.
February 1886	W.E. Gladstone Liberal	First Irish home rule bill.
August 1886	Marquis of Salisbury Conservative	1887: Crimes Act (Ireland); Land Purchase Act for Irish tenants. 1888: County Councils Act. 1891: free elementary education.
August 1892	W.E. Gladstone Liberal	1893: Second Irish home rule bill.
March 1894	Earl of Rosebery Liberal	1894: Local Government Act.
June 1895	Marquis of Salisbury Conservative	1896: Irish Land Purchase Act. 1897: Workmen's Compensation Act. 1899: Board of Education Act.
July 1902	A.J. Balfour Conservative	1902: Education Act. 1903: Irish Land Purchase Act.
December 1905	Sir Henry Campbell-Bannerman Liberal	1906: Trade Disputes Act (protection of union funds); school meals; Workmen's Compensation Act; Merchant Shipping Act; Haldane's army reforms. 1907: school medical inspection; probation system.
April 1908	H.H. Asquith Liberal	1908: Pensions (old age) Act. 1909: Labour exchanges; Trade Boards Act (minimum wages in certain trades); People's Budget. 1911: Parliament Act; National Insurance Act (health and unemployment); payment of members of parliament. 1912: Shop Act. 1913: Trade Union Act (political levy legalised); Cat and Mouse Act. 1914: Irish Home Rule Act, Defence of the Realm Act.
May 1915	H.H. Asquith Coalition	1915: MacKenna duties; Ministry of Defence set up. 1916: conscription.
December 1916 (to December 1918 Coupon election)	D. Lloyd George Coalition	1917: Departments of Shipping, Labour, Food, National Service, Food Production set up. 1918: Ministry of Information set up; Representation of the People Act; compulsory education to age of 14.

universities of Manchester, Liverpool and Leeds. Sheffield and Bristol universities followed in 1905 and 1909. In addition there were six university colleges in different parts of the country by 1914. In 1899 Ruskin Hall was established at Oxford for workingmen. In 1904 the Workers' Educational Association (WEA) was founded.

Social legislation

In 1903 Joseph Chamberlain, colonial secretary, suggested a system of imperial tariff preference which would create a great British economic unit dominating world trade. 'Tariff reform means work for all', said Chamberlain. But the Liberal argument of 'the big loaf' (cheap bread under free trade) and 'the little loaf' (expensive bread under protection) remained more popular, as was proved in the elections of 1906. A long period of Conservative rule had ended.

When the Liberals 'floated into parliament on the river of free trade', under the leadership of Henry Campbell-Bannerman, a new period of reforming activity began. The driving force behind this was Lloyd George, who as a child had known poverty.

In 1906 a Workmen's Compensation Act improved on a Conservative act of 1897 by extending protection to more workers and by covering certain industrial diseases as well as accidents. In the same year (see p. 51) the Trade Disputes Act gave full protection to union funds against claims for damages. A Merchant Shipping Act extended the protection given by Samuel Plimsoll's 1876 act against the overloading of ships. In 1906, at the initiative of Labour members, an act provided for meals for needy schoolchildren. In 1907 an act introduced medical inspection for schoolchildren and the Probation of Offenders Act established the probation system. The next year the Borstal system was introduced and the imprisonment of children under fourteen was forbidden. A licensing bill to deal with the 'monstrous evil of intemperance' by cutting down the number of public houses was rejected by the Lords.

In 1907 Churchill, who had left the Conservatives because he disagreed with protectionism, wrote: 'Minimum standards of wages and comfort, insurance in some effective form or another against sickness, unemployment and old age – these are the questions, and the only questions, by which parties are going to live in the future.' In 1909, as president of the board of trade, he set up labour exchanges. He was assisted by William Beveridge, a Fabian whom he had met at one of Beatrice Webb's dinners. By no means all Labour men or all unionists approved the scheme. However, Churchill and Lloyd George were intent upon providing a state system of unemployment insurance, and without the help of the labour exchanges, which kept records of the unemployed, this would not have been practicable.

Women and children working in such sweated industries as tailoring had no union to fight for them. Some London seamstresses made a penny (less than $\frac{1}{2}$p) an hour for stitching away in garrets at clothes for ladies of fashion. Two exhibitions of sweated labour arranged by the *Daily News*, a Liberal paper, shocked many people. In 1909, at Churchill's instigation, a Trade Boards Act set up boards to fix minimum wages in the tailoring, lacemaking and other specified trades. The Shop Act of 1912 made one half-day holiday a week compulsory and obliged employers to provide certain facilities for shop assistants. However, their condition remained unenviable until a further Shop Act was passed in 1928.

The beginning of the welfare state

In 1908 Campbell-Bannerman died and Asquith became prime minister. The great achievement of the Liberals under Asquith was the initiation of the welfare state.

After 1834 the aged, the unemployed and the destitute – all classed as 'paupers' – could get relief only in the workhouses which were paid for out of rates. The system was harsh and extremely unpopular – to go to the workhouse was the ultimate indignity.

The first step away from the workhouse system was the introduction in 1908 of pensions for men and women at the age of seventy. A couple with a yearly income of under £39 received 7s. 6d. (37$\frac{1}{2}$p) weekly. A single person with an income of under £26 yearly received 5s. (25p). When bread cost about 1$\frac{1}{2}$p per kilogram, 5 Edwardian shillings, though not a generous pension, was quite a useful sum. The scheme, introduced by Lloyd George, chancellor of the exchequer, was non-contributory. The fear of the workhouse, so hated by old people who had been self-supporting, receded.

Lloyd George was determined to build a 'parapet' against the hazards of unemployment and sickness. With increased expenditure on the services, as the naval race with Germany grew fiercer (see p. 89), there were no funds available for welfare projects. So in 1909 Lloyd George presented his People's Budget, his War on Poverty Budget. Thereupon there was an uproar in the Commons as well as in the Lords (see p. 53). Death duties (imposed on all classes of property in 1894) were to go up, income tax to go up, alcohol and tobacco to cost more – and a new land value (capital gains) duty! When in 1910 the People's Budget was passed by the Lords funds were made available for health and unemployment insurance schemes.

The National Insurance Act of 1911 made health insurance compulsory for manual workers, but anyone earning under £160 a year could join. The scheme gave free medical treatment and 10s. (50p) a week for a maximum of six months. Unemployment insurance was restricted to some two and a quarter million people, mainly in the engineering and building trades. Employers, employees and the state contributed to both health and unemployment insurance. Various unions, friendly societies and insurance companies that had provided cover against sickness and unemployment were absorbed into the state scheme.

No other state had as yet introduced unemployment benefits. Many people enjoyed a security they had never known before. Yet there was at first considerable opposition, not only from employers. The less moderate workers claimed that as unemployment was not the workers' fault they should not have to contribute. Many doctors at first protested against the health scheme. The first payments under the National Insurance Act were made in 1913. Such was the welfare state in embryo.

The Irish problem

For much of the period 1870 to 1914 'politics were Ireland' at Westminster. Conquered and colonised by the British, the Irish had endured much. There were bitter memories of rebellions and massacres on both sides. By the Act of Union the United Kingdom of Great Britain and Ireland came into being in 1801. Thereafter the Irish were represented at Westminster, losing their Dublin parliament and such independence as their British rulers had allowed them. The Irish problem became more acute as national spirit became more demanding. Whereas many Irish people in the earlier years of the nineteenth century wanted only a degree of fair play, later in the century some were convinced home rulers. Some were determined to end all connection with Britain.

After the famine caused by the potato blight in 1846–48 Ireland's population had dropped from over eight million to six and a half million. Nearly a million people had died. The rest had emigrated, most of them to America – the New World, many to England. In their new homes rancid memories stirred them to support, financially and by word, nationalists left behind in Ireland.

The Fenians, a militant Irish group set up in the USA, also worked among Irish immigrants in England. In London in December 1867 a barrel of gunpowder was blown up against the wall of Clerkenwell prison during an attempt to rescue two Fenians. The Fenians did not gain a real hold over the Irish. They did, however, bring the Irish problem into the open in England and by so doing may have convinced Gladstone of its acuteness.

'My mission', said Gladstone before he took office as prime minister in 1868, 'is to pacify Ireland.' Resolutely he waded into the morass of Irish politics. In 1869 the Anglican Church of Ireland, to the satisfaction of its many Catholic tithepayers, was disestablished. Gladstone then tackled land reform. The condition of tenants, worst on the estates of absentee owners where harsh stewards held sway, was unsatisfactory almost everywhere. Eviction of tenants was an everyday occurrence; worse still, tenants who had spent money on improvements received no compensation if they were evicted. By the Land Act of 1870 an evicted tenant was to be paid for his improvements and was also to receive compensation for eviction – even for non-payment of rent, provided the rent had been exorbitant. However, this did not satisfy the Irish, who wanted fixity of tenure and a 'fair' rent. In the 1870s falling prices for agricultural products made the situation of Irish tenants almost intolerable.

Gladstone's concessions seemed to encourage nationalist demands. In 1870 in Dublin Isaac Butt founded a home rule movement. This movement, unlike that of the Fenians, was parliamentary. Irish tenants had been subject to much pressure from landlords at elections, but the Ballot Act of 1872 (see p. 48) left them free to cast their votes as they wished. The result was a strengthening of an Irish Home Rule Party at Westminster.

In 1875 Charles Stewart Parnell, a dynamic nationalist, more militant than Butt, entered the House of Commons. In 1878 he became leader of the Irish Party. Business at Westminster was hampered by Parnell's tactics. Interference and interruptions by Irish members forced the Commons into all-night sittings in an attempt to get its business done.

Harvests were poor in 1879. That year an ex-Fenian leader, Michael Davitt, formed the Irish National Land

Eviction of an Irish tenant farmer in Kilrush, County Clare, in 1888. With the passing of the Land Acts the position improved

League, which planned to take direct action against evictions and exacting landlords. In 1880 many tenants were unable to pay their rent and there were over 10,000 evictions. Land League members began burning hayricks and mansions, assaulting landlords and stewards, stealing and maiming cattle. Captain Boycott, agent for a landowner who had taken over from an evicted tenant, gave a new word to the language; he was to be treated, said Parnell, 'as if he were a leper of old'. He was. Eventually volunteer Protestants from Ulster, escorted by troops and policemen, had to help Boycott with his harvesting. Funds came in to help the Land League from Australia and from the USA.

Gladstone in his second ministry struggled on trying to solve the Irish problem. On the one hand the British tried to coerce Ireland into obedience. The Habeas Corpus Act and normal legal processes were suspended. On the other hand in 1881 another Land Act gave Irish tenant farmers the Three Fs – fixed tenure, fair rent (to be fixed by rent tribunals) and free sale. These concessions put fresh spirit into the home rulers – especially as they seemed to have been made in response to the violence of the Land League. Nor were the concessions altogether successful; rent tribunals' idea of a fair rent was very different from that of tenants.

As Parnell continued to urge agitation, he was arrested and imprisoned in Kilmainham gaol where he was allowed various privileges. His imprisonment not only made him a martyr. It also gave him the opportunity of disassociating himself from the embarrassing tactics of the Land League, whom he could not afford to antagonise while he was at liberty.

An obstacle to a solution of the land problem was the fact that 100,000 farmers owed arrears of rent. Until arrears were paid a farmer remained liable to eviction under the old law. At the initiative of Joseph Chamberlain, then a Liberal, a secret agreement, the so-called Kilmainham 'treaty', was made with Parnell in May 1882. He and two companions were released from prison. In return for a bill assisting farmers to meet their liabilities Parnell promised to urge the Irish to co-operate. A few days later Lord Frederick Cavendish, newly appointed to the cabinet as chief secretary for Ireland, and the under-secretary were hacked to death with surgical knives in Phoenix Park in Dublin. The murders, which Parnell strongly condemned, were the work of the Invincibles, a revolutionary secret society. More murders followed and a Coercion Act giving the police wide powers of arrest and suspending trial by jury was passed.

With the entry of Joseph Chamberlain into the House of Commons (1876), the Liberal Party acquired its bothersome radical wing, whilst the Conservatives had their activist group, the Tory Democrats, led until 1886 by Lord Randolph Churchill. With his sizeable Irish Party, Parnell was able to take advantage of the divisions that at times threatened to split both the Liberal and Conservative parties. Thus harassed, the Conservatives, during Salisbury's first brief administration, partly fulfilled the Kilmainham agreement by passing an Arrears Act (1885). This gave Irish tenants some help with their debts and a period of relative calm followed. Coercion was discontinued and a scheme for the state-assisted purchase of land was introduced.

At elections held in November 1885 Parnell's agents directed all Irish voters in England to support the Conservatives. The Liberals won eighty-six more seats than the Conservatives. There were also eighty-six Irish home rule members. As these Irish members were expected to support the Conservatives Lord Salisbury remained in office as prime minster.

Then came the surprising news that Gladstone had become a home ruler. In January 1886 the Irish members joined with the Liberals to defeat the Conservatives in a matter of little importance. Salisbury resigned and Gladstone became prime minister. In April 1886 he introduced a bill for Irish home rule but was opposed both by the Conservatives and by many of his own party. His 'right wing' left him whilst he failed to convert Chamberlain and his radical followers to home rule. Thus, despite the votes of the Irish Party, the first home rule bill was defeated in the Commons. The Liberal Unionists, the Liberals who for one reason or another had opposed the home rule bill, left the party. Parliament was dissolved. In the elections that followed the Conservatives came to power, with the Liberal Unionists supporting them.

There was renewed turmoil in Ireland. Firmly opposed to home rule, Salisbury's government set out to sweeten firmness with economic concessions. Said Salisbury: 'What Ireland wants is government – government that does not flinch, that does not vary.' His nephew, Arthur Balfour, who became chief secretary for Ireland in 1887, said: 'I shall be as relentless as Cromwell in enforcing obedience to the law, but, at the same time, I shall be as radical as any reformer in redressing grievances.' A new and drastic Crimes Act was balanced by a law giving useful concessions to Irish tenants (1887).

For some years Parnell had been living with Mrs Katherine O'Shea, the wife of an Irish Liberal member of parliament. The affair became public when in 1890 O'Shea won a divorce suit on the ground of his wife's adultery with Parnell. Such an affair was then regarded as disgraceful. It was made clear that Gladstone would not co-operate with the Irish Party while Parnell remained its leader. The Irish clergy, who had supported Parnell, though he was not a Catholic, had to withdraw their assistance. Feuds between Parnellites and anti-Parnellites split the Irish Party. In 1891 Parnell died. Feuding continued until 1900 when John Redmond became leader of the Irish Party.

The Liberals returned to power and Gladstone to office in 1892. In 1893 the Grand Old Man introduced a second home rule bill. This bill was passed by the Commons but was defeated by a huge majority in the House of Lords. In 1894 the prime minister, aged eighty-four, resigned. Lord Rosebery succeeded him.

Neither of Gladstone's home rule bills attempted to deal with the problem of Ulster, large parts of which were Protestant. Yet Protestant Ulstermen were already drilling to resist home rule when Gladstone introduced his first bill. In 1886 Randolph Churchill, at a meeting in Belfast, warned that if the Protestant Loyalists of Ireland were to be handed over to 'their hereditary and most bitter foes ... Ulster at the proper moment will resort to the supreme arbitrament of force; Ulster will fight, Ulster will be right. ...'

In 1895 the Conservatives under Salisbury returned to power and tried to win Ireland over by renewed doses of sweetness – 'killing home rule with kindness'. Effective Land Purchase Acts passed in 1896 and 1903 enabled Irish farmers to buy their land with government help. In place of the great landowners in their mansions a body of yeomen farmers was built up.

Meanwhile, extremists who went beyond the home rule aims of Redmond were at work. In 1905 Arthur Griffith established a new party, Sinn Fein (We Ourselves), which demanded independence and a republic for Ireland.

> And we'll have little children,
> And rear them neat and clean,
> They'll shout 'Up the Republic' and talk about
>   Sinn Fein,
> To emulate their old fellas
> Who England's laws defied,
> And to turn their guns against the Saxon Huns
> Down by the Liffey side.

The revival of the Irish language and the works of such poets and playwrights as W.B. Yeats and J.M. Synge fostered nationalist feeling.

In 1910 the Liberals, wanting the support of the Irish Party to ensure the passage of their parliament bill (see p. 53), promised to take up the cause of home rule again. In 1912 the third home rule bill was introduced. By this Ireland, including Ulster, was to control its domestic affairs. A two-house parliament was to sit in Dublin and forty-two Irish members were to sit at Westminster. The upper house exercised its power to delay the home rule bill, but in May 1914, when it was passed for a third time by the Commons, further opposition by the Lords was impossible.

For some Irish people the concession was too little and came too late, whilst to most Protestants in Ulster an end to their union with Britain and 'rule' by Dublin was totally unacceptable. In 1912 some half a million anti-Catholic Orangemen, under the leadership of Sir Edward Carson, signed a Solemn League and Covenant:

'We ... men of Ulster ... do hereby pledge ourselves in solemn covenant throughout this our time of threatened calamity to stand by one another ... in using all means which may be found necessary to defeat the present conspiracy to set up a home rule parliament in Ireland. ...'

Some signed the covenant in their own blood. A hundred thousand men (the Ulster Volunteer Force) offered themselves for service. The next year, taking their cue from Ulster, another army, the Irish Nationalist Volunteers, began drilling around Dublin.

In March 1914 there occurred the so-called Curragh mutiny. Officers at the Curragh barracks outside Dublin declared themselves unwilling to take up arms against Ulster should they be ordered to do so. When the prime minister, insisting that politics could never be the province of the army, told the officers that they would obey any order given, the 'mutiny' petered out. The next month arms for the Ulster Volunteer Force were successfully landed in Ulster.

With Ireland on the verge of civil war, and with the home rule bill due to receive the royal assent in September, the government redoubled its efforts to arrive at a compromise over Ulster. In July 1914 King George V tried to mediate in the deadlock but a conference at Buckingham Palace achieved nothing. No agreement could be reached as to whether any part of Ulster should be excluded from the authority of the proposed new Irish parliament.

Two days after the Buckingham Palace conference ended and barely a week before the outbreak of the First World War the Irish Nationalist Volunteers attempted to land arms near Dublin. The Volunteers got most of the arms away but soldiers who fired on a crowd throwing stones killed three civilians. This provoked great anger, especially as there had been no interference when arms had been landed by Protestants three months before in Ulster.

In September 1914, a month after the First World War broke out, the home rule bill became law. It was agreed that the act should not come into effect until the war ended. Special provision was then to be made for Ulster. Redmond expressed his loyalty to Britain. Over the years 135,000 Irishmen, both Catholics and Protestants, volunteered for service with the British – some perhaps with mixed feelings:

> Those that I fight I do not hate,
> Those that I guard I do not love;
> My country is Kiltartan Cross,
> My countrymen Kiltartan's poor,
> No likely end could bring them loss
> Or leave them happier than before.

The Irish problem, Churchill said, 'faded back into the mists'. But Ireland was to emerge from the mists in dramatic fashion during the course of the war, for a nationalist minority remained committed to a revolutionary policy.

7 The United States, 1870–1914

The constitution

In 1870 the United States of America was recovering from a civil war (1861–65) in which some 600,000 lives were lost. In 1861 the issues of slavery, tariffs, state rights and certain social and economic differences had caused eleven southern states to withdraw from the union. The war that followed was fought because the northern states were determined 'to preserve the union'.

The USA was the first country in modern times to have a written constitution setting out the powers and duties of its government and the rights of its citizens. The makers of this constitution, drawn up in 1787, were deeply suspicious of political power and its tendency to grow at the expense of individual freedom, and so devised a system of checks and balances. The power of the federal (central) government was balanced against that of the states. The federal government was responsible for foreign policy, defence, the regulation of trade, postal communications, currency and so on. The states kept all powers not specifically granted to the federal government. However, with the passage of time the balance of power has changed to the advantage of the federal government. The president, elected by the people for four years, could not be removed from office (except by impeachment). An elected Congress, which the president could not dismiss, was to make the laws and supervise his activities. As commander in chief of the armed forces the president was given unlimited power in the conduct of war; but as he could not raise taxes without the consent of Congress his power in the conduct of war was nicely balanced. Congress contained its own checks and balances. The Senate, consisting of two senators elected from each state for six years and retiring by rotation, was to represent state interests; the House of Representatives, elected every two years, was to represent more popular interests. The Senate was given wide powers to check the activities of the lower house. Finally a Supreme Court, independent of both president and Congress, had power to settle disputes concerning the constitution. The Supreme Court could thus act as a check on the activities of both the president and Congress.

After the abolition of slavery (1865) a Civil Rights Act gave all men born or naturalised in the USA (including Negroes) legal and political rights, including the right to vote. (Negroes were later discriminated against.) Women were not given the vote until 1920. In such respects American democracy was incomplete. But by 1870 the American people could boast a succession of presidents who were no more than common people elected by common people.

Throughout its history the two party system has operated in the USA. The two present day parties, the Democrats and the Republicans, have in general represented less divergent policies than, for example, the British Conservative and Labour parties. To a great extent they have been associated with different regions within the United States.

Political parties have had exceptional influence in that large numbers of officials – even judges – are elected and so subject to party control. The practice of electing officials was based on the democratic belief that any citizen should be capable of performing the various functions of government. Under the spoils system, which no longer prevails, large numbers of non-elective government jobs, even of a very humble nature, changed hands whenever there was a change of party in power.

Imperialism

Expansion coast to coast

In 1783 the United States consisted of thirteen states strung out along the Atlantic coast and certain territories extending as far west as the Mississippi. By 1870 there were thirty-seven states including California and Oregon on the Pacific coast and vast territories which included Alaska, bought from Russia for 7 million dollars in 1867.

American expansion towards the Pacific (see map opposite) was assisted by the fact that the territories occupied were geographically continuous with the original thirteen states. Russia had a similar advantage in her expansion across Asia. As with Russia, American expansion was helped by the relative emptiness of the territories overrun. Where there were only half-civilised

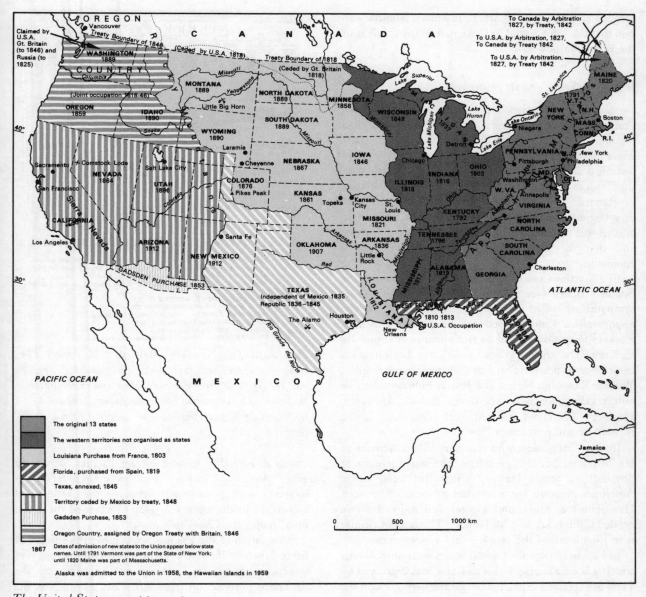

The United States: coast to coast

nomadic tribes opposition to the onward march could at most be sporadic. However, as with Russia, there were in certain areas existing governments. With these the Americans dealt according to their relative strength and the prevailing circumstances.

The advance across the North American continent was openly imperialist. The Americans excused themselves with the doctrine of 'manifest destiny' – the occupation of the continent from the Atlantic to the Pacific it was held was the 'undoubted destiny of the American people'. Manifest destiny was complemented by the exclusion of European states from the Americas. In 1823 President Monroe declared that North and South America were 'not to be considered as subjects for future colonisation by any European powers' and that any intervention by European states would be regarded as 'unfriendly'. This exclusive attitude, usually referred to as the Monroe Doctrine, has remained a basic principle of American policy. In general the European powers have abided by the Monroe Doctrine and have avoided entanglement in American affairs. Monroe also said that the USA would not take part in the conflicts of the European powers.

War with Spain and its consequences

In the era of European imperialism, when the United States had recovered from the Civil War and had digested the territories fairly recently acquired, there was a new phase of expansion and a fresh declaration of 'manifest destiny'. In 1890, the year the last battle with the American Indians was fought, Captain A.T. Mahan proclaimed: 'Whether they will or no, Americans must now begin to look outward.' Mahan, a naval historian, argued that command of the seas was the key to fortune and that the United States must acquire such a command.

In 1895 the Cubans began a rebellion against their Spanish rulers (see map p. 65). Americans, while sympathising with the Cubans, were aware of the opportunities Cuba offered for investment and as a market. They coveted Cuba's rich sugar plantations. By this time the cheap 'yellow press' was beginning to exercise great power. Through their newspaper empires William Randolph Hearst and Joseph Pulitzer raised an outcry calling for assistance to the Cubans. However, President Cleveland resisted such demands, as he resisted demands to annex Hawaii.

In 1897 McKinley, who represented the interests of big business, became president. He soon gave in to demands to annex Hawaii, which had been under American pressure for a number of years. 'We need Hawaii just as much and a good deal more than we needed California', said McKinley. 'The taste of empire is in the mouth of the people', said a newspaper.

In February 1898 the United States battleship *Maine*, which was on a courtesy visit to Cuba, was destroyed by a still unexplained explosion in Havana harbour with the loss of 260 lives. In the United States there was a popular outcry for war. Though Spain agreed to the terms of an ultimatum war was declared in April. By August 1898 Spain had been defeated in Cuba and in the Philippines (see map). By the Treaty of Paris (December 1898) Spain withdrew from Cuba, which became an independent republic. However, as a condition of American troops being withdrawn, Cuba had to accept a virtual protectorate by the USA. Spain ceded Puerto Rico, Guam and the Philippines to the United States. For the Philippines America made a payment of 20 million dollars. In 1899 the USA

Front page of the New York Journal, *2 May 1898. The American sailors, it is said, got up early and destroyed half the Spanish fleet before breakfast and the rest after breakfast. The invitation above the paper's title to 'all friends of aggressive Americanism' suggests the power of the press*

obtained a further footing in the Pacific: Samoa, in which Americans had for some time been taking an interest, was partitioned between the USA and Germany. In the same year Hay proclaimed the 'open door' policy for China (see p. 19).

Annexation of the Philippines became the subject of fierce debate in the USA. To many Americans rule over foreign territory was contrary to the spirit of 'the American purpose' (of freedom). This, as much as the desire to escape poverty, had lured millions across the seas to settle in America. But louder voices prevailed. A popular orator talked of 'American expansion until all the seas shall bloom with that flower of liberty, the flag of the great republic . . . the trade of the world must and shall be ours.' 'Manila with its magnificent bay is the prize and pearl of the East.' And there were fears that the Philippines might fall into the hands of Germany. Eventually the Senate voted by a narrow margin for annexation of the Philippines.

For some thirty years an independence movement had been active in the Philippines. In 1898 the Filipinos,

THE UNITED STATES, 1870–1914

under the leadership of Emilio Aguinaldo, declared their independence and joined the Americans in attacking their Spanish rulers. When the Americans decided to annex the Philippines, although they were promised 'the amplest liberty of self-government', Aguinaldo resumed the struggle against foreign rule. Soon numbers of American troops were engaged in a guerilla struggle. In 1901 Aguinaldo was captured. He signed an oath of loyalty to the USA and called on the Filipinos to end resistance. For another year there was savage fighting in the northern Philippines. The Muslims of Sulu and Mindanao in the south fought on for another ten years. Twice several hundred Muslims committed mass suicide on the slopes of an extinct volcano.

In 1916 the USA promised withdrawal from the Philippines as soon as a strong democratic government had been established. Arrangements to honour this promise had been made when the Second World War intervened. The islands never became the great channel for trade with China that had been hoped for.

Cuba's relations with the USA were complex. The Americans repeatedly intervened in its political and economic affairs until in 1935 they gave up their special rights, except that of maintaining a naval base.

A great power

In 1889 the first Pan-American Congress was held in Washington with the object of encouraging closer relations among the American states – with the USA playing the role of elder sister. The congress agreed to establish a Pan-American Union; this proved to be little more than an information bureau. Over the next decades 'closer relations' were marked by the growth of Yankee imperialism and dollar diplomacy in Latin America – and resentment towards the 'Yanquis' (see p. 265).

In September 1901 McKinley, re-elected on a policy of imperialism, was assassinated. His place was taken by Theodore Roosevelt, who remained president until 1909. Roosevelt, though he promoted the growth of the army and navy, annexed no territory. He brought much prestige to America in world affairs. 'Speak softly and carry a big stick', said Roosevelt. He mediated between Russia and Japan in 1905 (see p. 21) and in 1906 helped bring about the Algeçiras conference (see p. 33).

In 1895 President Cleveland had invoked the Monroe Doctrine to force Britain to settle a boundary dispute between British Guiana and Venezuela by arbitration. In 1903 a dispute with Britain over the Alaskan boundary

The manifest destiny of the USA

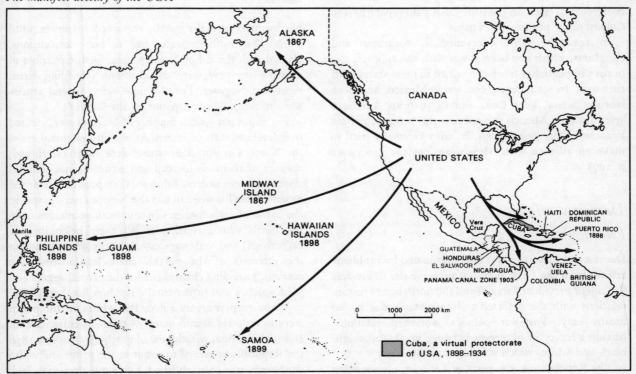

Cuba, a virtual protectorate of USA, 1898–1934

with Canada was settled. Between 1902 and 1903 Britain, Germany and Italy blockaded Venezuelan ports in an attempt to make Venezuela pay her debts. Roosevelt handled the sabre-rattling kaiser skilfully and the matter was submitted to arbitration. In 1904, when a similar situation arose in the Dominican Republic, Roosevelt pronounced an extension of the Monroe Doctrine: when an American state behaved in such a way as to provoke foreign intervention, it was the duty of the USA to intervene, to act as a sort of policeman to enforce good behaviour. American marines then invaded the Dominican Republic, as they did again in 1916.

The Spanish-American War made Americans more aware of the advantages of a canal linking the Atlantic and Pacific oceans. In 1901 Britain gave up a treaty right to share with the USA in building a Panama canal. The USA then bought up the rights of the French Panama Canal Company (see p. 73). But Colombia, through whose territory the canal was planned to run, hesitated to grant the land necessary. When the part of Colombia that is now Panama rebelled the USA prevented Colombian forces from putting down the rebellion and recognised Panama as independent (1903). On payment of considerable sums of money Panama granted the USA the use of a 16-kilometre-wide canal zone. Construction of the canal began in 1907 and was completed in 1914. In 1921 the USA paid reparations to Colombia for her loss of Panama.

In 1912 the USA intervened in Nicaragua and Honduras, which had been at war with one another, and in 1915 in Haiti; her troops remained in these states until the 1930s. In 1914, during civil war in Mexico, American marines seized Vera Cruz and in 1916 an American army invaded Mexico to suppress the bandit chieftain Francisco Villa (see p. 260). In 1917 Germany tried to make an alliance with Mexico against the USA (see p. 107).

Domestic affairs

Reconstruction

Domestic policies were for long dominated by problems arising from the Civil War. To preserve the union was the aim of President Lincoln and the north but to restore relations with the defeated southern states was by no means easy. Post-war policies worsened relations, leaving a legacy of bitterness between north and south, black and white, which is evident to this day.

The Republicans, the party of Lincoln, representing

A cartoon from Harper's Weekly, *1873, condemning the Ku-Klux Klan and other white terrorist organisations.* 'A band of wild and desperate young men ...', Harper's Weekly *reported*, 'masked, armed and supplied with horses and money by the Democratic candidates ... ride over the country at midnight, and perpetrate unheard of enormities.'

big business and the north, remained in power until 1884. The southern states had to hold conventions, elected with the aid of Negro voters, for the purpose of drawing up new state constitutions providing equal rights for Negroes. For the time being federal armies were to remain in occupation of the south.

For about ten years a number of Negroes were elected to federal and state positions. At one time 98 members of the South Carolina legislature were Negroes, though only 22 of them could read and write – a not unusual state of affairs: Andrew Johnson, then president, learned to write from his wife. In fact the Negroes were pawns in the hands of carpetbaggers (Republican politicians from the north who arrived with all their belongings in carpetbags) and scalawags (southerners who worked in the interests of the north). State legislatures were corrupt, providing champagne for the carpetbaggers and gold watches and ornamental cuspidors for themselves.

While carpetbaggers ruled, the whites in the south were heavily taxed and many of them disenfranchised. But with the final withdrawal of northern troops in 1876 the Republicans ceased to count in the south and white supremacy was re-established. Economic pressures, lack of education and the brutal violence of such societies as the Ku-Klux-Klan brought 'the niggers' to heel. Negroes dared not use their political and social 'rights'.

Immigration

Between 1865 and 1880 four and a half million immigrants, mainly from the United Kingdom, Scandinavia and Germany, arrived in the USA. Until 1882 there was considerable immigration from China. Between 1880 and 1920 twenty-three million immigrants arrived. After 1890 about 70 per cent came from Austria-Hungary, Russia, Poland, Italy and the Balkans. By 1900 the Italian population of New York exceeded that of Naples.

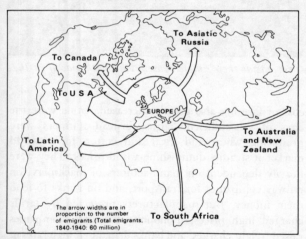

Migration from Europe, 1840–1940

To these migrants the United States was an Ark of Refuge into which Uncle Sam welcomed them with the words: 'No oppressive taxes, no expensive kings, no compulsory military service, no knouts [Russian whips] or dungeons.' Not all found a welcome. To some Americans the newcomers were German socialists, Russian anarchists, Italian brigands or English convicts. Cheap fares offered by steamship and railway companies – from Europe to the mid-west of the USA for £25 – assisted immigrants. Once in America they were often exploited. They swelled the proletariat of New York and Chicago – while native born Americans went west. Although the USA was a land of opportunity many Americans were born poor – and remained poor. It was a curiously mixed society – democratic and egalitarian, yet full of racial prejudice and quick to exploit the ignorant and weak.

Big business

The Civil War had accelerated industrial development. The construction of transcontinental railways hastened the process. In ten years 32,000 kilometres of track were laid by armies of Irish labourers and coolies from China. (Coolie, a word now out of favour, sounds like two Cantonese words meaning 'bitter toil'.) An unrestrained desire to make money dominated life. Accepting *laissez-faire* principles, governments stood back and individuals made their fortunes by good means or bad. John D. Rockefeller and a penniless lad from Scotland, Andrew Carnegie, and others too, made fortunes out of iron and steel, railroads and oil. Protected by tariffs and with a large home market, manufacturers flourished. Cheap immigrant labour, European inventions adapted to American conditions, the development of abundant resources of land and raw materials, brought about an economic miracle.

Until the turn of the century the industrialists of the north were the dictators of the nation's life. The politicians danced to their tune. Under a system known as 'pork barrel legislation' they distributed jobs, pensions, contracts, and enacted laws favouring sectional interests – in return for support. The law was used to protect the interests of employers but not the interests of workers. Employers, while preaching the virtues of competition for others, themselves built up monopolies, especially trusts that restricted output and raised prices. By 1890 half of the nation's wealth was in the hands of 125,000 men. In 1901 the banker John Pierpont Morgan controlled half the nation's output of pig iron, coke, steel rails and industrial steel – and almost all the barbed wire, nails, tinplate and steel tubes.

Farmers suffered severely from high tariffs, workers from the ruthless methods of employers and the lack of union organisation. While migrants provided an apparently inexhaustible reservoir of cheap labour employers could safely reject the demands of their workers. Slums proliferated.

Farmers and their problems

The railway companies were assisted by grants of land which they sold to settlers who then used the railways for the transport of supplies and of their farm products. The frontier of permanent settlement pressed steadily westward. Settlers were assisted by the introduction of barbed wire for cheap fencing and of windmills for pumping water. The settlers soon caught up with the

Farmers in the mid-west state of Nebraska pose in their Sunday best outside their simple house – built with sods of earth, grass grows from its roof!

cattle pioneers and miners who had pushed on ahead – the days of the wild west were relatively short. Cattle raising and mining had, by the 1890s, become big business. The Red Indians, too, were soon overrun, though they occasionally had spectacular successes, as when the Sioux ambushed General Custer at Little Big Horn. The slaughter of bison which accompanied the advancing line of settlement made the decline of the Indian way of life inevitable. In 1887 an act was passed for the assimilation of the Indians into American society. For the most part confined to reserves, they did not acquire full legal rights and citizenship until 1924.

By 1890 there ceased to be a frontier of settlement. However, the frontier outlook continued to influence American life. For the frontier called for a high degree of self-reliance, a characteristic still held in the highest esteem. And the challenge of the unknown continued to fascinate Americans. The astounding endurance and physical feats of the pioneers who crossed rivers and mountains, canyons and bitter wastes, surviving drought and loneliness and every kind of privation, were a challenge to future generations.

The farmers who pioneered the west made increasing use of machinery. The labour cost of producing corn fell dramatically. Four men and a threshing machine could do work formerly done by 400 men. Thus, while agricultural output increased enormously, the capital cost of farming also greatly increased. Gone were the days of self-sufficient farms; instead, farmers were producing wheat and meat and cotton for a world market at steadily diminishing world prices. They were heavily dependent on manufacturers of machinery, on railway companies for transport, and on banks to lend them money. But manufacturers protected by tariffs charged high prices; monopolistic railway companies raised freight charges; and banks demanded high rates of interest. And farmers had to face the competition of Canadian and Russian wheat, of beef from Argentina, wool from Australia and cotton from Egypt and India. By the 1890s the farmers who had pioneered the USA were in serious difficulties. At times it was more profitable to burn grain for fuel than to sell it. The southern states, predominantly agricultural, remained poor and backward. In the Deep South not only the Negroes languished; the Poor Whites were pitiable too.

The problems of labour

There was a rapid growth in the size and number of cities. In 1871 a fire destroyed the whole of Chicago's business centre and 18,000 houses. Twenty years later, with a population of over a million, Chicago was a city of skyscrapers. But the new cities emphasised the differences between riches and poverty, between weakness and power.

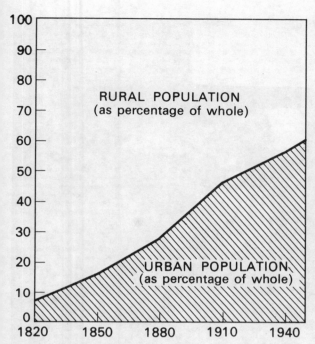

The diagram shows the growth of urban population in the USA. Cities with a population of over 100,000 numbered 5 in 1850, 50 in 1910 and 92 in 1940. In 1850 only New York had a population of over 500,000. By 1910 New York, Chicago and Philadelphia had populations of over 1,000,000; by 1940 Detroit and Los Angeles also had populations of over 1,000,000. Similar urbanisation occurred in other industrialised countries

The most ruthless means were adopted to keep labour subservient. Conditions were made worse by the great numbers of uneducated immigrants. In 1890 in steel and paper mills, in oil refineries and other heavy industries, men worked twelve hours a day for six or seven days a week. Factories employed large numbers of women and children. Conditions of work were often dangerous. Outside the cities workers were often forced to live in company-owned houses and were paid not in money but with coupons which could only be used in company-owned stores.

Trade unionism was slow to develop. A few craft unions were formed and some of these came together to form the National Labour Union, but this did not survive the depression of the 1870s. At times there were open battles between strikers and police or the army. A semi-secret society, the Knights of Labour, was founded in 1869. In 1885 it won a victory over a railway company. But in the same year a bomb killed seven policemen during a strike at the McCormick harvester works in Chicago. The Knights of Labour, who were implicated in the affair, thereafter lost support. Vague ideas of brotherhood could not bind together the opposing interests of skilled and unskilled workers.

In 1886 the American Federation of Labour (AFL), led by Samuel Gompers, was founded. It confined its activities to the development of craft unions; the organisation of unskilled labour did not occur until after the First World War. The AFL concentrated on day-to-day bargaining for an eight-hour day, higher wages, health and sanitation regulations and child labour laws. It used the strike weapon only as a last resort. By 1900 its membership was only half a million.

The progress of labour was limited by the frontier tradition of individualism and violence. To the employers, an organised labour movement appeared 'un-American, illegal and indecent'. Moreover, labour legislation was a responsibility of the states. So labour had to fight the same old battle in state after state, where industry, often supported by the legislature and the courts, used every possible weapon to resist its claims. A state that legislated favourably to labour simply caused industries to move away.

Education

Before the Civil War the principle of free public education for all children was well established. After the war it was the great achievement of schools to 'Americanise' a population of increasingly mixed origins. By the end of the nineteenth century it was customary for children to receive twelve years of schooling. In spite of the great influx of immigrants and an increase in population from fifty million in 1880 to seventy-five million in 1900 the rate of illiteracy had fallen by 1900 to 11 per cent. But whereas the illiteracy rate among whites was 6 per cent it was 45 per cent among non-whites. Booker T. Washington, born a slave in Virginia, developed Tuskegee Institute into an educational centre for Negroes. He believed that education, especially industrial education, rather than political agitation, was the best means of advancement for the Negro community.

In the churches of all denominations there was a strong movement towards 'socialised Christianity', a Christianity which would concern itself with the problems of an urban, capitalist society, substituting Christian principles for ruthless competition. Socialised Christianity led to demands for social legislation.

Did these Bohemian immigrants making cigars in New York in 1889 go on to make a fortune?

The return of the Democrats

Gradually the Democrats recovered from the eclipse they suffered after the Civil War. The Republicans, by their corruption and selfish policies, were discredited. In 1884 Grover Cleveland, a Democrat, was elected president. By this time *laissez-faire* policies were under attack by liberal groups wanting greater government control and social reforms. Monopolies were attacked. Under Cleveland an attempt was made, through the Interstate Commerce Act, to regularise railway charges, but court decisions made the act ineffective. In 1890 an Anti-Trust Law was passed; ironically, this was used more effectively against labour unions than against industrial monopolists. Attempts were made to eliminate corruption and improve the efficiency of the civil service.

In the 1880s a Farmers' Alliance was founded to 'obtain for the farmer and the labourer equal privileges with the manufacturing and commercial classes'. In 1891 a National People's (Populist) Party was founded. This aimed at a fairer distribution of the nation's wealth by means of a graduated income tax, government ownership of railways, an eight-hour day, and so on. Cleveland was elected president for a second time in

1892. A severe depression marked the beginning of his term of office. Over 150 railroad companies and 600 banks went bankrupt. An army of unemployed marched to Washington. Apart from trying to check the outflow of gold, Cleveland took no action, believing that, like storms, depressions should be left to wear themselves out without government interference. However, when strikers threatened a Carnegie steel plant and Pullman's railway works, state and federal troops were ordered to intervene and there was considerable bloodshed. Under Cleveland tariffs were substantially reduced – only to be restored under the next president, McKinley.

In 1896 the Populists joined the Democrats in nominating William Jennings Bryan for the presidency. 'You shall not crucify mankind upon this cross of gold', said Bryan. His defeat and the victory of the Republican, McKinley, marked the end of Populism, but a new movement was by then taking shape – Progressivism.

Progressivism

Whereas Populism was agrarian and the product of despair in a period of depression, Progressivism was the product of middle-class indignation in a period of growing prosperity. The Progressives were found in both political parties and in every section of the community, often organising themselves in leagues or associations to attack some specific abuse. They fought – against monopolies, child labour, drunkenness, injustice towards Negroes and Indians, bribery, slums, police brutality and the savage treatment of prisoners. Because of the limited powers of the federal government they had to work through the individual state and city legislatures. They won considerable press support but the party bosses (such as those who met at Tammany Hall in New York) were slow to give way. La Follette, a Progressive who later as governor of Wisconsin turned his state into a laboratory of social reform, fought the party bosses three times before they agreed to his nomination for election to the state legislature. Other outstanding Progressives were Theodore Roosevelt in New York City and Woodrow Wilson in New Jersey. Nevertheless progress was slow. Not until 1903 was there any effective state law limiting the hours of work for children. And as late as 1930 only thirty-seven states had enforced a forty-eight-hour week for children in factories.

German migrants brought with them Marxist socialism but this made little impact in the USA though for a time the First International (see p. 41) had its headquarters in New York. Socialists and Progressives later co-operated over particular issues, but Progressivism, which attacked specific abuses with specific remedies but offered no scheme for reorganising society, was more in keeping with American attitudes.

McKinley was elected president in 1896 as the 'Advance Agent of Prosperity'. Prosperity did return and with it came a multiplication of industrial and financial trusts and combines. McKinley, re-elected in 1900, was assassinated the following year and was succeeded by his vice-president, Theodore Roosevelt. Roosevelt, the advocate of soft speech and a big stick in foreign relations, acted firmly but cautiously in domestic matters also. He championed civil service reform and extended the use of examinations as against pork barrel favouritism (see p. 67) for making appointments. He enforced the law against 'bad' trusts, including a very powerful group of railway companies. In his second term tobacco, beef and fertiliser trusts were broken. In 1902 he used federal troops against the employers in a great coal strike. Roosevelt took action to preserve national resources of timber, water, minerals and so on, which unrestrained individuals and companies had wasted or destroyed. Taft, another Republican, who followed Roosevelt, tried to continue his policies but with limited success. In 1912 Roosevelt, who had called Taft 'a traitor to the Progressive cause', campaigned against him. In the upshot, a Democrat, Woodrow Wilson, was elected twenty-eighth president.

Wilson, a former president of Princeton University, believed that twentieth-century conditions called for the restoration of the freedom of the small man. 'There has been something crude and heartless and unfeeling in our haste to succeed and be great', he said. Under the New Freedom, he urged, government must protect individual rights against the power of bankers, employers and monopolists. This to a substantial degree he succeeded in doing. He forced through the first genuine tariff reduction since the Civil War. He introduced a graduated income tax. The Federal Reserve Bank Act gave the government control of the currency and indirectly the whole banking system. In 1914 the Anti-Trust Act was considerably strengthened, but labour and farmers' organisations were freed from its operation.

Wilson's programme of Progressive legislation was halted after the outbreak of the First World War. In August 1914 he proclaimed United States neutrality but American bankers were soon lending money to the Allies and American farmers and industries were supplying them with immense quantities of goods. The United States thus had an increasing financial interest in an Allied victory. Meanwhile, she had taken over markets, notably in Latin America, formerly dominated by Europe. Some Americans, especially those of German origin, were sympathetic to Germany, whilst to Irish Americans Britain was a tyrant. And Britain's determination to search neutral vessels during her blockade of Germany was resented. However the underlying sympathies of most Americans were with the Allies.

In December 1916, having just been re-elected president, Wilson called on the nations at war to state their war aims and to devise arrangements to guarantee the world against further wars. But in April 1917 the USA was drawn into the war on the Allied side (see p. 107). Wilson organised the American war effort admirably. American troops arrived in France just in time to tip the scales of battle. But Wilson is chiefly remembered as the founder of the League of Nations, the man who rejected imperial Germany's philosophy of force and joined the Allied side to 'make the world safe for democracy'.

8 Western and central Europe: progress and domestic problems, 1871–1914

France

The economy

France made limited economic progress in the years 1871–1914. With her population growing very slowly the home market offered little stimulus. The loss of Alsace-Lorraine (see p. 4) took from her many of her best cotton factories and coal and iron ore deposits. After higher tariffs were introduced in 1892 there was more rapid growth but in 1914 less than half the population lived in cities. Almost half the French merchant marine consisted of sailing ships. Heavy industries remained relatively undeveloped. However, stimulated by demand for armaments, steel production substantially increased. Despite backward farming methods France was almost self-sufficient in agricultural products; only the USA and Russia grew more wheat and only Italy produced more wine. French banks accumulated considerable funds and lent large sums abroad – in particular to Russia. Banks and the coal, iron and steel cartels (monopoly organisations) had considerable political influence.

Threats to the Third Republic

In 1876 the first elections after the formal establishment of the republic returned a good republican majority in the Chamber of Deputies. In the so-called coup of Seize Mai (16 May) 1877, MacMahon, the monarchist president, forced the premier to resign and later dissolved the Chamber of Deputies, as in fact he was entitled to do. However, despite trickery in the ensuing elections, victory went to the republicans. After the

With gas lights, a few motor vehicles and pedestrians crossing at leisure, Paris at the turn of the century was typical of other European cities. Tiffanys the jewellers can be seen at the right and Thomas Cook is across the road

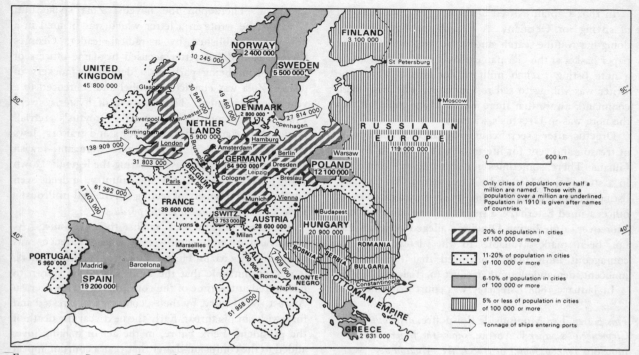

Europe 1910. Between 1850 and 1910 the growth of industry and a rising population were accompanied in western Europe by rapid urbanisation. In 1850 in England and Wales 20% of the population were living in towns of 100,000 or more. In 1850 London, Paris and Constantinople had populations of over half a million. Trade also had grown. In 1850 tonnage of shipping entering Britain was 12m., France 4m., Russia 2m.

failure of further attempts to force a conservative prime minister on the Chamber of Deputies, MacMahon had to appoint a prime minister who had the support of the majority in the chamber. In 1879 MacMahon resigned and Grévy, a moderate republican, became president.

From the time of Seize Mai until 1913, when war was threatening, French presidents were content to keep the ship of state on a safe course. Real power lay with the Chamber of Deputies to whom the prime minister was responsible. However, it was often not clear just who in the Chamber of Deputies exercised control for government tended to be in the hands of uneasily based coalitions.

However, in the 1880s it seemed that the French people might again turn to a popular hero, another 'Bonaparte'. The strong man of the day was General Boulanger, a striking figure who rode a big black horse and who had won popularity by his reforms as minister of war. A Boulangist 'party', which aimed at changing the constitution by giving wider powers to the president, attracted supporters of varying views – some radical, most strongly conservative. In January 1889, following

Boulanger's election to the chamber, demonstrators in Paris urged him to stage a coup. However, Boulanger, when it came to the point, proved unwilling to make the attempt. 'It was Bonapartism without a Bonaparte.' Boulanger fled and later committed suicide upon the grave of his mistress in Brussels.

In 1889 the French Panama Canal Company (see p. 66), with its employees hard hit by yellow fever, became bankrupt. Later it was found that politicians had been bribed to support a bill allowing shares in the company to be sold by lottery. Groups hostile to the republic (conservatives found chiefly among certain religious orders, in the upper crust of society and in the higher ranks of the army) were glad to make capital of this scandal, which reached its climax in 1892–93. Such strongly nationalist groups were feverishly eager to recover Alsace-Lorraine and to gain colonies. They were also hostile to Jews. An influx of Jews, seeking refuge from the repression under which they lived in eastern Europe, added fuel to the fire. A wave of anti-semitism was one result of the Panama affair, in which Jewish financiers were involved.

In 1894 Captain Alfred Dreyfus, a Jew, was accused of spying for Germany. A French intelligence agent doing her routine search among the contents of a waste paper basket at the German embassy in Paris had found a note listing French military documents which the writer was willing to sell to Germany. The army high command, aware that there were leakages, alleged that the note was in Dreyfus's writing.

Dreyfus, after a secret court martial, was found guilty of treason and sent for life to Devil's Island in French Guiana. There, sometimes in chains, he was kept alone in a stone hut. Meanwhile it transpired that the note listing the documents was almost certainly written by an officer named Esterhazy, a spendthrift and a debauchee. Moreover, a file listing Dreyfus's alleged activities had not been made available to the defence. A few courageous individuals, convinced that Dreyfus was innocent, demanded another court martial.

In January 1898 Esterhazy was court martialled and

This poster, Les Moutons de Boisdeffre, *distributed by Clemenceau's paper* L'Aurore, *shows the frenzy of the* moutons (sheep, fools) *of Boisdeffre. Mouton de Boisdeffre, French chief of staff, was covering up for the army – at Dreyfus's expense. By Théophile Steinlen, a pioneer of poster design (1898)*

acquitted. Thereupon the novelist Zola spoke out: '*J'accuse*', he wrote in a letter which was printed in a newspaper published by a radical leader, Georges Clemenceau. Zola's letter accused by name officers of high rank of being party to a deliberate mockery of justice. Zola was convicted of libel and sentenced to a year's imprisonment. Then a wave of hysteria swept France. 'Revisionists' demanded Dreyfus's retrial. Nationalists clamoured against Jews and traitors. Jews were attacked and in Algeria there were anti-Jewish riots. Ladies carried parasols bearing the legend: 'Down with Jews.' *L'affaire* split the country, indeed even families. The intensity of feeling is reflected in Proust's novel *A la recherche du temps perdu*.

The army fought back against the revisionists. As embarrassing enquiries were made, evidence was fabricated by a Major Henry. To him, as to many others, it was unthinkable that the army should be shown to have erred at the time of the court martial. However, in August 1898 Henry, by then a colonel, was arrested and forthwith cut his throat. Early the next year the death of the president, Félix Faure, in the act of making love, added to the confusion. Later that year a court of appeal ordered the retrial of Dreyfus.

So Dreyfus, a pitiful ghost, was brought back from Devil's Island to face a second court martial. He was found guilty but with 'extenuating circumstances'. This verdict, so obviously a lame attempt to appease the revisionists without discrediting the army, shook freedom lovers the world over. Queen Victoria was stupefied. 'What remains of the historic tradition that once made us champions of justice for the whole of the earth?' thundered Clemenceau. However, the prime minister, Waldeck-Rousseau, poured oil on the waters by having Dreyfus pardoned. Gradually the mad excitement died away. In 1906 an appeal court 'broke' the verdict of the second court martial. Dreyfus was reinstated and later served in the First World War.

L'affaire showed that many people were willing to accept forgery and perjury in order to protect the army; the end justified the means however devious. It revealed too that thousands of others were passionately attached to justice. It evidenced the feverish quality of political life in France. It revealed the power for both good and evil of the French press. In the event the republic did not yield to reaction and falsehood. Its enemies vented their spleen in fresh tirades against all Jews.

1898, the year when Zola spoke out, saw the birth of the Comité d'Action Française, which attracted numerous writers to its disreputable ranks. It was passionately and scurrilously anti-Dreyfusard. To some extent it had student support and stirred up under-graduate 'riots'. It included too disgruntled nobles, professional men and numerous lower middle-class supporters. It was above all anti-Jewish, anti-republican and more revengeful against enemies at home than against enemies abroad – the republic appeared in its journal as 'The Slut'. From 1908 its newspaper, *Action Française*, appeared daily. The paper was a hate machine, remarkable for its powerful invective. The movement had the blessing of numerous clericals, though a number of bishops strongly opposed it. Other right-wing movements tried in similar fashion to undermine the republic.

Education and the church

Republicans regarded church schools with suspicion. In 1882 Jules Ferry, minister of education, introduced free and compulsory primary schooling. State school teachers were forbidden to give religious instruction. Normal (teacher training) schools for women were founded, so that the education of girls, hitherto largely in the hands of nuns, might be entrusted to lay teachers.

Some religious orders, the authorised orders, were entitled to own property. Some, among them the Jesuits, were tolerated but legally could not hold property. Ferry expelled the unauthorised orders so as to exclude them from teaching. Some members boarded themselves up in their houses in an attempt to remain. Then for a time the expulsion decrees were allowed to lapse.

During the papacy of Leo XIII (1878–1903) there was hope of a rapprochement (reconciliation) between church and state. In 1892 in the encyclical *Au Milieu des Sollicitudes* (Amid Anxieties) Leo XIII urged French Catholics to work with the republic and take part in political life. Under the influence of his 1891 encyclical *De Rerum Novarum* (Concerning New Things), which outlined the church's teachings on modern industrial relationships, some parish priests went 'out to the people' to work for better social conditions. But in general there was little interest in reforms – and it was not forgotten that under a new pope the attitude of the Vatican might change. On the whole the church remained hostile to the republic.

The moderate republican government of Waldeck-Rousseau, which held office from 1899 to 1902, was probably the most talented of the administrations between 1875 and 1914. The cabinet included a leading socialist, Alexandre Millerand. Millerand's acceptance of office in a bourgeois government led to violent disputes among socialists. Under Waldeck-Rousseau the control of the church in education was further reduced. But in 1902 Waldeck-Rousseau, disliking the extremism of some anti-clericals, resigned. Emile Combes succeeded him. Under Combes, the narrowest of anti-clericals, the law against unauthorised orders was vigorously enforced and the Jesuits, among others, were expelled from France. The philosopher-priest, Teilhard de Chardin, for example, sought refuge in the Channel Islands. Some 1,500 religious houses were closed. Convents also were shut down. In 1904 education came completely under state control.

Disputes with Pius X shortly after he became pope (1903) resulted in France breaking off relations with the Vatican. Combes then decided upon the separation of church and state. The Law of Separation was in fact passed after Combes, following a scandal, had resigned (1905). Aristide Briand, a socialist, piloted the bill through the chamber. The Law of Separation ended the centuries-old connection between the Catholic Church and the French state. The state ceased to appoint bishops; one result of this was to increase the pope's influence in such appointments. Clergy were no longer paid by the state. The Law of Separation in the end won acceptance, not least because it was applied with restraint and even sympathy. Freedom of religion was preserved and in time clericalism and anti-clericalism ceased to arouse passions. Republicanism was strengthened by the secular education provided in the state schools. Meanwhile, French missionaries continued to be active overseas.

Working-class movements

As the horrors of the Paris Commune (see p. 5) faded workers began organising to improve conditions. In 1884 syndicats (trade unions) were legalised, though government employees were forbidden to be members. A depression that caused widespread unemployment in the later 1880s quickened the growth of the working-class movement. The syndicalists chose the *Internationale* (first sung in 1895) as their song. May Day was their day. On May Day in 1891 troops fired on demonstrators demanding an eight-hour day and nine people were killed. Anarchists and other extremists were active with bombs. In 1894 President Sadi-Carnot was stabbed to death by an Italian anarchist.

By 1899 half a million French workers were syndicat members. In general they took little interest in parliamentary activity, preferring direct action, particularly the general strike, as the instrument that would best serve their ends. This revolutionary syndicalism (see p. 52), influenced by anarchism (see p. 37), and intolerant of intellectual leadership, had an immediacy, a personal appeal that attracted workers – the workers would occupy their own factories or workshops and run them for their own benefit. The English Fabians (see p. 49), with their avoidance of strife and their programme of piecemeal reforms, had little in common with the syndicalists.

However, working-class representation in parliament was growing; forty-eight socialists were elected to the Chamber of Deputies in 1893. In 1904 Briand and Jean Jaurès founded the socialist paper, *L'Humanité*. Jaurès was willing to work within the constitution to win reforms; though he did not always admit it, he was prepared to take half now and hope for more later. Others, in particular the unyielding Jules Guesde, were more doctrinaire, more 'pure' in their theory. Briand was probably willing to work in with anyone. In 1905 a number of French socialists united as a party under Jaurès's leadership. The next year the politically supple Briand was expelled from this party for having taken office in a coalition government.

In general the working-class movement achieved little. The triumph of republicanism did not mean the triumph of social reform. The republicans were in fact the protectors of the rights of the propertied classes. Small shopkeepers and peasant proprietors and independent craftsmen were doing fairly well, making a little more money, getting small comforts, even small luxuries. With their little stake in the country they were not in favour of invading property rights. Like richer people they opposed any system of taxation by which the better off would pay for the welfare of the poorer. They welcomed tariff protection of manufactures. The imposition of duties on imports of food pleased the peasants of a big wheat growing country but for the workers it was a 'stomach tax'.

The Third Republic, it is often said, was politically left but socially right. The more definite party line that was a feature of English politics was not apparent. Governments were shifting combinations, a series of coalitions and groupings often uncomfortable in partnership and achieving little. With right wing and left wing fairly well balanced, the centre more or less kept control of the situation.

In these circumstances only minor reforms were won by the working classes – and even these were not effectively enforced. This applied for instance to the eleven-hour day introduced in 1900; again its reduction to ten hours in 1904 was not strictly enforced. Clemenceau who in 1906 became prime minister in a parliament that included 200 socialists – of varying views – promised much but achieved little. His chief concern was the suppression of a succession of strikes by revolutionary syndicalists. A neat solution to the problem of such strikes was found by Briand, France's first socialist prime minister, when in 1910 he called up striking railwaymen for military service. This of course put the strikers under military discipline so that refusal to work was a serious offence. Yet in earlier days Briand had regarded the general strike as the workers' most effective weapon.

The left wing in France was strongly pacifist. It opposed France's alliance with tsarist Russia (see p. 87) and believed that French workers would never fight against workers of other nations; class, it believed, would triumph over nationalism. In 1913–14 socialists opposed extending the period of military service from two to three years; they yielded when the imposition of an income tax was agreed to in principle.

At the outbreak of war in 1914 Jaurès, most influential of French socialists, went off to Brussels and called on German and other workers to resist mobilisation orders. On his return to Paris he was shot dead by a young super-patriot. Soon all the divisions in French society disappeared – for the time being – as though a magic wand had been waved. Socialists went off to shoulder their rifles with feelings apparently no different from those of other citizens. A French syndicalist who left with other reservists for the battle front later wrote:

'I did not have the strength of character not to go, although I did not recognise frontiers or fatherlands. . . . But at the front, thinking of my family, scratching the names of my wife and son on the bottom of the trench, I said: "How is it possible that I, anti-patriot, antimilitarist, who acknowledge only the International [see p. 41], come to be attacking my companions in misery . . .?"'

Italy

The new kingdom

In 1870, during the Franco-Prussian War, a French garrison that had been guarding papal territory around

Rome was withdrawn. Victor Emmanuel II, who had been proclaimed king of Italy in 1861, then seized the opportunity to add Rome to his kingdom. The area known as Italia Irredenta (in particular South Tyrol and Trieste (see map p. 81) which were still under Habsburg rule) was not yet part of the kingdom. With this exception Italy, which a few years before was still 'a geographic expression', had by 1870 come into being.

Economic development was confined mainly to the north. Swift flowing rivers favoured the production of hydro-electric power. Such power being well suited to textile manufacture, production of silk and cotton goods went ahead rapidly. Railways grew from 6,000 to 17,000 kilometres in 1914. A large merchant marine was built up.

The new Italy began her career with two severe drawbacks. The first was the economic and social division between north and south. The south suffered from lack of resources, poverty and illiteracy. From the south an endless stream of emigrants poured across the Atlantic, leaving behind the less enterprising. And it was the south that was dominated by vicious secret societies such as the Mafia. The introduction of farm machinery on some of the great estates in the south resulted only in unemployment among landless labourers. Roads, railways and telegraphs were only partially successful in welding the south into the Italian national state.

Secondly, Italy, essentially a Catholic country, had unhappy relations with the Vatican. After Victor Emmanuel II seized Rome in 1870 Pope Pius IX retired to the Vatican Palace. There the popes remained – Prisoners in the Vatican – until 1929 (see p. 179).

Italy was a parliamentary monarchy, though the crown had certain powers to legislate by decree. Government was responsible. However, at first the franchise was narrow. In 1881 it was extended from about half a million to two million men. In 1912 the electorate was trebled, bringing almost total manhood suffrage. Politics tended to be corrupt and to fall under the influence of party bosses. 'Parties' counted far less, a 'leader' and his henchmen far more, than in England. In the south there was considerable manipulation of votes, achieved by a combination of bribes and punches.

In 1877 primary education was made compulsory, though only for children aged from six to nine years. Every township that could afford to do so was required to build a school. However, this law was not enforced. The scope of primary education was extended later and by 1914 more than half the people of Italy were literate.

Social unrest

Francesco Crispi, prime minister of Italy from 1887 to 1891 and from 1893 to 1896, was anti-clerical and antagonised the church by his education policy. From 1874 to 1903 loyal Catholics were forbidden by the Vatican to vote, let alone hold government office: 'Neither elect nor be elected.' After the accession of Pius X (1903) Catholics considering whether to join in political life were told by the pope to 'do as their conscience orders'. The new policy of the Vatican was in part prompted by fear of the 'red tide of revolution' that seemed to be threatening Italy.

A socialist party appeared in 1892. By 1900 socialists had won 32 of the 500 seats in the lower house. Meanwhile anarchists and syndicalists and other extremists were disturbing the peace. In 1894 Crispi imposed martial law in Sicily following uprisings. For a time socialist bodies were banned. Eighty people were killed when troops fired during bread riots in Milan in 1898. In 1900 the conservative King Humbert I was assassinated by an anarchist, an Italian who had come from the USA to translate his ideas into action.

Victor Emmanuel III, who followed Humbert, was more liberal. Serious industrial unrest continued but the government, although less authoritarian than that of Crispi, managed to keep order and to see, for example, that non-strikers were not intimidated by militants. In 1903 Giovanni Giolitti became prime minister. In 1904, when a general strike was threatening disruption, the government made ready to act. However, it held its hand and the strike came to an end without its intervention. In 1905 trade unions were legalised and various factory laws were passed.

Giolitti, though not continuously in office, remained prominent in political life until after the First World War. Government continued to be by 'transformist' majorities: in the absence of any party with a clear majority, groups of 'parties' acted together for the time being. Policy thus shaded across (trans) from right to left, with the centre holding the balance. Transformism hindered the development of definite policies. As clericals after 1904 increased their representation Giolitti prevailed on them to act with him. In 1913 a rise in the socialist vote forced him into coalition with the clericals.

In 1914 the right-wing government of Antonio Salandra took office. When the First World War broke out Italy was in no condition economically or politically to join in. A succession of bitter strikes in which Benito

Mussolini (see p. 177) took an active part divided the country and revolution seemed to threaten. Giolitti and many others, aware of Italy's weakness, opposed entry into the war. But nationalist groups were eager to join in. On 3 August 1914 Italy declared her neutrality.

Imperial Germany

Economic background

The formation of the empire (see p. 7) brought with it a large and growing market with a uniform customs and administrative system. Railways, roads and canals were already well developed in 1871. After that railways were co-ordinated under an imperial office – partly because of their military importance. Many of the senior posts in railway administration were held by generals, and railwaymen were not allowed to form trade unions. The Rhine with its connected waterways became one of the great highways of the world. And by 1914 Germany's merchant marine was second only to that of Britain.

Germany had abundant coal and iron, especially after she obtained Alsace-Lorraine. By 1900 she was the second largest steel producer in the world (the USA occupied first place). The possession of rich deposits of salt and potash and of scientists of great ability resulted in rapid development of the chemical industries.

Von Siemens in 1867 invented the dynamo and applied electricity to the needs of transport. The use of electricity in a number of industrial processes became widespread. Soon there was a considerable export trade in electrical appliances. By 1914 the electrical industry was employing well over 100,000 men.

Industrial development was reflected in the growth of towns and cities. In 1871 about two-thirds of the people of Germany lived on farms or in villages. By 1914 two-thirds of the population lived in towns and cities. Her growing population and concentration on industrial production forced Germany to import considerable quantities of food and raw materials.

Bismarck and the church

The form of government established in 1871 (see p. 7), an autocracy behind a facade of democratic forms, survived relatively unshaken until 1918. Though centrifugal forces, particularly in Bavaria, pulled against Prussia, they did not dislodge her from her commanding position.

Until 1890 Bismarck piloted the new Germany towards security. Whilst tolerating parliamentary institutions, Bismarck, by holding a balance between the various parties, always managed, or if need be manipulated them in what he considered to be the interests of the state. In June 1888, after the death of Kaiser William I (March 1888) and the very brief reign of the liberal Frederick III, William II succeeded to the throne. Within two years the new kaiser, young and arrogant, dropped his pilot.

Bismarck at the outset regarded Catholicism as hostile to the newly established empire. Catholics, most of them in Bavaria and other southern states, comprised a third of the population. They resented the dominant status of Prussia, a largely Protestant state. Moreover, the minorities under German rule in Posen (Polish Poznan) and Alsace-Lorraine were Catholic. And many German Catholics desired the inclusion of Austria within the empire, for if she were a member state Catholic influence would be substantially increased.

In 1870 the Vatican Council pronounced the dogma of papal infallibility, whereby all official statements of the pope concerning matters of faith and morals were declared infallible (incapable of error) – and so had to be accepted by loyal Catholics. This assertion of papal authority was everywhere regarded as a threat to the authority of the state. In Germany, and elsewhere, some Catholics opposed the dogma of infallibility which, they claimed, was 'new'. These 'Old Catholics' tended to support Bismarck against the papacy. On the other hand the Catholic Centre Party, formed in 1871, aimed to defend Catholic interests. As this party shaded through from a right to a left wing, it had wide connections.

In 1872 penalties were imposed upon priests who wove politics into their sermons. Church schools were brought under government control and certain religious orders, among them the Jesuits, were expelled. Other orders were later dissolved. From 1875 no marriage was valid unless a civil ceremony was performed. In May 1873, 1874 and 1875 laws later known as the May Laws were introduced in Prussia with the object of bringing the training, appointment and work of priests under state control. To these policies all but a handful of priests were totally opposed. Some were exiled or imprisoned for resisting the May Laws – and became martyrs.

The campaign against the Catholic Church, usually known as the *kulturkampf* (the struggle of beliefs) was part of Bismarck's policy of thwarting any body that might undermine the solidarity of the state. The *kulturkampf* did not have entirely the results he wished. It left many Catholics mistrustful of the state. It antagonised many liberals. After a time even Bismarck's Lutheran supporters found the application of his anti-clerical policies distasteful. With the accession of Pope Leo XIII in 1878 relations with the Vatican were less strained. After 1879 most of the anti-Catholic laws were either ignored or repealed. Moreover, by then Bismarck needed the support of the Catholic Centre Party in campaigns against free trade and socialism. However, laws hostile to Catholic Poles under German rule continued to be enforced.

Bismarck and socialism

The mid-nineteenth century saw the triumph of free trade policies in much of Europe. In the last quarter of the century the tide turned towards protection. In Germany a nationalist outlook, Bismarck's desire to secure an income over which the states would have no control, the difficulties faced by agriculture and the demands of industrialists for protection resulted in the Tariff Law of 1879. This protected both manufactured goods and primary products and won support from conservatives and the Catholic Centre Party.

Rapid industrial growth was accompanied by proletarian ills and discontent. Marx had regarded Germany as the state that would be in the forefront of world revolution. At the Gotha congress of 1875 two German socialist groups joined to form the German Social Democratic Party. The Social Democratic Party soon became popular and in 1877 won half a million votes.

Though the German Social Democrats sought to bring about changes only through parliament – they were criticised by Marx for their mildness – it seemed to many people that socialism was threatening the basis of society. In 1878 there were two attempts to assassinate the kaiser. Bismarck used these incidents as a pretext for a violent attack on the Social Democrats, although the party was not involved on either occasion. An anti-socialist newspaper campaign was followed by the Exceptional Laws, which banned all socialist meetings and publications (1878). By 1890 900 socialist 'agitators' had been removed from their houses to other areas, 1,500 imprisoned and over 1,000 publications banned. Yet the Social Democrats' following grew. (The Exceptional Laws did not prevent Social Democrats being elected to the Reichstag.)

Bismarck also sought to undermine the basis of

socialism by offering workers counter-attractions. In 1883, 1884 and 1888–89 state schemes were introduced providing first insurance against sickness, then against accident and lastly relief in old age. The schemes were contributory, the cost being met by the state, the employers and the workers themselves. It was over twenty years before similar protection for workers was introduced in Britain, still longer before it was adopted in France and various other countries.

Despite the double-headed axe of repression and protection of workers the Social Democrats in 1890 won thirty-five seats in the Reichstag. It was in the same year that William II brought about the resignation of old Bismarck. One point on which they disagreed was Bismarck's insistence that the Exceptional Laws should be renewed. When he went the Exceptional Laws were dropped.

1890–1914, Germany under Kaiser William II

The Social Democrats won fifty-six seats in the 1900 elections. By 1912 they formed the largest party in the Reichstag. At the outbreak of war they were the largest socialist group in Europe. Their growth was evidence that many Germans desired if not revolution, substantial social changes. However, though in 1891 the Social Democrats had officially adopted Marxist theory, their aim was the gradual dissolution of capitalism by peaceful methods, not the overthrow of the system by revolutionary violence. They were therefore willing to work through parliament. They did, however, refuse to accept office in the various 'bourgeois' coalition cabinets by which Germany was governed.

William II made himself master over a succession of chancellors and ministers, men of much lesser talent and authority than Bismarck. General Caprivi, Bismarck's successor, though a conservative, was responsible for various 'leftist' laws which William II, 'the Labour Emperor', hoped would turn the workers from socialism. Arbitration courts were set up. The hours of work for women and children were limited, though they were still very long. Sunday was made a workers' holiday and factory inspection was made effective. In 1892–94 the lowering of tariffs on primary products from certain countries benefited workers by easing the price of food. But despite the various reforms that 'cossetted' the workers Germany was troubled, as were France and Italy at this time, by anarchists.

From 1894 to 1900 Hohenlohe was chancellor. From 1900 to 1909 Count von Bülow held office. Germany

The Krupp works at Essen, 1912. Krupp's production of steel plates expanded rapidly with the building up of the German navy. By 1902 Krupp employed 40,000 workers. The firm was noted for its workers' welfare programme

under the kaiser's direction was then dangerously nationalist. An ambitious naval policy (see p. 89) necessitated large additional revenue and to this end in 1902 high tariffs were imposed on agricultural imports.

In 1906, following a struggle with the Catholic Centre Party, which had held the balance in the Reichstag for some years, Bülow arranged a coalition of Conservatives, National Liberals and Progressives. Known as the Bülow Bloc, this government opposed both Catholic Centre and Social Democrats. However, concessions continued to be made to workers. Though the religious orders expelled by Bismarck were still legally barred in Germany, individual Jesuits were allowed to carry on their work there.

From 1909 to 1917 Dr Bethmann Hollweg was chancellor. In 1911 Alsace-Lorraine was granted considerable autonomy – though this failed to win the support of the people. From 1912 co-operation between radicals and socialists increased and a coalition that shaded from National Liberals to Radicals and on to the Social Democrats took shape in opposition to the forces of the right. A Finance Law passed in 1913, when huge sums of money were required to pay for army increases, imposed a special national defence levy on both property and income. This tax, which fell most heavily on the rich, was a concession to the socialists and their allies. In

1914 class feeling was submerged in the Reichstag, as throughout Germany, by a tide of patriotism.

Fear that the instability of society might bring the left to power seems to have affected Germany's foreign policy in the pre-war years. Her aggressive policies and her attempt to win world predominance may have been intended to turn the attention of the masses from grievances at home to thoughts of grandeur abroad. So the changing social conditions that accompanied Germany's industrial growth probably played a part in bringing about the First World War.

The Dual Monarchy of Austria-Hungary

The Ausgleich

The Habsburgs of Austria ruled a hotchpotch of peoples (see map opposite). However, the map does not show the Germans scattered in small groups in various parts or the Jews found throughout the empire. And in many places small groups of different nationalities lived side by side.

In the early nineteenth century Habsburg rule was

The multi-national Dual Monarchy. National groups are shown in bold lettering

autocratic and conservative – if not positively reactionary. So unchanging seemed the Austrian empire that it was nicknamed the China of Europe. After nationalist revolutions (1848–49) in almost every part of the empire had failed, Vienna seemed to control every move. But from then on the Habsburg empire was subjected to rude shocks from without and to severe internal strains. It lost Lombardy (1859) and Venetia (1866) to Italy. Defeat by Prussia (see p. 1) excluded Austria from German affairs. And in Hungary iron repression did not dampen the ardour of Magyar nationalists.

In 1867 the Habsburgs were obliged to come to terms with the Magyars – a proud people who before 1848 had enjoyed certain privileges unknown to other Habsburg subjects. By the *Ausgleich* (Compromise) of 1867 the former Habsburg empire became the Dual Monarchy of

Austria-Hungary. The Habsburg emperor as king of Hungary was to be a personal link between the two states. Francis Joseph, who had ruled the Austrian empire since the Year of Revolutions (1848), thus became emperor of Austria and king of Hungary. The two parts into which the former Austrian empire was divided by the *Ausgleich* were separated by the River Leith; the empire of Austria lay west, the kingdom of Hungary east, of the river. Both states were equal in status and constitutional, though not democratic, rule was granted in both. Each state had full control of its domestic affairs. Each had its own prime minister. Foreign policy, defence and finance were jointly administered. There was one army and one foreign minister. Yearly sixty delegates from the Austrian Reichsrat and sixty from the Diet of Hungary met to discuss matters of joint concern. The Austrian

The farther east one travelled in Europe the fewer cities there were. Nomadic herdsmen such as these roamed the plains of Hungary until towards the end of the nineteenth century when much of the land came under wheat. An engraving of 1855

delegation sat in Vienna, the Hungarian in Budapest; only if there was a deadlock were the two delegations to sit together.

Francis Joseph survived until 1916. By that time he had suffered many tragedies – his brother, the emperor of Mexico, was shot; his only son, the Crown Prince Rudolf, killed himself because of an unhappy love affair; his wife, the beautiful Empress Elizabeth, was assassinated by an Italian anarchist. The assassination of his heir by a Serb nationalist (see p. 85) was followed by the First World War and, two years after the old emperor's death, by the dissolution of the Dual Monarchy.

Minorities in Hungary

If to some extent the *Ausgleich* satisfied the Magyars, it did nothing for the minorities of the Dual Monarchy. Germans remained dominant in Austria and Magyars in Hungary. Together they made up about half the population of the Dual Monarchy – and the Magyars and to a less extent the Germans continued to regard the Slav, Romanian and other minority groups as backward and 'uncivilised'.

Count Andrassy, who became prime minister of Hungary after the *Ausgleich*, sought to co-operate both with Austria and with the Slavs in Hungary. But his concessions to the 'barbarians' were strongly opposed by followers of Francis Kossuth, the spokesman of Magyar nationalism in its narrowest form. The franchise in Hungary was weighted in favour of Magyar representation in the Diet. Moreover elections were manipulated. From 1875 Hungary was subjected to a policy of rigid Magyarisation. Magyar, a difficult tongue, became virtually the official language; even in primary school all children had to do their lessons in Magyar. The autonomy which Andrassy had promised to the Croats was whittled away. In an attempt to arouse enmity against the Croats, the government tended to favour the Serb minority in Croatia. In due course these two Slav groups made common front against their Magyar masters. The Magyar nationalists, proudly determined that Vienna should never dictate to Budapest, were also pulling against Austria.

Austria and her minorities

Hungary with its Diet had some tradition of representative government. For Austria it was a new experience. From 1867–79 a nationalist and anti-clerical party was prominent. The régime became, at least for Germans, relatively liberal. Censorship was less rigid than before. Primary schooling was made free and compulsory. The influence of the Roman Catholic Church was reduced. After 1870, as in Germany, the *kulturkampf* created problems for Catholic subjects.

In Austria ministers were responsible not to the Reichsrat but to the emperor. From 1879–93 Count Taaffe, a conservative and clerical, and a boyhood friend of the emperor, was prime minister. Little interested in the new-fangled parliament with its rather elementary party system, Taaffe simply tried to keep the parties 'in a balanced state of mild dissatisfaction'. Though in general the outcome was lack of any really constructive policy, concessions were made to the minorities. In Bohemia and Moravia from 1880 the Czech language was used in all official communications. In 1882 the widening of the franchise enabled the minorities to secure stronger representation in the Reichsrat.

Meanwhile a Young Czech Party whose aim was full autonomy for all the lands once ruled by King Wenceslas emerged. Tomàš Masaryk, son of a coachman, appointed professor of philosophy at the new Czech university, was elected to the Reichsrat as a Young Czech in 1891. He soon resigned to further his plans for Czech independence outside parliament.

A Social Democratic Party was founded in Austria in 1888. Early in the twentieth century old age and sickness insurance schemes were introduced by decree. In Vienna the Christian Socialists, a party with *petit bourgeois* (lower middle-class) support, had by then done much to transform the city. Green parks were laid out, schools built, slums cleared and great blocks of flats constructed. Utilities were transferred from private to municipal ownership. (Among those living in the doss houses of Vienna was Adolf Hitler. He arrived there in 1909 when he was twenty.)

In 1897 a law requiring civil servants to be proficient in Czech as well as German aroused such an uproar that the prime minister – himself a Pole – resigned and the ordinance was revoked. Reichsrat elections in 1901 returned Young Czechs and their opponents, the Pan-Germans, in strength. From 1903–07 Czechs and Germans were at loggerheads in Bohemia. In Galicia the Poles were quarrelling with the Ruthenians whilst in the South Tyrol there were feuds between Germans and Italians.

Hungarian separatism

Meanwhile, relations between the partners in the Dual Monarchy became more strained. Towards the close of

The Emperor Francis Joseph (centre) attends an industrialists' ball in Budapest, 1902. By then even in Hungary there were industrialists rich enough to break their way into a 'feudal' society

the nineteenth century Francis Kossuth was leading a Magyar separatist party. These extreme nationalists demanded that Hungarian regiments in the joint army should fly the Hungarian flag and that Magyar should be the language of command. (The army of the Dual Monarchy was multi-national; some of its best commanders, for example, were 'barbarian' Croats. Troops spoke their native tongue among themselves but all had to learn some sixty German words of command.)

The *Ausgleich* provided for a customs union between Austria and Hungary, renewable every ten years. Whenever the time came for discussions, disputes, largely Magyar-instigated, arose. In order to be independent of Austria's port, Trieste, Hungary developed Fiume (Rijeka) as her outlet to the sea.

In 1913 the franchise was extended, but even then only about a quarter of adult males became eligible to vote. The great estates of the nobles still sprawled across the plains. Hungarian society was still feudal in 1914.

The Dual Monarchy in 1914

In Austria the vote was given to men of twenty-four and over in 1907. This was a bid for support from those who opposed the extreme German nationalists; it was thus a bid to preserve unity. For a time the minorities in Austria were less restive. But by 1914 the outlook for the Dual Monarchy was bleak. The Austrian Reichsrat, which had at least been a meeting ground for men of various races, was in abeyance. In Hungary the policy of the government was to oppose Austria. In Bohemia Masaryk was leader of a small group whose aim was to make their homeland fully independent. However, most

Czechs would then have been satisfied with a 'Triple Monarchy' in which Slavs were the equals of Germans and Magyars. Francis Ferdinand, the heir to the thrones of Austria and Hungary, favoured some such scheme – though he inclined more to the south (Yugo) Slavs and the Romanians than to the Czechs. However, his ideas were not acceptable to Francis Joseph. The southern Slavs within the monarchy, many of whom were Serbs, could look for leadership to Serbia – small but independent and fiercely nationalist. So southern Slav leaders favoured absorption into Serbia rather than becoming part of a new federal system within the monarchy. The oppressed Romanians of Transylvania had independent Romania to look to. But before the war, even among the southern Slavs and the Romanians, the majority perhaps wanted security and an end of oppression rather than independence.

There were displays of patriotism at the outbreak of war in 1914. But in Austria social problems soon caused serious disturbances. Hungary continued pulling against her partner, by, for example, withholding supplies of corn. The high degree of control allowed during the war to the military authorities increased the resentment of the minorities. Vague hopes of autonomy hardened into a determination to be free of Austria-Hungary and the House of Habsburg. People who had sat on the fence came down in favour of independence. As the war went on representatives of these peoples won more and more support from Allied leaders. At the end of the war Austria and her uneasy partner Hungary dwindled into insignificance. The Habsburg bastion that had once dominated central Europe tumbled to the ground.

9 To world war: 1871 to August 1914

Sarajevo, 28 June 1914: the match that lit the bonfire

In the years following the Franco-Prussian War the European powers were like children standing by a heap of dry wood with an oil-soaked rag beneath it.

In 1908 Austria had annexed Bosnia and Herzegovina (see p. 93), both inhabited by Serbs. On 28 June 1914 the heir to the thrones of Austria and Hungary, the Habsburg Archduke Francis Ferdinand, visited Sarajevo, the capital of Bosnia. The feelings of Serb patriots were always high on 28 June – the anniversary of Kossovo, the Field of Blackbirds, a great battle fought between Serbs and Turks in the fourteenth century. At Sarajevo on 28 June 1914 Gavrilo Princip, a Bosnian Serb belonging to a nationalist group called Young Serbia, assassinated the archduke and his wife. This was not just another tragedy for the old Habsburg emperor, Francis Joseph; it was the match that lit the fire of war.

Bismarck, just before he died, had said that 'some damned foolish thing in the Balkans' would bring war to Europe. Though the archduke and his wife were shot in Bosnia, part of the Austrian empire, by a Bosnian Serb, Austria a month later declared war on Serbia. Other wars in the Balkans – for example, the Russo-Turkish War of 1877 – had been localised. The war between Austria and Serbia had by August 1914 widened into the Great War which in time became worldwide. And this First World War that ended the years of armed peace was to alter the balance of power in the whole world. How did this Great War come about?

The division of Europe into two camps

Bismarck's fear of a two front war

By 1907 the great powers of Europe were divided into the two camps which clashed in 1914. Though the division of the powers may for a time have helped to keep the peace it was an explosive situation. How did this division come about?

Bismarck was aware that the German victories in the Franco-Prussian War had aroused apprehension among the powers. After 1871 his concern was to protect the

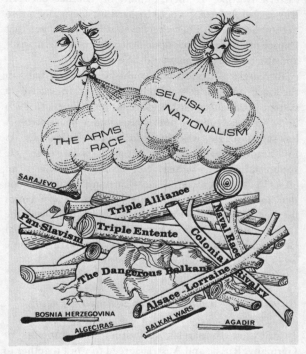

This drawing helps to explain the causes of the First World War. There was a heap of dry wood and an oil-soaked rag. The matches at the bottom had gone out, but in 1914 the match of Sarajevo lit the fire. The winds fanned the flames

German reich, 'the new giant in the heart of Europe'. 'What we gained by war in six months we must protect by arms for fifty years, unless it is to be torn from us again', said Count von Moltke the Elder, who had led Prussia's armies to victory.

The German army was large and efficient enough for Bismarck not to fear any other power – on its own. 'We Germans', he said, 'fear God and nothing else.' But he admitted to suffering from one nightmare – a coalition of powers that could force Germany into a two front war: Germany, a central European power, was open to attack from both the west and the east.

To Germany's west was France, humiliated by defeat, angered by the loss of Alsace-Lorraine and, more than any other power, alarmed by the creation of 'the new giant'. France, Bismarck once said, would always be hostile to Germany. In the east there was the possibility that Russia's policy in the Balkans might bring her into conflict with Austria whose exclusion from Italy and from German affairs had increased her interest in south-eastern Europe. If there should be conflict between Russia and Austria it would be hard for Germany not to become involved. Then there would be the danger that France might seize the opportunity to attack Germany – and the two front war would be a reality.

Bismarck, a juggler who could keep several balls in the air at once, dealt with the problem in the east by a system of alliances and understandings aimed to keep both Austria-Hungary and Russia under his control. A less skilful juggler was bound to run into difficulties. As for France, he set out to try and isolate her. He supported her in Tunisia (see p. 29) not only in an effort to divert her from Alsace-Lorraine but in the hope that an ambitious colonial policy would make enemies for her. The Anglo-French rivalry that followed the British intervention in Egypt (1882) (see p. 28) suited Bismarck's interests well – though Britain in his time was not likely to tie herself to any power.

Bismarck's system of alliances and understandings

In 1873, at Bismarck's suggestion, the emperors of Germany, Russia and Austria agreed to work together to ensure their mutual security. But this Three Emperors' League (*Dreikaiserbund*) proved of little strength when in 1875 a Franco-German dispute threatened hostilities. Nor was it of much avail during the Balkan crisis that preceded the Congress of Berlin in 1878 (see p. 12).

In 1879 Germany entered into an alliance with Austria-Hungary. Under this Dual Alliance, negotiated by Bismarck, the two powers bound each other to mutual assistance if either were attacked by Russia or by another power supported by Russia, and to friendly neutrality if attacked by any other power. The Dual Alliance clearly promised support to Germany in the event of a joint attack by France and Russia. From the Dual Alliance, made in peacetime, regularly renewed and still in force in 1914, sprang further alliances and understandings – and the eventual division of Europe into two camps. 'It was the first thread in a network of alliances that was soon to cover Europe.' And though the terms to which Bismarck agreed in 1879 were strictly defensive, the Dual Alliance made Austria dangerously reckless.

In 1881 Bismarck was able to renew the Three Emperors' League. The emperors pledged themselves to neutrality in the case of war between one of them and a fourth European power. Thus Russia would be bound to remain neutral if there were a war between France and Germany. The emperors also promised to consult in matters concerning the Balkans. Bismarck hoped thus to put Germany in a position to prevent a confrontation between Austria and Russia.

In 1882 Italy, at loggerheads with France over the latter's policy in Tunisia, joined Germany and Austria-Hungary in the Triple Alliance. Germany and Austria-Hungary agreed to help Italy if she were attacked by France. Italy agreed to help Germany if she were attacked by France. Each of the powers agreed to help if either of the others were attacked by any two or more powers and to remain neutral if either of the others were attacked by a single power. Italy would thus remain neutral in for example a war between Austria-Hungary and Russia. As the price for joining this alliance Italy for the time being gave up her claims to Austrian-ruled territory in the South Tyrol and around Trieste. Later Italy came to an understanding with France over Morocco and Tripoli and in 1902, at the very time she was renewing the Triple Alliance, secretly agreed not to join in a war against France.

In 1885 Austria and Russia were in dispute over Bulgaria, who was refusing to toe the Russian line (see p. 13). Again the Three Emperors' League seemed in danger of falling apart. But Bismarck refused to support Austrian provocations, thus improving Russo-German relations. In 1887, when the *Dreikaiserbund* expired, he was able both to renew the Triple Alliance and to negotiate a secret treaty with Russia. By this Reinsurance Treaty Germany and Russia agreed to remain neutral in a war waged by either against a third power – but the treaty did not apply if Germany attacked France or if Russia attacked Austria.

At about this time Bismarck began seeking collaboration between Britain and the members of the Triple Alliance. In 1887 he was able to use British influence to make the Russians moderate their attitude to Bulgaria. At the same time the German government forbade the Reichsbank (the state bank) to make loans to Russia. Such policies left the Russians disillusioned with their German 'partner'. In 1888 they turned for financial help to France.

Still, in 1890, the year when Bismarck fell from power, the Russians seemed anxious to renew the Reinsurance Treaty. But the new German chancellor, Caprivi, refused renewal. Hopeful of forming ties with Britain he was willing to weaken relations with her

With the Franco-Russian alliance soon to be concluded, the Russian fleet received a rapturous welcome when it visited Toulon in 1893. Contrast these ships, which still carried sail, with the Dreadnought on p. 88

traditional enemy, Russia. Bismarck's successors, less capable than he of running with the hare and hunting with the hounds, succeeded only in antagonising Britain as well as Russia – and eventually drove Britain into partnership with France and then Russia. And whereas Bismarck had avoided unlimited guarantees, his successors led Austria to believe that the Dual Alliance, on paper still purely defensive, gave her the support of Germany in virtually any circumstances.

The Franco-Russian Alliance, 1894

As France and Russia began drawing together the nightmare of a two front war threatened Germany. France made her first loan to Russia in 1888, the year when the Dual Alliance of Germany and Austria-Hungary became public. Yearly, until 1917, French loans helped develop Russian industry and communications. Capital for the Trans-Siberian and Chinese Eastern railways came from French investors. And Russia herself was able to make loans to China, thus gaining more influence in the Far East.

Just as France and Russia were moving towards a full alliance Bismarck, 'the uncrowned king of Germany', was asked to resign (see p. 79). The Iron Chancellor, as he was called, was then seventy-five. Though his control of affairs could not have continued for much longer, he might, while he remained in office, have managed to keep Russia and France apart. Under his leadership the new Germany had sought security. 'We are surfeited', Bismarck had said in 1872 – and seems to have meant it. Under William II Germany, it seemed, wanted to dominate the world. World power, the kaiser said, was Germany's 'historical mission'. To what extent he wanted territorial gains or merely prestige is uncertain. Believing in his own divine right, he was arrogant, inclined to make melodramatic speeches and much less cool and calculating than Bismarck.

The Franco-Russian Alliance, the terms of which had been worked out by August 1892, was concluded early in 1894. The alliance, to continue for as long as the Triple Alliance was in force, provided that Russia would support France if the latter were attacked by Germany or by Italy with Germany's help. France was to support

Russia if the latter were attacked by Germany or by Austria with Germany's help. If any member of the Triple Alliance mobilised, France and Russia were to mobilise immediately. This provision was dangerous for mobilisation could have much the same effect as a declaration of war, especially when the idea of the swift 'knockout' war was accepted (see p. 92). The result of the alliance was that Germany would have to fight on two fronts if she attacked either France or Russia.

There were great differences between republican France and autocratic Russia. 'Beauty', it was said, 'was dancing with the Beast.' For the tsar to uncover his head for the playing of the *Marseillaise* (the French national anthem with its revolutionary associations) might have seemed impossible – but he did. To some extent ties with France affected tsarist domestic policy – the tsar's acceptance of the Duma, for example (see p. 43).

Great Britain and Germany

'Splendid' isolation

For much of the time since Napoleon Bonaparte's defeat Britain had preferred to be in 'splendid' isolation from European affairs. She controlled the seas and had an extensive empire. Her trade flourished. She seemed to

want no help from anyone and had intervened in European affairs only when her own interests were involved. But towards the end of the nineteenth century there were signs of change.

As a result of rivalry in Africa and South-east Asia relations with France were not good. France had refused to act with Britain when Alexandria was bombarded in 1882 and the subsequent British occupation of Egypt was not acceptable to her. The Fashoda affair (see p. 31) provoked an alarming crisis; though relations improved, the possibility of further crises remained.

Britain's predominant position during the nineteenth century was based on industrial supremacy – and on sea power. France and Russia had powerful fleets but Britain throughout the nineteenth century made sure that her navy was larger than their combined navies. Towards the end of the century the United States and even Japan were building large fleets. Though a review at Spithead in 1897, during Victoria's Diamond Jubilee, gave an impression of overwhelming might, Britain's naval supremacy was already being challenged.

The naval race

Bismarck was always careful not to antagonise Britain without reason. And Bismarck had been content with land power. In 1890 the kaiser said: 'Our future lies on

HMS Dreadnought; not all her ten big guns can be seen

the water.' He was a firm believer in the popular doctrine that sea power is the basis of world power. He referred to himself as the Admiral of the Atlantic. In 1895 the Kiel Canal, linking the Baltic and North seas, was completed. Under Admiral von Tirpitz Navy Laws in 1898, 1900 and 1908 announced great shipbuilding programmes. The British, thus challenged, in 1906 launched HMS *Dreadnought*, a battleship of an altogether new design. Built in a year and a day, she was capable of 21 knots and had ten 305-millimetre guns that could fire while she was beyond torpedo range. All existing battleships thus became virtually useless. Then Germany began to build battleships of the dreadnought class. The British public then demanded more of these vessels: 'We want eight [more battleships] and we won't wait', they sang.

Not all Germans approved of the kaiser's naval ambitions; for example, Bülow, chancellor from 1900 to 1909, did not. But in the years before the First World War the kaiser tried to keep policy in his own hands. And many Germans had a genuine fear of British sea power. What would happen if Britain should behave as Japan had done at Port Arthur in 1904 (see p. 20)? *The Times*, praising that attack, had said: 'The Japanese have opened the war by an act of daring which is destined to take a place of honour in naval annals.'

The average Englishman's views were expressed by Churchill, first lord of the admiralty from 1911 to 1915: 'Whereas a large navy was a necessity for England', with her far flung empire and dependence on imports, 'it was a luxury for Germany'. People wondered whether the kaiser would have intervened in the Boer War if his fleet had been larger. He had said then: 'I am not in a position to go beyond the strictest neutrality. . . . In twenty years time, when my fleet is ready, I can use different language.' The cruising range of the German ships was reported to be short. Against whom then – except Britain – could their guns be aimed? From 1904 to 1910 (and from 1914 to 1915) Sir John Fisher, a terrifying figure at sight of whom 'the deck and the sailors shook', commanded the Royal Navy. Fisher was determined that Britannia should continue to rule the waves. He named one of his ships *Ut veniant omnes* (Let them all come). While Germany went on building ships he spent his vast energy on plans for new and better vessels for Britannia. So the naval race went on, arousing fear and suspicion and making any Anglo-German understanding unlikely. Meanwhile, the expansion of German industry and of her merchant marine aroused jealousy if not hostility in Britain.

Negotiations between Britain and Germany

Earlier it had seemed that Britain might end her isolation by coming to an alliance or at least an understanding with Germany. The 1890 treaty concerning German and British boundaries in Africa (see p. 31) was not ungenerous to Britain – and may have been intended to coax her into friendship. But Salisbury was unwilling to tie Britain on the terms offered by Germany. Germany also tried to frighten the British into friendship. At the time of the Jameson raid (see p. 27) the kaiser sent his congratulatory telegram to Kruger. This, with its veiled threat, perhaps brought home to the British their isolation, but they were not to be threatened into friendship.

Kaiser William II, although he was a grandson of Queen Victoria, was intensely jealous of Britain. He claimed that his uncle, Edward VII, was plotting the encirclement of Germany. 'Edward', he once said, 'is Satan. You cannot imagine what a Satan he is.' 'My colleagues, the rulers of Europe, have never paid attention to what I have to say. Soon, with my great navy to support my words, they will be more respectful', he said to the king of Italy.

In 1901 negotiations with Lord Lansdowne, British foreign secretary, came to nothing. By then the desire of many Germans to dominate the world was becoming apparent in England. It was about then that propaganda fiction describing a German invasion of England replaced stories of a French invasion. Anglo-German relations became less and less friendly. In 1911, at the time of the second Moroccan crisis, the British fleet was prepared for action, whilst Lloyd George warned that Britain would not 'surrender' to German threats (see p. 33). In 1912 German negotiations with Lord Haldane, British secretary of state for war, came to nothing. By that time, as Bethmann Hollweg, the German chancellor noted, Germany had upset Russia over the Berlin to Baghdad Railway (see p. 93), Britain over her fleet and France over Morocco.

Yet in 1914 Germany and Britain made an agreement about the Baghdad Railway. And the Anglo-Iranian Oil Company came to an agreement with German interests in the Persian Gulf – though British warships were then converting from coal to oil. Britain, though she had arrived at an understanding with Russia in 1907 (see p. 91), probably regarded Germany as less of a threat than Russia to her interests in the Persian Gulf. When Princip fired at the archduke in Sarajevo British warships were visiting Kiel.

May 1913: Kaiser William II (left) and his cousin, King George V, ride to review troops at Potsdam Palace near Berlin

The Triple Entente

France and Britain: the Entente Cordiale, 1904

In January 1902, shortly after Lansdowne's negotiations with Germany collapsed, the world was startled by the signing of the Anglo-Japanese Alliance (see p. 20). Though this related only to the Far East, it was clear that the alliance might make Japan confident enough to attack Russia. What then might be the position of France, Russia's ally? Might Britain be drawn into a war on Japan's side, and France on Russia's side? In these circumstances it seemed desirable for France to settle differences with Britain.

In 1901 Edward VII had succeeded his mother, Victoria. When in 1903 he visited Paris for the first time after his accession the crowds shouted: 'Long live Fashoda. Long live the Boers.' By the end of his visit they were shouting: 'Long live our king.' Edward's popularity in France increased. When he died (1910) Paris lamp posts and shop windows were draped in black. Cab drivers tied black bows on their whips.

Shortly after Edward's visit to Paris in 1903 conversations which led to the signing of the Entente Cordiale (Friendly Understanding) began. The hard work of British and French diplomats was responsible for the Entente Cordiale. But Edward's popularity in France made it easier for the British and the French to settle their differences.

The entente was signed in April 1904, soon after the outbreak (February 1904) of the Russo-Japanese War. Unlike the Triple Alliance, the Entente Cordiale was not directed against specific foes – nor was it a military alliance. All it did was to clear the way for Britain and France to co-operate. It did this by settling various disputes concerning overseas territories. In particular, it promised France a free hand in Morocco, whilst Britain's occupation of Egypt was not to be opposed. The understanding covered also lesser affairs – frontiers in West Africa, Madagascar, the remote New Hebrides and fishing rights in Newfoundland. It dealt also with Siam, which lay between the French in Indo-China and the British in Burma and Malaya. Britain's chief concern seemed still to be for her empire. So Germany had had less to offer than France.

From 1904 Britain and France drew closer together though neither party really knew how far the other would support her in a crisis. Germany, when she intervened in Morocco in 1905 (see p. 33), was trying to test the strength of the entente; Britain, by supporting France, showed that the understanding was real. In January 1906, a day after the Algeçiras conference opened, Anglo-French military talks began. In 1911, after the crisis at Agadir, naval talks began. Following the failure of Haldane's mission to Berlin in 1912 the French fleet was concentrated in the Mediterranean, whilst the Royal Navy withdrew to home bases. A full military alliance between France and Britain was made only after the First World War had begun.

France, Russia and Britain: the Triple Entente, 1907

It seemed unlikely that Britain would ever come to an understanding with Russia, France's partner by the 1894 alliance. British suspicion of Russian moves in the Balkans, in Persia, Afghanistan and the Far East was traditional. In 1901 an Anglo-Persian oil concession was granted. The increasing use of oil made British power in the Persian Gulf vital. Moreover, Britain's ally, Japan, had made war on Russia in 1904. And liberal Britain disapproved of Russian despotism. 'Long live the

Duma', shouted the prime minister in 1906 when parliamentarians from more than twenty countries met in London.

In 1904 Russian warships on their way from the Baltic to defeat at Tsushima fired on British fishing vessels in the North Sea – believing that they were Japanese torpedo boats! A number of British ships were sunk during this tragic little battle of the Dogger Bank. However, the crisis that resulted was settled peacefully.

Mistrust of Germany and fear of her naval power, French pressure after the Algeçiras crisis, and apprehension lest Germany and Russia might again come to an understanding, led Sir Edward Grey, British foreign secretary from 1905–16, to begin talks with Russia. In August 1907 British and Russian negotiators agreed that Persia should be divided into three spheres of influence. The northern sphere, including Tehran, was to be under Russian influence, and the southern sphere under British influence. The middle zone was to be neutral. Persia in effect was partitioned. Afghanistan was to be a British sphere of influence. Tibet, of interest to both Russia and Britain, was declared to be neutral and China's sovereignty there was recognised.

The removal of such obstacles to friendship in 1907 enabled Britain, France and Russia to come to the understanding known as the Triple Entente. Again there was no military alliance, just an agreement to work together – though Britain suspected Russia of cheating her in Persia.

So from 1907 the major states of Europe were drawn up in two camps – the Dual Alliance of Germany and Austria-Hungary and the Triple Entente. Italy, allied to Germany and Austria-Hungary by the Triple Alliance, stood watching on the sidelines.

The armed peace

The two camps year by year increased their strength. The armies ready for war on the continent were the largest ever formed in Europe in time of peace. Behind the professional armies conscription provided great reserves of manpower. Britain, relying on her naval power, did not introduce conscription until 1916. Between 1899 and 1914 Russia, France, Germany and Austria-Hungary greatly increased their armies. In 1913 a German Army Act decreed great increases in expenditure during the next eighteen months. And so it went on.

From 1911, as first lord of the admiralty, Churchill, who had earlier opposed expenditure on the navy, was

Population (in millions), 1870–1914

	1870	1900	1914
Austria-Hungary	36	45	51.6 [1]
Britain	31	42	46
France	38	39	40
Germany	39	57	68
Italy	27	32	35
Russia	78	112	142
USA	40	76	98

[1] Excluding Bosnia-Herzegovina

Coal production (in million tonnes), 1880–1914

	1880	1900	1914
Austria-Hungary	15.0	39.0	47.0
Britain	149.0	228.0	292.0
France	19.4	33.4	40.0
Germany	59.0	149.0	277.0
Italy	—	0.5	0.9
Russia	3.2	16.2	36.2
USA	64.9	244.0	455.0

Steel production (in million tonnes), 1880–1914

	1880	1900	1914
Austria-Hungary	—	1.2	2.7
Britain	1.3	5.0	6.5
France	0.4	1.6	3.5
Germany	0.7	6.7	14.0
Russia	—	1.5	4.1
USA	1.3	10.0	32.0

(Steel production in Italy was insignificant.)

Germany's growth in population and industrial might is apparent from these tables. However, United States growth was even more rapid

obliged to follow a policy of expansion. In 1913 he suggested that Britain and Germany should take a 'naval holiday' by building no more ships for a time. Germany ignored the suggestion. So new ships continued to be built and old ones were scrapped or modernised. Scapa Flow and Cromarty, facing Germany across the North Sea, were fortified. Germany raced on. By 1913 she was widening the Kiel Canal to allow passage of her dreadnoughts.

Munitions firms, some with international connections, increased their output. Krupps, the German armaments firm, was the greatest single business in Europe. In the United States the Carnegie Steel

Corporation between 1896 and 1900 increased its annual profits from $6 million to $40 million. In Britain Armstrong-Whitworth made immense profits building ever bigger battleships. In France Schneider built up a great armaments industry. In Sweden Nobel made a fortune from the manufacture of explosives. Between 1867 and 1897 annual production of dynamite rose from 11 to 66,500 tonnes.

The manufacturers of arms profited by selling their wares to 'both sides of every quarrel'. By inventing new weapons they drove the nations into competitive arming at ever increasing cost. While all governments were saying that war must be avoided, all were busy amassing arms. A conference called by Tsar Nicholas II for the limitation of armaments proved abortive (see p. 117). Nobel in 1892 said: 'One already hears in the distance war's hollow rumble.' The Norwegian dramatist Ibsen wrote: 'We are sailing with a corpse in our cargo.'

The various powers drew up their war plans. Germany had a plan drawn up by Count Alfred von Schlieffen, chief of staff from 1891 to 1906. This secret plan was based on the assumption that Germany would be fighting France and Russia simultaneously. If war came relatively few divisions were to be sent to the eastern, Russian, front. Another small defensive force was to hold the Franco-German frontier. The remainder of Germany's troops, seven-eighths according to the original plan, were to march into neutral Belgium and make a concentrated attack on France with the aim of capturing Paris. Then it would be Russia's turn for a full-scale attack. Speed and strict adherence to a detailed timetable were essential to the success of the Schlieffen plan. The Germans were to cross the Belgian frontier on the twelfth day after mobilisation. Brussels was to be taken on the nineteenth day, the French frontier was to be crossed three days later and Paris was to be captured on M39 – the thirty-ninth day after mobilisation.

The other European powers, too, had plans of a sort. The Russian plan initially was to attack only Austria and to carry on a defensive war against Germany. But the French, afraid of being overwhelmed by German numbers, were determined if war came to force Germany to fight on two fronts from the first moment. So they persuaded the Russians to promise to attack both Germany and Austria as soon as war should come. Meanwhile the English and French were making their plans. Anglo-Russian naval talks began only after the outbreak of war.

So Europe, divided by alliances and ententes, was well prepared for war. 'The reservoirs of power were full.' When the 'vials of wrath overflowed' in the Balkans an explosion occurred that was to bring Europe down in ruins.

The Balkans

The oil-soaked rag

The extension of Bulgaria's territory by her union with Eastern Rumelia (see p. 13) had angered Serbia. And Bulgaria, Serbia and Greece all wanted a share in Macedonia and Albania, which were Turkish territory. But the most serious threat to peace was enmity between Austria-Hungary and Serbia. Serbia had been angered when the Congress of Berlin allowed Austria to administer the Turkish provinces of Bosnia and Herzegovina, with their Serb population. Serb nationalists were determined that Bosnia and Herzegovina should be united with Serbia (see map p. 81) to form a Yugoslav (South Slav) state.

However, towards the end of the nineteenth century Serbia was relatively quiet. The king, an Obrenovitch, did not antagonise Austria. But in 1903 the king and queen of Serbia and some twenty of their attendants were murdered during a palace coup and the Karageorgevitch dynasty – and with it an aggressively anti-Austrian and pro-Russian policy – was restored. A tariff dispute between Austria and Serbia, the so-called Pig War, increased hostility. Meanwhile Serbia was buying arms from France.

For her part Austria wanted to expand farther into the Balkans. Unlike Britain, France and Germany she had no 'place in the sun' in Africa. Bismarck had excluded her from German affairs. And after the loss of Venice (1866) the empire's only ports were Trieste and Fiume on the Adriatic – to both of which Italy laid claim. So the Austrian desire to reach the Aegean Sea at Salonika was strong. But instead of being able to expand into the Balkans, Austria-Hungary, it seemed, might contract or even split apart because of Balkan nationalism. Above all, Austria was fearful that Pan-Slav and Pan-Serb propaganda from Serbia would disturb the hotchpotch of peoples under Habsburg rule. Some Austrian statesmen felt that Serbia should be broken before she became too strong.

Towards the end of the nineteenth century Germany interested herself in the Balkans, a policy of which Bismarck would never have approved. Germany became friendly with Turkey, still ruled by Sultan Abdul

Hamid, Abdul the Damned and Unreformed. In 1896 a German company completed a railway from the Bosphorus to Konia in Asia Minor. In 1898 after the kaiser, untroubled by the sultan's massacres of Christian Armenians, paid a visit to Constantinople, the sultan agreed that the line to Konia should be continued to Baghdad. In 1903 the Germans were given the right to extend the Baghdad Railway to the Persian Gulf. They also had railway concessions in Serbia and Bulgaria; these in turn linked up with railways in Germany. The whole scheme was known as the Berlin to Baghdad Railway. 'With a bow to the British lion and a curtsey to the Russian bear, we will worm our way little by little down to the Persian Gulf,' Bülow boasted. In fact the Baghdad Railway had only reached Mosul when the First World War began. German interest in Iraq (Mesopotamia), where oil had been found, and in Persia, displeased both the French and the British.

Russia necessarily remained interested in the Straits, giving entrance from the Black Sea to the Mediterranean. Half her total exports and nearly all her exports of grain were carried in vessels sailing from Black Sea ports. Imports of machinery came through these ports. In 1912, when Turkey closed the Straits during her war against Italy, trade was disrupted.

Britain and France were less interested in the Balkans after they had acquired territory in North Africa. The British occupation of Egypt protected the Suez Canal and guaranteed the route to India.

Austria annexes Bosnia and Herzegovina, 1908

In the late nineteenth century a number of young Turkish army officers, calling themselves the Secret Society of Union and Progress, began meeting in Geneva and then in Paris. Claiming to be liberals these Young Turks demanded the restoration of the constitution that had had so brief a life in 1876 (see p. 11) and promised equality to all Turkish subjects, rayas and Muslims.

In 1908 the Young Turks won over troops in Salonika. Soon there were uprisings in many parts of the Ottoman empire. In 1909 the Young Turks captured Constantinople. They forced Abdul Hamid to leave his palace – and the St Bernard dogs that guarded him day and night. Muhammad V then became sultan. He promised such revolutionary changes as a parliament and civil liberties. It seemed that the Young Turks might be the saviours of their country and that even for the rayas life might improve.

Amid the confusion of the Young Turk Revolution, Austria in October 1908 annexed Bosnia and Herzegovina. This was the first of three crises that occurred after the division of the powers had been completed in 1907. Britain proposed that an international conference should be called. But Austria, confident of the support of Germany, ignored this suggestion. Turkey agreed to accept compensation for her two provinces; in addition, the sanjak of Novibazar, garrisoned by Austria-Hungary since 1878, returned to Turkish control.

The anger of Serb nationalists rose to boiling point after the annexation of Bosnia and Herzegovina. Serbia's path to the Adriatic was blocked. Her dream of union with Bosnia and Herzegovina, the dream of a Yugoslav state, seemed to be ended. Serbia prepared to mobilise her army. But she was too small for her protests to be effective without outside support.

Russia would have liked to support Serbia. Defeat by Japan, by checking tsarist ambitions in the Far East, had made Russia's interest in south-eastern Europe, and her desire for prestige, greater. But weakened by war with Japan and the 1905 Revolution she did nothing.

The kaiser boasted that he had stood by Austria 'in shining armour' during the tense days that followed the annexation. He had indeed: Bülow had warned Russia that if Serbia did not accept the annexation Austria would make war on Serbia with Germany's full support. Britain and France, whilst not recognising the annexation, were not prepared to help Russia or Serbia. The Triple Entente did not appear at that time to be a very firm association.

Bulgaria and Italy took advantage of Turkey's weakness. In 1908 Bulgaria declared herself fully independent with Ferdinand, the Long Nosed Fox of the Balkans, as her tsar. And in 1911 Italy declared war on Turkey. In 1912, on the defeat of Turkey, Italy received Tripoli (Libya). She also occupied the Dodecanese Islands, though these were supposed later to be returned to Turkey.

In 1911 came the second of the three pre-war crises, the Agadir crisis (see p. 33). Here the German threat to France and fear for her own naval power drove Britain closer to France. The German military chiefs, feeling they had been outmanoeuvred, were determined there should not be a second such climbdown.

The Balkan Wars, 1912–13

The administration set up by the Young Turks proved

The Balkans, 1913; after the treaties of London and Bucharest

to be narrowly nationalist, the reverse of liberal. Life for rayas in Macedonia and Albania did not improve with the departure of Abdul the Damned and Unreformed, for the promises the Young Turks had made were all broken, as similar promises had been in the past. In 1915 some 600,000 Armenians were massacred.

For their own reasons the major powers had from time to time either supported or tried to weaken the Sick Turk; now the little Balkan states were to knock him right over. In 1912, while the Turkish army was engaged against Italy, a Balkan League was formed that showed a new and threatening unity. Venizelos, the prime minister of Greece, did much to help the formation of the league. The Russians too played a major part. The league's aim was not only to support the rayas still under Turkish misrule. All the Balkan states had hopes of getting a share of Macedonia and Albania. Desires for territorial gains combined with the brutality of the Turks thus drove the Balkan states into a temporary union.

In October 1912 the Balkan League (Bulgaria, Greece, Serbia and Montenegro) went to war against Turkey – and had remarkable success. By 1913 the sick man was virtually gone from Europe; not much more than Constantinople was left to him.

Following an armistice the great powers met in London and again tried to settle Balkan affairs. In May 1913 they agreed that nearly all Turkey's European territories should be shared between Serbia, Montenegro, Greece and Bulgaria. But a decision that Albania, instead of being shared out, should be independent, was highly displeasing to Serbia and her neighbour Montenegro, for Albania blocked Serbia's path to the Adriatic. In compensation Serbia was to receive, at Bulgaria's expense, a large slice of Macedonia.

Soon the Balkan League was divided by disputes. In June 1913 Bulgaria, who had done most of the fighting against Turkey, attacked Serbia and Greece. Then Romania and Turkey joined the war against Bulgaria. Bulgaria was overwhelmed. In August 1913 the Treaty of Bucharest made a fresh division of territory (see map). Macedonia, the prize for which both Balkan Wars had really been fought, was divided between Serbia and Greece, whose share included Salonika. Greece was also to have the long sought after island of Crete. Romania, who had seized part of the Bulgarian Dobruja, kept it. Turkey got a reward – Bulgaria had to restore Adrianople to her. Montenegro, whose ruler had fired the first gun against the Turks, took no part in the Second Balkan War but kept the territory taken in the first war.

After the Second Balkan War the great powers still insisted on the independence of Albania. An Austrian ultimatum forced the Serbs, who had twice invaded this new state, to withdraw. The Greeks had to leave southern Albania. Beyond this the powers did not intervene after the second war.

Nationalism at white heat

The 'vials of wrath' were full in the Balkans. Nobody's satellites, the Balkan states sought allies who could be useful to them. Serbia and Montenegro, flushed with victory and eager to try their strength against Austria-Hungary, looked to Russia. The Bulgars, brooding over their 'intolerable wrongs' and furling 'their glorious standards for the days to come', were inclined to seek sympathy from Austria and Turkey.

In Serbia anti-Austrian feeling was kept at white heat by the Unity or Death Society, often known as the Black Hand. Nationalism became more intense as Serbia, her territory much enlarged after the Balkan Wars, grew in strength. The Black Hand spread hatred of Austria. Whether Austria had real reason to fear Pan-Serb agitation is hard to say, but many Austrians, confident of German support, felt that troublesome Serbia should be suppressed or even destroyed. To such people the idea of war against the state that was 'the heart and centre' of Pan-Serb propaganda was welcome, for from Serbia might come a South Slav rebirth that would drive the Austro-Hungarian empire out of all its Serbian, Croat and Slovene territories.

28 June–4 August 1914

The Habsburg empire, it had long been said, would collapse as soon as Turkey collapsed. Turkey, it seemed, had collapsed, her European territory after the Balkan Wars being limited to the area around Constantinople and Adrianople.

Then on 28 June 1914 the Austrian archduke and his wife, herself a Slav, paid their visit to Sarajevo. The gun which Gavrilo Princip fired that day was supplied by the Serbian Black Hand. Berchtold, the Austrian chancellor, welcoming an excuse for war, claimed that the Serbian government had planned the assassinations. Though this was not so, the Serbian authorities probably knew an attack was intended.

On 5 July a war council called by the kaiser promised 'faithful support' if action by Austria against Serbia provoked Russian intervention. Not all Germans wanted to give such strong support to Austria. The chancellor, Bethmann Hollweg, disagreed with a policy which in effect changed the Dual Alliance of 1879 from a defensive into an aggressive alliance. Even the kaiser was alarmed at the prospect of real war. But the attitude of the military high command was different. And in Germany 'a wilful army' could get its way. The attitude of the army was of course affected by the fact that if war was coming it needed to act speedily. For the Schlieffen plan depended for its success upon speed.

On 23 July Austria-Hungary sent Serbia an ultimatum that had to be replied to within forty-eight hours. So harsh were the terms that Sir Edward Grey said that submission in full would end Serbia's existence as an independent state. Serbia's answer was reasonable, as the kaiser for example admitted, though she did not yield to all Austria's demands. A British proposal for a conference of the powers was of no effect. The decision taken at the kaiser's war council had given Austria 'a blank cheque' and Austria was recklessly determined to fill it in and cash it.

So Serbia's reply to the ultimatum was rejected.

28 June 1914: the Archduke Francis Ferdinand, and his wife, leave the city hall at Sarajevo to step into an open car. Earlier that morning a bomb had been thrown at them. Yet there were few security arrangements and a few minutes after leaving the hall they were assassinated. The men wearing fezzes are Muslims

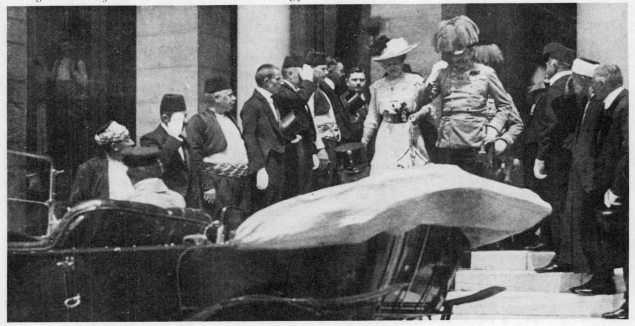

Meanwhile Serbia had mobilised her forces. On 28 July 1914 the Emperor Francis Joseph declared war on Serbia. The next day Austrian troops marched into Serbia and bombarded Belgrade.

> An Austrian army awfully arrayed
> Boldly by battery besieged Belgrade.
> Cossack commanders cannonading come –

For Russia, having promised to support Serbia, and unwilling to let Austria and Germany win domination over an area that might include the Black Sea and the Straits, then mobilised. On 31 July she refused a German ultimatum to demobilise.

On 1 August Germany mobilised and declared war on Russia. France then mobilised as the Franco-Russian Alliance obliged her to do. When she refused a German demand to remain neutral, Germany, on 3 August, declared war on her. French soldiers, as they joined their regiments, were shouting: 'We must have Alsace and Lorraine – Oh! Oh! Oh!' But it was not to recover Alsace-Lorraine that France went to war.

For a few days the intentions of Britain, not bound by strict military alliance to any of the powers concerned, had not been clear. Anything Britain might have done in the days following Austria's declaration of war would almost certainly not have prevented the spread of the war. But in later years France claimed that an early and definite declaration from Great Britain might have stopped the war from spreading. Britain did inform Germany that she would not allow a naval attack upon France in the Channel. And Churchill on 1 August ordered the fleet to mobilise.

Then at 7 a.m. on 4 August Germany, having been refused passage through neutral Belgium, marched her troops into that country with the object of invading France. Britain mobilised at 4 p.m. that day and from 11 p.m. was at war with Germany. Germany had dishonoured the 1839 Treaty of London guaranteeing the neutrality of Belgium – 'a scrap of paper' Bethmann Hollweg called it. The people of England had not been much interested in the war until then. 'To hell with Serbia', one newspaper said. But when Belgium was invaded almost everyone was in full support of the declaration of war.

It had long been British policy to resist any power that attempted to attack Belgium, whose ports face London: 'Hands off Antwerp', was a traditional cry. So, in addition to honouring the 1839 treaty and their moral obligation to support France, the British were protecting their own interests – as indeed were all the powers.

Conclusion

In due course Austria-Hungary declared war on Russia. France and Britain declared war on Austria-Hungary. With Britain were swept into the war Canada, Australia, New Zealand, the Union of South Africa, India and Britain's entire colonial empire. The peoples of Canada, Australia, New Zealand and many in South Africa were eager to help the 'mother country', but millions in India and Africa were involved in a war 'of which they understood nothing against an enemy who was also unknown to them'. The peoples of France's colonial empire also found themselves at war. Other states – European, American and Asian – joined in the contest. Japan supported her ally, Britain. The Sick Turk and disappointed Bulgaria joined Germany and Austria-Hungary. Italy, Romania, the United States, Greece, China, Brazil and others joined the Entente powers.

'Some damned foolish thing in the Balkans' had blazed up into a general war. Selfish national interests and memories of old quarrels and recent disputes fanned the flames. So there was plenty of wood to keep the bonfire going. The many people who in August 1914 thought the war that interrupted their summer holidays would be a brief one, the kaiser who said his troops would be home 'before the leaves fall', were mistaken. As he watched the street lights being lit in Whitehall Sir Edward Grey said: 'The lamps are going out all over Europe; we shall not see them lit again in our lifetime.'

Was any power more to blame than others for the dark years of war? Historians have for long debated the degree of responsibility of the major powers. Austria was clearly determined to crush Serbia, whatever the consequences. But was it only because of Germany's support that she was bold enough to act so recklessly? The Germans bitterly resented the implication in the Treaty of Versailles (see p. 113) that they were 'guilty' of causing the First World War. Beyond doubt their bold policy of world supremacy helped to bring the Entente powers into line. But was Germany's responsibility greater than this? As fresh facts come to light some historians, among them Germans, have come to believe it was much greater. Many Germans, they say, were willing to risk a major war breaking out, perhaps even to provoke a major war, in order to win world predominance. To these historians the First and Second World Wars were consecutive acts in one tragic drama.

As for Gavrilo Princip, he died of tuberculosis in an Austrian prison in 1918. He was nineteen when he fired the shots in Sarajevo.

10 The First World War, 1914–18

The Great War

The First World War, entered into almost light-heartedly by some, but with dreadful premonitions by others, became a long drawn out agony. The exhilaration of Rupert Brooke's 'Now God be thanked who has matched us with His hour' fell, as the slaughter dragged on, into the bitterness of Wilfred Owen's 'What passing bells for these who die as cattle?' There had been longer struggles. But there had been none so total as this Great War, as it used to be called, involving so many countries and so many people. Millions died before the guns ceased firing on 11 November 1918. Owen, killed a week before the armistice, described one of those who lived on:

Now, he will spend a few sick years in Institutes,
And do what things the rules consider wise,
And take whatever pity they may dole.
Tonight he noticed how the women's eyes
Passed from him to the strong men that were whole.
How cold and late it is! Why don't they come
And put him into bed? Why don't they come?

The early battles

German mobilisation was near perfect. At stations and sidings built along the Belgian and Luxembourg borders vast hordes of men, under the command of Count von Moltke the Younger, a nephew of William I's chief of staff, swarmed out of German trains. After meeting unexpected resistance from the Belgians in such fortresses as Liège and Namur, the German armies of the right wing swung south and east into France. Atrocities committed with the object of breaking Belgian resistance, for example the destruction of Louvain with its ancient library, hardened the will of the Allies. (From September 1914 when the Entente powers entered into full military alliance they were known as the Allied powers; those who joined them later were called the Associated powers. Germany and her allies were called the Central powers.)

French mobilisation too was speedy. An offensive in Alsace-Lorraine failed to drive the Germans back, but continued to engage large German forces urgently required on the right (western) flank of the invading armies. And although Schlieffen had insisted that the right flank must be kept strong, Moltke reinforced the left flank at the expense of the right. Meanwhile, the Russians, having mobilised more quickly than had been expected, were invading East Prussia. Moltke therefore switched two corps from the French front to the Russian front – thus disastrously weakening the armies invading France. Nevertheless the French armies on the German right were forced to retreat towards Paris.

The British Expeditionary Force (BEF), which had advanced into Belgium, had to retreat from Mons, where for one day it had stemmed the German advance. The BEF was a highly trained but small army of about 80,000 – a 'contemptible little force' the kaiser called it. Some sixty aeroplanes of the Royal Flying Corps were used for reconnaissance with the BEF.

By 2 September one German army was close enough to Paris to see the Eiffel Tower. But the Germans were nearing exhaustion and losing contact with their supplies. On 6 September the French commander, General Joffre, counter-attacked. A great front of French troops, assisted by the 'Old Contemptibles', as the BEF proudly called themselves, turned about. From the River Marne, on a line running from Verdun to Paris, they drove the Germans north. On 13 September they came to a halt on the River Aisne (see map p. 98). This Allied counter-attack, the first battle of the Marne, may have sealed Germany's fate. She had control of Belgium and much of northern France (including valuable industrial areas) but the possibility of the knockout victory over France was gone. After the Marne, Moltke, ill and depressed, is said to have told the kaiser that the war was 'lost'. He was relieved of his command and replaced by General Erich von Falkenhayn.

The Belgians held out until early October 1914, when Antwerp fell to the Germans; thereafter Belgian forces fought on the western sector of the Allied lines. From early October to November the Germans and the Allies raced towards the coast, to reach the vital Channel ports. From the end of October to late November the BEF,

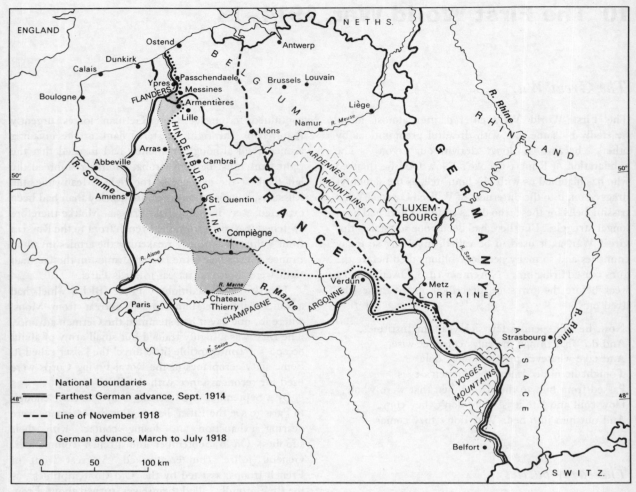

The western front, 1914–18

aided by Indian troops, fought the first of three great battles around Ypres. They fought doggedly and held Ypres, or what was left of it. Control of the Channel ports remained in Allied hands, but a tenth of the men of the BEF had been killed.

On the western front, in Belgium and northern France, there followed years of trench warfare. Lines of parallel trenches, stretching from the Alps at the Swiss frontier to the sea at Ostend, were dug and fortified. At one point the German line was only about 100 kilometres from Paris. From their lines the forces of the Allied and Central powers tried to advance across the no man's land between – to be killed in artillery barrages or by machine gun or rifle fire, or to be caught on the barbed wire that protected their enemies' dugouts, or sometimes to drown in mud. Initially the troops were ill

equipped for trench warfare. The British did not use steel helmets until the autumn of 1915. They had few telephones, but great numbers of horses – requiring shiploads of hay. The lines of trenches remained almost stationary though from time to time hundreds of thousands of men fought for a few square kilometres of land.

The eastern front was more mobile. At one time the line thrust deep into German East Prussia and Austrian Galicia (see map p. 99); later it was swept back far to the east into Russia. In the early weeks of the war the Russians won a considerable victory in Galicia; among the prisoners taken were Habsburg subjects who were happy to join the Allies. The Serbs too won victories against the Austrians who never really recovered from these early defeats. Meanwhile two Russian armies

The eastern front, 1914–18

The Japanese also occupied Germany's island colonies in the northern Pacific.

German Togoland fell in August 1914. New Zealand troops took Samoa in the same month and in September the Australians captured German New Guinea. South African troops led by the Boer general, Botha, took German South-west Africa in 1915. The Cameroons, and German East Africa, where Jan Smuts was for a time Allied commander, held out until 1917. Survivors from the East African campaign continued fighting in Portuguese Mozambique until the armistice.

Before the war began Churchill had withdrawn the British Grand Fleet to its bases at Scapa Flow, Cromarty and Rosyth, for the real threat from Germany was believed to be in home waters. When the war began merchant ships were requisitioned and with the navy took over the maintenance of supplies and the transport of troops from England and the dominions. In November 1914 the German China squadron, which left Tsingtao when war broke out, destroyed a smaller British force at Coronel, off the coast of Chile. In December the Royal Navy destroyed this squadron off the Falkland Islands, a British coaling station. And in November 1914 the Australian cruiser *Sydney* sank the German raider *Emden* in the Indian Ocean. Save for submarines and stray raiders, Britain had command of the seas. The German High Seas Fleet, after a minor defeat in the Heligoland Bight, remained at its bases. But the loss of three old cruisers to a German U-boat (submarine) in September 1914 and the mining of a battleship in October were ominous signs.

Gallipoli, the Middle East and Balkan fronts

Under pressure from Germany the Turks, who had acquired two German warships, in October 1914 threatened Russia's Black Sea coast. At the end of the month these warships, still manned by Germans, bombarded Odessa and Sebastopol. Thereupon Russia, then Britain and France, declared war upon Turkey, who then attacked Russia in the Caucasus.

In England there were fears for Allied vessels in the eastern Mediterranean and for the Suez Canal. In December 1914 the British began landing troops in Egypt and proclaimed a protectorate there. Egypt remained an Allied base throughout the war. In February 1915 a Turkish force attacked the canal but was driven off.

drove into East Prussia, causing Moltke to transfer the two corps so vitally needed in France. At the battle of Tannenberg (August 1914) the Germans, after bringing down troops that had been advancing towards the more northerly Russian army, virtually annihilated the southern army; Samsonov, its commander, shot himself on the field. Then the Germans turned and at the battle of the Masurian Lakes (September 1914) defeated the northern force. In East Prussia General Paul von Hindenburg and Major-General Erich von Ludendorff covered themselves with glory and laid the foundation of their domination of German policy. Thereafter the Russians were largely on the defensive. Their manpower was vast but they lacked supplies. At one time their forces were firing more shells daily than Russia was producing in a month.

Japan joined the Allies on 23 August, though her alliance with Britain did not oblige her to do so. Her entry into the war relieved the Russians of the necessity of keeping forces in the Far East, but Japan's war effort benefited chiefly herself. In November 1914 Tsingtao, the German stronghold in China, fell to the Japanese.

Gallipoli: construction work at Suvla Bay following a fresh British landing in August 1915. Among the troops at Suvla Bay were the Royal Dublin Fusiliers and the Royal Irish Fusiliers

On the western front, where the opposing forces were evenly balanced, frontal collisions achieved nothing. With the opposing trenches barred at one end by the sea, at the other by the Alps, there was no enemy flank capable of being 'turned'. In these circumstances a group known as the Easterners, prominent among whom were Churchill and Lloyd George, suggested a bold new strategy: Germany's props, as Lloyd George called her allies, should be knocked out first.

Churchill proposed that warships should force a passage through the Dardanelles and land an army to assist Russia and turn the enemy's flank. The French and many in England opposed this plan. Where, they asked, were the troops to be found? The argument that an attack on Turkey by way of Gallipoli could open a supply line to Russia was reinforced when in January 1915 the Grand Duke Nicholas, Russian commander in chief, appealed for help against Turkey. Britain and France themselves were then short of supplies. It is unlikely that they could have sent much to Russia. But

there were other arguments in favour of the Easterners. Though Serbia had had some successes against the Austrians in 1914, the other Balkan states had stood on the sidelines, wondering which side to support – or whether to remain neutral. An attack upon Turkey, said the Easterners, might rally these states to the Allied side and open a back door against the Central powers.

In March 1915 an Allied attempt to force the Dardanelles was abandoned when several ships, all more or less obsolete, struck Turkish mines in the Narrows. Warned of impending attacks, the Turks, directed by their German adviser, Liman von Sanders, reinforced the Gallipoli peninsula. On 25 April 1915, having lost the advantage of surprise, Allied troops landed at Gallipoli. The terrain gave them little cover. Men wading ashore from small boats were mown down by machine guns fired from the heights or became entangled in the barbed wire that covered the beaches. Further landings were made and disputes concerning the campaign went on at home. Gallipoli too knew the horrors of trench warfare. Despite the courage of the troops on Gallipoli, prominent among whom were the Australian and New Zealand Army Corps (Anzacs), no progress was made. In December 1915 and January 1916 the peninsula was evacuated. The Straits, Russia's lifeline, remained closed. The dead in the gullies of Gallipoli had, it seemed, been sacrificed in vain.

In 1915 troops from India entered Mesopotamia and pressed towards Baghdad, but in April 1916, besieged in Kut el Amara, they surrendered to superior Turkish forces.

The British hoped Arab nationalists in Syria and Arabia would revolt against Turkey. In 1915 Sir Henry McMahon, British high commissioner in Egypt, trying to stir up Arab nationalism, gave Hussein, Sherif of Mecca, assurances concerning the future independence of Turkey's Arab territories. The exploits of Lawrence of Arabia, Colonel T.E. Lawrence, an archaeologist with much knowledge of Arab ways, put life into the revolt against Turkey. His desert raids (1917–18) were a romantic interlude, but the McMahon Pledge with its promises of Arab independence later complicated relations in the Middle East.

Meanwhile, in October 1915, Bulgaria, after negotiating with both sides, joined the Central powers. Greece, bound by treaty to assist Serbia against a Bulgarian attack, hesitated. The pro-German king, Constantine, a brother-in-law of the kaiser, thought it unlikely that the Allies would win the war, whilst Venizelos, the prime minister, was in constant touch with Britain and France. At his suggestion the British and French sent troops to Salonika. Reinforcements did not arrive until October 1915. By then it was too late to help the Serbs for in that month the Germans and Austrians from the north and the Bulgars from the east invaded Serbia and Belgrade fell. Montenegro, another associate of the Allies, was also overwhelmed in 1915. Greece remained on the sidelines. Though the occupation of Salonika was to have been temporary, the army of the Orient, about half a million men, was kept at the base there. Salonika, said the Germans scornfully, was 'an Allied internment camp'.

Wartime ambitions of the powers

Italy had refused to join the Central powers as her obligations under the Triple Alliance were limited to a defensive war and Austria had attacked Serbia. The desire for territorial gains dictated Italian policy. After declaring her neutrality Italy attempted to bargain with the Central powers. But in April 1915 she concluded the secret Treaty of London with the Allies. This promised her Austrian-ruled territory in the southern Alps and on the Adriatic. She was to keep the Dodecanese Islands, taken from Turkey in 1912. There were also promises of Turkish Adalia (Antalya) and southern Anatolia and of an interest in former German colonies. The Treaty of London was kept secret from one ally, Serbia – for nearly a million southern Slavs lived in territories promised to Italy. In May 1915 Italy declared war on Austria and later on Germany.

As the war dragged on more people began thinking of gains of one kind or another. France, for example, would not have accepted a peace that did not restore Alsace-Lorraine to her.

In 1917 the Bolsheviks published secret agreements made between Britain, France and tsarist Russia after the war began. These promised France and Britain a free hand in drawing up Germany's western frontiers. France was to acquire the Saar coal district. Russia was to have a free hand in drawing up the eastern frontiers of Germany and Austria-Hungary. She was to have special rights in Poland. She was to acquire Constantinople and other Turkish territory – a strange reversal of British policy – though Britain and France were to keep 'their special rights' within these territories. Britain was to extend her sphere of influence in Persia.

Lesser powers had their ambitions. The Serbs looked for the establishment of a great southern Slav state. Greece had ambitions in Asia Minor. Japan had considerable territorial and commercial ambitions in China and the Pacific.

The greatest gains were sought by Germany – and not only by the military. In September 1914 Bethmann Hollweg noted that the 'general aim of the war [was] security for the German Reich in west and east for all imaginable time'. For this purpose, he said, 'France must be so weakened as to make her revival as a great power impossible for all time. Russia must be thrust back as far as possible from Germany's eastern frontier.' He also envisaged colonial gains and territorial acquisitions in Europe. Others in Germany had grander aims.

Blockade and counter-blockade

Britain carried on a successful blockade of Germany. The British searched neutral as well as enemy vessels bound for Germany and by the end of 1915 the

This German cartoon of February 1915 shows how Britain was expected to suffer from the intensified U-boat campaign then announced but soon called off

Germans were short of almost everything. By producing *ersatz* (substitute) goods they made a brave attempt to overcome shortages.

For a time German U-boats hunted down neutral as well as Allied shipping in an effort to blockade Britain. In May 1915 the sinking of the *Lusitania*, a British liner whose passengers included over a hundred Americans, aroused strong protests in the USA. Bethmann Hollweg, aware of the risk of pushing the USA with her vast resources into the war, then insisted that U-boats should not attack neutral vessels. Until early in 1917 there was a decline in German submarine activity.

1915–16: Ypres, Verdun, the Somme and Jutland

On the western front 1915 and 1916 were marked by tremendous battles. In April–May 1915 the British fought a second desperate engagement around battered Ypres. The German attack did not effect a breakthrough to the Channel but British losses were heavy. Poison gas was used by the Germans for the first time during this battle.

Another novel weapon was the zeppelin (a type of airship named after Count von Zeppelin). In 1915 zeppelins began bombing London and Yarmouth. As zeppelins proved easy to shoot down the Germans began using aeroplanes in rather ineffective raids over England.

With the two opposing forces more or less balanced in the west, frontal attacks were achieving little. Yet the high commands continued to order men 'over the top'. Siegfried Sassoon, a British officer, wrote:

'Good-morning; good-morning!' the general said
When we met him last week on our way to the line.
Now the soldiers he smiled at are most of 'em dead,
And we're cursing his staff for incompetent swine.

A supreme Allied offensive on the Somme was forestalled by a German assault on Verdun. The intention was to bleed France white, to strike her where she would defend to the last. For five months, from February to July 1916, the French, under the command of General Pétain, endured. 'Ils ne passeront pas', said General Nivelle. The Germans did not pass. The French might have been wiser to have withdrawn after the Germans had paid 'a sufficient price'. The series of battles around Verdun cost the Germans and the French about a million casualties each. Of these two million men over half a million were killed.

Throughout the last week of June 1916 the British bombarded the German lines east of Amiens. Then, from 1 July until mid-November, when winter mud and a blizzard turned the whole battlefield into a wasteland in which no animal lived, no tree grew, the Allies fought the series of battles known as the Somme – a stupendous attempt to break through the German lines on both sides of the river. Vance Palmer, an Australian, remembered:

The mud and the misty figures endlessly coming
In file through the foul morass,
And the grey flood water lipping the reeds and grass,
And the steel wings drumming . . .
. . . all that my mind sees
Is a quaking bog in a mist – stark, snapped trees,
And the dark Somme flowing.

French losses at Verdun made the Somme more of a British undertaking than had been planned. As the enemy trenches were too deep for artillery fire to bombard them effectively the British were mown down as they advanced on the Germans. In one day they suffered 57,000 casualties, of whom a third were killed. Still the generals directed them to fight on. From the

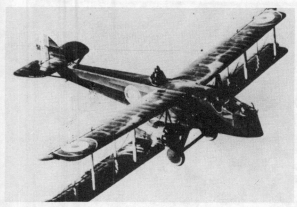

De Havilland fighter with two 320 h.p. engines. Large numbers of fighters were needed to protect scout planes from the German Fokkers until in 1916 de Havillands proved their match. Several rich Hong Kong Chinese contributed sums for the purchase of such planes – they cost about £2,000 in 1917!

German lines sewage was pumped downhill into the British trenches. By mid-November the Germans had been forced off the high ground. Their armies had been greatly worn down, their casualties including many of their most highly trained men. Only by visiting the war cemeteries in this area can one begin to comprehend the slaughter, on both sides, of this 'battle', of which the result was an 11-kilometre thrust forward by the Allies.

On 15 September the first tanks went into action. Churchill had been quick to realise the potential of this invention – sketched in rough by Leonardo da Vinci – against barbed wire and machine guns. But the tank crews had had only a short training before the Somme. Some of the tanks broke down before reaching the battlefield, others were bogged in mud. Only twenty-four went into action – too few to have much effect.

As the war went on there was progress in aeronautics. Aeroplanes were at first used for scouting. Then fighter planes were used to protect the scout planes and many air battles were fought. At Verdun and at the Somme aeroplanes were used in support of the land forces: 'And the steel wings drumming.' By 1918 aeroplanes were bombing communications and munitions factories.

In August 1916, after the failure of the Verdun offensive, Hindenburg replaced Falkenhayn as chief of staff. Germany's hero soon proved more powerful than kaiser or chancellor. With Hindenburg was Ludendorff, his chief assistant since the battle of Tannenberg.

The German fleet in the spring of 1916 began making sweeps into the North Sea. On 31 May 1916 the High

Seas Fleet and Britain's Grand Fleet met in their one major battle of the war. Who won the battle of Jutland (Skaggerak) is disputed. Although the Grand Fleet suffered greater losses the British remained in command of the seas. The High Seas Fleet never again left its base; inactivity helped to sap the morale of the German sailors. But with the German fleet so close the British had to keep strong naval forces in the North Sea.

1915–16: the Italian and eastern fronts

On the Austro-Italian front, in the Isonzo valley north of Trieste, a series of inconclusive battles was fought during 1916. A surprise Austrian offensive from the Trentino failed to break through the Italian lines.

On the eastern front the line was pushed well back by the Germans and Austrians in 1915. In May they drove into Russian Poland and by August had taken Warsaw; by September Russia had lost all Poland, Lithuania and western Latvia.

The plans for the Somme offensive had included a simultaneous forward drive by the Russians. The desperate situation of the French at Verdun led to the Russian attack being brought forward. By then munitions and other supplies from Russia's allies were coming in through Murmansk and Vladivostok. From June to September 1916 a huge Russian army commanded by General Brusilov drove west against Austria. It reached the Carpathian Mountains, on the Hungarian frontier, and took 500,000 prisoners. The Austrians were again hampered by nationalist movements within their ranks. Many Czechs defected to Russia. Russian losses were, however, very heavy.

In 1916 Francis Joseph's long reign over the Dual Monarchy ended. His successor, Carl, unsuccessfully attempted a negotiated peace with the Allies.

In August 1916 Romania, encouraged by Brusilov's victories, joined the Allies, who promised to reward her with Transylvania (Hungarian) and Bukovina (Austrian) territory. By the end of the year German forces had knocked Romania out. Romania, a small power, lost, including those wounded, about a million men in 1916. Her capture gave Germany access to fresh supplies of oil and wheat.

The home front in Britain

As the war dragged on it demanded total effort on the

DON'T IMAGINE YOU ARE NOT WANTED

EVERY MAN between 19 and 38 years of age is WANTED!

Ex-Soldiers up to 45 years of age

MEN CAN ENLIST IN THE NEW ARMY FOR THE DURATION OF THE WAR

"YOUR COUNTRY NEEDS **YOU**"

RATE OF PAY: Lowest Scale 7s. per week with Food, Clothing &c., in addition

1. **Separation Allowance for Wives and Children of Married Men when separated from their Families** (Inclusive of the allotment required from the Soldier's pay of a maximum of 6d. a day in the case of a private)

For a Wife **without** Children	-	12s. 6d. per week
For Wife with One Child	-	15s. 0d. per week
For Wife with Two Children	-	17s. 6d. per week
For Wife with Three Children	-	20s. 0d. per week
For Wife with Four Children	-	22s. 0d. per week

and so on, with an addition of 2s. for each additional child.
Motherless children 3s. a week each, exclusive of allotment from Soldier's pay

2. **Separation Allowance for Dependants of Unmarried Men.**

Provided the Soldier does his share, the Government will assist liberally in keeping up, within the limits of Separation Allowance for Families, any regular contribution made before enlistment by unmarried Soldiers or Widowers to other dependants such as mothers, fathers, sisters, etc.

YOUR COUNTRY IS STILL CALLING. FIGHTING MEN!   FALL IN!!

Full Particulars can be obtained at any Recruiting Office or Post Office.

Nº 0200 DAVID ALLEN & SONS LTD HARROW LONDON

Within a few days of the outbreak of war Kitchener posters appeared in Britain. Note the pay rates and the amount of separation allowances part of the warring nations. There had to be total national involvement. The consequent political, economic and social strains necessitated various changes.

Britain, though a few socialists and Labour Party members opposed the war, took up arms with its people firmly united. Women now demanded not the franchise but 'the right to serve' their country. And serve they did, in offices, on the land, as bus conductresses and in munitions factories. But if supplies were to be adequate, planning, it became clear, was essential. 'Dora', the Defence of the Realm Act (1914), gave the government wide powers. People gradually became accustomed to a great growth of government activity.

In the 1915 budget McKenna increased taxes, especially on war profits. He took also the revolutionary step of introducing duties to keep out such luxury imports as cars and watches. The sacred Liberal principle of free trade was thus sacrificed to the needs of a wartime economy.

Kitchener, who on the outbreak of war had been made secretary of state for war, conducted a recruiting campaign which brought in more men than the army could train. The army which engaged the Germans in the battle of the Somme was an army of volunteers – the cream of Britain's manhood.

No elections were held during the war. For a time the Liberals, who since 1910 had had a bare majority, carried on. In May 1915 there were complaints that the government had failed to provide sufficient munitions. There was also dissatisfaction over the Gallipoli campaign. The Conservatives under Bonar Law successfully demanded a coalition government. Asquith remained prime minister. Churchill, who was blamed for the Gallipoli failure, had to resign from the admiralty. Lloyd George – an Easterner but not directly concerned with the Gallipoli campaign – became head of a new ministry of munitions. The Conservatives held various posts, including the admiralty. Arthur Henderson of the Labour Party became president of the board of education.

The vast energy of Lloyd George did much to ensure adequate supplies of munitions. 'Convert your machinery into battalions', he told workers. The supply of men for the front remained the subject of debate. Though two and a half million had answered Kitchener's call for volunteers, by the end of 1915 ultrapatriots were demanding conscription and women were presenting white feathers to men not in uniform. In January 1916 Asquith hesitantly agreed to compulsory service for unmarried men aged between eighteen and forty-one. Three months later conscription was extended to all men aged eighteen to forty-one, with exemptions for munitions workers, coal miners and others in 'essential occupations'. Some provision was made for the relief of conscientious objectors. Conscription was not extended to Ireland until 1918. Though conscription did not greatly add to Britain's forces it was a tidier method of maximising her war effort. In the last months of the war the age for conscription was raised to fifty. None of the older men called up served overseas.

But neither increased munitions nor conscription were winning the war. In 1916 the bruising battle of the Somme was fought. The inconclusive battle of Jutland caused disappointment. And at Easter 1916 there was an uprising in Ireland (see p. 150). In Parliament in issue after issue Asquith had to give way. The rising star was Lloyd George, the Welsh Wizard. In June 1916, after Kitchener was drowned while on his way to Russia, Lloyd George became secretary of state for war. He recognised the need to regulate the whole economy. If the war were to be won the Liberal system of free enterprise would have to give way to 'war socialism'.

In December 1916 a crisis of leadership split the Liberals. Lloyd George proposed the formation of a war council, with himself as chairman, to run the war more efficiently. Asquith would have none of it. Lloyd George forced Asquith's hand by resigning from his cabinet. Asquith, who had the support of leading Conservatives, also resigned. But backbench Conservatives supported Lloyd George. Many Liberals were willing to desert Asquith in favour of Lloyd George. Labour members too were willing to support him. So Lloyd George, contrary to Asquith's expectations, was able to form a government. Conservative leaders on whom Asquith had relied came – some sooner than others – to Lloyd George's support. Balfour, the former Conservative prime minister, became foreign secretary. Bonar Law was chancellor of the exchequer. Churchill – still a Liberal – after two years in the political wilderness returned to office as minister of munitions. Henderson, representative of the 'people', on whom victory ultimately depended, was one of the five members of the war cabinet which Lloyd George set up. This cabinet had a secretariat and records of proceedings were kept for the first time.

Lloyd George was virtually a dictator. To streamline the economy he set up five new departments – shipping, labour, food, national service and food production.

These departments exercised control as much by co-operation as by direction. For example, the minister of shipping brought all merchant ships under public control but employed the former owners as managers. When food rationing was, somewhat unnecessarily, introduced early in 1917 it was largely operated by shopkeepers. Meanwhile, prices and rents had been controlled, so there was little change in the cost of living until after the war. A subsidy to wheat importers kept bread at a stable price and in sufficient supply without rationing. And national control of coal mining kept that important industry in steady operation.

It took some time for the new controls to come into effect. Shortages of food and fuel made 1917 a bad year. A rise in wages helped to check popular unrest, but news of revolution in Russia (see Chapter 13) aroused some excitement, for the proposal for a negotiated peace with no annexations and no indemnities put forward by Russia's provisional government stirred opponents of the war to new efforts. At a convention in Leeds in June 1917 1,100 delegates from the Independent Labour Party and other groups, among them Ramsay MacDonald and Philip Snowden, supported the Russian peace proposals and called, not very resoundingly, for councils (soviets) of workers' and soldiers' representatives to be set up. Such proposals found little support in Parliament. Nor was there much support for a proposal by Henderson to send a Labour delegation to a conference of socialist parties in Stockholm. British seamen refused to take delegates to Stockholm. Henderson himself had to resign from the war cabinet.

The publication by the Bolsheviks of the secret treaties made by the Allies caused much disquiet, for it was apparent that annexations and indemnities were very much in the minds of some of Britain's allies. To dispel disquiet – and perhaps to forestall President Wilson (see p. 109) – Lloyd George in January 1918 made a statement of war aims. He proclaimed the need for an international organisation as an alternative to war. He called for the return of Alsace-Lorraine to France, for the independence of Belgium and Poland and for self-government for the minority peoples under Austro-Hungarian rule. Germany would lose her colonies, he said, and Turkey would lose her territories in the Middle East. When the terms of the Treaty of Brest-Litovsk (see p. 126) became known in March 1918 Lloyd George's moderation was apparent.

Early in 1918 the Royal Air Force (RAF) was founded as an independent force – with the object of bombing Germany into submission and so, it was believed,

avoiding the mass casualties of land battles. The RAF never had enough planes to test this theory. The theory lived on and was brought to the test in the Second World War.

In February 1918 a ministry of information was created to give publicity at home and in enemy countries to British war aims and ideals. The first minister of information was Lord Beaverbrook. The first director of propaganda was Lord Northcliffe. Both were great newspaper men.

In June 1918 the Representation of the People Act extended the suffrage to all males of twenty-one and to all women over thirty, provided the woman or her husband was a householder. Special provision was made for servicemen who had reached the age of nineteen to vote. The act redistributed seats on the basis of population, one member for every 70,000 people. And it virtually accepted the principle of one man one vote. The right to vote more than once survived for the university (Oxford and Cambridge) seats. Where a person had business premises outside the electorate in which he lived he had one additional vote. Voting was to take place on a single day, instead of being spread over several weeks. Another act made women eligible to sit in the House of Commons. In 1918 schooling became compulsory for all children to the age of fourteen.

In spite of propaganda, and franchise and other concessions, unrest increased. In the summer of 1918 there was a wave of strikes over such matters as dilution of labour and the recognition of certain unions. The resentment felt by workers at the wartime profits made by 'the bosses' threatened class conflict in the future. And the extension of conscription to Ireland deepened the rift with the Irish.

There had been various disputes between Lloyd George and the generals, whose strategy he regarded as unnecessarily costly in lives. In the crisis of near defeat in March 1918 (see p. 109) Lloyd George acted with dramatic speed. He took personal control of the war office. Reserves which normally would have taken several weeks to reach France were there ready for action in a week. And Lloyd George, aware that American troops could swing the balance, persuaded President Wilson to put into action forthwith troops who were then in training. (The USA had joined the Allies in April 1917.)

The tragedies and effort of the long war to some extent brought classes closer together. The rich with higher taxes were less rich than before. The sacrifices made by humble people won them respect. But between those who had experienced war on the western front and those who had not there was a great gulf.

1917: entry of the USA; withdrawal of Russia

In March 1917 revolution overthrew the tsarist régime in Russia. In November a second revolution established the Bolsheviks in power. In December 1917 Russia withdrew from the war and in March 1918 concluded the Treaty of Brest-Litovsk with Germany. In the spring of 1917 the United States of America ended her so-called isolation and entered the war on the side of the Allies. So as one giant, weak and disorganised, drifted off the battlefield, another giant, his strength fresh and untried, marched on.

In 1916 Woodrow Wilson was re-elected president of the USA on the slogan: 'He kept us out of war.' In December 1916 he tried to mediate between the Allied and Central powers. Why did the USA some four months later join the Allies?

In January 1917 Germany announced that her submarines would again wage unrestricted warfare, attacking neutral and enemy vessels alike. Bethmann Hollweg, realising the danger of pushing the USA into war, opposed this. But Germany was drifting towards a dictatorship under Hindenburg and Ludendorff and the military were willing to gamble on being able to knock Britain and France out before the United States, if she joined the Allies, could give effective help. The chancellor's warning was ignored. And in January 1917 Zimmermann, Germany's foreign minister, sent a telegram to the German ambassador in Mexico, directing him to seek an alliance; in return the ambassador was to promise that Texas and other American territory would be ceded to Mexico. Relations between the USA and Mexico were already poor. The British decoded the telegram and informed the United States of its contents. This was the third startling telegram from Germany since 1870: Ems, Kruger, Zimmermann. Then in February and March 1917 several American ships were sunk by German U-boats.

So it was that on 6 April the United States declared war on Germany. She was followed by a string of lesser states. The first American troops landed in France in June 1917. Their arrival greatly encouraged the Allies and had a depressing effect on the war weary Germans.

A Russian military hospital on the eastern front: lack of equipment and supplies hampered Russia's war effort – and increased the sufferings of her forces

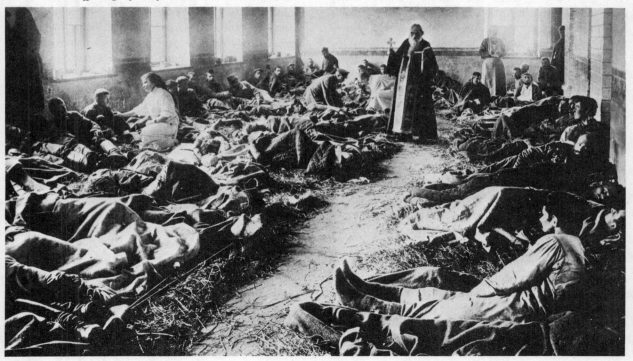

However, it was not until the summer of 1918 that American troops began to arrive on the western front in sufficient numbers to influence the fighting. American casualties were relatively light but the United States did swing the balance of war against Germany.

Meanwhile, as millions were dying and vast material destruction was being done the supremacy of western Europe was dying too. Not long after the war three women missionaries, journeying through north-west China and Mongolia, met Russian refugees begging their way to Peking. 'From this time', the ladies noted, 'European prestige was entirely shattered [in the East].'

Since the Second World War two super-powers, the USA and the USSR, have dominated the world. Their predominance had been foreseen by some people long before the First World War. By the end of that war the power of one giant, the USA, was apparent, though it was soon to be masked by her withdrawal – for a time – from world affairs. The other giant, in a state of revolution after 1917, seemed an unlikely contender for world power. But Russia was only in eclipse.

1917 : military operations

As the U-boat campaign developed in 1917 British shipping losses reached alarming proportions. They were at their peak in April of that year. By then Britain's stores of food were perilously low. However, it was in April 1917 that at Lloyd George's insistence the admiralty agreed to provide naval escorts for convoys of merchant ships. Gradually, with ships travelling in armed convoys and escorts using depth charges for attacking submarines, the U-boat threat was overcome. In 1918 Allied shipping losses fell by more than half and tonnage of new ships built exceeded the tonnage sunk.

In March 1917 the Germans had retired to their shorter, more easily defensible Hindenburg line, 'a masterpiece of concrete and armour', built between the winter of 1916, when the battle of the Somme dragged to its end, and the spring of 1917. The Allies were unaware of its construction until the Germans withdrew, leaving a wilderness behind them.

The British in July 1917 won the half victory of Passchendaele, the battle fought against 'boue and Boche' (mud and German). This third engagement around Ypres lasted several months and cost the British 400,000 casualties. It was a valiant attempt to break out from Ypres, get through to the coast, attack the U-boat bases and then in a supreme effort 'roll up' the Germans.

But the only advance was from Messines Ridge to Passchendaele. A British general who saw the mud of Passchendaele after the fighting was over said: 'Did we really send men to fight in that?' – and burst into tears.

In November 1917, with the aid of the Tank Corps, the British were victorious at Cambrai, south of Ypres. A triumphant peal of bells rang out in London to announce this victory. But ten days later the Germans recovered the little territory won at Cambrai; indeed they gained ground.

In May 1917 the vast casualties suffered under the command of Joffre and his successor Nivelle resulted in serious mutinies in the French army – to whom Nivelle was known as 'the drinker of blood'. Strangely, knowledge of the mutinies did not reach the Germans. Pétain, hero of Verdun, replaced Nivelle. He decided to wait until 'Yanks and tanks' should strengthen his striking power. In November 1917 Clemenceau became prime minister of France, with near dictatorial powers.

In October 1917 several German divisions were switched to the aid of the Austrians in the hope of dealing Italy a knockout blow. France and Britain had given Italy little help in men or material. At Caporetto, the last of a long series of battles in the Isonzo valley, the Italians were disastrously defeated and withdrew to the Piave line near Venice.

In June 1917 Allied pressure led to the abdication of King Constantine of Greece. Under Venizelos Greece, tempted by a promise of gains in Asia Minor, entered the war against the Central powers. Greece took little part in the fighting until the final campaign of 1918.

In the Middle East, largely a British theatre, Kut el Amara was taken by the British in January 1917. In March they entered Baghdad. In December 1917 General Allenby, with a force that had come from Egypt, rode triumphantly into Jerusalem. The Muslims greeted him as Al Nebi, The Prophet. The following year, operating with Lawrence, Al Nebi took Damascus and drove the Turks from Syria.

The operations in the Middle East were sowing seeds of trouble. In England Chaim Weizmann, a Jew whose wartime assistance had won him good contacts, aroused sympathy for Zionism (a worldwide movement to secure for the Jews a national home in Palestine). In November 1917 Balfour, the British foreign secretary, declared Britain's support for the Zionist programme. In view of the McMahon Pledge the Balfour Declaration promised to uphold the rights of non-Jews (that is, Arabs) in Palestine.

1918: collapse of the Central powers

Meanwhile the people of Germany had suffered greatly. Problems of munitions and manpower, earlier effectively tackled by Walther Rathenau, were by the end of 1916 again acute. Coal, food and clothing were in short supply. In April 1917 the cutting of the bread ration was followed by the first major strikes of the war. There were complaints about profiteering and inequalities of rationing – and demands for greater political rights. In July Bethmann Hollweg, who had attempted to exercise some check on the military, was forced to resign. Hindenburg and Ludendorff were then virtually dictators. But strict military control did not stop discontent. Nor did the military manage to suppress all political opposition. The Germans knew that the Emperor Carl had made secret peace overtures to the Allies (see p. 103). In July 1917, a few days after the resignation of Bethmann Hollweg, Matthias Erzberger of the Catholic Centre Party and Friedrich Ebert of the Social Democrats persuaded the Reichstag to declare itself in favour of a peace without annexations. However, the drift towards military dictatorship continued and the military were determined on total victory and annexations. The Reichstag resolution was ignored. A Fatherland Party under the leadership of von Tirpitz drummed up renewed support for the war.

In November 1917 Hindenburg and Ludendorff planned a series of blows on the western front. Their aim was to break the British and French or, failing that, to destroy their 'war will' before the Americans arrived in sufficient numbers to swing the balance against Germany. So 1918 brought a burst of furious activity. Though the Germans kept large garrisons in the areas ceded to them at Brest-Litovsk, they were able to switch some troops to the west. For the time being they outnumbered the Allies there.

The Germans began their offensive in March 1918. The first action, against the British on the Somme, resulted in a bulge forward of the German line. The Germans were halted only 8 kilometres from the vital railway centre of Amiens and a way seemed open to Paris. They struck again near Ypres and took the Messines Ridge and Armentières. Next they crossed the Aisne and drove a 64-kilometre wedge into the French line. The Allies fought on as Sir Douglas Haig, the British commander, ordered with their 'backs to the wall'. By 30 May the Germans were about 60 kilometres from Paris. Shells from their long-range guns fell on the city. However, their offensives in June had little success.

Casualties on both sides were enormous – 700,000 in forty days – but Germany's losses were heavier than those of the Allies and she was short of reserves.

The Germans failed to destroy the 'war will' of the Allies. Earlier, jealousy had made unified command of the Allied forces impracticable. But in April 1918 Marshal Foch of France was accepted as Allied commander in chief. This brought greater efficiency in operations. And by June American troops were pouring in – a quarter of a million men a month were landing in France. More tanks were available: Yanks – and tanks to clear the way. And the Allies had won air superiority.

From mid-July to early August French and American forces were making counter-attacks. At the second battle of the Marne the Germans were forced to withdraw behind the river. On 8 August, the Black Day of the German army, British and dominion forces broke the German line in the battle of Amiens. The Germans, some of whom were captured without resistance, could make no counter-attack. A whole series of attacks by the British in Flanders, the French farther south in Champagne and the Americans in the Argonne were coordinated in a general Allied offensive.

By the end of September the Germans had lost all their 1918 gains. On 29 September Ludendorff told the government that it must seek an armistice at once. Six days later the Hindenburg line was breached. As morale declined many men deserted. Ludendorff, disguised by coloured glasses and false whiskers, escaped to Sweden.

Meanwhile German workers had been on strike – half a million in January 1918. The British naval blockade and other factors had squeezed much of the life out of the German economy. Everyone was tired of shortages and tasteless *ersatz* food. Workers fainted in factories. Few children had enough to eat.

In January 1918 President Wilson outlined the Fourteen Points (see p. 111) on acceptance of which he would be willing to make peace. The German military leaders, still aiming for victory, rejected the Fourteen Points. They were then at the height of their self-confidence and their ideas of gains in Europe, Africa and the Far East were at a peak. But by October the position had changed. On 4 October Prince Max of Baden, a liberal, became chancellor. On the same day, at the insistence of the military chiefs, he cabled Wilson asking for an armistice on the basis of the Fourteen Points.

Prince Max introduced sweeping constitutional reforms but events were soon to overtake these. While negotiations concerning the evacuation of occupied territory, the future of the kaiser and other matters went

9 October 1918: body of a German medical orderly beside trenches hastily dug by the Germans in a vain attempt to defend a town near St Quentin

on the Allies continued to advance. In October the U-boat bases at Zeebrugge and Ostend fell to the British. However, there was no invasion of Germany; her people were spared that. The devastation lay behind the Germans, who continued to destroy as they retreated.

Germany's props were collapsing too. In October the Italians captured the Austrian headquarters at Vittorio Veneto and took 500,000 prisoners. Early in November they captured Trieste and Fiume.

In September the army of the Orient came out of its 'internment camp' in Salonika and attacked the Bulgars. Air attacks harassed columns of enemy soldiers marching through the Balkan valleys. On 30 September Bulgaria made a separate armistice, enabling the Allies to attack the Central powers in the rear. On 30 October the Turks signed an armistice and early in November 1918 an Allied fleet steamed into Constantinople.

By October there were mutinies in the Austrian army, especially among Czech and other non-German troops. On the Piave front Austrian troops not in combat were shivering in their underclothes. There were strikes in Vienna. Czechs were fighting with the Allies in France and Italy. The Hungarians too were going their own way. Late in October the Czechoslovaks and then the southern Slavs declared their independence.

On 3 November 1918 Austria signed an armistice with Italy. Hungary made a separate armistice on 7 November, whereupon parts of her territory were occupied by Allied forces – among them soldiers belonging to various minorities within the Dual Monarchy. On 11 November the Emperor Carl renounced 'all participation in the affairs of state'; he signed his declaration with a pencil. Austria and, a few days later, Hungary declared themselves republics.

While her armies retreated Germany was torn by unrest and threatened by revolution. Early in November a sailors' mutiny that began in Kiel spread to Hamburg and through north-western Germany. A soviet republic was proclaimed in Bavaria. Hindenburg had to tell the kaiser that the army could no longer be relied on and advised him to abdicate. On 9 November a republic was proclaimed. A few hours later the kaiser abdicated and fled to neutral Holland.

On 11 November 1918 Erzberger signed the armistice in the presence of Marshal Foch in a railway carriage at Compiègne in northern France. So at 11 a.m. on 11 November the guns ceased firing. But the new quiet was an uneasy one.

11 The post-war settlement

The peace conference: January, 1919

Woodrow Wilson's Fourteen Points, which were accepted as the basis for making peace, demanded:

1. an end to secret diplomacy;
2. freedom of navigation on the seas;
3. removal of economic barriers to trade;
4. guarantees to reduce armaments to a level consistent with domestic safety;
5. the settlement of colonial claims with proper regard for the interests of the inhabitants;
6. German evacuation of Russian territory;
7. restoration of Belgian sovereignty;
8. return of Alsace-Lorraine to France;
9. adjustment of Italy's frontiers on national lines;
10. independence for the subject peoples of Austria-Hungary;
11. restoration of Serbia, Montenegro and Romania, with access to the sea for Serbia;
12. independent development for the subject peoples of the Ottoman empire and the opening of the Dardanelles under international guarantee;
13. independence and access to the sea for Poland;
14. the formation of an international organisation securing the independence and territorial integrity of all nations.

France and Britain also demanded payment by the Central powers of reparations (compensation for damage done to civilians and their property during the war). To this demand Wilson had yielded.

The peace conference opened in Paris on 18 January 1919. Wilson, so prominent in the armistice negotiations, had little understanding of the problems of European politics and geography. However, with Clemenceau, prime minister of France, Lloyd George and Orlando, the Italian prime minister, Wilson was a dominant figure at the conference.

The voice that made itself heard over all others was that of Clemenceau, the Tiger, who presided. 'Père la victoire', as he was called, represented the determination of Frenchmen 'never to let it happen again' – that never again should the Germans invade the fair land of France. The photograph on page 112 shows one among the host of towns and villages destroyed during the First World War. Such sights were common all along the western front – and on the eastern front too. And France had lost well over a million citizens killed; four million had been wounded. Clemenceau had twice seen the Germans invade his country; he was about thirty when the Franco-Prussian War was fought. Behind Clemenceau were the French people, complaining that he was too mild. It was hardly likely that they would think back to the havoc done by Napoleon Bonaparte's armies in the German states. The British too were almost hysterical in the months after the armistice. The British general election of 1918 was won on promises of revenge against Germany.

Orlando's chief concern was to obtain from Austria the Alpine and Adriatic territory known as Italia Irredenta – Unredeemed Italy – the 'national' territory which the Treaty of London had promised in 1915 in return for Italy's entry into the war. Orlando, at the outset one of the Big Four at Paris, soon found himself excluded from the inner circle of Clemenceau, Lloyd George and Wilson. Not all the Italian claims could be justified on national lines, and so conflicted with point 9. Italy, touchy because of her humiliation at Caporetto, yet the more proud of her victory at Vittorio Veneto, for a time withdrew her delegation from the conference.

There were many other delegates, of varied dress and tongue and race. In all thirty-two states, among them Japan and China, Brazil and Uruguay, the Hejaz and Siam, India, the dominions of Canada, South Africa, Australia and New Zealand, were represented. The dominions, India (whose casualties had been heavy), and Asian states, notably China, grew in stature with their representation at the conference. Russia, torn by civil war and threatened by foreign intervention, was not represented. The Treaty of Brest-Litovsk, which conflicted with point 6, was automatically cancelled when Germany accepted the Fourteen Points as the basis of her armistice. The secret wartime agreements made with tsarist Russia (see p. 101) were regarded as having lapsed with the overthrow of the tsar.

Various other arrangements made by the Allies during the war complicated affairs. There were the gains promised to Italy by the Treaty of London. And in 1916

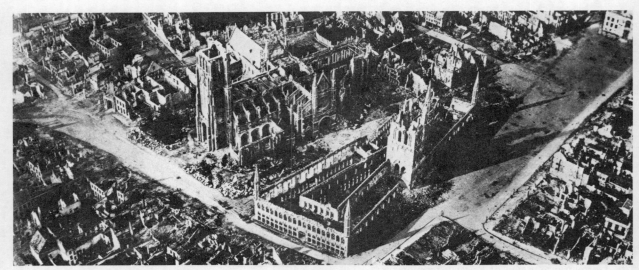

Ypres in ruins, August 1915. In France too, and on the eastern front, cities, towns, farms were in ruins when the war ended

a secret Anglo-French agreement, the Sykes-Picot Note, had in effect provided for the partitioning of the Ottoman empire: France was to have special rights in Syria and Lebanon, whilst the British were to have a favoured position in Mesopotamia and Palestine. This was scarcely consistent with the pledges of Arab independence given by McMahon in 1915. Relations with the Arabs were further complicated by the Balfour Declaration with its promise of a national home in Palestine for the Jews. China's partial acceptance of the Twenty-one Demands (see p. 22) and secret allied promises to Japan presented further complications.

National movements among European peoples had also to be considered. As early as 1916 the Allies had informed the USA that they wanted Czechs, Poles and other non-Germans freed from Habsburg rule. Wilson's agreement was naturally influenced by the large numbers of Polish, Czech and other Slav voters in the USA. The Poles, Czechs and Southern Slavs declared their independence in October 1918, but the boundaries of the new states were not easy to determine. Soon newly established or restored states were trying to extend their territories by force of arms.

The atmosphere of the conference was darkened by the background of post-war suffering. Millions were starving. In Serbia a third of the surviving population in 1919 had tuberculosis. Polish peasants were eating grass and heather and acorns. An epidemic of influenza that began in the East reached Europe in 1918 and caused millions of deaths.

Though with Russia facing counter-revolution and foreign intervention (see p. 128) the survival of communism was uncertain, fear of the red tide of revolution overhung victors and vanquished alike. There was severe unrest in Germany. In victorious France and England strikes seemed to threaten the social order. Harold Nicolson, a member of the British delegation, said of the conference:

'[It was like] a riot in a parrot house ... newspapers screaming in headlines against the Dawdlers of Paris, the clamour for demobilisation, "Get the Boys Back", the starving millions of central Europe, the slouching queues of prisoners still behind their barbed wire, the flames of communism flaring, now from Munich, and now from [Budapest]. ... '

So amid suffering and hatred, greed and fear, amid aspirations too for a Brave New World that might dispense with bravery in battle, the Big Four set out to arrange the affairs of the post-war world.

Germany: the Treaty of Versailles, 1919

The major treaty was that with Germany, the Treaty of Versailles. Later, propaganda based on the allegation that this was 'dictated' to Germany and therefore not binding upon her proved highly effective. Yet Germany had been happy to 'dictate' peace terms to Russia at

Brest-Litovsk – and earlier to France at Frankfurt (see p. 4). And Germany, though not allowed to send representatives to the conference, was permitted to submit points for discussion after receipt of the draft treaty. However, the amendments were very minor.

On 28 June 1919, exactly five years after the Sarajevo assassinations, representatives of the new republic of Germany signed the Treaty of Versailles in the long Hall of Mirrors, overlooking the fountains and formal gardens of the palace built by Louis XIV, the Sun King. There the German Empire had been proclaimed nearly fifty years before.

The Treaty of Versailles (see map p. 115) returned Alsace-Lorraine to France. The Saar, with its rich coal mines, was placed under international control for fifteen years, after which a plebiscite (referendum) was to decide its fate. Meanwhile, the French were to control its mines. Two small frontier areas, Eupen and Malmédy, passed to Belgium. Holstein and southern Schleswig remained with Germany, but northern Schleswig after a plebiscite went to Denmark (1920). The East Prussian port of Memel (Klaipeda) was ceded to the Allies for disposal and eventually became autonomous under Lithuania (see p. 121). The Kiel Canal was opened to the shipping of all nations and the Rhine was internationalised. The Polish territory acquired by Prussia during the eighteenth century and a small but valuable area in Upper Silesia became part of the reconstructed state of Poland. (The Silesian territory passed to Poland after a plebiscite in 1921.) Danzig (Gdansk), a largely German-populated city, became a free city under League of Nations' control; its foreign policy and customs were to be regulated by Poland. Poland also received a strip of Prussian territory, the Polish Corridor, giving her access to the sea at Danzig. This corridor, which contained a number of German-speaking people, divided East Prussia from the rest of Germany and caused much antagonism. The former German colonies became League of Nations' mandates, held by one or other of the Allies in trust for the inhabitants (see p. 119). Germany surrendered her extra-territorial and other rights in China. Her leased area in Shantung remained for the time being under Japanese control (see p. 162).

Germany was forbidden to conscript men for service. Her army was limited to 100,000 men to serve for twelve years. She was to have no tanks or heavy artillery, military aircraft, major warships or submarines.

To give security to France the right (eastern) bank of the Rhine was to be permanently demilitarised for 50 kilometres beyond the river. The part of the Rhineland lying west of the river was to be demilitarised and occupied by Allied forces, who would be evacuated over a period of fifteen years.

France had wanted greater security against future attack. Foch had urged that only if the Rhineland were taken from Germany could France be secure. André Tardieu, later prime minister of France, who helped to draw up the Treaty of Versailles, said:

'France has a unique experience of Germany. No one has suffered as she has. . . . What happened in 1914 was possible only for one reason: Germany, because of her mastery over offensive preparations . . . on the left bank of the [Rhine], thought herself capable of crushing the democracies, France and Belgium, before the latter could receive the aid of the Overseas Democracies, Great Britain, the Dominions, and the United States. . . . It is therefore this possibility which must be done away with, by depriving Germany of the means which permitted her to believe in the success of her plan.'

Wilson and Lloyd George believed that to detach the western Rhineland from Germany would cause such resentment that another war might follow. Britain was less concerned than France about a German threat. It was Germany's naval power that had alarmed her – and this was gone. The High Seas Fleet, interned at Scapa Flow in 1918, was scuttled by order of its commander when the peace terms became public.

Germany was to pay reparations for loss and damage suffered by the Allies. A reparations commission was to assess the amount payable (see p. 180). Meanwhile, Germany was to hand over the greater part of her merchant navy and a quarter of her fishing fleet to the Allies. She was also to build a number of ships for them and to supply them with coal over a period of years. J.M. Keynes, an economist who was a member of the British delegation at Paris, argued that reparations should be fixed at a sum within Germany's capacity to pay. But Keynes was overruled. He left the delegation and in *The Economic Consequences of the Peace* criticised Allied policy. Reparations at most provided bitter fruit. As well as burdening Germany, for a time they disrupted the entire European economy.

Payment of reparations was based on article 231 of the Versailles treaty: 'Germany accepts the responsibility of Germany and her allies for causing all the loss and damage to which the Allied and Associated Governments and their nationals have been subjected as a consequence of the war imposed upon them by the aggression of Germany and her allies.' This 'war guilt' clause was bitterly resented by the Germans – though there were similar clauses in the other peace treaties. The German signatories of the treaty were regarded as traitors. The Germans also resented a demand that the ex-kaiser and others – among them Hindenburg, still a super-patriot to many of his countrymen – should be surrendered for trial as war criminals. This for various reasons proved impracticable; for example, the Dutch were unwilling to extradite the kaiser.

The treaties with Austria, Hungary, Bulgaria and Turkey

The Big Four left the settlement of the remaining peace treaties to a council of statesmen. Like Versailles, the names of the other treaties come from places near Paris.

In September 1919 the Treaty of St Germain-en-Laye was signed with the republic of Austria. It took from Austria all her non-German territory and some of her German territory too (see map opposite). Her population dropped from nearly thirty million to less than eight million. The South Tyrol, peopled in the south (the Trentino) by Italians and in the north (Bolzano) by Germans, went to Italy. Istria, including Trieste and some of the Dalmation Islands also passed to Italy. Bosnia-Herzegovina, Slovenia and Dalmatia went to the new South Slav state later named Yugoslavia. Bohemia and Moravia, numbering about three million Germans among their inhabitants, became part of Czechoslovakia. Romania received Bukovina. Galicia returned to Poland. The treaty limited Austria's army to 30,000 men and obliged her to pay reparations.

The Treaty of Trianon with Hungary was signed in June 1920. Hungary lost about two-thirds of her territory; her population dropped from twenty to eight million. Romania received Transylvania, promised her when she joined the Allies; this area was peopled by Romanian peasants but the town folk were mostly Magyars. Burgenland passed to Austria. Yugoslavia obtained Croatia, whilst Slovakia and Ruthenia went to Czechoslovakia. The new frontiers of Hungary left a number of Magyars under foreign rule. On the other hand some Germans were left in Hungary. However, to draw boundaries disentangling the peoples of these areas would have been impossible. Hungary's army was limited and she undertook to pay reparations.

By the Treaty of Neuilly, November 1919, Bulgaria lost western Thrace – and with it her access to the Aegean Sea – to Greece. Bulgaria also lost a small area to Yugoslavia. She had to reduce her armed forces and to pay reparations.

Constantinople and much of Turkey's Asian territory were in Allied occupation at the time of the peace conference. In accordance with the Treaty of London (see p. 101) an Italian landing was made in Adalia in April 1919. By another wartime understanding Greece sent troops to occupy Smyrna (Ismir), a city with many Greek inhabitants.

In August 1920 the Treaty of Sèvres was signed with Turkey. By this eastern Thrace was to pass to Greece. Turkey-in-Europe was thus reduced to a small area surrounding Constantinople. In Asia Anatolia was left to Turkey so the Italians had to leave Adalia. The Greeks were to administer Smyrna for five years, after which there was to be a plebiscite. But the Treaty of Sèvres was never ratified and in 1923 was replaced by the Treaty of Lausanne (see p. 192).

In the Middle East the non-Turkish territories of the Ottoman empire were placed under the control of France and Britain, who were to administer them as mandates. Despite the McMahon Pledge the only Arab territory that became independent was the kingdom of the Hejaz (which under Ibn Saud later became part of Saudi Arabia). (The kingdom of the Yemen was recognised as independent before the peace conference.)

Romania, besides getting Transylvania and Bukovina, kept the Dobruja, taken from Bulgaria after the Second Balkan War. She also received Bessarabia. Romania, like Greece, was thus well rewarded for having joined the Allies. With the loss of Bessarabia, Russia, like Austria, was excluded from the Balkans after the war.

Serbia, where in a sense the war had begun, swelled to three times her pre-war size – becoming the kingdom of the Serbs, Croats and Slovenes (Yugoslavia). Montenegro voted for union with her and the extended 'Serbia' at last had access to the Adriatic. Included in her borders was Bosnia with its capital Sarajevo. On the spot where Gavrilo Princip had fired at the Austrian archduke, a monument was set up. By placing a pair of Princip's shoes on wet cement the footprints of the assassin were preserved.

The Baltic states and Poland

With the cancellation of the Treaty of Brest-Litovsk Russia's western frontiers had to be fixed. The western powers, as well as upholding the principle of national

Changed frontiers in post-war Europe

independence, aimed to create out of former tsarist territories a buffer zone – a *cordon sanitaire* – a quarantine area to protect themselves from being infected with Russian Bolshevism. Finland, where Germans had been fighting against Bolshevik forces, became independent in 1919. In 1920 Estonia and in 1921 Latvia and Lithuania, all formerly under Russian rule, were recognised as independent.

The line of the *cordon sanitaire* was continued by the restoration of Poland, in eclipse since the partitions of the eighteenth century. The new Poland consisted in the first place of the territories seized by Austria, Prussia and Russia in these partitions. No natural feature marks off 'Poland' either on the west from Germany or on the east from Russia. Her frontier with Germany was fixed by the Treaty of Versailles, though certain areas were left for determination by plebiscites. Substantial numbers of Germans came under Polish rule. After an enquiry by the British foreign secretary, Lord Curzon, Poland's eastern frontier was fixed on the 'ethnic' line separating Polish-speaking people from Russian-speaking people. However, following a Russo-Polish War, the Treaty of Riga (1921) shifted the Russo-Polish boundary well to the east of the so-called Curzon line, with the result that several million Ukrainians and Byelorussians passed under Polish rule. In 1920 Poland extended her territory northward by seizing Vilna (Vilnius) and the surrounding area from Lithuania.

Conclusion

Perhaps there were two practicable alternatives at the peace conference – to make a stern peace with provisions for securing it or to risk a milder settlement. Neither of these alternatives was followed. The peace concluded with the Central powers was relatively hard. It was also inadequately secured.

It was perhaps unrealistic to expect a mild peace, especially in the case of Germany. She had dictated a harsh peace to Russia. And, until late in 1918, her intention was to force a hard peace on the Allies. Germany had perhaps reason to complain of the reparations imposed on her; these were perhaps unduly heavy, indeed unrealistic. Beyond this she probably had no valid cause for complaint. But the fact that the peace terms were relatively hard and 'dictated' gave German nationalists excuse for complaint – and later many people outside Germany were convinced that she had been treated too harshly.

As well as resenting the 'war guilt' clause, the Germans claimed that the transfer of their colonies even as mandates was inconsistent with Wilson's point 5. They argued that the principle of national rights, implicit in points 6–13, had been ignored in their case, for example by the setting up of the Polish Corridor. Moreover, their peace treaties forbade Germany and German Austria to unite, except with the consent of the council of the League of Nations.

The Germans, determined to undo what they regarded as the injustices of the Versailles treaty, remained a threat to peace. Although the other Central powers too resented the terms imposed on them, they were not powerful enough to be a serious threat to peace. But post-war Germany, though stripped of certain territory and subjected to military and other disabilities, remained large and powerful. She lost some six million subjects – but still had a population of fifty-eight million as against France's forty million. The military restrictions were virtually impossible to enforce; she soon began rearming in secret. A promised Anglo-American guarantee of the demilitarisation of the Rhineland lapsed when in 1920 the Americans refused to accept it. And with the setting up of an independent Poland and with Russia in disorder after the 1917 revolution, Germany no longer faced the danger of a two front war against France and Russia. So the peace, as well as being hard, was inadequately secured.

Certainly mistakes were made at the peace conference, but the difficulties were great. Lloyd George, who had tried to exercise moderation, was criticised for being too mild and, especially later, for being too severe. What should have been done? Keynes would have put his faith in a milder settlement. In 1922 he wrote: 'That [France] has anything to fear from Germany in the future which we can foresee, except what she herself may provoke, is a delusion.' Duff Cooper, British diplomat and statesman, wrote in March 1939: 'If Germany had been left stronger in 1919 she would sooner have been in a position to do what she is doing today.' Was he only being wise after the event? Who was right?

Acceptance of the right of European peoples formerly under foreign rule to determine their own future and the setting up of new national states gave impetus to Asian and later African nationalism. It is significant that the first true Pan-African congress took place in Paris in 1919. The movement for independence in India gained momentum; soon Gandhi's protesting voice echoed far and wide.

12 Attempted co-operation and the League of Nations

Arbitration and proposed disarmament before 1914

When the lights went out over Europe in 1914 international co-operation was not unknown. The idea that disputes between nations, as between individuals, can be settled by arbitration had won some acceptance. In 1872 Britain and the USA settled a dispute by arbitration. Later the USA and other states settled various disputes over frontiers and quarrels concerning the treatment of their citizens by arbitration. The dispute following the unfortunate battle of the Dogger Bank (see p. 91) was so settled.

In 1899 Tsar Nicholas II called a conference to discuss arbitration and the limitation of armaments. Twenty-six nations sent representatives to the conference, which met that year at The Hague. A Permanent Court of Arbitration was established; meeting at The Hague it has continued to function under various names and with judges drawn from many nations. No provision was made for compulsory arbitration. 'You cannot', said a German statesman, 'submit great questions to arbitration; that is for little states and little problems.' The tsar was, it seems, genuinely anxious to limit the arms race. But the reason for this may have been that Russia was behind the other powers in the race. Rudyard Kipling, for one, warned that the Russian bear was only trying to get time to sharpen his claws. In fact none of the great powers was willing to disarm. Germany most strongly resisted disarmament. Sir John Fisher, representing Britain, said: 'I fought – but not for peace – at that conference.' However, declarations were made prohibiting bombing from balloons (aeroplanes had not yet been invented) and the use of poison gas and expanding (dumdum) bullets.

In 1907 a second Hague conference, called by the tsar at the suggestion of President Theodore Roosevelt, was no more successful in limiting arms. The declarations prohibiting the use of gas and of expanding bullets were not renewed. The declaration prohibiting bombing from balloons was renewed – perhaps the invention of the aeroplane four years earlier was overlooked! Rules made in Geneva in 1864 for the conduct of wars were redrawn

and extended to naval warfare. The representatives of the forty-four states who attended this conference agreed to meet again in 1915. That meeting never took place!

In 1891 an International Peace Bureau was founded in Berne. In 1897 a Russian Jew wrote a book in which he correctly predicted the more terrible nature of future wars. In 1910 Norman Angell's *The Great Illusion*, whose theme was that war can benefit no one, was published; soldiers, like pirates, he said, were colourful but out of date. Many people believed that a large-scale war would be so devastating that no state would dare start it. Pacifists of many races swore that they would never take up arms on behalf of their homelands. Though most of them did in due course take up arms many suffered indignity and imprisonment on account of their beliefs.

The growth of internationalism

Socialist theory held that economic or class barriers were more important than national differences. The Second International (see p. 41) made the preservation of world peace one of its aims. In 1912 it issued an anti-war manifesto. But once war broke out in 1914 most socialists fought with their fellow countrymen, of whatever class or income. The Marxist tie with workers in other lands was disregarded. However, as the war dragged on, socialists tended to remember that tie. In 1915 Swiss and Italian socialists arranged a conference in Switzerland. This meeting, which Lenin attended, called for peace without annexations or indemnities. Another socialist conference held in Switzerland in 1916 asserted that there could be no lasting peace until the peoples of all nations had overthrown capitalism. Dutch and Scandinavian socialists tried to arrange a conference in Stockholm in 1917, but this proved abortive. In December 1917 the Russian Bolsheviks appealed to the peoples of the world, in particular to the proletariat in Germany, France and Britain, to make an end of war. It was in an attempt to discredit war, a 'bourgeois institution', that they published the secret 'partitioning' treaties and bargains made between tsarist Russia and her allies during the war.

The development of trade and communications seemed to promise the world something better than nationalism. Business houses with capital invested in foreign lands would, it was said, oppose war, for war would ruin their prosperity. In fact as trade grew competition tended to increase national rivalries. And powerful munitions firms saw that they would prosper, if not from war, then from preparations for war.

Hopes that increasing travel and the internationalism of scholars who met at congresses and exchanged information in learned journals might help to prevent wars proved unfounded. The International Olympic Games were instituted in 1896 – but the internationalism of the athletes did not help much either. Attempts to achieve world brotherhood by the creation of a universal language, for example Esperanto, accomplished little.

The success of several international organisations established during the nineteenth century – the International Red Cross (1864), the Telegraph Union (1864) (now the International Telecommunications Union), and the Universal Postal Union (UPU) (1875) – proved that people of different nations could work together for the common good. The UPU perhaps did little to prevent wars – but it has added immeasurably to human convenience and happiness. The International Copyright Convention was signed at Berne in 1887. In 1890 delegates from eighteen states drew up regulations aimed at ending the last traces of the African slave trade (see p. 30). There was international co-operation also in dealing with the white slave traffic to Latin America.

Christian leaders, both Catholic and Protestant, joined in the struggle against war. Well before the First World War the papacy had supported the principle of arbitration. Pope Leo XIII (1878–1903) was himself the arbitrator in a dispute between Germany and Spain and in other international disputes. On 2 August 1914 Pope Pius X appealed for peace. In 1917 Benedict XV proposed that peace be concluded on the basis of the restoration of the 1914 frontiers. The Salvation Army, founded by General Booth in 1864, was international in operation and worked for peace on earth, goodwill among men.

The World Student Christian Federation, the YMCA and YWCA and the Boy Scout Movement brought together young men and women of many nations. Carnegie, the American millionaire, gave great sums of money to the cause of peace. Nobel, the Swede who had made a fortune from dynamite, established the Nobel peace prize.

The consciences of some people had been awakened before Princip fired at the archduke in Sarajevo. The horrors of the years that followed made many more people anxious to outlaw war. Their aspirations resulted in the formation of the League of Nations. But those who supported the League failed to realise that in the last resort their support needed to be forcible.

The League of Nations

Its establishment

At the insistence of Woodrow Wilson the covenant (solemn constitution) of the League of Nations was included in each of the peace treaties. Not all the credit for the establishment of the League belongs to Wilson; others, among them Lord Robert Cecil and Sir Edward Grey from England, Smuts from South Africa and Venizelos from Greece share the honour. But it was Wilson's firmness that won the covenant a place in the peace treaties. To secure this, he had to yield on certain matters. In particular he had to agree to terms which he thought foolishly harsh (for example, payment of reparations). Fearing that such terms might lead to further conflict, he hoped that when tempers were cooler statesmen would agree to change them. Provision was made to revise the treaties if the League thought fit. Though the League itself never revised any treaties, various changes were made by member states.

The League of Nations began its existence in January 1920. It was never a universal organisation. The United States, despite the efforts of Wilson, never joined, for the Senate refused to ratify the Treaty of Versailles. With her vast economic power the USA's absence from the League perhaps doomed it to ultimate failure. When Hitler was threatening the peace of the world, Stanley Baldwin, formerly prime minister of Britain, said: 'Fifty per cent of the power and influence of the League vanished when America retired.'

At the outset none of the defeated powers was a member. Russia, which was in violent disorder, was not an original member. Germany was admitted to the League in 1926, the USSR in 1934.

Included among the initial members were Asian states – in particular China and Japan. From the extreme isolation of earlier years these countries had become members of a world organisation. Australia, Canada, New Zealand, South Africa and India were also League members. Other states could join on getting the votes of two-thirds of the member states. In 1933 total membership was fifty-seven. In that year Japan and Germany resigned from the League.

The League was in no way concerned with internal politics. It concerned itself solely with the international relations of members. As open diplomacy was regarded as safer than secret dealings the covenant bound members to register all treaties with the League.

The machinery of the League

The League had its headquarters in Switzerland, in a great white building beside Lake Geneva. Some people, scornful of the new organisation, called the building the Great White Elephant. The League had a permanent secretariat, an assembly and a council. The secretariat was drawn from all member nations. All member states were represented on the assembly, which met annually. Every state had one vote and all decisions of the assembly had to be unanimous – this made it difficult to take any strong action. But the powers, unwilling to restrict their independence, had agreed to join the League only on this basis. The council met three times yearly and whenever an emergency arose. It consisted of representatives of the larger powers, who were permanent members – Britain, France, Italy and Japan and, after 1926, Germany – and four (later nine) others; the assembly elected the additional members from among the minor powers in turn.

Collective security and sanctions

The covenant guaranteed the political independence and territorial integrity, and so the existing frontiers of the League members. Violation of the frontiers of any member was to be regarded as an act of war against all member states. The League thus offered its members a system of collective security against aggression. When disputes arose they were to be submitted to the League for decision. League members bound themselves not to go to war within three months of a decision with which they disagreed – there was to be time for tempers to cool. The Permanent Court of International Justice at The Hague, successor to the Permanent Court of Arbitration, was empowered to decide any international dispute submitted to it. The council and assembly of the League appointed the judges of this court.

If any state committed an act of aggression or disobeyed a League decision, all members were to apply economic sanctions, that is, to cease trading with that state. If economic sanctions failed the council of the League could recommend that the members should take military action. But the League had no armed forces of its own – without police to call into action against lawbreakers it depended entirely on the good faith of its members. As for economic sanctions, their effect was not likely to be great without the USA.

Whilst pacifists opposed the League because of its basis of force, more realistic people criticised its lack of force. Baldwin, then prime minister, speaking when the Ethiopian army was facing destruction by Italian forces (see p. 201), said:

'To a great extent sanctions are slow in action, [and] lose a great deal of their force unless they can be supported by the ultimate sanction, which is blockade or force. . . . Collective security will never work unless all the nations that take part in it are prepared simultaneously to threaten with sanctions and to fight if necessary an aggressor. . . .'

Mandated territories

At the end of the First World War Germany's colonies and, with the exception of the Hejaz, Turkey's non-Turkish territories were regarded as not yet fit for independence. They became mandated territories of one or other of the Allies, under the control of the League of Nations. In accordance with point 5 of the Fourteen Points each mandatory bound itself to administer its mandates as a trustee for the benefit of the inhabitants in preparation for independence. Britain held mandates over Iraq, Palestine (of which Transjordan was part until 1922) and Tanganyika. France was mandatory for Syria, Lebanon, Togoland and part of the Cameroons. The Union of South Africa was mandatory for Southwest Africa (Namibia). Australia held the mandate over German New Guinea, New Britain and the German Solomon Islands, and New Zealand that over Samoa. German colonies north of the equator (the Marshalls, Marianas and Carolines) became Japanese mandates.

Reports on mandated territories had to be sent every year to the League. Although criticisms were made, for instance concerning French administration of Syria, the League's mandates commission could not enforce its wishes. Not all mandates were faithfully administered; Japan illegally fortified her mandates.

Disarmament – little is achieved

The League covenant included provisions for the general reduction of armaments by its members. Clemenceau in June 1919 told the German foreign minister: 'The Allied and Associated powers wish to make it clear that their requirements in regard to German [disarmament] ... are also the first steps towards that general reduction and limitation of armaments which they seek to bring about as one of the most fruitful preventives of war.'

In 1921–22 at the Washington conference (see p. 162) five naval powers set certain limitations on naval armaments and fortification of bases in the Pacific. In 1930 three of these powers agreed to further naval limitations (see p. 163). With these exceptions there was no general decision to disarm between 1919 and 1939. The argument against disarmament was of course the need for security. League members could protest that if they disarmed they would be open to attack – and unable to fulfil any military obligations that might arise under the covenant.

In 1924 Ramsay MacDonald drew up the Geneva Protocol, in an attempt to strengthen collective security and pave the way for disarmament. The protocol defined aggression and provided for compulsory arbitration. However, the Geneva Protocol never came into effect (see p. 139). Then the relaxation of tension that followed the Locarno pacts of 1925 (see p. 198) and the Kellogg-Briand pact of 1928 (see p. 198) seemed to open the way for general disarmament.

From 1925 two non-League members, the USA and the USSR, took part with League members in pre-parations for a disarmament conference which opened in 1932. The USSR came out in favour of disarming but her motives were suspect for she was then poorly armed and support for disarmament was good socialist propaganda. France proposed the formation of an inter-national security force. Germany, claiming she was insecure until other states disarmed, wanted the doubling of her army and the removal of the ban on her possession of certain weapons. Eventually it was agreed that Germany should have equal rights under an arrangement that aimed to provide 'security for all'. Britain, impressed by Hitler's dove-like speeches, argued that Germany should reach equality with France in five years. France, alarmed by growing Nazi power, wanted Germany to postpone rearming for four years and to reach equality with her in eight years.

In October 1933 Hitler, who by then was chancellor of Germany, finally withdrew from the conference and Germany left the League. By this time most states were thinking in terms of rearmament. In 1934 the conference fizzled out. At most it could be said that some people by this time regarded armaments as a matter for consul-tation not for independent action. Germany proceeded to rearm. Japan withdrew from her obligations under the Washington agreements as from 1937 (see p. 163). Britain had considerably reduced her armaments in the 1920s to save money, and to help preserve peace. As the other powers, with the exception of Denmark, did not disarm with her, she found herself in a dangerous position in the 1930s and began to rearm.

The ILO and other League activities

All League members belonged to the International Labour Organisation (ILO), to which governments and employers and workers sent representatives. The ILO debated such matters as workers' compensation, hours of work, conditions of service of merchant seamen and so on. Though its recommendations were not binding, much was done to improve conditions. Even today not all the ILO's recommendations apply, even in the more advanced countries – thus many women are paid at lower rates than men. However, the ILO, a meeting place for people of many races and of different classes, gave valuable experience in practical co-operation. Non-League members, including the USA, joined the ILO.

The League also set up a health service. This did valuable work during the epidemics that struck mankind in the post-war years, killing more than were killed in the Great War. It also gave assistance to needy states and provided famine relief.

The League helped with the resettlement of prisoners of war and refugees; Fridtjof Nansen, a Norwegian who was high commissioner for refugees, was prominent in this work. Homes were found for White Russians who had fled after the Bolshevik revolution, for over a million Greeks repatriated from Turkish territory in Asia Minor and for some half a million Turks moved from Greece (see p. 192).

Treaties signed by various powers guaranteed to mi-nority peoples (for example Germans in Czechoslovakia) the right to practise their own religion, to speak their own tongue and so on. Reports on minorities were sent to the League minorities commission. The commission's attempts to see that minority rights were respected tended to be blocked by the objections of the ruling powers to 'interference' in their affairs.

The League also established international control over opium and other dangerous drugs and worked to abolish all forms of slavery.

The successes and failures of collective security

In its early years the League had some success in settling small disputes between small states. It managed to get German-Polish co-operation in the vexed area of Upper Silesia. It provided a high commissioner for Danzig, another trouble spot, and for fifteen years supervised the administration of the Saar basin.

In 1921 a quarrel arose between Finland and Sweden concerning the Aaland Isles. The dispute was submitted to the League, which ruled in favour of Finland. Sweden, who had tried to take over the islands in 1918, protested, but submitted. Swedish inhabitants of the islands were recognised as a minority and so came under League supervision.

In 1923 Lithuania accepted a League decision that Poland should retain Vilna (see p. 116) – though the two countries remained in a near state of war. In 1923 Lithuania drove the Allied garrison from Memel (see p. 113) and seized the port. In 1924 she accepted a League proposal that Memel should be self-governing under Lithuania.

In 1923 some Italian officials, who were delimiting the Greek-Albanian border, were murdered on Greek territory. Italy then bombarded and occupied the island of Corfu. Claiming that her 'honour' was involved, Italy refused to have the matter submitted to the League. However, she accepted a decision made by the council of ambassadors and on receipt of compensation withdrew from Corfu. Though the League itself did not bring about this compromise, a quarrel that might have led to war was ended.

In 1925, after a frontier quarrel between Greek and Bulgarian soldiers, Greek forces crossed into Bulgaria. The League council ordered the Greeks to withdraw, and told the Bulgars not to oppose the invading forces. Both Greece and Bulgaria did as they were told. As this quarrel had passed beyond words into action when the League intervened success in restoring the peace was the more obvious.

Later the League failed to stop aggression. When in

THE HANDS OF THE LEAGUE:
OR, HER FIRST GREAT TEST.

In 1931 Bernard Partridge, the Punch *cartoonist, expressed the hope that the League would prove able to keep Japan (right) and China apart*

1931 Japan attacked Chinese territory and when in 1937 she stepped up her attacks on China no effective action was taken. Sanctions were imposed on Italy after she attacked Ethiopia (Abyssinia) in 1935, but these failed to stop Italy and no further action was taken. Nor did the League prevent Italy from invading Albania in 1939. When Germany occupied Austria in 1938 there was no League action. The League was powerless to stop Germany's aggressions against Czechoslovakia in 1938 and 1939 and her invasion of Poland in September 1939. When in November 1939 the Russians attacked Finland, the Finns appealed to the League which in a last burst of activity expelled the USSR.

Though the League failed to end war it benefited millions of people of many races. The palace beside Lake Geneva was not altogether a Great White Elephant. The League of Nations was formally dissolved in April 1946.

13 The USSR: from revolution towards communism

The February Revolution, 1917

The first days

Revolution, which had long threatened to overwhelm Russia, came in 1917. There were in fact two revolutions – the February Revolution and the October (Bolshevik) Revolution. (The Julian calendar used in Russia until 1918 was thirteen days behind the Gregorian calendar used in western Europe; according to the latter the revolutions occurred in March and November. In this chapter the Gregorian calendar is followed.)

The February Revolution came when mass discontent boiled over in Petrograd. In January and February 1917 there had been disorder in the city. On 3 March men in the Putilov metal works went on strike. On 8 March the tsar left Petrograd for army headquarters while socialists were celebrating Women's Day. Women from the textile factories were swarming about the streets. Bread rationing had just been introduced but on 8 March there was no bread to buy. Women and boys, tired, cold and hungry, stormed the bakers' shops. The Putilov

workers, who by then had been locked out, joined these mobs. The next day the police fired on the crowds. Factories began closing and workers began rioting.

Order might have been restored, perhaps with relative ease, had not the army proved to be largely on the side of the rioters. On 11 March crowds did disperse when soldiers opened fire. But some of the troops disobeyed orders when told to fire; some simply shot into the air. On 12 March the city garrison joined the mobs; by the evening there were over 60,000 mutineers. Martial law was proclaimed but so great was the confusion that no glue could be found to paste up the proclamation. By nightfall on 12 March Petrograd was in rebel hands, though there were still some loyal troops in the city. Bread riots had, with the aid of the army, become revolution. Though only a small section of 'His Majesty the Russian people' had rioted 'only the tongues of machine guns' would have silenced them. 'Only lead

A bread queue in Petrograd shortly before the outbreak of the February Revolution

could drive back into its lair the terrible beast that was escaping.' For tsarist rule rested on armed force. When the loyalty of the army broke down tsarist power broke down with it.

On 15 March, while en route from army headquarters to his summer palace in Tsarskoe Selo (Tsar's Village), not far from Petrograd, Nicholas II was forced to abdicate. As his son was an invalid Nicholas named as his successor his own brother, the Grand Duke Michael. On 16 March Michael, told that he could not rely on the army, 'abdicated'. Nicholas and his family were placed under house arrest. In April 1918 they were taken to Ekaterinburg (Sverdlovsk) in the Ural Mountains.

The provisional government and the Petrograd soviet

On 11 March, at the height of the riots, Nicholas had dismissed the Duma. The following day Duma members set up a provisional committee to try to restore order. On the tsar's abdication a provisional government was set up. It was intended to hold office until a Constituent Assembly could be elected. The provisional government was far from wanting revolutionary changes. Though the tsar had abdicated it did not proclaim a republic. Its head was Prince Lvov, who inclined to the conservative Octobrists rather than to the more liberal Cadets (see p. 44). Only one socialist, Alexander Kerensky, a lawyer, held office, as minister of justice. Formerly a Trudovik (Labour) member of the Duma, Kerensky admitted now to being a Socialist Revolutionary.

On 12 March, the day the provisional committee was set up, military and industrial establishments elected deputies to a Petrograd soviet of soldiers' and workers' representatives. The Petrograd soviet, which included some Bolsheviks, was controlled by Socialist Revolutionaries and Mensheviks. Its policies were therefore much more radical than those of the provisional government. Soviets began forming throughout Russia. Though the Petrograd soviet was nominally only a local body other soviets deferred to it and it acquired a dominant position. Its executive committee took control of railways, posts and telegraphs and organised food supplies. It was the Petrograd soviet which issued 'Order No. 1' which relaxed military discipline, thus contributing to a further breakdown of authority in the army. However, though the soviet had greater influence than the provisional government its members were unprepared for the work of government.

The Allies recognised the provisional government, which promised to continue the war against Germany. It abolished the death penalty and gave an amnesty to political offenders. Beyond this it achieved little. It proposed labour laws but did not carry them into effect. Industrial relations became chaotic and the Petrograd soviet of its own initiative arranged an eight-hour day. The Moscow soviet followed suit. Nor did the provisional government grapple with peasant unrest. It tended to defer all problems until the Constituent Assembly met – but this was not to be elected until September (later postponed to November). To most people September seemed far away.

Many Russians had no idea what was happening in those confused months. The residents of one town, hearing talk of revolution, wrote to Petrograd asking for 'Revolution's portrait'; they wanted to hang a picture of their 'new ruler' in a place of honour.

Lenin and the Bolsheviks

At the time of the February Revolution there were few Bolsheviks in Petrograd, indeed in all Russia. They had no hold upon the people and their leaders were mostly in exile. But they had in Lenin a leader who was determined that an élite of revolutionaries, an intellectual spearhead, should make another revolution – against the wishes of the dumb masses, if need be. But Lenin was still in exile in Switzerland in March 1917.

Then, believing that the Bolsheviks could further disrupt Russia's war effort, Ludendorff arranged to smuggle Lenin and some thirty other revolutionaries, mostly Bolsheviks, by train through Germany and from Sweden into Russia. 'It is as right to attack Russia with Lenin as with poison gas', said Ludendorff.

So Lenin arrived in Petrograd on 16 April 1917. He immediately outlined his programme in the 'April Theses', published in the Bolshevik paper, *Pravda* (Truth). In the 'April Theses' Lenin said there should be no further co-operation with the government; all power must go to the soviets. The errors of the socialist majority (the non-Bolsheviks) in the Petrograd soviet, he said, must be shown up and the soviet must follow Bolshevik policy. He demanded an end to the war, the control of industry by workers' committees and the nationalisation of land. He said that a new Communist International should be formed to work for world revolution. The Petrograd soviet showed little interest in the 'April Theses'. Nor were Lenin's fellow Bolsheviks in the least confident that his programme could succeed.

Marxist dogma 'bound' Lenin to oppose the 'capitalist, bourgeois' war – but Lenin, the political opportunist, also gambled on a peace policy winning popular support. His call to end the war led some people to regard him as a traitor, but won support from those who were weary of the war. Brusilov's victories (see p. 103) had been great but in 1916 two million Russians were killed or wounded and a third of a million taken prisoner. Bolshevik agitators were sent to the front to work on the troops. Within a few weeks of the February Revolution there were about a million deserters.

As Russia was primarily an agricultural society peasant support seemed necessary to Lenin. Though in the 'April Theses' he had just demanded the nationalisation of land, now, to attract the masses, he coined a new slogan – Land, Peace and Bread. About three-quarters of Russia's farmland was already peasant owned but *Pravda* urged peasants to go ahead and seize land, as many were doing. Soldiers, hearing rumours of a handout of land, hurried back to get their share. In July 1917 Brusilov's last great offensive ended in defeat. Soon another million men had deserted. Russia was signing peace 'with the feet of her soldiers'. Lenin's new land 'policy' was in fact the policy of his hated opponents, the Socialist Revolutionaries – but his opportunism was bearing fruit.

The July days and the Kornilov affair

Meanwhile there were disputes between the provisional government and the Petrograd soviet. During the early months of the revolution, the period of dual control, the soviet kept watch on the government to ensure that conservatives did not undo what had already been achieved. Torn by disputes, the soviet could do little more than this and indeed had few plans.

In mid-July a mob of Bolshevik supporters – workers, soldiers, and sailors from the Kronstadt naval base – rushed on the Tauride Palace where both the government and the soviet met. 'Down with the government; all power to the soviets', they shouted. Some 400 people were killed before order was restored. Whether the Bolshevik leaders incited the uprising or whether it was the work of over enthusiastic supporters is not clear. The government's claim that Lenin had tried to stir up trouble because he was in the pay of Germany led to an outcry against the Bolsheviks. *Pravda*'s offices were wrecked. Lenin in disguise escaped to Finland. Other Bolsheviks were imprisoned. Among them was Leon Trotsky who after his return to Russia in May 1917 had

gone over from the Mensheviks to the Bolsheviks. After the July days support for the 'pro-German' Bolsheviks declined. In July Kerensky, who was a member of the soviet as well as the provisional government, replaced Prince Lvov as prime minister. He included numerous socialists in his government.

Early in September General Kornilov, whom Kerensky had appointed commander in chief in place of Brusilov, ordered cavalry to advance on Petrograd. Bent on restoring order in the army, Kornilov intended to suppress both the soviet and the Bolsheviks. Whether he also intended to set up a military dictatorship is not clear. However, Kerensky took fright and accepted support from the soviet and even the Bolsheviks. Bolshevik leaders, among them Trotsky, were released from prison. Arms were supplied to their followers. Meanwhile, agitators had undermined the morale of Kornilov's troops and railwaymen had refused to assist him. The march on Petrograd fizzled out. The general himself was arrested.

Following the Kornilov affair Russia became a republic. Fear of a counter-revolutionary takeover led to a rapid increase in Bolshevik influence in the Petrograd and other soviets.

The October (Bolshevik) Revolution

The Bolsheviks overthrow the provisional government

In mid-September Trotsky became chairman of the Petrograd soviet, which soon had a Bolshevik majority. Late in October Lenin returned in disguise to Petrograd. His headquarters were in Smolny, a working-class suburb where there were many Bolshevik supporters. Here, at the Smolny Institute, formerly a college for young women of aristocratic birth, the Petrograd soviet had been meeting since August. In 'The Eve of October' Lenin wrote: '[Our] majority in both the [Petrograd and Moscow] soviets was created only by . . . the experience of ruthless punishment meted out to the Bolsheviks [after the July disturbances], and by the experience of the Kornilov affair.'

However, it was by no means certain that the Bolsheviks would have a majority in the National Congress of Soviets, due to meet on 7 November. To forestall any opposition, the Petrograd soviet, on 23 October, the day after Lenin's return, decided on an armed uprising. A military revolutionary committee

Petrograd, November 1917: women on guard facing the Winter Palace. With a few young officers they were the last of Kerensky's bodyguard to yield when the Bolsheviks swept through the Admiralty Arch at the rear to swarm into the palace

under Trotsky, Lenin and Joseph Stalin drew up plans to overthrow the provisional government. Trotsky armed workers with rifles coaxed from soldiers in the Peter and Paul fortress.

Some of the Bolsheviks thought it was too early for action. But Lenin had the support of the city garrison. Soldiers had turned bread riots into the February Revolution. Now soldiers and sailors were to make the October Revolution. And small volunteer groups, the red guards, some with weapons supplied by Kerensky's government during the Kornilov affair, were acting as revolutionary cells throughout the city. On 6 November Lenin said: 'Questions that are not solved by conferences or by congresses (even by congresses of soviets) [are] on the agenda.'

On 7 November 1917 the siren of the cruiser *Aurora* gave the signal for the second revolution, the Bolshevik or Communist Revolution. It all happened very quickly. Bolsheviks seized Petrograd's railway stations, bridges, powerhouses and telephone exchanges. Kerensky's headquarters, then in the Winter Palace, were seized; red guards rushed from behind an archway and stormed their way into the palace. Kerensky got away in a car belonging to an American diplomat but most of his

ministers were arrested. Meanwhile schools and offices in Petrograd had remained open as usual. In the evening there were the usual theatrical performances. A statue of Catherine the Great stood outside one theatre. Somebody placed a little red flag in her hands.

At 11 p.m. the National Congress of Soviets met. Fighting was still going on around the Winter Palace but the overthrow of Kerensky's government was announced. The congress then entrusted power to a Sovnarkom, a council of people's commissars (ministers), the new government of Russia. The Sovnarkom, formed from the committee that had planned the October uprising, was led by Lenin and Trotsky. All its members were Bolsheviks. It was empowered to govern and legislate by decree. However, its power was in theory provisional, granted until the Constituent Assembly met. And in theory the Sovnarkom was subject to the Congress of Soviets.

Orders poured out from the Bolshevik headquarters. Decrees on peace and land were issued forthwith. All social, military and naval ranks were abolished and Russian citizens became comrades (*tovarishchi*). Bolshevik appointees took over the offices left vacant by officials of the provisional government. Alexandra

Kollontai, later a Soviet ambassador, recalled how on 9 November she met Lenin, 'squeezed into a little side room with a plain table'. 'Go immediately and take over the ministry of social security', he told her. She made her way past a 'porter in gold braid' who 'did not sympathise with the Bolsheviks'. 'As we went upstairs, we were met by a flood of people coming down – clerks, typists, accountants, heads of departments. . . . We came in and the staff went out. . . . Typewriters had been abandoned, papers were lying about everywhere. . . . And no keys. . . . ' After the safe keys turned up a peasant came with a note signed by Lenin himself: 'Pay him out of the social security fund whatever is due to him for his horse.'

A week after their victory in Petrograd, the Kremlin, Moscow's old walled city with its palaces and churches, fell to the Bolsheviks.

The Cheka

On 9 November 1917 all newspapers opposed to the new régime were ordered to stop publication. On 20 December the Cheka (All Russia Extraordinary Commission against Counter-revolution and Sabotage) replaced the tsarist secret police, the Okhrana. The Cheka's task was to destroy all critics of the Bolsheviks – counter-revolutionaries (Whites), outspoken editors, saboteurs, strikers, Socialist Revolutionaries and all other non-Bolshevik socialists. The Cheka had the right to arrest, even to pass sentence of death. It was the all-seeing eye, the all-hearing ear, of the Bolsheviks. It was their mailed fist, their 'heavy punishing hand that would mercilessly fall' on the head of anyone who dared to oppose them. The Bolsheviks soon outdid tsarist officials in their brutal repression and terror.

The Treaty of Brest-Litovsk

In December 1917 the Bolsheviks published the secret treaties made by tsarist Russia with her allies (see p. 101). In December too they signed an armistice with Germany. Germany required Russia to cede to her Finland, Estonia, Latvia, Lithuania, Poland, part of Byelorussia, the bread-basket of the Ukraine and oft-disputed Bessarabia. Part of the Transcaucasus was to go to Turkey. While the Bolsheviks were discussing these terms, Germany renounced the truce and moved troops towards Petrograd. Russia had no bargaining power. So in March 1918 the 'shameful treaty' of Brest-Litovsk was concluded.

There was considerable opposition to the treaty within Russia. The German ambassador was shot in July 1918. In August Lenin was wounded by a Socialist Revolutionary – in revenge the Cheka killed 500 people in Moscow on the same night. The next day 500 people were executed for the killing of a Cheka official in Petrograd. With Germany's acceptance of the Fourteen Points (see p. 111), the Treaty of Brest-Litovsk lapsed.

Overthrow of the Constituent Assembly

The Bolsheviks did not upset arrangements for the long awaited Constituent Assembly. In the elections the Right Socialist Revolutionaries (Socialist Revolutionaries who continued to oppose the Bolsheviks) won far more seats (375) than Lenin's followers (175). In January 1918 the Constituent Assembly held its first and only meeting at the Tauride Palace in Petrograd. Bolshevik troops opened fire on a crowd that had come to see the opening of the assembly. The non-Bolshevik deputies, hissed by the troops, entered the palace carrying packets of food and candles – brought in expectation of a Bolshevik siege. 'Thus democracy entered upon the struggle with dictatorship heavily armed with sandwiches and candles', said Trotsky. When the assembly rejected a Bolshevik resolution Lenin's followers walked out. The Bolsheviks, more sure of their position than they had been in November, dissolved the assembly and posted troops outside the palace to stop the deputies re-entering. Trotsky, with blunt truthfulness, said: 'The simple, open, brutal breaking up of the assembly dealt formal democracy a finishing stroke from which it has never recovered.'

The overthrow of the assembly made it clear that Russia was to be a one party state. The Sovnarkom's power was now absolute and the word provisional was struck out of its title. Some Bolsheviks had had nobler ideals but Lenin's hard line triumphed. The Socialist Revolutionaries, despite their large following, offered no real resistance at this time. Bolshevik power, they dreamed, would burst 'like a soap bubble'.

In March 1918 the capital was transferred to Moscow. At the same time the Bolshevik Party took the name Communist Party (though Bolshevik was an alternative name until 1952).

The Comintern

In March 1919 the Comintern or Third Communist

On 7 November 1918, first anniversary of the Bolshevik Revolution, Lenin spoke at a ceremony marking the opening of a temporary memorial to Marx and Engels in Red Square, Moscow

International was established in Moscow to replace the Second International which had virtually come to an end in 1914. The Comintern aimed to spread communism to every corner of the earth to prepare for world revolution. Lenin and his associates at this stage believed that the revolution must spread if communism was to survive in Russia – and indeed at the end of the First World War unrest was widespread. Hungary was for a time in the hands of communists. And Germany, where Bolshevik agitators had had considerable success, was seriously disturbed. In 1920 the Comintern laid down rigid rules for membership; all non-communist socialists were excluded. The Comintern also saw that affiliated communist parties followed its strict party line.

It is hard to say for how long Russia's leaders and communists elsewhere believed that the revolution was spreading. But it is certain that among non-communists fear of revolution persisted for a long time. The Comintern was disbanded in 1943, during the Second World War, with the object of assuring the USSR's allies that she was not acting subversively.

Over the years the ideas of Marx, modified and put

into practice by Lenin, have found support in every continent. But neither the USSR nor any other country has achieved the ideal communist state depicted by Marx. The dictatorship endures; the millenium is not yet reached.

Civil war and foreign intervention

The Communists forced themselves into power relatively easily and with relatively little bloodshed. Maintaining their power cost millions of lives. In 1917 communist doctrine was not acceptable to many Russians. The abolition of private trade (see p. 130) made enemies of shopkeepers and others with small businesses. The peasants, who had to hand over surplus corn to the government, were angered. Many people were disgusted by the Treaty of Brest-Litovsk. Again, the Russians were a devout people, whereas Marx had called religion the 'opiate of the people'. Christianity may indeed have had a narcotic effect upon the poor of Russia – but this did not turn them against it. There

Trotsky on the platform of the train he used during the civil war while organising and encouraging the Red army. The war train was so long that it took two engines to pull it. It carried a printing press, an electric generator, radio and telegraph equipment – and cars for Trotsky and his staff

were many Muslims, too, who had to be coaxed or forced into the communist fold. Minority peoples recently colonised by the Russians were hostile to the new régime.

In May 1918 Trotsky, commissar for war, organised the Red (later Soviet) army to fight against counter-revolution. Many tsarist officers joined the Red army, where their experience was of great value – though Trotsky was later blamed for using them. Over each commander a Bolshevik commissar watched, counter-signing every order, maintaining morale and indoctrinating the troops.

A revolt by the Don Cossacks in December 1917 was the beginning of a civil war that spread over much of Russia (see map p. 132). A red terror, waged by the Cheka and the Red army, killed off whole classes of people. It raged throughout the land, destroying not only bourgeoisie and reactionaries, but moderate socialists who opposed communism. By 1921 the Socialist Revolutionaries and the Mensheviks had ceased to exist. Communism had brought to Russia a new dictatorship that allowed no opposition – in theory the dictatorship of the proletariat, in fact the dictatorship of a handful of people in the Communist Party.

Foreign powers intervened in the Russian Civil War

both before and after Germany's defeat. The wars fought by the counter-revolutionaries and their foreign allies against the Bolsheviks were savage and widespread and left bitter memories. To what extent they left a genuine fear of foreign intervention is hard to know.

Initially intervention was intended to bring Russia back into the war against Germany. Later there was fear of the Comintern with its threat of world revolution and its aim of stirring up rebellion in colonial areas. The Japanese had territorial ambitions in the Far East.

In March 1918 British forces landed at Murmansk. Other forces, mainly from the French and British army of the Orient, operated from the Black Sea. In May 1918 a Czech legion, defectors from the Austrian army, was on its way to Vladivostok with the object of joining other Czech units fighting in France. East of the Urals, the Czechs clashed with Austro-Hungarian prisoners of war who were travelling west to be repatriated following the Brest-Litovsk treaty. Trotsky ordered the Czechs to be disarmed, but the Tcheko Sobaki – a nickname coined from the Russian *sobarka* (dog) – seized a large section of the Trans-Siberian Railway between the Volga and Irkutsk. The USA had been unwilling to intervene but in August 1918 agreed to go to the rescue of the Czechs and even dropped opposition to Japanese intervention.

Soon numbers of Japanese troops landed at Vladivostok.

In August 1918 a Bolshevik proclamation appealed to the 'toiling masses' of Europe, America and Japan:

'Like a vicious dog loosed from its chain, the whole capitalist press of your countries howls for the "intervention" of your governments in Russian affairs. ... The Anglo-French bandits are already shooting Soviet workers on the Murmansk railway. ... [Czecho-Slovaks in the Urals] are cutting off the Russian people from bread in order to force workers and peasants to put their necks once more in the noose of the Paris and London stock exchanges.'

Counter-revolutionaries, among them many socialists as well as tsarist supporters, dreamed of a three-pronged attack that would meet at Moscow – White (counter-revolutionary) and Allied forces would converge on the capital from Murmansk and Archangel, from Siberia and from the Caucasus.

For a time the Communists were hard pressed by the Whites and their allies. In the summer of 1919 General Anton Denikin led a White army close to Moscow. An Anglo-Japanese force defeated the Reds on the Ussuri River, thus establishing control over the Maritime Province. At the end of 1918 thousands of Japanese were holding strategic points in eastern Siberia and the Maritime Province, Americans were protecting the Trans-Siberian and Chinese Eastern railways and British and Czech troops were based on Omsk. In November the White leader in Omsk, Admiral Kolchak, proclaimed himself supreme ruler 'of the Russias'. For a time his government held sway in Siberia.

Meanwhile, in July 1918 Tsar Nicholas II, his wife, his son and his four daughters were shot by order of the Ekaterinburg soviet who were afraid Czechs advancing towards the town might rescue the royal family and provide a rallying point for anti-Bolshevik forces. This was but one of the tragedies that stained the years when Reds and Whites contended for control of Russia.

In November 1919 the Red army forced Kolchak to retreat east to Irkutsk. There, after a quarrel, the Czechs handed him over to a revolutionary committee who had him shot. Denikin, commander of the Whites in the south, who had retreated to the Crimea, then became supreme ruler.

Gradually the White dream faded. The three counter-revolutionary forks did not meet. The last important battles were fought late in 1920. The Whites had thought that the neck of land joining the Crimea to the mainland was too strongly held for the Reds to break

A Bolshevik recruiting poster, 1920; 'Have you volunteered [to fight in the civil war]?' Did the Bolsheviks get their idea from the Kitchener poster (p. 104)?

through, but a violent night attack overcame them. Odessa, the last White stronghold, fell. Over 100,000 refugees escaped to eastern Europe.

In 1919 foreign forces had left Archangel. In 1920 all except the Japanese withdrew from Siberia. The Japanese did not leave until October 1922. Until 1925 they remained in northern Sakhalin.

Separatism in border areas and among minority groups

Resistance to communist rule was especially strong in border areas and among minority groups. All, whatever they might think of Bolshevism, saw its coming to power as a triumph for the Russians and particularly the Great Russians, their oppressors.

After the First World War ended German forces with Allied consent had remained in Lithuania, Latvia and Estonia to contain the Reds. With aid from Britain's Royal Navy these states rid themselves of Germans, Reds and Whites – and were recognised as independent. Finland also made itself independent. Finland and the Baltic states, along with Poland, Czechoslovakia and Romania, formed the *cordon sanitaire* (see p. 116) around the new Red Russia – 'the Great Wall against Bolshevism' as Lenin called it.

When the Germans left the Ukraine a civil war raged. The Ukraine knew 'an unparalleled diversity of régimes' until finally the Communists established their control.

In Byelorussia, where Russia faded into territory ethnically Polish, German withdrawal was followed by a war of Red against White. As in the Ukraine the problem was complicated by nationalist agitation. The Poles, taking advantage of this situation, attacked the Russians (see p. 116). By the Treaty of Riga (1921) part of Byelorussia passed to Poland. The rest came under Communist Russian control.

By 1922 Turkestan was virtually absorbed into the Communist fold. However, Muslim partisans, opposed to both Communists and Russians, fought on there until 1926. The Transcaucasian states (Georgia, Armenia and Azerbaijan), which had been ceded to Turkey at Brest-Litovsk, declared their independence in March 1918. British, White and Red forces fought there. Turkey also threatened them. But in due course, with the exception of western Armenia (Russian only since 1878), these areas were gathered back into the Communist Russian fold.

The USSR: its constitution

In July 1918 the constitution of the Russian Soviet Federated Socialist Republic – still the largest and most important republic in the Soviet Union – was drawn up. The word federated implied that certain minorities in this Moscow-centred republic were to have some autonomy. In December 1922 the Union of Soviet Socialist Republics (USSR or Soviet Union) was formed. The constitution of this union was drawn up in 1923. It provided for the election, by indirect and open voting, of an All Union Congress of Soviets. This congress, a large, unwieldy body that was theoretically the supreme power in the USSR, then elected a central executive committee consisting of a union council and a council of nationalities. These two councils elected the presidium, a small permanent committee, from among their members.

Even the presidium was not all-powerful. Only the Communist Party could nominate candidates for election to the Congress of Soviets and all elected members had to follow the party line. So the highest authority was in fact that of the top party officials – those who were members of its political bureau, the politburo. (After 1952 the politburo was called the presidium of the Communist Party.) Members of the politburo could hold key posts in the government presidium, though not all did so.

The USSR is a federal republic. The 1923 constitution gave member republics autonomy in local affairs and the right to leave the union. In 1936 the Union of Soviet Socialist Republics included the Russian Soviet Federated Socialist Republic (the nucleus of the union), and the Ukrainian, Byelorussian, Armenian, Georgian, Azerbaijan, Kazakh, Uzbek, Turkmen, Kirghiz, and Tadzhik Soviet Socialist Republics. To these in 1939–40 were added the Karelo-Finnish, Lithuanian, Estonian, Latvian and Moldavian Soviet Socialist Republics. The union thus welded together more national groups than the Habsburgs or the sultans of Turkey had ruled in their heyday. To what degree any republic had real autonomy in domestic affairs it is hard to say. None would have been allowed to exercise its 'right' to leave the union.

From war communism to the NEP

From mid-1918 to March 1921 was the period of war communism in Russia. Private property was abolished and an attempt was made to do away altogether with markets and money. Factories and banks were nationalised and in 1920 farmers were ordered to deliver surplus crops to the government for distribution. Meanwhile Russia was laid waste by civil war and had lost valuable territory. A scorched earth policy – the destruction of everything that could be of value to the other side – made the devastation greater.

By the end of the Civil War Russia's economy was right out of gear. Under war communism farmers grew enough for their own needs (subsistence farming) and no more. Industrial output fell to less than 15 per cent of its pre-war figure. Foreign trade came to a standstill. Transport broke down entirely. With the virtual disappearance of a money economy a black market flourished. In 1921–22 Russia suffered a most terrible famine.

Bands of starving children roamed like animals through the country. Some four million people died despite assistance from the League of Nations and the United States.

In February–March 1921 sailors at the Kronstadt naval base mutinied in support of striking factory workers. They demanded, as well as economic reforms, freedom of speech and of association for all socialists – an end in fact to the dictatorship of the Communist Party. After much bloodshed the Red army suppressed the mutiny. The Bolsheviks had come to power with the support of the armed forces; Red Kronstadt had been a valuable ally in 1917. So the Kronstadt mutiny was especially alarming. Lenin was already aware that war communism was not working. The Kronstadt mutiny gave him the opportunity to convince his more dogmatic followers that changes were essential.

In March 1921 Lenin, by a temporary retreat from communist principles, tried to restore the economy and win popular support. War communism, having failed, had to end; dogma had to yield to hard facts. So it was that from March 1921 Russia followed the New Economic Policy – NEP.

The peasants had bitterly resented the requisitioning of their corn, often taken at gun point by the Cheka or party officials. Under the tsars, they said, 'The land was God's, but the rye was the peasants'. Under war communism the land was the peasants' – but all the rye went to God.' Under the NEP the peasants handed over only a percentage levy of their harvest. The levy was later commuted to a money payment. The peasants, being now allowed to sell their surplus grain, grew more. They sold their surplus to private traders, the NEPmen. Many nepmen did very well.

Soon 'capitalism' spread from farms to factories and commerce. Privately owned shops appeared in the cities. By 1924 four-fifths of Russia's smaller factories were privately run. Heavy industry, banks and transport remained under state control. But the economic concessions of the NEP were accompanied by tighter party control. Party officials moved into every office, every workshop and every village. The party was a pyramid whose broad base touched the roots of Soviet society.

Gradually, under the NEP, the economy began to recover and the standard of living to rise a little. But problems did not vanish overnight.

Stalin in power

The defeat of Trotsky

Lenin died in January 1924. Petrograd was renamed Leningrad. Lenin's reputation, unlike those of many

Starving children in Russia, October 1921, six months after Lenin abandoned war communism. At this time typhus and cholera broke out

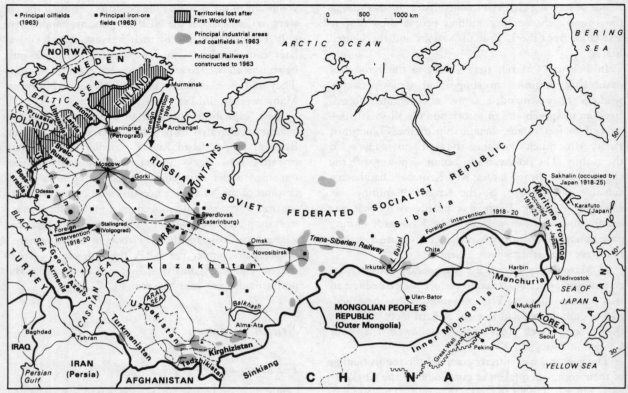

The Union of Soviet Socialist Republics

communist leaders, survives unscathed. Daily thousands of people come to Moscow's Red Square to offer homage in his mausoleum, solid, imposing, austere. On little Siberian railway stations or peering through washing machines in a Samarkand shop window the face of Lenin continues to dominate the Russian people.

After Lenin's death Trotsky and Stalin contended for the leadership. Stalin, man of steel (*stal*), born in 1879, was the son of a Georgian cobbler. In a seminary in Tiflis (Tbilisi), an industrial town full of revolutionary talk, he turned to Marxism. Several times arrested and exiled, he attracted attention by writing for *Pravda*, of which he became editor in 1912. A member of the original Sovnarkom, he held a number of key posts. In the Civil War he defended Tsaritsyn and organised the Red offensive in the Crimea. (Tsaritsyn, renamed Stalingrad, became Volgograd after Stalin's disgrace (see p. 248).) In 1921, as commissar for nationalities, he suppressed his fellow Georgians with vigour. Later as secretary of the Communist Party he built up a wide following. Like Lenin, Stalin was willing to discard dogma; practical politics and above all national interests

were to him supreme. His overriding aim was to make the USSR a great power. Lenin's will, published only in 1956, suggests he might have liked to ease Stalin from power. Stalin lacked, he said, patience and politeness – a description of Stalin that is more than polite.

Trotsky, architect of the Red army and a brilliant Marxist theoretician, believed that the USSR should work actively for world revolution; only when world revolution was achieved, Trotsky said, could the USSR itself be safe. He wanted greater freedom of opinion within the Communist Party. Freedom of opinion was anathema to Stalin. And Stalin was not prepared to work for world revolution unless, in his opinion, it suited the Soviet Union to do so. In 1925, at the fourteenth party conference, he spoke of 'socialism in one country' as practicable. In the same year he engineered Trotsky's dismissal as commissar for war. The next year Trotsky ceased to be a member of the politburo. In 1927 Stalin's victory was complete: the fifteenth all union congress of the party said there could be no deviation from the party line as he interpreted it. From then until his death in 1953 Stalin maintained an iron grip on the USSR.

In 1928 Trotsky, by then expelled from the Communist Party, was exiled to Alma Ata in Kazakhstan, and later from the Soviet Union. In 1940 he was 'eliminated' by a Stalinist agent – stabbed to death with an ice pick in Mexico while writing a history of Stalin. In exile he had tried to set up a Fourth International to work for world revolution.

A planned economy

In 1921 Gosplan, a state planning commission, was set up. However, a planned economy was embarked on only in December 1928 when Stalin decided to abandon the NEP and drive towards socialism again. Under the first five-year plan a tremendous drive towards collectivisation of agriculture began. 'Annihilate the kulaks', was the party cry. The relatively prosperous kulaks (see p. 44), though not numerous, controlled much of the land and were naturally conservative. During this so-called Second Bolshevik Revolution the peasants too lost the land 'given' to them in 1917. Nepmen were disposed of and the state took over their assets. Many farmers burned their crops. But those who resisted collectivisation risked firing squads or prison camps. Perhaps some five million people were 'liquidated' between 1932 and 1933. In those years there was famine. Livestock numbers fell by about 50 per cent. On the collective farms each family kept a small private plot.

Meanwhile, development of roads and railways and the production of tractors under the first five-year plan aided agriculture. Though targets were not always reached, heavy industries made considerable advance. Mines were developed and the Urals area became industrialised. Wage differentials increased in the years of planning and 'ants', the toiling masses, were soon much worse off than the 'lucky fellows' at the top. Labour in heavy industries was often virtual slave labour.

In 1933 the second five-year plan came into operation. While the capitalist world suffered its depression (see p. 173) Russian heavy industry forged ahead. The output of steel increased fourfold. Seven times more electricity was generated. Consumer goods remained in short supply but the number of hospital beds quadrupled. In 1935 a miner named Stakhanov by his prodigious efficiency earned a month's wages in a day. Soon there were numerous Stakhanovites in mines and factories. In 1938 the Hero of Socialist Toil medal, the supreme reward for workers, was first awarded.

A literacy campaign begun after the Civil War was speeded up under the five-year plans. Between 1929 and 1938 the number of schools more than doubled. Education was used for state purposes. Literacy was politically important, for it made indoctrination easier. Thus the Communist Party was able greatly to strengthen its hold. However, among the more-than-literate there seem always to have been critics of the régime. Many intellectuals resented the stifling of thought by its subjection to the state.

Repression and the purges

By 1922 there were twenty-two corrective labour camps in the USSR. In that year the GPU (State Political Administration) replaced the Cheka. Later the GPU became the OGPU (Union State Political Administration). In 1934 the OGPU was merged with the NKVD (All Union Internal Affairs Commissariat). Changes of name however did not alter the character of the security system, which continued to terrorise the entire population.

The security police had almost unlimited powers against anyone, high official or peasant, who even appeared to go against the party. Against people described as 'socially dangerous' or 'unreliable' – members of minority groups, nepmen, bourgeois scientists and engineers, kulaks and peasants who opposed collectivisation – the authorities could act without even the formality of a trial. Untold thousands of people were sent – usually for ten years – to labour camps in remote parts of the USSR. Prisoners were usually employed where conditions were too severe for free labour. Inadequately clothed, underfed, overworked and brutally treated, unknown numbers died. Many who survived long sentences were immediately sentenced to further terms.

Stalin ended what little freedom of expression remained within the party. One after another he destroyed his former associates, as well as opponents of the system. In 1933 party membership, which had grown considerably, was cut down by a bloodless purge. Foreign technicians working in the USSR were arrested. Then in December 1934 Sergei Kirov, whom Stalin had appointed chief of the party in Leningrad, was murdered by a party member. Leningrad, which had tended to follow a somewhat independent line, was to have been kept on the right tracks by Kirov.

It may be that Kirov's murder was seen as evidence of a plot, within the party, against Stalin. It may be, as Nikita Khrushchev (see p. 248) suggested in 1956, that Stalin himself was behind the assassination. Whatever the facts, Stalin, neurotically fearful and suspicious, set out to eliminate all possible opponents. Some eight million people were arrested by order of the man of steel. Estimates of the number killed range from two million to six million. Many others were exiled to Siberia. All classes suffered – politicians, army chiefs, comrades of no apparent importance.

Show trials were staged in open court, mockeries of justice in which the brainwashed accused 'confessed' their 'errors'. There was no possibility of defence. This rabbit joke illustrates the position:

'"Why", said the Polish rabbit to the Russian rabbit, "have you fled to Poland?" "Because", said the Russian rabbit, "Comrade Stalin is preparing a bear hunt." "But you are not a bear", said the Polish rabbit. "No, but I can't prove I'm not a bear", the Russian rabbit replied.'

In 1935 Zinoviev, a close associate of Lenin and the first president of the Comintern, was accused of being a Trotskyite. With another prominent Communist he was sentenced to ten years in the labour camps. The next year he and fifteen others 'confessed' and were executed. At the trials of The Seventeen in 1937 and The Twenty-one in 1938 prominent Communists were accused of Trotskyism; all but four were executed. Hundreds of senior army officers were executed. These included eight generals of the highest rank who 'confessed' during a secret trial to conspiring with the Germans and Japanese. The Great Purge, the years of the Yezhovshchina (from 1936 Yezhov was the head of the NKVD), lasted until December 1938. Then, like his predecessor, Yezhov fell from power and was executed.

The Stalin constitution

In 1936, at the height of the Yezhovshchina, the USSR received a new constitution. In theory this Stalin constitution marked the end of the period of dictatorship and introduced a democracy of workers and peasants. The All Union Congress of Soviets was replaced by the Supreme Soviet, which appointed the presidium. The constitution provided for universal franchise and secret voting. In fact the Supreme Soviet, which met twice a year, merely confirmed the decisions already made by the Soviet leaders. As before, control lay with the Communist Party, still the only party allowed. As before, only the Communist Party could nominate candidates for election to the Supreme Soviet. The first elections under the new constitution were held in 1937.

The constitution guaranteed the usual civil liberties.

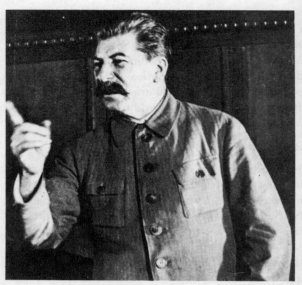

Stalin

In practice such rights were worth little. For example, with the right to attack religion being guaranteed, freedom of religion was more or less meaningless, though some churches continued to function. To some extent a Lenin cult encouraged by Stalin acted as a substitute for religion. In 1943, to win support in the war against Germany, the USSR gave state recognition to Orthodox Christianity and to Islam.

With the elimination of the old party leaders under the Yezhovshchina, new officials, less inclined than some of the older Bolsheviks to criticise, came to the fore. However, criticism did not end. The victims of the Soviet security system, as they were rounded up, tortured, given secret trials, shot or despatched to ten years in the prison camps, must have smiled grimly at the Stalin constitution's 'guarantee' of freedom of speech and freedom from arbitrary arrest.

The democracy of the new constitution was like the gilding which adorned the splendid Metro stations built in Moscow in the 1930s. Perhaps the granting of the constitution was intended to gain goodwill abroad at a time when the Comintern was encouraging the formation of popular front governments in which communists joined with non-revolutionary socialists. But if some foreign communists and fellow travellers were hoodwinked by the 'democracy' of the Stalin constitution, others found Stalin's ruthless purges an embarrassment. Stalin remained in power to lead his people to victory in 1945 in the Great Patriotic War and to see the USSR emerge as a super-power.

14 Britain, 1918—39

The 'coupon election', 1918

The Parliament elected in December 1910 sat well beyond the term fixed by the Parliament Act of 1911, being dissolved just after the armistice. The electorate had by then been almost trebled by the Representation of the People Act, 1918 (see p. 106).

In May 1918 General Maurice, who had been director of operations at the war office, alleged that Lloyd George had misled the House of Commons as to the number of British troops in France in January of that year. Lloyd George was able to clear himself but the split (see p. 105) between his followers (the Georgian Liberals) and the Squiffites (followers of Asquith) became much sharper. Lloyd George appeared to be a leader without a party. However, Bonar Law, the Conservative leader, agreed to fight the election in coalition with the Georgian Liberals and under the leadership of Lloyd George. Coalition candidates were identified by a letter signed by Lloyd George and Law – the 'coupon', Asquith sarcastically called it, referring to the coupons in wartime ration books. Labour fought the election independently.

In the 'coupon election' (December 1918), fought amid cries of 'Hang the kaiser' and 'Make the Germans pay until the pips squeak', the Coalition Conservatives won 339 seats, the Georgian Liberals 136 and the Squiffites only 26. Labour had 59 seats. So in January 1919 Lloyd George, 'the Welsh Wizard who had won the war', returned to office but remained dependent on the support of the Conservatives – and on his own remarkable ability to manoeuvre and manipulate. At the peace conference Lloyd George tried to exercise moderation and was accused of being too mild – though he was later called a 'hater of Huns'. At home there was social unrest – and fear of the red tide of revolution, then flowing in parts of Europe. The outbreak of influenza that killed 150,000 Britons in 1918–19 – and laid Lloyd George low – heightened tension.

Post-war problems

Demobilisation

A decision that key industrial workers should be the first to be demobilised led to near mutiny, for in general these men had been the last taken into the services. In January 1919 Churchill, appointed secretary of state for war, announced that the longest in were to be the first out. By summer 1919 four-fifths of the men in the forces had been peaceably demobilised. They were given free though not permanent insurance against unemployment and allowances were paid to their dependants.

Unemployment

Most of those demobilised found work, for 1919 was a boom year. But the boom had ended by the autumn of 1920. Soon one and a half million men were without work. From then until the outbreak of war in 1939 there were never less than a million unemployed.

When peace came manufacturers rushed to sell their products overseas. But the primary producing countries, as a result of falling prices, lacked the means to buy British goods. Goods from the USA and Japan, where industrial growth had been rapid, offered sharper competition in markets formerly regarded as British. And there was much structural unemployment – unemployment arising from a general decline in demand, abroad and at home, for the products of long-established industries, such as coal, iron and textiles.

Structural unemployment was most evident in the north of England and South Wales where the old staple industries were located. The relative prosperity of areas where new industries were developing and standards of living were rising showed up the stark poverty elsewhere. Yet despite the experiences of wartime controls, there was no attempt to overhaul and restructure the economy. Rather there was a determination to return to 'normal' (pre-war) ways: 'Business as usual'. New ministries remained – labour, pensions, health, air and transport. The civil service continued to grow. But controls on prices, production, shipping, transport and so on soon ended.

Housing

The social achievements of the first post-war government were not dramatic. It had promised servicemen

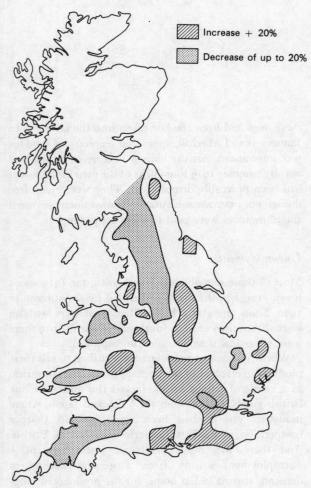

Increase + 20%

Decrease of up to 20%

Population changes in England and Wales in the first half of the twentieth century: in the south and midlands the growth of the chemical, electrical, motor and aircraft industries was accompanied by an increase in population and relatively low unemployment – for example, in 1934 6.4% in Birmingham, 5.1% in Coventry and Oxford. Elsewhere a decline in population accompanied the decline in shipbuilding, coalmining and the steel and cotton industries and a high rate of unemployment – for example in 1934 61.9% in Merthyr, 44.2% in Newcastle and 67.8% in Jarrow

'homes fit for heroes' and in 1919 launched a massive housing scheme. Price controls had ended and the houses that were built, financed from local rates and a government subsidy, cost the state too much. The programme ended in 1922–23. However, at least some of the heroes were decently housed at rents they could pay. More important, by undertaking the scheme the government had admitted the state's obligation to house people – housing became a right of the citizen and later administrations recognised this.

Industrial action, 1920–21

In May 1920 London dockers, opposed to Lloyd George's policy of aiding the Poles in their frontier war with the Bolsheviks (see p. 130), refused to load munitions on to a ship bound for Poland. When later the prime minister appeared determined to give military support to the Poles preparations were made for a general strike. The prime minister then yielded. This apparently successful opposition was acclaimed by Labour as proof of the power of working-class solidarity. But was there real solidarity – or just war weariness? And was it only because Poland was then less hard pressed that Lloyd George 'bowed' to his opponents?

Other strikes gave evidence of social unrest. In 1919, when threatened wage cuts led to a strike of railwaymen, the prime minister yielded to the workers. And following industrial action by the miners legislation was passed giving them a seven-hour day and obliging employers to provide certain amenities. In 1920 the dockers won better working conditions.

The mines had been under government control during the war. With their return to private ownership in 1921 there was a threat of wage cuts and of district agreements (men working pits with poor seams getting less than those in more profitable mines). When the miners refused to yield there was a lockout by the employers (1 April 1921). The miners called on their allies of the Triple Alliance – the railwaymen and transport workers (including the dockers) – who agreed to come out on strike in sympathy. But on 15 April, at the last minute, they backed down. Friday 15 April 1921 became Black Friday, the day of the Cripple Alliance. The miners had got nowhere and bitterness remained. Following their defeat wages throughout industry fell.

The post-war Labour Party

In 1918 the Labour Party came out with a programme based on Sidney Webb's *Labour and the New Social Order*. Its plans, now bolder and more definite, included the socialisation of industry and a controlled economy: 'To secure for the producers by hand or by brain the full fruits of their industry, and the most equitable distribution . . . possible, upon the basis of the

Election results and ministries, 1900–1935

Elections	Seats won by the major parties				
	Conservatives	Liberals	Irish Nationalists	Labour	Ministry
1900	402	184	82	2	Salisbury; 1902, Balfour (Conservative)
1906	157	377	83	29 LRC 24 Lib-Lab	Campbell-Bannerman; 1908, Asquith (Liberal)
1910	273	275	82	40	Asquith (Liberal)
1910	272	272	84	42	Asquith (Liberal); 1916, Lloyd George (Coalition)
1918	339 Coalition 48 non-Coalition	136 Coalition 26 non-Coalition	7 Nationalist 73 Sinn Fein	4 Coalition 59 non-Coalition	Lloyd George (Coalition)
1922	345	116	—	142	Bonar Law; 1923, Baldwin (Conservative)
1923	258	159	—	191	MacDonald (Labour)
1924	419	40	—	151	Baldwin (Conservative)
1929	260	59	—	288	MacDonald (Labour)
1931	473	35 National 33 non-National	—	13 National 52 non-National 4 ILP	MacDonald (National)
1935	432 [1]	21	—	154 4 ILP	Baldwin; 1937, Chamberlain (National); 1940–45, Churchill (Coalition)

[1] National Conservatives (including a few National Liberals and National Labour)

common ownership of the means of production and the best obtainable system of popular administration and control.' Labour declared its opposition to aggressive foreign policies and support for international co-operation. Party branches were to be set up in all constituencies and individual members were to be admitted. Links with the TUC were tightened. The socialist newspaper, *Daily Herald*, founded in 1912, made an increasing number of people aware of Labour's programme.

Nearly all the Labour members elected to Parliament in 1918 were working-class men. In 1923 a bare half were workers. However, though Labour had more non-unionists in Parliament and in its leadership, it drew its votes predominantly from the working classes. In general the middle class shunned it. Some of the middle-class intellectuals who did join Labour were attracted for political rather than social reasons – thus, middle-class pacifists found its idealist foreign policy attractive. And some middle-class intellectuals were aware that they could 'get on' more quickly in the Labour Party than with the Conservatives or Liberals, for many workers still had an exaggerated respect for academic qualifications. Whether the sturdy trade unionists who were midwives at the party's birth would have felt at home among some of these intellectuals is difficult to answer.

In 1920 the British Socialist Party amalgamated with other groups to found the Communist Party of Great Britain, which was linked with the Comintern (see p. 126). Membership of this party was never large. And if its speech was violent at times the party was not revolutionary in action. However, the Labour Party, 'born out of the bowels of' a relatively mild TUC, refused it affiliation and even the more leftist ILP (see p. 51) refused to associate itself with it.

Unemployment insurance and the dole

In 1920 unemployment insurance was extended to further categories of workers, so that most of those earning under £5 weekly were included. However, insurance payments covered only the first fifteen weeks in a year out of work. After that an insured man was dependent on poor law relief. By 1921 the long-term unemployed were too great a burden for the poor law, which depended on rates (especially as relief was most needed where rates brought in relatively little). So from 1921 the state provided all insured workers (most of Britain's workers) with 'uncovenanted benefit' during additional periods of unemployment. This benefit, paid for entirely out of national funds, was in fact a 'dole'. Allowances were paid to dependants of unemployed workers. Thus, perhaps, Lloyd George insured against class war – for the grant of relief, little though the individual received, did much to allay bitterness. In 1927 a Conservative administration gave everyone genuinely seeking work the right to relief for an indefinite period. By the 1930s the pressure of long-term unemployment was so great that the dole more or less took the place of insurance payments.

To some extent, perhaps, the dole, by 'patching over' the unemployment problem, made the government, employers and unions less active in seeking a cure. And some workers were less inclined to seek employment in new and more rewarding industries when their old trades rejected them. However, a man sure of getting his dole was less likely to accept lower wages in desperation.

The fall of Lloyd George, 1922

Criticism of Lloyd George's handling of affairs at the peace conference continued. There was talk of corruption. The Lloyd George Political Fund was built up by what was in effect the sale of honours – £12,000 for a knighthood, about four times that amount for a peerage.

In September 1922 Lloyd George's proposed intervention against the Turks during the Chanak crisis (see p. 192) aroused much opposition among the public and in Parliament. Bonar Law, who had resigned from office on account of ill health, in a letter to *The Times* said: 'We cannot act alone as the policemen of the world.' Four days later Lloyd George, believing he had popular support and expecting the coalition with the Conservatives to continue, decided to call a general election.

With two exceptions the Conservative leaders intended to continue the coalition. But at a meeting at the Carlton Club on 19 October 1922 Conservative members of parliament voted to end the coalition and contest the election independently. Lloyd George resigned and Bonar Law, re-elected leader of the Conservatives, became prime minister. Since the Carlton Club meeting the Conservative Party has had its 1922 Committee, which aims to make known to party leaders the views of other Conservative members of parliament.

Tariffs and the fall of the Conservatives

The elections of November 1922 returned an outright Conservative majority. In May 1923 Stanley Baldwin succeeded Bonar Law, who was dying. Baldwin, a steel manufacturer, first held office in 1917 and had been Bonar Law's chancellor of the exchequer. Suddenly the new prime minister raised that spectre of English politics – protection of trade by tariffs. The imposition of duties, he claimed, would solve the problem of unemployment. Having decided in favour of protection, Baldwin felt obliged to call a general election (December 1923). Fought on the free trade against protection issue, it returned 191 Labour members, 159 Liberals (reunited against protection) and 258 Conservatives. When Parliament met in January 1924 Labour and Liberals, united by opposition to tariffs, defeated the Conservatives on a minor measure.

The first Labour government

Ramsay MacDonald, the Labour leader, was invited to

Blackpool in 1920. Note the bathing boxes for swimmers. In the post-war years the holiday business grew rapidly. Billy Butlin's first holiday camp opened in 1935

form a government. He had lost his seat in 1918 but had been re-elected in 1922 and again in 1923. He had never held ministerial office.

A minority government dependent on Liberal support, the first Labour government had to tread cautiously – and perhaps wanted to do no more than that. Its administration was orthodox. In general, relations with the unions were not satisfactory. No radical attempt was made to deal with unemployment. Unemployment benefits were increased – that was all. Perhaps, as a minority government, Labour could have done no more. And like others it had little idea of what to do. Its main domestic achievement was a further housing scheme, for which John Wheatley, at the ministry of health, was responsible. (Formed in 1919, the ministry of health had taken over the responsibilities of the local government board (see p. 54).) Philip Snowden, once a clerk, was an orthodox and in non-Labour eyes 'respectable' chancellor of the exchequer. His budget produced nothing as alarming and spectacular as the People's Budget of 1909. The McKenna duties imposed during the war were ended but were restored when the Conservatives returned to power.

MacDonald showed more interest in foreign than in domestic affairs and in this first Labour administration was foreign secretary. Unlike some Labour members, who disapproved of the League of Nations' supposed 'basis of force', he believed enthusiastically in collective security. British mediation helped to win acceptance of the Dawes plan (see p. 182) for reparations. The Geneva Protocol on arbitration (see p. 120) was MacDonald's

brain child but had not been ratified when Labour fell and was disowned by the Conservatives.

Labour held aloof from the British Communist Party and in 1924 drew up rules to prevent the infiltration of communists. However, Labour displayed a cautious interest in the USSR and favoured an understanding with that isolated state. Britain recognised the USSR in 1924 and arranged to assist her with a loan. This alarmed many people – the 'respectable' Labour Party seemed to be showing its true red colour. Then the Campbell 'affair' burst upon the public. Campbell, editor of the communist *Workers' Weekly*, was charged with having published a letter 'inciting to mutiny in the forces'. When the attorney general, with MacDonald's support, dropped the prosecution, the government was accused of interfering with the course of justice. A motion of censure that followed was carried comfortably. Labour resigned and a general election was held in October 1924.

Just before this election the *Daily Mail* published a letter which provoked an anti-communist outburst. The letter, allegedly signed by Zinoviev, then president of the Comintern, was addressed to the British Communist Party and urged it to 'stir up the British proletariat'. It said capitalism could not be overthrown peacefully. The letter was perhaps forged – but from then on Labour was more than usually wary of communists whilst many electors looked on Labour with renewed suspicion.

At the elections there was a big swing to the Conservatives, who won 419 seats. Labour, with 151 seats, excused its failure by blaming the publication of the Zinoviev Red Letter – overlooking the fact that it had achieved nothing distinctive while in office. Against this it could argue that lacking a majority – 'in office, but not in power' – it could not have taken positive action. It was in fact the Liberals who failed most dismally in 1924; their seats fell from 159 to 40. Their organisation was less effective than it had been and they ran fewer candidates than previously. The once great Liberal Party no longer occupied a central position in British politics.

Conservative government

The general strike, 1926

Baldwin again took office. This was the Locarno period (see p. 198) when Germany and France seemed to be reconciled. And at home it seemed auspicious that in 1925 days lost in strikes were the fewest since the war. But whereas home industries were doing well, unemployment in the old export trades was serious. Exports were lower than in 1913. The gold standard, aimed at keeping the value of the pound sterling stable, had been abandoned in 1919. In 1925 Britain returned to the gold standard. One result was that British goods became more expensive in foreign markets. Manufacturers, bent on cheapening their exports to regain overseas sales, began thinking in terms of wage cuts.

Coal remained the biggest employer. In 1924, when the Ruhr occupation (see p. 181) resulted in a scarcity of coal, British miners had won better wages. When German and Polish production increased British pits began losing money. In June 1925 the owners gave notice of termination of the 1924 wage agreement. The miners were totally unprepared to accept lower wages. On Friday 31 July 1925, Red Friday, shortly before a lockout was to begin, the government yielded – or so it seemed. It agreed to continue for nine months a subsidy to support the miners' wages – and the owners' profits.

Meanwhile, a commission was to report on the mines. The miners, it seemed, had won a great victory on Red Friday. In fact the government was buying time. During the next nine months it made plans for ensuring minimum disruption if there should be widespread strikes.

In March 1926 the Samuel commission made certain recommendations pleasing to the miners – such as the amalgamation of lesser pits and the provision of pit-head baths. But these were for the future. For the present all the Samuel report suggested was wage cuts. And the owners were clamouring for longer hours. 'Nowt doing', said a miners' leader. 'Not a penny off the pay, not a minute on the day.'

The miners made plans for a strike, and hoped for general support from the unions. The home secretary, Joynson Hicks, believing that communists were 'behind it all', indulged in a red witch hunt. Churchill, who had rejoined the Conservatives and was chancellor of the exchequer, seemed to be spoiling for a fight.

The miners struck on 1 May 1926 and a lockout followed. The TUC decided on a 'general' strike, in fact

The 1926 strike: unperturbed and well escorted, a volunteer driver sets out from the depot. Many such 'blackleg' buses had their windows broken by stones

on a progressive sympathy strike. However, what the TUC wanted was conciliation, not by crippling the economy to bring the government to its knees. It probably agreed to a general strike so as to be in a better position for negotiating a compromise.

The general strike began at midnight on 3 May 1926, after Baldwin had broken off negotiations with the TUC. All those called out by the TUC – transport, railway, dock, gas and electrical workers and printers – responded, a solid turnout of some two million workers. There was little disorder. The government's emergency plans worked well.

On 12 May, when it was clear that the government would not yield, so that there was no prospect of conciliation, the TUC called an end to the strike, though the miners stayed out. Some employers were unwilling to take back men who had been prominent in the strike. This provoked further unrest but the government intervened and, save for the miners, industry settled down again. George V was among those insistent that there should be no victimisation. The miners held out for six months. Then, extremely bitter, they returned, to longer hours, less pay and district agreements.

For a time union membership dropped, so that funds, already depleted by the strike, were further reduced. However, in time membership recovered and funds built up again. To some extent the 1926 strike brought revolutionary syndicalism (see p. 52) into greater disfavour. To some extent the way of parliamentary pressure and reform won renewed support. Perhaps, too, the strike warned employers of the folly of cutting wages – and so averted trouble in other industries. Whatever the reasons, strikes substantially decreased after 1926. A few people saw the possibility of linking wages to productivity. Sir Alfred Mond of Imperial Chemical Industries (ICI), for example, set up committees of management and labour to investigate means of increasing efficiency. By 1929, except in the mines, the average British worker was better off than ever before – provided he was not unemployed.

In 1927 the Trade Disputes and Trade Union Act made sympathy strikes, and consequently general strikes, unlawful and forbade civil servants to join any union affiliated to the TUC. And whereas the Trades Union Act of 1913 had allowed union members to contract out of paying a political levy the 1927 act allowed the levy to be collected only from members who had contracted in.

The general strike increased fear of communism. India was disturbed by nationalists at this time and the Comintern was suspected of trying to create trouble there. In 1927 there was a raid on the London premises of Arcos, the Soviet trading agency. Nothing improper was found but diplomatic ties with the USSR were for a time severed.

Poplarism, local government, electricity and the flapper vote

Local authorities with a Labour majority often made unemployment relief and other payments in excess of the amounts fixed by the ministry of health. The London borough of Poplar was notorious for this. Neville Chamberlain, 'Radical Joe's' son, made a frontal attack on Poplarism. Three times Chamberlain, using powers given to the minister of health by a 1926 act, took over the responsibilities of authorities who disregarded the ministry.

The Local Government Act of 1929 abolished the boards of guardians which administered health and public relief and transferred their duties to the county and county borough councils. These councils were now responsible for education, public health, housing, slum clearance, roads, town and country planning, public assistance and welfare. The county boroughs also looked after gas, electricity, water and local transport. As their activities were financed by grants from the central government as well as from rates, the councils were the more inclined to comply with government wishes.

In 1926 a Central Electricity Board (CEB) was set up to end confusion of voltages and frequencies and to create a national grid to provide cheaper electricity for industry and homes. The completion of the grid in 1933 led to a great increase in the use of home electrical appliances. In 1930 a third of all houses were wired for electricity; by 1940 two-thirds were wired. However, in 1939 60 per cent of houses in rural areas still used oil lamps. Set up not to destroy capitalist control but for better regulation of the industry, the CEB was an early experiment in nationalisation.

In 1928 the franchise was extended to women of twenty-one and over – the 'flapper' (young woman) vote. In the same year Emmeline Pankhurst (see p. 52) died, a Conservative candidate for Parliament.

Lloyd George fails to make a comeback

In the 1929 elections each of the parties ran a large number of candidates. Lloyd George, who had become

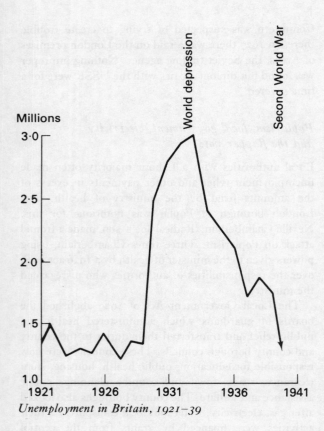

Millions

World depression

Second World War

Unemployment in Britain, 1921–39

labour. In foreign affairs Labour was preoccupied with disarmament. In domestic affairs its achievements were slight. A Coal Mines Act in 1930 reduced the miners' day from eight to seven and a half hours – half an hour longer than when the 1926 strike began. Schemes for amalgamation of the less productive pits were proposed but not put into effect. Mine owners were empowered to fix minimum prices. The Housing Act of 1930 granted a subsidy for slum clearance. (Between 1934 and 1939 more slums were cleared than in the preceding fifty years.)

In 1929 Lord Beaverbrook, campaigning for free trade within the British empire, formed the United Empire Party. In 1930 Oswald Mosley, a Labour member, proposed public direction of industry and the use of credit to encourage economic growth and conquer unemployment – proposals not unlike those made by Lloyd George in 1929. Labour refused to adopt Mosley's schemes and in 1931 he founded the New Party. Rich and aristocratic, he was never quite accepted by Labour. Neither party attracted significant support.

By 1930 Britain was feeling the effects of the world depression triggered off by the Wall Street crash of October 1929 (see p. 157). Factory after factory stopped production. Splendid ships, their paint peeling, lay idle. By Christmas 1930 nearly two million men were out of work. Unemployment remained particularly serious where such heavy industries as shipbuilding and coal mining were predominant. By contrast light industries were still doing reasonably well.

The 1930s

1931: a National government

By the middle of 1931 Britain's financial position was very unsound. A run on sterling (panic selling of sterling pounds in exchange for gold) decreased the Bank of England's gold reserves alarmingly. In August 1931, in a bid to balance the budget and attract foreign credits, cuts in unemployment payments and in civil service salaries were proposed. The TUC was highly critical and nearly half the cabinet threatened to resign.

On 24 August 1931 a National government of Conservatives, Liberals and a few Labour members was formed to 'save the pound'. MacDonald remained prime minister and thereby incurred the contempt of Labour. He himself seems to have thought that he was acting in the national interest – and did not expect the coalition to

Liberal leader again after Asquith entered the Lords in 1925, announced a programme based on startling new economic theories – a planned economy and extensive public works to be paid for by borrowing, without balancing the budget. 'We can conquer unemployment' was Lloyd George's electoral slogan. Such ideas were advocated by Keynes: a deficit for the present, prosperity in due course.

Such policies, which later experience suggests might then have been effective, got little support in 1929. The Liberals won 59 seats, the Conservatives 260. Labour with 288 seats emerged as the largest party, though again without a clear majority. The 'dragon of unemployment' continued to consume the economy.

The second Labour government

In June 1929 MacDonald was sworn in as prime minister for the second time. For the first time a woman sat in the cabinet – Margaret Bondfield, minister of outlast the crisis. However, MacDonald, hopping in and out of comfortable limousines, talking with ladies of rank and fashion, by then perhaps cared more for high office than for the party that had brought him to office – and which he had served from its birth. The Irish playwright Sean O'Casey perhaps expressed the thoughts of some workers when he wrote of him: 'Oh workers on the march, pause here a while, and lay a wreath of part-forgiveness on the lonely grave ... forgetting the grey-haired man who did not stay the strife; remembering only ... the gallant ragged lad of Lossiemouth.'

MacDonald, once Labour's 'disc of gold', now 'Labour's Love Lost', was expelled from the party. Henderson succeeded him as leader. Defeated in the elections of October 1931, Henderson was succeeded by George Lansbury, pacifist and former editor of the *Daily Herald*. Henderson, who won a considerable reputation as foreign secretary in the second Labour government, increased this reputation as president of the disarmament conference (see p. 120).

A few Labour members joined MacDonald in the National government, but his real support came from Conservatives. Snowden increased income and other taxes and made the economies he had earlier proposed as Labour chancellor of the exchequer. Civil service salaries were cut; the police lost 5 per cent, the armed forces 10 per cent and teachers 15 per cent. Unemployment relief was cut by 10 per cent and a much resented family means test (as distinct from a personal means test) was introduced for those on transitional benefits (the dole).

Foreign credits came in but the run on sterling was only halted. In September 1931 a near mutiny by sailors at Invergordon led the government to agree that wage cuts would not exceed 10 per cent. Following the Invergordon 'mutiny' there was a further run on sterling. On 21 September the National government rushed through an act to take Britain off the gold standard, out of 'the gold cage'. So the National government, formed to 'save the pound', in less than a month abandoned it. The value of sterling fell by about a quarter on foreign exchanges but the run on the pound was stopped. As Keynes had predicted, the fall in the exchange rate encouraged exports.

The doctor's mandate

At a general election in October 1931 the National government asked for a 'doctor's mandate', a free hand to do whatever it saw fit to cure the nation's ills. The coalition of Conservatives and a handful of National Liberals and National Labour won a huge majority. Labour was reduced from 288 in 1929 to 52 seats. MacDonald remained prime minister.

Neville Chamberlain replaced Snowden as chancellor of the exchequer. Soon he was to see adopted the protectionist policies advocated by his father. In 1932 an Import Duties Act imposed a 10 per cent tariff on certain manufactured goods. By a quota system preference was given to countries admitting British goods. No taxes were imposed on food but subsidies were granted in aid of agriculture. Following a conference in Ottawa in 1932 a complex series of preferential agreements was made with the dominions. The colonies also enjoyed preferential treatment. Thus issues which during the previous hundred years had shattered parties and governments were decided almost overnight. Ministers opposed to tariffs were allowed to express their views while remaining members of the cabinet.

With the growing number of cars on the road more people could visit the beaches and countryside

The Jarrow crusade, 26 October 1936. Marchers from Jarrow, 'the town they killed by the closure of a shipyard', approach Bedford on their way to London. They took with them a petition which their MP, Ellen Wilkinson, presented in Parliament

Employment and unemployment

In January 1933 unemployment reached nearly three million. Gradually the economy recovered – less perhaps because of government action than because the home market went on growing and there was a slow recovery in world trade. Construction of council houses and still more private houses led to a building boom in the later 1930s; this assisted the furniture and electrical industries. The motor industry grew. Hire purchase helped to expand the home market. However, some older industries continued their long decline and the neighbourhoods in which they were located remained depressed areas. Men began drifting away from the textile factories, the mines and shipyards, though more

often it was their children who went over to the new industries – and often enjoyed marked prosperity. Gradually the pay of government and other employees was restored.

In 1934 the cuts in payments to the unemployed were ended. In the same year Chamberlain's Unemployment Act placed relief on a more orderly basis. A statutory committee, of which William Beveridge was secretary, was set up to manage unemployment insurance on an actuarial, self-supporting basis. Unemployment insurance was to be paid for a period of twenty-six weeks and was not to be subject to a means test. Unemployment assistance (supplementary aid or the dole) for the long-term unemployed and for the non-insured was placed under a national unemployment assistance board. This relief remained subject to the means test, for assistance was to be 'proportionate to need'. The local councils were left to deal with a remnant of people who for one reason or another were not eligible for either insurance or assistance – tramps, for example. After exactly a century the poor law lay dying as it were from lack of customers – though there were plenty of customers for insurance and national assistance. The workhouses had already been handed over to the public health authorities.

The 1920s and 1930s – the days of jazz and the movies – were not all gloom. People had their fun too. The saxophone was what the electric guitar is now. Harold Lloyd, the Marx brothers and Laurel and Hardy films filled the cinemas. The unemployed were as likely to save a few pennies to go to the movies as to march with Mosley or the communists. An American asking un-employed men in Greenwich what attracted them to the pictures was told: 'The pictures help you to live in another world for a little while. I almost feel I'm in the picture.' At the cinema, he said: 'For three hours [the unemployed man] rides the plains of Arizona, tastes the night life of Paris or New York, makes a safe excursion into the underworld, sails the seven seas or penetrates the African jungle.'

Socialism

If the 1920s had attempted to recapture the world of 1914, in the 1930s there was a growing inclination to look towards the future. Labour, after the 'treachery' of its leader, and having failed in its attempt 'to make capitalism work', was taking a harder, more definitely socialist line. In 1932 it bound itself to introduce 'definite socialist legislation' immediately it came to office – majority or no. This did not satisfy the Independent Labour Party which ceased to be affiliated with Labour. Meanwhile the unions collaborated with the employers.

In the 1930s intellectuals were increasingly interested in the USSR and its five-year plans and some advocated a planned economy for Britain. Hewlett Johnson, Canterbury's Red Dean, wrote *The socialist sixth of the world*, praising the achievements of the USSR. The Left Book Club, founded by Victor Gollancz in 1936, had considerable influence and a much larger membership than the British Communist Party. On the other hand many influential people had an intense dread of

Bolshevism and its apparent threat to western civilisation.

In 1937 the Labour Party showed its dislike of extremism and its fear of 'a party within a party' by expelling members of the Socialist League, a left-wing intellectual group that had begun as a research circle.

The British Union of Fascists

To expose the failure of capitalism communists organised hunger marches of unemployed workers to demonstrate in London. At the other extreme Mosley in 1932 founded the British Union of Fascists, which won some 20,000 black-shirted followers. In 1934 there was an outburst of fascist violence at Olympia in London. The government, fearing such disorders as marked the rise of the fascist dictators in Europe, passed the Incitement to Disaffection Act and in 1936 passed the Public Order Act. The wearing of uniforms by political parties was prohibited and the police were empowered to forbid political processions. This was virtually the end of Britain's small fascist movement.

Baldwin and Neville Chamberlain: gathering shadows

In June 1935 Baldwin succeeded MacDonald, who was in poor health, as prime minister. General elections that year returned a substantial majority for the National government, a sizeable Labour group (154), and a handful of non-National Liberals. Baldwin said that 'for good or evil the days of non-interference [in domestic affairs] by governments are gone. We are passing into a new era.' But by this time foreign affairs were of paramount importance, for Germany, with Hitler at the helm, was boldly resurgent. Chamberlain's 1932 budget had had the lowest armaments expenditure of the inter-war years. But from about 1935 Britain began to rearm. It was in 1935 that Hitler told Sir John Simon, Britain's foreign secretary, that Germany's air force was as strong as that of Britain. Hitler was exaggerating but Britain's air chiefs, convinced that air power could of itself win a war, called loudly for bombers. The growth of the armaments industry helped to reduce unemployment in Britain.

In the 1930s there was much discussion of the merits and demerits of pacifism, the League of Nations, rearmament and disarmament, the rights and wrongs of Germany and the Versailles treaty. The Oxford Union won notoriety when in 1933 it resolved that 'the house'

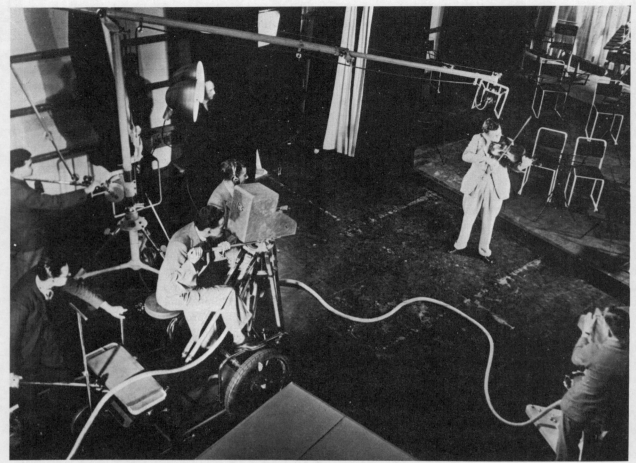

Studio at the first high-definition TV station at Alexandra Palace, London, in August 1936, the year the BBC inaugurated its public TV service

would not fight for king and country. In the same year a Conservative who favoured rearmament was resoundingly defeated in a by-election. Labour members of parliament tended to be both pacifists and upholders of the League and of collective security – which in the final resort depended on force. But in 1935, following the resignation of Lansbury, a pacifist, Labour chose Clement Attlee, who had fought in the First World War, as its leader. To some extent the Spanish Civil War (see Chapter 20) turned leftists from pacifism. From 1937 Labour members ceased to vote against allocations of money for rearmament.

George V had won increasing respect and affection in Britain and throughout the Commonwealth. This affection was more marked after he began his Christmas broadcasts in 1932. The Silver Jubilee of his accession was celebrated with enthusiasm in 1935. In January

1936 the king died and Edward, the popular if rather unorthodox Prince of Wales, succeeded as Edward VIII. His determination to marry an American woman, Wallis Simpson, who had been twice divorced, proved unacceptable to Baldwin and Cosmo Lang, Archbishop of Canterbury, who probably represented the views of the majority of people in a not yet permissive society. In December 1936 Edward abdicated and his brother, the Duke of York, succeeded him as George VI. Edward married Wallis Simpson and took the title Duke of Windsor. George VI was to prove equally popular, equally a man of social conscience. More orthodox than Edward, he was perhaps a more suitable monarch for Britain.

In May 1937 Neville Chamberlain succeeded Baldwin as prime minister. Baldwin, who liked to be thought of as the pipe-smoking country gentleman with literary inclinations and an interest in pigs, had shown skill in piloting the country in a period of changing social relations. For fifteen years Chamberlain had played second fiddle to Baldwin – yoked to him as it were by mutual dislike of Lloyd George and Churchill, the two political volcanoes of their age. By the 1930s Lloyd George was an extinct volcano. He died in 1945. Churchill, who had opposed Conservative policy over India and who supported Edward VIII in the abdication crisis, continued to rumble warnings of the growing power of Hitler. But in 1937 he appeared to be another extinct volcano.

Chamberlain was an experienced administrator of great ability. 'Nearly all the domestic achievements of Conservative governments between the wars stand to his credit . . . yet he was a man, in Napoleon's phrase, of No Luck.' He surrounded himself with professional administrators who carried through a useful programme of domestic legislation. In 1938, as Hitler's upsurge gained momentum, provision was made to direct industries to war manufactures. At the same time TUC leaders agreed to ease restrictive practices which might hamper the manufacture of arms. By the time of the Czech crisis in September 1938 (see p. 206) arms production had reached a substantial level and continued to accelerate.

Neville Chamberlain and 'appeasement'

Chamberlain was less sure in his dealings with other countries. In 1937 he did not protest when Eamon de Valera declared the Irish Free State independent (see p. 152). Under nationalist pressure from Arabs he restricted the entry of Jews into Palestine (see p. 330). De Valera paid tribute to his handling of the Irish Free State but neither in Ireland nor in Palestine did his policy bring about a final settlement. In February 1938 Anthony Eden, a supporter of collective security, who had been foreign secretary since the Abyssinian (Ethiopian) crisis of 1935 (see p. 201), resigned because of the government's weak policy in the Spanish Civil War – the War of the Spanish Obsession as he called it. Viscount Halifax then became foreign secretary.

Chamberlain himself was increasingly alienated from his foreign office advisers, who warned him of the dangerous situation developing in Germany but could offer him no solution. In this dilemma Chamberlain adopted a policy generally referred to as 'appeasement'. But in negotiating with Hitler his intention was not blindly to yield to force. He intervened in the belief that by offering what he thought were reasonable concessions to Germany he could avert war. In his determination to avert war he was willing to strip 'faraway' Czechoslovakia of substantial territory. Was it wrong to bring pressure on the Czechs so that he could offer concessions to Hitler? The British people, the dominions and certainly the USA would not have supported a stronger policy at the time. Would France? Chamberlain seems to have been unaware of the insatiability of Hitler's appetite – as were most people in 1938. On the other hand he foresaw the danger of Soviet domination in the future. With his great dislike of communism he found the idea of negotiating with the USSR distasteful. The true judgement of the prime minister may be that he was an insufficient man to direct the nation's affairs in a time of crisis. However, until 1939 his policies met with general approval. On his return from meeting Hitler in September 1938 (see p. 207) most people received his promise of 'peace in our time' with wild enthusiasm.

At least until the Czech-German dispute reached its climax in that September of 1938 few people had thought that war would come in their time. The *Daily Express* every day printed on its front page: 'There will be no war in Europe this year or next!' But as Hitler continued to make his 'final' demands there was growing recognition that only force could stop him – and that appeasement was a failure. Soon the man who hated war and who had promised 'peace in our time' was to be scorned. His policy had failed.

15 The British Commonwealth

The colonies of temperate settlement

By 1870 Britain's empire included the temperate regions of Canada, Australia, New Zealand and South Africa, monsoonal India, Ceylon and much of Burma. In the four temperate regions exploration and initial settlement were by then more or less complete. The years after 1870 saw economic, political and cultural developments – and the rise to nationhood of these communities.

Canada was the first to approach maturity. The granting of responsible government to Canada was the seed from which dominion status, independent nationhood and the dissolution of the British empire were to grow. Soon after responsible government was granted to Canada it was extended to the Australian colonies

(1850). New Zealand, formally occupied by the British in 1840, had responsible self-government from 1856. In South Africa the white settlers in the Cape Colony and Natal had representative and responsible government after 1872.

The second step towards political maturity in Canada came when the British Parliament passed the British North America Act (1867) which gave Canada a federal government. The six Australian colonies federated to form the Commonwealth of Australia in 1901. As with Canada, the larger unit created by federation was able to speak with far more authority than the individual states had ever done.

Emigrants leave Liverpool for a new life in Australia, 1871. (Illustrated London News)

In Canada fear of American aggression promoted federation. In Australia German expansion in New Guinea and neighbouring islands was one factor promoting federation. As in Canada, economic development, which to a great extent meant railway construction, helped to bring about federation. In 1885 the Canadian Pacific Railway, from the Atlantic to the Pacific, was completed. In Australia the completion of the transcontinental railway in 1917 linked Perth in the west with Brisbane in the north-east. In the decisions leading to the formation of the Union of South Africa (see p. 28) railway development also played a part.

In Canada there was little social legislation until 1935 when R.B. Bennett's Conservative government introduced a minimum wage, limitation of working hours, social insurance and so on. The governments of Australia and New Zealand were more radical. Labour parties were founded at an early stage and exercised effective power earlier than in England –thus Australia had a Labour cabinet in 1904 and Labour held a clear majority in the federal parliament in 1914. In these circumstances both state and commonwealth governments were early noted for social legislation. South Australia gave the vote to women in 1894 and was soon followed by the other states and by the federal government (1902). In 1895 Victoria adopted wages boards and in 1901 New South Wales set up courts for settling industrial disputes and provided non-contributory old age pensions.

In New Zealand wars with the Maoris, the by no means backward original inhabitants, had ended by 1870. A combination of Liberals and representatives of labour, led by Richard Seddon, from 1891 to 1906 made their country 'the social laboratory of the world'. Votes for women (1893), old age pensions (1898), conciliation and arbitration in labour disputes, limitation of hours in shops and offices, state provision of secondary and technical education, state coal mines (1901), state fire insurance (1903), laws to protect mothers and children and the homes of workingmen were all pioneered in New Zealand.

The colonies of white settlement were in their early years mainly primary producers. The discovery of gold and other minerals and the development of railways changed the scene. But the main effect of railways and steamships and, from the 1880s, of refrigerator ships was to open up the interiors to agricultural development and to facilitate the transport of bulky and perishable cargoes, such as wheat and meat, to Europe. Industrial development followed slowly. Tariffs to protect infant industries were a major battle ground in politics. Industrial development accelerated after the First World War but became of major significance only after 1939.

Though responsible government did not initially include responsibility for defence, foreign relations and tariffs, these gradually passed from the control of Westminster to the 'colonies'. First to go was control of tariffs; it was agreed that the colonies might even impose duties on goods made in Britain. Towards the end of the nineteenth century and as international tension heightened in the early twentieth century, the colonies took a greater interest in their own defence and began to establish their own military and naval forces. The Royal Canadian Navy and the Royal Australian Navy were both founded in 1910. Moreover, the colonies began to offer military assistance to Britain. In 1885 cavalry from New South Wales helped in Britain's Sudan campaign (see p. 28). Many men from Canada, the Australian colonies and New Zealand came to the help of Britain in the Boer War (see p. 27).

In 1887 and at fairly regular intervals thereafter colonial or imperial conferences were held in London (and in 1894 in Ottawa) to discuss tariffs, communications, defence and, later, foreign policy. For a time there was some interest in Joseph Chamberlain's proposal for imperial preference (see p. 57) but nothing came of it. One thing was clear; the colonies did not want some form of super-government binding them and Britain together. Rather there was growing recognition that they were equal in status with Britain. The notion of a mother and daughter relationship was discarded in favour of a relationship among sisters. By 1914 it was customary to refer to the former colonies of temperate settlement as dominions.

Yet in 1914 the self-governing 'dominions', still not fully independent, found themselves, like the rest of the British empire, automatically involved in the war. Their contribution was considerable. 'To the last man and last shilling' said the Australian prime minister. From a population of barely five million a third of a million Australians volunteered for service overseas.

Responsibility for defence, the cost of war in blood and material, drew the dominions into the field of foreign affairs. They could not be expected to expend their lives and treasure on issues in which they had no say. During the First World War Smuts of South Africa and W.M. Hughes of Australia attended meetings of the British war cabinet. At the war's end the dominions insisted on individual representation at Paris. They signed the peace treaties as independent states and were founder members, equal in status with Britain or any other power, of the League of Nations. Australia, New Zealand and South Africa held mandates over former German colonies. In 1922 at the time of the Chanak crisis (see p. 192) Canada made it clear that she would not support British intervention. Nor were the dominions very agreeable to commitments which Britain accepted at Locarno (1925).

At an imperial conference in 1926 the Balfour Declaration defined Great Britain and her dominions as self-governing 'communities within the empire, equal in status, in no way subordinate to one another – though united by a common allegiance to the crown, and freely associated as members of the British Commonwealth of Nations'. In 1931 the Statute of Westminster repealed acts which might restrict the authority of the dominions. It declared that no future British law should apply to them and they could make any laws that seemed good to them.

Conferences between Britain and the dominions continued to be held for co-operation in matters of mutual interest. A conference at Ottawa in 1932, during the world depression, resulted in a system of imperial preferential tariffs. The conference of 1937 was mainly concerned with defence and foreign affairs. After the Second World War the conferences, attended by growing numbers of independent Asian and African states, were called Commonwealth conferences. Following the Statute of Westminster a dominions office was set up. After 1945 the dominions (or Commonwealth) office and then the colonial office were wound up, their responsibilities being taken over by the foreign office. A Commonwealth secretariat was set up to facilitate co-operation among members.

Ireland: to independence

The Irish question came into the limelight again during the First World War. The problem had become one of pure national feeling. The Catholics had long since been emancipated, the Anglican Church disestablished and land reforms effected. But as Parnell had said: 'No one can set bounds to the march of a nation.' A minority with old hatreds smouldering in their hearts wanted to end all connection with England.

May we never taste of death nor leave this vale of
    tears

Until we see the Englishry go begging down the
    years,
Packs on their backs to earn a penny pay
In little leaking boots – as the Irish in their day.

During the war Irish extremists sought support from Germany. Late in 1914 plans were being made for an Easter Rising in 1916. On Good Friday 1916 Sir Roger Casement, a former member of the British consular service, was landed by a German U-boat in Kerry – though he came to call the rising off. However, on Easter Monday Irish nationalists seized the GPO and other buildings in Dublin, declared a provisional government and proclaimed a republic.

The British suppressed the revolt within a few days, though not without considerable bloodshed.

And such a broth of love and hate
Was stirred ere Monday morn was late
As Dublin town had never seen. . . .
He cracked up all the town with guns
That roared loud psalms to fire and death,
And houses hailed down granite tons
To smash our wounded underneath.

Four hundred and fifty Irishmen and a hundred British troops had lost their lives.

Casement was found guilty of treason and was executed, as were all the leaders of the Easter Rising except Eamon de Valera who was sentenced to life imprisonment. People less prominent in the rising were imprisoned or interned. The rebels became martyrs to an increasing number of people who had before not been sympathetic to the Sinn Fein cause. John Dillon, for a time the Irish leader at Westminster, said in the House of Commons:

'Thousands of people in Dublin, who ten days ago were bitterly opposed to the whole of the Sinn Fein movement and to the rebellion, are now becoming infuriated against the government on account of these executions [of ringleaders of the rebellion] and . . . that feeling is spreading throughout the country in a most dangerous degree. . . . '

De Valera and others were granted amnesty in 1917. As the only surviving leader of the Easter Rising de Valera became the leader of the republican group. Animosity increased when in 1918 conscription was extended to Ireland, though this was not to come into force until home rule (see p. 61) became operative. In April 1918 a short general strike in southern Ireland closed down even the bars. De Valera and other extremists were again imprisoned and Sinn Fein won more followers.

At the general election in 1918 virtually all constituencies in southern Ireland returned Sinn Feiners, though this was partly the result of vote rigging. The Sinn Fein members thus elected declared themselves an independent Irish parliament – Dail Eireann – and again proclaimed a republic. So it was that the first woman elected to Parliament in the United Kingdom, Constance Gore-Booth (Countess Markiewicz), never took her seat at Westminster. At the peace conference in 1919 delegates from the Dail asked, unsuccessfully, for recognition of Ireland's independence.

Virtually disregarding the British administration in Dublin Castle, a government of Dail members carried on the affairs of Ireland. Former members of the Irish Nationalist Volunteers set up the Irish Republican Army (IRA) of which Michael Collins was the effective head. Before long Collins, who was also a minister in the Dail 'government', had a price of £10,000 on his head.

Money sent by Irish immigrants in the United States and elsewhere enabled the IRA to buy arms and these were smuggled into the country. At Easter 1920 IRA attacks on British barracks and police stations began a period of guerilla warfare. The British reinforced the Royal Irish Constabulary with a force of ex-servicemen known as the Black and Tans – their uniform was part police (black belt) and part military (khaki jacket). The nickname had other overtones, for the Black and Tans was a famous pack of hounds in Tipperary. During 'the troubles' both sides showed brutality – particularly brutal were the Auxis, auxiliary police recruited by Britain from ex-army officers. Following an IRA ambush the Auxis set the centre of Cork on fire.

Meanwhile, a new Government of Ireland Act (1920) set up separate home rule parliaments in Dublin and Belfast. The six counties of Ulster with a Protestant majority (Northern Ireland) were to have their parliament in Belfast. The other twenty-six counties of Ireland, including Ulster's three Catholic counties (Donegal, Cavan and Monaghan), were to have their parliament in Dublin. The six counties accepted the act. In June 1921 George V opened the parliament of Northern Ireland in Belfast. Westminster continued to control Northern Ireland's defence, foreign affairs and similar matters. But at elections for·the Dublin parliament all except four of the members returned were Sinn Feiners. Like the Sinn Feiners elected in 1918, they regarded themselves as elected to the Dail Eireann. The legal parliament set up in Dublin by the 1920 act

The centre of Cork after being fired by the Auxis, December 1920. Cork had been a centre of resistance against the British

thus had only four members – all returned by the University of Dublin.

Gradually both the British and the IRA became aware of the futility of continuing the guerilla war. Following a truce (June 1921) Lloyd George proposed dominion status for southern Ireland – an idea suggested by Smuts and supported by George V, who throughout did his utmost to bring about a non-violent settlement. In December 1921, with Lloyd George threatening outright war, articles of agreement for a treaty constituting an Irish Free State were accepted. The new state was to include all Ireland, but the six counties of Ulster were to be free to contract out. Three ports in the south were kept by Britain for use by the Royal Navy. The Dail, by a small majority, ratified the treaty in January 1922 and in December 1922 the Irish Free State came into being.

De Valera had wanted full independence and continued to oppose more moderate leaders, such as Arthur Griffith and Collins, who had negotiated the articles of agreement with Britain. In 1922 civil war broke out between extremists and moderates – de Valera against the treaty, Collins for the treaty. Both sides were guilty of many excesses. Collins was ambushed and killed in a glen in his own beloved Cork. He had foreseen his death when he concluded the negotiations with the British in 1921. 'The shadow of the end [was] on him.'

The civil war petered out in April 1923 but for some years extremists continued to pester the government of the Irish Free State. Acts of violence were frequent – and severely punished by the Irish authorities.

The day after the Irish Free State had been established the six northern counties contracted out. So Northern Ireland (Ulster) continued to have its own parliament and to send representatives to Westminster. Neither the Free State nor Northern Ireland was happy with the new situation. Religious differences remained acute. From time to time there were outbursts of violence. In general the Protestant minority in the south was better treated than the Catholic minority in the north.

The Irish Free State was a member of the British Commonwealth, but the tie was very loose. The governor-general was appointed by the crown and Dail members had to take an oath of allegiance – that was virtually all. De Valera, because of his refusal to take this oath, was unable to sit in the Dail until 1927.

In 1926 de Valera formed a new republican party,

Fianna Fail (Soldiers of Destiny). In 1932 Fianna Fail won elections and de Valera became prime minister of the Irish Free State. He further reduced the ties with Britain. Separate Irish citizenship was granted and the oath of allegiance was no longer taken. For a time relations between Britain and the Irish Free State were very strained. Britain imposed a 20 per cent tariff on Irish goods, the Irish following suit with a duty on imports from Britain. The tariff war dragged on until 1936.

In 1937 the Dail, taking advantage of the powers given by the Statute of Westminster, enacted a new constitution whereby the Irish Free State became the independent state of Eire. Neville Chamberlain accepted the inevitable (see p. 147). Financial problems inherited from the land purchase acts (see p. 61) were settled and the three ports that Britain had retained in 1922 were surrendered. Relations improved considerably and economic ties became stronger after severance than before.

India: neither colony nor dominion

By 1870 the whole of India was under British rule.

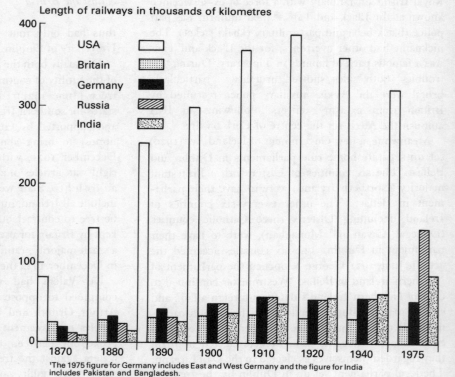

Length of railways in thousands of kilometres

As late as 1910 India, despite her size, had fewer kilometres of railways than Britain and Germany. At that time railways were still a barometer of economic progress. In recent years, with the development of road and air transport, railways have declined in importance. However, in India, as in the USSR, railway construction has continued. In China railways increased from 16,000 kilometres in 1935 to 48,000 kilometres in 1975

¹The 1975 figure for Germany includes East and West Germany and the figure for India includes Pakistan and Bangladesh.

From a Sikh woodcut of about 1870. Such woodcuts were very popular in the Punjab. The tender carries wood for firing the engine. Note the carriage for women at the rear

Within this immense region there was peace, the *pax Britannica*. To the north India was protected by the Himalayas, but the north-east and north-west frontiers were insecure. After the third Burmese War (1885) Britain controlled the whole of Burma. But beyond Burma were the French in Indo-China and the occasionally troublesome Chinese in Yunnan province. There was rivalry with the Russians and the Chinese over Tibet.

The north-west presented a more dangerous situation. Russia's advance deep into central Asia threatened Afghanistan, the traditional invasion route to India. Diplomatic and military activity indicated the intense rivalry between Britain and Russia.

'We shall get there – we shall creep on and on [towards India] ... and then some day when you English are unprepared we shall strike the blow. Why of course we all want India! ... We can't touch you anywhere, thanks to your silver streak [the Channel]. But by advancing towards India we obliterate that silver streak, and at last when we are near enough you will become vulnerable.'

So said a Russian general to a British officer in 1878. In that year the ruler of Afghanistan, after accepting a Russian mission in Kabul, refused to accept a British mission. The British then invaded Afghanistan and secured a favourable treaty. When the British resident in Kabul and his staff were murdered General Roberts occupied Kabul (1879) and the next year led a 500-kilometre march over wild country in extreme temperatures to Kandahar to rescue a British force besieged there. The British then withdrew from Afghanistan but continued to exercise some control. In 1907 the entente with Russia (see p. 91) recognised Afghanistan as a British sphere of influence. In 1919 the British drove back an Afghan attack on India. But

Britain was then so busy dealing with Indian nationalists that she gave up her claim to direct Afghanistan's foreign policy.

Within India there was peace, though scarcely peace and plenty. However, the construction of railways made famines somewhat less disastrous as food could be moved rapidly from better off districts. Irrigation works helped to increase food supplies. The importation of manufactured goods, for example cotton textiles from Lancashire, resulted in a decline in domestic industries. But a rapid increase in population under the *pax Britannica* (from 200 million in 1800 to nearly 300 million in 1900 and nearly 400 million in 1940) was chiefly responsible for a decline in living standards.

Under the British sanitation and medical services were improved. The creation of a western education system was undertaken. But sanitation and education touched only a fringe of the population. Ignorance and squalor were the lot of the myriad villages which dot the Indian countryside.

In 1858, following the Indian Mutiny, the British East India Company was abolished. British India was then administered directly by the crown. Besides British India there was the India of the princes, occupying about a third of the sub-continent but with a population less than a third of the total. These princes had at various times made treaties with the British, whereby in return for British protection they were obliged to rule with British advice – though this left them considerable freedom to rule and live in autocratic luxury.

When the education system was inaugurated in 1833 it was decided that instruction should be in English. Perhaps this was inevitable where there were so many different languages. Perhaps the English language gave the Indians a degree of unity which British arms and government could not have achieved. Instruction in

India, 1919: serene amid the troubles, the headmaster and a few members of staff sit with the Bareilly High School Hockey Eleven

English provided a ready supply of English-speaking officials. The Indian village system had always had strong elements of democracy. However, an English education introduced to Indians new ideas of liberty and national dignity. It is not surprising that Indians, educated perhaps at Oxford or Cambridge, were frustrated when they returned to find themselves excluded from positions of authority; or that numbers of 'failed BAs' from Indian institutions were embittered when they were unable to get employment, or at most held minor ill-paid posts.

In 1853 competitive examinations for entry into the Indian civil service were introduced. From 1861 Indians could be appointed to provincial and central legislative and executive councils and as magistrates. Thereafter, apart from minor changes, Indian political organisation stagnated. In 1877 Queen Victoria was proclaimed Empress of India; this added a certain glamour to the British connection but otherwise had little significance. Of greater significance was the first meeting in 1886 of

the Indian National Congress which agitated for greater Indian participation in government and eventually for *swaraj* (self-government). In 1905 the Muslim League was founded to protect Muslim interests against the Hindu majority. In 1909 an Indian Councils Act increased Indian representation in government but did not offer Indians any of the realities of power.

When war broke out in 1914 India found herself automatically involved. For a time political agitation ceased and Indians co-operated whole-heartedly in the war effort. The Indian army served loyally on various fronts. Such service merited political reforms. In 1919 the Government of India Act declared that self-government was the ultimate objective of Britain. For the time being a system known as dyarchy was introduced in eight provinces: certain matters (for instance education) were 'transferred' to the control of Indian ministers, while other matters (police and security for instance) were 'reserved' for the governor's control. The majority of legislative councillors in the provinces was to be elected. The representative element in the central government was also greatly increased but still had no responsibility for administration.

To many Indians dyarchy was quite unacceptable. And during 1919 two disasters occurred. The influenza epidemic killed sixteen million Indians. And in April, amid mounting tension and violence in the Punjab, a British general, Dyer, ordered troops in Amritsar to fire on a mob that disobeyed an order to disperse. The British were not aware that the mob, who were in a cul-de-sac, had no means of escape. Nearly 400 people were killed and many more were injured. The incident not only left an indelible impression on Indian minds but provoked intense controversy at Westminster. In the end Dyer was retired.

By 1919 Gandhi was in control of the Indian Congress Party. When he was eighteen Gandhi had gone to England to study law. In 1893 he went to practise in South Africa. Within a year he had founded the Natal Indian Congress and for twenty years carried on a non-violent campaign against discrimination against Indians. Having successfully concluded this campaign Gandhi returned to India in 1914.

Under Gandhi's leadership non-violent non-co-operation became the guiding principle behind Congress opposition to British rule. For years there was a seemingly interminable round of strikes, *hartals* (days of mourning or protest when shops closed), mass meetings and seditious speeches, extremist newspaper propaganda, boycotts of British goods and institutions, assassinations, defiance of British law – and Indian leaders going into or coming out of prison.

Gandhi always insisted that there must be no violence. He himself was never violent. But he was unable to control the violence which his demands for non-co-operation aroused. Nor could he control the growing communal strife between Hindus and Muslims.

Progress towards self-government was complicated by the existence of minority groups for whom the British felt responsible, for example the untouchables or out-castes whom Gandhi called Harijans or Children of God, the Christians, and the Eurasians. There were too the princely states to whose rulers Britain was bound by treaties. Above all there was the ever growing strife between the two chief religious communities, the Hindus and Muslims. The task of ruling India seemed too difficult to hand over to inexperienced politicians who were often intolerant of each other.

In spite of Congress hostility, there were liberals who co-operated with the British in implementing the 1919 Government of India Act. And the British government prepared further reforms, as promised, by various means (including three round table conferences in London). In 1935 another Government of India Act gave eleven provinces full responsible government and increased the number of electors in the provinces. It also provided for a central federal government which the princely states might join if they wished. Negotiations for admission of the princely states were not complete in 1939 and the federal government never came into being.

Congress was not at all satisfied with the new act and refused to co-operate in implementing it. In four provinces responsible government worked smoothly. In the remaining seven, where there were non-co-operating Congress majorities, there were inevitable difficulties. In these years two leaders came into prominence: Jawaharlal Nehru of the Congress Party, and Mohammed Ali Jinnah of the Muslim League. Around these leaders there crystallised the forces which were to lead to the partitioning of the Indian sub-continent.

In 1939 India was neither a dominion nor a colony. She had signed the Treaty of Versailles and was a foundation member of the League of Nations. Indian representatives had attended imperial conferences alongside representatives from the dominions. But in September 1939 India could exercise no choice when Britain declared war on Germany. She made a tremendous war effort, but Congress resentment towards Britain and hostility between Muslims and Hindus continued. The Japanese entry into the war and a threatened invasion of India failed to break the political deadlock.

16 The United States between the wars

Retreat from reality

Isolationism

During the First World War the United States had, as it were, tried on the cloak of a super-power. Then for a time she withdrew into 'splendid isolation'. When Wilson asked the Senate to ratify (confirm) the Treaty of Versailles, which included the covenant of the League of Nations, he said: 'The question is whether we can refuse the moral leadership that is offered us, whether we shall accept or reject the confidence of the world.' The Senate had a Republican majority, many of whom were antagonistic to Wilson, a Democrat, or distrustful of the new international organisation. Wilson set out on a nationwide tour to win support for the League. But in September 1919 he had a paralytic stroke. His opponents then had the upper hand. In March 1920 the Senate refused to ratify the treaty. By refusing membership of the League the USA rejected the role of world leadership to which she was being driven. In 1920 Warren G. Harding, soon to be president, declared that the USA needed 'not submergence in internationality, but sustainment in triumphant nationalism'.

There could not however be complete isolation from the world outside. At times the USA took positive action. At times she withdrew again into isolation. In 1921 she called the Washington Conference (see p. 162) and took part in the London (1930) and Geneva (1932) disarmament conferences (see p. 199). Secretary of state Kellogg's proposal for a pact to outlaw war (see p. 198) resulted in the Kellogg-Briand pact (1928). In 1933 the USA recognised the USSR. In the same year the World Economic Conference in London came to a virtual standstill when President F.D. Roosevelt declared that the United States must be free to manage its currency as it saw fit. Following a Reciprocal Trade Agreement Act of 1934, Cordell Hull, secretary of state, negotiated trade agreements with various states. In 1935 the USA rejected membership of the Permanent Court of International Justice.

Meanwhile, the USA was no more willing to cancel the war debts of her allies than France was to forego reparations. But American tariffs hindered repayment of loans in goods, and repayment in gold was equally impracticable. Twice American experts, Dawes and Young, drew up plans for the settlement of reparations (see pp. 182–3). The strange triangular situation arose by which American loans enabled Germany to make her reparations payments to France, whilst France and Britain staggered under the burden of paying off their debts to the United States. No one benefited from this mad movement of money. The United States, it has been said, might as well have moved the money from one treasury building to another. But during the world depression both reparations and debts were cancelled. Many Americans, convinced that they had been duped, were all the less willing to see their country involved in European affairs.

Isolationism expressed itself in suspicion of immigrants and in racialism. To many Americans immigrants from eastern Europe were Bolsheviks bringing revolution in their baggage. Acts passed in 1921 and 1924 greatly restricted immigration. In the pre-war years about a million immigrants a year were entering the USA. The 1924 act set the yearly total at about 150,000. Negroes suffered from the savage lynchings of the Ku-Klux Klan. The Poor White members of the Klan were also violently hostile to Jews and Catholics.

Theodore Roosevelt's interpretation of the Monroe Doctrine (see p. 66) in effect gave the USA the right to interfere in the affairs of any American state. However, the period of 'armed imperialism' ended about 1928. Marines, instead of being sent off to intervene in other American states, were called home. From 1933 Cordell Hull actively practised the 'good neighbour' policy. One practical result of this new approach was the construction of the Pan-American highway, which eventually ran from Alaska to Chile.

Business as usual and prohibition

Presidents Harding (1921–23), Coolidge (1923–29) and Hoover (1929–33) were Republicans. Under Harding with his cityslicker supporters there was a return to the pork barrel (see p. 67) – with party bosses in the saddle and corruption and scandal on a grand scale. Under Coolidge it was 'business as usual', unchecked by the controls built up by the Progressives (see pp. 70–71). 'The man who builds a factory builds a temple. The man who works there worships there', said Coolidge. Monopoly flourished as never before. Captains of industry were the heroes of the day. Tariffs were raised in 1922 and 1929 to ever higher levels. On the surface all was well: Europe may have been impoverished but American living standards were rising, business flourished and wealth multiplied. Mass production and new inventions seemed to offer a future of unlimited abundance.

But the apparent prosperity of the 1920s was very uneven. The pie was big – but some people had such large slices that there was little left for others. Amid all the prosperity of the 1920s the farmers languished. A farmer whose income was a quarter that of a clerk was doing well. Agricultural output had grown greatly during the war. But in the post-war years farmers were competing with Canada, Argentina and Australia in a world market with falling prices. Tariffs only made farm operating costs higher. Laws to assist the farmers were opposed because they restricted that unlimited economic freedom to which America was dedicated. Co-operative marketing schemes and loans introduced in 1929 were little help when world prices continued to fall. Poorest among the farmers were the American Indians on their reservations. And the Negroes in the cotton belt of the Deep South were desperately poor – poorer even than the Poor Whites there. In the 1920s most Negroes still lived in the southern states.

In 1860 a National Prohibition Party, whose aim was to prohibit the drinking of alcohol, had been organised. Many Progressives were hostile to drink. An Anti-Saloon League was founded in 1893. Women were exercising growing influence and support for prohibition increased. In 1919, the year before American women received the vote, prohibition was introduced to the USA. By the 18th Amendment to the Constitution and the Volstead Act the manufacture, sale or transport of alcoholic liquor was forbidden in the United States.

For fourteen years, from 1 January 1920 until the end of 1933, the United States was legally 'dry' – but in practice the wettest it had ever been. Morality by legislation proved disastrous. It was the age of jazz, Rudolph Valentino, short skirts and the Charleston. Drink became a national obsession. The law was flouted and racketeers and gangsters flourished in a carnival of crime. In Chicago Al Capone and his thugs with their 'typewriters' (machine guns) grew rich on the proceeds of bootlegging (making and selling alcoholic liquor) and virtually ruled the city. Nor was Capone the only bootlegger with a private army. In countless speakeasies (illegal drinking saloons) people drank dangerous home-distilled spirits. So unpleasant was much of the gin that the mixed gin, 'gin and it', became the fashion. So drunkenness and armed thugs were the fruit of 'the noble experiment' of prohibition. Prohibition, like isolationism, offered a way of escape from reality, from personal responsibility. In the end Americans had to come to terms with both. In 1933 the 18th Amendment was repealed and prohibition ended.

The great depression

Its causes

President Herbert Hoover took office early in 1929 in a period of unbounded prosperity and optimism. Before the year was out he was facing an economic blizzard. What caused this blizzard which before long was sweeping the world? The Wall Street crash of 1929 is always regarded as its starting point.

In the 1920s, when credit was readily available, Americans invested heavily on the stock exchange. Many, by speculating, made huge gains, sometimes overnight. In 1929 prices on the stock market rose higher and higher. Fluctuations in share prices aroused alarm among investors, and many began selling, not to reinvest, but to realise their cash. By the autumn of 1929 there was frantic selling. Confidence in the market melted away. Then, the bubble burst: on 19 October 1929, Black Saturday, prices on the Wall Street exchange in New York tumbled. On 24 October, Black Thursday, millions of shares were sold. Prices tumbled farther down. Investors who sold at a loss could not pay brokers who had given them credit. Brokers could not pay banks which had given them credit. A run on the banks – panic withdrawal of money – followed. Banks, unable to meet the demand for cash, began closing their doors. And so the credit spiral collapsed.

Whether the Wall Street collapse was a cause or only the herald of the great depression is difficult to answer. It was certainly not the only cause. There had been booms and depressions before – for which economists offered a variety of explanations. The boom of the 1920s had been kept going by a substantially new practice – credit buying on instalments, hire purchase. More and more goods were produced to satisfy the seemingly

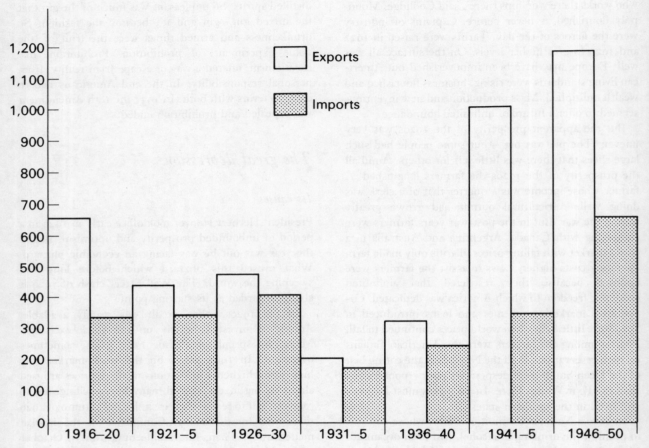

Value of U S exports and imports:
annual averages in millions of U S dollars

☐ Exports

▨ Imports

The severe effects of the world depression are clearly seen in this chart. Much of the later growth in exports represents
wartime and post-war aid; thus in 1944 exports were about $17,000 million of which three-quarters was lend-lease aid

endless demand, until there was a glut – and no longer a
home market worth producing for. The high exchange
rate of the US dollar made it difficult to sell American
goods in foreign markets. And American tariffs had
caused other countries to raise their tariffs against goods
from the USA. Employers began laying off labour.
Demand further declined and unemployment increased.

Hoover and the depression

From October 1929 economic conditions steadily
worsened throughout the world. The lowest point in the
United States was reached in 1933, when some thirteen

million people, almost a quarter of the work force, were
unemployed. Wages were down 60 per cent, production
down 40 per cent. National income between 1929 and
1932 fell by more than half.

In this period of dwindling world trade the best
Hoover could do was to raise tariffs even higher (1930).
To this twenty-five European states responded by
raising high barriers against American goods, resulting
in a further strangulation of the trade on which all
depended.

The depression, said Hoover, would soon be over.
Like Cleveland before him (see p. 70) he believed that
business should be left to solve its own problems. In

'Dusted out' and on the road, Oklahoma 1938. Some of the 'Okies' whose plight John Steinbeck described in The Grapes of Wrath. *Erosion caused by over-cultivation and drought had turned rich wheat-growing land into a wasteland of dust*

general he followed a deflationary policy of balanced budgets similar to that of the National government in Britain (see p. 143). There was then no unemployment insurance in the USA. In 1932 Hoover did provide aid for the states to assist their unemployed, but very little money was paid out.

These were the years when mothers competed with stray dogs to snatch up spoilt goods on the docks of a great industrial nation. Thousands of people picked over rubbish bins. Some developed pellagra or rickets or other deficiency diseases. Some committed suicide. A few died of starvation. Charity in soup kitchens kept some alive.

There was poverty but in the midst of plenty. Except in the dust bowl of Oklahoma, Kansas and Arkansas, farmers were producing a surplus but got nothing for it. For a time there was a trek from the cities to the countryside in search of food or relations with whom to stay – and from 1934 a pitiful trek from the dust bowl to California. Negroes moved from the Deep South to the northern cities, where conditions were rather better. On

the fringes of the cities the unemployed built shanty towns, huts of corrugated iron and cardboard and sacking tents. They called them Hoovervilles. In 1932 veterans of the First World War set up a Hooverville outside Washington and asked for their wartime bonuses, due in 1945, to be paid. They called themselves the BEF (Bonus Expeditionary Force). The authorities panicked and met the BEF with tear gas, bayonets and tanks, and burned down the shanties.

F.D. Roosevelt and the New Deal

In 1933 one of the outstanding presidents of the United States took office – Franklin D. Roosevelt, the former Democrat governor of New York state and a distant relation of Theodore Roosevelt. Crippled from polio when he was thirty-eight, he always had difficulty in standing.

Roosevelt was elected president for four successive terms. In his first two terms he led the USA from depression towards renewed prosperity. In his third term he led his country to the brink of victory in the Second World War. He died in April 1945, a few weeks after the commencement of his fourth term.

The new president had no precise course mapped out, no clear programme for dealing with the depression. But he had great drive and determination. Above all perhaps he gave hope to the people of the USA. Under Roosevelt things got moving.

In his 1932 election campaign Roosevelt promised a 'new deal' for the American people. His New Deal was perhaps the culmination of Progressivism – he set out to do nationally what earlier had been done by individual states. He was assisted by having a Democrat majority in both houses of Congress. Until 1933 presidents took office in March, not January. In Roosevelt's Hundred Days from March to July 1933 laws to combat the depression were passed one after the other. The Emergency Banking Act eased credit restrictions. Various acts regulated farm finances, production and prices. A law to regulate stock market practices, aimed at preventing another Wall Street crash, was passed. Agencies to combat the depression and relieve unemployment, the 'alphabetic agencies', were set up one after another.

The Civilian Conservation Corps (CCC) gave thousands of young men out of door work and a small wage. The Federal Emergency Relief Administration (FERA) helped the states to provide unemployment relief – virtually a dole – in return sometimes for rather unproductive work. The Tennessee Valley Authority (TVA), set up in 1933, provided a pattern for future national undertakings; its activities extended across seven states where unemployment was particularly high. The Farm Credit Administration (FCA) and the Home Owners' Loan Corporation helped some people to keep up mortgage payments. The Public Works Administration (PWA) provided employment building hospitals, schools, harbours, tunnels and so on, whilst the Civil Works Administration (CWA) gave temporary work to about four million people in the winter of 1933–34. When the CWA ended the Works Progress Administration (WPA), which provided more lasting work, though at low wages, gave work to about a third of those unemployed.

All the letters of the alphabet were being used up, complained those who felt that Roosevelt was moving dangerously far left. Under a socialist government, they said, the man who has two cows must give one to his neighbour, but under the New Deal the farmer shoots

The New Deal. Young unemployed men set off for work camps in California in the 1930s

both cows and milks the government.

By 1934 recovery seemed to be on its way and Roosevelt turned to social legislation. The Social Security Act of 1935 provided for contributory old age pensions and helped the states to set up unemployment insurance schemes and to care for needy mothers and children and certain handicapped people.

In 1935 a National Labour Relations Act provided for collective bargaining in industry and set up machinery for settling disputes. In the shelter of this act the American Federation of Labour (AFL) (see p. 69) grew steadily. More spectacular in growth and achievements was John L. Lewis's Congress of Industrial Organisations (CIO) for unskilled workers. The AFL stuck to its craft exclusiveness and friction between the CIO and the AFL continued until in 1955 they combined. In 1938 an act fixing a minimum wage and maximum hours was passed.

At times Progressive legislation (see p. 71) had been declared unconstitutional. But gradually Supreme Court justices Oliver Wendell Holmes and Louis Brandeis established the principle that an interpretation of the constitution which took account of prevailing conditions was correct. One effect of this was to widen the powers of government. Nevertheless several of Roosevelt's earlier acts were invalidated by the Supreme Court, for example, acts regulating farm production and setting up codes of fair competition in industry. As the court gradually accepted the views of Holmes and Brandeis – and as retiring justices were replaced by men sympathetic to the New Deal – Roosevelt reintroduced legislation earlier invalidated by the court.

Roosevelt, though some critics regarded him as a 'dangerous communist', aimed to preserve capitalism by reforming it. Other critics argued that he was not radical enough. Little was done for the Negroes – yet it was in the 1930s that the Negroes began voting Democratic. Doubtless they saw Roosevelt, with his 'concern for people', if not as a champion of the underdog, at least as showing interest in the underdog.

The chief characteristic of the New Deal was the great extension of federal authority in social and economic affairs. And by providing for greater social justice, some people say, Roosevelt – although claiming to be an individualist – was inaugurating the American welfare state.

Others had had plans of a sort to overcome the depression. Senator Huey (Kingfish) Long set up a Share our Wealth movement which for a time had many supporters. God, he said, had called to all Americans 'Come to my feast'. But in 1935 the Kingfish was assassinated. Father Coughlin, a Catholic priest, led a right-wing, virtually fascist movement. 'The new deal is the Jew deal', Coughlin said. Dr Townsend's Old Age Revolving Pensions Ltd had the ground cut from under its feet by the Social Security Act of 1935 – introduced in part to counteract Townsend's growing popularity. And his partner was found lining his pockets with Revolving Pensions funds.

Although the New Deal put the USA on the road to recovery, there was a serious recession in 1937. In 1939 several million were out of work and national income was still below the 1929 level. But war expenditure changed all this; by 1944 national income was more than double the 1929 figure.

From cautious isolation to world war

When Japan attacked China in the 1930s the USA was unwilling to take positive action to restrain her. Italy's invasion of Ethiopia in 1935 and the rise of Nazism in Germany provoked Congress to pass a series of Neutrality Acts (1935–37). These forbade Americans to supply money or munitions to countries at war and refused protection to Americans sailing in ships belonging to such states.

In 1937, after referring to the epidemic spread of lawlessness in the world, Roosevelt said that positive endeavours must be made to preserve peace. But even in 1939 he could not persuade the Senate to modify the Neutrality Act of 1937. Later that year the Second World War broke out. Roosevelt, convinced that the only way to keep the USA out of the war was to give aid to Britain and France, then persuaded Congress, while retaining other provisions of the Neutrality Act, to allow the sale of arms to non-aggressors.

Thereafter the USA aided Britain and her allies by, for example, selling arms on a cash and carry basis (see p. 213). In September 1940 an embargo was placed on the sale of scrap metal to Japan. And selective service was introduced for men between the ages of twenty-one and thirty-five – though Roosevelt at this time said: 'I have said this before, but I shall say it again and again and again; your boys are not going to be sent into any foreign wars.' Early in 1941, still hoping to keep the USA out of the war by making her the 'arsenal of democracy', Roosevelt persuaded Congress to agree to lend-lease (see p. 213) and a massive rearmament programme began. When Japan attacked the American fleet in Pearl Harbour in December 1941 the United States was not altogether unready for war.

17 China and Japan 1919–41

The peace conference, 1919

At the peace conference after the First World War China had three goals: the return by Japan of Kiaochow Bay in Shantung, release from the obligations forced upon her by Japan's Twenty-one Demands, and the ending of the unequal treaties (see p. 14).

The USA suggested that Allied powers should control Kiaochow. The Japanese opposed this. Their position was strong for in 1917 France, Britain and Italy had promised to uphold their rights in Shantung. And in 1917 notes exchanged between Viscount Ishii, a Japanese diplomat, and Lansing, the American secretary of state, whilst supporting the open door policy, recognised 'special Japanese rights' in China. Again, on paper at least, China had in 1915 accepted Japan's demands concerning Shantung. However, Japan agreed to return Kiaochow Bay in due course, though she was to keep mining and railway rights in Shantung. In China national feeling expressed itself in boycotts of Japanese goods and nationals.

The unequal treaties made with Germany and Austria were ended and the German concessions (areas reserved for the use of and controlled by foreigners) at Hankow and Tientsin were returned to China. Treaties signed with states set up after the war gave no special rights to their nationals in China. Though China's gains seemed small they heralded the ending of the privileges which foreigners had enjoyed since 1842 And as a member of the League of Nations China acquired a new status.

Germany's colonies in the north Pacific became Japanese mandates. Japan's control was virtually unlimited. The strategic value of the islands, whose economic worth was not great, was proved during the Second World War when Japan used them as stepping stones in her southward advance.

The Washington conference, 1921–22

After the First World War the USA became increasingly suspicious of Japanese ambitions. The Anglo-Japanese Alliance (see p. 20) was due for renewal in 1921. However much Britain explained that the alliance enabled her to curb Japan, Washington saw it as strengthening Japanese imperialism. Meanwhile, relations between the USA and Japan were strained by problems concerning Japanese immigration. Both Japan and the USA were building up their navies to new strengths. Britain too was engaged in a naval construction programme.

Against this background the USA issued invitations to a conference to meet in Washington on 11 November, Armistice Day, 1921 to discuss limitation of armaments and Pacific and Far Eastern problems. Eight powers joined the United States at the conference – Britain and her empire, France, Italy, Belgium, the Netherlands, Portugal, China and Japan. Charles Evans Hughes, American secretary of state, Balfour, British foreign minister, and Japan's Viscount Kato were the Big Three at the conference.

On the opening day Hughes made two bold proposals. He suggested:

1. that no battleships or battle cruisers be built by the USA, Britain or Japan for ten years – the 'naval holiday' proposal;
2. that a ratio for battleships and battle cruisers of 5 (USA), 5 (Britain), 3 (Japan), 1.67 (France) and 1.67 (Italy) should be accepted, and that a maximum of 520,000 tonnes should be set for Britain and the USA.

The five powers eventually agreed to these proposals. Japan in return won concessions limiting the building of naval bases in the Pacific, though this was advantageous to Britain and the USA as well. Hawaii, Alaska and Singapore were not covered by the agreement. No decision was made to limit smaller naval vessels or land forces. The agreements were to last until December 1936 but after December 1934 any of the five powers could, by giving two years notice, terminate them.

The Anglo-Japanese Alliance was not renewed. Instead the USA, Britain, France and Japan promised to respect one another's rights in the Pacific region.

Under pressure from the United States and Britain the Japanese agreed to fulfil their promise to return Kiaochow Bay to China. And the nine powers represented at the conference promised to respect China's territorial and political integrity. However, this

Nine Power Treaty did nothing to cut down privileges previously granted to foreigners; it concerned only the future. And as no provision was made for enforcing the treaty everything depended on the sincerity of the signatories.

China's representatives asked for the ending of extra-territoriality and of the conventional tariff. Limited concessions were made. A commission was set up to study the question of extra-territorial rights and to prepare for their ending. A commission to study tariffs was agreed upon and certain increases in duties on imports were authorised.

By further involving the USA in the Pacific area the Washington conference made likely an eventual clash with Japan. However, for some years Japan was relatively co-operative. In 1930, at Ramsay MacDonald's initiative, Britain, the USA and Japan made further agreements limiting naval strength. But in 1931 Japan attacked Manchuria (see p. 169). In December 1934 Japan gave notice of withdrawal from the Washington agreements. So from 1937 the various powers were free to build up their navies and to fortify their Pacific possessions.

China

The Nationalists come to power, 1928

The confusion which followed the 1911 revolution (see p. 22) continued in the post-war years. In Peking governments came and went. In Canton there was Sun Yat-sen's rival administration. Until 1928 the Peking administration was the one recognised by foreign powers. To that extent it was the 'government' of China. In so far as it controlled China it did so by military force.

Peking's orders were accepted or more often ignored according to the changing attitudes of the warlords who controlled large armies and ruled, in bandit fashion, whole provinces. The chief warlords made their own arms and ammunition and coined their own often worthless 'dollars'. They made and broke 'alliances' with one another and withdrew their support of the central government as they pleased. Peasants were taxed unmercifully and forced to plant opium instead of less profitable rice. When luck was against them the warlords retired for the time being to the shelter of some foreign concession.

Sun Yat-sen's Kuomintang (National People's Party

or KMT) was for some years hardly a party, so poorly was it organised. But in 1922 plans were made to reorganise the Kuomintang. A manifesto in 1923 affiirmed that the KMT upheld Sun's Three Principles of nationalism, democracy and 'livelihood'. In 1924 the first party congress stressed that there must be one party government, with complete obedience to the party and its leader. Party offices were to be set up and a propaganda network and a party army built up.

In 1923 Sun came to an agreement with a Soviet diplomat, Adolph Joffe, who promised that the USSR would supply the KMT with arms and send military and political advisers. It was agreed that members of the newly established Chinese Communist Party (see p. 164) could join the KMT. Chief among the advisers who came to China were Michael Borodin and General Galin. Soon arms were being supplied to the KMT and a soviet-style military academy was established at Whampoa near Canton. Chiang Kai-shek, a young general who had trained with the Red army in the USSR, was appointed head of the Whampoa Academy; Chou En-lai (Zhou Enlai), a communist, was in charge of its political department.

In March 1925 Sun Yat-sen died. By 1926 there was tension between Chiang Kai-shek, who by then was virtually leader of the KMT, and the communists. Matters were smoothed over for the time being. In June 1926 the Nationalist armies swept northwards from Canton with Chiang in command. A propaganda campaign promising a new order in China won many sympathisers. As the KMT army advanced it was joined by great numbers of peasants and by many of the troops sent by the warlords to oppose it. Whole provinces declared themselves in favour of the Nationalists. Chiang's troops soon controlled much of the Yangtse valley and such key cities as Nanking (March 1927) and Shanghai (April 1927). Nanking replaced Canton as the Nationalist capital.

In June 1928 KMT forces captured Peking. With the fall of Peking the Nationalist government in Nanking was recognised by foreign powers. Peking (Northern Capital) was for the time being renamed Peiping (Northern Peace).

The Nanking régime was based on control by a single party, the KMT. It used such slogans as 'The rights of the KMT are superior to all rights.' A democratic constitution was promised when the people of China were fit to exercise political rights, but the KMT showed little intention of giving up its one party rule. A decision in 1930 to concentrate power in the hands of

Chiang Kai-shek turned the government into almost a personal dictatorship.

For a time there was progress in education, health and communications. But land reforms proved ineffective, being undertaken less than halfheartedly. Plans were drawn up – but they remained plans. Land reforms were essential if the power which the KMT had won by military strength and propaganda was to endure. A Hunanese folk song makes the position clear:

> Tillers of the soil, always under threat –
> Like three swords over the head – high interest, rent, and debt.
> Tillers of the soil before them only three choices to make –
> Prison, beggar's stick, or home to forsake.

Though Chiang's control over China seemed secure the communists were establishing their power.

The Chinese Communist Party and the KMT

In July 1921 the Chinese Communist Party (CCP) was founded. Thirteen delegates, among them Mao Tsetung (Mao Zedong) and two Comintern envoys, attended the first meeting, held in secret in a girls' school in the French concession in Shanghai. In 1922 Chou En-lai, who had gone to France as a member of a work-study group, set up a branch of the CCP in Paris. Chou was from an official's family. Mao's father, a Hunanese peasant, had managed to acquire a few hectares of land.

With two other Hunanese Mao worked among labour unions, trying to combat illiteracy and to organise strikes. He was strongly nationalist. From childhood his heroes had been the strong men of history. He delighted in such Chinese romances as *The Water Margin*.

When in 1923 Sun Yat-sen accepted help from the USSR, members of the CCP began working with the KMT. If Sun was suspicious of the Russians, the Chinese communists were suspicious of the KMT. Each party regarded the other as a tool to be used for its own purposes. In March 1927 Shanghai workers, under the direction of Chou En-lai, captured key points throughout the city. When Chiang Kai-shek's forces arrived the workers surrendered the city to Chiang's control but were unwilling to give up their arms. Chiang decided to smash the communists. In April 1927, three weeks after the KMT army entered Shanghai, a white terror, in which Chiang had the support of the city's financiers – and of its powerful underworld – purged this great city of its communist sympathisers. Among those who made dramatic escapes was Chou En-lai. Communist sympathisers lived for years in peril. Three years after the Shanghai purge Mao Tsetung's wife and sister were executed by the KMT. Mao wrote the poem beginning: 'My proud poplar is lost to me and to you your willow' in memory of his wife and of a comrade's husband killed in battle against the Nationalists.

Mao Tsetung in the Chingkangshan and Kiangsi

After the Shanghai purge the communists attempted several uprisings. All were unsuccessful. Mao, who had escaped hatless and shoeless from a KMT firing squad, remained active in Hunan. Unlike some communists Mao had realised that only the peasants could bring the communists to power in China: 'Several hundred million peasants will rise like a mighty storm, like a hurricane, a force so swift and violent that no power, however great, will be able to hold it back.'

In September 1927 Mao led a peasant army in an Autumn Harvest uprising but was forced to withdraw. He led the survivors to a mountain hideout in the Chingkangshan (Jinggangshan). The next year Chu Teh (Zhu De), father of the Red army, with survivors from another uprising, joined Mao in the Chingkang Mountains. There, on the borders of Hunan and Kiangsi (Jiangxi), among mountain bandits, Mao and Chu set up soviets of peasants, workers and soldiers. They suffered untold hardship in their little base area. The 'officers' of the infant Red army shared their food and even their cigarettes with their men. At first their only 'weapons' – apart from those they managed to take from KMT troops – were made out of farm tools. Yet the Chu-Mao army, as it was called, became a disciplined force. Lin Piao (Lin Biao), Lin the Tiger Cat, who had trained under Chiang Kai-shek at Whampoa, made rules for the army: soldiers must pay for any supplies obtained from the local people; latrines must be dug at a distance from dwellings. And so on. While in the cities the communists had to remain underground, their red flag flew boldly in the Chingkang Mountains.

In 1929 Mao and Chu came down from the Chingkangshan and established a base in Kiangsi. Local soviets were again set up and disciplined communist cadres indoctrinated the peasants. Mao followed the guerilla tactics which had enabled him to survive on the Chingkangshan: 'Divide our forces to arouse the masses, concentrate our forces to deal with the enemy. The enemy advances, we retreat; the enemy camps, we attack; the enemy retreats, we pursue.'

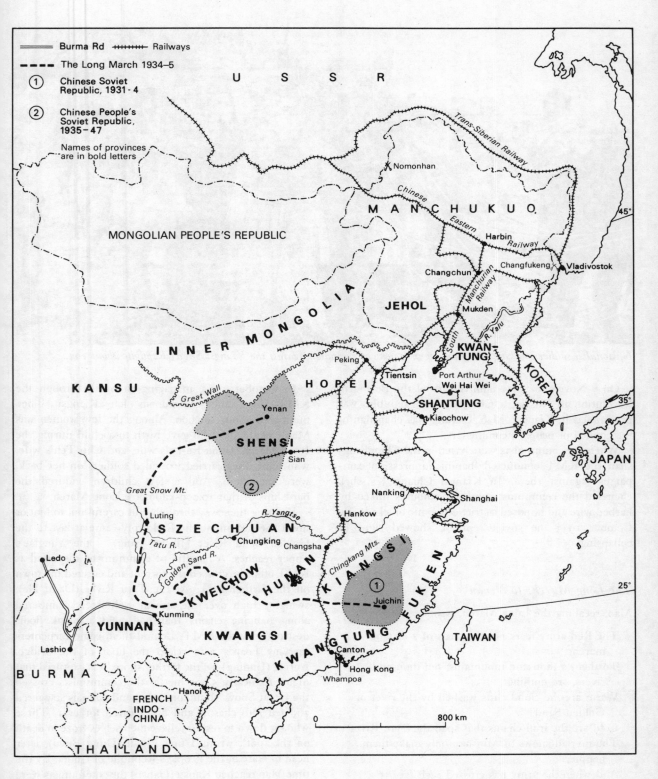

Burma Rd ═══   Railways ┼┼┼┼┼┼┼

- - - - The Long March 1934-5

① Chinese Soviet
Republic, 1931-4

② Chinese People's
Soviet Republic,
1935-47

Names of provinces
are in bold letters

U S S R

MONGOLIAN PEOPLE'S REPUBLIC

M A N C H U K U O

Trans-Siberian Railway

Chinese

Eastern

Nomonhan

Harbin   Railway

Changchun   Changfukeng   Vladivostok

I N N E R   M O N G O L I A

JEHOL

Manchurian
Railway

Mukden

KWAN-
TUNG

South

R. Yalu

KOREA

KANSU

Great Wall

Yenan

HOPEI

Peking

Tientsin   Port Arthur
Wei Hai Wei

SHENSI   ②

Sian

SHANTUNG

Kiaochow

JAPAN

Great Snow Mt.

Luting

Nanking

Shanghai

R. Yangtse

Hankow

SZECHUAN

Tatu R.

Chungking   Changsha

Golden Sand R.

Chingkang Mts.

KIANGSI

Ledo

KWEICHOW   HUNAN

FUKIEN

① Juichin

Kunming

YUNNAN

KWANGSI

TAIWAN

Lashio

KWANGTUNG

Canton

BURMA

Hanoi   Hong Kong
Whampoa

FRENCH
INDO-
CHINA

0   800 km

THAILAND

China in the 1930s

Nationalist soldiers making ready for an encirclement campaign against the Kiangsi Soviet Republic about 1932

On 7 November 1931, anniversary of the Bolshevik Revolution in Russia, a Chinese soviet republic was proclaimed in Kiangsi. Mao Tsetung was chairman of the council of people's commissars.

When the communists were based in the Chingkang-shan the KMT conducted 'bandit suppression campaigns' against them. In Kiangsi Chiang Kai-shek encircled the communists with blockhouses linked by barbed wire and imposed a strict economic blockade. By October 1933 the soviet republic showed signs of collapsing.

The Long March: to Yenan

Mao, recalling the Long March, wrote:

The Red army fears not the trials of a distant
  march;
To them a thousand mountains, ten thousand
  rivers, are nothing ...
Warm are the cloud cliffs washed by the river of
  Golden Sand.
Cold are the iron chains that span the Tatu River.
The myriad snows of Minshan only make them
  happier
And when the army has crossed each face is
  smiling

In October 1934, managing to break through the KMT lines, the communists left Kiangsi. They numbered about 100,000. Among the few women was Mao's new wife, who gave birth to a child during the Long March. Chou En-lai's wife, and Chu Teh's wife, who sometimes carried wounded soldiers on her back, were there too. And a few children endured the hardships of that 10,000-kilometre Long March.

Fighting their way through, but careful not to loot or upset the peasantry, the Red army came at last to the Golden Sand River (Jinsha Jiang) – the Yangtse's upper reaches. A handful of communists, disguised as KMT officials, crossed the torrent and entered the town on the farther bank. At the Tatu River (Dadu He), swinging high over the stream, volunteers clambered along hanging chains that had held a plank floor, destroyed by the KMT. Behind them came carpenters carrying boards who relaid the floor of the bridge. Luting (Luding), on the farther shore, was captured that night. At nearly 5,000 metres the communists crossed the Great Snow Mountain. 'Men and animals staggered and fell into chasms and disappeared for ever. Those who sat down to rest or relieve themselves froze to death on the spot', wrote T'ung Pi-wu (Dung Biwu), later head of state of the People's Republic of China. By the time Mao reached Kansu (Gansu) the communists were eating their horses, their belts and their shoes.

In the autumn of 1935 Mao Tsetung led about 8,000 men and a few women into Shensi (Shaanxi) where communist supporters welcomed them. In December 1936 a soviet republic, with its base in Yenan (Yan'an), was set up. This town built into the loess cliffs was the communist headquarters for some years. The Yenan régime showed great drive in producing food, in manufacturing weapons under the most primitive conditions and in turning the people of the north towards communism – and in resisting both the Japanese and the KMT. Mao showed increasing independence of the Comintern and Moscow. In Yenan he married Chiang Ch'ing (Jiang Qing), a former film actress from Shanghai.

Sino-Western relations

The chief problem troubling Sino-Western relations in the 1920s was the demand to end the conventional tariff and extra-territoriality. The promises made at the Washington conference by no means satisfied the Chinese. Boycotts and assaults on foreigners revealed China's national spirit. The situation was particularly serious in 1925–26 after a British officer ordered police in Shanghai to shoot at a crowd of demonstrators.

The British surrendered two concessions to China and in 1930, as promised at Washington, their leased territory at Wei Hai Wei. The Boxer indemnity payments, suspended when China joined the Allies in the First World War, were used on projects helpful to China. The USA had earlier decided to spend its share of the indemnity on educating Chinese students. The USA also led the way in allowing China to fix her own tariffs. By 1930 all agreements restricting China's control of her own tariffs were ended.

As promised at Washington, a commission to study extra-territoriality was set up. In the late 1920s the Nationalists demanded the immediate ending of extra-territorial rights. To this the USA, Britain and France would not agree, as conditions in China were still unstable. Then the Nanking government announced that all extra-territorial rights would end as from January 1930. By then about half the foreigners in China were already subject to Chinese law. The Manchurian crisis of 1931 (see p. 169) delayed settlement of the matter. Britain and the USA gave up their extra-territorial rights in 1943.

In 1924 – at the same time as they were working hand in glove with Sun Yat-sen's régime in Canton – the Russians entered into formal relations with the Peking government. It was agreed that Russians resident in China – mostly White refugees in whom the Soviet Union had little interest – should no longer have extra-territorial rights. Russian concessions in Chinese cities were given up. China's sovereignty over Inner Mongolia (Nei Monggol) was admitted. Outer Mongolia, where in 1921 a soviet republic had been set up with Russian help, was rapidly passing from Chinese control. In 1924 it became the Mongolian People's Republic. Later, relations between Chiang Kai-shek's government and the USSR deteriorated. In 1929 clashes on the Manchurian border ended with the breaking off of diplomatic relations.

Japan

Decline from liberal government

In 1912 Mutsuhito, the Meiji Emperor, symbol of the transformation of Japan, died. Under Yoshihito Japan continued to flourish. Then in 1926 Hirohito, a young man with scientific interests, who had been regent since 1921, became emperor. His reign title was Showa – Enlightened Peace. But war not peace marked the earlier years of Hirohito's long reign.

Until 1929 Japan continued to prosper and was more conciliatory towards China and other powers than before. Under liberal leadership she seemed to be moving towards responsible party government. In 1925 the franchise was extended. But even in the 'decade of liberalism' (1921–31) diehards were criticising Japan's 'weak' policy at the Washington conference. Twice attacks were made on the lives of liberal prime ministers.

In the 1930s the reactionary influence of the upper house of the Diet was more noticeable. Through their ministers the army and navy continued to have unusual influence in the cabinet. After 1929 the world depression caused severe difficulties. The population was growing rapidly. National wealth had increased but there was no corresponding rise in living standards. As the depression widened Japan's overseas markets shrank. High tariffs shut out her products. There seemed little hope that trade could expand to provide better living standards.

Many Japanese, convinced that party government and non-imperialist policies had failed, said 'some other way out' must be found, that Japan must follow a policy of expansion to obtain markets and raw materials. Young officers talked of establishing a military dictatorship. Assassination tended to take the place of the ballot box.

As seen from the International Settlement in Shanghai, the Chinese city after a Japanese air raid appeared to be one big bonfire (January 1932). Smartly dressed and well equipped Japanese soldiers seek out Chinese infantry. The Odeon was the biggest Chinese cinema

Japanese aggression: the China 'incident' Act I, 1931

Just as the Japanese were looking for 'some other way out' the way forward seemed to be blocked. They had looked to Manchuria as a source of coal and other raw materials, a market for manufactures and a place for settlement. Railways had brought a great influx of Chinese settlers into this fertile region. With the establishment of China's relatively strong Nationalist government Japan's position in Manchuria appeared threatened. Swift action seemed necessary if Japan was to maintain her position in Manchuria.

For some time officers of the Kwantung army (see p. 21) had been planning a coup in Manchuria. An opportunity came while Chiang Kai-shek's army was engaged in an encirclement campaign against the communists. On 18 September 1931, in Mukden, hostilities which the Japanese for long referred to as the China 'incident' began. These hostilities did not end until Japan's defeat in the Second World War.

According to Japanese accounts, Chinese soldiers on the night of 18 September attempted to blow up a section of the South Manchurian Railway (see map p. 35). Thereupon Japanese troops fired on the saboteurs. However, if the Chinese were the first to take action, Japanese officers immediately put into operation their plan to occupy Manchuria. The commander of the Kwantung army ordered troops from Port Arthur and Korea to occupy Mukden and Changchun. Soon the Chinese forces in Manchuria, under Chang Hsueh-liang, known as the Young Marshal, were retreating south of the Great Wall. By February 1932 the conquest of Manchuria was virtually complete. The Japanese government appeared embarrassed by its runaway army. The emperor declared: 'The army's interference in domestic and foreign politics and its wilfulness is a state of affairs which ... we must view with apprehension.' However, though the Kwantung army leadership had in effect mutinied, to many Japanese the headstrong officers were patriots.

In January 1932, again on the Kwantung army's initiative, Japanese marines landed at Shanghai, where boycotts were hindering business. The Japanese government claimed that its forces were 'restoring order'. After weeks of fighting and heavy air raids the Chinese agreed to end the boycotts and the marines left Shanghai. Beyond this the government of Japan did nothing to check the army. In 1933 the area between Peking and the Manchurian border became a demilitarised zone.

Throughout this zone Japan soon had economic and political influence.

Manchukuo and the League of Nations

In February 1932 Japan announced the birth of a new national state, independent Manchukuo (Manchuland). The people of Manchuria, Japan claimed, desired to be free of Chinese rule, so she had helped them to win their freedom. But the people living in Manchuria were predominantly Chinese and most had no love for the Japanese. (The Manchus themselves had almost ceased to exist as a national group.) Nor was Manchukuo anything but a Japanese puppet.

The Japanese installed China's ex-emperor Hsuan T'ung (see p. 22) as regent and then emperor of Manchukuo. Better known as Henry P'u I (Puyi) the emperor of Manchukuo was the puppet of the Japanese army. The commander of the Kwantung army – who was also Japanese ambassador to Manchukuo and commander of Manchukuo's 'own' army – ruled the puppet state. Chinese collaborators held high posts in the government but Japanese colleagues controlled them at every step. In 1933 Manchukuo was extended to include part of Hopei (Hebei).

There was no effective resistance to Japan's aggression, though the Chinese people showed hostility and the communists in Kiangsi made protests. The Nationalist government seemed willing to let Japan control north China.

However, China did appeal to the League of Nations. The League appointed a commission under Lord Lytton, a British statesman, to enquire into the matter. Meanwhile Japanese forces went unchecked. The Lytton report stated that the Japanese had not been acting in self-defence in Manchuria and that Manchukuo was not independent. It recommended that Manchukuo should have self-government under Chinese sovereignty but that Japan's economic rights should be recognised. In March 1933 Japan announced her resignation from the League of Nations.

Two non-League members, the USA and the USSR, were concerned with Japan's aggression. In January 1932 Stimson, American secretary of state, sent notes to the signatories of the 1922 Nine Power treaty (see p. 162). Gains acquired by armed force, said Stimson, should not be recognised. As Britain, in the grip of the world depression, would give no firm promise of support against Japan the USA, also hard hit by the depression, did little to back up its protests. The USSR, which had a common frontier with Manchukuo, resumed diplomatic relations with China (see p. 167). Beyond that she did nothing, but fear of the Soviet Union forced Japan to keep large numbers of troops in Manchukuo.

Nationalism and militarism

To some extent the occupation of Manchuria eased Japan's economic problems. To offset the gains there was the burden of military expenditure and consequent taxation. In Japan there was a steady shift towards military control of the government. Fanatical nationalism found expression in further assassinations. In 1932 the prime minister, who was suspected of intending to restrain the army, was shot by a gang of young officers.

From 1936, in Japan, as in Germany and Italy, there was violent nationalist propaganda and rigid censorship of press, radio and films. There was the same subjection of education to political and military ends. Japan had her secret police – but there were no purges such as occurred in Nazi Germany. Moderate elements fought back longer than in Germany or Italy; the extremists finally gained control only a few weeks before the Japanese attack on Pearl Harbour in December 1941. Nor was there in Japan a one man dictatorship. Instead of a Mussolini or a Hitler Japan had her emperor, a man who was perhaps no admirer of militarism. But about half of Japan's budget was spent on preparations for war.

The Sian incident began at 5 a.m. on 10 December 1936 when Chiang Kai-shek, hearing shots, leaped from this bed. In his nightshirt, without his false teeth and shoes, he tried to escape his kidnappers by jumping through the window and scrambling up the rocky hillside behind

A united front for China; the Anti-Comintern pact for Japan

Chiang Kai-shek seemed more interested in suppressing the communists in China than in resisting the Japanese. At his order an army commanded by the Young Marshal, Chang Hsueh-liang, went into action against the communists in Yenan. Meanwhile, the communists began thinking of uniting with the KMT against the Japanese. A united front also appealed to the Young Marshal, who until 1931 had governed Manchuria. In December 1936 the Sian incident occurred: Chiang Kai-shek, while visiting the Young Marshal's headquarters in Sian (Xi'an), was kidnapped by officers of Chang's army. Negotiations between the Young Marshal and Chou En-lai for the communists followed. What happened is not clear but Chiang Kai-shek was released and the next year the Nationalist government agreed to co-operate with the communists in resisting the

Japanese. The communists made various concessions to obtain the united front but the coalition was naturally uneasy. There could not be 'two suns in the sky', as Mao Tsetung said – except for a specific purpose and for a limited period. As for Chang Hsueh-liang, after the Sian incident he became a prisoner of Chiang Kai-shek – and remained such until his death many years later.

The announcement of the united front was not made until September 1937 but the Japanese were aware before that of its likelihood. Again their position in China seemed threatened and renewed action seemed necessary. By 1937 the Japanese were less concerned than before about the possibility of Russian intervention in China. The signing in November 1936 of the Anti-Comintern pact with Germany encouraged Japan (see p. 201). In the end the pact proved little more than a paper tiger, its only common denominator being fear of communism and the USSR. Hitler openly expresssed his contempt for the Japanese. However Germany gradually cut down on the arms she had been supplying to Chiang Kai-shek through Hong Kong. Of more importance than the Anti-Comintern pact in freeing Japan's hands was the USSR's concern with the growing threat of Nazi Germany. In 1937 the USSR countered the Anti-Comintern pact by signing a non-aggression pact with China. But a month before that Act II of the China 'incident' began.

The China 'incident', Act II, 1937

On 7 July 1937 there was a night clash between Chinese and Japanese troops. The Japanese soldiers, part of a garrison force stationed in Peking under the Boxer Protocol, were manoeuvring at the Marco Polo bridge. If officers of the Kwantung army had planned the Mukden incident, the action at the Marco Polo bridge seems to have been unexpected. However, Japanese militarists were quick to take advantage of it.

A few days after the clash at the Marco Polo bridge, the killing of some Japanese near Peking provided further excuse for action. The Japanese sent troops from Manchukuo and Korea and before the end of July Peking and Tientsin were in Japanese hands. Hostilities then moved to Shanghai which fell after three months of savage fighting.

China again appealed to the League of Nations, which declared that the Japanese had broken the terms of the 1922 Nine Power Treaty. A conference of these powers was called but Japan sent no representative and the meeting proved useless.

Nanking, which the Nationalist government had evacuated, fell to the Japanese in December 1937. Its capture was marked by brutal conduct, strikingly different from the chivalry of the Japanese during their war with Russia (1904–05).

For the time being Japan was able to ignore the growing antagonism of the USA and Britain. With the USSR there were greater problems. In July 1938 there was a serious clash at Changfukeng, near Vladivostok, but at their emperor's order the Japanese withdrew.

In October 1938 the Japanese captured Canton, the port through which China received supplies of arms, and Hankow, a great railway and industrial centre. Yet China was by no means conquered. Japan held only the ports and cities of the east and some of the railways. And her control of these areas was much disturbed by Chinese guerillas.

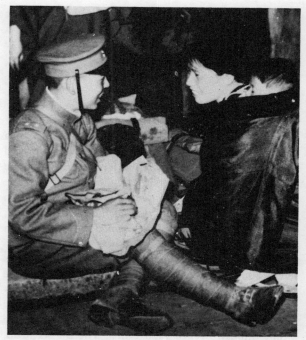

The war between China and Japan. A smiling farewell: but will this Japanese soldier return from the battlefront to his wife and child?

In November 1937 Chiang Kai-shek made Chungking (Chongqing), in the remote south-west of China, his capital. Though the city was the target for merciless air attacks, the Chinese streamed into Chungking. Millions of patriots, most of them arriving on foot, some in carts or on bicycles, packed the provinces of Szechuan (Sichuan), Kweichow (Guizhou) and Yunnan. They came from all walks of life – professors, students, peasants and beggars. They took with them the equipment of entire factories, scientific apparatus and whole university libraries. They set up schools and universities in cave shelters. With the crudest of equipment they manufactured munitions. They built roads, carrying the earth in baskets slung on bamboo poles. They suffered from heat and from cold, from malnutrition, tuberculosis, often hunger, sometimes starvation, and death from the air. But they refused to yield, to be 'liberated' as the Japanese said.

And in the north-west of China Japanese aggression was fiercely resisted by communist guerillas. In occupied areas the communists chalked up on walls the words of a general who had fought against Tartar invaders: 'Let all the rivers and mountains be recovered.' 'We, the Chinese nation, have the spirit to fight the enemy to the last drop of our blood, the determination to recover our lost territory by our own efforts and the ability to stand on our own feet in the family of nations', said Mao Tsetung.

Stalemate in China

The Japanese made no significant advances in China after the end of 1938. Towns and villages were captured and recaptured, held now by the Japanese, now by the Chinese. But the Kuomintang was increasingly inactive. Believing that the western powers would be drawn into the war, Chiang Kai-shek waited; he sold, it is said, space to buy time. A paralysis seemed to descend upon Chungking. The administration was grossly corrupt. Civil and military promotions depended on personal ties not on ability. However, though some groups within the KMT wanted a negotiated peace, Chiang Kai-shek refused attempts by Japan to come to terms. After the fall of Canton aid came in along the Burma Road and for a time through French Indo-China. The Burma Road, constructed by immense gangs of Chinese labourers, was completed early in 1939. Some 1,100 kilometres long, it ran through wild mountain country from Lashio in Burma to Kunming in Yunnan.

Japan: towards world war

In May 1939 border disputes between Inner Mongolia, which was under Japanese control, and the Mongolian People's Republic, a Soviet satellite, led to heavy clashes at Nomonhan near the border of north-western Manchukuo. The Russians won a decisive victory. In August of that year Germany and the USSR entered into a non-aggression pact (see p. 208). This was a blow to Japan. On 1 September 1939 German forces invaded Poland. By June of the following year Germany had conquered most of western Europe. In 1938 the Japanese had begun referring to a Great East Asian Co-prosperity Sphere which would include Manchukuo and China and dominate East and South-east Asia. In March 1940 Japan set up the 'True Government of Free China' in Nanking – the second puppet state she had established in Chinese territory. In July 1940, France having collapsed, Japanese troops occupied bases in the north of French Indo-China. In September 1940 a Tripartite pact (the Rome–Berlin–Tokyo pact) was signed. By this ten-year pact Germany, Italy and Japan promised full military support if any one of them was attacked by a 'fresh' enemy.

There was little sign of Britain's being able to resist Japan at that time for her forces were fully engaged elsewhere. Indeed, at Japan's request, about the time of the battle of Britain (see p. 214), the British, who still ruled Burma, briefly closed the Burma Road over which 5,000 tonnes of supplies were being carried into China every month. In April 1941 the Japanese signed a neutrality pact with the USSR. This freed them from concern over Manchukuo. Then in June 1941 Germany invaded the USSR (see p. 216).

In July 1941 the Japanese seized airfields and bases in southern Indo-China. The USA and Britain then cut off all trade with Japan and gave more aid to China. Military equipment was rushed to Kunming along the re-opened Burma Road. And the USA speeded up defensive measures in the Pacific. By then war against the USA and Britain was probably inevitable. And by then there was serious tension again between the Chinese Nationalists and communists.

18 Western Europe, 1918–39: democracy and totalitarianism

Introductory

After the First World War state intervention increased throughout western Europe. On the whole this was beneficial to the poorer classes, bringing improved social services and greater regulation of industry in their interests. The status of women improved. Educational opportunities increased. There was a slow but steady improvement in the standard of living in most European countries between 1918 and 1939. This was interrupted by the depression which began in the USA in 1929 and spread rapidly to other countries – to Europe and Japan, to remote Australian ports and Brazilian villages. There was an almost complete stoppage of international trade. So the depression was most severe in countries that were most industrialised or depended most on foreign trade. In such countries year after year long lines of men waited hopelessly for work.

> No man has hired us
> With pocketed hands
> And lowered faces
> We stand about in open places
> And shiver in unlit rooms . . .
> . . . In this land
> There shall be one cigarette to two men,
> To two women one half pint of bitter
> Ale. In this land
> No man has hired us.

Though in the 1980s unemployment has become all too familiar, the misery of these men and their families is hard to imagine. Every country made some attempt to help those who were out of work through no fault of their own, but protection was much less adequate than today. After 1934 the effects of the depression grew less. The growth of armaments and of the motor and aircraft industries was important. By 1939 the depression was virtually over. But by then a number of states had come under authoritarian rule. In Germany and Italy totalitarian régimes were threatening to overwhelm the democracies, to exile freedom from the world.

Democracy preserved

Britain faced prolonged unemployment and other problems in the years between the wars (see Chapter 14). But this did not destroy the hold of parliament or respect for liberty. Britain was democratic in form in 1918. By 1939 the democratic spirit had taken a strong hold on the British people. Britain became more democratic not only in its government but in the way people treated one another.

In Holland and Belgium, in Switzerland, in Denmark, Norway and Sweden, democratic government continued to flourish, in spite of difficulties. In all these countries socialist parties were strong. As in Britain, heavy taxation provided greater economic and social equality and relative security for everyone in sickness, old age and unemployment.

Democracy in difficulties: France

1919–26: governments of the right and of the left

When British and American guarantees against German aggression failed to materialise and the USA failed to join the League, France felt a sense of desertion – a feeling understandable in view of her five million war casualties, of whom over 1,250,000 were killed. Her male population was soon to be relatively old. By 1939 her population, including some three million immigrants, was about the same as in 1913.

As before the war power shifted rapidly from one ministry to the next, with the Chamber of Deputies acting as 'kingmaker' or 'un-kingmaker'. The resulting instability made it difficult for ministries to follow firm policies. Though from time to time there were bursts of effort, government was in general ineffective.

The Chamber of Deputies elected in 1914 was dissolved in November 1919. The seventy-nine-year-old Clemenceau, 'père la victoire', then formed the *Bloc National* – anti-communist, pro-Catholic, anxious for the security of property, anxious for security against Germany. In January 1920 Clemenceau retired from political life. He was succeeded by Alexandre Millerand. Shortly after Millerand became president in September 1920, Briand became prime minister.

In the early post-war years the work of restoring the northern departments, with their wrecked machinery and burnt-out farms, was undertaken. But how was this to be paid for? The war had largely been paid for by borrowing. Unwilling to increase taxation, post-war governments relied on reparations – the magic money they expected to receive from Germany.

In 1922 Poincaré became prime minister with power to rule by decree. In January 1923, when Germany failed to pay reparations then due, Poincaré sent troops across the Rhine to occupy the Ruhr coal mining districts (see p. 181). The occupation of the Ruhr, in which the Belgians took part but which was opposed by Britain, created fresh difficulties. France herself suffered from inflation. In 1924 she had to accept the Dawes plan (see p. 182) for payment of reparations.

Elections in 1924 resulted in the formation of an uneasy coalition of socialists and radicals, the *Cartel des Gauches* (Combination of the Left). United by little except anti-clericalism, this government of the left failed to introduce social reforms – or even to balance the budget. The *petit bourgeoisie*, a large and influential section of society, would not have tolerated increased direct taxes. Increased indirect taxes would have been a burden on the government's own supporters, the working classes. By 1926 continued borrowing and consequent inflation had made the franc almost valueless.

The government had other problems. A rebellion that began in Morocco in 1921 smouldered on until 1926. In 1925 the Druze of Syria, a French mandate, rose in a revolt that lasted over ten years. Anti-clerical measures in Alsace led to a demand for autonomy, though not for re-union with Germany.

In 1920 a French Communist Party was founded and affiliated itself to the Comintern. But most French socialists refused to accept the undeviating obedience required by the Comintern. The party of Jaurès, it was said, must not go to Moscow 'with a cord round its neck and ashes on its head'. 'One must be a patriot', said Léon Blum, a brilliant Jewish socialist; Moscow's control in all matters could not be accepted. So communism failed to win much political support. However, for a time communism was strong in the trade unions. In 1924 France recognised the USSR.

On the extreme right Action Francaise (see p. 74) attacked Jews, communists and anyone who favoured reconciliation with Germany. In 1926 Pope Pius XI denounced Action Française. (Diplomatic relations with the papacy, broken off in 1904, were resumed in 1921.)

The Croix de Feu, an ex-servicemen's association, was anti-socialist and anti-internationalist. These and similar groups received support from rich manufacturers as well as from the *petit bourgeoisie*. They also had the support of anti-foreign, anti-republican newspapers, whose campaigns of slander against politicians of the centre and left weakened the will of the people to resist fascism, at home and abroad.

Poincaré's Government of National Union, 1926–29

In the financial crisis of 1926 Poincaré formed a Government of National Union. With power to rule by decree Poincaré increased taxes, cut expenses and 'saved the franc', though it had to be devalued in 1928. In 1928 and 1930 contributory insurance schemes protected workers against sickness, accident and death.

With greater financial stability at home and the atmosphere of greater security abroad that followed the Locarno treaties of 1925 (see p. 198), industry made substantial progress. The return of Alsace-Lorraine had added to manpower and material resources. Heavy industries and mining developed rapidly. Mass production and large factories replaced many of the small plants which had characterised French industry. However, agriculture, protected by high tariffs, remained predominant.

In 1923 France had cut the period of military service from two years to eighteen months. Under Poincaré it was reduced to a year (1928). But between 1929 and 1934 the heavily fortified Maginot line was built, running from the Swiss border and westward along the frontier with Luxembourg. Maginot was minister of defence.

Years of instability

The world depression affected France relatively late. And to some extent unemployment was cushioned by immigrants returning to their home countries. However by 1933 there were 1,300,000 unemployed. Meanwhile, after Poincaré's resignation in 1929, ministries came and went in rapid succession.

The government cut salaries, reduced ex-servicemen's pensions, closed down public works and taxed consumer goods. Such policies failed to get parliamentary support and France remained in a state of on-going crisis – with both communists and fascists mocking the incompetence and corruption of parliamentary democracy.

Paris, February 1934. Right-wing demonstrators in the Champs Élysées just before disturbances broke out

In December 1933 Stavisky, a financier of Russian-Jewish origin, who had connections in high places, apparently committed suicide after floating a fraudulent loan. Newspapers claimed he had been murdered to prevent him betraying his protectors. The prime minister and other ministers were forced to resign. High-ranking police officers were accused of being involved. Extremists of both the left and the right used the Stavisky scandal to discredit the government. In February 1934 an attempted right-wing coup led to rioting in Paris. A few days later there were communist disturbances and a call for a general strike. Daladier, the prime minister, was forced to resign. A coalition Government of National Union then took office.

The Popular Front

At the disarmament conference in 1932–34 (see p. 120) French resistance to German rearmament reflected the alarm caused by the growing power of the Nazis. And the French communists, under Comintern instructions, began in 1934 to seek alliance with other forces of the left. On 14 July 1935, Bastille Day, socialists, radicals and communists marched together to show the solidarity of

their newly formed Popular Front movement. In June 1936 a Popular Front government came to office with the socialist Blum as prime minister. The communists co-operated with the new government but no communist took office. The Popular Front government dissolved the rightist leagues, though some re-emerged as 'constitutional' parties.

An outbreak of strikes, with workers occupying their factories and claiming the right to manage them, revealed the urgency of social problems. The socialist trade union organisation, the *Confédération Générale du Travail* (CGT), and the communist organisation, the *Confédération Générale du Travail Unitaire* (CGTU), amalgamated in a popular front of their own. Thereupon management and labour met at the Hôtel Mâtignon, the prime minister's residence. By the Mâtignon agreement of June 1936 the government established control over the Bank of France. Wage increases were decreed and annual paid holidays made compulsory. A forty-hour working week was instituted but was later modified. Munitions factories were nationalised. The Mâtignon agreement bitterly antagonised men of property. Though the wave of strikes that had led to the agreement abated, industrial unrest did not end. The franc fell in value and Blum, though he had said the gold standard would be maintained, devalued. In 1937 the financial crisis forced him to call a halt in his reform programme. A few weeks later he was forced to resign.

Down the slippery slope

In April 1938, after various changes of government, Daladier, a socialist farther to the right than Blum, became prime minister again. By now defeatism was apparent in France. A sickness in society led to strange movements on the left as well as on the right. Socialist factions broke away from their party and turned towards authoritarianism. Like some of their right-wing compatriots, some of the straying socialists later collaborated with Germany. Well before the outbreak of war the French right had shown itself not unfavourable to Nazism. Right-wing journals heaped abuse upon the government. 'Better Hitler than Blum', they had said. '*A bas la guerre*' (Down with war), shrieked the newspaper *Action Française*. In October 1938 the Popular Front ended when socialists and communists, opposed to appeasing Germany over Czechoslovakia (see p. 206), and aware that Daladier was moving farther to the right, withdrew their support. Daladier, however, retained sufficient support to remain prime minister. In March 1939, when Britain and France guaranteed the independence of Poland (see p. 208), he was given power to rule by decree and was thus able to provide for rearmament and for mobilisation.

Democracy in defeat: Italy

Disillusionment and unrest

Italy too faced war debts, unbalanced budgets, rising prices and considerable unemployment. And Italy was much poorer than France, especially in the south. After the war her landless labourers were in greater difficulties than ever.

Despite the gains she made in the Tyrol and Istria (see p. 114), the legend grew up that Italy had won the war but lost the peace. There was resentment that she had not obtained Dalmatia and had won no 'colonial prizes' – not even a mandate. Hopes of getting Turkish territory in Asia Minor had come to nothing. There was disappointment that Fiume (Rijeka), whose population was mainly Italian, was not given to Italy. In September 1919 Gabriele d'Annunzio, a violently nationalist poet,

led a band of black-shirted men to capture Fiume and proclaimed himself commandant of the city. Meanwhile the Italian government had proclaimed a protectorate over Albania.

Elections were held in November 1919. From then until 1922 there was a succession of liberal prime ministers. But no government had a secure majority. Two new parties had appeared. The People's Party, supported by trade unionists and farm workers, had Catholic affiliations. (In 1919 the pope, fearing the advancing tide of Bolshevism, allowed Italian Catholics to participate fully in political life.) And in 1919 Benito Mussolini founded the Fascist Party. In the 1919 elections the People's Party did well. The Fascists did not win a single seat. Within three years the Fascists were to become the rulers of Italy. The People's Party disappeared from history. Early in 1921 those socialists who were prepared to subject themselves to the Comintern formed the Italian Communist Party.

In June 1920 Giolitti again formed a government. He gave up the claim to a protectorate over Albania. And in November 1920 the Treaty of Rapallo was made with Yugoslavia; Italy gave up her claims to Dalmatia and agreed that Fiume should become a free city. Giolitti then sent a battleship to Fiume to bombard d'Annunzio's palace. D'Annunzio and his followers made a rapid escape.

In the autumn of 1920 Italy appeared to be engaged in an all-out class war. Workers occupied factories and set up committees to operate them. Giolitti eventually persuaded them, in return for concessions, to return to work. Meanwhile farm labourers were banding together against their employers. In some areas they seized land. Landlords began to offer armed resistance. Some of the land leagues in turn began to form armed squads. Meanwhile the restrictions on immigration to the USA (see p. 156) removed an important safety valve. Before the war half a million Italians every year had migrated to North and South America.

Parliament was dissolved in April 1921. Giolitti retired from political life. In the elections which followed the People's Party and the socialists did well. There was a good number of liberals but they were disunited. And there were fifteen communists and thirty-five Fascists in the new parliament. Again government was in the hands of a feeble liberal coalition.

Mussolini and the Fascist Party

In these circumstances Benito Mussolini, a former

socialist agitator, rose to power. Born in 1883, Mussolini was named after Benito Juárez, a Mexican reformer (see p. 260). He became a schoolteacher and journalist. He was frequently in trouble on account of his socialist activities. In 1912 he became editor of the socialist newspaper *Avanti!* (Forward!). Mussolini at that time was an opponent of war. When Italy seized Libya in 1912 he said: 'The Fatherland is a spook.' But once the First World War began he resigned from *Avanti!* and ran a paper called *Il Popolo d'Italia* (The People of Italy), whose front page carried two slogans: 'The man who has iron has bread.' 'Bayonets turn ideas into revolution.' When Italy joined the Allies in the First World War Mussolini enlisted and was wounded – and drew attention to himself by stumping about on crutches well after he was able to walk.

The disorders of post-war Italy gave Mussolini his opportunity. Unwilling to commit himself to any political creed until he had a sufficient following, he only gradually abandoned socialism. His pre-war ties with the left continued to gain him followers. The fact that as a blacksmith's son he was 'of the people' was, he said, 'a trump card' for him.

Mussolini's Fascist Party was composed of *fascio* (groups) *di combattimento*. The party name had connections with the idea of force; the *fasces* were bundles of rods carried before a magistrate in ancient Rome. Fascist Party members wore a uniform, from which came their name Blackshirts. From the start they were strongly nationalist.

During the disorders of 1920 Fascists and socialist 'red guards' frequently fought against one another. The Fascists with their better organisation usually won. They built up a nationwide organisation – in 1920 there were 120 Fascist squads, a year later there were 2,300. They burned down the offices and printing presses of the socialists. They terrorised their opponents by forcing them to drink bottles of castor oil or swallow live toads. Sometimes they beat them with rubber hoses. Occasionally they murdered them. By such means they crushed trade unions – and set up rival syndicates in their stead.

A general strike in the summer of 1922 gave the Fascists the opportunity to 'restore order' – and to seize control of such cities as Milan, Genoa and Leghorn (Livorno). In Milan they burned down the offices of *Avanti!* and drove the socialists out of the town hall. As the government was too weak to deal with the strike the illegal actions of the Fascists won them popular support. Landlords and industrialists sympathised with a movement which stood for strike breaking and lower wages and hostility to communism.

Meanwhile Mussolini decided to abandon anti-clericalism and republicanism and so won support among Catholics and the military. Demobilised officers, unemployed white collar workers, hoodlums from all sections of society flocked to the support of Fascism. The middle class, fearing revolution from the left, showed little awareness of the dangers of revolution from the right. By the autumn of 1922 the Fascists were a very large political army.

The 'March on Rome'; Fascist government

In October 1922 Mussolini demanded a share in the government of Italy. For a few hours the prime minister considered ordering the army into action against the Fascists. Meanwhile thousands of well armed Black-shirts guarded the roads to Rome and other strategic places. The prime minister resigned. On 28 October Mussolini, wearing a black shirt, spats over his shoes, and a bowler hat, went by train from Milan to Rome. There he accepted Victor Emmanuel III's invitation to become prime minister. So this so-called 'March on Rome' was peacefully concluded. Only four Fascists held office in Mussolini's first cabinet. He himself was given dictatorial powers for a year.

By a law passed in 1923 the party gaining the largest number of votes in an election was to occupy two-thirds of the seats in the Chamber of Deputies. In 1924 the Fascist Party swept to victory in the elections; the days of ineffective coalitions were over. However, all opposition was not stilled. In 1924 Giacomo Matteotti, a rich socialist deputy, published *The Fascists Exposed*. Soon after, Matteotti was murdered by Fascist agents. Mussolini, it seems, was not directly involved. The outcry caused by Matteotti's murder seemed to threaten the Fascist régime. Opposition newspapers were therefore suppressed or taken under Fascist control. Most of the non-Fascists then quit the Chamber of Deputies. Their withdrawal is known as the Aventine secession. (In early Roman times the plebs withdrew from Rome to the Aventine Hill in protest against despotic rule.) After the Aventine secession only a handful of liberals and communists remained in opposition.

During 1925 and 1926 four attempts were made on Mussolini's life. Il Duce (the Leader), as he became known, showed cool courage. On the second occasion it was a woman who shot at him – the bullet just grazed his nose. 'Fancy', said Mussolini, 'a woman!' After his face had been bandaged, he shouted: 'If I go forward, follow me! If I go back, kill me! If I die, avenge me!' A Fascist official called to the cheering crowds: 'God has put his finger on the Duce. He is Italy's greatest son, the rightful heir of Caesar.' The crowds replied: 'Duce! Duce! We are yours to the end!'

After the fourth attempt on Mussolini's life censorship was strengthened, 'anti-national' parties (socialists, communists, republicans) were dissolved and secret societies forbidden. Opponents of Fascism were packed off to the inhospitable Lipari Islands off the coast of Sicily. In 1926 Mussolini was again given power to govern by decree; no time limit was imposed. His few remaining opponents in the Chamber of Deputies withdrew.

In 1928 the franchise was much reduced, though as the Chamber of Deputies no longer had any power this was of little significance. At the same time the Grand Council of Fascism became an official organisation which nominated all parliamentary candidates and was consulted on all important matters. At elections in 1929 only a few thousand people dared to vote against the government. The Chamber of Deputies, shorn of all authority, survived in name until 1938.

Special tribunals which met in secret and from which there was no appeal dealt with political crimes. In fact most opposition leaders went into voluntary exile. The Fascist squads became a security militia. In 1938, by which time Italy was under the shadow of Germany, the Grand Council recommended excluding Jews from the army, the civil service and certain professions, but not much was done about this.

Totalitarianism

Mussolini, whilst preserving the monarchy, had created a new political form. Democracy, he claimed, was a sham; party government and freedom of expression divided and weakened the state; authority and strong leadership were needed to restore Italy. But his state was more than authoritarian; it was totalitarian, for it concerned itself with the total of things, with the total activities of its citizens – their work, their religion, their culture, even their private lives. 'The state', said Mussolini, 'is absolute, whereas groups and individuals are relative.' To the state, said Mussolini, the citizen owes total and unquestioning obedience. Totalitarianism is a form of absolutism that magnifies the importance of the state at the expense of the individual. Mussolini claimed that his totalitarian rule was based

Mussolini and Hitler, the dictators of Italy and Germany – Hitler half a pace ahead

on popular approval. But mostly the 'popular support' was won by Fascist propaganda – and, when propaganda failed, by Fascist force. Like many dictatorships, Fascism was established in time of crisis. But the Fascist state was intended to outlast the crisis in which it was born, indeed, to endure for a thousand years.

The Fascists supplemented the old weapons of absolutism – secret police and censorship – with modern propaganda that used the popular press and school textbooks, the radio and cinema to indoctrinate the citizens of Italy. Il Duce himself exercised a hypnotic power. The Italians thought as he thought. To some he was a god. His photograph adorned every home.

Fascist achievements

Outside Italy, until the war against Ethiopia (see p. 201), there was considerable praise for Mussolini. Churchill, for example, admired the order and discipline he gave Italy.

Mussolini claimed to have developed an alternative to both communism and capitalism, what he called the corporative state in which private enterprise remained important but in which the state intervened as it thought fit. From 1934 there was emphasis on a planned economy. State participation in industry resulted in a top heavy bureaucracy and was enormously expensive.

Mussolini aimed to make Italy economically self-sufficient, for example in wheat. But 'the battle for wheat' involved the destruction of vineyards and olive orchards which had taken years to grow and the production of wheat at artificially high prices. The production of textiles and of hydro-electric power advanced. But the development of heavy industry sometimes required the protection of uneconomic cartels (combines).

Great public works helped to reduce unemployment. Highways, the *autostrade*, were built. The railways were electrified. Millions of trees were planted. Near Rome the draining of the Pontine marshes, formerly useless because of the presence of malaria-carrying mosquitoes, brought much land under cultivation. In general the south remained desperately poor, though roads and railways were built in an attempt to reduce its isolation.

One of Mussolini's first actions was to make both strikes and lockouts illegal. Hours of work were increased. On the other hand, rent and price controls helped workers. In 1926 corporations formed of representatives of management and labour were set up to fix wages and hours of work. Trade unions then became illegal. Disputes were settled by compulsory arbitration. An organisation called *Dopo Lavoro* (After Work) provided interest for leisure hours and trained workers to be good Fascists. Youth organisations had similar aims.

A high birth rate was encouraged. Large families were given economic assistance but bachelors had to pay a special tax. Babies were valued as an addition to the nation's manpower. And overpopulation was a useful argument when trying to persuade other countries of Italy's need for colonies. In fact the birth rate declined.

A partial economic recovery was followed by the world depression. Mussolini then turned to foreign adventures to distract a discontented people.

Catholic unions and parties had been dissolved along with others. However, Il Duce wanted the support of Catholicism. Though he himself was superstitious rather than religious – he once referred to Christ as 'insignificant' – religious instruction was made compulsory and a crucifix was placed in all schools. In 1929 the Lateran treaties were signed with the pope. Catholicism was recognised as the state religion. The papacy recognised the Italian state, whilst Italy recognised the sovereignty of the tiny Vatican City state (see p. 77). The church accepted compensation for property acquired earlier by the Italian state.

Over the years Mussolini became increasingly intolerant of criticism. He was unaware of his limitations. At one time he held the posts of prime minister, foreign minister, minister of the interior, president of the Grand Council of Fascism, minister for corporations, commander in chief of the militia and minister of the army, navy and air force.

There was often a wide gap between what was set down on paper and what was achieved under Fascism. Fascism became increasingly unwieldy corrupt and inefficient. Among the discontented people who left Italy in the 1930s was her greatest scientist, Enrico Fermi (see p. 225).

Germany: democracy in difficulties

The establishment of the Weimar Republic

Imperial Germany came to an end on 9 November 1918 when a republic was proclaimed with Ebert, one time saddle maker and union organiser, as chancellor (see p. 110).

Ebert was a Social Democrat, a parliamentary socialist. The more extreme socialists were the Spartacists, led by Carl Liebknecht and Rosa Luxemburg. (Spartacus was the leader of a Roman slave revolt.) In January 1919 the Spartacists became the German Communist Party.

In the early months of the republic armed mobs roamed the streets. Soldiers' and workers' soviets claimed the right to direct affairs. Bavaria and other states set up revolutionary governments. Meanwhile, until July 1919 Germany remained in the grip of the Allied blockade. Thousands of people were close to starvation and thousands of children were suffering from tuberculosis.

So great was the unrest that Ebert decided to use armed force to restore order. As the army itself was in disorder he turned to the free corps, volunteer units led by former army officers which had sprung up all over the country. The free corps were ill-trained and undisciplined. They were violently opposed to communism. In January 1919 they quickly put down a Spartacist revolt in Berlin. Liebknecht and Luxemburg were brutally murdered. In March 1919, during a general strike, the free corps were let loose in Berlin; over a thousand people were killed. In May 1919 free corps units overthrew the Bavarian soviet. For weeks a white terror raged in the streets of Munich.

In January 1919 elections for a National Constituent Assembly were held. In this assembly Social Democrats predominated. Because of the disorder in Berlin the assembly met in Weimar, Goethe's old town.

The constitution drawn up at Weimar in February 1919 gave its name to the new Germany – the Weimar Republic. The Weimar constitution guaranteed civil liberties to all citizens. Women were enfranchised. The president, elected by popular vote, held office for seven years and appointed the chancellor. The cabinet ministers, selected by the chancellor, were responsible to the lower legislative house, the Reichstag. However, the president could assume special powers, including the suspension of civil liberties, during a national emergency. Like the empire, the republic was a federation, though the powers of the central government were wider than before – in particular it now had the right to impose direct taxes. The second house, the Reichsrat, in which state representatives sat, could only delay legislation. The first president of the Weimar Republic was Ebert, the moderate socialist.

Troubles of the Weimar Republic

The Weimar Republic never had the full support of the German people. Businessmen, army officers and the Prussian *junkers* had no wish to see the republic endure. The educational system remained a stronghold of uncritical nationalism. In 1919, during an enquiry into the causes of Germany's defeat, Hindenburg asserted that 'a British general' had said that German politicians – 'the November criminals' – and revolutionaries in Kiel, Hamburg and Berlin had 'stabbed the reich in the back'. The army, said Hindenburg, disregarding the facts, had not been defeated. Scorn for 'the defeatists and traitors' who sent the kaiser into exile and accepted the armistice and the Treaty of Versailles became widespread. In 1921 Erzberger, a signatory of the armistice, was murdered. Rathenau was assassinated in 1922 because as foreign minister he recognised that the Treaty of Versailles must be complied with – and he was a Jew.

Social unrest and fears of a communist revolution continued to trouble Germany. The middle and upper classes remained uncomfortably aware that Marx had said that Germany would be the leader in world revolution. Army cuts required by the Treaty of Versailles left many officers and men without occupation and discontented.

In March 1920 Wolfgang Kapp attempted a right-wing coup. Kapp was supported by free corps units that were about to be disbanded. Some of them wore the swastika, the hooked cross badge. As the army was unwilling to fight against fellow servicemen Ebert withdrew from Berlin. The free corps marched on Berlin, proclaimed Kapp chancellor and urged the restoration of the kaiser. However trade unionists called a general strike and the Kapp putsch was thwarted. In Munich another right-wing coup attempted to set up a separate Bavarian government. In Berlin the failure of right-wing activities was followed by fresh communist activity. The army showed no objection to dealing with this.

At elections in 1920 the Social Democrats, who had protected Germany from extremists of both right and left, lost ground. After that government was by unstable coalitions, the Catholic Centre Party uniting either with socialists or with more conservative groups supported by the army.

In 1922 Germany and the infant USSR signed the Treaty of Rapallo which established diplomatic relations and commercial ties between the two countries. Under cover of these ties Germany was able to re-arm secretly in the USSR. With the connivance of Hans von Seeckt, German commander in chief, tank and air force units trained in the USSR. The German right wing favoured the tie with the USSR. The link between the two states was hostility to Poland – who had taken territory from both Germany and the Soviet Union (see p. 113).

Reparations

Germany, had she won the First World War, would doubtless have demanded heavy reparations. The Allies were in some confusion on the subject. An American expert said: 'Some ... wanted to destroy Germany, some wanted to collect reparations, and others wanted to do both ... to take all her capital, destroy her and then collect a large reparations bill.' In 1921 the Allies fixed reparations at £6,600 million – a sum which may now sound trifling but which was then crippling. It included not only compensation for damage to civilians and their property but the cost of pensions to ex-servicemen. Payable over thirty years, the bulk of reparations was to go to France. But no one had thought out how payments were to be made. Meanwhile the USA and Britain were

Inflation: one billion mark bank note issued in Cologne (Köln) and signed by Adenauer (see p. 285). Issued on 25 October 1923, shortly before the rentenmark was introduced

insisting on repayment of war debts by France and other states.

During 1922 Germany found it increasingly difficult to meet her reparations commitments and in January 1923 was in default with coal deliveries from the Ruhr. French and Belgian troops then occupied the Ruhr in an attempt to force delivery. Ebert decided on a policy of passive resistance. German workers in the Ruhr went on strike, leaving the French and Belgians to work the mines themselves. The French then imposed an economic blockade, cutting off the Ruhr and most of the Rhineland from the rest of Germany.

The Ruhr occupation proved disastrous to both Germany and France. By the end of 1923 only 29 per cent of the German work force was fully employed. The government resorted to 'borrowing' to meet its liabilities – in fact to printing money. The German mark fell catastrophically until even a postage stamp cost millions of marks. The inflation was felt particularly by the middle class whose savings became worthless; their support of the Weimar Republic, already grudging, declined. Skilled workers with modest savings and

people on pensions were also hit – and withdrew their support from the republic.

By the summer of 1923 a mood of despair filled Germany. A general strike threatened. There was an upsurge of communism. In August 1923 Gustav Stresemann, an industrialist and leader of the People's (Liberal) Party, became chancellor. With Ebert's support, he took the courageous step of ordering the Ruhr strikers back to work and accepted Germany's responsibility for reparations. With the establishment towards the end of 1923 of a new currency, the rentenmark, economic recovery began. At the same time negotiations began for the withdrawal of the French and Belgians from the Ruhr.

Adolf Hitler and the Munich putsch

Adolf Hitler was born in Austria in 1889. He lived a drifting life until the First World War. He served as a corporal in a Bavarian regiment, was twice decorated with the Iron Cross and almost blinded by gas. After his discharge he took up political work in Munich with the object of overthrowing the Versailles settlement. By 1921 he was leader (Führer) of a small party called the National Socialist (Nazi) German Workers' Party. (Nazi is the German pronunciation of the letters NS.) The use of socialist in the party name was a sop to attract the gullible; Hitler in fact hated socialists. The Nazi badge was the swastika. Nazis wore brown shirts – hence the name Brownshirts. By the autumn of 1923 Hitler had some 15,000 followers. His most eminent supporter was Ludendorff, who had taken part in the Kapp putsch. Others were Hermann Goering, an air force ace, the crippled Joseph Goebbels, doctor of philosophy, and Ernst Röhm, a former free corps officer.

Munich was the headquarters of a Bavarian rightist separatist movement. Army units stationed in Bavaria were forced to take an oath of loyalty to the state government. Amid the difficulties of 1923 Hitler tried to take advantage of this situation. On the evening of 8 November 1923 he attempted to force the hands of the Bavarian leaders. In their presence, in a Munich beer hall, surrounded by 600 of his followers, Hitler proclaimed a provisional national government. But during the night the Bavarian nationalists withdrew their halfhearted support. In the morning the local army commander, submitting to orders from Berlin, surrounded Nazis assembled outside Munich. Meanwhile, Hitler, Ludendorff and about 2,000 supporters set out from the beer hall for the centre of Munich. Police who blocked their way opened fire. Ludendorff alone did not quail. Goering, badly wounded, escaped to Austria. Hitler, with a dislocated shoulder, and Ludendorff were arrested.

Following the Beer Hall putsch Hitler was sentenced to five years imprisonment for treason but was released after eight months. In his comfortable prison room he received numerous visitors to whom he aired his views on the future of Germany. And he began writing the book, *Mein Kampf* (My Struggle), in which he set forth his political ideas. It later became a best seller.

In *Mein Kampf* Hitler looked forward to the establishment of a Third Reich (so called as the successor to Charlemagne's Holy Roman Empire and Bismarck's *reich*) which would restore Germany to her dominant place in Europe. He took up the legend of the stab in the back (see p. 180) and argued that Germany was encircled by her enemies, that she was the 'Have-not state' in a world of greedy 'Haves'. Yet the Germans, he said, were by right the master people, the *Herrenvolk*, supreme among the Aryans – who in turn were superior to all other races. The *Herrenvolk*, he claimed, should have *lebensraum*, room to live and develop and grow in number. He attacked the Jews, of whom there were many in Germany. They were 'an inferior race' who profited while Germans suffered. At the same time he equated these 'rich and crafty' Jews with communism.

After the Munich putsch Hitler and his associates built up the hard core of the Nazi Party. While Hitler engaged in propaganda Röhm organised strong-arm squads, the SA (*Sturmabteilungen*, Stormtroopers), to protect party meetings and attack socialists, communists and Jews. To outsiders the Nazis appeared little more than a lunatic fringe.

More hopeful years: the Dawes and Young plans

After 1923, uneasily balanced coalitions in which various parties had to be represented paid little regard to the national interest. And early in 1925 President Ebert, who had exercised a steadying influence, died. Nationalist opponents of socialism and the Versailles settlement managed to bring about the election of Field Marshal Hindenburg, then aged seventy-seven, as president. At heart a monarchist, Hindenburg loyally served the republic.

In 1925 Germany entered a period of relative prosperity. This was based on Stresemann's commitment to a policy of fulfilment: only by fulfilling the terms of the peace treaty, he argued, could Germany hope to negotiate any bettering of those terms. This statesmanlike policy, constantly under attack from nationalists, brought a relaxation of Franco-German relations. Stresemann, chancellor for a few months in 1923, continued as foreign minister until his death in 1929. He was supported by Briand, French foreign minister almost without a break from 1925 to early in 1932, and by Austen Chamberlain, British foreign secretary from 1924 to 1929. All three were awarded Nobel peace prizes.

Stresemann's decision to end resistance in the Ruhr led to a British proposal to reconsider reparations. General Dawes, an American, was appointed to head a team of financial experts. In 1924 the Dawes plan was accepted. This was a businesslike scheme for Germany to meet her reparations, and at the same time to receive large loans from the USA. American credit, in addition to enabling Germany to comply with the Dawes plan, provided money which was used, for example, for municipal development. Such amenities as health services were extended; indeed, Germany at this time fared better than some of the victor states. The fact that the president of the Reichsbank, Hjalmar Schacht, was able to borrow abroad more money than was required for reparations did much to secure the support of the businessmen who dominated German political life.

With Germany's acceptance of the Dawes plan the French and Belgians withdrew from the Ruhr. The next step forward was Stresemann's proposal for an international guarantee of existing frontiers in western Europe. The Locarno pact which resulted in 1925 (see p. 198) was followed by Germany's admission to the League of Nations, with a permanent seat on the council (1926). Said Hans Luther, the chancellor: 'We were a people of helots, and today we are once more a state of world consequence.'

Stresemann's next objectives were the early evacuation of the Rhineland by the Allies and a further review of reparations. In 1929 an international board, headed by an American banker, Owen D. Young, prepared a new plan. The Young plan reduced the sum fixed in 1921 by about three-quarters and provided for instalment payments until 1988. Hindenburg said the new agreements were 'a step forward . . . along the hard path of Germany's re-establishment and liberation'. But acceptance of the plan in itself implied renewed acceptance of war guilt. This caused a tremendous outcry by the Nationalist Party, led by the newspaper and film magnate Alfred Hugenberg. In compensation Stresemann demanded the withdrawal of occupation forces from the Rhineland by 1930. Snowden, Britain's representative at the talks, who was anxious to reduce military expenditure, persuaded France to give way. A few weeks later Stresemann died.

Economic crisis: Brüning

During 1929 an economic crisis had been building up in Germany. By spring a million and a half men were on unemployment relief – and the cost to the state was proving excessive. In the autumn came the Wall Street crash. The flow of loans from America which had enabled Germany to meet her reparations liabilities and to expand her economy dried up. For almost a year a political struggle went on – the Nationalists demanding lower rates of unemployment relief and a means test, the Social Democrats unwilling to take such steps but unable to increase taxes. In the spring of 1930 Müller, the Social Democrat chancellor, gave up the struggle. Unlike Ramsay MacDonald about a year later he was unable to cling to power in the new government which emerged.

Heinrich Brüning, leader of the Catholic Centre Party and organiser of the resistance in the Ruhr in 1923, formed a crisis government. As chancellor (1930–32) Brüning showed an increasing inclination to work with big business and the nationalists of the right and to make the president use his emergency powers to force through legislation. In an effort to win support by going one better than the Nazis and other extremists he demanded the return of the Saar, remilitarisation of the Rhineland, abolition of the Polish Corridor and so on. When in 1931 Brüning proposed a customs union with Austria, France and other states objected (see p. 116). When the disarmament conference began in 1932 the French were still suspicious of Germany's intentions (see p. 120).

Germany: democracy defeated

The Nazis in the ascendant

In elections in 1928 the Nazis won twelve seats in the Reichstag. The Social Democrats and the communists did much better. In 1929 Hitler's fortunes began to improve. A compact with Hugenberg during the anti-Young plan campaign gave him respectability, and an outlet for propaganda through Hugenberg's films and newspapers. And money for the Nazis came from a powerful Ruhr industrialist, Fritz Thyssen, to whom aggressive nationalism – Nazi-style or otherwise – offered a cure for socialism.

The economic crisis that began in 1929 brought disillusionment with the policy of fulfilment. The Germans began to renew their faith in the old gods – nationalism and militarism. Following elections a few months after Brüning became chancellor the Nazis became the second largest party in the Reichstag with 108 seats.

In June 1931 Germany announced that she could not pay the instalment of reparations then due. President Hoover then proposed that payment of all international debts should be postponed for a year. To this France had to agree. Later that year the reparations committee reported that further payments were inadvisable and impossible. No payments were made after 1931 – though Nazis and other nationalists clamoured for the formal abolition of reparations. In all, Germany had paid an eighth of the original amount fixed. She had received in loans, mostly from the USA, more than she had paid out.

In 1931 Hugenberg, Schacht and others, fearing revolution from the left, made an alliance with Hitler in opposition to Brüning. The *Stahlhelm* (Steel Helmets), a nationalist ex-servicemen's association, and Hitler's Brownshirt army gave the alliance physical support. Hitler and his propaganda chief, Dr Goebbels, continued to stir up resentment against the 'dictated peace'. They pointed out the dangers of being disarmed and encircled by well armed neighbours. Once Germany was powerful again, Hitler told the workers, they would be better off. But the workers mostly remained loyal to socialism; some turned to the communists. It was more affluent people who, in their fear of unemployed workers with communist leanings, fell for Nazi propaganda. In happier times sober Germans might have restrained Hitler's excesses. In those unhappy years they applauded him and voted for him. And terrorism silenced those who disapproved.

The presidential election, 1932

In 1932 there was a presidential election. Hitler entered the contest. Brüning persuaded Hindenburg to stand for re-election. Hindenburg disliked Hitler, the arrogant former corporal, who was not even born in Germany. During the election campaign there was bloody fighting between the 'armies' of the left and right. Hindenburg had the support of Brüning's Catholic Centre Party, of the Social Democrats, the trade unions and the Jews. Hitler was supported by the upper classes of the Protestant north, by the industrialists of the Ruhr and the Rhineland, by conservative agriculturists – and by the former crown prince. Hindenburg won nineteen million votes, Hitler won thirteen million and the communist candidate nearly four million.

Von Papen and the Nazis

Within a few weeks of the elections Brüning, who had banned the activities of the Stormtroopers (SA) and of Hitler's bodyguard, the élite *Schutzstaffeln* (Defence Squads), the black-shirted SS, was forced to resign. The new chancellor, Fritz von Papen, was supported by the Nationalist Party, which represented big business and the old aristocracy. Lacking a majority in the Reichstag, von Papen sought Nazi support by lifting Brüning's ban. The effect was seen in elections in July 1932 when there was violent street fighting between Nazis, and communists and socialists. Hitler set a precedent during the campaign by touring the country in an aeroplane.

After the elections the Nazis were the largest party in the Reichstag, with 230 seats. The communists had 89 seats, von Papen's Nationalist Party won only 44. But Hindenburg refused to have Hitler as chancellor. 'That man for a chancellor', he said, 'I'll make him a postmaster and he can lick the stamps with my head on them.' Von Papen carried on until November 1932 when the threat of a Nazi vote of no confidence forced him to call another election. This time the Nazis won 197 seats. The communists increased their seats to 100. General von Schleicher, who had intrigued against Müller, Brüning and von Papen one after the other, became chancellor – but only for a few weeks.

The Nazis, in addition to losing ground in the Reichstag, were short of money. There were insufficient funds even to pay Hitler's bodyguard – who briefly mutinied. But Hitler's luck held. Von Papen and Hugenberg negotiated with him for an alliance. In return Hitler demanded the chancellorship for himself and enormous funds for his party. Von Papen concluded the bargain early in January 1933. 'We have hired him', said von Papen. 'Within two months we will have pushed Hitler so far into the corner that he'll squeak.'

Chancellor Hitler: the Enabling Act

At the end of January von Schleicher was forced to resign. Hindenburg refused to send for Hitler. Von Papen was ordered to negotiate with him. Hitler would consent to nothing less for himself than the chancellorship – as von Papen had promised. He demanded also a promise that the president would consent to an enabling act that would empower him to rule by decree. He demanded an early dissolution of the Reichstag and elections. Von Papen apparently convinced Hindenburg that under Hitler the old Germany would live again, would again be a power in the world. Hitler might even restore the Hohenzollern dynasty. And Hitler would stop the communists. So the old man gave way and on 30 January 1933 Hitler became chancellor of Germany. There were two Nazis in his cabinet: the minister of the interior with control of the police and Hitler's chief aide, Goering.

Another election campaign got under way. The Stormtroopers, armed as auxiliary police, carried violence into the streets, breaking up the meetings of other parties with complete disregard for the law.

In the early hours of 27 February 1933 someone set fire to the Reichstag building. Was the fire the work of the half-witted van der Lubbe, a Dutchman caught

Adolf Hitler, chancellor of Germany, with President Hindenburg and Hermann Goering in 1934

loitering near by and later tried and executed? Or was it the work of the SS? The facts are still not clear. What is clear is the use to which the Nazis put the Reichstag fire. Within twenty-four hours the Communist Party had been abolished and 4,000 of its members arrested. And Hitler secured from the president an emergency decree suspending the basic rights of citizens and giving the government unlimited powers to arrest, imprison or execute without trial.

The elections were held in March 1933. In spite of the emergency decree and a decree giving the government complete control of the press and radio, the Nazis did not get overwhelming support. With the support of von Papen's Nationalists Hitler had a bare majority of 52 per cent in the Reichstag.

But the Nazis were in power. The police forces, which had been under the control of the states, were brought under the reich minister of the interior. The SA were then free to wreak their vengeance on all opponents – socialists, Jews, communists, pacifists – high or low. Brüning was hunted from house to house. Concentration camps were opened into which 'enemies of the third reich' were to be thrown – without trial, and with little hope of release.

When on 23 March the Reichstag met in a Berlin opera house the streets were filled with yelling SA and SS men. Communist deputies who had so far escaped arrest did not attend. The socialists alone dared oppose the enabling bill that Hitler put before the Reichstag. The Enabling Act transferred the power to make laws and even to amend the constitution from the Reichstag to Hitler. The Enabling Act in effect destroyed the Weimar constitution. The Third Reich with Hitler as dictator came into being. The one remaining check on Nazi power was Hitler's promise to consult the president.

Germany: the totalitarian state

Terror and propaganda

'No enabling act', said the chairman of the Social Democrats, 'can give you the power to destroy ideas that are eternal and indestructible.' Hitler did his utmost to destroy such ideas, to destroy liberty as well as his opponents. After the passing of the Enabling Act he acted with speed to establish his totalitarian state in which everybody and everything were subject to his will.

Already freedom of speech and freedom from arbitrary arrest had been suspended. Already the government had control of the press and radio. In April 1933 Goering set up the Secret State Police, the Gestapo (*Geheime Staatspolizei*) – political spies with power to arrest and punish without trial. The Germans lived in dread of the midnight hammering on the door that was followed by the swift disappearance into the bottomless pits of the concentration camps. Sir John Wheeler-Bennett, an historian who was in Germany during Hitler's rise to power, wrote:

'The technique of conducting a successful system of terror is to terrorise the maximum number of people with the minimum amount of effort. . . . The art lies in the use of the spot-check. . . . One closed the door carefully and conducted conversations in a whisper. One looked over one's shoulder in a public place before speaking. One did not trust the mails. One chose with great care the rendezvous where one met one's friends.'

In 1934 the cruel and pitiless Heinrich Himmler, who already controlled the SS, took control of the Gestapo. In 1936 the Gestapo was freed from any control by the courts.

The Nazis used every device of propaganda. In March 1933 Hitler made Goebbels minister of enlightenment and propaganda. For Goebbels no falsehood was too blatant. He imposed the strictest of censorships. By the end of 1934 newspapers printed only the Nazi version of the news. Every office, factory, restaurant and public place – and most homes – had its radio through which Goebbels or Hitler himself sought to control the minds of the German people. At party rallies in Nüremberg young and old, mesmerised by Hitler's voice, screamed their blind adulation.

The concentration of power

In April 1933 the civil service came under Nazi control. Officials who were not 'politically reliable' or who could not prove they were of pure Aryan descent were dismissed. Even judges were expected to obey party instructions. From time to time there were show trials with pre-arranged results. In 1934 people's courts, presided over by party members, were empowered to try all cases of treason – a word given a wide definition.

In May 1933 trade unions were abolished and their funds seized. Later a Labour Front which included representatives of employers and employees was formed to control industry – under Nazi orders.

In July 1933 the Nazis became the only legal political party. The Communist Party had already been abolished whilst the Catholic Centre Party had dissolved itself. Now the Social Democrats and even the Nationalist Party ceased to exist. The Reichstag became nothing but a stage for Hitler.

During 1933 the powers of the state governments were undermined. In January 1934 their parliaments were dissolved and the state governors, Nazi appointees, were given power to rule by decree. The Reichsrat was abolished.

The Night of the Long Knives

By 1934 the SA had increased to well over a million men and had absorbed the Nationalist Party's strong arm, the *Stahlhelm*. Hitler was aware that the army was jealous of the power of the SA and its ambitious leader, Röhm. The army was more important to him than the SA. And Hitler, once in power, no longer needed the SA for mob control and street fighting. He had Himmler's smaller but more efficient SS to support him. Moreover, Röhm and other SA leaders were homosexuals and so anathema to many Nazis. Many SA members for their part were disillusioned by Hitler's failure to carry out the 'socialist' programme of the National Socialist (Nazi) Party.

On the night of 30 June 1934, the Night of the Long Knives, Hitler with three companions flew to Munich. There, at the head of a party of SS, he drove to the house of his close friend, Röhm. Within a few hours Röhm and many other SA leaders had been seized and shot. Meanwhile Goering and Himmler had carried out a similar operation in Berlin. Among the victims was General von Schleicher, who had been plotting with Röhm. One former Nazi leader was taken away from dinner with his family; his ashes were later delivered at their front door. Von Papen, who had made a bold speech attacking Nazi methods, was spared but some of his associates were arrested. Altogether about a hundred people – not all of them SA members – were murdered. After the purge Hitler said: 'In those twenty-four hours I was the supreme court of Germany.' Such he was to be for another eleven years.

Himmler, as well as controlling the SS and the Gestapo, later took charge of the police throughout Germany. He also controlled the concentration camps. A special section of the SS, the Order of the Death's

Head, was put in charge of the camps. With all the weapons of terror at their command the SS were the effective rulers of Germany.

Hitler, the Führer

President Hindenburg's death in August 1934 removed the last check on Hitler's power. No new president was elected. Hitler, still chancellor, simply took for himself the title Führer (Leader). Every officer and man in the armed forces then gave a solemn oath of 'unconditional obedience to the Führer of the German reich and volk (people)'. To the very end officers and men felt themselves bound by their oath. And in a plebiscite held two weeks after Hindenburg's death 90 per cent of the people accepted Hitler as head of the German state.

Hitler, with an element of truth, later said: 'My pride is that I know no statesman in the world who with greater right than I can say that he is the representative of his people.' The Weimar Republic that he overthrew was a democracy. Democracy, rule by the people, is today a catch-cry the world over. More than two thousand years ago Aristotle warned that democracy can easily slide into despotism, for especially in a time of emergency a democracy may vote away its powers to a despot. That is what the Germans did. Already disillusioned, they were hoodwinked by propaganda and terrorised by strong-arm tactics into voting away their democratic liberties to Adolf Hitler, their Führer.

Economic recovery

Under Hitler Germany appeared to prosper. The world depression was receding. Great public works, not unlike those started by Roosevelt in the USA, were undertaken – for example the *autobahnen*, the national network of highways. Private industry, especially the manufacture of machinery, was assisted. The building industry was encouraged. In 1934 a rapid expansion of the armaments industry began. Production of synthetic fuel, rubber and other products was undertaken so that Germany would not be dependent on imports. Agreements were made with twenty-five states, mainly in South America and the Balkans, to buy German goods in exchange for credits. The introduction of conscription in 1935 eased unemployment. By 1936 there was little unemployment in Germany.

Rearmament was accomplished with no noticeable reduction in living standards. Wages were strictly controlled but so were prices. By 1939 many people had

radios and vacuum cleaners and various electrical appliances. Many workers were thinking of buying a Volkswagen. The Germans seemed able to have both 'guns and butter'. But were they? Germany was less well armed than was then realised. For Hitler, it seems, kept the workers contented at the expense of deficiencies in armaments. And because of a decline in agriculture it was necessary to import more food, mainly from eastern Europe. However, until well after the outbreak of war in 1939, particularly as loot from conquests continued to flow in, living standards remained high.

Women, children and workers

Unlike other west European states Germany under Hitler had a rising birth rate. Marriage loans were offered, there were tax allowances for dependent children and other benefits were given to mothers. The task of girls, the Nazis taught, was to bear healthy children for Hitler.

From birth the upbringing and education of children came under Nazi control. Children were taught to spy on their parents and teachers. They were taught that might is right and that they belonged to the master race. They were taught to live and die for their Führer. Textbooks – especially history books – were rewritten to conform with Hitler's beliefs. Intensive physical training 'hardened [children] for the demands to be made on them in later years'. In 1936 membership of the Hitler Youth organisations became compulsory between the ages of ten and eighteen.

By 1939 a decline in educational standards was apparent. Admission to universities depended more upon enthusiasm for Nazism than upon scholastic ability. Many older teachers resigned, went abroad or were replaced by young Nazis who showed little devotion to learning. 'We don't want to think', said their students, 'only to believe and do.'

In 1933 in Nüremberg – and later in other cities – there was a spectacular burning of books and pictures that offended Nazi beliefs. With a few exceptions, writers, artists, musicians, scientists who did not toady to the Nazis found themselves in trouble – or left the country. The only art that flourished was the cinema which had the special protection of Goebbels.

The German Labour Front formed after the trade unions were abolished set out to educate workers in devotion to National Socialism. The Strength through Joy movement gave them all sorts of recreational opportunities – sports and cultural programmes, travel

Hitler Youth saluting their Führer during a parade in Berlin. They sang: 'We march for Hitler through night and through need, With the flag of youth for freedom and bread, And the flag leads us into eternity . . .'

including cruises to Majorca and Norway, loans for buying the Volkswagens that came into production just before the war.

The Jews

After Hitler came to power anyone who had a Jewish parent or grandparent was excluded from government employment, from the universities and from practising law or medicine. (In Berlin about half the lawyers and doctors were Jews.) Jewish music and musicians were banned. For a time Jews were able to continue in business and physical attacks were stopped for fear of provoking boycotts of German goods abroad. The lesser humiliations continued – the shop assistants who refused to serve Jews, the notices in parks 'No Jews allowed here', the Jewish children who had to listen while the class read out 'The Jew is our greatest enemy. Beware of Jews.'

In 1935 the Nüremberg laws stripped Jews of their German nationality and so of such protection as the law still provided. Jews were not allowed to marry German citizens. Attacks on Jews were checked with the approach of the 1936 Berlin Olympic Games. After the games Hitler decreed that the whole Jewish community would be responsible for the actions of individual Jews. This led to a series of laws which eventually stripped Jews of all their property.

But the full weight of anti-semitism was not felt until 1938. When Austria came under German control in March 1938 (see p. 205) the Jewish community there was looted 'with honest joy'. The Austrians, said the SS newspaper, 'in a fortnight [did what the Germans had] failed to achieve in the slow moving ponderous north up to this day'. The Germans had their turn in November after a young Polish Jew murdered a German diplomat in Paris. On *Krystallnacht* (Crystal Night), 9 November 1938, the SA, the SS, the Gestapo and the Hitler Youth in evil association set fire to Jewish homes and synagogues. Jews were assaulted and thousands were thrown into concentration camps.

Krystallnacht was the beginning of the end for the Jews. A fine of a billion marks was collected from the Jewish community. Jews were excluded from almost every kind of employment. Their businesses were taken over by those of pure 'Aryan' blood. Doctors and lawyers who had survived earlier anti-Jewish decrees had three months to liquidate their practices.

But such measures, said Reinhard Heydrich, Himmler's assistant, were only a half solution. Jews, he said, should do forced labour in concentration camps or be driven out of the country. By the beginning of 1939 Hitler was talking of 'the destruction of the Jewish race in Europe'.

The concentration camps were filling up, not only with Jews. Liberals, pacifists, socialists, all who in any way offended the Nazis, were in danger of being carried off to the camps without a moment's warning. Those who could fled the country. By 1939 some 370,000 Jews and 30,000 others had escaped from Germany and Austria. The 'useless' – beggars, alcoholics, homosexuals and others – were also tidied away in the camps. Euthanasia dealt with many of the handicapped – though protests from the Catholic Church resulted in some modification of this programme.

Opposition to Hitler

Organised opposition to Nazism was eliminated. With the banning of political parties their members were dispersed. Trade unionists too could work only underground. The press and universities had been brought under control. The churches offered only limited protests. By a concordat with the papacy in 1933 Catholic schools and organisations were to be tolerated but priests were not to take part in politics. In fact the Nazis frequently interfered with Catholic activities. In 1937 Pope Pius XI condemned Nazi beliefs and actions, but in general the Catholic bishops took the line of least resistance. Hitler's attempts to establish a new German 'Protestant religion' under a 'bishop' chosen by him failed after it was denounced in the churches. But after that relatively few pastors dared to adopt a strong line. Pastor Martin Niemöller, once a U-boat commander, was an outstanding critic – and spent from 1937 to 1945 in a concentration camp. His associate Bonhoeffer, and Lichtenberg, the Catholic bishop who prayed for the Jews, paid for their opposition with their lives.

Most Germans kept their thoughts to themselves. However, by 1939 300,000 Germans were political prisoners. By 1945 over a million Germans had suffered

Hitler talks of peace
And prepares for war!
Shall millions die again?
Shall Germany be devastated?
Make peace secure!
Away with Hitlerism!

Freedom

Only the overthrow of Hitler
Will bring freedom and bread!

Freedom

Facsimiles of stickers placed on pillar boxes and lamp posts by opponents of the Nazi régime. Germans who put up such stickers risked torture and death

in concentration camps. Of the 11,881 civilians formally executed in Germany between 1933 and 1944 over half were Germans who opposed Nazism. And many officers and men in the armed services were executed following court martials because of their political views. 'Forty thousand is a very conservative estimate of the number of Germans executed or otherwise murdered [between 1933 and 1945] because of their religious or political views.'[1]

[1] Figures published by Informationszentrum West Berlin

19 Eastern Europe, 1918–39: democracy in disorder

Czechoslovakia

Tomáš Masaryk, the Slovak who was president of Czechoslovakia from 1919 to 1935, was a statesman to whom right was more important than might. Beneš, president from 1935, was also wise and tolerant.

The Czech inhabitants of Bohemia, a highly industrialised area, and the Germans living to their north and west in the Sudetenland, were progressive, industrious and well educated. Their standard of living was relatively high. Slovakia and Ruthenia in eastern Czechoslovakia were more backward.

Czechoslovakia's problems were the existence of dissatisfied minority groups and the ambitions of neighbouring states. Minority groups were treated better than elsewhere. But religious differences led to tension between the dominant Czechs, many of whom were Protestant and anti-clerical, and the Catholic Slovaks. During the world depression the Slovaks blamed the Czechs for all hardships. The Ruthenes were resentful when falling farm prices hit them. The three million Sudeten Germans, though near the German frontier, seemed contented in Czechoslovakia's early years. When the depression struck, the Sudeten Germans, stirred by propaganda from Germany, became restless. In 1934 Conrad Henlein, with financial help from Germany, founded the Sudeten German Movement which soon was the second largest party in Czechoslovakia. Sudeten Germans sat in coalitions, but worked against the government. From 1936 Nazi propaganda in Germany accused the Czechs of ill-treating them. By 1938 most Sudeten Germans probably wanted union with Germany. There were also frontier disputes with Poland and Hungary. A dispute with Poland, which concerned Teschen (Cieszyn), an area rich in iron and coal (see p. 206), had led in 1919 to border clashes. And in 1919 Hungary declared war on Czechoslovakia in an unsuccessful attempt to recover territory.

In spite of such difficulties, the republic of Czechoslovakia stuck fast to the democratic institutions with which it began. Socialist and communist parties, as well as the Sudeten Movement, were tolerated.

Poland

Poland's existence largely depended on the goodwill of Germany and the USSR. The Polish Corridor (see p. 113) was highly irritating to the Germans. The German minority in western Poland and the Russian minority in the east were also a problem.

In 1926 Marshal Pilsudski, who had played the leading part in the immediate post-war years, returned to power in a coup carried out with left-wing support. As prime minister and minister of war Pilsudski remained an unofficial dictator until his death in 1935. From that year parliament virtually ceased to represent the people and still wider powers were given to the president. Poland became a 'conducted democracy' – certain democratic forms were followed but the government was in fact authoritarian.

Austria

The republic of Austria – the small German remnant of a multi-national empire – was like a head without a body. Vienna made up a third of the total population. From the outset there was a strong movement for union with Germany. In 1931 a proposed customs union with Germany was not permitted (see p. 116).

The chief parties were the Social Democrats, strong in Vienna, and the Christian Socialists who had ties with the countryside and with the conservative clericals. Each party had its own political 'army', the *Schutzbund* and the *Heimwehr*. In 1933, the year Hitler came to power, Engelbert Dollfuss, the Christian Socialist chancellor of Austria, suspended parliamentary government in an attempt to suppress the political armies (see p. 204). Later that year the Austrian Nazi Party was made illegal. Soon Austria was in effect a dictatorship with rulers no less autocratic than the Habsburg emperors. In 1934 a party of Austrian Nazis murdered Dollfuss. Kurt Schuschnigg, another Christian Socialist, then became chancellor. Pressure by Italy for the time being prevented Germany from absorbing Austria.

Hungary

Hungary too was reduced by her peace treaty to a relatively small size. Walls in Budapest were covered with the slogan '*Nem! Nem! Soha!*' (No! No! Never!) in opposition to the terms of the treaty. Hungary, we saw, tried to regain territory from Czechoslovakia. Meanwhile the Romanians invaded Hungary with the object of gaining territory. After looting the country for three months and occupying Budapest they withdrew.

For a few months after the war a communist administration under Bela Kun, an associate of Lenin, ruled in Budapest. Kun had some happy if impractical ideas; he declared for instance that private bathrooms were to be available for public use on Saturday nights. And no one was to have more than two pairs of socks. Then conservatives representing the great landowners set up a government under Admiral Horthy, who at least initially was regent for the former king, Carl. In 1922 Hungary was admitted to the League of Nations.

A carefully restricted electorate secured conservative rule. Radical disorders were put down and Jews were persecuted. Hungary suffered severely during the world depression. The government became more authoritarian but reacted strongly against Nazi agitation by its half million Germans. In 1937, when fascist and Nazi groups united, the government arrested their leaders and introduced land reforms. Yet, hoping to recover some of her lost territory, Hungary tried to maintain good relations with Germany and Italy. The persecution of Jews increased. In 1939, under Nazi pressure, the premier was forced to resign – because he had a Jewish great-grandfather. Hungary in fact tried to travel on two roads at once – playing with and opposing fascism. In 1938 the members of the Little Entente (see p. 198) agreed to her rearmament. In elections in 1939 Nazis increased their strength.

The Balkan states and Greece

The kingdom of the Serbs, Croats and Slovenes, later Yugoslavia, began its career with frontier disputes with neighbours – in particular with Italy concerning Fiume (see p. 176). And there were disputes between the dominant Serbs and the Croats, who wanted a federal state, with Croatian autonomy. In 1928 Stepan Radić, the Croat leader, was shot dead in parliament. The kingdom was so divided that in 1929 King Alexander I dissolved parliament and abolished all political parties.

The name Yugoslavia was adopted in an attempt to end the differences between Serbs, Croats and Slovenes. In 1934, after Alexander's assassination (see p. 200), relations between the Serbs and the Croats became more bitter than ever until 1939, when the state was reorganised on a federal basis. Meanwhile, the Communist Party formed an underground movement.

Albania became a kingdom in 1928 with its former president, Zog, as king. With dictatorial powers, Zog set about modernising his small state. He opposed Italian influence but in April 1939 Italy occupied Albania (see p. 202).

The kingdom of Romania, almost double its pre-war size, retained parliamentary government, but after 1933 this was threatened by the growing power of the Iron Guard, whose main policy was hostility to Jews. In 1938 King Carol II established his own dictatorship and set about stamping out the Iron Guard and making concessions to minority groups.

Bulgaria had lost much territory and was cut off from access to the Aegean Sea. Discontent resulted in violence and repression, murder and revenge. The liberal, limited monarchy became more authoritarian and from 1934 to 1938 there was a military and royal dictatorship. In 1938 the members of the Balkan pact (see p. 200) agreed to Bulgaria's rearmament – which had in fact already begun. In 1939 Bulgaria was demanding revision of the territorial settlement made in 1919.

In 1922 Greece suffered humiliating defeat in a war with Turkey (see below). In 1924 Greece became a republic under the leadership of Venizelos. In 1935 the monarchy was restored. The next year parliamentary rule was overthrown by a military dictatorship, with the usual results – the abolition of political parties, the persecution of opponents and strict censorship. On the other hand wages were increased and social services extended. There was also a rapid increase in armaments.

Turkey

The Greek occupation of Smyrna (Izmir) and the terms of the Treaty of Sevres (see p. 114) aroused Turkish national spirit. In 1920, while Constantinople was occupied by Allied forces, Mustafa Kemal, who had commanded the Turks at Gallipoli, set up a provisional government for Turkey-in-Asia in the small town of Angora (Ankara). Kemal set out to win back all Turk-inhabited territory. 'Turkey for the Turks' was his aim.

With the aid of the government's poster (1929) an old Turk, a street seal engraver, learns the Latin alphabet he has to use instead of Arabic letters. He wears a cloth cap, not a fez

In 1921 Mustafa Kemal defeated the Greeks in a twenty-two-day battle. In the following year, after setting fire to Smyrna, he expelled over a million Greeks from Asia Minor. He then prepared to move into eastern Thrace, ceded to Greece at Sèvres.

In September 1922, as Turkish cavalrymen drew close to British forces at Constantinople, Lloyd George sent reinforcements to Chanak, on the Asian side of the Dardanelles, to help the Greeks. France and Italy opposed this move and withdrew their forces from the Straits. Nor, with the exception of New Zealand, were the dominions willing to support Lloyd George's policy. Following this exercise in 'brinkmanship', the British and Turks came to an agreement that formed the basis of the Treaty of Lausanne (1923).

The Treaty of Lausanne returned eastern Thrace to Turkey, whose territories on the European side of the Dardanelles were thus restored to approximately their 1914 boundaries. The Straits and the Graeco-Turkish frontier were demilitarised. (In 1936, following Italian aggression in Ethiopia, Turkey was permitted to fortify the Straits.) The Greeks gave up their claim to Smyrna but kept certain Aegean islands. Italy kept the Dodecanese Islands and Britain's possession of Cyprus was affirmed. Legal and financial privileges which Europeans trading in Ottoman lands had long enjoyed were ended.

Turkey formally became a republic in 1923. Mustafa Kemal, given the name Ataturk (Father of the Turks), was president until his death in 1938. Having won Turkey for the Turks, he embarked upon modernisation. He ended the sultanate and in 1924 abolished the office of caliph, supreme head of all Islam. Islam ceased to be the state religion and ties between Turkey and Pan-Islamism weakened. Children were educated in lay schools instead of mosques. The Koran was translated from Arabic, official tongue of Islam, into Turkish, and a Latin script was adopted. Atatürk's anti-clerical policy led to changes even in dress; men were forbidden to wear the fez and women were encouraged not to veil their faces. Women began entering professional and later public life.

20 Spain: conflict of ideologies

Political chaos, 1873–1930

Spain, once mistress of a vast empire, entered the twentieth century as a lesser state. In general she was backward and her people desperately poor. Early in the nineteenth century most of her territories in Latin America had won independence (see Chapter 27). In 1898 came the loss of Cuba, Puerto Rico and the Philippines (see p. 64).

In the nineteenth century periods of constitutional rule alternated with periods of dictatorship. In 1873 a republic was proclaimed but in 1876 the monarchy was restored with Alfonso XII as a constitutional ruler.

In 1886 a baby, Alfonso XIII, became king. From about this time Spain was much troubled by anarchists and syndicalists, to whom direct action, 'the propaganda of the deed', was all important.

Spain remained neutral during the First World War and to some extent benefited, for her iron and munitions were in demand. The chief industrial areas were around Barcelona, in the mining districts of Asturias and around Bilbao, a Basque city (see map p. 2).

Government remained weak. In the post-war years industrial unrest increased. A Berber rebellion in the Spanish zone of Morocco strained finances and humiliating defeats caused discontent at home. In 1923 General Primo de Rivera established a virtual dictatorship in Spain. His régime, despotic but paternal, was not unmarked by reforms. However, the vital problem of land reform was not attended to. In 1927 the long Moroccan rebellion was put down and for a time Spain enjoyed some stability. But in 1930 loss of army support and increased unrest accompanying the world depression led Primo de Rivera to resign.

Background to the civil war

In 1931, after local government elections had shown strong anti-monarchist feeling in the cities, King Alfonso left Spain. Following parliamentary elections later that year moderate socialists established a second republic. The republic was harassed by enemies on its left and on its right. A one chamber parliament, the Cortes, was established and a liberal but anti-clerical constitution framed. Provision was made for authoritarian rule in time of emergency; so wide were the powers of the home secretary that at times the government of the republic was more authoritarian than Primo de Rivera's dictatorship had been. An attack on the church aroused much opposition, though the majority of Spaniards were no longer practising Catholics. Separatist forces were strong, particularly in Catalonia and the Basque area. Navarra, though largely Basque-inhabited, was not separatist. In 1932 Catalonia was granted autonomy. This antagonised conservatives. Nor did land reforms endear the republic to landowners. But to the extreme left the government was too conservative. In January 1932 there was an unsuccessful communist rebellion. A right-wing coup was staged later that year but it too failed.

From November 1933 a centre-right government tried to restore order. In 1934 miners in Asturias proclaimed a communist régime independent of the central authority. Their revolt was suppressed by the Spanish Foreign Legion, commanded by General Francisco Franco. Severe reprisals followed.

In 1936 hitherto divided groups on both right and left combined in two opposing fronts. At the suggestion of the small Communist Party a left coalition, the Popular Front, was formed. On the right monarchists, Carlists, clericals and Falangists combined in a National Front. The Carlists supported a pretender to the throne. The Falange was a fascist group formed by José Antonio Primo de Rivera, son of the former dictator; its membership in 1936 was not large but it had been prominent in right-wing disturbances.

At elections in February 1936 the Popular Front came to power by a comfortable margin and set out to implement the anti-clerical policy of the republic's first days and pledged itself to social reform. Its programme was too extreme for the National Front to tolerate, yet not speedy or radical enough to satisfy the far left. Spain plunged into anarchy. Strikes, the firing of churches and political murders were more than frequent. There were serious clashes between right- and left-wing forces. Absence of discipline was the central fact of life.

The Spanish Civil War, 1936–39

In July 1936 a group of right-wing generals made plans for a rebellion against the government. On 17 July troops in Spanish Morocco mutinied. The next day Andalusia rose in revolt and within two days there was civil war in Spain. In garrison towns well planned revolts broke out. Franco, who was then commanding Spanish forces in the Canary Islands, proceeded to Morocco and thence to Spain, taking with him Spanish and Moroccan troops of the army of Africa. Italian and German aircraft helped transport these forces. Italy and Germany at once recognised the rebels as the legitimate government of Spain.

Within a few days the rebels, who were known as the Nationalists, were in more or less effective control of two large wedges of territory. Republican forces, the forces loyal to the government, held most of southern and central Spain, including Madrid, and the north-east including Barcelona. They also held a northern coastal strip that included the Basque provinces with Bilbao, and most of Asturias. Burgos became the Nationalist 'capital'. In October 1936 Franco, the *caudillo* (leader) of the Nationalists, assumed the title of head of state. His aim, he said, was to establish 'a broadly totalitarian' state.

In general the army, the church, the nobility and the bourgeoisie supported the Nationalists, the forces of vested interests. When four Nationalist columns approached Madrid Nationalist sympathisers within the city – a fifth column – tried to undermine the Republican government. And in other cities held by the Republicans a fascist fifth column – a term first used by one of Franco's generals – assisted the Nationalists. In general the Republicans had to rely on militia forces and worker volunteers to combat the regular soldiers in the service of the Nationalists.

Both sides were guilty of frequent atrocities. In one

Scene in a subway during the long siege of Madrid. A poster says 'Venceremos!' – 'We shall overcome!'

Republican-held area rosary beads were pushed through the eardrums of monks; a woman with two sons in the Society of Jesus had a crucifix thrust down her throat. On the other hand a priest in Estremadura had five Republicans – one a girl – buried alive after they had dug their own graves. On both sides too there were idealists and men and women of great courage. The war became a jihad, a holy war. For outsiders too the civil war became charged with emotion, a battlefield of conflicting ideologies, a war of passion and poetry.

The conflict of ideologies led to foreign intervention. Help given to the Nationalists by Italy and Germany and to the Republicans by the USSR caused acute problems. Blum, then prime minister of France, was sympathetic to the Republicans and, though he was a pacifist, was inclined to give support. But others – notably France's own fascist groups – opposed giving aid. So too did the British government, which feared that intervention might lead to an international war. In Britain and France many feared that a Republican victory might result in the establishment of a communist state in western Europe. The threat from Germany following the remilitarisation of the Rhineland (see p. 203) made Blum anxious not to estrange Britain – and equally anxious to avoid a widening of the Spanish war. In September 1936 a non-intervention committee was set up in London. The committee was supposed to make sure that no foreign aid reached Spain, but signature of a non-intervention pact failed to restrain either Germany or Italy, or the USSR, from giving aid. And controls arranged in an attempt to enforce adherence to the pact – controls in which Germany and Italy 'took part' – were a fiasco. After Republican aircraft attacked a German battleship Germany and Italy withdrew from the non-intervention committee. However, after a conference held in Nyon, from September 1937 measures taken against Italian submarines that had been attacking British, French and Russian vessels proved successful.

Italian aid to the Nationalists was more substantial than that given by Germany, though the Italians scarcely covered themselves with glory. The German *Luftwaffe* is considered to have played a decisive part in the ultimate Nationalist victory. For its part the *Luftwaffe* obtained valuable practical experience; its Condor Legion won an unenviable reputation by bombing defenceless towns. The artist Picasso recorded for all time the horror of the legion's 'carpet' bombing of Guernica, a town sacred to the Basques, on a market day – over 2,000 people were killed or maimed. Edgell

Rickword, an English communist who opposed Britain's policy of non-intervention, recorded horrors in Barcelona:

> On Barcelona slums he rains
> German bombs from Fiat planes.
> Five hundred dead at ten a second
> is the world record so far reckoned;
> a hundred children in one street,
> their little hands and guts and feet,
> like offal round a butcher's stall,
> scattered where they'd been playing ball.

Portugal had since 1932 been under the authoritarian and efficient rule of Dr Salazar. Salazar, afraid that the establishment of a liberal republican Spain might weaken his own régime, allowed the Nationalists to import arms through Portugal.

Though Britain and France followed a strictly neutral policy, their nationals were among those who joined the unofficial International Brigades directed by the Comintern. Some 2,000 British subjects, mostly workers and intellectuals, fought in Spain; about 500 were killed. Germans and Italians unsympathetic to the totalitarian régimes in their homelands, men from the east of Europe, Irishmen, Americans, Arabs and others also fought with the brigades. Josip Broz, the Yugoslav communist better known as Marshal Tito, helped organise these forces.

In 1938 the brigades were withdrawn in the hope of inducing Germany and Italy to withdraw their forces. Dolores Ibarruri, the eloquent communist known as La Pasionaria, the Passionflower, said in her farewell speech:

'Mothers! Women! When the wounds of war are staunched ... tell your children of the International Brigades ... coming over seas and mountains, crossing frontiers bristling with bayonets ... these men reached our country as Crusaders for freedom. ... Many of them ... are staying here with the Spanish earth for their shroud.'

There had always been divisions among the Republicans. In May 1937, after severe disputes, Juan Negrín, a former professor of philosophy, a man of relatively little political experience, became the Republican leader. He sought further help from the USSR and worked more closely with the communists than his predecessor – though he himself was a socialist. Negrín's hope was less for victory in Spain than to continue fighting until the Spanish conflict should

P.S.U.

FEIXISME NO!

A Republican poster says 'No to Fascism' – 'Feixisme No!'

merge into another war – a war in which totalitarian Germany and Italy would have to face Britain, France and the USSR.

Victory of the Nationalists

The Republican strongholds in the north, Asturias and the Basque areas, were early cut off from other government-controlled regions. (Navarra had sided with the Nationalists.) Bilbao was captured by the Nationalists in June and Gijón in October 1937. The war in the north was thus brought to an end. In April 1938, by a drive through to the Mediterranean, Nationalist forces severed Valencia, which for a time had been the Republican headquarters, from Catalonia. Elsewhere quick Nationalist thrusts were followed by weeks of near stalemate. In January 1939 Barcelona, the seat of the Republican government since October 1937, fell to the Nationalists. In February Negrín withdrew to Madrid, which had been under siege for over two years. In the same month Britain and France recognised Franco's administration as the government of Spain. The non-intervention committee ceased its farcical activities. Nearly half a million refugees streamed across the Pyrenees into France. Britain, having recognised Franco's government, showed a marked reluctance to help the refugees.

In March 1939 Negrín was forced from office. Then for a week communists and other Negrín supporters in Madrid fought against the Republican council of defence, headed by General Miaja. The communists were overcome. But Miaja was unsuccessful in attempts to obtain a compromise peace with Franco, whose terms were total surrender.

By that time Madrid was without any form of heating. The daily food ration was down to 60 grammes. At the end of March 1939 Nationalist forces finally entered Madrid. The Spanish Civil War was over. A million people had lost their lives. Of these perhaps 200,000 died of disease. Estimates of those executed – by one side or the other – vary from some 30,000 to 100,000.

Franco's régime, reactionary and repressive, made harsh reprisals. Republican sympathisers were sent to prison or internment camps or to their death.

In April 1939 Spain joined the Anti-Comintern pact (see p. 201). When the Second World War began Franco declared Spain's neutrality. But until the defeat of Germany and Italy seemed likely he showed sympathy towards them. After Germany invaded the USSR (see p. 216) a division of Spanish volunteers fought with the Germans in the Ukraine.

21 The failure of collective security: totalitarian aggression

The post-war years

The violence of the struggles that followed the 'peace' of 1918 is sometimes overlooked. There was the Allied intervention in Russia (see p. 128), the Russo-Polish War (see p. 116), the fighting between Hungary and her neighbours (see p. 191) and the Graeco-Turkish War (see p. 192). The Turks also fought successfully against Russia for Kars and western Armenia.

After 1922, except for the minor conflicts between Italy and Greece in 1923 and Greece and Bulgaria in 1925 (see p. 121), Europe enjoyed a period of peace. Africa and much of Asia remained largely colonial areas to which Europe's peace extended – though the French had to deal with rebellions in Morocco and Syria and the British had trouble in their mandated territories of Iraq and Palestine and with the Pathans in the north-west of India.

Western Europe still appeared to dominate the world. In fact 'Europe's century' had ended. She had exhausted herself in the battles of the Great War. And whereas her

share of the world's population had grown from a fifth to a quarter in the nineteenth century, in the twentieth century her rate of population growth fell whilst in Asia and Africa population was increasing more rapidly (see table below). But Europe's diminished status was

Estimated world population in millions

	1800	1850	1900	1952
Africa	90	95	120	205
America (North and South)	25	59	144	344
Asia	602	749	937	1357
Europe	187	266	401	549
Oceania	2	2	6	14
World	906	1171	1608	2469

masked by the withdrawal into isolation of the unexhausted USA and the preoccupation of the USSR with internal problems.

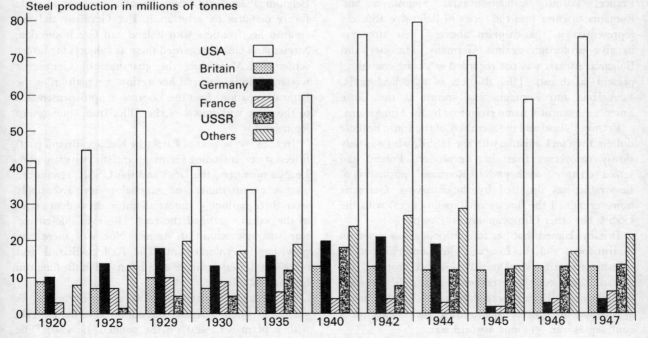

Steel production in millions of tonnes

Legend: USA, Britain, Germany, France, USSR, Others

The changing fortunes of peace, war, revolution, prosperity and depression may be traced in this chart

The European security system: a network of alliances

France felt that at the Peace Conference in 1919 she did not get sufficient security against Germany – no alliance of the victorious powers, just hopes of collective security under the League of Nations, no annexation of the Rhineland, just its demilitarisation and Allied occupation of its western part for fifteen years (see p. 113). With the Rhineland demilitarised France held a kind of hostage for Germany's good behaviour, for the French could march in if Germany made trouble. Nevertheless the French continued to feel insecure.

Poland, Czechoslovakia, Yugoslavia and Romania, having made gains at the expense of neighbours, were afraid of losing newly acquired territories. Like France, they placed little confidence in the League. In the immediate post-war years their feelings of insecurity led France, Poland, Czechoslovakia, Yugoslavia and Romania to enter into the series of defensive alliances represented in the diagram above. Their aim was to give protection against Germany, Hungary and Bulgaria. Austria was not regarded as strong enough to present a threat. The alliance of Czechoslovakia, Yugoslavia and Romania was known as the Little Entente – a scornful name given to it by the Hungarians.

France, Poland and the members of the Little Entente did not then seek alliance with the USSR, who was only slowly recovering from her revolution. Poland had seized territory from her whilst Romania's possession of Bessarabia was disputed by the Russians. Germany however signed the Treaty of Rapallo (1922) with the USSR, the other European outcast (see p. 180).

Britain claimed that her foreign policy was based on disarmament and the League. The Conservatives, by refusing to ratify MacDonald's Geneva Protocol (see p. 120), suggested that even her League policy was not wholehearted. Britain was dominated by the 'never again' school – never again must she engage in a continental war, let alone a world war.

Italy did not enter the system of alliances, but made treaties of friendship with most of her neighbours – Spain, Romania, Albania, Hungary, Austria, Greece and, in Africa, Ethiopia (Abyssinia). Between 1935 and 1940 Italy was to attack three of these states. Her dispute with Yugoslavia was settled in 1924 when Yugoslavia recognised Fiume as Italian, though she kept the adjacent Susak.

The Locarno period

From 1925 to 1932 Briand, 'apostle of peace', attempted to find security for France by making a rapprochement with Germany. Whether Stresemann for Germany was equally sincere is doubtful, but he co-operated (see p. 182). Austen Chamberlain, British foreign secretary, was happy to help unite the two powers.

In October 1925 following the 'settlement' of the reparations issue by the Dawes plan and the evacuation of the Ruhr (see p. 183), a series of pacts that seemed to guarantee the peace of Europe was made at Locarno. Chief of the Locarno treaties was that by which Germany, France and Belgium confirmed their existing frontiers; their promises were guaranteed by Britain and Italy, who were to intervene if the pact were violated. Germany also reaffirmed the demilitarisation of the Rhineland. In a further treaty Germany, France, Belgium, Poland and Czechoslovakia promised to settle future disputes by arbitration. But Germany did not confirm her frontiers with Poland and Czechoslovakia; Stresemann clearly regarded these as subjects for future settlement. Meanwhile the guarantee of Germany's western frontier secured her against a repetition of the Ruhr occupation. And the Locarno rapprochement led to the early withdrawal of the Allies from the western Rhineland.

In 1928 by the pact of Paris (the Kellogg-Briand pact) fifteen states, including Germany and the two giant non-League members, the USA and the USSR, renounced war as an instrument of national policy. Eventually sixty-three nations – almost all the independent states in the world – ratified the pact. However, 'defensive' war was not within its terms. Nor was there any provision for enforcement. The Kellogg-Briand pact merely indicated a climate of opinion and in the long run had no real effect.

'At Locarno', Briand said, 'we spoke European.' A year later, when Germany was admitted to the League, with a permanent seat on the council, he said: 'The cannon and the mourning weeds are behind us.' By 1928

France had reduced the period of conscription to one year. In 1929 Briand went so far as to propose a European federal union. But although France was persuaded to withdraw from the Rhineland in 1930, ahead of schedule (see p. 183), she was by then on the defensive. The construction of the Maginot line, 1929–34 (see p. 174), was an attempt to make up for insufficient manpower. It was also an attempt to buy a double insurance for French security. Meanwhile, as Germany secretly rearmed, armoured cars camouflaged as farm wagons stood about her countryside. The Indian summer of Locarno was short-lived; it did not outlast Brüning's term of office.

Disarmament and rearmament

At the beginning of the 1930s Europe's peace depended on collective security under the League, on the Locarno treaties and the network of alliances described above. There was also the possibility of 'that general reduction and limitation of armaments' that Clemenceau had said the Allied and Associated powers wanted (see p. 120).

Five powers had agreed at Washington (1921–22) to limit their naval forces and a further naval agreement was made in 1930 (see pp. 162–3). Meanwhile Britain had of her own accord also reduced her land and air forces.

The long-awaited world disarmament conference that met in Geneva in 1932 proved a prelude to rearmament. When in 1933 Hitler came to power Germany withdrew from the conference, only to return when promised equality in a system that would give security to all nations. In October 1933, following disputes as to when she should achieve equality, she withdrew from the conference and from the League. The disarmament conference came to its dismal end in 1934.

Meanwhile Hitler had appointed Goering air minister. Soon Germany had the beginnings of an air force while expenditure on forces permitted by the Treaty of Versailles was doubled. In March 1935 Hitler, using the excuse that other states had failed to disarm, declared that Germany would no longer observe the restrictions imposed in 1919. Conscription was introduced and the formation of an armoured division was begun. In June 1935 Britain agreed to the construction of a German navy, limited to 35 per cent of British strength. In 1936 Goering introduced a four-year plan for the expansion of the armed forces, including the fortification of the Siegfried line, fronting the Maginot line. Meanwhile

Hitler by rhetoric and bluster convinced people that Germany was much better armed than she really was.

While Germany took the initiative, Britain slowly followed. By 1939 she had a sizeable air force. But she failed to maintain her early lead in aircraft carriers and tanks. She introduced conscription in April 1939 but only for six months, for men aged twenty and twenty-one. France also neglected tanks and the strategy of mobile warfare. A young staff officer, Charles de Gaulle, who said that aircraft and tanks were needed, not the immobile defences of the Maginot line, was laughed to scorn by his superiors. Mesmerised by the immensely powerful Maginot line and the conviction that no force could outflank it by an advance through the Ardennes – the hilly region of Luxembourg and south-eastern Belgium – the French were ill-prepared for modern war. (The German staff itself did not regard an advance through the Ardennes as practicable until forced to plan for it by Hitler.) Italy after 1930 built up her naval and air forces but the ineffectiveness of her armed forces was exposed during the Spanish Civil War. In 1939, when Germany and Italy signed 'the pact of steel' (see p. 208), Mussolini warned Hitler that Italy would not be ready for war until 1942. The USSR built up her forces during the 1930s but no one outside the Soviet Union knew their real strength.

Outside Europe the Japanese had a large though not highly mechanised army. They were however advanced in the development of aircraft carriers. And, contrary to her undertakings as a mandatory power, Japan developed her Pacific mandates as naval and air bases. The USA maintained a large navy but in 1941 had scarcely any land forces and an inadequate air force.

A tangle of alliances

In the early 1930s, with Hitler's rise to power and the relative recovery of the USSR, some states began to look for support to the Russians, who in turn were seeking closer ties with western Europe. By 1934 fear of the spread of communism had sufficiently weakened for the USSR to be admitted to the League.

Litvinov, Soviet foreign minister from 1930 to 1939, was genuinely interested in promoting collective security. The Comintern, previously hostile to noncommunist socialist parties, encouraged the formation of popular front coalitions – as in France and Spain and in China too. It also agreed that communists could vote for expenditure on arms in their national parliaments.

- Little Entente
- Balkan Pact
- .... Frontier guarantees

Pacts of aggression

It needed a strong will and determined action to make the League of Nations, the Locarno treaties and the network of defensive alliances effective and this was what was lacking. No one proved willing to take action to back up these agreements. In Germany and Italy however a determined will found expression in pacts of aggression (see diagram below).

Mussolini was at first scornful of his fellow dictator, Hitler. The Germans, he once remarked, were illiterate when Caesars ruled in Rome. In 1933, wanting to keep a buffer between Italy and Germany, he made an alliance with Austria. The next year, by the Rome Protocols, he linked Italy with Austria and Hungary. Disarmed and isolated in the post-war years, Austria and Hungary now appeared with Italy as possible rivals to the Little Entente. When later in 1934 Nazis murdered Dollfuss, Mussolini marched troops to the Brenner Pass (leading from Italy into Austria) in support of the Austrian government. Hitler then met Mussolini in Venice and promised not to intervene in Austria. When Hitler denounced the military clauses of the Treaty of Versailles, Italy joined Britain and France in the Stresa front.

However, after the league condemned her attack on Abyssinia in 1935 (see p. 201), Italy drew closer to Germany. When in 1936 Germany remilitarised the Rhineland (see p. 203) Italy took no action. Then their joint intervention in the Spanish Civil War drew Germany and Italy together. In October 1936 they made a pact for joint action and friendly collaboration – which Mussolini called the Berlin-Rome axis. Italy agreed not to interfere with the Nazi movement in Austria whilst

Meanwhile in France Jean Barthou, who became foreign minister in 1932, was revitalising the French system of alliances. In 1934 Barthou and King Alexander of Yugoslavia, who had been conferring about the Little Entente, were assassinated. By 1935 there had grown up the tangle of treaties of friendship, alliances, mutual assistance and non-aggression pacts illustrated in the diagram above. The link between Turkey, Romania, Yugoslavia and Greece was known as the Balkan pact. (The diagram does not show the Locarno pacts. Nor does it show a ten-year non-aggression pact made in 1934 between Germany and Poland.)

In April 1935, a month after Hitler announced the rearmament of Germany, representatives of Britain, France and Italy met at Stresa in northern Italy. They mildly condemned Germany and agreed to follow 'a common line of conduct' on German rearmament. They renewed their Locarno obligations and affirmed that Austria must remain independent. But the 'Stresa front' was a paper tiger. France took more effective action by making an alliance with the Soviet Union (May 1935) by which each state promised to help the other in case of unprovoked aggression. At the same time the Soviet Union agreed to help the Czechs, provided France had already taken up arms on their behalf. Hitler protested that Germany was being encircled. The French certainly regarded Czechoslovakia, with her large army, highly developed armaments industry and excellent fortifications, as the linchpin in her system of alliances. Britain, still mistrustful of the USSR and critical of France for entering into an alliance with her, made the agreement limiting German naval forces – implying that Germany's strength on land was no concern of hers. France blamed 'perfidious Albion' for entering into an agreement with Germany. On the other hand France and the USSR did not make their alliance effective by making military plans.

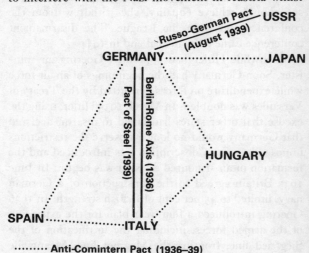

Germany recognised Italy's conquest of Abyssinia. From this time Hitler and Mussolini began threatening their neighbours, demanding colonies, the restoration of territories, 'living room'. And Italy's growing subservience to Germany became apparent. The Italian army even adopted the German goose-step, 'il passo Romano' as they called it – after all, said Mussolini, geese had saved Rome in ancient times. More significantly, anti-Jewish laws were proclaimed though they were not enforced with vigour.

In November 1936 Germany and Japan made their Anti-Comintern pact. This, they claimed, was aimed at preventing the spread of communism. In fact, along with the Berlin-Rome axis, it was intended to counter the Franco-Russian pact of 1935. In November 1937 Hitler invited Mussolini to Germany. Italy then joined the Anti-Comintern pact.

Successful aggression: Japan

In 1931, when Japan attacked Manchuria, the other powers who had signed the Nine Power Treaty at Washington did nothing to make her honour her promises. Nor did the League do anything effective to get her out of Manchuria (see p. 169).

Japan's unchecked aggression weakened the position of both Britain and the USA in the Far East. And it weakened the authority of the League throughout the world. Collective security seemed to have no real strength. The Anti-Comintern pact of 1936, by securing Japan against a Soviet attack, encouraged her to renew her war against China in 1937 (see p. 171). At a time when Hitler was becoming dangerously defiant this distracted world attention from Europe.

Successful aggression: Italy

To some extent Mussolini and the Fascist Party depended on an aggressive foreign policy to win support. They aimed at least to dominate the Mediterranean – 'Our Sea' as Mussolini called it.

Mussolini needed to match words with action. Italy, with colonies in Eritrea and Somaliland, had long been interested in Abyssinia (Ethiopia). Her defeat at Adowa in 1896 (see p. 34) left bitter memories. After Adowa Italy concentrated on the economic exploitation of Abyssinia. In 1923 she supported her admission to the League and in 1928 made a treaty of friendship with her.

Haile Selassie, who became negus (emperor) of Abyssinia in 1930, was hostile to Italian penetration. In December 1934 a dispute on the border of Italian Somaliland resulted in the death of about 100 Abyssinians and 30 Italian soldiers. Haile Selassie appealed to the League to settle the crisis that followed. The question of responsibility for the clash was submitted to arbitration. But a request that the League should investigate Italian preparations for an attack on Abyssinia was fruitless.

Abyssinia, Mussolini claimed, offered commercial opportunities and land for settlers. War would absorb unemployed men into the forces and the production of munitions. In October 1935, without any declaration of war, Italy invaded Abyssinia. The League council promptly declared Italy an aggressor. All but four members of the League then imposed economic sanctions against her. But sanctions allowed Mussolini to justify himself at home: Italy was being victimised by the 'have' powers. And the imposition of sanctions helped to move Italy closer to Germany, who continued trading with her. The USA, under its Neutrality Acts (see p. 161), refused to sell arms to either side.

The fact that most League members agreed to apply sanctions indicated a desire to maintain peace by collective security. But oil, steel and iron were excluded from sanctions. Imposition of oil sanctions, Italy said, would be 'an unfriendly act' that might provoke retaliation. Britain did not want to risk her navy in an attempt to enforce oil sanctions. France, rather than antagonising Italy, wanted her support against Germany. So Pierre Laval, the French prime minister, and Sir Samuel Hoare, the British foreign minister, entered into secret negotiations with Italy. In December 1935 their proposals – which involved handing over two-thirds of Abyssinia to Italy – became known. There was an indignant outcry and both Laval and Hoare were forced to resign. Anthony Eden, who favoured effective sanctions, became Britain's foreign secretary. But no agreement to impose oil sanctions was reached – and in March 1936 Germany's remilitarisation of the Rhineland gave statesmen new problems to think about.

In May 1936, with the advantages of air power and mechanised equipment – and poison gas – the Italians overcame the brave resistance of the Abyssinians and captured Addis Ababa, the capital. Victor Emmanuel III was proclaimed emperor of Ethiopia and Haile Selassie went into exile in England, where he lived in Bath. Sanctions were lifted and Italy resumed normal relations with the rest of the world. Victory reconciled

BARBARISM | **CIVILIZATION**

The British cartoonist David Low, at the time of the Abyssinian campaign asks if aggressive civilisation is superior to peaceful barbarism

critics at home to Mussolini. Italian administration of Abyssinia was in many respects admirable. But the new territory brought poor returns in wealth and settlement. And the cost in inflation and compulsory loans was high. As for the League of Nations, its authority was totally undermined. And Hitler's policy of bluff was confirmed.

When in July 1936 the civil war broke out in Spain, Germany and Italy were quick to give aid to the Nationalist rebels. Italy, instead of taking part in a short and glorious war, lost in prestige, men and materials. Her difficulties in Spain forced her to rely more heavily on Germany. The war in Spain to a great degree polarised the world into two camps – those who were for fascism and Nazism and those who were against.

In December 1937 Italy withdrew from the League. Count Ciano, her foreign minister and Mussolini's son-in-law, was expecting the Mediterranean soon to become an Italian lake and thought a German–Italian war against the west 'in the spring of 1939' was inevitable. In 1938 Italy was clamouring for a share of French colonies – and for Nice, Savoy and Corsica. Not

wanting to alienate Britain, the claim she made to Malta was more cautious.

Having given up their claim to a protectorate over Albania in 1920, the Italians adopted a policy of political and economic penetration. In 1926 they made their treaty of friendship with Albania. King Zog, like Haile Selassie, wanted to modernise his country without Italian interference. In 1934 an Italian fleet frightened his government into giving Italy various privileges. In April 1939, shortly after the second partition of Czechoslovakia (see p. 207), the Italian navy bombarded Albanian coastal towns. Troops were landed and overran the country. Zog escaped to Greece. An Albanian assembly then voted for union with Italy.

Successful aggression: Germany

Remilitarisation of the Rhineland

In January 1935 the Saar plebiscite (see p. 113) was held.

Some Saarlanders would have preferred to remain under League control so long as Hitler ruled Germany. But a Nazi propaganda campaign, coupled with threats of reprisals for those who voted against return to Germany, thwarted the efforts of League officials to secure a free vote. Ninety per cent of Saarlanders voted for return to Germany. Germany then became less dependent on the goodwill of France and Britain and two months later Hitler announced his decision to rearm – to which Britain, France and Italy lamely responded with the Stresa front (see p. 200).

The Treaty of Versailles bound Germany never to remilitarise the Rhineland. If Versailles was a 'diktat', Germany voluntarily accepted demilitarisation at Locarno. In good faith in 1930 the Allies completed their withdrawal from the Rhineland. In 1935 Hitler himself voluntarily declared Germany's adherence to the Locarno pact. But in March 1936 some 35,000 German soldiers marched into the Rhineland. Hitler attempted to justify this, claiming that the Franco–Russian–Czech alliances of 1935 were encircling Germany. Whilst proclaiming that he had no more demands to make, he offered France and Belgium a twenty-five-year non-aggression pact. But clearly treaties, freely negotiated or dictated, were all one to Hitler – 'scraps of paper'. His offer was not accepted.

When France appealed to the League the council merely condemned the German action. As for Britain's and Italy's Locarno guarantee of the demilitarisation of the Rhineland, no thought had been given as to how to enforce this. And by 1936 Italy had rejected collective security. In Britain the Germans, it was argued, were 'only going into their own back garden'. Labour made it clear that they would not support sanctions, economic or military, against Germany. Baldwin, the prime minister, 'tearfully' it is said, told the French that Britain had no forces with which she could help. This let the French off the hook. Their chief of staff, General Gamelin, claiming that 300,000 Germans had poured into the Rhineland, opposed action. Belgium, now totally exposed to a German attack, withdrew from the Locarno system and proclaimed her neutrality – which Germany guaranteed in the following year. The Maginot line, which extended only as far west as the Belgian frontier, was thus left hanging in mid-air. (Belgium had opposed its extension along her frontier as being likely to provoke Germany.) The Germans for their part got on with building the Siegfried line.

March 1936 was perhaps the last occasion on which Germany could have been halted on the path that led to

THE GOOSE-STEP.
"GOOSEY GOOSEY GANDER,
WHITHER DOST THOU WANDER?"
"ONLY THROUGH THE RHINELAND–
PRAY EXCUSE MY BLUNDER!"

E.H. Shepard's cartoon of 1936 shows a heavily armed Nazi goose, 'German peace' in his mouth, goose-stepping into the Rhineland, trampling underfoot the Locarno pacts

world war. The remilitarisation of the Rhineland had not been favoured by the German general staff. If opposed, they said, they could hold out for at most six weeks. And a military defeat at this stage, they warned Hitler, would result in his downfall. However, it was a gamble that came off. Economic and political problems, misinformation and miscalculation, led France and Britain to hesitate. Their hands were already full, they complained, with Italy. Their people were war weary. They seemed to lack the will to resist.

The 'liberation' of Austria: the Anschluss

After the remilitarisation of the Rhineland Hitler set out to absorb all Germans into his Third Reich. The largest German group outside the reich were the Austrians. In 1931 the proposal for a customs union between Germany and Austria was rejected.

For some years Austria was troubled by clashes

between the two political armies, the *Schutzbund*, supporters of the Social Democrats, and the *Heimwehr*, nationalist and reactionary, who supported the Christian Socialists. Later the Austrian Nazi Party won considerable support. After Dollfuss became chancellor (1932) he set up a Fatherland Front on the fascist model in an attempt to end party strife. He used the *Heimwehr* to suppress the *Schutzbund*. A socialist housing estate in Vienna was bombarded and several hundred died.

In 1933, as we saw, the Austrian Nazi Party was banned. This infuriated Hitler. When in 1934 Dollfuss was murdered during an unsuccessful Nazi plot to exterminate the entire cabinet, Mussolini marched troops to the Brenner Pass to prevent a Nazi takeover. Many Austrians who had once wanted the *Anschluss* (union) with Germany now opposed it.

Schuschnigg, who succeded Dollfuss, tried to carry on the Fatherland Front. In 1936, contrary to the Treaty of St Germain, Austria introduced conscription. In the same year Hitler, in return for the release of Nazis held in prison, promised to respect Austria's independence. He declared he was finished with the 'policy of surprises'. But by then Nazis were boring their way into Austria like worms into wooden furniture. Schuschnigg was forced to make concessions. Nazi newspapers were allowed to circulate in Austria and two pro-Nazis joined the cabinet. By this time Mussolini was on Hitler's hook and had proclaimed the Berlin-Rome axis.

In November 1937 Hitler announced to his generals that Austria and Czechoslovakia were to be absorbed into the reich. Early the next year he dismissed his independently minded war minister and placed the three

Europe 1939: the pre-war aggressions of Nazi Germany

armed services under his direct command. Any officers who might have opposed him from caution or any other reason were eliminated.

In February 1938 Schuschnigg was summoned to meet Hitler at Berchtesgaden, the Führer's mountain residence near the Austrian border. After much bullying the Austrian chancellor agreed to legalise the Nazi Party and to appoint Seyss-Inquart, a pro-Nazi, as minister of the interior in control of the police. The Austrian Nazi Party, as soon as it was legalised, grew bolder. Early in March there were Nazi disorders in Graz. The chancellor then announced that a plebiscite would be held to show Austria's determination to remain independent. Hitler demanded that the plebiscite should be postponed and that Schuschnigg should resign. As German troops concentrated on the frontier Schuschnigg submitted and Seyss-Inquart became chancellor. Claiming that unrest was threatening Austria's security, he invited the Germans to enter and restore order. So on 12 March 1938 German soldiers marched into Austria. Hitler received a tumultuous welcome. In Linz, the town where he had gone to school, he said: 'If Providence once called me forth from this town to be the leader of the reich, it must . . . have charged me with a mission, and that mission could be only to restore my dear homeland to the German reich.'

Seyss-Inquart proclaimed the *Anschluss*, the union of Austria with Germany. Hitler, the former Austrian corporal, took formal possession of Vienna, the old Habsburg capital. He was later to receive the regalia of Charlemagne, first Holy Roman Emperor. In April 1938 a plebiscite, not unlike the one held in the Saar, gave a virtually unanimous vote in favour of the *Anschluss*. Austria thus became part of Hitler's reich. Austrians who had opposed the union were thrown into concentration camps and tortured. Jews were especially harshly treated.

In spite of the Berlin-Rome axis and the Anti-Comintern pact Mussolini was still afraid of a strong Germany facing Italy across the Brenner Pass. But involvement with Spain left Italy isolated from Britain and France and dependent on Germany. So Mussolini did not dare oppose the *Anschluss*. The French government resigned. The British government said the occupation was a fait accompli so there was nothing they could do. Nothing came of a Russian proposal for a meeting with France, Britain and the USA to discuss collective security. Powerful groups, not only in Britain, still feared Hitler less than the threat of communism.

The occupation of Austria followed a pattern soon to become all too familiar. First Goebbels's propaganda machine shouted against the injustices done to Germany. Its screams convinced most Germans and more than half convinced many others – in Britain, for example, there was much sympathy for Germany. When propaganda had divided Hitler's opponents force was applied with dramatic suddenness. Within hours Europe was faced with a fait accompli it was powerless to resist.

The absorption of Czechoslovakia

Clemenceau at Locarno said: 'He who holds Bohemia controls central Europe. . . . If Germany is allowed to fortify the Rhineland then she will move against Bohemia, will be free to raise the issue of the [German minority] in the Sudetenland, settle the question of the *Anschluss*, and take off in any direction she may decide.'

Hitler was determined that Germany should find living space in the rich black soil region of the Ukraine. Between this region and Germany lay Czechoslovakia with its Bohemian heartland. Soon after the *Anschluss* he said that Czechoslovakia was to be removed from the map. He was aware that action against Czechoslovakia would have the sympathy of Poland and Hungary, both of whom had claims on Czech territory. And he was willing to gamble that Britain and France would not attack his still weakly defended Rhine frontier.

'You have only to look at a map to see that neither Britain nor France could help Czechoslovakia. . . . I have abandoned any idea of giving guarantees to Czechoslovakia or to the French in connection with their obligations to Czechoslovakia', wrote Neville Chamberlain. And the Russians he suspected were 'stealthily and cunningly pulling all the strings to get [Britain] involved in war with Germany.'

We saw that in 1936 German propaganda began accusing the Czechs of ill-treating the Sudeten Germans. The Czechs were also accused of being too friendly with the USSR. German propaganda asserted that the Czechs were harbouring Russian planes and constructing airfields for the Russians. In 1937 Henlein (see p. 190) demanded virtual autonomy for the Sudeten Germans.

Industrial development had made it possible for the Czechs to build up a powerful army. They had constructed fortifications along the German border. Their alliances with France, the USSR and with the other members of the Little Entente gave them confidence. They replied to the German threat by increasing their armaments and improving their fortifications. But

Czechoslovakia's apparently secure position was dramatically altered by the *Anschluss*. The German frontier now extended far beyond the fortified western rim of Bohemia and the Sudetenland. Czechoslovakia now had a long, exposed and unfortified frontier on her south, along the former border with Austria. She found herself surrounded on all sides by unfriendly powers – Hungary, Poland and Germany. She soon discovered that her system of alliances offered her as little protection as her outflanked fortifications.

In April 1938 Henlein in the Carlsbad programme claimed what amounted to full independence for the Sudetenland. Throughout the summer of 1938, while the Germans built fortifications along the Czech frontier, negotiations dragged on between the Czech government and the Sudeten leaders. Britain and France urged the Czechs to make concessions. In August Britain sent Lord Runciman, a Liberal supporter of Chamberlain, to mediate. And indeed President Beneš did yield on many points, but as Henlein was under instructions not to come to terms negotiation was useless.

On 30 May 1938 Hitler had informed his staff that Czechoslovakia must be smashed by 1 October at latest. Early in September he announced that the Sudeten Germans, 'these tortured and oppressed creatures', must determine their own future. Thereupon riots broke out in German-speaking areas of Czechoslovakia. The Czech government imposed martial law. Though disorders in the Sudetenland increased as Hitler and Henlein made fresh demands the Czech authorities proved able to cope with the situation. Henlein and many of his followers fled to Germany.

Chamberlain and Daladier believed it would be better to take the Sudetenland from Czechoslovakia – a 'faraway country' – than to risk starting a European war. On 15 September 1938 Chamberlain flew – his first air journey – to Munich and from there went to Berchtesgaden to discuss the crisis with Hitler. After the meeting Chamberlain promised Daladier that if the French would consent to the partition of Czechoslovakia, Britain would join them in guaranteeing the remainder of her territory. The French brought pressure on the Czechs to consent to partition by saying they would not be able to defend them – as required by their mutual aid treaty – for lack of British support. The Franco-Czech treaty thus had as little effect as Britain's League of Nations policy. And the Russians, according to the terms of their pact with Czechoslovakia, would not come to her aid without the French. Chamberlain, refusing

Soviet assistance or even participation in the negotiations, said: 'I must confess to the most profound distrust of Russia.' On 21 September, while Poland and Hungary too were making claims for Czech territory, the Czechs agreed to yield the Sudetenland.

On 22 September Chamberlain again flew to Germany, and met Hitler at Godesberg. There Hitler announced that Germany must occupy the Sudetenland not later than 1 October. This indecent haste, leaving no time for preparations by Czechoslovakia, provoked a fresh crisis. Half a million Czech soldiers stood to arms whilst the Germans called up 750,000 men. While British statesmen issued warnings and the fleet prepared for action a million Frenchmen were under arms.

On 28 September, fearing that Britain and France might resist, Hitler accepted a proposal from Mussolini for a four power conference the following day. So on 29 September Hitler, Mussolini, Chamberlain and Daladier met in Munich. Czechoslovakia was not represented. At midnight an agreement promising Hitler almost everything he had demanded was signed. Czechoslovakia, abandoned, was obliged to consent. On 1 October the Germans were to move into the Sudetenland as the Czechs withdrew. The operation was to be completed within a week. The four powers represented at Munich were to fix the new frontier between Germany and Czechoslovakia. France and Britain guaranteed the new frontier against aggression.

Thus the rich and heavily fortified Sudetenland was lost without a blow. Moreover, Czechoslovakia had to yield a large part of Slovakia to Hungary whilst the Poles, despite their defensive treaty with the Czechs, took Teschen (see p. 190 and map p. 204). (In 1919 Poland kept the town of Teschen but had to yield the neighbouring territory to Czechoslovakia. It was this area which Poland acquired in 1938.) Of a population of fifteen million and a territory of 145,000 square kilometres Czechoslovakia lost five million inhabitants and 43,000 square kilometres. What remained was further divided by the grant of semi-independence to Slovakia and Ruthenia. Beneš resigned and left the country. Henlein, who became governor of the territories annexed by Germany, demanded that Czech refugees from the Sudetenland should be forcibly returned. This, said Wheeler-Bennett, the historian, who was then in Prague,

'was tantamount to a death warrant. . . . [In the Sudetenland] the Sudeten Legion and the Henleinist Storm-troops were going from house to house with lists,

October 1938. A Czech woman, forced to salute German troops, weeps for her country

arresting former political foes. ... On the platform of the Masaryk railway station [in Prague I saw] the refugee trains come in – only to be turned back – I [saw] heads swathed in bloody bandages, bruised and broken faces. ... '

After the Munich meeting Chamberlain returned to England with a paper signed by himself and Hitler, stating that Germany and Britain wanted never to go to war against one another. Consultation, it said, was the correct method of settling disputes. Chamberlain, waving his paper to an enthusiastic crowd, said: 'I believe it is peace in our time.'

Chamberlain believed that Germany had good reason for dissatisfaction. He had a sincere desire for peace – and a greater dread of war. His visits to the lion in his den were widely acclaimed (see p. 147). From 3 to 5 October the House of Commons debated the Munich settlement. Chamberlain said: 'Everything depends upon there being sincerity and goodwill on both sides. I believe that there is sincerity and goodwill on both sides ...'. But Duff Cooper, who had resigned as first lord of the admiralty, pointed out: 'When Herr Hitler broke the treaty of Versailles he undertook to keep the treaty of Locarno, and when he broke the treaty of Locarno, he undertook not to interfere further ... '. Attlee perhaps summed things up best:

'There was enormous relief that war had been averted, at all events for the time being; [but] there was a sense of humiliation and foreboding for the future. ... Without firing a shot ... [Hitler] has achieved a dominating position in Europe which Germany failed to win after four years of war. ... The cause [of the crisis] was ... not that the position of the Sudeten Germans had become intolerable. It was not the wonderful principle of self-determination. It was because Herr Hitler had decided that the time was ripe for another step forward in his design to dominate Europe.'

Churchill predicted: 'All the countries of central and eastern Europe will [now] make the best terms they can with the triumphant Nazi power. The system of alliances in central Europe upon which France has relied for her safety has been swept away ... '. And indeed the Little Entente, which had been powerless to help when the great powers themselves deserted Czechoslovakia, forthwith collapsed. And when Yugoslavia made a treaty with Italy the Balkan pact too was undermined.

Following the Commons debate only 150 members voted against the government. In France the Popular Front ended as socialists and communists opposed Daladier (see p. 176). A spirit of inertia deadened France. '*A bas la guerre*' was a rallying cry for right-wing nationalists, pro-Nazis and defeatist parties.

Italy was still not totally committed to Germany. Whilst clamouring for colonies and territory from France she tried not to antagonise Britain. Early in 1938 Britain had agreed to recognise Italy's Abyssinian empire in return for an Italian withdrawal from Spain. In January 1939 Chamberlain visited Mussolini in Rome – better Mussolini than Stalin. But in April 1939 Italy, throwing caution to the winds, overran Albania.

As for Hitler, appeasement had made him despise the men who had accepted his demands. The men he got to know at Munich, he said, were not the kind who would dare to start a war. He said he had made his 'final territorial demands' at Munich but in March 1939, under a threat of bombing Prague, he compelled the Czechs and Slovaks to accept German 'protection'. The whole Czech heartland was thus absorbed into what had now become Greater Germany. In theory Slovakia remained autonomous but in fact was little more than an extension of the reich. And Hungary was allowed to overrun Ruthenia. When the Germans entered Prague on 15 March 1939 nothing was left of the rump state that Britain and France had guaranteed at Munich to protect.

A will to resist: negotiations with the USSR

By the end of 1938 the European 'security system' had collapsed. Collective security and the post-war system of alliances had proved of no effect. The totalitarian powers had made agreements and then dishonoured them, whilst the non-aggressive states, the 'satisfied' powers, seemed to lack the will to resist. But after March 1939, when it became clear that Hitler desired more than to bring all Germans into the reich, a will to resist appeared. France and Britain gave guarantees that were not mere scraps of paper – though Hitler thought they were.

As Hitler began threatening Poland and the Italians overran Albania, Britain and France guaranteed the independence of Poland, Romania, Greece (March–April 1939) and Turkey (May–June 1939). Full powers were given to Daladier for the arming of France and Britain introduced conscription. Hitler responded by denouncing the 1934 non-aggression pact with Poland and the 1935 naval agreement with Britain. Earlier in the year Hungary and Spain had joined the Anti-Comintern pact. In May 1939 Germany and Italy made a military alliance, the 'pact of steel'. Assistance under this pact was not limited to a defensive war. It was at this time that Hitler ordered his forces to be ready for an attack on Poland by 1 September 1939.

Without Soviet co-operation the Anglo-French guarantee to Poland was unrealistic. To go to the aid of Poland without the USSR, Lloyd George said, was to walk into a trap. In spite of the red spectre of communism Britain and France negotiated for an alliance with the USSR, though with little enthusiasm. The horror aroused by the recent purges in the Soviet Union (see p. 134) did not make her an attractive ally. And the elimination of many of her military leaders reduced confidence in her army. The Russians in turn put little reliance on the strength of British and French forces. In fact British rearmament had by 1939 reached the point where opposition to Hitler was practicable. Everyone at that time overestimated German strength.

All through the summer of 1939 negotiations between Britain, France and the USSR went on. A major difficulty was Poland's refusal to allow Russian forces to enter her territory. That, said the Polish foreign minister, would be as good as agreeing to a new Polish partition. Once in, he said, the Russians would never leave Poland. But by the end of July it seemed agreement had been reached. Then the Russians began stalling.

The Nazi-Soviet pact

Perhaps Chamberlain was justified in his distrust of the USSR. In May 1939 Litvinov, a strong supporter of collective security, was dismissed and Molotov became Soviet foreign minister. And between 1934 and 1937 Stalin had been secretly negotiating with Germany. Hitler, who despised all Slavs, hated communism and cast envious eyes on the living space in the Ukraine, had rebuffed his advances. But in 1939 the Bismarckian nightmare of a two front war had reappeared. So the USSR had to be won over to the German side.

In May 1939 the Germans informed the Soviets that they were ready to negotiate. The Russians kept the Germans waiting until early in August Molotov suggested making a trade agreement and then a non-aggression pact. Hitler, having set his date for attacking Poland, was in a hurry. On 21 August the trade agreement was concluded. Ribbentrop, the German foreign minister, was then sent posthaste to Moscow. He arrived on 23 August. Before the day was over a Nazi-Soviet pact had been signed. Hitler told his generals that he and Stalin would carry out 'a redistribution of the world'. He told them to shut their hearts to pity and act brutally. As for Mussolini, he was not even informed that Hitler was negotiating with the USSR.

The Nazi-Soviet pact, often known as the Molotov-Ribbentrop pact, was to last for ten years. The USSR and Germany agreed not to join any group of powers aimed against the USSR or Germany. If Germany or the USSR was attacked by a third power, her partner was to remain neutral. But there were also secret clauses for the partitioning of Poland by Germany and the USSR. Finland, Estonia, Latvia and Bessarabia were to be Soviet spheres of influence and Lithuania, including Vilna, was to be a German sphere. (By a later agreement Lithuania was to be part of the Russian sphere.) The Anti-Comintern pact – to the consternation at any rate of Japan – naturally ceased to have any effect. And what of the Franco-Russian pact (see p. 200)? Above all, what of the Russo-Polish pact?

Poland: Hitler's 'final demands' and the outbreak of the Second World War

Between 1933 and 1937 Danzig (Gdansk) came under the control of its own Nazi Party. In October 1938 Germany began to make 'suggestions' to Poland on the subject of Danzig and the Polish Corridor (see p. 113). Poland, said Hitler, should yield control of Danzig to Germany and should allow her to build a railway and a road across the corridor. Poland, though she had a comparatively small army and little modern equipment, was not willing to discuss these matters. Instead, she reaffirmed her non-aggression pact with Russia, and when invited to join the Anti-Comintern pact refused to do so.

In March 1939, after the final breakup of Czechoslovakia, Lithuania had to surrender Memel (see p. 121), which lay close to the East Prussian frontier, and its hinterland to Germany. This, said Hitler, was his 'final demand'. Then his 'suggestions' to Poland concerning Danzig and the corridor became his 'final demands'.

During August the pressure on Poland was increased. The Poles held fast to their refusal to negotiate. As the month drew to an end there were warnings and appeals from all sides, whilst military preparations were hurried on. On 29 August Hitler said that a Polish representative must come to Berlin within twenty-four hours to conclude the matter. But no Polish representative came.

On the night of 31 August German Stormtroopers dressed as Polish soldiers attacked a German radio station on the frontier at Gleiwitz (Gliwice). The Germans claimed that Poland had attacked German frontier posts and the next morning German troops marched into Poland. Before breakfast the *Luftwaffe* was flying over Warsaw. So on 1 September 1939 the Second World War began.

For two days, while there were still faint hopes of a last minute agreement, France and Britain hesitated. On 3 September 1939, their demands that Germany should withdraw from Poland having been rejected, Britain and France declared war on Germany.

Gone are the days when madness was confined
By seas or hills from spreading through Mankind

For now our linked-up globe has shrunk so small,
One Hitler in it means mad days for all.
Through the whole World each wave of worry
  spreads,
And Ipoh dreads the war that Ipsden dreads.

So wrote a scholar-poet, Martyn Skinner, who was farming at Ipsden in Oxfordshire as he thought of a friend in Ipoh, a Malayan mining town.

22 The Second World War, 1939–45

Lightning war: Poland

At dawn on 1 September 1939 some 1,700,000 Germans swept across the Polish frontiers. The heroism of the Polish cavalrymen charging German tanks and the courage of the people of Warsaw were of no avail against the German *blitzkrieg* – the lightning war in which tanks and Stuka dive-bombers reduced cities to heaps of rubble. The Polish air force was destroyed on the ground. Civilian refugees swarming on the roads impeded military operations. On 27 September Warsaw, 'without ammunition, food, water and light', surrendered.

On 17 September the Russians, astonished by the speed of the German advance and apprehensive of having the Germans too close to them, overran the Ukrainian and Byelorussian areas of eastern Poland. At the end of the month Germany and the USSR divided Poland between them as the Nazi-Soviet pact 'allowed' them to do. A Polish government in exile was set up in London.

Polish sailors, soldiers and airmen who escaped continued the war against Germany from abroad. In Poland the home army fought a war of resistance against the Germans and Russians and suffered fearful retaliation. In the winter of 1939–40 some 14,000 Polish officers vanished without trace. When in 1943 the bodies of several thousand of these men were found in the Katyn Woods, near Smolensk, the Germans accused the Russians of having carried out a mass slaughter. The German accusation it seems was correct. The Russians were responsible for many atrocities against the Poles. And the Germans were responsible for the deaths of perhaps six million Poles. But the slaughter in the Katyn Woods aroused particularly bitter feelings (see p. 222).

Finland: the Winter War

On 30 November 1939, following Finland's refusal to yield territory around Lake Ladoga that covered the sea approaches to Leningrad, the USSR declared war on Finland. For over three months the Finns, led by Marshal Mannerheim, held out against the might of the Soviet Union. But in March 1940 Finland had to

September 1939: a Polish peasant carries on ploughing as German tanks rumble past

surrender the territory around Lake Ladoga. Later in 1940 Soviet forces occupied Estonia, Latvia and Lithuania. The USSR also took back Bessarabia from Romania and occupied northern Bukovina. When in 1941 Germany attacked the Soviet Union Finland entered the war on the German side.

Phoney war

In Britain memories of the Somme and Flanders mud were still fresh. The terrors of the Spanish Civil War, just ended, the old horrors of gas warfare and the menace of aerial bombardment hung like shadows over Britain. Yet there was relief that the indecisions of the previous months were over.

In expectation of immediate aerial attack householders and municipalities hastily built shelters. An irritating blackout was imposed. Mothers and children were evacuated to the countryside. Reservists were called up. But the call up of men conscripted for service (see p. 199) was slow in coming into operation.

However, after the conquest of Poland Germany was too busy building up the *Luftwaffe* and constructing tanks to attack France and Britain. A million French soldiers occupied the Maginot line (see p. 174); facing them were the Germans along the Siegfried line. West of the French, along the unfortified Belgian frontier to the English Channel, was the British Expeditionary Force, some 300,000 men. All was quiet on the western front. In English bars and schools the popular song was: 'We'll hang out the washing on the Siegfried line . . . '.

The war, it seemed, was a phoney war – except at sea. Within twelve hours of the outbreak of war a German submarine had sunk the British liner *Athenia* off the Irish coast. In December 1939, far away in the South Atlantic, the Royal Navy did such damage to the German pocket battleship *Graf Spee* that she limped to refuge in Montevideo. There her crew scuttled her.

Lightning war again: Denmark and Norway

Denmark and Norway refused to accept German 'protection', although in Norway a fascist movement led by a Major Quisling offered its support to Hitler. The word 'quisling' soon came to mean traitor. On 9 April 1940 Hitler attacked Denmark and Norway. On Norway's Atlantic coast he could set up submarine bases. And the Royal Navy threatened communications

with Sweden, from which Germany obtained iron ore. Denmark, who alone among European states had disarmed, was overrun in a day. Oslo and the chief centres of southern Norway fell to the invaders within twenty-four hours. However, the Royal Navy sank a large German destroyer force at Narvik and a British army landed there. But with Germany in control of Norway's airfields the British were forced to evacuate Narvik. The Germans recovered Narvik on 8 June.

The king and queen of Norway escaped to England and set up a government of Free Norway. Men and women, daring the dangers of the North Sea and German naval patrols, set out in small craft to join the forces of Free Norway. Most of Norway's large merchant marine joined that of Britain – and suffered like losses. In Norway a war of resistance was carried on.

Lightning strikes again: Holland, Belgium and France

On 10 May, before the war in Norway was over, Hitler struck at Holland, Belgium, Luxembourg and France. The conquest of Holland was completed in five days. Queen Wilhelmina escaped to England and set up a government in exile. Holland's navy and large merchant marine went over to Britain. Thousands of Dutchmen were taken as slave labourers to Germany. Others waged a war of resistance. Belgium, who had relied on the German guarantee of her frontiers (see p. 203), fought a staying action until on 28 May King Leopold III surrendered. The Belgians, ignoring the surrender, later set up a government in London.

The French and British had based their strategy on the belief that an advance into France through the Ardennes and across the River Meuse was not possible. (In 1914 the Germans had advanced through low-lying Flanders.) But on 10 May 1940 German mechanised forces swept through the Ardennes and, after crossing the Meuse on 13 May, came out behind the British and French in Flanders. The Allied forces then raced towards the Channel. German troops also swept seawards and the Allies found themselves in a trap.

Britain: Churchill comes to power

On 7 May 1940, during a Commons debate on the failure of the Norway campaign, Leopold Amery, then a backbencher, in words used by Oliver Cromwell, demanded that Chamberlain should go: 'In the name of God, go.' On 10 May Winston Churchill, first lord of the admiralty, became prime minister of Britain. He formed a Coalition government. Several labour leaders, among them Attlee, Bevin, Morrison and Greenwood, took office in Churchill's cabinet.

Churchill, who had begun his career as a Conservative, was a leading Liberal between 1904 and 1922. He rejoined the Conservatives in 1924, but later quarrelled with them over India and defence. For years he had been a lone voice crying for rearmament – and warning of the threat from Nazi Germany. He was not trusted by Labour who had not forgotten his attitude during the 1926 general strike. The military chiefs thought he was over interested in strategy and too likely to interfere. A former cavalry officer, he tended to fancy wide flanking movements – for example, the Gallipoli campaign in 1915. But whatever the true assessment of Churchill may be, his resolve and zest in that desperate hour of 1940 fired imagination and gave hope. On 13 May, addressing the Commons, he said: 'I have nothing to offer but blood, toil, tears and sweat.' His policy was to wage war 'by sea, land and air' 'with all our might and with all the strength' that God could give. The aim was to be victory 'at all costs'.

Dunkirk and the fall of France

The British army that had been trapped in Flanders completed its withdrawal to the Channel. The encircling Germans took Calais and Boulogne. Only Dunkirk remained in Allied hands. In six days at the end of May and early in June over 300,000 men, among them 140,000 French soldiers, were picked up from the beaches of Dunkirk by British destroyers and a host of small craft and taken to England. Hitler had lost perhaps the biggest prize of the war. But the RAF, providing cover for the evacuation, suffered heavy losses. And the British Expeditionary Force had lost its guns and mechanised equipment.

In France all was disorder. Torrents of refugees impeded the movement of armies. The armies that had manned the Maginot line retreated towards Paris and the south. On 14 June the Germans occupied Paris. For a few days the government, operating from Bordeaux, carried on the struggle. Churchill hoped that the French would carry on the war from their African empire. But on 22 June 1940, in the same railway coach in which the Germans had signed their surrender in 1918, French representatives signed an armistice with Germany.

Nearly two million French prisoners of war remained in German hands. Two-thirds of France, including Paris and the industrial north, came under direct German rule, whilst the departments of the south-east, and the French empire, were administered by a puppet government with its capital at Vichy. The aged Marshal Petain, hero of Verdun, became the official head of the Vichy government. He perhaps compromised to prevent the Germans from taking even more than they did. The Vichy government was anti-left, anti-semitic and authoritarian. Pétain's belief was that only authoritarian rule could restore the morale of France.

Thousands of Frenchmen were taken to work in Germany. Other joined resistance movements. In the south of France one sees simple memorials to these men and women who from cellars and mountain hideouts carried on the war against – as some of the plaques say – 'the barbarous Germans'.

Meanwhile Colonel Charles de Gaulle (see p. 199) had escaped to England. On 18 June 1940, the day he arrived, de Gaulle, broadcasting over the BBC, called on the French to resist, 'We have lost a battle but not the war', he said. The Vichy government condemned him and his supporters to death as traitors. De Gaulle later became the leader of the Free French, who pledged support to the Allies and assisted them in various operations, for example an attack on Dakar and the occupation of Syria. De Gaulle regarded the limited recognition given him by the Allies as an affront; he felt he should be treated as the equal of their leaders.

The armistice with Germany bound the French navy to await demobilisation in specified ports. One fleet was at Mers el Kebir, the French base at Oran in Algeria. The British had little faith in a German promise to the French not to make use of their navy during the war. So in July 1940, after the commanders at Oran had refused a British ultimatum to sail to British or American ports or to scuttle, the Royal Navy opened fire on the French ships. An important part of the French fleet was destroyed. But more than a thousand French sailors were killed and an angry Vichy France broke off relations with Britain. Churchill, however, tried to maintain ties with the people of France, 'comrades still though in eclipse'.

Britain – not altogether alone

By the summer of 1940 Germany was triumphant from

King George VI and Queen Elizabeth, with workers demolishing buildings after an air raid on London, September 1940. An air raid warden stands to the left of the king. The queen's presence is typical of one who has given a lifetime of devoted service to her country

the North Sea to the Mediterranean and from the English Channel to the Danube. Sweden and Switzerland remained neutral. Spain, recovering from civil war, was in no condition to join the conflict, though Franco's sympathies were with Hitler. Portugal was isolated. On 10 June 1940, when France was collapsing and the end of the war seemed near, Mussolini declared war on France and Britain. More afraid of than sympathetic to Hitler, Il Duce had waited to see how events would turn out. Now he feared that unless he joined Germany, apart from having no share in the spoils of victory, Italy would be left isolated.

So in the summer of 1940 Britain stood alone. As she confronted Hitler's 'Fortress Europe' Churchill, in defiant mood, said this was her 'finest hour'. Yet she was not quite alone. At the outbreak of war Canada, Australia, New Zealand and South Africa had declared war on Germany. The British government of India also declared war, though Gandhi's Congress Party (see p. 155) withheld its support. The colonies were swept automatically into the war. By June 1940 there were many Commonwealth soldiers and airmen in England

and others were training overseas. The navies of the Commonwealth were operating with the Royal Navy. Eire remained neutral and refused Britain use of her ports.

The USA was beginning to lend support. Under her Neutrality Acts (see p. 161) arms from the USA could not be supplied to any of the states at war. Yet in November 1939 Congress approved the sale of arms on the 'cash and carry' basis – an arrangement clearly to the advantage of Britain, who alone was in a position to send ships to 'carry' arms from the USA. In September 1940 President Roosevelt agreed to give Britain fifty old warships in return for the use of British naval and air bases in the Caribbean and Newfoundland. By then Britain's cash was running low. In November 1940 Roosevelt was re-elected president. In March 1941 Congress approved his scheme for the system of aid known as lend-lease: the USA was to supply Britain with equipment without payment; at the end of the war what was not consumed or destroyed was to be returned. 'If your neighbour's house was on fire', said Roosevelt, 'you would lend a hose to help put it out without expecting payment.' Vast supplies were thus provided for Britain and her associates without the piling up of the debts that bedevilled the world economy after 1918. The USSR in due course also benefited from lend-lease, for the scheme applied to any state whose defence was regarded as vital to the USA's safety. And at his meeting with Churchill in August 1941 (see p. 220) Roosevelt agreed that the USA would protect British as well as American shipping as far west as Iceland.

The battle of Britain, 1940

In Britain throughout the summer of 1940 everyone wondered 'When will the invasion begin? Will this be the day?' Yet a curious calm prevailed. Nearly everyone had some task – manufacturing equipment to replace that lost in France, building aeroplanes and ships, constructing fortifications, growing food, drilling in the home guard with weapons ranging from scythes to sporting guns, patrolling the beaches, watching nightly for parachutists who never came. The king practised pistol shooting in the grounds of Buckingham Palace.

In July 1940 the Germans occupied the Channel Islands. Along the French coast Hitler prepared an armada of landing craft. The Nazi army was massed ready for the invasion of Britain – Operation Sea Lion. But Sea Lion could not proceed until the Germans had air supremacy over the Channel.

Goering, who commanded the *Luftwaffe*, was given the task of destroying the Royal Air Force. In August and September 1940 tremendous battles were fought in the skies over southern England. Day after day hundreds of German bombers, escorted by fighter planes, flew in from France. The pilots flying the British Hurricane and Spitfire fighters were assisted by a secret device, radar, invented by Robert Watson-Watt in the 1930s. Day after day the Germans were driven back with heavy losses. In all they lost some 1,700 aircraft; British losses were about 1,000. More significant – for both Britain and Germany – was the loss of airmen. On 17 September 1940, Goering having admitted that the battle of Britain could not go on, the Führer postponed Operation Sea Lion.

War in Africa and complications in the Balkans

In October 1940 Mussolini declared war on Greece. The Greeks resisted stubbornly and forced the Italians back into Albania.

Meanwhile, British armies were engaged against the Italians in Abyssinia, Somaliland, Eritrea and Egypt. In September 1940 an Italian attack on Egypt was launched from Libya but in December the British under General Wavell counter-attacked. By mid-December Egypt had been cleared of Italian troops. Early in 1941 Tobruk and Benghazi surrendered to Wavell's forces. In the Mediterranean the Italian navy suffered serious defeats. The reconquest of Abyssinia was completed in May 1941 and Haile Selassie, the Lion of Judah, emperor of Ethiopia, returned to his throne.

In September 1940 Germany, Italy and Japan signed their Tripartite pact (see p. 172) with the declared object of establishing a 'new order'. Various Balkan states were invited to join the pact. Romania had earlier lost territory to the USSR (see p. 211) and also to Hungary and Bulgaria. In October 1940 German troops occupied what was left of Romania to 'protect' its oil fields. Hungary, Romania and Bulgaria joined the Tripartite pact. But the people of Yugoslavia defied Hitler: 'Sooner war than the pact; sooner death than slavery.'

By the spring of 1941 Hitler was preparing to attack the USSR. He decided first to win control of the rest of the Balkans, on his southern flank. In April 1941 he launched a *blitzkrieg* against the defiant Yugoslavs. In three days German Stukas bombed Belgrade to ruins. German troops swept down through Yugoslavia into Greece. The British had occupied Crete in November 1940. Now in 1941 British and Australian forces withdrawn from North Africa were landed in Greece. But by early June their remnants had been evacuated in another 'Dunkirk', first from Greece and then from Crete. Except for resistance movements the whole of south-east Europe was in the grip of the Nazis.

Meanwhile Hitler sent one of his ablest generals, Erwin Rommel, with his Afrika korps, to rescue the Italians in Libya. In the desert war which followed tanks and armoured cars operated almost as though they were ships and the desert the sea. For eighteen months the battle swung to and fro along the African coast. In April and May 1941 Rommel drove the British back towards Egypt, but they managed to hold on at Tobruk. The Tobruk garrison, supplied by sea from Malta, threatened the German flank. In January 1942 the British, after a brief counter-offensive, were halted at Benghazi. In June Rommel drove them back. Tobruk's gallant stand ended that month. The German advance was checked at El Alamein, about 100 kilometres from

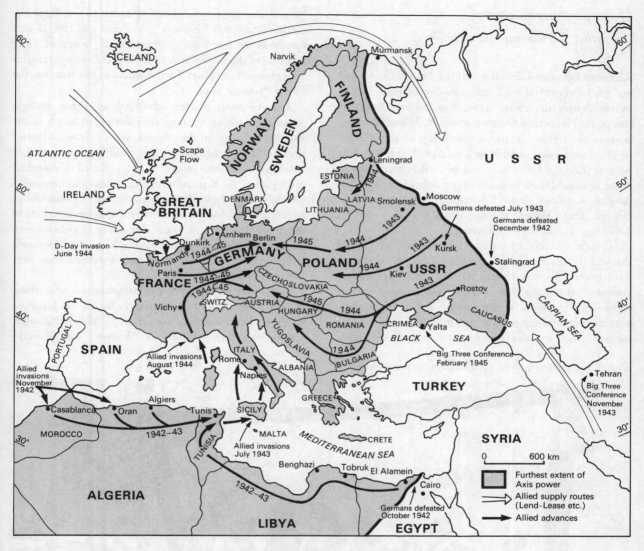

The war against the Axis powers: Europe and North Africa

Alexandria. In October–November 1942 the Germans and the Italians were defeated in a tremendous tank, air and infantry battle at El Alamein. Air superiority and better supplies played a large part in this British victory.

In December 1941 Germany and Italy had declared war on the USA (see p. 217). In November 1942 American armies under General Dwight D. Eisenhower landed in Morocco, whilst the British landed in Algeria. The Vichy French garrisons were quickly subdued and Admiral Darlan, the Vichy representative in Africa, came over to the Allies. The Germans then took direct control of Vichy France. As German mechanised units

raced through Toulon to seize the French warships there they heard explosions – the French were scuttling their ships.

From El Alamein British forces under General Bernard Montgomery advanced rapidly westwards. Rommel, caught between Montgomery in the east and Eisenhower in the west, withdrew to Tunis. As the Allies converged on Tunis Rommel received no further reinforcements. In May 1943, after desperate battles, Tunis fell to the Allies. The western entrance to the Mediterranean was thus cleared. In England church bells rang out. The war in Africa was over.

Germany turns east

Operation Barbarossa: the invasion of the USSR

Relations between Germany and the Soviet Union had not really improved with the Nazi-Soviet pact. Soviet moves against the Baltic states, Finland and Romania (see p. 211) increased German mistrust. Hitler had long coveted the fertile Ukraine – the 'living room' referred to in *Mein Kampf*. And if he could push the Russians back beyond the Urals into Asia he could obtain oil and other resources for a final assault on defiant Britain. But despite warnings from Churchill, Stalin refused to believe that Hitler would attack, and went on delivering supplies to the Germans.

Hitler's decision to reduce Yugoslavia and Greece delayed the planned attack on the USSR by what may have been a decisive month. On 22 June 1941 Hitler, claiming that Russian troops were massing on Germany's frontiers 'in preparation for an onslaught', sent an army of three million men into the Soviet Union. Among the invaders were Italians, Hungarians,

Romanians and Finns. Hitler intended to use *blitzkrieg* methods to reach Leningrad, Moscow and the oil-rich Caucasus before winter, 'Russia's ally', set in. The invasion of the USSR was code named Barbarossa, after a Germanic hero king. To the Russians the war was the Great Patriotic War.

The German armies advanced in three prongs. Attacking without warning they destroyed much of the Russian air force on the ground. With control of the air they advanced rapidly – the middle prong was at Smolensk in three weeks. Stalin ordered a scorched earth policy. By September the Germans had blockaded Leningrad. Early in December isolated German troops advancing on Moscow could see the glistening towers of the Kremlin – just a tram ride away. Farther south 700,000 Russians were encircled in Kiev. The Germans swept on to the Crimea; by the end of the year they were at Rostov on the Don.

Hitler was within an ace of attaining his objectives. But on 5 December 1941, two days before the Japanese attack on Pearl Harbour (see p. 217), Marshal Zhukov counter-attacked in front of Moscow. The Russian

Bodies of Russians hanged by the Germans near Moscow, 1941

winter, an all-out scorched earth policy, the magnificent resistance of the Russian people, the vast resources and spaces of their country were to defeat Hitler. Any advantage the Germans might have gained from discontent within the Soviet Union was lost by their brutal treatment of her people. And in July 1941 Britain and the USSR had bound themselves not to make a separate peace with Germany. 'Their danger is our danger', said Churchill. Over the years the USSR received some 13,000 planes and much other material aid from Britain and the USA. For her part in 1943 the USSR, in evidence of good faith, dissolved the Comintern.

Stalingrad and further Russian victories

Throughout the winter of 1941–42 the Germans held their lines. The Russians moved factories east to Siberia and built up fresh forces. Early in 1942 Hitler determined on an all-out offensive towards the Volga and the Caucasus. Rostov fell in July. In August the Germans attacked Stalingrad (now Volgograd) on the Volga.

The battle of Stalingrad lasted for six months. By November 1942 the German Sixth army was trapped between Russian forces on the Don and those on the Volga. Hitler forbade General von Paulus, the German commander, to withdraw. In cruel cold, fighting street by street, both Russians and Germans went through indescribable suffering. The Russians lost more men at Stalingrad than the USA lost in the whole war. On 31 January 1943 the remnants of an army of a third of a million men, among them twenty-four generals, surrendered to the Russians.

In the spring of 1943 the Russians were driving the Germans back – a few kilometres from Leningrad, about 160 kilometres from Moscow, several hundred kilometres from Stalingrad. In July 1943 the Germans counter-attacked at Kursk. In one of the decisive battles of the war, in which over a million men and some 3,000 tanks were engaged, the armies of Nazi Germany in seven days suffered a crushing defeat. By the end of 1943 the Germans were almost out of the Soviet Union. In 1944 relentless pressure drove them farther and farther back. The 900-day siege of Leningrad was ended and the rest of Russian territory was liberated.

By the end of 1944 the Russians had wrested Bulgaria, Romania, most of Hungary and more than half of Poland from Nazi control. In October Yugoslav partisans led by the communist Josip Broz – Marshal Tito – linked up with the Russians in Belgrade. About the same time the Russians recovered Estonia and Latvia.

Japan: war in the Pacific

To Pearl Harbour, 7 December 1941

For some years Japan had hoped, by expanding beyond Manchuria or into South-east Asia, to gain resources that would enable her to complete the conquest of China and establish her Greater East Asian Co-prosperity Sphere (see p. 172). By 1941 the policy of expansion into South-east Asia had been accepted by Japanese leaders.

Her neutrality pact with the USSR in April 1941, and above all the German invasion of the USSR in June of that year, relieved Japan of fear of Soviet interference. In July 1941 Japan overran what remained of French Indo-China. The Dutch government in exile that ruled the Netherlands East Indies could offer little resistance to Japanese plans. However, following this further aggression in Indo-China, the Dutch as well as the British and the USA (see p. 172) cut off trade with Japan who therefore could not get oil from Borneo or Sumatra.

In October 1941 General Tojo, the Razor, became prime minister of Japan. In Washington the Japanese ambassador was negotiating with the Americans. As the Americans insisted that Japan should withdraw from China as well as Indo-China there was no hope of agreement. In Japan civilian ministers, aware of the strength of American resources, urged caution, but the army was confident – and the army controlled affairs. On 26 November a fleet of Japanese aircraft carriers and battleships proceeded towards Hawaii.

On Sunday 7 December 1941 Japanese carrier-based planes launched an assault on the United States fleet in Pearl Harbour, Hawaii. The same day Japanese troops attacked Hong Kong. Others began to advance on Malaya and the Philippines (see map p. 219). On 8 December the USA and Britain declared war on Japan. China formally declared war on Japan the following day. On 11 December Japan's partners in the Tripartite pact, Germany and Italy, declared war on the USA. Hitler hoped that the Japanese would respond by declaring war on the USSR – but this they had no intention of doing.

Japan's swift advance

The Japanese were initially brilliantly successful. Hong Kong, after a splendid staying action, fell on Christmas Day. On 10 December 1941 torpedo bombers sank HMS *Prince of Wales* and *Repulse*, which had gone up the east coast of Malaya to prevent Japanese landings.

A drawing made by a Japanese airman shortly before he was shot down over Pearl Harbour. The aircraft carriers he expected to find were not there

By February 1942 the Japanese had conquered Malaya, crossed the Straits of Johore and captured Singapore – whose supposedly impregnable defences faced seawards. There 80,000 troops surrendered. Singapore, the proud Lion City, was renamed Shonan, Light of the South.

Following their defeat of an Allied fleet in the Java Sea the Japanese occupied Java in March 1942 and thereafter the rest of the Netherlands East Indies. They overran the Philippines; though a small force held out on the island of Corregidor until May 1942. From Thailand (see p. 316) the Japanese invaded Burma and took Rangoon on 12 March and Mandalay a few weeks later. The British withdrew into India which then came under threat of invasion. The Burma Road (see p. 172) was closed but American planes were soon flying supplies over the Hump (the Himalayas) for Chiang Kai-shek. None of this aid stirred Chiang from his lethargy. He preferred to wait for the Americans to win the war. The Chinese communists, carrying on their guerilla war, were more active.

Difficulties of Japan

Japan's initial successes had used up much of her resources. She lost many of her best airmen in the early assaults. Nor was the attack on Pearl Harbour as successful as the Japanese had hoped. Several American battleships were put out of action but three aircraft carriers were delivering planes to island bases and escaped harm. This was crucial, for the war in the Pacific was to be largely a carrier war – as Admiral Yamamoto, who had planned the Pearl Harbour attack, had foreseen.

'We are all in the same boat now', Roosevelt said to Churchill after Pearl Harbour. There was no one else in Japan's boat. She got no direct help from Germany or Italy – though their declaration of war on the USA diverted American effort from Japan. Japan won no real allies in Asia though she continued to claim she was establishing her Co-prosperity Sphere. Some nationalist leaders did co-operate with her – but for their own purposes. Burma and the Philippines were granted 'independence'. In some areas Japan imposed military rule. But in independent Burma or non-independent Java, indeed anywhere within the Co-prosperity Sphere, there was little prosperity. When food in Hong Kong became scarce the Japanese dumped Chinese on nearby islands 'to look after themselves' – to die of starvation.

Everywhere there were beatings and torture and conscription of workers. It is understandable that the Japanese treated prisoners of war harshly, for to them the one alternative to victory was death. But this does not explain their treatment of civilians whom they claimed to be liberating.

Japan's resources of men and materials were spread out over a vast area. Her extended lines of communication, mainly across the sea, could be easily attacked. She had made scarcely any preparation for anti-submarine warfare. In their conquered territories the Japanese had to rely almost entirely on local resources. Supplies of oil were almost totally cut off. Japan was unable to replace ships at the same rate as the Americans. While American shipyards turned out fleet aircraft carriers by the score and light carriers by the hundred, the Japanese built only a handful. Many of their planes were sub-standard – the mobile coffins as Japanese airmen called them.

The turn of the tide in the Pacific

By April 1942 the Japanese advance directly threatened Australia. But in May 1942 the advance towards Australia was halted at the Coral Sea when American carrier forces, with the aid of the Royal Australian Navy, turned back a Japanese task force heading for Port Moresby.

In June 1942 the Japanese made a thrust towards Midway Island, within striking distance of Honolulu.

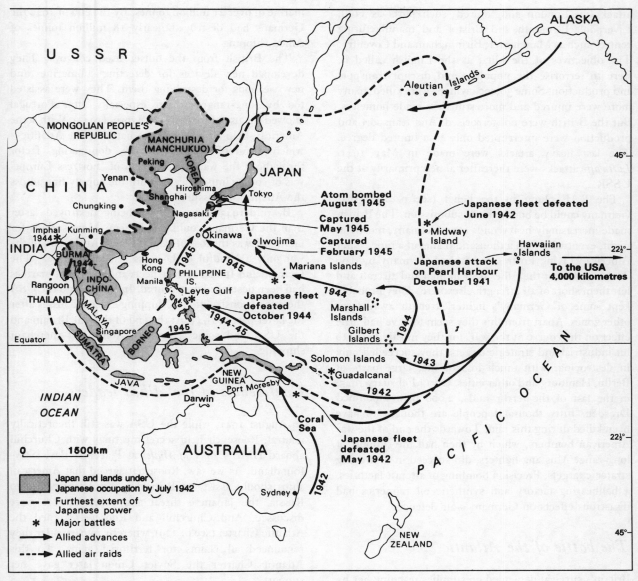

The war against Japan, 1941–1945

The Americans, who had broken the Japanese codes and so knew their plans, won a decisive victory at Midway. The Japanese navy never recovered from the loss of the four carriers sunk at Midway.

Guadalcanal, an island in the Solomon group, was the most southerly point occupied by the Japanese. There, in August 1942, the Americans made a landing. Roosevelt wrote to Stalin: 'We have gained, I believe, a toehold in the south-west from which the Japanese will find it very difficult to dislodge us.' The sea and land battles fought for control of Guadalcanal lasted until

early 1943 when the Japanese gave in.

The autumn of 1942 marked a turning point in the war. While the Americans held the Japanese on Guadalcanal the Russians held the Germans in Stalingrad. And at El Alamein the British defeated the Germans and Italians.

War in the air

After the battle of Britain ended the *Luftwaffe* continued

attacks on London and 'toured' such ports as Hull, Liverpool, Plymouth and Bristol and manufacturing centres such as Manchester, Birmingham and Coventry. The objectives of the blitz, as the English called it, were to terrorise the populace and disrupt transport and production. Some 30,000 civilians were killed, many more were injured and more still were made homeless. But the British were not terrorised. And transport and production were interrupted only to a limited degree. The last heavy attacks were made in May 1941. *Luftwaffe* attacks were thereafter aimed primarily at the USSR.

The RAF clung to the belief (see p. 106) that Germany could be bombed into submission. The British made increasingly heavy raids over Germany, mostly at night, eventually with a thousand planes at a time. Later American Flying Fortresses bombed Germany by day. These raids cost the Allies dear in men and aircraft and left them short of air strength elsewhere. They probably kept some of Germany's fighter strength away from other zones. Apart from this they seem to have had little effect on the course of the war, for they mostly failed to hit industrial and strategic targets; they succeeded only in destroying, with much loss of life, large parts of Berlin, Hamburg and other cities. On 14 February 1945, in the last of the terror raids, 2,000 planes bombed Dresden. Fifty thousand people are thought to have been killed during this raid. Towards the end of the war American bombers, which by then had the support of long-range Mustang fighters, did succeed in destroying strategic targets. Precision bombing of aircraft factories, a ballbearing factory and synthetic oil refineries had disastrous effects on Germany's air defences.

The battle of the Atlantic

Britain's survival depended on supplies reaching her by sea. By attacking Allied ships Germany hoped to bring about the defeat of Britain. In 1939, when the Germans had only twenty-two long-range U-boats, most of their attacks were made in the seas around Britain. Later, with over 1,000 ocean-going submarines, they attacked far out in the Atlantic and in Arctic waters and even along the United States coast. For a time U-boats operating in groups or 'wolf packs' had great success. German raiders disguised as merchant vessels attacked freighters as far afield as the coast of Australia. In the Atlantic lone battleships and cruisers raided ships and convoys. When the war began Britain had a merchant marine of over 21 million tonnes. By the end of 1942 the Germans had destroyed nearly 18 million tonnes of Allied shipping.

The British from the outset used convoys. They developed new devices for detecting submarines and new weapons for destroying them. They were assisted too by long-range aircraft especially after Portugal allowed the use of bases in the Azores (1943). With some American help Britain won the battle of the Atlantic – which Churchill said was the dominating factor throughout the war. An invasion of 'Fortress Europe' was of course impracticable until the supply line across the Atlantic was assured.

By mid-1943 U-boats were being destroyed faster than the Germans could build them. More serious for Germany was the loss of skilled crews. At the end of the war only a handful of U-boats remained at sea. The German and Italian surface fleets and merchant marines had been destroyed or captured. In Britain and the USA the rate of construction of shipping exceeded losses after the latter part of 1943. At the end of the war Britain and the USA had some 43 million tonnes of merchant shipping.

Conferences of the Allied leaders

In August 1941, while the USA was still theoretically neutral, Roosevelt held secret meetings with Churchill aboard HMS *Prince of Wales* at Placentia Bay, Newfoundland. As we saw, Roosevelt agreed that American ships should assist the British in the Atlantic. Aid to Russia, the Japanese threat and other matters were discussed. And Churchill and Roosevelt signed the Atlantic Charter (see p. 229), whereby in particular they renounced all claims for territorial gains. To this Atlantic Charter the Soviet Union later gave her support.

After the attack on Pearl Harbour Churchill hastened to America. He and Roosevelt agreed that their first objective was the defeat of Germany. They agreed to the establishment of a joint Anglo-American command and that the bulk of American resources should be directed against Germany. In fact considerable resources were from the outset made available in the Pacific.

In January 1943 Churchill and Roosevelt met at Casablanca in Morocco and decided on an Allied invasion of Italy that year. They also agreed that bomber raids on Germany and aid to Russia should continue until 1944, when an invasion would be mounted from the west against Germany's 'Fortress Europe'. Roosevelt reassured the Russians by promising there would be no negotiations with Germany; the USA and Britain would accept only unconditional surrender.

In November 1943, after a conference in Cairo, Churchill, Roosevelt and Chiang Kai-shek signed the Cairo Declaration. This declared that the war against Japan would continue until she made an unconditional surrender and that she would be stripped of all the territories she had taken, including Manchukuo and Taiwan. Korea was to become independent.

Later in November Roosevelt and Churchill met Stalin in Tehran. Stalin made clear his view that 'Germany is to be broken up and kept broken up'. He continued to insist that his allies should open a second front in France. Roosevelt and Churchill agreed – though their stipulations concerning the time required for preparations seemed unconvincing to Stalin. Stalin opposed a plan put forward by Churchill for Allied forces not engaged in Italy to occupy the Balkans; except in the case of Greece Stalin was determined to do this himself.

Second fronts

Italy

On 10 July 1943 American, British and Canadian forces under Eisenhower invaded Sicily. Meanwhile Italy's humiliating defeats in Africa and domestic problems had led to growing resentment against Mussolini. On 25 July he was forced to resign. After an audience with Victor Emmanuel III he was whisked into an ambulance and placed under arrest. Amid wild rejoicing people shouted: 'Fascism is dead.' Mussolini was succeeded by Marshal Badoglio. On 3 September 1943 Badoglio agreed to Italy's unconditional surrender. On the same day the Allies invaded mainland Italy.

Meanwhile German forces took control of northern Italy. In mid-September, at Hitler's order, Nazi paratroopers rescued Mussolini from the mountain top where he had been secluded. A Fascist republic was proclaimed in northern Italy and Mussolini again declared war on the Allies. In October 1943 Badoglio's government declared war on Germany. German opposition in Italy remained strong and the Allies made slow progress. Rome, declared an open city, was captured by the Allies only in June 1944. By the winter of that year they were within 160 kilometres of the River Po in northern Italy.

Operation Overlord

6 June 1944 was D-Day for Operation Overlord, the invasion of Normandy by the western allies. Eisenhower was in supreme command. Much of the success of Operation Overlord was the result of detailed preparation. An artificial harbour, Mulberry, was created by sinking ships filled with concrete off the shores of Normandy. Pluto (Pipe Line Under the Ocean) carried oil from England to the beachhead. In the hundred days after D-Day more than two million men and 4 million tonnes of supplies were landed.

Again Rommel, who now commanded the German defences in Normandy, confronted Montgomery, who was in immediate command of the invading forces. Rommel's communications were so disrupted by Allied air and naval bombardment that movement behind the German lines was almost brought to a standstill. And behind the lines the French resistance, outraged by Nazi ruthlessness, was active. On 12 June Rommel wrote: 'The material equipment of the Anglo-Americans . . . is far superior. . . . Parachute troops and airborne troops are used in such large numbers and so effectively that the troops attacked have a difficult task in defending themselves. . . . The Luftwaffe has unfortunately not been able to take action.' By the end of July the German defences in Normandy were broken.

In August an Allied army under the American General Patch landed in the south of France, advanced up the Rhône valley and linked up with troops from Normandy. On 24 August Paris was liberated by the French resistance assisted by a Free French armoured division. At the end of August de Gaulle led a triumphal procession through Paris.

On 20 July some of Hitler's officers had made an unsuccessful attempt to assassinate him. 'With Hitler we can never have peace', they said. In October 1944 Rommel, who was involved in the plot, was arrested, took poison and was then given a splendid military funeral.

The drive towards Berlin

The Germans fought on. As the autumn of 1944 approached they were defeated, but by no means beaten. Brussels was liberated early in September but an attempt to outflank the Germans through Holland failed when a British airborne division was destroyed at Arnhem. In December 1944 a German army again drove through the Ardennes. The Allies were forced back and the German line bulged forward. But the Americans could not be driven from their key positions and the battle of the Bulge ended in defeat for the Germans. The Allies renewed their advance to Berlin, which they hoped to reach by Christmas 1944. But by Christmas they had not reached the Rhine.

The Russians had continued to drive forward. By 1 August 1944 they were on the outskirts of Warsaw. Encouraged by broadcasts from Moscow the Polish home army in Warsaw rose against the Germans. There followed two months of savage fighting – while the Russians looked on. They later claimed that it had not been possible for them to help the Poles. This was probably so – but as the 'rebels' were not communists the Russians were perhaps content to see them destroyed. Whatever the truth of the matter, some 300,000 Poles were killed and Warsaw was reduced to ruins. The Germans remained in control.

Yalta, February 1945

In February 1945 Churchill, Roosevelt and Stalin met at Yalta in the Crimea. They agreed that Germany should be disarmed, demilitarised and divided into zones, to be occupied by the three major allies. France was to occupy part of the American zone if she wished. Germany was also to pay reparations 'to the greatest possible extent', of which half would go to the Soviet Union. Arrangements were to be made to try war criminals. The Allies agreed that their only duty towards Germany was to provide her people with a minimum level of subsistence.

In accordance with the Atlantic Charter (see p. 220) the countries occupied by Germany (including her allies) were to be free to elect their own governments.

Although the Atlantic Charter had renounced territorial gains the Big Three – Churchill, Roosevelt and Stalin – now agreed that the USSR should get Polish territory east of the Curzon line. This was the territory Poland had acquired from Bolshevik Russia in 1921 (see p. 116). In compensation Poland was promised German territory to her west. There was also the problem of the two Polish 'governments': the London government in exile, which the western allies supported, and the Polish Committee of National Liberation in Lublin in Poland, which the USSR recognised. The London Poles, particularly mistrustful of the Russians after the discovery of the Katyn Woods massacre (see p. 210), and more mistrustful after the Warsaw uprising, opposed any cession of territory to the USSR. However, Stalin promised that London Poles would be included in the Lublin 'government' and that there would be free elections.

The Big Three also agreed that the USSR should sign a treaty of friendship and alliance with China and should join the war against Japan after the defeat of Germany – in return for concessions in Manchuria. All this was kept secret from the Chinese. The USSR was also to get southern Sakhalin and the Kuriles.

Roosevelt, it has been said, was so preoccupied with the need for Britain to dismantle her empire that at Yalta he did not seriously consider the possibility of the Russians building up their 'empire' in eastern Europe. However, Russians already occupied all eastern Europe, except Greece, which was liberated by British forces, and Yugoslavia. No amount of pressure by the USA or Britain was likely to have altered the consequences of that hard fact. The scheme put forward by Churchill at Tehran for the western allies to invade eastern Europe might have altered the situation, but was not supported by the Americans. Roosevelt was certainly anxious to placate Stalin at Yalta as he wanted the USSR to join in the war against Japan, whose early defeat then seemed unlikely.

Roosevelt was not to know the consequences of the decisions made at Yalta. The great statesman died on 12 April 1945, less than a month before the defeat of Germany.

Victory in Europe

In January 1945 the Russians liberated Warsaw and moved ruthlessly towards Berlin. Soviet soldiers were given a propaganda sheet which read: 'Kill. Nothing in Germany is guiltless, neither the living nor the yet unborn. Follow the words of Comrade Stalin and crush for ever the fascist beast in its den. Break the racial pride of the German woman. Take her as your legitimate booty. Kill, you brave soldiers of the victorious Soviet army.'

By this time the Luftwaffe had suffered such losses that British and American planes could attack factories, communications and military stores almost without opposition. By the war's end for every tonne of bombs dropped on Britain over 300 tonnes had fallen on Germany.

The western allies reached the Rhine in February 1945. The first troops crossed the river early in March – Americans in the south, British and Canadians in the

VE Day: the end of the war in Europe. Piccadilly Circus, with the statue of Eros boarded up, 8 May 1945

north. On 11 April American troops were on the River Elbe and approaching Berlin. They agreed to wait there while the Russians pressed on to Berlin from the east.

From 19 April to 1 May Russians and Germans fought the battle of Berlin. The Germans would not yield a single building without a fierce struggle. Shells and bombs rained down on the ruined city. On 30 April Hitler, who had moved to Berlin, committed suicide in his bunker, not far from the Reichstag whose overthrow had brought such havoc to Germany. The day before he died he had married Eva Braun, the woman with whom he had been associated for a number of years. She too committed suicide. The bodies of Adolf Hitler and Eva Braun were soaked with petrol and burnt. But to this day mystery surrounds the last frightful hours of the

man who for years had terrorised the world.

Two days before Hitler's death the Germans in Italy surrendered. Italian partisans seized Mussolini as he attempted to flee. He was shot and his corpse was taken to Milan. There a mother who had lost five sons in the war shot five bullets into Il Duce's body. Mussolini was then hung by his ankles from a shopfront. Beside him dangled the corpse of his mistress; she too had been shot by the partisans.

In Germany what little authority survived Hitler's death passed to Admiral Doenitz. The Third Reich was breaking up piecemeal. On 4 May German forces in north Germany surrendered to Field-Marshal Montgomery. On 7 May Eisenhower accepted Germany's unconditional surrender at Rheims. VE Day, Victory in

The Burma campaign. British soldiers advance cautiously from a Buddhist temple, January 1945

Europe Day, was celebrated on 8 May 1945. On the same day the Germans formally surrendered to Marshal Zhukov in Berlin.

The approaching defeat of Japan

After the capture of Guadalcanal (see p. 219) the Americans captured one after another of the Japanese-held Pacific islands; other islands were deliberately by-passed. Throughout 1943 and 1944 this island-hopping campaign continued. In June and October 1944, in two battles fought off the Philippines, all but the last remnants of the Japanese navy were destroyed. 'I shall return', General MacArthur, who escaped from the Philippines in 1942, had said. In October 1944 he waded ashore at the head of American forces that had come to recover the Philippines.

A Japanese plan to invade India, the March on Delhi (March 1944), had ended in failure. The British under

General Slim then invaded Burma. Chinese forces came into Burma from the north. The Burma Road was reopened. The reconquest of Burma was completed in May 1945.

Meanwhile the fanaticism of the Japanese expressed itself in kamikaze attacks. (Kamikaze, divine wind, was the typhoon that shattered a fleet sent by Kublai Khan to invade Japan.) The kamikaze pilots set out with sufficient fuel only to reach their objective. Singing,

> We go to battle shielded by a divine force
> And as we die we salute our Emperor God,

they threw themselves – planes, bombs, pilots and all – against their targets in certain suicide.

The Japanese had fought with fanatical bravery and on island after island had to be searched out and killed to the last man. Only a handful of Japanese prisoners was taken – and these were regarded by their families as dead and dishonoured. In February 1945 the Americans landed on Iwojima, 1,200 kilometres from Tokyo.

Iwojima cost 4,000 American lives. Soon after, the capture of Okinawa cost 12,000 American and 120,000 Japanese lives. If the Japanese fought thus for outlying islands, how would they fight for Japan itself, the Americans wondered. That 7,000 Japanese prisoners were taken at Okinawa was an indication of weakening.

After the conquest of Burma the British planned an invasion of Malaya. The Australians recovered Borneo. British carriers and supporting ships linked up with American fleets to make bombing raids upon Japan itself. Japanese houses had no air raid shelters. On one day in March 1945 some 80,000 people in Tokyo were killed. As the Japanese navy and air force had almost ceased to exist battleships could approach the coast and shell cities with little danger to themselves.

Scientific discoveries during the war

Throughout the war scientists and engineers were at work. Great advances were made. In the First World War a high proportion of men wounded in battle died. In the Second World War the proportion was relatively low. The sulpha drugs, and penicillin (discovered in Oxford by Alexander Fleming and developed by an Australian, Howard Florey) saved many lives. Radar equipment used early in the war looked old fashioned by 1945. The planes of 1939 were relatively cheap and simple; by 1945 they were costly and sophisticated. Jet aeroplanes, pioneered in England by Frank Whittle, had ushered in the jet age.

The Germans succeeded to a greater extent than the British and Americans in developing rockets. They invented a pilotless jet-propelled bomb, V1, and a rocket-propelled bomb, V2 (Vengeance weapons 1 and 2). Late in the summer of 1944 V1 flying bombs, the doodlebugs, were used to bombard England. In September southern England was attacked by V2s. Fired over 300 kilometres from their targets, these rockets travelled at 1.6 kilometres a second carrying a 1-tonne bomb. These secret weapons had little effect on the course of the war but the work on V2 was the basis for post-war developments in the USA and the USSR of rockets – for space research as well as for weapons.

In 1920 Ernest Rutherford, a New Zealander working at Cambridge, demonstrated the nuclear reaction of particles. His discovery was followed up by other scientists. Foremost among these were Enrico Fermi in Rome and Otto Hahn in Berlin. In 1938 Fermi escaped to the USA. In the same year a German refugee scientist told a Danish physicist, Niels Bohr, that Hahn had succeeded in bringing about the fission of uranium atoms. This news Bohr took to Washington, where he attended a conference of physicists in January 1939. Fermi and a Hungarian refugee scientist, Leo Szilard, passed on this information to Albert Einstein, the foremost physicist and mathematician in the world. Einstein, a Jew, had left Germany in 1932. In a letter to Roosevelt he warned of the danger of Germany producing a bomb based on the principle of atomic fission. Roosevelt then made money available for secret atomic research in the USA.

In December 1942, under Fermi's direction, a chain reaction fission of uranium was brought about in Chicago. British and Canadian scientists joined in the research. At 5.30 a.m. on 16 July 1945 an atomic bomb was exploded at Alamogordo air base in New Mexico. The tower from which the bomb was exploded was turned to vapour and the desert sand for over 700 metres around was reduced to glass.

Hiroshima and Nagasaki: enduring the unendurable

On the death of Roosevelt in April 1945 Vice-president Harry S. Truman became president of the USA. To him fell the responsibility of deciding whether to use the atomic bomb against Japan. Was Japan so weakened that she would soon surrender? A strong and fanatically brave army still defended the home islands. It seemed that an invasion might meet prolonged resistance, with great loss of life, both Allied and Japanese. Although some of his military advisers said it was not necessary, Truman decided to use the atomic bomb.

On 6 August 1945 black smoke mushroomed over Hiroshima. On 8 August the USSR declared war on Japan and invaded Manchuria (Manchukuo). On 9 August an atomic bomb was dropped on Nagasaki.

Meanwhile, at Potsdam (see p. 233) the Allies had demanded Japan's unconditional surrender. The events of 6–9 August led Emperor Hirohito himself to insist that the struggle must end. So the Potsdam demands were accepted, with a plea that the emperor's position should not suffer. At midday on 15 August 1945, in a radio broadcast, the ordinary people of Japan for the first time in history heard the voice of an emperor: 'We have resolved to pave the way for a grand peace for all generations to come by enduring the unendurable and suffering what is insufferable.'

Hiroshima has been rebuilt, but the immediate area where the bomb fell has been left as it was – a memorial, a warning and a challenge to future generations the world over. In a museum near by there is a piece of stone with the outline of a human figure seared on to it like a strange shadow. And there is a watch, apparently little damaged, its hands stopped for ever at the moment at which the atomic bomb exploded over Hiroshima.

The cost of total war

The Second World War affected the lives of entire nations – by conscription, by rationing, by control of employment, by evacuation. As victims of bombing, as refugees, by the ruthless demands of conquerors, by starvation, as prisoners, as partisans, countless people suffered. The disruption of lives and the destruction and waste of material resources are beyond assessment.

The cost of the war in lives has been variously assessed. A conservative estimate is that over 15 million

servicemen were killed. Probably one out of every 22 Russians, one out of every 25 Germans, one out of every 46 Japanese, one out of every 150 Britons and one out of every 450 Americans was killed. There is some truth in Stalin's remark that Britain's contribution towards victory was time, the United States' contribution was goods – and the Russian contribution was lives.

The loss of civilian lives – certainly greater than that of servicemen – is impossible to assess. For China, estimates range from three to thirteen million. Bombing accounted for only a fraction of the civilian deaths. Brutal treatment of civilians by their conquerors caused millions of deaths. To quote one instance: the inhabitants of the Czech village of Lidice were suspected of complicity in the murder of a German official renowned for his brutal cruelty. Thereupon every male in Lidice, young or old, and fifty-six women were executed. The remaining women and girls were taken to concentration camps and the village was levelled to the ground.

Some eight million slave labourers were taken to work

Brother kills brother, 1941 : bodies of French soldiers after a Free French attack in Vichy-controlled Syria

Polish Jews being rounded up in the Warsaw ghetto, April 1943. The small boy was one of the 'lucky' ones – he survived and in 1983 was living in America

in Germany; another four million were transferred to occupied territories. Working under appalling conditions, millions of these people died. The Germans themselves admitted that over three and a half million Russians died in their hands. The Poles suffered unspeakably at the hands of both Germans and Russians; 15 per cent of Poland's population, among them many Jews, were killed or murdered.

The concentration camps to which the Nazis sent opponents and suspected opponents of their rule were places of cruelty, horror and death. Survivors of the camp at Theresienstadt (Terezin) in Czechoslovakia said of conditions there: 'We sweat and starve. We work half naked. We dig throughout the night. In the morning . . . a piece of black bread [is thrown to each of us]; it soars through the air and we catch it like wild cats behind iron bars, eat it avidly within a few minutes and go on digging. . . . ' Speaking of prisoners who had been moved from Theresienstadt they said: '[The fate of all of them is] the same, though each sounds different: Gas,

shot, died of hunger, air raid, typhus, electric current, scores of deaths, each in a different form.'

During the war, camps at Treblinka, Auschwitz (Oswiecim) and other centres in Poland became extermination camps, where Hitler arrived at his 'final' monstrous 'solution' of the Jewish 'problem'. To these camps were consigned for mass extermination Jews from every corner of Europe where the Nazis were in control. Gas chambers were constructed into which 2,000 people at a time were herded. Children about to be led into the gas chambers were told that they were going to have a shower. Young Jews, after working as slave labourers, were forced to dig their own graves before being shot. Some six million Jews were thus destroyed. By similar methods many of the gypsies of eastern Europe were eliminated.

Only after the war did the world – and many people in Germany – learn the full extent of this horror. The war had added another word to our vocabulary – genocide, the killing of a race.

23 The post-war world: the United Nations Organisation

A world in ruins

The material destruction of the First World War was confined to relatively limited regions. At the end of the Second World War much of Europe and Asia lay in ruins. There were shortages of the most elementary requirements – food, clothing, warmth and shelter. In Germany the daily wage of an unskilled worker was enough to buy half a cigarette. In Poland 'coal was sold by the kilogramme and in some places people lived in clay huts. . . . Even in the centre of Warsaw mines blew up and day after day collapsing walls caused further deaths.' In western Russia some 2,000 towns and 70,000 villages had been destroyed. In Japan the destruction was complete.

Across the wasteland of Europe millions of 'displaced persons', for example slave labourers used by the Germans, struggled towards their homes. Millions of prisoners of war, and survivors of concentration camps, waited to be repatriated. More millions of refugees fled from persecution or political pressure, whilst other millions of 'settlers' poured in to take their places. In parts of Asia millions of refugees returned to shells of cities and towns and villages that had been their homes.

Out of such chaos order eventually emerged. Ironically, where destruction was most complete, for example in Germany and Japan, reconstruction with all its advantages was correspondingly complete. Such was not the position in Britain, or in France, which was relatively unscathed.

A changed world

After the Second World War western Europe ceased to be the centre round which the rest of the world even appeared to revolve. In 1945 Hitler predicted:

'With the defeat of the reich and pending the emergence of the [Asian], the African and perhaps the South American nationalisms, there will remain only two great powers capable of confronting each other – the United States and Soviet Russia. The laws of both history and geography will compel these two powers to a trial of strength either militarily or in the fields of economics and ideology.'

A German family, from Frankfurt on Oder, in the Russian zone of Germany, in a street in Berlin, September 1945. In some cities refugees were eating human flesh. Packs of wolves roamed over once prosperous farms

Western Europe was overshadowed by these two giants: the USSR, totalitarian and in theory egalitarian; and the USA, champion of individual liberty and multi-party democracy. The clamour for independence apparent in Asia and to some extent in Africa by 1945 was to lead to the emergence of a 'third world' that would have to be taken into account by the great powers.

The industrial revolution spread its net ever wider. Quiet kampongs (villages) in faraway Borneo began to be lit by electric light. Kampong children began to go to school and farmers, abandoning their buffalo-drawn ploughs, began using tractors and rotary cultivators and pesticides. In remote parts of China immense industrial cities sprang up. Brazil, once heavily dependent on one crop, coffee, became a major shipbuilder and in 1981 was the world's seventh largest exporter of arms. Everywhere 'king' coal and steel became less important, whilst oil, and plastics and other synthetics, grew in importance. Inventions, new techniques, education were transforming society in every continent and making possible greater wealth – at least for some. New technology opened up undreamt-of opportunities – even of reaching out beyond the earth to explore the universe – and greater destruction in the event of war.

After the war many parts of the world looked to the USSR rather than to western Europe or the USA for their model. The experience of the Second World War had shown how the resources of a community, both human and material, could be fully utilised. The idea of a planned economy gained widespread favour.

Nationalism, often a very aggressive nationalism, remained powerful but there was a growth in international activity. There was immense growth in international trade and communication. In the extended industrial society the Fiat company of Italy builds cars in the USSR to sell in Hungary. In Argentina the Ford company builds cars for Latin America. An English company manufactures shoes in Shanghai and American companies build hotels in Peking. A holiday abroad has become common for millions the world over.

The welfare of society as a whole, rather than of the individual or some section of the community, seemed more important – or at least lip service was given to that idea. And there was growing awareness of the gulf between the stark poverty in developing lands and the comfort and even luxury in economically advanced states. The population explosion (see table above) that accompanied improved conditions of health and the pollution that accompanied the spread of industry threatened the security of rich and poor nations alike.

The population explosion 1967–77: world population in millions and average annual percentage growth

	1967	1977	1967–77
Africa	328	440	3.4
Asia (excluding USSR)	1907[1]	2352[2]	2.3
Europe (excluding USSR)	452	478	0.6
Latin America (including Cuba, Dominican Republic)	259	322	2.4
North America (including West Indies)	220	254	1.5
Oceania	20	22	1.0
USSR	226	259[3]	1.5
World	3412	4127	2.1

[1]720 million in China, 511 million in India
[2]866 million in China, 626 million in India
[3]191 million in Europe, 68 million in Asia

World production of staple foods in million tonnes 1955–77

	1955–57	1965	1967	1977
Wheat	218	257	301	387
Rice	215	255	282	367
Meat	52	68	74	122

Comparison of rates of growth of food production per head in developed and developing countries 1948–76

	1948–52	1956–60	1961–65	1971–76
Developed countries	81	94	100	115
Developing countries[1]	89	98	100	102

[1]Excluding China

Whilst overall food production has scarcely kept pace with the population explosion, consumption per head is far from even – for although the base figure 100 (in the last table), representing average annual production per head, is the same for developed and developing countries, actual production per head 1961–65 was much higher in the former.

The United Nations Organisation

The League of Nations for all practical purposes ceased to exist in 1939. Its final act had been to expel the USSR when she invaded Finland. On 1 January 1942 twenty-six Allied and friendly nations accepted the principles of the Atlantic Charter, drawn up the previous August

Rubber and jute from UNRRA, sent by river and canal, reach Prague

by Churchill and Roosevelt. The signatories of the pact, who called themselves the United Nations, included Britain, the USA, the Soviet Union, China, eight European states whose governments were in exile, five members of the British commonwealth and nine Latin American states. The United Nations bound themselves to recognise the principles of self-determination (the right of peoples to choose their own form of government) and of territorial integrity. Churchill and Roosevelt had also declared the hope that 'all the men in all the lands may live out their lives in freedom from fear and want'. The United Nations therefore bound themselves to abandon the use of force and to co-operate in establishing social, economic and political freedom.

In November 1943 the United Nations Relief and Rehabilitation Administration (UNRRA) was set up. Financed mainly by the USA and Britain, its function was to provide immediate aid – food, clothing, medicine,

agricultural equipment, transport – in liberated areas. In the five years of its operation UNRRA did valuable work in Europe and the Far East. The International Refugee Organisation between 1946 and 1952 gave help to some 1,500,000 refugees left in Europe after the first post-war mass movements of people were completed. Later the UN high commissioner for refugees assisted Arabs, Kampucheans, boat people from Vietnam, Afghans and many others. The UN International Children's Emergency Fund (UNICEF), organised in 1946, was later set up on a permanent basis. In 1944 the UN Organisation for Educational and Cultural Reconstruction, now the UN Educational Scientific and Cultural Organisation (UNESCO), came into being. UNESCO has engaged in a variety of tasks, from the review of textbooks to exclude nationalist propaganda to the rescue of Egyptian monuments threatened by flooding. In 1944 the International Monetary Fund (IMF), which concerns itself with the exchange and stability of currencies, and the

International Bank for Reconstruction and Development (the World Bank) were founded. The World Bank has provided capital for developing countries to undertake major projects in irrigation, power supplies, communications and so on.

From August to September 1944 delegates from the USA, the Soviet Union, the British Commonwealth and China met at Dumbarton Oaks, near Washington, to prepare plans for an international organisation, the United Nations Organisation, to replace the League of Nations. The outline scheme was approved at Yalta (February 1945) – including a provision that each permanent member of the security council (see below) should have the right of veto.

At a conference held in San Francisco from April to June 1945 arrangements were finalised. On 26 June fifty nations signed the United Nations Charter and on 24 October 1945 the United Nations Organisation came into being. The charter makes clear that its chief aims are the maintenance of peace and the development of friendly relations among nations.

Like the League of Nations, UNO is not permitted to intervene in the domestic affairs of its members. However, it seeks international co-operation in economic, cultural and humanitarian matters. In 1948 it adopted a universal declaration of human rights – including such positive rights as the right to education, and to work. Yet some UNO members, whether of the left or the right, continue to abuse human rights.

UNO members are required to be 'peace-loving states' willing to assist in any action the organisation takes under the charter. Unlike the League of Nations UNO has become an almost universal organisation. By 1958 there were 82 member nations, including Japan and all Germany's former allies. With the grant of independence to colonial areas membership grew rapidly. By 1961 Afro-Asian members were in a majority. In 1983 there were 157 members. Certain states were permanent observers – for example neutral Switzerland, divided Korea and little Monaco. The admission of East and West Germany (see p. 253) to UNO followed a treaty (1972) by which these states recognised one another; until then both claimed to represent Germany.

UNO has a general assembly in which each state, large or small, has one vote. The assembly meets every September and at other times if required to discuss affairs and to supervise the activities of dependent organisations. It votes on the admission of members to UNO, elects the non-permanent members of the security council and arranges the organisation's finances. The security council meets whenever required – in an emergency it can assemble at very short notice. This council has the special responsibility of preserving peace. It has five permanent members (Britain, France, China, the USA and the USSR) and six, later ten, elected members. Until 1971 China was represented by the Republic of China (Taiwan) and then by the People's Republic of China. Decisions in the security council were made by seven, now nine, votes which because of their power of veto must include the votes of all five permanent members. By the end of 1949 the USSR had used its veto forty times.

Because action was so often blocked the security council lost some of its authority, whereas the assembly gained in stature. In January 1950, after the USA had vetoed a Russian proposal, the Russians withdrew from the council for some months; in particular they were absent during the early part of the Korean crisis (see p. 245). During this crisis the assembly acquired the right, if the council failed to reach agreement, to recommend by a two-thirds vote suitable action in case of a threat to peace.

The secretariat of UNO with its headquarters in New York is responsible for day-to-day administration. Officials are chosen from all the nations of UNO. The chief officer is the secretary general. In this post the Norwegian Trygve Lie (1946–52), Dag Hammarskjöld from Sweden (1953–61), the Burmese U Thant (1961–71) and the Austrian Kurt Waldheim (1972–81) at times exercised considerable influence. A Peruvian, Javier Perez de Cuellar, became secretary general in 1982. The expenses of the organisation are met by members according to their size and ability to pay. Many small states and some larger ones have not kept up with their payments.

UNO has a number of subsidiary agencies. At the head of these is the Economic and Social Council which is assisted by three regional commissions (Europe, Asia and the Far East, and Latin America) and by functional commissions concerned with particular activities. Other agencies, for example the World Health Organisation (WHO), and the Trusteeship Council, which took over responsibility for mandated (trust) territories (Tanganyika for example) carried on the work of League of Nations bodies. The International Labour Organisation (ILO) continued to be active; thus in 1981 ILO was advising Panama, under whose flag a large merchant marine is registered, on wages and working conditions of seamen. New agencies are the Food and Agricultural

20 October 1971: the Security Council votes in favour of UN members showing disapproval of South Africa's presence in Namibia (see p. 324). Council members then included Belgium, Burundi, Japan, Nicaragua and Somalia. At the right in the foreground is a Namibian representative

Organisation (FAO) and the International Atomic Energy Agency (IAEA). The latter has been used to monitor the use of atomic energy for peaceful purposes. All UN agencies have permanent secretariats, chosen from among UN members. They have headquarters in various capital cities and regional offices in many parts of the world. Closely connected with UNO is the International Court of Justice, successor to the tribunal founded before the First World War.

Like the League of Nations, UNO can require its members to impose economic sanctions. It has used this power against, for example, Rhodesia (see p. 320). UNO can also call on its members to supply armed forces. The use of UN forces against aggression in Korea, to restore order in the Congo (Zaïre) and to enforce truces in the Middle East has carried UNO an important step beyond the League of Nations.

At times the high ideals of the UN have been brushed aside by power politics, rapaciousness and folly. Since 1945 some ten million people have died in over a hundred conflicts. In recent years the UN has not made the USSR budge over Afghanistán (see p. 254) – or small but resolute Israel over the Palestinians (see p. 335). In 1982 the security council's order to Argentina to withdraw from the Falkland Islands (see p. 263) was ignored by the Argentinians though it gave legitimacy to Britain's expulsion of the invaders. Whilst the secretary general attempted to negotiate between Britain and Argentina, much of the hard bargaining, the hurrying and scurrying to and fro of diplomats that preceded the conflict, was carried on independently of UNO. Still, the authority of UNO has been considerable. On occasions – in particular in the Middle East and Cyprus – it has halted conflict by demanding a cease-fire. And through its subsidiary agencies UNO may bring into existence a true world community. By co-operating in economic and social affairs the nations may learn to co-operate in political affairs.

24 Potsdam and the Allied occupation of Germany

Background to the Potsdam conference

After the war the whole of Germany (except areas taken by Poland and the USSR) and Austria came under Allied occupation. The boundaries of the zones which the USSR, the USA, Britain and France occupied had been fixed after Yalta. Each zone had a commander in chief who maintained economic life and carried out the duties of government. Control councils consisting of the zone commanders were supposed to co-ordinate activities.

From 17 July to 2 August 1945 the Russian, American and British leaders attended a conference at Potsdam, outside Berlin. President Truman was chairman. Churchill represented Britain until shortly before the conference ended he was replaced by Attlee, the new Labour prime minister (see p. 267). 'Generalissimo' Stalin, heavily guarded, was the last of the leaders to arrive.

On the evening before the conference opened Truman received a cable from Washington: 'Top Secret Urgent: For Colonel Kyles's eyes only. Operated on this morning. Diagnosis not yet complete but results seem satisfactory and already exceed expectations....' Colonel Kyles was Truman's code name. The operation was the explosion of the test bomb in New Mexico. Truman soon received more details: 'Doctor has just returned. Most enthusiastic and confident that the little boy [the bomb for use against Japan] is as [strong] as his big brother [the test bomb]. The light in his eyes is discernible [400 kilometres away] ... '.

The day after the explosion of the test bomb Churchill was told of the successful experiment. Several days later Truman said to Stalin: 'We have a new weapon of unusual destructive power.' Stalin learned the nature of the 'new weapon' only after an atom bomb had fallen on Hiroshima, just after the Potsdam conference ended.

It has been said that the dropping of the atom bombs on Japan was less the last act of the Second World War than the first act of the Cold War that followed. After Hiroshima Truman and Churchill hoped that fear of atomic warfare might cause the Russians to withdraw from eastern Europe. The intense fear felt by the Russians after Hiroshima did not lead them to withdraw – but it contributed to the Cold War. Their fears intensified when they learned that some of Truman's military advisers had said there was 'no need' to use the bomb against Japan.

At Yalta Roosevelt had made concessions to Stalin whose help he wanted against Japan. Truman, with 'the bomb in his pocket', wanted to delay or even prevent Russian entry into the Far Eastern war. He did not want the USSR to receive 'fruits of victory' such as the right to an occupation zone in Japan. And Roosevelt had trusted Stalin. At Potsdam there was an atmosphere of mistrust. After Germany's surrender there was an abrupt cancellation of lend-lease aid. American ships on their way to the USSR were recalled. On the other hand the Russians, not wanting the war against Japan to end before they could take part, kept secret the fact that Japan had asked them to help in negotiating an end to the war. The Americans, who had intercepted the message asking for Russian mediation, thus had good grounds for suspecting Soviet intentions.

At Potsdam Stalin informed his allies that the USSR would join the war against Japan as agreed at Yalta. On 26 July the USA and Britain, in the Potsdam Declaration, demanded that Japan should surrender unconditionally. China was not represented at the conference but consented to the Potsdam Declaration by telegram.

Poland

At Yalta the Soviet Union had promised that freely elected governments would be set up in the countries from which her armies had driven out the Germans – Poland, Hungary, Romania and Bulgaria. By the time the leaders met at Potsdam it was apparent that the Soviet Union was not honouring this promise. Churchill had already referred to 'the steel curtain' that separated Russian-dominated eastern Europe from the west. In Romania and Bulgaria representatives of the British and Americans were being ignored. Even in Yugoslavia, which had liberated itself without Russian help, Churchill complained, 'administration is under the control of the party police, and the press is also

Territorial changes in Europe after the Second World War

controlled'. Stalin accused the British, who had liberated Greece, of rigging elections there.

The USA and Britain unwillingly recognised the governments established in Hungary, Romania and Bulgaria. They hoped to get greater freedom for Poland. Britain in particular felt a special responsibility for Poland, the invasion of whose territory had been the occasion of her entry into the war. The USSR on the other hand had twice since 1914 been invaded by German troops advancing through Poland and once by the Poles themselves (see p. 116). Stalin complained that the British were trying to restore the *cordon sanitaire* by establishing a government unfriendly to the Soviet Union in Poland. In fact Truman and Churchill had to accept the provisional government of national unity, the Lublin government (see p. 222). Following the agreement made at Yalta, this had been joined by Mikolajczyk, the leader of the London Poles. The most Stalin would do was to declare that the provisional government would hold free elections in which all democratic and anti-Nazi parties could take part.

Over the location of Poland's frontier with Germany the western powers faced a fait accompli. Russian armies had been followed into Germany by the Poles, who got as far as the Oder and Western Neisse rivers. The Poles thus occupied eastern Pomerania and Silesia. They were also in occupation of much of East Prussia, including the former free city of Danzig (Gdansk). The USA and Britain wanted the Poles to withdraw to the Eastern Neisse River. But the German inhabitants of the disputed area had already fled. 'If they return', Stalin said, 'the Poles will hang them.' All the USA and Britain could do was to express hopes that a final decision on Poland's western frontier would be reached later. Disputes over this frontier provided fuel for the Cold War but all the territory Poland had occupied in 1945 was eventually recognised as hers. East Germany accepted the Oder-Western Neisse line in 1950; West Germany recognised it in 1970. In 1975 Poland's frontiers received international recognition at a conference in Helsinki (see p. 254).

By advancing the Russian frontier west to the Curzon line and setting up a Russian-dominated government in a Poland stretching farther west than before, Stalin aimed to increase the security of the USSR.

Reparations

At Yalta it was agreed that Germany should make compensation, by reparations, 'for the loss and suffering she had caused'. To avoid the problems caused by reparations payments after the First World War the Allies at Yalta decided to take reparations in goods – chiefly capital equipment such as factories, machinery, rolling stock. Such reparations were also to be taken from Germany's allies. By the time of Potsdam a large part of Germany had passed into Polish or Russian hands. Reparations could therefore be taken only from the diminished 'Germany' that was under Allied (including Soviet) occupation.

The USSR, as the main claimant, wanted to take heavy reparations from the zones occupied by the western allies. The latter opposed this and, in return for the concessions made concerning Poland and eastern Europe, the Russians had to accept their views. It was agreed that reparations due to the USA, Britain, France and other western states, and to Czechoslovakia and Yugoslavia, should be taken from the western-occupied zones of Germany and Austria. Reparations due to the USSR and Poland were to be taken from the Russian-occupied zones in Germany and Austria and from Bulgaria, Romania, Hungary and Finland. In addition the USSR was to get 15 per cent of the industrial equipment 'available' in the western zones. But the Russians had to supply the equivalent value of food, coal and other raw materials to the western zones. The USSR was also to receive a further 10 per cent of the equipment 'available' in the western zones; for this she did not have to supply goods in exchange. Decisions concerning what was 'available' were left to the zone commanders. All transfers of equipment were to be completed within two and a half years.

The Potsdam Proclamation

The Potsdam Proclamation, 29 July 1945, said: 'The German people shall be given the opportunity to prepare for the eventual reconstruction of their lives on a peaceful and democratic basis and in due course to take their place among the free and peaceful peoples of the world.'

An earlier American plan for reducing Germany to a weak pastoral society was dropped though at Potsdam the breakup of German industry and the development of an agricultural economy were still being discussed. In fact the loss of territory, the removal of capital equipment and Germany's effective division into eastern and western sections left her seriously weakened.

While the conference was going on German refugees

were fleeing westwards, driven from their homes in Poland, Czechoslovakia, Hungary, Romania and Yugoslavia, and from the parts of Germany transferred to the USSR and Poland. Refugee 'men, women and children wandered aimlessly [about Berlin] carrying, pushing or pulling what was left of their belongings'. At Potsdam it was agreed that the transfer of Germans expelled from farther east should be 'orderly and humane'. But it was impossible to transfer millions of people from their homes 'humanely'. Many of the refugees from eastern and central Europe were treated with great brutality. Thousands died on their way westward. Many died of starvation or disease after they reached their destinations. Between 1945 and 1948 sixteen million Germans were driven from their homes. Germans are no longer found scattered throughout eastern Europe.

A council of foreign ministers was to settle remaining problems and conclude peace treaties with Germany and her allies. France and China were invited to send ministers. In fact China did not take part.

On 2 August 1945 Truman said: 'I declare the conference adjourned – until our next meeting, which I hope will be in Washington.' Stalin, with a smile, said: 'God willing.' But the Cold War was already so advanced that a further meeting between the leaders of the USSR and the western powers was unlikely. They did not come together again until 1955.

Territorial changes

The council of foreign ministers could not reach agreement about Germany. The USSR wanted to establish its own kind of Germany; the western powers wanted to establish their kind of Germany. By the time the council met in Moscow late in 1947 it was clear neither side would 'dare run the risk that an eventual united Germany might carry its strength into the other camp'. Germany was to be left divided, without a peace treaty.

The making of treaties with Italy, Hungary, Bulgaria, Romania and Finland was completed early in 1947. All had to pay reparations, mostly to the USSR, Yugoslavia and Greece. All had to reduce their armed forces. Italy had to accept UN control of her colonies in Africa and to cede the Istrian peninsula, including Fiume (Rijeka), to Yugoslavia. Trieste was made a free territory but in 1954 it was partitioned between Italy and Yugoslavia – a method of settling territorial disputes adopted on various occasions since the war. The Dodecanese Islands were given to Greece. Romania ceded southern

Dobruja to Bulgaria and yielded Bessarabia, which had been the subject of so many transfers, and northern Bukovina to the USSR. Transylvania, taken by Hungary in 1940, was returned to Romania. The USSR kept territory taken from Finland after the Winter War and received Finnish territory farther north.

The USSR retained Estonia, Latvia and Lithuania, annexed in 1940. She also acquired Ruthenia, the easternmost part of Czechoslovakia, thus gaining direct access to Hungary, and annexed the northern part of East Prussia, lying next to Lithuania. The Soviet Union had also acquired substantial territory from Poland, and from Japan (see p. 306).

The Teschen area acquired by Poland in 1938 (see p. 206) was returned to Czechoslovakia. The Saar (see p. 203) was under French control from 1945 to 1955 but was integrated with West Germany in 1957.

Occupied Germany after Potsdam

At Yalta and Potsdam the Allies agreed to carry out a programme of demilitarisation, de-nazification, de-industrialisation and decentralisation. There was little uniformity in the methods adopted in applying these principles. Administration was initially little more than makeshift. And everything was made more complicated

Salvaging bricks to rebuild Germany. Old people working voluntarily on a Sunday

for the western allies by the arrival of millions of refugees from eastern Europe (most of whom made their way to the western zones), by the loss to Poland and the USSR of a quarter of Germany's agricultural land as well as important coalfields, and by the transfer of vast quantities of industrial equipment as reparations.

Demilitarisation was relatively straightforward. De-nazification presented greater problems. There had been about seven million members of the Nazi Party, many of them young people – a number far too great to punish, even if punishment could cure. And many party members had been unwilling or halfhearted Nazis. The Russians were the most severe in their treatment of former Nazis – many of those who were not useful were simply sent to Siberia. The Americans were the most systematic, bringing vast numbers to trial.

The most spectacular act in de-nazification was the Nüremberg trials conducted jointly by the four occupying powers. Leading Nazis – among them Goering, Hitler's closest adviser and the *Luftwaffe* chief; Ribbentrop, the foreign minister; Seyss-Inquart, the ruthless governor of Austria and the Netherlands; Admiral Raeder, responsible for submarine warfare, and Julius Streicher who persecuted the Jews – faced innumerable charges. Day after day, for almost a year, their cruelties and excesses were revealed to the world. Twelve of the accused were sentenced to death, seven were imprisoned and three were acquitted.

Since the Nüremberg trials ended in October 1946 their significance has been debated. Were they a warning to future war-makers? Did they simply indicate it is a mistake to be defeated? Perhaps they succeeded in making the Germans themselves aware of many terrible things done under the Nazi régime. Later West Germany voluntarily paid out large amounts of money in an effort to 'compensate' for the Nazis' treatment of Jews and others.

Some attempt was made, especially by the Americans, to re-educate the German people – for instance by removing ideas of racial superiority from textbooks. But there was a shortage of teachers, particularly as former Nazis were disqualified; in any case the task seemed too complex to deal with in the time available.

De-industrialisation was largely the product of reparations policies. The British and Americans, faced with feeding a population greatly inflated by the influx of refugees, and believing that to take heavy reparations would harm the whole European economy, took little. They did however attempt to break up the industrial cartels, such as Krupps, I.G. Farben Industries, and

Siemens, which had for long dominated the economy. The Russians and initially the French were determined to take all they could as reparations. The Russians of course were free to take almost anything they wanted from their own zone – and did so. Indeed the stripping of the Russian zone continued until 1953 – though it was sometimes difficult to make use of the equipment removed. Quantities of German machinery were left rusting in the USSR and Poland – and in France too. Perhaps more useful to the USSR were the scientists and technicians she took from Germany – including atomic scientists and experts in rocket technology. The USA also benefited from the arrival of German scientists. Wernher von Braun, who supervised the American moon exploration programme, had been Germany's leading rocket specialist.

The British and American zone commanders were soon disputing with the Russians concerning reparations. Everything hinged on the words used at Potsdam, according to which the Russians could take a percentage of what was 'available' in the western zones. In the opinion of the western zone commanders only what was not essential to the economies of their zones was 'available' – and that amounted to considerably less than the Russians demanded. So there was plenty of room for dispute. The western zone commanders resisted the Russian demands and tried to get greater supplies of food from the Russian zone. The disputes that developed provided fuel for the early stages of the Cold War. And the subsequent poverty of East Germany and the rapid recovery of West Germany are traceable to the difference in the reparations policies adopted by the Soviet Union and by the western allies.

Decentralisation was brought about by the establishment of state governments similar to those which had existed before Hitler came to power. Political parties were formed and elections for state parliaments were held. In the western zones the leading parties were the Christian Democrats (conservative in outlook) and the Social Democrats; the communists never won much support. In the Russian zone the communists were in control. In the west democratic institutions soon took root. From the outset there was little real democracy in the eastern zone.

Under Allied supervision the new state governments carried on much of the administration of Germany. Meanwhile there was a slow economic recovery as the German people worked with determination to clear away the rubble of war and make a new start.

25 The Cold War

Super-powers in rivalry

The Second World War had resulted in a considerable extension of Soviet territory both in Europe and the Far East. Moreover Soviet armies remained in occupation of the satellite states in eastern Europe. In the Far East the Mongolian People's Republic was a Soviet satellite whilst Russian forces occupied northern Korea. Yugoslavia, though liberated by its own partisans, appeared to belong to the Soviet camp. In France and Italy, where there was economic unrest, the communists, popular because of their underground opposition to the Nazis and the Fascists, had increased their strength. At Potsdam Truman was suspicious that Stalin was aiming at world conquest. In the following months, with the Russians little inclined to co-operate over Germany and other problems, his suspicions appeared to be confirmed. Had the threat of Nazi domination been replaced by the threat of Russian communism? It was not unnatural to see the outward thrust of Russian communism as tsarist imperialism in a more powerful form. That certainly became the view of the Chinese.

To Stalin 'everyone beyond the control of [his] police was a potential enemy'. His fears and enmity were not allayed at Potsdam, where the British and Americans seemed bent on removing Russian influence from eastern Europe, and were intensified when he discovered the nature of Truman's 'new weapon' (see p. 233). He was aware that Russian soldiers fighting abroad had seen higher living standards and greater freedom than they were accustomed to at home. The USSR, having lost perhaps twenty million lives in the war, was scarcely in a position to embark on fresh campaigns in 1945. The Russians were primarily concerned with conserving their gains. But control of eastern Europe seemed essential to protect themselves against a resurgent Germany – of which they had a justifiable fear. The west had built a *cordon sanitaire*, a 'Chinese wall', against the spread of Bolshevism (see p. 116). Now Stalin was determined to build his 'Chinese wall' to protect the USSR – and communism.

Did the Soviet Union want more than security? Stalin had opposed Trotsky's call for world revolution (see p. 132) and had appeared content with 'socialism in one country'. But at that time the USSR had been too weak to try to extend communist influence to the world outside. Now Stalin, flushed with victory, appeared no longer satisfied with 'socialism in one country'. From an apparently impregnable position he appeared to be leading the world in spreading communism.

Was the United States guiltless of power hunger? With the bomb 'in her pocket' and assuming that all the world was anxious to adopt her way of life (or, if it was not, should be) the Americans too seemed bent on dominating the globe. With an enormously expanded economy and having suffered relatively little loss of life and no material damage, the Americans were buoyant. However, the primary objective of the USA was her own security and prosperity.

With the Russians unable to intervene in western Europe where relatively conservative régimes were established, and with the Americans unable to dislodge the Russians from eastern Europe, there developed a kind of tit for tat chain reaction. Each incident, each claim, each argument produced a response which in turn provoked a further response. Such was the nature of the Cold War which dominated international relations until a thaw developed in the 1960s. The Cold War then changed its character. But it did not end.

The Cold War, dominated by the two super-powers, emphasised the decline in western Europe's status. But it was the Cold War that led the USA to involve herself in the affairs of western Europe – and so to strengthen it. The Cold War also helped western Europe to move towards unity.

The Cold War was marked by the intervention of the super-powers, directly or indirectly, in almost every part of the world. For the Cold War extended far beyond the 'battle line' in Europe. The Atlantic Charter's affirmation of the right of nations to self-determination was frequently ignored. And national leaders seeking power or security took advantage of super-power rivalry, playing off one side against the other.

The Cold War was mostly a war of words. The Americans opposed Russian domination of eastern Europe and wanted revision of Poland's frontier with Germany, but were not willing to fight over these matters. On the other hand they would not tolerate a Russian takeover of West Berlin, or Soviet nuclear bases in Cuba. But the USSR was not willing to fight over these issues. The USSR was at first weaker than her rival. However, she made more moves in the Cold War game; in general the USA made the counter-moves.

Advances in nuclear and rocket technology made the threat that the Cold War might develop into a hot war more terrifying. The USA and soon the Soviet Union were far ahead of the rest of the world. In July 1949 the USSR exploded an atom bomb. In November 1952 the USA exploded a hydrogen (nuclear) bomb – far more destructive than any atom bomb. The Russians exploded their hydrogen bomb in August 1953. Though for some years the USA had a larger nuclear arsenal than the USSR this did not make the threat of nuclear war any less alarming.

If the Cold War had its origins at Potsdam or even earlier its birth was announced by Churchill in March 1946 during a public lecture at Fulton, in Missouri, Truman's home state. Churchill said:

'From Stettin [Szczecin] in the Baltic to Trieste in the Adriatic, an iron curtain has descended. . . . Behind that line lie all the capitals of the states of central and eastern Europe – all are subject in one form or another not only to Soviet influence but to a very high and increasing measure of control from Moscow.'

Churchill, though not in office, went on to say he hoped that the close political and military association between the USA and Britain would continue.

Soon after Churchill's speech the USA had its first 'success'. During the war Russian and British troops were stationed in Iran to protect the flow of lend-lease supplies into the USSR. British and American oil interests took the opportunity to get concessions in Iran. The USSR was refused similar concessions. After the war the British withdrew their troops but Russian forces stayed on and put pressure on the Iranian government by supporting a revolt. Iran appealed to UNO and in May 1946 the Russians withdrew. As they left the Americans moved in, 'not with troops and revolution . . . but silently with dollars and advisers'. The Russians were not pleased by this activity near their own frontier by Americans 10,000 kilometres from home.

The USSR tightens her hold over eastern Europe

After this American success the Russians exercised tighter control over their satellites. The east European governments in whose formation the Russians had played a major part were subservient to Moscow and not genuinely representative. However, they were initially coalitions that included agrarians, whose aim was the redistribution of land, and socialists of various kinds as well as communists. From 1946 the coalition governments began to crumble. Local leaders, some of them communists, and many lesser figures, too nationalist in outlook to be entirely subservient to Moscow, were in one way or another got rid of. Elections based on a 'single list' communist ticket (listing only the Communist Party's candidates) produced their inevitable results and 'people's republics' were set up.

In Romania, Juliu Maniu, the leader of the National Peasant Party, had the support of the majority of the people. But in 1947 he was sentenced to life imprisonment and his party was dissolved. The king abdicated and Romania became a people's republic. A Soviet-style constitution was adopted in March 1948. The Orthodox Church became subject to the state and independently minded clergy, Catholic as well as Orthodox, were arrested. In 1946 Simeon, the nine-year-old tsar of Bulgaria, a grandson of the Long Nosed Fox of the Balkans, went into exile. Thousands of Bulgarians had already been eliminated, among them the regent – condemned to death and ordered to dig his own grave by a people's court. In 1947 there was a further purge in Bulgaria. Early in 1947 the Hungarian premier gave up his post – by telephone – while 'on holiday' in Switzerland, thus avoiding arrest or perhaps death. Meanwhile, his little son had been held hostage in Budapest. Later that year communists formed a government and all other parties were dissolved. There was strong opposition from the Catholic Church. In 1949 Cardinal Mindszenty, who spoke openly against communism, was sentenced to life imprisonment for 'espionage'. Communist success in elections that year was followed by party purges and Hungary was soon firmly penned within the Stalinist fold. In Poland the promised free elections were never held. Mikolajczyk, the representative of the London Poles (see p. 222), fled in October 1947 to avoid arrest. His opposition Peasant Party was dissolved and Poland too became a people's republic. But in Yugoslavia Tito refused to adopt a Stalinist line. 'I will lift my little finger', said Stalin, 'and there will be no more Tito!' 'Do you think after all we have been through we shall throw away our hard won independence?' said Tito. Attempts to split the Yugoslav Communist Party and to dislodge Tito were unsuccessful. Yugoslavia was expelled from Cominform and became the black sheep of the communist fold.

Cominform, the Communist Information Bureau, was set up by the USSR in October 1947 as a means of direct communication, or of subordination, between the Kremlin and other communist parties, including those of France and Italy. The Cominform manifesto declared that 'the world is divided into two fronts, one imperialist, the other socialist and democratic, and there must be no [appeasement] with the imperialists'. Soon after the formation of Cominform a Soviet leader urged that 'the time had come for the colonial people to expel their aggressors'. This speech triggered off the communist rebellion in Malaya (see p. 311) besides encouraging anti-colonialists in for example the Gold Coast (Ghana).

The Truman Doctrine: Greece, Turkey and Czechoslovakia

Meanwhile Turkey and Greece were under communist pressure. Stalin wanted the USSR to have permanent bases in the Dardanelles and Aegean. He also wanted Turkey to yield certain territory formerly under tsarist rule. As the USSR continued pressing Turkey the Americans in August 1946 sent warships to Istanbul. In Greece the British had since December 1944 been supporting a harsh and unpopular monarchy against communist partisans. The communists received help from Yugoslavia and Albania but not, it seems, directly from the USSR. Early in 1947 the Greek government appealed to Britain for further assistance. Britain's difficulties at that time were so great that she turned the matter over to the USA.

So it was that in March 1947, a year after Churchill made his iron curtain speech, Truman announced what became known as the Truman Doctrine:

'At the present moment in history nearly every nation must choose between alternate ways of life. The choice is too often not a free one. One way of life is based upon the will of the majority and is distinguished by free institutions. . . . The second way of life is based upon the will of a minority. . . . It relies upon terror and oppression . . . fixed elections and the suppression of personal freedom.'

With such stark simplicity he divided the sheep from the goats. He went on: 'I believe it must be [our policy] to support free peoples who are resisting attempted subjugation by armed minorities or by outside pressure.' The Truman Doctrine made it clear that the USA was not prepared to withdraw into isolation but would assert itself anywhere to 'support free peoples' – which came to mean assisting them when threatened by communist takeovers. Reactionary régimes in Spain, Cuba, the Dominican Republic and so on had no need to be alarmed – for they had the merit of being anti-communist. Truman's speech, said a British diplomat, seemed 'hardly less than a declaration of war on the Soviet Union'.

In Greece American support enabled the government to reconstruct the economy and by the end of 1949 the communists were defeated. American assistance enabled Turkey to withstand Russian pressure. But when in 1948 a crisis occurred in Czechoslovakia the Americans did not intervene. The Russians had liberated Czechoslovakia in 1944. Many Czechs in free elections in 1946 supported the communists. The party leader, Klement Gottwald, became prime minister and communists soon dominated political life. Czechoslovakia thus fell into Stalin's grasp – and Stalin was not one to let a captive go. However, in 1947 the communists began to lose popularity. Most of Czechoslovakia's trade was with the west. And the Czechs were angered by Stalin's refusal to allow them to accept American aid, which was helping to restore the economy of western Europe (see below).

Threatened with defeat at a time when communists were being squeezed out of coalition governments in France and Italy, the Czech communists in February 1948 staged a coup. President Beneš, who had survived the tragedy of Munich and the war years, was forced to accept a government that admitted no anti-communists. Liberals were 'tried' and severely punished. A few non-communists fled; others committed or tried to commit suicide. Jan Masaryk, liberal son of the first president, who had stayed on as foreign minister, died in mysterious circumstances. Single list elections in May 1948 produced a solid 'national front' (communist) vote. Beneš resigned and Gottwald became president. Clearly Czechoslovakia was on the side of the iron curtain that was beyond the aid of the Truman Doctrine. However, the Czech coup strengthened the hands of extreme opponents of the USSR in the United States and elsewhere.

The Marshall Plan and economic recovery

After cleaning up the destruction of war and reorganising their economies to meet civilian needs the

'Noses left!' orders headmistress Molotov (Soviet foreign minister) when her young ladies (the Russian satellites) are attracted by the tempting smell of Marshall Aid. A Low cartoon of 1947

European states made little progress. Trade remained at a low level and shortages of necessities continued. In these circumstances communist parties grew rapidly, in France and Italy especially.

The winter of 1946–47 was particularly severe, making shortages of food, clothing and housing all the harder to bear. But in June 1947, soon after the announcement of the Truman Doctrine, General Marshall, American secretary of state, outlined a plan by which the USA would help Europe to help itself. Marshall said his plan was directed against 'hunger, poverty, desperation and chaos'. The Russians eyed it with suspicion, as nothing more than an extension of the Truman Doctrine – and so far as Truman himself was

concerned that was not far from the truth. It certainly had the effect of tying the recipients of aid more closely to the USA.

Under the European Recovery Programme, generally known as the Marshall Plan, the countries of Europe were invited to join in asking the USA to provide them with what they needed to get their economies moving. The USSR denounced the plan as foreign intervention. As Marshall Aid would have weakened her hold on her satellites she would not allow these states (including Czechoslovakia) to accept it. The representatives of seventeen states (Austria, all the Scandinavian states including Iceland, Turkey, Greece, Eire and all the states of western Europe except Spain) met in Paris and gave the Americans details of their needs. Aid received had to be matched by contributions from the governments that received it. By 1952 billions of dollars worth of American machinery, fertilisers, transport equipment and so on were supplied. Marshall Aid was a 'blood transfusion' given to a Europe that might otherwise have bled to death. It also protected America from the effects of an economic collapse in western Europe.

When Marshall Aid ended in 1952 the west European economy was rapidly gaining momentum. The worst of the shortages were over. With substantially full employment the level of pre-war production was recovered and soon surpassed.

Having rejected Marshall Aid, the USSR later in 1947 made trade agreements with her satellites and in 1949 offered them assistance under the Molotov Plan. Her refusal of Marshall Aid and her counter Molotov Plan clearly marked the division between eastern and western Europe. The idea of communism in one country had been extended to communism in one bloc of states.

The Cold War in Germany

The Russians, fearful of a revived and powerful Germany, wanted a divided and weakened Germany – or an undivided communist Germany. The French too, though only initially, wanted to keep Germany decentralised and weak. Britain and the USA at their own expense had to import millions of pounds worth of food to prevent mass starvation in their zones. The continued stripping of these zones by the Russians left them unable to pay for the food they needed to import. And it was to these zones that most of the German refugees had fled. In these circumstances the western zone commanders opposed Soviet reparations demands and sought larger supplies of food from the Russian zone. Eventually they decided that the economy of their zones must be restored.

In 1947 production in these zones was 27 per cent of what it had been before the war. To hasten economic recovery in January 1947 the British and American zones were combined in one economic unit – Bizonia. The western zones received Marshall Aid but their share was relatively small.

In June 1948 the three western allies moved farther towards establishing a unified economy by announcing plans for setting up a West German government. As the existing currency was almost worthless they introduced a new currency, the deutsche mark.

The Berlin airlift

Berlin lay well within the Russian zone but each occupying power held a sector there – the vodka sector (now East Berlin), the whisky, champagne and coca cola sectors (now West Berlin). When the Russians began introducing their own new currency into all the sectors of Berlin the USA, Britain and France introduced the deutsche mark into Berlin.

The Russians were greatly displeased by the western allies' plans. When the deutsche mark was introduced into Berlin they decided to cut West Berlin off from the rest of Germany until the western powers abandoned their plans for setting up a West German state. West Berlin depended for all its supplies on communications passing through the Russian zone. From March 1948 the Russians had interfered with communications to West Berlin. Late in June 1948 they blockaded the city. Six days after the introduction of the deutsche mark to Berlin there was a complete stoppage of communications between West Berlin and the outside world – except by air. 'If we mean . . . to hold Europe against communism, we must not budge', said General Clay, the American commander in chief in Germany. So the USA and Britain decided to supply their garrisons and the two million civilians in West Berlin by air. In spite of great difficulties, including the building of new runways, they succeeded in doing this. The Russians did all they could to interfere with the Berlin airlift, though they did not actually attack the transport planes. In the winter flying and landing conditions grew worse. However, by March 1949 about 8,000 tonnes of goods, including coal and potatoes, were being brought in every day. Meanwhile the Americans and British imposed a counter-blockade against the Russian zone.

In May 1949, after a siege of eleven months, the Russians reopened all land and water routes into West Berlin. In the same month the Federal Republic of Germany (West Germany), with its capital at Bonn, was set up. The military government ended four months later, though the western allies retained certain powers until 1955, when West Germany became fully independent.

In October 1949 the Russians, who refused to allow any party other than the Communist Party in their zone, converted this zone into a communist state, the German Democratic Republic (East Germany). This comprised a third of Germany's post-war territory but only a quarter of her population.

The crisis of the Berlin blockade concluded the separation of Germany into two states. It also strengthened the solidarity of West Germany and West Berlin with the western powers. And the crisis provoked an escalation of military expenditure in the United States.

No further advances into Europe were made by the Soviet Union. Rather, the rapid economic, political and military progress made in western Europe tended to set the pace for the states on the Russian side of the iron curtain. In 1949 East Germany's economy was virtually at a standstill, whereas in West Germany an economic miracle had begun. In the 1950s the only country whose economy was growing faster than West Germany's was Japan.

The North Atlantic Treaty Organisation

In 1947 Britain and France signed a fifty-year treaty of alliance, known appropriately as the Treaty of Dunkirk. In 1948, following the communist takeover of Czechoslovakia, Britain, France, Holland, Belgium and Luxembourg signed the Treaty of Brussels, setting up the Western Union. By this Western Union they agreed to co-ordinate their forces against the danger of 'an armed attack in Europe'.

However, it was clear, not only in Europe but also in North America, that the Western Union was not powerful enough to resist the might of the USSR. It was equally clear that the United Nations Organisation, whose actions were repeatedly vetoed by the USSR, could not provide security against major aggression. Soon after the signing of the Brussels treaty representatives of the Western Union and representatives of Canada and the USA met in Washington. They were later joined by representatives of Italy, Norway, Denmark, Iceland and Portugal. Sweden, Switzerland and Ireland, with their traditions of neutrality, did not join them. Spain remained aloof.

In April 1949 the twelve states meeting in Washington signed the North Atlantic Treaty. The Czech coup (see p. 240) and the Berlin blockade had caused the USA for the first time in her history to enter into a peacetime military alliance. Said a French leader: 'We have today obtained what we hoped for in vain between the two wars – the recognition by the USA that her security depends on the security of Europe.'

The signatories to the North Atlantic Treaty agreed

This Soviet cartoon of 1950 expresses the USSR's suspicion and fears of the North Atlantic Treaty. On the surface Truman, bearing the peace banner of the 'North Atlantic Treaty (doubly peaceful and purely defensive!!)', swims forward at the head of his team – Churchill, Bevin, Schuman, Spaak and others. Below the surface is a torpedo labelled 'Aggressive Pact' and powered by the American dollar

that 'an armed attack against one or more of them shall be considered an attack against them all'. In exercise of the right of self-defence recognised by the charter of the United Nations they promised to assist one another to maintain the security of the North Atlantic area – by armed force if necessary. The treaty included promises to develop free institutions and co-operate in economic affairs.

In 1950 the North Atlantic Treaty states formed an organisation that made their alliance militarily effective. In spite of the many difficulties involved they agreed to a system of military co-operation under unified commands and with a single commander in chief. The first commander in chief of the North Atlantic Treaty Organisation (NATO) was General Eisenhower. In 1951 Greece and Turkey joined NATO. From the outset it was thought necessary to deploy substantial forces in West Germany, the region which seemed most likely to come under attack. Before long it became apparent that German manpower was needed to strengthen these forces.

26 The Cold War continues

The upsurge of communism in Asia

In October 1949 the communist People's Republic of China was set up under Mao Tsetung. Chiang Kai-shek withdrew to the island of Taiwan, which became the seat of the Nationalist government of the Republic of China.

The establishment of a communist régime in China was regarded as a disastrous defeat by the USA, who had provided the Nationalists with billions of dollars of aid. Suddenly – or so it seemed to Americans who had failed to observe the portents – 'democratic' China had slipped from their control into the communist camp. When early in 1950 the People's Republic signed a thirty-year treaty of alliance with the USSR, the Americans found themselves confronted by a massive communist bloc extending from eastern Europe to the China Sea. Communism, which appeared to be contained in eastern Europe, was now rearing its head in East and South-east Asia. By 1949 there were communist threats in Malaya, the Philippines and Indo-China (see p. 312). To the Americans communists appeared to be springing up like the fruit of the legendary dragon's teeth – everywhere. And in July 1949 the Russians had exploded their atom bomb – far sooner than had been expected.

War between North and South Korea

At Potsdam it was agreed that Korea, formerly under Japanese rule, should be occupied by the Russians in the north and by the Americans in the south until fit for independence. The 38th parallel was the dividing line.

Once they had occupied North Korea the Russians refused to allow any communication with the south. When the Americans called for free elections for the whole of Korea the Soviet Union rejected the proposal. The matter was put before the UN security council but the Russians vetoed any discussion. So elections were held in South Korea only (May 1948). Dr Syngman Rhee, a strong opponent of communism, became president of the Republic of Korea (South Korea). In the north the Russians set up the People's Democratic Republic of Korea under the leadership of Kim Il-sung.

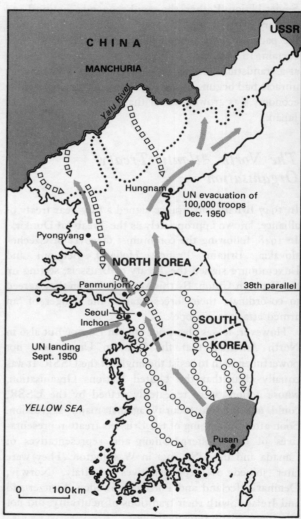

○○○○○○▷   North Korean offensive 25 June to Sept. 1950

▰▰▰   Area held by UN forces Sept. 1950

➤➤➤   UN offensive 15 Sept. to Nov. 1950

••••••••   Northern limit of UN offensive Nov. 1950

▭▭▭▭▭▷   Chinese offensive 3 Nov. 1950 to Jan 1951

------   Southern limit of Chinese offensive Jan. 1951

------   Armistice line between North and South Korea July 1953

The Korean War

Korea, December 1950: civilian refugees hoping to get to the south, mass on the Hungnam beach

In 1948 the Russians withdrew from Korea and in 1949 the Americans left. But the iron curtain had in effect been extended to the Far East.

South Korea, with its capital at Seoul and a population of twenty-one million, was predominantly agricultural. North Korea, with its capital at Pyongyang and a population of nine million, had at that time more industry than the south. Both Kim and Rhee claimed to represent the whole of Korea. Both were anxious to unify Korea – under their own leadership. The North Korean Army was large, well trained and equipped with Soviet tanks and planes. The South Korean army was relatively small, ill-trained and poorly equipped.

Early in 1950 electoral defeats suggested that Rhee's rule was unpopular. It was perhaps this that prompted a North Korean army to invade the south in June 1950. The USA claimed that the North Koreans were acting under Russian instructions and probably with Chinese connivance. 'Communism', said Truman, 'has passed beyond the use of subversion to conquer independent nations and will now use armed invasion and war.' Perhaps the account given by Khrushchev, later first secretary of the Russian Communist Party, is nearer the mark: 'The war wasn't Stalin's idea. Kim Il-sung was the initiator. Stalin of course didn't try to dissuade him.' During the Cold War the super-powers, avoiding direct confrontation, have sometimes fought by proxy. The Korean War was perhaps the USSR's first proxy war.

On 28 June 1950, three days after the North Korean army crossed the 38th parallel, Seoul fell to the invaders. On 27 June Truman had ordered American air and naval forces in Japan to support the South Koreans. On the same day the UN security council recommended that member states should give military aid to South Korea. (The USSR, having temporarily withdrawn from the security council, was unable to veto this resolution.) Within a week American forces had landed in Korea. Eventually troops from seventeen countries joined the conflict. By far the largest effort however was made by the USA. MacArthur, then commander of the occupation forces in Japan, was in supreme command.

After capturing Seoul the North Koreans continued their swift advance. They were stopped only at Pusan, in the extreme south. In September MacArthur landed troops at Inchon (Chemulpo) behind the enemy lines. Two weeks later UN forces were established on the 38th parallel. By then the North Korean army had almost ceased to exist. MacArthur was authorised to cross the 38th parallel with the object of uniting Korea by force.

China was understandably afraid of an invasion of Manchuria through Korea. In October 1950 the Chinese warned that if the Americans crossed the 38th parallel they would intervene. Early in November 'volunteers' from the Chinese People's Liberation Army clashed with UN troops on the Yalu River, China's Manchurian frontier with Korea.

A 'great human wave' of Chinese forced the UN troops to retreat so rapidly that 100,000 had to be evacuated by sea from Hungnam. By the end of 1950 the UN troops had been driven south of the 38th parallel. Though the People's Republic of China was not officially at war the United Nations denounced her as an aggressor and placed an embargo on the export of strategic goods to China. MacArthur wanted more drastic action – the bombing of Chinese railways and production centres. Rather than risk extending the war, in April 1951 Truman dismissed MacArthur. General Ridgway, who succeeded him, first held and then defeated the Chinese without moving out of Korea. The Russians meanwhile lost interest in a conflict which had become increasingly a Chinese affair. In July 1951 peace talks began but not until July 1953 was an armistice signed at Panmunjom. The armistice virtually restored the arbitrary dividing line on the 38th parallel. In 1983 United Nations units were still supervising the truce line, which was frequently violated by the north.

Consequences of the Korean War

There were some three million Korean casualties, many of them civilians. Seoul, four times overrun by the contending armies, was almost totally destroyed. About 142,000 Americans and 17,000 other UN servicemen were casualties. The Chinese who, lacking modern weapons, had adopted 'human wave' tactics, lost perhaps 900,000 men.

The consequences of the war extended far beyond Korea. When Truman ordered American troops to assist South Korea he announced that the USA would intervene militarily against any extension of communist rule in the Pacific area – a strong reaffirmation of the Truman Doctrine. Aid to the French in Indo-China and to the Philippines, both contesting communist uprisings, was extended. The American fleet protected Taiwan from a possible Chinese invasion and in 1954 the USA guaranteed her security. The conclusion of a peace treaty with Japan was hurried on. There were longer-term results too. After the Korean War the Russians were less inclined to risk a resort to arms by proxy or otherwise. China gained in prestige as the preserver of North Korea but had used in war resources desperately needed for reconstruction. Isolated from the rest of the world China showed implacable hostility towards the USA and her allies – thus convincing the Americans of the existence of a hostile bloc from the Baltic to the China Sea. The USA responded with an enormous increase in arms. This in turn provoked the USSR into an arms race which she could not afford.

Perhaps the greatest significance of the Korean War was that servicemen from many countries, all wearing the badge of the United Nations, fought under one commander to resist aggression.

Co-existence?

After the USSR exploded her hydrogen bomb (H-bomb) in 1953 she was technologically equal to the USA, though until about 1970 her stockpile of nuclear weapons was smaller. The super-powers became increasingly concerned with developing effective means of delivering nuclear bombs. In 1954 the Americans launched a nuclear-powered submarine, USS *Nautilus*. Nuclear submarines were capable of remaining submerged for weeks. (In 1958 *Nautilus* submerged in the Pacific, emerged briefly at the North Pole, where her crew played football, and eventually surfaced in the Atlantic.) In 1960 an American nuclear submarine, USS *George Washington*, fired a Polaris missile, a rocket missile with a nuclear warhead. Meanwhile, in 1957 the Russians launched the first space satellite, *Sputnik*, proving they had rockets capable of delivering nuclear warheads to the USA.

In 1952 Stalin said that war between the capitalist and socialist powers was not inevitable; they could co-exist side by side. After his death (1953) the Soviet leaders seemed increasingly inclined to co-existence. Meanwhile, in January 1953 Eisenhower became president of the USA. His secretary of state, John Foster Dulles, an implacable opponent of communism, supported a policy not only of containing communism but of liberating peoples under communist rule. He favoured massive (nuclear) retaliation – a policy which Russian possession of the H-bomb soon made unrealistic.

Dulles gained a reputation for brinkmanship – for pushing opponents to the brink of open conflict. 'If you are scared to go to the brink you are lost', he said. An example of brinkmanship occurred in 1955 when the Chinese communists began a daily bombardment of the islands of Quemoy (Jinmen) and Matsu (Mazu Dao), which lie between China and Taiwan. When the USA threatened nuclear war the Chinese ceased the bombardment.

After Stalin's death the USSR took several steps towards co-existence. In May 1953 Russian military control of East Germany ended, as did the collecting of reparations. Somewhat greater economic freedom was allowed to the satellite states, though an uprising over wage cuts in East Germany was put down by Soviet tanks in June 1953. In July 1953 came the Korean armistice, made possible partly by Russian influence. About the same time the USSR gave up her territorial claims against Turkey. In July 1954 an agreement at Geneva brought the French war in Vietnam to an end (see p. 312), though the Americans regarded this as a victory for communism. In May 1955 the USSR consented to a peace treaty with Austria, on condition that she remained a neutral state. As in 1919 union with Germany was forbidden.

Containing the USSR?

Meanwhile Dulles was building up alliances to contain the USSR. In 1951 Australia and New Zealand had thrown in their lot with the USA by entering into the ANZUS pact. In 1954 Australia, New Zealand, the Philippines, Thailand, Pakistan, Britain, France and the USA joined to form the South-east Asia Treaty Organisation (SEATO). In 1953 American aid to the shah of Iran enabled him to overthrow a revolutionary régime to which the USSR was giving aid. In 1955, with American prompting, Iran, Pakistan, Iraq, Turkey and Britain joined in the Baghdad pact which set up the Central Treaty Organisation or CENTO. (In 1958 Iraq withdrew.) Intended to develop along the lines of NATO, SEATO and CENTO were but pale shadows and soon faded away. Dulles also negotiated defensive treaties, for example, with South Korea, Japan, Taiwan and Turkey. In return for aid to Franco's Spain the Americans were given the use of bases in Spanish territory. They also acquired bases in Morocco, Libya, Turkey and Saudi Arabia.

At the time of the Korean War NATO forces in Europe were outnumbered by those of the eastern bloc. And the forces of some NATO members were heavily committed outside Europe – the Americans in Korea, the British in Korea and Malaya (see p. 311) and the French in Vietnam (see p. 312). West German participation in the defence of western Europe seemed essential. (West Germany then had no army, though she had been permitted to raise internal security forces.) In 1950 the French prime minister, René Pleven, called for the establishment of a European Defence Community with what would have been a genuine European navy, army and air force which would not be under the control of

individual governments and in which West Germans would take an active part. West Germany and the Benelux countries (see p. 280) favoured Pleven's proposal but it ran into various difficulties. Instead in 1954 it was agreed that the Federal Republic of Germany should be allowed to raise armed forces and should join NATO in May 1955. However, all forces raised by West Germany were to be under NATO command and forces from other NATO members were to remain in West Germany. West Germany's admission to NATO was an important advance towards containing communism in Europe. The Russians naturally saw this strengthening of NATO as a threat to the eastern bloc.

The Warsaw pact

In May 1955, a few days after West Germany's admission to NATO, the USSR entered into a defensive pact, the Warsaw pact, with her satellites. Poland, Czechoslovakia, Hungary, Bulgaria, Romania, Albania and East Germany agreed to the stationing of Russian forces within their territories and the appointment of a Russian general as supreme commander of all their forces. (East Germany became an effective member of the pact early in 1956. Albania later quarrelled with the USSR and ceased to be a member.)

It was estimated at the time of its creation that the Warsaw pact forces numbered six million. Like the North Atlantic Treaty, the Warsaw pact stated that its signatories were acting in accordance with the peaceful principles of the United Nations. The pact was to remain in force until a system of collective security for both eastern and western Europe together was created. Indeed, after 1955 the USSR repeatedly called for the dissolution of both NATO and the Warsaw pact organisation in favour of a Europe-wide system of security. How sincere the Soviet proposals were is hard to say. Certainly the USSR was genuinely afraid of West Germany and the possibility that she might acquire nuclear arms.

During 1954–55 Khrushchev, by then at the head of affairs in the USSR, visited Peking, Delhi, London – and Belgrade. A Holy Roman Emperor had once had to eat humble pie at the feet of the pope in Canossa. Belgrade was Khrushchev's Canossa. Marshal Tito and Yugoslavia were the black sheep of the communist world, an acute embarrassment to Moscow. In 1948 Tito had declared Yugoslavia's neutrality in the Cold War. Yugoslavia gave the lie to the Soviet accusations of

Khrushchev's Canossa: Tito (on left) meeting
Khrushchev at Belgrade airport, May 1955

western aggressiveness; it was not the western powers but the USSR which threatened her independence. From the western powers Yugoslavia obtained loans. And Yugoslavia was standing proof that there may be more than one road to socialism. Khrushchev was able to normalise relations with Yugoslavia – but at the price of dissolving Cominform. And Tito did not come back into the Soviet camp.

Bandung and non-alignment

In April 1955 a conference of newly emerged states, mostly Asian and African, met at Bandung at the invitation of President Sukarno of Indonesia. The object was to present a united front to the rest of the world. At Bandung these states declared their support for the *Panchasila* (Five Principles), framed by Chou En-lai of China and Nehru of India. Of these principles the chief were non-alignment (refusal to adhere to either of the two great power blocs) and non-interference. It was partly to woo the uncommitted nations of the third world that shortly after Bandung Khrushchev went to Belgrade to meet Tito, a firm supporter of non-alignment. Later meetings of the 'non-aligned' states

were not as uncommitted as Nehru had desired. They were often distinctly anti-western in outlook.

The two Germanys

The Berlin blockade (1948–49), followed by the establishment of the Federal Republic of Germany and the German Democratic Republic, left Germany – and Berlin – divided. Few people then thought Germany would remain divided. Throughout the 1950s the powers tried to end the division. Each side wanted to end it in its own favour. But the position remained as it had been: 'Neither side [dared] run the risk that an eventual united Germany might carry its strength into the other camp.'

In 1952 the USSR proposed the formation of a unified Germany. By then East Germany had substantial armed forces, whereas West Germany had none. Fearing a Czech-style takeover by the communists, Adenauer, the West German chancellor, rejected the proposal. In 1953 the German Democratic Republic acquired independence within the Soviet system. Her independence was formally acknowledged in a treaty of 1955. By that time, with the full independence of the Federal Republic of Germany and her admission to NATO, what amounted to an irreversible situation was created. The admission of the German Democratic Republic to the Warsaw pact set the seal on the situation.

In July 1955 the leaders of the USA, the Soviet Union, Britain and France met in Geneva. The leaders of the two blocs were at least on speaking terms with one another. The western powers hoped that steps might be taken towards German unification. But Khrushchev was unyielding. A stalemate had been arrived at. Adenauer, like Rathenau and Stresemann a generation earlier, accepted the inevitable instead of futilely resisting it. In September 1955 he went to Moscow and won Soviet recognition for West Germany. West Germany soon received general international recognition but only the Soviet bloc recognised East Germany.

Ups and downs of co-existence, 1956–61

In February 1956 Khrushchev made an astonishing denunciation of Stalin (see p. 290). Perhaps he wanted to show how smiling the face of the Soviet Union had become by contrasting it with the despotism of Stalin. Perhaps he wanted to impress on the third world that the Soviet Union had abandoned the goal of world power seemingly sought by Stalin in his later years. Perhaps he wanted to woo the satellite states by his admission that there are various roads to socialism.

The last admission had dramatic results, first in Poland and then in Hungary. Whereas in Poland the Russians compromised (see p. 293), in Hungary a more serious threat to the solidarity of the communist bloc led to armed intervention (see p. 293). The Hungarian crisis coincided with the Suez crisis (see p. 331). The latter left Britain and France rather sore with their American allies. The suppression of the Hungarian uprising renewed the western powers' distrust of the Soviet Union and the smiling face of Khrushchev.

When in October 1957 the USSR launched *Sputnik* the day of the inter-continental ballistic missile (ICBM) dawned. The arms race between the super-powers accelerated. Before long they had the capacity to destroy one another from their home bases.

The refusal of the western powers to recognise East Germany and the continued occupation of West Berlin by the USA, Britain and France were an affront to the USSR. This was exacerbated by the contrast between drab, down-at-heel, socialist East Berlin, and glittering capitalist West Berlin. Between 1949 and 1958 2.2 million East Germans out of a population (in 1949) of 17 million – many of them young professional people, technicians and so on – 'voted' against communism by crossing the border into West Germany. By 1958 the East Germans had closed their frontier with West Germany by building fences protected by mine-fields, dogs and armed guards. But fugitives continued to escape through Berlin. Apart from the humiliation of the situation, East Germany could not afford to lose so much of her youth and talent.

In 1958 the Russians began pressing for withdrawal of the western powers from Berlin which they described as a centre for espionage (which it was) and a 'smouldering powder keg'. They proposed to set up instead a free city of Berlin. When asked how they felt only 2 per cent of West Berliners voted in favour of the proposal. The western powers insisted on maintaining the status quo.

In 1958 Congress gave Eisenhower renewed authority to aid any nation requesting help against communist aggression. In 1959 Dulles, arch-opponent of communism, died. Later that year Khrushchev visited the USA. Eisenhower got on well with Khrushchev; he liked his rough humour – when addressing the UN assembly Khrushchev enforced his point by hammering on the rostrum with his shoe. The two leaders declared that 'all outstanding international questions should be settled . . . by peaceful means through negotiation'. But an 'atoms for peace' plan which Eisenhower concocted met with limited success.

In 1960 Eisenhower arranged for Khrushchev, Macmillan and de Gaulle to meet with him in Paris in May. Shortly before the meeting Khrushchev announced a planned reduction of Soviet forces by a third – he did not mention a planned buildup of nuclear arms. He also offered not to conduct further tests of nuclear weapons if the western powers would agree to do the same. This countered an earlier 'open skies' proposal by Eisenhower, involving air and ground inspection of Russian and American bases. The Russians had rejected this proposal.

The Paris summit meeting was not a success. Two weeks before the leaders were due to meet an American U-2 spy plane was shot down inside Soviet territory. At Paris, Khrushchev said he could not take part in other business until the United States government agreed to cancel further flights and apologised for past incursions. Eisenhower said the flights had been cancelled but refused to make an apology.

Eventually Khrushchev left in a violent huff for East Berlin. Fear of a surprise move by the Russians was so great that American forces were put on a worldwide alert. But nothing happened. Khrushchev returned to the policy of peaceful co-existence – perhaps because he knew that Soviet relations with the People's Republic of China had gone sour (see p. 303).

Since 1958 East Germans had continued to flock to the west through Berlin. In the first half of 1961 103,000 'voted' in this way. In June 1961 Khrushchev met President Kennedy in Vienna. He made renewed demands about Berlin. He thought the young and inexperienced Kennedy was soft. In July Khrushchev announced an increase in military expenditure. Kennedy responded in kind. Threat and counter-threat followed. Then on Sunday 13 August 1961 East German soldiers began erecting barbed wire fences between East and West Berlin – 'to keep out spies and saboteurs'. Four days later the East Germans began building a wall. The wall is still there. So are the western allies in West Berlin – 'the island in the Red Sea'. There were incidents along the wall at the time of its building but nothing more. Some East Germans have managed to scramble across the wall. Many have been killed while trying to do so.

This stretch of the Berlin Wall, seen from West Berlin in 1983, bisects what was once the splendid hub of Berlin. The wasteland across the wall is deliberately kept levelled. On the extreme left was the bunker in which Hitler and Eva Braun spent their last hours

The Cuban crisis, 1962

In the early 1960s the USA heavily outnumbered the USSR in all kinds of nuclear weapons and in rockets, planes and submarines for delivering them. Moreover Britain and France, both relatively close to the Soviet Union, had nuclear weapons. The USA had bases in Britain with nuclear-armed planes on constant alert. She had nuclear-armed rockets in Italy, and in Turkey, on the doorstep of the USSR. In 1962 the USSR made a bold attempt to counter this situation.

In 1959 Marxists and liberals had overthrown the dictatorship of Fulgencio Batista in Cuba (see p. 264). The new régime of Fidel Castro confiscated American-owned sugar plantations and mills. The USA responded by banning the importation of sugar from Cuba and early in 1961 broke off diplomatic relations with her.

In 1954 exiles from Guatemala, supplied with arms from the USA, had succeeded in overthrowing a leftist régime. But an American attempt in April 1961 to overthrow Castro by backing Cuban exiles who landed at the Bay of Pigs proved a disastrous failure. Kennedy justified the United States part in the operation by referring to the earlier Soviet intervention in Hungary. The landing at the Bay of Pigs was a humiliation for the USA, and pushed Cuba into the Soviet camp. The USSR gave Cuba aid and bought up the sugar crop that had lost its market in the USA.

On 8 September 1962 a Soviet missile ship arrived in Cuba. But it was not until mid-October that photographs from American U-2 planes showed that the Russians were preparing missile sites and were stationing missiles in Cuba. The Russians denied any unusual activity in Cuba but, while photographic evidence was accumulated, America made preparations for action.

The Americans estimated that the first missiles would be ready to use by 28 October. On 22 October the USA announced to the Soviet Union and to the world that the American navy was about to blockade Cuba. Kennedy, referring to the events of the 1930s, said that unchecked aggression ultimately leads to war and begged Khrushchev to 'move the world back from the brink of the abyss'. Meanwhile preparations were being made for an air attack and/or invasion of Cuba.

On 24 October two Soviet ships and a submarine were approaching the blockade limits set by the USA. They slowed down, stopped and finally turned back. The next day the Soviet representative at the United Nations made fresh denials of missile activity on Cuba but was given the lie by American photographs.

On 26 October Khrushchev sent a message to Kennedy offering to remove the missiles in return for an American promise not to invade Cuba. On 27 October Kennedy accepted this proposal but warned that American forces were ready to invade Cuba on the 29th. Early on 28 October Khrushchev announced over Radio Moscow that the weapons would be dismantled. Three hours later Kennedy over the Voice of America accepted the Russian offer. Within weeks there was no trace of missiles or missile sites on Cuba.

Said Kennedy's secretary of state: 'We looked into the mouth of the cannon. The Russians flinched.' The world had flinched too – but the greatest crisis of the Cold War had been surmounted. The Cuban crisis was a turning point in the Cold War. Hopes of co-existence, of living together without conflict, were succeeded by the greater hope of détente, of coming closer together.

The methods of communication available during the Cuban crisis were clumsy and dangerous. A step forward was the installation of a direct telephone link between the leaders of the super-powers, a 'hot line' between the White House and the Kremlin.

The 1960s: Vietnam, China, and space research

The years following the Cuban crisis saw the American involvement in Vietnam (see p. 313), the USSR's private cold war with China, the development of space exploration and a period of détente.

In Vietnam an American commitment to advise the government of South Vietnam in its struggle to prevent a communist takeover rapidly escalated into a major though undeclared war. This war cost the USA dearly in men and resources and effectively tied her hands until 1973. To what extent the Vietnam conflict was part of the Cold War is hard to assess. Certainly the USA regarded the communist threat to Vietnam as a threat to the whole of South-east Asia. On the other hand neither the USSR nor China was directly responsible for provoking the communist attack. And the amount of aid they gave to the Vietnamese communists was small compared with what the USA poured into South

Vietnam. Perhaps the USSR was content to let the Americans use up their resources while she concentrated on an enormous arms programme. By 1970 the USSR had substantially closed the gap between her own and the American nuclear forces. And caught at the time of the Cuban crisis with an inadequate navy she rapidly increased her sea power. On the other hand, by the 1970s the USA may be said to have secured the stability of South-east Asia. For with the exception of Cambodia and Laos (see p. 315) the other South-east Asian states were not knocked over like 'dominoes' after the victory of the communists in Vietnam. This may have been because during the Vietnam War these states had had time to stabilise their governments and economies.

While American hands were tied by the war in Vietnam, Russian hands were tied by their cold war with China (see p. 303). After ten years of 'unshakeable friendship' China from 1960 became the USSR's most bitter foe and critic. She condemned the Soviet Union for yielding to American imperialism, over the U-2 spy plane incident, over Cuba, over reaching an agreement with the USA on nuclear testing (see p. 252). She resented the Soviet Union's lack of support in her confrontation with the USA over Taiwan. She resented the Soviet Union's adopting India as a protégé. She attacked the 'gangster logic' of the USSR in invading Czechoslovakia in 1968 (see p. 294). She claimed that the treaties by which tsarist Russia acquired territories from China in the nineteenth century ought to be revised. Above all she attacked the USSR as a 'revisionist country' sneaking back onto 'the capitalist road' and set herself up as an example for revolution among the oppressed nations of the third world. And China in spite of all her difficulties was not without muscle. In 1967 the Chinese exploded a hydrogen bomb. In 1970 they put a satellite into orbit, thus giving evidence that they had rockets capable of firing deep into the USSR.

The USSR was thus obliged to divert a considerable proportion of her military resources towards China. A large part of her land forces was stationed on the Chinese frontier. In 1962 and 1969 there were border clashes. And while the Soviet Union was kept on the defensive the USA drew closer to China who began to regard the Americans as less of a threat than the Russians. The Americans, recognising that it was impossible to contain China and aware of her potential threat to the USSR, began to show a willingness to reduce their commitments in South Korea, Taiwan and South-east Asia. After 1969 the American trade and travel embargo

Yuri Gagarin, photographed in 1967

Americans orbited the moon. Seven months later, while Michael Collins circled the moon in a command module, Edwin Aldrin and Neil Armstrong landed and brought back specimens of moon rock. In the next few years the Americans made further moon landings.

Meanwhile the Russians concentrated on earth satellites which offered more immediate returns in defence, communications and weather forecasting. Space research resulted in the development of new weapons by both super-powers. The use of satellites enabled them to keep a closer watch on one another's activities.

Détente: nuclear control

'Although we competed', President Nixon once said, 'we seemed compelled to co-exist.' In 1963 the USSR and the USA signed a treaty banning the above-ground testing of nuclear devices, thus protecting the world from nuclear fallout. Britain associated herself with this treaty. France, the only other nuclear power at the time, refused to do so. China, after she became a nuclear power, also refused to sign the treaty. In 1967 the USA and the USSR signed a treaty banning nuclear weapons in outer space.

By the mid-1960s some twenty nations had the capacity to make nuclear weapons. The signing of a Nuclear Non-proliferation Treaty by the USA and the USSR in 1968, which other nations were invited to sign, was an attempt to check smaller states developing nuclear weapons. The signatories promised not to exchange military nuclear information or hardware. Within a year Britain and eighty-three other countries had signed the treaty. Its policing was entrusted to the International Atomic Energy Agency.

The Brezhnev Doctrine

In the 1960s the USSR showed no inclination to relax her hold over her satellites. In 1961 Albania, mistrustful both of the USSR and of her neighbour Yugoslavia, established close relations with China. The Soviet navy had to give up its Mediterranean base at Valona. In 1968 Albania formally withdrew from the Warsaw pact. The USSR, having no common frontier with Albania, was not in a position to assert military control there.

When in 1968 Czechoslovakia showed signs of independence (see p. 294) it was a different matter. In August 1968 forces of the Warsaw pact countries (other

imposed on China in 1949 was gradually lifted. In 1971 the USA ceased to veto the admission of the People's Republic of China to UNO. The People's Republic took her seat on the security council and Chiang Kai-shek's Republic of China was driven into limbo. The Soviet Union's loss of an 'unshakeable' friend had provided the United States with an immense strategic gain.

Soon after the launching of *Sputnik I*, *Sputnik II*, with the dog Laika on board, went into orbit. The Americans responded by setting up the National Aeronautics and Space Agency and soon were placing a variety of 'hardware' into orbit. However, the administration, aware of the needs of more earth-bound projects, planned a cautious, orderly development with limited objectives. But when on 12 April 1961 the Russians put Yuri Gagarin into space orbit the Americans were dismayed to discover they were still running second. A week later came the humiliation of the Bay of Pigs. Kennedy reacted dramatically. 'Regardless of cost', he said, 'if we can get to the moon before the Russians, we should ... within the decade.' In 1962 John Glenn was put into orbit. On Christmas Day 1968 three

Nuclear military power

1945	(August)	USA drops atomic (fission) bombs on Hiroshima and Nagasaki
1949	(July)	Russian atomic bomb exploded
1952	(October)	British atomic bomb
	(November)	US hydrogen (fusion) bomb
1953	(August)	Russian hydrogen bomb
1954	(January)	US nuclear-powered submarine, USS *Nautilus*, launched
1957	(May)	British hydrogen bomb
	(August)	Russian Intercontinental Ballistic Missile (ICBM)
	(October)	Russian launching of *Sputnik I*
	(December)	US Atlas ICBM
1960	(February)	French atomic bomb
	(July)	US submarine *George Washington* fires Polaris missile with nuclear warhead
1963	(August)	Nuclear Test Ban Treaty between USA and USSR
1964	(October)	Chinese atomic bomb
1966	(September)	First British nuclear submarine fitted with Polaris missiles becomes operational
1967	(June)	Chinese hydrogen bomb
1968	(July)	Nuclear Non-proliferation Treaty between USA and USSR; within a year joined by Britain and eighty-three other nations
	(August)	French hydrogen bomb
1974	(May)	Indian atomic device exploded

than Romania) invaded Czechoslovakia under Russian command. China, Albania, Yugoslavia, Romania and the western powers condemned the invasion but were powerless to help the Czechs. Leonid Brezhnev, who by then had come to the head of affairs in the USSR, proclaimed the Brezhnev Doctrine of limited sovereignty. In effect Brezhnev said that a threat to socialism in one country was a threat to all socialist countries, who therefore had a duty to intervene.

Ostpolitik

Meanwhile the thaw in east-west relations continued. Germany was central to the situation. West Germany had refused to have diplomatic relations with any country (except the USSR) that recognised East Germany. When in 1966 a new coalition government was formed in West Germany Willy Brandt, the foreign minister, followed a policy of reconciliation and adjustment with east (*ost*) Europe. This *ostpolitik* he believed would lead to a general European détente. The first steps

were taken when in 1967 and 1968 West Germany established relations with Romania and Yugoslavia – both states that recognised East Germany. In September 1969 Brandt became chancellor. When in the next month West Germany signed the Nuclear Non-proliferation Treaty the Soviet Union felt she was less of a threat.

In March 1970 Brandt went to East Germany, where he received a tumultuous welcome. The prime minister of East Germany was cautious but the ice in East-West German relations had been broken. A number of agreements followed.

In August 1970 the Federal Republic made a non-aggression treaty with the USSR; this also provided for greater trade between the two countries. In December 1970 West Germany signed a non-aggression pact with Poland and formally recognised the Oder-Western Neisse frontier (see p. 235). In Warsaw Brandt knelt before the memorial to Jewish victims of Hitler's Germany.

In September 1971 a four power agreement gave formal recognition to the status quo in Berlin. Links between West Berlin and the Federal Republic were to remain unchanged. And West Berliners were soon to have greater freedom to visit East Berlin and East Germany. Meanwhile the USA, the USSR, Britain and France continued to exercise their residual rights and responsibilities in Berlin. In 1983 these four powers were still taking turns in guarding the sole inmate of Spandau Allied Prison in West Berlin – Rudolf Hess. Once Hitler's deputy, Hess was sentenced to life imprisonment at Nüremberg (see p. 237). The left of the four flags flying at Spandau showed which power held the guard for the month.

In December 1972 the Federal Republic and the German Democratic Republic signed a treaty providing for increased trade, cultural and personal contacts and respect for one another's frontiers and alliance obligations. The existence of the two Germanys, traceable back to Yalta and Potsdam, thus received formal recognition.

The 1970s
Limitation of arms?

In the 1970s economies were expanding more slowly or even contracting. Military expenditure – generally at the cost of welfare – was less and less welcome, at any rate in the west, which also felt less threatened than in previous decades. In the USA, after Vietnam and under the influence of détente, there was a reduction in military expenditure until in 1979 a greatly expanded arms programme was undertaken. Meanwhile the USSR during the 1970s overtook and then surpassed the USA in both nuclear and conventional weapons.

In 1971 an international pact banned nuclear weapons on the sea-bed outside territorial waters. In 1972 an international treaty banned the use of biological weapons and toxins. In 1972, after five years of discussion, Nixon and Brezhnev signed a Strategic Arms Limitation Treaty (SALT 1) limiting the number of intercontinental land- and submarine-based launching weapons possessed by either side. (As the number of nuclear warheads possessed is difficult to verify, limitation of launching weapons was the only practicable arrangement.) An anti-ballistic missiles treaty at the same time limited the defensive missiles systems of both sides. After SALT 1 strategic arms limitation talks (SALT 2) continued. In 1979 a second SALT treaty was signed. This aimed at establishing nuclear parity between the two super-powers by setting ceilings to the number of land-, submarine- and bomber-launchers available to them. It also set limits on multiple warhead missiles. A standing committee (a joint USA–USSR body) was set up to supervise adherence to the treaty.

Limitation of conventional forces was discussed during more general talks concerning security and co-operation. In 1973 representatives of the USA, USSR, Britain, France and thirty-one other states met in Helsinki to discuss co-operation and security in Europe (CSCE). Shortly afterwards a conference on mutual and balanced force reduction (MBFR) met in Vienna. Neither conference made any progress – mutual, balanced or otherwise – towards limiting conventional arms. Both power blocs wanted to reduce their forces, if only on account of cost, but neither was willing to diminish its 'security'. Another obstacle was Russian unwillingness to accept any system of inspection.

At Helsinki the western powers insisted that respect for individual liberty and human rights was a condition of genuine détente. To this the eastern bloc paid lip service in a joint resolution on human rights (1975). It is doubtful whether this Helsinki Human Rights accord has had much effect in any part of the world where individual freedom is disregarded – whether by forces of the right or of the left. In keeping with the accord was an undertaking made at the Vienna meeting to 'facilitate the movement of people and information across national frontiers' – for example there was to be no jamming of foreign radio broadcasts.

All the powers attending the Helsinki meeting formally accepted all existing frontiers in Europe – in particular those of East and West Germany and of divided Berlin.

Continued rivalry

While these discussions went on the USA and the USSR continued to exert their influence as time and opportunity offered. Besides conventional diplomacy, undercover agents and the supply of arms and other aid were used with varying degrees of success – sometimes with unexpected results. Such was the case when Muslim extremists (1979) turned out the shah of Iran, who had been heavily subsidised by the USA, and held some fifty Americans hostage for over a year, or when Somalia allowed the Americans use of naval and air bases built by the Russians!

For some years neither the USA nor the USSR intervened directly in other states. The USA did not want to repeat its experience in Vietnam. The USSR used Cuban troops as proxies in Angola (see p. 323) and the Horn of Africa (Ethiopia, Eritrea and Somalia) and supported Cuban agents in Latin America. Over the docking of the Apollo and Soyuz spacecraft (1975), in the provision of trading facilities, in medical research, the super-powers showed some capacity for working together. Then in December 1979 a Soviet army invaded Afghanistan in support of a revolutionary movement. 'All the old fears of Soviet imperialism came flooding back.' The United States Senate refused to ratify SALT 2 and negotiations for SALT 3 came to a halt. The USA, West Germany, China and a few lesser states refused to take part in the 1980 Olympic Games in Moscow. The USA embarked on a huge rearmaments programme. And the Soviet Union found itself involved in an expensive struggle with Afghan guerillas, many of whose officers had trained in the USSR.

In 1975, shortly before his death, that wise statesman, Chou En-lai of China, found little to choose between the super-powers; their rivalry he regarded as a continuing danger to the world. If the Russians have a strong presence in, for example, the Baltic and the Indian Ocean, the Americans have a strong presence in the Gulf of Mexico and the Mediterranean. Of some significance has been the growing importance of the third world – to which, along with lesser states, oil-rich Middle Eastern countries and the People's Republic of China with its immense population and potential claim to belong.

27 The United States and Latin America

The USA

President Truman, 1945–53

Truman, who succeeded Roosevelt as president in 1945, was elected for a further term in 1948. The Truman Doctrine (see p. 240) was characteristic of the hard line he took in combating the advance of communism.

The American economy, which had doubled its output between 1939 and 1945, entered the post-war years with a vast momentum for growth. By the end of Truman's presidency it was estimated that the American standard of living was three times that of Britain, six times that of Italy and forty times that of Indonesia.

Having 'won the war' Americans looked forward to a period of plenty at home and non-involvement abroad. When Marshall put forward his plan for bolstering European economies in 1947 (see p. 241) they showed little enthusiasm. The communist takeover of Czechoslovakia in 1948 resulted in a new attitude. The Berlin blockade and the Korean War set the seal on that. By the end of Truman's presidency Americans were committed to the defence of western Europe and the security of the Far East.

In 1947 the National Security Act set up a department of defence responsible for all three armed services, a National Security Council to advise the president and a Central Intelligence Agency (the CIA) to organise a worldwide information gathering and spy network. Truman ordered a loyalty check on government employees. By early 1950 checking on loyalty had become a national preoccupation. Senator Joseph McCarthy, a Republican, claimed that the communist victory in China was the result of advice given in the state department by pro-communist American officials. He and his sympathisers were soon arguing that every post-war problem at home or abroad was the product of the activities of American communists and their sympathisers. Such views were fuelled by the trial of Alger Hiss, a former state department official accused of treason but convicted of perjury, by spy trials in Canada and the conviction in Britain of Klaus Fuchs, a physicist who sold atomic research secrets to the USSR. (McCarthy and his friends would have been even more alarmed had they known the full extent of the Fuchs spy ring revealed during the next thirty years.)

In 1950 a judge of the Supreme Court ruled that the American Communist Party was a conspiracy rather than a political party. In many states the party was outlawed. In the House of Representatives a committee was set up to investigate un-American activities. Teachers, film stars, government officials, universities, publishers, trade unions – anyone and any organisation that McCarthy and his cohorts accused – were investigated by this and similar state committees. Unrestricted by the rules of evidence, the committees listened to truths, half-truths and lies. Though there was no guillotine and no Siberia, heads rolled. Many lives, many careers, were ruined in the nationwide witch hunt. Even the president, who had taken such a hard line against communism, was smeared.

President Eisenhower, 1953–61

The election in 1952 of Eisenhower, a Republican, ended twenty years of Democratic rule. Although Eisenhower scorned McCarthy the Republican Party took advantage of his widespread popularity to gain votes. For a time McCarthy and his 'multiple untruths' continued to flourish. Then common sense and diminished tension abroad began to have their effect. In 1954 McCarthy made attacks on the army. A series of television programmes investigated his accusations and convinced millions of viewers of the viciousness of his methods and the falsity of his claims.

Eisenhower's vice-president was Richard Nixon. His secretary of state was Dulles (see p. 246). As a result of the Cold War the draft (compulsory enrolment in the armed services) became an apparently permanent feature of life – but under Eisenhower there was no war for servicemen to fight.

Peace and prosperity provided a good platform for Eisenhower when he was re-elected in 1956 – this time without Nixon. There was little outstanding legislation during his presidency. In 1959 Hawaii and Alaska were admitted as the forty-ninth and fiftieth states of the Union. Meanwhile the western states, especially

California, were growing more rapidly in population and economic importance than the rest of the USA.

In 1948 Truman had desegregated the armed forces. A decision made in 1954 by the Supreme Court, in *Brown* v. *Topeka Board of Education*, made racial discrimination in schools illegal. Discrimination had for long been the practice in schools, especially in the southern states. In 1957 there was a dispute in Little Rock, Arkansas, when seventeen Negroes who had been accepted by a school board insisted on their right to attend. This spotlighted the struggle for racial equality. Eisenhower, who sent in federal troops to enforce a federal court order, won a significant victory for equality – and places in college for the young Negroes. A Civil Rights Act designed to protect Negro voting rights, and the establishment of a civil rights commission to investigate discrimination were further proof of Eisenhower's determination to secure Negro rights.

Presidents Kennedy, 1961–63 and Johnson, 1963–69

Eisenhower was succeeded by a much younger man, the Democrat John F. Kennedy. In November 1963 Kennedy was assassinated. Lyndon Johnson, the vice-president, then became president. In 1964 Johnson was elected president by a huge majority.

When Kennedy became president Vietnam (see p. 312) was only a small cloud on the horizon. By the end of Johnson's presidency it dominated politics. And by then the USA had seen the worst domestic violence it had known since the Civil War. Conscription for service in Vietnam was widely resented and often evaded. Johnson in 1965 had promised a 'great society'. But revenue needed for welfare was diverted to the war, thus adding to the resentment of the underprivileged. Tensions that had remained submerged during the previous decade surfaced in open conflict in the 1960s. A youth culture of protest emerged, leading to violent and prolonged clashes with authority. A tragic by-product of protest was the use of drugs by the young, the not-so-young and by servicemen.

The dissent of the 1960s was not directed only at the Vietnam War. It was also directed against racial inequality. Between 1940 and 1960 there had been a great increase in the Negro population, accompanied by a steady movement to seek work and a brighter life in the glittering cities of the north. Soon ghetto districts disfigured many cities. In these ghettoes Negroes ate well enough but lived in squalor. In 1961 Washington,

DC, became the first American city with a majority of Negro inhabitants.

The rapid growth of cities had not been paralleled by an increase in their representation in the legislatures, state or federal. However, following a 1962 Supreme Court ruling, urban areas were given a fairer share of representatives. In 1965 Congress passed an effective Voting Rights Act that prescribed penalties for preventing Negroes from voting.

In 1957, the year of the Little Rock dispute, about 6 per cent of Negro children in the south attended desegregated schools; by 1963 the proportion was nearly 80 per cent. The struggle for desegregation had spread to restaurants, public transport, cinemas and to those churches where segregation was the rule. The movement was at first peaceful, under the leadership of Martin Luther King, a Christian of deep convictions and great courage. In 1963 King led a civil rights protest march through Birmingham, Alabama. The police dispersed the marchers with hoses, dogs and electric cattle prods. Such harshness and the quiet dignity of King and his followers brought nationwide publicity and added support for desegregation. By boycotts and other non-violent methods King and his supporters, Negroes and whites, went on trying to achieve social equality. 'There were sit-ins at segregated restaurants, wade-ins at segregated swimming pools, walk-ins at segregated theatres, even kneel-ins at segregated churches. Freedom riders tested desegregation on buses and trains in the south.' In 1964 Congress passed an act banning racial discrimination in hotels and restaurants. In 1954 the Supreme Court had ruled that desegregation in schools should be carried out 'with all deliberate speed'. In 1969 it ruled that desegregation should begin 'at once'.

But relatively more Negroes than whites were unemployed and lived in squalid conditions. It became clear in the 1960s that not paper civil rights but only full equality would satisfy the Negroes. They wanted an end to all discrimination – in housing, employment and opportunities generally – an end in fact to the days of second-class citizenship. Harsher leaders than King came to the fore. A civil rights movement active mainly in rural areas in the south and under Christian leadership gave way to a Black Power movement, 'urban, secular, militant', in the cities in the north. While one after another of the African states was achieving independence, in the USA the Black Panthers and similar groups seemed bent on all-out war against the whites. Black became the only name acceptable to the Negroes –

Martin Luther King addressing a civil rights rally attended by 70,000 people in Chicago, 21 June 1964

a very proud name. Stokeley Carmichael, a black student leader, urged his followers to buy black, sell black, vote black and above all think black – to see beauty in 'a broad nose, a thick lip and nappy hair'. In city after city riots, often triggered off by some minor incident, developed into violent clashes in which blacks fought against those who represented the authority and power of white America. The Vietnam War, however many protests it brought, was accustoming thousands of young people to senseless violence. Television revealed the glossy life of white Americans and made the blacks more conscious of their underprivileged status.

In 1965 riots in the Watts district of Los Angeles caused thirty-five deaths. In 1967–68 there were serious riots in many cities throughout the USA. In 1965 Malcolm X, a black leader, was killed. In 1968 Martin Luther King and two months later Senator Robert Kennedy, John Kennedy's brother and a candidate for the presidency, were assassinated.

A rebellion on the Berkeley campus of the University of California (December 1964 to January 1965) triggered off a period of student revolt – in the USA, Japan, Australia, Germany, France and Britain. Students

seized control of campuses in protest at anything and everything – Vietnam, racial and social injustice, administrators and professors with whom they did not see eye to eye. Sometimes they seemed to be protesting for protest's sake. The last serious disorders in the USA were in 1970. Then for a variety of reasons the steam went out of the protest movement. Those protesters whose careers and personalities had survived settled down to relatively orthodox lives – to suits and ties, wedlock even. Some had fallen by the wayside.

One discovery of the 1960s was that not all Americans, even white Americans, were well off. The USA with 6 per cent of the world's population had 40 per cent of its income. The American farmer who in 1940 grew enough food for ten people in 1960 grew enough to feed twenty-five. Yet there was still real poverty, especially in the Deep South. Uncontrolled urbanisation threatened to strangle society.

Kennedy had introduced bills for federal aid to education, limited medical care and the control of urban development. (The federal government was able to enter the field of education under the doctrine of implied powers.) These bills were rejected by Congress but won assent under Johnson. Indeed in social legislation Johnson's régime was one of the most fruitful in American history. Nevertheless, the 'great society' which he had promised was far from attainment when he left office. There were still large areas of deprivation and misery in wealthy America. Yet the 1970s saw the decline of protest. The Republican administration of Nixon was harsh in its enforcement of law and order. The conclusion of the Vietnam War and successes won in the struggle against racial inequality left the protesters without their two main platforms. And protest had had a surfeit of itself and left the protesters exhausted. The generation born in the baby boom of the post-war years was growing up and growing conservative. Women's liberation and pollution became the 'in' things in the 1970s. Only extreme feminists could discover much to protest about. The noise of Concorde and nuclear contamination caused more of a stir.

Presidents Nixon, 1969–74, Ford, 1974–77 and Carter, 1977–81

In 1951 an amendment to the constitution prevented a president seeking election for a third successive term. Johnson, having succeeded to the presidency in 1963 without election, was eligible to stand for re-election in 1968. But bewildered by his unpopularity over Vietnam he refused to stand. Nixon, a Republican, followed him. His presidency was notable for de-escalation of the Vietnam War and, paradoxically, both for détente with the USSR and for rapprochement with the People's Republic of China. And during Nixon's presidency man took his 'first small footsteps on the moon'. These achievements go far to explain Nixon's re-election in 1972. Early in his second term the ending of the Vietnam War (1973), largely as a result of the diplomacy of his secretary of state, Henry Kissinger, was a triumph of a kind. It resulted at any rate in the ending of the draft for military service. Later that year Nixon's vice-president, Spiro Agnew, was found to have taken bribes and submitted false tax returns. Agnew was forced to resign. About the same time the Watergate scandal erupted.

In June 1972, prior to the elections of that year, the Democratic Party's headquarters in the Watergate building in Washington were broken into. Early in 1973 the Watergate burglars and two accomplices were convicted on various charges. Persistent investigations by newspaper reporters led them to believe that Nixon's assistants and even the president himself were in some

way involved. It became known that some of Nixon's conversations with his assistants concerning the Watergate breakin were recorded on tapes. After long delays Nixon was forced to hand over the tapes. These revealed that he had almost certainly authorised the burglary. The judiciary committee of the House of Representatives then adopted articles of impeachment for debate by the house. But a few days later, on 8 August 1974, Nixon, who had stubbornly clung to power, resigned. Gerald Ford, vice-president since Agnew's resignation, then became president. Soon afterwards he pardoned Nixon for his presumed offences. But Nixon's close associates were imprisoned for their part in the Watergate affair.

The 1970s were marked by mounting economic difficulties. Full employment was a thing of the past. By 1975 there were seven and a half million unemployed (8.2 per cent of the work force, the highest percentage since 1941). The steep rise in the price of oil that followed the Yom Kippur War in 1973 (see p. 333) stoked the fires of inflation. It was with such problems and with the restoration of the integrity of the presidency that Ford and his successor, Jimmy Carter, a Democrat, were especially concerned. In foreign relations Carter was preoccupied with human rights and a solution of the Arab-Israeli problem. Détente was interrupted by the Soviet invasion of Afghanistan (see p. 254). Congress for its part took action to curb presidential power which had been growing since the time of F.D. Roosevelt. In 1981 Ronald Reagan, a Republican, took office as president. He was the first president to come from California. California and the other western states continued to grow in wealth and importance.

Latin America

Latin America, stretching from Mexico to Tierra del Fuego and including Cuba and the Dominican Republic, consists of lands ruled until the nineteenth century by Spain and Portugal. Spanish remains the language of Latin America except in Brazil where Portuguese is spoken. And as the people of the USA are not altogether unlike the British, so the people of Latin America, despite its mixture of races, are not unlike the Spaniards and Portuguese in outlook, habits and culture.

In some parts, for example Cuba, the native Indians were wiped out in early colonial times. Other states, Peru and Bolivia for example, have a large proportion of

Indian inhabitants. In other parts mestizos, people of mixed European and Indian blood, form a substantial part of the population. In Mexico the mixture of people is so complex that statisticians have given up the attempt to classify them by racial origins – they are just Mexicans. In Brazil and Cuba, where large numbers of African slaves were imported, a high proportion of the people is of Negro descent. In the nineteenth and twentieth centuries millions of immigrants – Italians, Germans, Poles, Japanese, Spaniards and others – settled in Latin America. In the city of São Paulo in Brazil there are more Italian-speaking Brazilians than there are Italians in Naples. Whole news-stands sell only Japanese magazines. South America has too its British-Irish communities which, though small, are important. Though the new arrivals added to the culture of Latin America they did not alter its basic Spanish–Portuguese character. There is a passionate interest in music, literature and art. Institutions of learning flourish. Men of letters are honoured. But there is much illiteracy.

Latin America's resources have been much developed in recent years. Feats of engineering have opened up the interior. Railways, many built by British engineers in the nineteenth century, climb seemingly impossible gradients and cross viaducts over terrifying gorges. Mexico City and São Paulo – which has more television channels than any city except New York – are among the world's largest cities. Brasilia, the new capital of Brazil, is a dream city of modern architecture.

Portuguese Brazil – almost the size of the USA including Alaska – did not fragment when it became independent and until 1889 was ruled by its own emperors, descendants of the royal house of Portugal. Spanish America broke up after independence into sixteen, and eventually eighteen, relatively small republics – though compared with European states some are large. (Argentina, for example, is five times the size of France.)

Subjected under colonial rule to the pervasive authority of Madrid or Lisbon, Latin Americans still tend to accept authoritarian rule as normal. Constitutional and democratic rule are much talked about, but those who rule and many of the ruled seem to agree that democracy tends to break down in disorder. So, they say, 'authoritarian rule is perhaps best for us.' Yet the great Latin American liberals of the past are revered. Constitutions that have been 'suspended' are honoured in ceremonies of almost religious piety. 'The framing of our constitution was a splendid achievement – but until it was suspended it wasn't safe to walk about at night',

said a young woman in Montevideo. In such circumstances 'democratorship' – a mixture of democracy and dictatorship, with the latter predominating – flourishes. And football and fiestas on which rich and poor spend money with abandon are more diverting than politics.

But there are those among the ruled to whom politics do matter. From the late 1960s urban guerillas with vague communist or anarchist ties or no ties at all troubled such cities as Buenos Aires, São Paulo and Montevideo. The activities of the Tupamaro guerillas in Montevideo led the army to suspend Uruguay's constitution. The guerillas showed special talent for holding governments to ransom by kidnapping foreign diplomats. The common factor among the urban guerilla groups was their belief in violence as 'the only way' to some vaguely envisaged end. Meanwhile, the leader of Latin America's one communist state, Castro of Cuba, had to some extent made his ideas known to the poor in the remotest areas. In 1961 a traveller noted 'only two faces were universally recognised throughout Latin America' – those of the Virgin Mary and Fidel Castro. 'Che' Guevara, an Argentinian, perhaps won a greater following overseas than among Latin Americans. He was unable to put across his ideas to the Indians of Bolivia, who deserted their would-be saviour. In 1967 Guevara was killed by Bolivian government troops.

The Catholic Church continues to exercise influence, though numerous faiths flourish in lands whose people are of diverse origin. The church has in recent years spoken out in championship of greater social justice. Young priests point out that the urban guerillas were stung to activity by bad government and an 'unvarnished capitalism that exploits the poor'. Though Latin Americans perhaps lack the earnest money-making zeal of the North Americans there are patches of extreme wealth. There are also squalid shanty towns in the cities, and deep in the interior are whole regions of poverty. In some parts there are indications of concern for public welfare. 'Little' Uruguay (it is as large as England and Scotland together) is top heavy with a welfare system it can scarcely afford.

Where generals are often politically active and streets, plazas and railway stations by the score are named after generals, war the proper trade of generals has not played a very important part. A Shanghainese who left China in 1949 remarked: 'For the first twenty-seven years of my life I knew nothing but war. Since I came to Brazil twenty-seven years ago there has been peace.' High on the border between Chile and Argentina stands the

Mexico City, 1914: Zapata (with sombrero) sits beside the bandit chieftain Villa (see p. 66) in the presidential palace

Christ of the Andes, a perpetual reminder that, though they bitterly dispute certain territories, there must never be war. There have been wars but in this century only one (the war between Bolivia and Paraguay for possession of the swampy Chaco region, 1932–35) has led to prolonged fighting. The Falklands campaign of 1982 (see p. 263) was sharply fought but brief. There have however been savagely fought domestic conflicts.

Under the shadow of the Monroe Doctrine (see p. 63), Latin America has been protected from the rest of the world. In the wake of the USA some of the Latin American states entered the First and Second World Wars. Latin American states joined the League of Nations and were later active in UNO – Brazil, for example, supplied troops for a peace-keeping force in the Middle East in the 1950s. Many states signed the Nuclear Non-proliferation Treaty of 1968 and also adopted their own protocol declaring Latin America a nuclear free zone.

Where régimes are often despotic and sometimes brutal and where generals are politically active, coups d'état are almost a way of life. But coups, with notable exceptions, have been conducted low key. Latin Americans, it is said, prefer to conduct their coups by telephone. But if most coups have been virtually blood-less violation of human rights – for instance, by torture

and imprisonment of opponents on remote islands without trial – is not uncommon.

In 1930 Latin America had a population of 109 million; 206 out of every 1,000 Chilean babies died in their first year. By 1975 the population was 324 million; the death rate for Chilean babies had fallen to 78. In 1930 out of every 1,000 people in the world 54 were Latin Americans; by 1975 the number had risen to 84.

Mexico

After independence (1821) there was conflict between urbanised people, mainly of Spanish origin, and near destitute Indian peasants who claimed restoration of their long lost lands. During these years of chaos Mexico lost vast territories to the USA (see map p. 63). In 1860 Benito Juárez, the liberal reformer after whom Mussolini was named, became president. But there was no order in Mexico until in 1876 Porfirio Díaz established a dictatorship. The twin pillars on which his rule rested were armed force and bribery. The *ley de fuega* (law of flight) – the prisoner was shot trying to escape – accounted for many opponents. Others were bribed into compliance. Lasting until 1911 Díaz's dictatorship gave Mexico more than thirty years of 'law and order'. Stability attracted British and American capital, especially after the discovery of oil. Díaz too late realised the unwisdom of allowing foreigners to gain a strong hold on the economy. 'Poor Mexico, so far from God and so close to the United States', he is alleged to have said. For the mass of the people his dictatorship did nothing.

In 1911 a peasant, Emiliano Zapata, who promised extensive land reforms, led the countryside in a rebellion which cost a quarter of a million lives. The war died down in 1917 when a constitution was drawn up. The constitution declared that land and natural resources belonged to the nation. It excluded the church from education and laid down a labour code. But the aims of the constitution were only very gradually carried out. In 1925 American and British oil companies had to exchange their titles of ownership for fifty-year leases. The closure of church primary schools in 1926 resulted in a three-year strike by priests. During the strike not a single mass was officially said in Mexico. In 1929 a National Revolutionary Party brought together numerous regional groups and under this party Mexico enjoyed a large measure of cohesion.

In 1934 General Cárdenas, of Indian birth, became president of Mexico. He nationalised the railways. He ordered the foreign oil companies to pay higher wages and train Mexicans for management – and when the companies did not comply he expelled them. He redistributed twice as much land as all previous governments had done and organised co-operative farms.

After Mexico declared war on the Axis powers (1942), with American help industries were modernised and agriculture improved. In recent years it has been to Mexico's benefit to be 'so near to the United States'. American tourists flock in, bringing hard currency. Many Mexicans, legally or illegally, migrate to work in the USA. The USA provides a convenient market for cheaply produced goods. Political stability has encouraged an inflow of American capital.

In 1983 Mexico remained a one party state but the party included varying shades of opinion and allowed considerable civil liberty. There was little social unrest although land reform was far from complete.

Brazil

From 1822 to 1889 under her two emperors Brazil was spared the rivalry for power which plagued the former Spanish lands. Dom Pedro II (1847–89) gave Brazil 'as much democracy as she could absorb at the time'. The vote was denied to the illiterate majority but there was freedom of speech. The abolition of slavery, long desired by Dom Pedro, came in 1888. In general slaves in Brazil had not been ill-treated and after emancipation were absorbed into the community without undue difficulty.

In the mid-nineteenth century Brazil had designs on Uruguay, whilst landlocked Paraguay also had territorial ambitions. Following the War of the Triple Alliance, 1865–70, in which Brazil, Argentina and Uruguay defeated Paraguay, Brazil acquired considerable territory from Paraguay, whose population had been decimated – of Paraguay's surviving population barely one in ten were men. Uruguay, fiercely proud of her independence, shook herself free of Brazil.

In 1889 an uprising led by ambitious army officers forced the emperor to abdicate. A new constitution provided for democratic and federal government, but like Spanish American constitutions it gave the president power to suspend constitutional rule and to intervene in the provinces. It was difficult to operate a democratic system in a vast country with a scattered and mostly illiterate population. To a great extent effective power remained with the military, supported by an oligarchy of rich families from the coffee plantations of São Paulo state and from the mining state of Minas Gerais.

After 1880 rubber brought great wealth. Manaus, 1,600 kilometres up the Amazon, became a little Paris with its *Teatro Amazonas* (Theatre of the Amazon), champagne and traders who lit their cigars with banknotes. But the forests were exploited and labour was exploited and the boom ended when Malaya began producing better quality rubber in efficiently run plantations. Then it was coffee which boomed. But demand stimulated production in other countries and when the world depression came Brazilians were dumping coffee in the sea. In 1942 Brazil declared war on the Axis powers and sent a division to fight in Italy. During the war manufactures grew enormously. Since the war Brazil has diversified her economy with manufacturing taking its place beside a variety of primary products. For example, the car industry by 1981 employed 133,000 workers.

Until Zapata roused the peasants of Mexico ' "revolution" in Latin America meant little more than the substitution of the "outs" for the "ins" in government; the life of the mass of the population was not greatly affected.' Brazil had its Zapata and Cárdenas in Gentilio Vargas. Supported by the army and the rapidly growing class of industrial workers, Vargas, 'Father of the poor', between 1930 and 1954 profoundly altered Brazilian society. A labour code forbade the exploitation of workers and provided a form of unemployment insurance. Education and medical services were developed. The steel industry was established and kept in Brazilian hands.

Architectural achievements are a striking feature of modern Brazil. It was at Vargas's inspiration that the architectural revolution – which influenced the whole continent – began. The next president, Kubitschek, was responsible for the creation of Brasilia. This was an expensive undertaking but booming Brazil could afford it.

Later weaker government and inflation caused economic difficulties. Fearing disorder, the army moved in. Another telephone revolution passed off peacefully. The new president, General Castello Branco, maintained a civilian government and after a period of austerity Brazil began to grow again with a grandiose scheme for the construction of a Trans-Amazonia highway opening up the interior. Brazil, they say, 'grows at night while the politicians are asleep'.

Latin America shows a remarkable degree of racial tolerance. Racial harmony in Brazil, where colour of skin ranges from white to black with a warm coffee colour predominating, is impressive. Attempts are being made, largely by the army, to bring the Indians of the Amazon basin into the mainstream of Brazilian life.

Argentina

After independence (1816) the rough-riding gauchos (cowboys) of the pampas, who had little liking for law and order, opposed a centralised government. However, by the mid-nineteenth century President Rosas, himself from the pampas, had imposed unity on the country.

Railways played an important part in unifying Argentina. By 1890 there were nearly 10,000 kilometres of railway and by 1912 32,000 kilometres. Most of these lines were built with British capital by British engineers using British equipment. Links with Britain were strengthened by the trade in beef. By 1900 nearly 300 refrigerator ships were operating between Buenos Aires and British ports.

During the late nineteenth century immigrants poured in – in 1895 one million out of a population of four million were 'foreigners'. Rapid economic development made Argentina richer – and more influential – than any other Latin American state, though the workers benefited little.

In general Argentinian presidents obeyed the consti-

tution only when it suited them. Whilst paying lip service to the constitution they frequently governed by decree. Economic progress and the growth of the middle class led to a demand for more democratic government. Electoral reforms led to the election of a radical president, Hipolitó Irigoyen (1916–22, 1928–30). Laws fixing minimum wages and maximum working hours were passed. As Irigoyen clung to power, reforming zeal waned and corruption flourished. In 1930, when Argentina was grappling with the world depression, he was politely removed from office and conservatives returned to power.

In 1943 a group of army officers seized power in Argentina. One of these officers, Colonel Juan Perón, aware of the power of the industrial workers, chose to be responsible for labour. He introduced collective bargaining and compulsory holidays. Workers' flats were built and so on. Perón patronised boxers, footballers, racing motorists – and especially the popular radio star, Eva (Evita) Duarte. In October 1945 his colleagues arrested him. But mass demonstrations by trade unionists resulted in his release – and he married Eva. In February 1946 the *Partida Laborista*, organised by his supporters, swept him to power as president. In the next six years under Perón and Eva Argentina moved into the era of urban industry and social security.

After Eva's death in 1952 Perón's régime began to fall apart. Corruption reached an unprecedented level, especially in state-owned industries. Perón also offended the Catholic Church which had initially supported him. As opposition grew there were rumours that he was planning to arm the trade unions. The army then moved in on Buenos Aires and the navy blockaded the River Plate. Perón took refuge in a Paraguayan gunboat and was allowed to go into exile (1955).

There was a clean sweep of Perón's supporters – the Peronistas. Military officers were put in charge of trade unions. And for most of the next eighteen years the army and navy remained in control. Nevertheless support for the Peronistas remained strong. In 1973 Perón, then aged seventy-eight, and married to Isabelita, was recalled from exile. He was again elected president, with his wife as vice-president. Within a year Perón died and Isabelita, as the constitution provided, succeeded him.

Under Isabelita's confused rule power slipped into the hands of the trade unions. But with headlong inflation real wages did not rise. Meanwhile the urban guerillas were at work. In 1976 there was another military coup. Isabelita was imprisoned. The power of the unions was broken. And in the so-called dirty war

A Buenos Aires Herald cartoon, 1 August 1981, just after the Prince of Wales's wedding. The Argentine foreign minister asks for his slice of cake. Already the Argentine press was demanding the return of the Malvinas (Falkland) Islands

which followed the coup guerilla terrorism was met with counter-terror and counter-terror won. Thousands of people, some of them innocent, disappeared into the 'black hole', never to reappear. Though in 1982 some 900 people were still unaccounted for ordinary people went about their business by day or night without fear. The bomb-proof limousines ordered by foreign embassies were no longer in use.

As a result of the War of the Triple Alliance (see p. 261) Argentina gained a new province. After that she lived at peace with her neighbours, although disputing with Chile over part of Tierra del Fuego and a slice of Antarctic territory, the latter already claimed by Britain – until in April 1982 she seized the Falkland Islands. Britain was caught unawares. Argentina refused to comply with a UN security council resolution demanding her withdrawal. A British task force recovered the Falklands in June after some loss of life on both sides and considerable loss of British ships and Argentinian planes. The chief aim of the Argentinian leaders may have been to quiet internal discontent by displaying the grandeur of the Colossus of the South.

Chile

After independence (1818) power was in the hands of a landowning oligarchy. The landless and illiterate had no political rights. The president directed the administration, controlled elections to the Congress and appointed his successor. Under such a simple system things went smoothly. After a civil war in 1891 the president became responsible to Congress but this remained under the control of the landowners.

From the mid-nineteenth century nitrates and British capital brought wealth – and railways to take the nitrates to the coast, telegraphs, a water supply in the desert and a mine to produce coal for ships and railway engines. Nitrates were worth fighting for. In the Pacific War (1879–83) Chile took from Bolivia and Peru coastal territory as far north as Arica and including Antofagasta, a nitrate centre. Bolivia was left without a coastline but Chile agreed to build a railway across the mountains to La Paz.

When, during the First World War, the Germans discovered how to make synthetic nitrates Chile's boom ended. Then it was the turn of copper mining, financed by American companies. In the inter-war years Chilean miners and factory workers began demanding parliamentary government and welfare legislation. But it was not until the 1960s that Eduardo Frei introduced reforms in land ownership and education and provided funds for electricity and water supplies.

In 1970, following electoral reforms, Salvador Allende, a Marxist, became president. Nationalisation of the mines was followed by a trade agreement with the USSR and the establishment of friendly relations with Cuba. The Chilean oligarchy was alarmed. The USA, fearing 'another Cuba', cut off aid. In 1973, following demonstrations against Allende, the military overthrew his government. To what extent the CIA encouraged the demonstrations which preceded the coup is not known. Allende was killed during the fighting of this non-telephone revolution – or perhaps committed suicide. A repressive régime took over, with grave abuse of human rights.

Cuba

Cuba's independence (1902) was limited by an agreement allowing the Americans to intervene to protect life and property or if Cuba was threatened from outside. The Americans also acquired the right to a naval base from which they could protect the Panama area. Meanwhile, between 1898 and 1902, the death rate in Cuba had been reduced by half, mainly by the elimination of yellow fever.

Sugar brought wealth, at any rate to the owners of plantations and mills. After 1902 American investment increased and there was some growth in prosperity though the short season during which cane was cut left many Cubans unemployed for many months. And government was as corrupt, inefficient and oppressive as in the days of Spanish rule.

American marines were frequently in Cuba preserving order. Though such intervention did not bring better government it did prevent bloodshed and insecurity. In 1933 Batista established the dictatorship that kept its grip on the country for twenty-five years. In 1934 the USA gave up her right to intervene in Cuba. However, Americans increased their hold over the economy.

In 1953 Fidel Castro and a few followers landed in Cuba with the object of overthrowing the Batista régime. Castro, son of a rich Cuban landowner, had studied law at the University of Havana. There he joined a movement demanding land for the landless and freedom from the control of foreign investors. Castro in 1953 had as little success as his nineteenth-century predecessors who had tried to overthrow Spanish rule. But in 1956 he landed again and set up a base in the mountains. From there he fought a guerilla war until on 1 January 1959 Batista resigned and fled from Cuba.

Castro in the hour of victory, 1 January 1959

By the end of 1960 land, industry and commerce were almost entirely in the hands of the state. Trade with the USA was at a standstill. Castro looked more and more to the Soviet Union for trade and aid, technical assistance and military equipment. The failure of the American-backed landing at the Bay of Pigs in 1961 resulted in still closer ties with the Soviet Union and the Russian attempt in 1962 to set up a missile base in Cuba (see p. 250).

Castro's régime brought no sudden rise in the standard of living – many Cubans were worse off. And the treatment of opponents was as harsh as under his predecessors or under the communist régimes of eastern Europe. And if Cuba had previously been tied to the apron strings of the USA she was now more firmly tied to the USSR. In 1972 she became a member of Comecon (see p. 292). In return for huge subsidies Cuba became the proxy of the Soviet Union in Africa and Latin America. Military adventures in Africa siphoned off domestic discontent. And while many Cubans fled to the USA, thousands of third-world youths were brought – often forcibly – to attend indoctrination and labour camps in Cuba.

Latin America and the USA

For a century and a half the USA has shown determination to allow no European interference in any American state. Since about 1900 the power of the American dollar has made itself felt in Latin America. More recently the USA has attempted to develop good neighbour relations.

Until the First World War and even afterwards Latin Americans, particularly Argentinians, were inclined to lean towards Britain politically and economically.

'In Buenos Aires [in 1908] ... American financial institutions are like the American merchant steamers, conspicuous by their absence. ... In England they talk familiarly of "B.A." [Buenos Aires] and the "River Plate" ... you might suppose they were speaking of something they owned, and you would not be so very far from the truth. ... '

Although in time Latin Americans had to allow American dollars to bridge the gap between their own resources and their desire for development, they have remained suspicious of Yanqui (American) intentions, fearing that overdependence on Yanqui dollars would keep them economically inferior. This has been especially so in the Argentine, the Colossus of the South. Looking on herself as the leader by right of the 'South American family of nations', Argentina has been the more jealous of the Colossus of the North. But though anti-Yanquiism has often been strong realism has compelled Latin Americans to recognise the benefits that the Yanqui connection can bring.

In 1947 the USA and the Latin American states made a pact at Rio de Janeiro declaring that an attack on any one of them would be regarded as an attack on all. In 1948 the Organisation of American States was formed to provide machinery for settling intra-hemisphere disputes and for the formulation of a joint military strategy. But the Latin American states insisted on a declaration that no state has the right to use coercion, political or economic, to impose its will on another state.

The Organisation of American States gave unanimous approval to the American blockade of Cuba during the 1962 missile crisis. But in 1965 American intervention – with 22,000 troops – in a civil war in the Dominican Republic aroused protests. President Johnson claimed that the troops had been sent in to prevent a Cuban-supported takeover, and proclaimed the USA's intention to prevent the spread of communism in Latin America. Since then reactionary régimes have tended to look for support from the USA – and have shown surprise and concern when she has taken up the human rights issue in for example Chile. And while left-wing groups, taking their line from Cuba, condemned the Americans for ignoring human rights, the USA in 1980 took in 140,000 refugees from Cuba.

Since 1945 American aid to Latin America has been considerable. There has been a corresponding gain for United States investors from Latin American agriculture, mining and industry. In the 1950s the progressive government of Bolivia received aid enabling it to carry out construction projects and develop health and education services. Although the Bolivians had nationalised their tin mines, giving them aid seemed to the USA preferable to allowing them to slip into chaos and communism. A different policy was adopted in Guatemala and later Cuba, both states in which American investments were more seriously involved than in Bolivia. During the 1960s, under Kennedy's Alliance for Progress programme, the USA spent vast sums supporting land and other reforms in Latin America. But the recipients of aid were required to spend four times as much out of their own revenue and much of the expenditure was on American manufactured goods. Kennedy established the Peace Corps whose members volunteer to serve people in underdeveloped third-world countries, especially in Latin America.

During the 1970s fear of communist penetration spearheaded from Cuba remained strong in many parts of Latin America, especially in Central America where predominantly military juntas resisted change. In 1979 savage fighting in Nicaragua ended with the victory of the Sandanista National Liberation Front. Nicaragua has since been variously described as being 'in the grip of pro-Moscow Marxists' and by a Catholic priest as 'a model other Latin American nations should follow after overthrowing dictators, [for it offers] the ideal combination between socialism and capitalism'. The USA responded to the success of the Sandanistas by trying to bolster pro-western leaders struggling for control in Guatemala, Honduras and in El Salvador where a full-scale civil war was being fought. Meanwhile, in Costa Rica, immediately to the south of Nicaragua, a serene calm prevailed and schoolteachers outnumbered soldiers.

By agreeing (1977) to hand over the canal zone to Panama and to give Panama control of the canal itself by the year 2000 the USA removed what had been the cause of much anti-Yanqui feeling in Latin America.

28 Post-war Britain

Preparing for a better future

With the formation of a coalition government in May 1940 party politics were put to bed. Churchill's Labour colleagues, Attlee, Bevin, Morrison and others, men of great renown, worked with unswerving loyalty in his war cabinet – and gained experience. War was showing what planning, government control, full employment, equality of sacrifice could do. The ideas of Keynes (see p. 142), set out in his *General Theory of Employment, Interest and Money* (1936), were being put into practice. Idle resources, especially of manpower, were brought into employment by expansion of credit. It seemed an expanding economy could lead to steady growth of wealth and rising living standards. The pitfalls, in particular inflation, of full employment and an expanding economy became apparent later.

In 1942 Beveridge's *Report on Social Insurance and Allied Services* provided a blueprint for the welfare state which aimed to ensure security for all 'from the cradle to the grave' after the war. Both Conservatives and Labour accepted the principles of this report. In 1944 Beveridge's *Full Employment in a Free Society* provoked fresh discussion and both Conservatives and Labour committed themselves to policies of full employment.

Early in the war thousands of children were evacuated to the country. Better off people were confronted with the realities of urban poverty – children who had no underclothes and shoes, children unaccustomed to drinking milk, children with skin infections from homes without baths. Then, while Britain was fighting for existence, the state began providing all children with free milk, free cod-liver oil, free immunisation and at nominal cost an extended school meals service. Children in wartime Britain were healthier than they had ever been! In 1941 the family means test for supplementary aid ended. In 1944 a ministry of town and country planning was set up and money was provided for building houses. In the same year the Education Act, the work of R.A. Butler, a Conservative, was passed. The Butler Act required local authorities to provide schooling for children from the age of five to fifteen (and eventually sixteen) 'suited to their age, aptitude and

Three prime ministers, Eden (left), Churchill and Attlee, on their way to a thanksgiving service at St Margaret's, Westminster, on the day Japan surrendered. On the right is Herbert Morrison

Post-war election results and ministries

Elections	Seats won by the major parties			Prime ministers
	Conservatives	Liberals	Labour	
July 1945	213	12	393	Clement Attlee
February 1950	298	9	315	Clement Attlee
October 1951	321	6	295	Winston Churchill
May 1955	344	6	277	Anthony Eden
				Harold Macmillan (January 1957)
October 1959	365	6	258	Harold Macmillan
				Alec Douglas-Home (October 1963)
October 1964	304	9	317	Harold Wilson
March 1966	253	12	363	Harold Wilson
June 1970	330	6	287	Edward Heath
February 1974	296	14	301	Harold Wilson
				James Callaghan (April 1976)
May 1979	339	11	268	Margaret Thatcher
June 1983	396	17	209	Margaret Thatcher

ability'. Thus local authorities had to provide free secondary schooling in schools established for the purpose. The heat had gone out of the religious arguments that had accompanied earlier educational reforms (see p. 55). William Temple, Archbishop of Canterbury, remarked: 'I believe that Our Lord is much more interested in raising the school leaving age to sixteen than in acquiring an agreed religious syllabus.' The act provided for special education for handicapped children and the extension of commercial and technical education and allowed local authorities to establish nursery schools. In the final months of the war allowances were paid to families with more than one child.

Post-war elections

When the war against Germany ended there had been no parliamentary elections for nearly ten years. In May 1945 the coalition government ended. Churchill then headed a caretaker government, prior to elections.

After the First World War many people had looked back to the good old days which had existed at least for some before the war – and had tried to recreate those days. In 1945 there were no good old days to recreate – only the nightmare days of unemployment and international insecurity. In 1945 the nation generally looked forward. During the election campaign Churchill seemed to ordinary people out of touch, insufficiently concerned with social reforms. Labour with its manifesto 'Let us face the future' and a more definite programme of full employment, nationalisation and improved social services seemed more forward looking.

The elections were held on 5 July but it took three weeks for the votes of servicemen to be collected and counted. On 26 July Churchill and Attlee, both at Potsdam, learned that Labour had won the election. Within twenty-four hours Attlee had returned to London, formed a government and was back at Potsdam for the final negotiations. For the first time a Labour government was not only in office but in power. Churchill was aggrieved, but Britain was ready for change.

The economic background, 1945–80

Expansion and contraction

In 1943 Churchill had warned about 'the hard facts of life'. Britain was planning, he said, to abolish unemployment, to improve health and education services, to build houses, to aid Europe and to assist the colonies – and by social insurance to abolish want. Could she afford so many commitments, he asked. As if in answer Labour in its 1945 manifesto declared: 'If the standard of life is to be high the standard of production must be high.'

The immediate post-war years were ones of great economic difficulty. But from about 1950 Britain entered a period of expansion, during which there was little to choose between the economic policies of Labour and the Conservatives. 'Butskellism' aptly described their policies. (Gaitskell, Labour chancellor of the exchequer from October 1950, was followed by Butler when the Conservatives came to power in 1951.) Both parties accepted the welfare state and a mixed economy in which certain enterprises were nationally operated. Both accepted the Keynesian doctrine that skilful manipulation of credit could maintain full employment. 'Growth' was the watchword. 'You have never had it so good', Macmillan told the people in 1959.

During the 1960s the economy continued to grow but more by fits and starts. The description 'stop-go' was apt for a period in which credit policies swung from expansion to contraction and back again. Nevertheless, even during credit squeezes, unemployment remained relatively low and the rate of inflation was by later standards moderate. But Britain was no longer at the head of the rich man's league in Europe. In the 1970s things began to go seriously wrong. For some years incomes in Britain had been growing twice as fast as output. And as elsewhere immense and abrupt increases in the price of oil (see p. 334) seriously upset the economy. Inflation accelerated and unemployment mounted. There were epidemics of strikes.

As inflation raised prices, workers demanded higher wages. As wages increased it was inevitable that prices would rise further – unless there was a corresponding increase in production. During the war there had been much talk of 'equality of sacrifice'. In the scramble of inflation it seemed the only consideration was 'equality of greed'. The weaker went to the wall. Governments advocated 'pay pauses' and 'pay restraints' or introduced 'incomes policies', voluntary or statutory, or manipulated the rate of interest – but with only limited success.

In the 1960s there had been fairly short periods of worldwide recession. In 1975 and in 1980 there began periods of severe international depression – not as severe as in the 1930s, when world trade was reduced to a trickle, but severe in terms of inflation and unemployment. During the 1970s 'stagflation' described Britain's condition of stagnation and inflation. Meanwhile, she was falling still farther behind other countries. The French, who had once looked enviously on Britain, could in 1980 boast they were much better off.

As inflation and unemployment reached crisis heights differences between the parties became sharper.

However, Labour and the Conservatives appeared to be in basic agreement that the Keynesian model was the right one. But when the Conservatives came to power under Margaret Thatcher in 1979 they introduced entirely different policies. These policies derived from 'orthodox economics', 'before Keynes'. The Conservatives aimed to reduce inflation by restricting the supply of money – even at the cost of increasing unemployment. They stressed the importance of private enterprise and tried to diminish the role of government.

The balance of payments problem

Britain's difficulties since 1945 have arisen largely because of her dependence on imports. She pays for imported food and raw materials by exporting manufactured goods, by lending capital and out of invisible earnings from such service industries as banking, insurance and shipping. More recently she has earned income by entertaining tourists and educating foreign students. As long as she exports goods and services worth more than she imports, the balance of payments is in credit. Once the balance of payments runs the other way, once there isn't enough to pay for imports, there is a trade deficit and trouble lies ahead.

Britain had had problems with the balance of payments in the inter-war years. After the war, with the loss of overseas markets, these problems were acute, at least until North Sea oil began to flow in the 1970s. In 1947 Labour had to raise a big loan from the USA and Canada. In 1961 the Conservatives, and in 1964 and 1977 Labour, had to borrow huge sums 'to pay the grocer' – on these occasions from the IMF, which laid down strict terms for making its money available. On occasions both Labour and the Conservatives manipulated interest rates with the object of encouraging exports or discouraging imports. And twice – in 1949 and 1967 – Labour devalued sterling (first by 30 per cent and then by 14 per cent). The element of 'dishonesty' in devaluation – creditors receive payment in a debased currency – makes governments extremely unwilling to devalue. Since 1972 sterling has been allowed to float – its exchange rate varies from day to day, though various means are employed to prevent too violent changes.

Underlying the balance of payments were more fundamental problems. The twentieth century has seen a steady decline in Britain's share of world trade. There was increasing competition from the USA, Japan, Germany, France and smaller countries. The rising cost of imported food and raw materials made British exports

Britain's declining share of world trade, 1870–1981

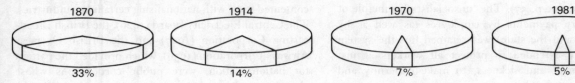

1870	1914	1970	1981
33%	14%	7%	5%

more expensive. But probably the main reason was that costs at home rose more steeply than productivity. Costs of management, costs of labour, costs of capital, were often higher than in other countries, making British exports relatively expensive. Antiquated machinery, restrictive labour practices, failure by management to adopt improved personnel practices, overmanning – these and other factors helped to make production inefficient and expensive.

Labour in power, 1945–51: the struggle to survive

Attlee headed an experienced cabinet in 1945. Bevin, a trade unionist who had directed manpower during the war, became foreign secretary. Hugh Dalton was at the exchequer. Morrison, Attlee's deputy, was responsible for the nationalisation programme. The flamboyant Aneurin Bevan was minister of health.

When Labour came to power Britain was impoverished. She was heavily in debt – to her own people (the national debt) and, in spite of lend-lease, to the USA. Investments abroad had been sold to pay for war materials. The railways and coal mines were run down and dilapidated. There was a shortage of shipping. Countless houses had been destroyed in the blitz. There were shortages of both capital and consumer goods. However, wartime organisations for control and planning were there ready for peacetime use and people had grown accustomed to regulations and controls.

In 1945 most people were engaged in war work. Labour's first task was to bring them back into production of goods for home consumption and even more for export. Food (including after 1946 bread and later potatoes), clothes and shoes, soap and sweets continued to be rationed – and rations were often pathetically small, an egg a week for example. Petrol too was rationed. Coal shortages and blackouts caused by power failures continued for several years. And many goods were simply not to be had.

The winter of 1946–47 was savage. The railways,

with their ageing rolling stock, were often at a standstill. This affected the delivery of coal on which factories and homes depended much more than now. Homes went cold and factories closed down. In February 1947 over four million people were temporarily laid off. By the end of 1947 the trade deficit had risen alarmingly.

In the autumn of 1947 Stafford Cripps became chancellor of the exchequer. He practised austerity himself and told the nation it too must practise austerity. He told the unions to keep down wages and urged workers to produce more, not for home consumption but for export. Without the incentives of wartime, austerity was not a popular diet. 'Fish and Cripps', people grumbled. Standard income tax stood at 9 shillings (45 pence) in the pound and in the 1948 budget there was a capital levy. Not that there was much to spend one's money on. Foreign exchange for travel abroad was not available. But prices, helped by subsidies for food, were kept relatively stable and Cripps did succeed in directing scarce raw materials to where they were most needed – into the export industries.

Meanwhile, other factors were turning the tide in Britain's favour. The General Agreement on Tariffs and Trade (GATT) worked out at Geneva in 1947 helped open up the channels of international trade. GATT, still in force in 1983, saved international trade from the strangling effects of excessive protectionism. In 1948 Marshall Aid became available. Gradually rationing was relaxed. The devaluation of the pound in 1949 helped exports, which by 1950 were 77 per cent higher than in 1946. By the end of Labour's period in office Britain was making a rapid recovery. In 1950 Seebohm Rowntree reckoned that 3 per cent of the people of York were living in 'primary poverty', compared with 31 per cent in 1935.

The welfare state

Meanwhile, the government had pushed on with reforms. The National Insurance and National Health Service Acts of 1946 brought into being the welfare state, which had had its beginnings before the First World War (see p. 57). The 'unsocialistic' principle of contributory payments by employees (as well as by employers and the state) was retained but the system was greatly extended to protect all workers against unemployment and sickness, to make maternity and funeral grants and to provide retirement pensions. Medical care was to be unconditionally free, the health service – as also child allowances – being a direct charge on taxation. Another act gave all workers protection in case of industrial accident. After prolonged negotiations Aneurin Bevan induced the medical profession to co-operate in establishing the health service. On the 'appointed day', 5 July 1948, the national insurance system and the national health service became operative.

In 1948 a National Assistance Act provided assistance (later called supplementary benefit) for anyone who slipped through the safety net of insurance. The poor law system finally died. Unlike national insurance benefits, national assistance was subject to a personal means test – as distinct from the old family means test with its accompanying injustices. From 1966 national assistance was administered by the department of social security (later the department of health and social security), which also became responsible for pensions and national insurance. By then social services, which in 1950 had cost some £1,500 million, were costing over £7,000 million annually (nearly 10 per cent of the gross national product). In 1981 unemployment, social security and other welfare benefits accounted for a quarter of all public expenditure.

Altered in detail from time to time (for example in 1961 by the introduction of graduated pensions), the system of social security created in 1946 undoubtedly transfromed life for the great majority of people. It is hard today to imagine the plight of parents unable to afford medical care for their children. The introduction of payment for prescriptions and spectacles and false teeth (necessitated by a rearmament programme at the time of the Korean War) aroused political storms out of all proportion to the charges involved.

Britain, famous for her inventions, cannot claim to have 'invented' the welfare state. But her comprehensive system of protection has been copied in many parts of the world.

Nationalisation

In its 1945 manifesto Labour promised the replanning of industry 'from the ground up'. But once in power it contented itself with nationalising certain key industries. The Central Electricity Board (1926), the British Broadcasting Corporation (1927) and the British Overseas Airways Corporation (1939), which provided the pattern for nationalisation, were public corporations whose chairmen and board members were appointed by the government. They depended on government for financial support, but were not under immediate government direction.

Between 1946 and 1948 the Bank of England, civil aviation, railways, canals and long-distance road haulage, coal, gas and electricity (generation as well as distribution) were 'nationalised'. They were brought under the control of boards appointed by the government but functioning independently. There had already been some control – for example gas under municipal authorities, coal mining and the railways under wartime direction – so nationalisation did not entirely revolutionise management, but only national funds could provide sufficient capital to restore the run-down mines and railways.

In 1949 an act nationalising certain iron and steel firms provoked great opposition. Its passage was delayed by the Lords, and before it had taken effect it was repealed by the Conservatives who also partly de-nationalised road haulage. A Labour government again nationalised steel (1966), though exempting certain smaller firms. Later Labour nationalised shipbuilding and aircraft construction and over a period of years established state control over a number of industries and firms of special importance, for example North Sea oil and British Leyland.

Nationalisation, if it eliminated 'jostling competition', did not always bring increased efficiency. Workers tended to assume that nationalisation simply guaranteed them security of employment and high wages. After 1979 the Conservatives restored certain businesses, such as Cable and Wireless, to private enterprise and tried to make state-controlled industries more efficient.

The achievements of Labour, 1945–51

The direction of Britain's economic recovery, the establishment of the welfare state and a programme of nationalisation were not the only achievements of Labour's astonishing post-war government. By 1950 Aneurin Bevan had organised the construction of three-

Women were increasingly prominent in public life. Here, in July 1946, shortly before the mines were nationalised, their MP, Jennie Lee, wife of Aneurin Bevan, discusses the problems of the miners of Norton Canes. Herself a Scottish miner's daughter, she became an MP at the age of 25 and was later a minister of state under Harold Wilson

quarters of a million low-rental houses on council estates. In 1947, in implementation of the 1944 Education Act (see p. 266), the school leaving age was raised to fifteen and an enormous programme of school building was undertaken. In 1946 the restrictions on unions that followed the 1926 general strike (see p. 141) ended. Sympathy strikes and the collection of a political levy from any union member who had not specifically contracted out were thus legalised. In 1948 plural voting and university representation in the Commons were ended. In 1949 an act reduced the delaying power of the House of Lords from three to two sessions (from about two years to about a year). And Attlee's government began dismantling the empire and creating a new Commonwealth, supported the USA in confrontation with the USSR (for example in the Berlin airlift), played a leading role in the formation of NATO, engaged in the Korean War – and set Britain on the way to becoming a nuclear power.

Conservatives and Labour in and out of office

Labour won the general election of 1950. But after five years of strain the Labour leaders were exhausted and their followers divided. The Korean War caused a new balance of payments crisis. In 1951 Attlee called for another election. The Conservatives won, with a majority of twenty-six.

There followed thirteen years of Conservative rule under Churchill, Eden, Macmillan and Douglas-Home. Churchill resigned in 1955 at the age of eighty. He died ten years later. Eden resigned because of ill health not long after the Suez fiasco (see p. 331). Macmillan also resigned on account of health. At elections in 1955 and 1959 the Conservatives increased their majority.

In 1952 George VI, held in universal esteem, died. He was succeeded by his daughter Elizabeth. Queen Elizabeth II and her husband Prince Philip have moved with the times. Their son Prince Charles, invested as Prince of Wales in 1969, is very different from earlier holders of that title.

In 1964 elections were again due. Bevin had died in 1951 and Cripps in 1952. Attlee resigned in 1955. Aneurin Bevan died in 1960. Gaitskell, who had followed Attlee as leader of the Labour Party, died in 1963. So a new Labour leadership with a new image faced the electors. Harold Wilson, who had read economics at Oxford, was Labour's new leader. He promised more efficient management of the mixed economy that had grown up since the war. The electorate, though fed up with Conservative stop-go policies, gave Labour a narrow majority. In 1966 Wilson called for fresh elections and Labour was returned with a much greater majority. But the problems of balance of payments, wages rising faster than productivity, living beyond the nation's means, did not vanish. In November 1967 James Callaghan, chancellor of the exchequer, who had repeatedly said there would be no devaluation, announced the 14 per cent devaluation of sterling. Roy Jenkins then became chancellor. The balance of payments improved but unemployment rose to over half a million. Bold plans for union reform (including restricting the right to strike) had to be abandoned. Price and income controls were likewise abandoned. Wages began to skyrocket. A decade of hyperinflation and of excessive union power was opening.

Wilson called for elections nine months before they were due. In June 1970 the Conservatives, led by Edward Heath, won with a comfortable majority. But the old difficulties recurred – wages chasing prices and prices chasing wages. Unemployment increased to a million by early 1972. The government, increasingly a hostage to the unions, moved first in one direction, then another and then apparently in two directions at once. When the miners banned overtime (November 1973) the government put the country on a three-day working week to conserve fuel (1 January 1974). When the miners went on strike (February 1974) Heath appealed to the country in a general election. Labour won only five more seats than the Conservatives and depended for survival on the support of minority parties – Scottish and Welsh nationalists, Ulster Unionists and the Liberals.

Wilson resigned in 1976 and was followed by Callaghan. Labour governed in consultation with the Trades Union Congress. Nevertheless there were prolonged strikes, especially in the winter of 1978–79. For a time the rate of inflation fell but unemployment remained about the million mark. As by-elections whittled away at Labour's 'majority' Callaghan entered into an agreement with the Liberals, led by David Steel, in return for their support. But in a vote of no-confidence in March 1979 Labour lost by one vote.

In the elections that followed, the Conservatives, led since 1975 by Margaret Thatcher, were returned with a clear majority. Thatcher had said that general prosperity

in a free economy is the way to rising living standards – but by December 1981 the base lending rate stood at $14\frac{1}{2}$ per cent and there were nearly three million unemployed. A year later, though the lending rate and inflation were substantially down, unemployment had risen to about three and a half million. Meanwhile legislation restricting union power had been introduced.

Changing class structure and the Social Democratic Party

The post-war period saw a marked decrease in the differentials (pay differences) that separated the white collar worker from the skilled blue collar worker and the blue collar worker from the labourer. Out shopping they all looked much the same and any one of them might have had a Mini – or something bigger. In 1922, when differentials were much greater, an Austin Seven cost eighty times the average weekly wage. By 1970 an Austin Mini cost eighteen times the average weekly wage. One consequence of the decrease in differentials was a decline in enterprise and effort – incentive was lacking. Another consequence was a great increase in the size of the middle class.

The broadly based middle class contains many of the swinging voters – voters without any firm attachment to one political party. Governments have increasingly depended on the support of swinging voters. The growth of a broadly based middle class was perhaps reflected in the choice of leaders of the Conservative Party: Heath, the talented son of a carpenter, and Thatcher, daughter of a small shopkeeper, who made their way to Oxford and from there to further heights.

The growth of a middle class, likely to distrust extremism, left or right, may account for the fear felt by some politicians for extremist policies. With Labour publicly in strife with its militant extremists, 1981 saw the emergence of the Social Democratic Party (SDP). The 'gang of four' who founded this party – Roy Jenkins, David Owen, William Rodgers and Shirley Williams – were all former Labour ministers and representatives of the broad middle class. With Labour calling for unilateral nuclear disarmament, withdrawal from the EEC and other extreme measures, and with the Conservatives divided – less publicly than Labour – over important issues, the Social Democrats sought to convince the floating voters that they were more level headed and 'conventional' than Labour, more flexible than the Conservative leadership. The new party, having allied itself with the Liberal Party, gave a jolt to the political machine.

The condition of the people

In the 1950s some one and a half million Britons migrated abroad. Their departure was matched by the arrival of an almost equal number of Commonwealth citizens. Between 1950 and 1975 the population increased by about 11 per cent. In 1976 for the first time in several centuries it showed no increase at all, although people were living longer.

By 1980 heart transplants, pioneered in South Africa by Christian Barnard, were not uncommon in Britain. Less spectacular medical and social advances continued to raise life expectancy (see table below). The problem of old age was by the 1970s almost as great as that of youth. And a greater proportion of handicapped people survived – and struggled for recognition of their rights.

British life expectancy at birth in years

1871	42 years	1931	61 years
1901	48 years	1961	71 years
1911	53 years	1981	73 years

During the war women were in the services, women were doing men's jobs. When the bombers came over women were in the front line. After the war women were determined to 'be equal'. The pill and various contraceptive devices gave them a new equality. Increasing use of electrical appliances (see table below) gave women relative freedom from housework. Such appliances were often bought from overtime earnings – or from a woman's earnings.

Percentage of British households owning electrical appliances

	Refrigerators	Washing machines	Vacuum cleaners
1938	3%	3.5%	27%
1963	33%	50%	77%
1980	93%	77%	93%

Legislation providing for equal payment for men and women doing the same work and making job discrimination on grounds of sex illegal gave in the economic field what franchise reforms had earlier given to women in the political field. Those few places and professions that had seemed obstinately shut to women were opened – almost all the Oxford and Cambridge colleges for example. In 1981 the Church of England synod passed a resolution allowing women to be made deacons. In 1983 London had its first woman Lord Mayor.

Macmillan, Churchill's housing minister, carried on Aneurin Bevan's work; in the 1950s 300,000 council houses were built every year. After 1952 it was possible for tenants to buy these houses, though most councils did not favour selling. With the growth of the middle class there was a rapid development of building societies and of private building.

Labour under Attlee set out to provide three kinds of secondary schools (see p. 267). Existing grammar schools were to provide free education for children with academic ability, with the prospect of going to a university. A few secondary technical schools were to provide for children with practical inclinations. The vast majority had to go to the new secondary modern schools. To select the appropriate type of school for each child the eleven-plus examination was devised. This soon became the nightmare of parents, pupils and teachers. To escape from the eleven-plus system comprehensive schools were developed in the 1960s. Strongly supported by Labour, comprehensive schools were almost universally adopted in the state system in the 1970s. The school leaving age was raised to sixteen in 1973. By then a much higher proportion of children in government schools was staying on to seventeen and eighteen and going to university, technical college or polytechnic. By then the voting age had been reduced (1969) to eighteen.

Between 1945 and 1960 eight new universities were set up. In 1963 the Robbins report recommended a great expansion of post-secondary education. Soon a whole new generation of universities, polytechnics, colleges of education and similar institutions was springing up. Government grants enabled any student with sufficient ability to receive further education.

The student unrest of the late 1960s did not pass Britain by. As elsewhere undue publicity perhaps both exaggerated and encouraged unrest. As elsewhere the demands of some students were incoherent and unrealistic; others had more definite aims or grievances; some were related to political movements. The student population was large enough to be conscious of its power and the mass media gave it hitherto unequalled opportunities of making itself heard. Gradually the

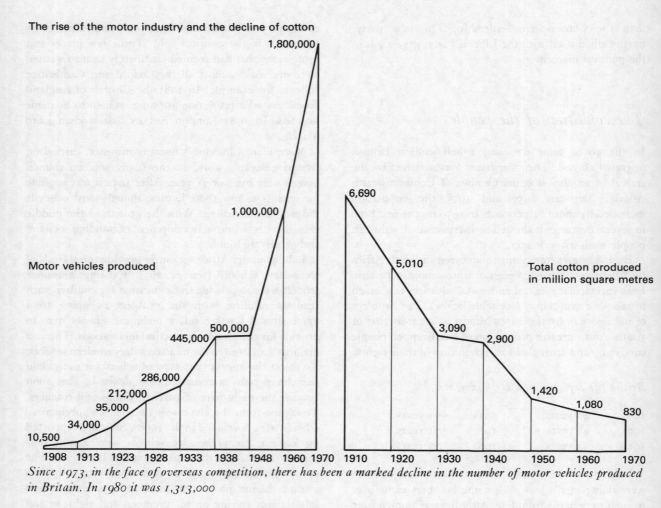

The rise of the motor industry and the decline of cotton

Motor vehicles produced

1,800,000
1,000,000
500,000
445,000
286,000
212,000
95,000
34,000
10,500

1908 1913 1923 1928 1933 1938 1948 1960 1970

Total cotton produced
in million square metres

6,690
5,010
3,090
2,900
1,420
1,080
830

1910 1920 1930 1940 1950 1960 1970

Since 1973, in the face of overseas competition, there has been a marked decline in the number of motor vehicles produced in Britain. In 1980 it was 1,313,000

unrest, raucous but in general unbloody, subsided. By 1980 university students in Britain seemed less addicted to protests – except in support of their grants.

On occasions there were violent protests in prisons. Many people, including prison governors and officers, agreed that some prisons were little better than 'festering slums' and that reforms were urgently necessary. As the crime rate grew one evil of the system, overcrowding, became worse. Plans for building new prisons were slow in coming into effect. Funds for education of prisoners remained inadequate. However in 1969 the death penalty for murder was abolished.

The churches continued to concern themselves with social problems. There was growing interest in church unity and greater understanding between the Anglican and Roman Catholic communions. But Pope Paul VI's encyclical condemning birth control in 1968 provoked much controversy – perhaps understandably when

population was growing in the less developed countries at astronomical rates.

Immigration: a multi-cultural society

In the 1950s and early 1960s large numbers of Asians, Africans, West Indians and other Commonwealth citizens took advantage of their right to settle in the United Kingdom. The immigrants were naturally attracted to a country which by then was a welfare state and where wages and conditions of employment were incomparably better than in their homelands. At that time Britain's economy was able to absorb the immigrants. Indeed they were encouraged to settle in Britain for it was a time of full employment and in general the immigrants were glad to accept jobs which other people were not prepared to take.

In 1962 the Commonwealth Immigration Act greatly restricted the right of entry into the United Kingdom by requiring immigrants from any part of the Commonwealth – for example Australians as well as Indians – to have jobs to go to or special skills to offer. Immigration of Commonwealth citizens was later further restricted. By 1980 if you could not prove that you were in some way a dependant of someone already living in the United Kingdom you were refused admission. But by 1980 Britain was a multi-cultural society, a land many of whose citizens are of African or Asian origin. (Among the Asian immigrants were Indians who had been forced to leave Kenya and Uganda after independence.) In 1980 some two million people (about 3 per cent of the total population of the United Kingdom) of New Commonwealth or Pakistani origin were living in Britain. About 40 per cent were born in Britain.

Most of the newcomers settled in the industrial centres of England – in London, Liverpool or other conurbations – where in the 1960s jobs were most easily found. They shared with the white population the crowded housing and poor welfare services of these sad, depressing 'inner city' areas. In such places strains, racial and otherwise, are swifter to surface than in comfortable middle-class areas and racial antagonism between the white community and their new neighbours soon became apparent. The problem of race relations provoked widely differing reactions. Thus in the 1960s a transport authority refused to allow a Sikh bus conductor to wear his turban, whilst the Marylebone Cricket Club (MCC) refused to send a team to South Africa which had discriminated against one of the MCC players who was Cape Coloured by origin (see p. 28). Whilst church leaders continued to make pronouncements aimed at promoting racial harmony, the racist National Front staged protests against the presence of blacks and Asians in Britain. In Parliament Enoch Powell voiced the resentments and perplexities of those among the white community who regarded people of different cultural origin as a threat to their way of life in suburb, school and work. In 1976 a Race Relations Act strengthened earlier laws aimed at preventing any discrimination based on race or colour. Racial discrimination, however, did not end with the passing of the 1976 act. How much discrimination there is today is debatable, but many people claim there is a great deal.

In the summer of 1981 hundreds of young people, both black and white, pitted themselves against the police and burned and looted in London, the Toxteth

In multi-cultural Britain, London's Central Mosque nears completion in Regent's Park (March 1977). It has a library, social centre, offices and a prayer hall accommodating 4,500 people

district of Liverpool and other areas. To what extent these riots were racial or simply a bursting out of frustrated, underemployed young people was not clear. But it would seem clear that most people, black or white, are opposed to the evils of extremist racialist activity. Most would prefer to live in a society in which 'no one is a second class citizen'.

Decentralisation

The growth of central and local government brought a rapid increase in the number of government employees and in government expenditure, which by the 1970s was about 40 per cent of the gross national product – compared with 15 per cent before the First World War.

As the business of government increased there was a need for more efficient administrative units. In 1963 the London County Council was replaced by the Greater London Council. In 1974 the counties were tidied up and the six largest cities became metropolitan counties. The police, medical and water authorities were organised in regions more convenient than the counties.

Opposition to over-centralisation was strong in Scotland and Wales. The Scottish Nationalist Party and the Welsh Plaid Cymru aimed at devolution, or limited self-government. They wanted Westminster to hand over certain powers to local assemblies. However, some Scottish Nationalists were committed to total independence. In 1974 eleven Scottish Nationalists and three Plaid Cymru members were elected to Parliament. Holding a balance of power, they were able to ensure the passage of Devolution Acts (1978). But by referendum both the Scots and more emphatically the Welsh rejected devolution.

Northern Ireland: still imprisoned by its history?

De Valera, believing formal proclamation of a republic could endanger Eire's claim to sovereignty over the whole of Ireland, did not take this step. But in April 1949 a coalition government that had replaced his Fianna Fail government proclaimed a Republic of Ireland that formally ceased to be a member of the Commonwealth. The United Kingdom and Ireland remained 'externally associated'. Free movement of people between the two states facilitated tourism on the one side and migration in search of employment on the

other. Economic ties remained close. In general formal severance resulted in improved relations. The republic claimed sovereignty over all Ireland, regarding its rule over the six counties in Ulster as simply being in abeyance, but showed no intention of enforcing that sovereignty. And the Dublin government dealt firmly with extremists such as the Irish Republican Army (IRA).

In 1949, in recognition of Northern Ireland's services during the war, an act of parliament promised that the six counties should remain part of the United Kingdom unless Northern Ireland's own parliament at Stormont should decide otherwise. The problem of the substantial Catholic minority in Northern Ireland remained unsolved, and indeed almost unnoticed, for some years. Stormont was controlled by Protestant Unionists, many of whom regarded the Catholics as traitors to Northern Ireland, the rightful home of the Loyalist Orangemen – an attitude reinforced when Eire remained neutral during the Second World War. As a result of gerrymandering Unionist control was particularly strong at the local government level – the level at which hard-hitting Protestant officials did most hurt to the Catholics. The neat new council houses and the skilled jobs were for the Protestants, the unskilled jobs and slums such as Londonderry's Bogside were for the Catholics.

When in the late 1960s discontent surfaced extremist republicans were quick to exploit the situation. In 1967 a non-sectarian civil rights association that sought to end discrimination was formed. In October 1968, defying an official ban, civil rights supporters organised a march in Londonderry. The Royal Ulster Constabulary (RUC), made up almost entirely of Protestants, broke up the march with unnecessary force. This proved to be the beginning of a new period of 'troubles'. In January 1969 more radical civil rights supporters set out to march from Belfast to Londonderry. This march had not been banned but provoked an attack, an ambush in fact, by Protestants. The RUC then 'restored order' by in effect siding with the Protestants.

In August 1969 the British government, in an attempt to contain civil strife – and indeed to protect the Catholic minority – moved troops into Northern Ireland. The troops were welcomed by the Catholics but resentment soon showed itself in attacks upon soldiers. Later that year a militant group, the Provisional IRA (naming themselves after the provisional government set up in Dublin at Easter 1916) split off from the 'official' IRA, who were to concern themselves more with social

Londonderry's Bogside and Belfast's Andersonstown, both Catholic areas, had for a time been 'no go areas' – areas controlled by the IRA. Here in August 1972 British troops in Operation Motorman clear the 'no go area' – 'Free Derry' – in Londonderry

reform. The aim of the Provisionals was to sever Northern Ireland from the United Kingdom, if need be by provoking civil war. In the same year the Protestants set up the Ulster Defence Force (UDF). Extremists on both sides continued to stir up old hatreds.

In February 1971 the first of many British soldiers to die in Northern Ireland was killed by the Provisionals in Belfast. There was increasing provocation of the troops by the Catholic community, even by children. The Provisional IRA moved in to 'protect' Catholic areas. Internment of suspected terrorists without trial was introduced. On 30 January 1972, during a civil rights march in Londonderry, British soldiers, then under much stress, killed thirteen Catholic civilians. Since that 'Bloody Sunday' Northern Ireland has 'been back in its ancient prison of history'. In March 1972 the British government, by its powers under the Government of Ireland Act of 1920, suspended the Stormont parliament and Northern Ireland came under the direct rule of Westminster. Reforms, for example in voting rights for local government elections, had already been made – but they were too late. Events had overtaken them.

In December 1973 the British and Irish governments and politicians from Northern Ireland took part in a conference at Sunningdale in Berkshire. The Northern Ireland delegation included representatives of the Ulster Unionist Party (Protestant), the Social Democratic and Labour Party (mainly Catholic) and the non-sectarian Alliance Party. The only major party not represented was the Democratic Unionist Party, led by a militant Protestant minister, Ian Paisley. Following Sunningdale a power-sharing Executive led by Brian Faulkner of the Ulster Unionist Party, with a Catholic, Gerry Fitt, of the Social Democratic and Labour Party, as his deputy, governed Northern Ireland for five months. But after a general strike by Protestant workers in May 1974 the Executive resigned and power sharing was finished in the province – at least for the time being. The storm clouds grew darker. The tale of horrors continued. A tale of funerals, funerals of soldiers and Provisionals, of civilians, Protestants and Catholics, prominent and humble, of children and old people; a tale of burnt-out shops and houses; of IRA bombs bursting in England, the Irish Republic and on the continent as well as in Northern Ireland; a tale of young men maimed and paralysed in wheelchairs.

In 1972 the Conservative government had granted 'special category status' to certain prisoners convicted for their part in the 'troubles'. In 1976 Labour stopped granting special category status. IRA prisoners protested in various ways – refusing to work or wear prison clothes, making their cells filthy – demanding what they called 'political status'. In effect this was a demand for privileges normally granted to prisoners of war. But the British government was unwilling to treat criminal terrorists, prisoners guilty of murder and appalling violence, as if they were soldiers captured in battle, though some concessions were promised in December 1980.

The protests culminated in a hunger strike – not the first – which began on 1 March 1981. Seven years previously the British government had decided not to force prisoners to take food. In May 1981 Bobby Sands, Republican 'commander' at the Maze prison in Belfast, died. While on hunger strike Sands had been elected to the Commons in a by-election in a Northern Ireland Catholic constituency. Nine other IRA hunger strikers followed him to death before the strike was called off in October 1981.

The autumn of 1981 saw more bombs in London, more deaths and communal strife in Northern Ireland. In November the British and Irish prime ministers agreed to set up an Anglo-Irish Council to facilitate discussions between their governments. Whilst most people in Northern Ireland seemed prepared to live in peace with their neighbours, the atrocities of republican extremists and the burning hatreds of diehard Protestant Unionists seemed to have a different goal.

Britain and her empire

Not only under pressure of circumstances, but because he believed it was morally right, Attlee was determined to liquidate as rapidly as possible Britain's empire in India. Labour took such decisive action over India (see p. 309) that its Conservative successors could scarcely adopt a different policy towards other territories. The dismantling of the empire went on steadily throughout the 1950s and 1960s, but apart from matters of timing and detail there was no great debate in Britain about the rightness and indeed necessity of granting independence. Over Rhodesia (Zimbabwe) (see p. 319) there was intense political concern in Britain – but that was because a white minority refused to accept black majority rule.

While the empire declined the Commonwealth grew. After 1949 it was no longer called British. A conference of Commonwealth prime ministers in 1949 agreed that India could become a republic yet remain within a Commonwealth of which the British monarch was head. What had been an empire became a loose association of friendly states.

In 1982 the ghost of empire briefly and spectacularly returned to life when the Falkland Islanders, who had for years insisted on retaining their connection with Britain, found their homeland occupied by Argentinian forces. Then the great grey ships sped to the South Atlantic and British sovereignty over the islands was asserted (see p. 263).

Foreign affairs

When Bevin became foreign secretary in 1945 he was anxious to co-operate with the USSR. But her provocative tactics made this almost impossible. In 1947 the Soviet foreign minister, Molotov, at a conference in London angered Bevin beyond endurance. 'Now 'e's gone too bloody far', said Bevin. Thereafter he turned towards more traditional allies. He signed the Treaty of Dunkirk and played a large part in arranging the conference that adopted Marshall Aid and in the formation of the North Atlantic Alliance (see p. 243). In 1950, in accordance with the UN resolution, Britain sent substantial forces to Korea (see p. 245).

Between 1951 and 1964 the Conservatives strengthened the 'special relationship' with the USA. Britain joined SEATO and CENTO (see p. 247) and allowed the USA to establish bases at which nuclear-armed aircraft were stationed. In 1956 the Suez crisis (see p. 331) gave the special relationship a severe jolt but before long it was resumed.

Until at least the end of the 1960s Britain had worldwide military commitments. Since 1945 she has taken part in the Korean War whilst rebellions in Malaya, Kenya and Aden (see pp. 311, 319) engaged large forces. Since the formation of NATO she has had to keep several divisions in West Germany and to maintain certain naval and air forces. Since 1969 British troops have been stationed in Northern Ireland. And in 1982 the Falklands campaign tested British forces and their equipment.

Britain exploded an atom bomb in 1952 and a hydrogen bomb in 1957. With her own planes carrying nuclear bombs she had an independent nuclear deterrent. In 1962 Macmillan agreed with President Kennedy for the supply to Britain of American Polaris missiles, to be based in British-built nuclear submarines under NATO command.

The Conservatives have on the whole maintained a steadfast attitude towards military commitments. Labour's left wing has urged disarmament, supporting, when out of office in the 1950s, the Campaign for Nuclear Disarmament (CND). Gaitskell, who opposed unilateral nuclear disarmament, healed the rifts within Labour and Wilson's government adopted conventional policies – though crying hard when defence costs cut into the demands of welfare. In 1968 Wilson decided to withdraw all British forces 'east of Suez'. By the early 1980s Labour, once more out of office, had returned to a policy of unilateral nuclear disarmament.

Britain and Europe

In 1946 Churchill said: 'We must build a kind of United States of Europe.' In 1948 he was one of the leaders who helped form the Council of Europe (see p. 280). But Britain did not join the movement for economic co-operation then developing in western Europe. In 1950 Britain (then the major coal and steel producer in western Europe) refused to join the European Coal and Steel Community (see p. 280). In 1950 Churchill called for a European army, yet he was reluctant to diminish Britain's independence and had a strong attachment to the Commonwealth and the USA. When the European Defence Community was being planned (see p. 247) he offered: 'All support short of membership.'

In 1956, when invited to be a founding member of the European Economic Community (see p. 281), Britain refused. She proposed instead that all the members of the Organisation for European Economic Co-operation (see p. 280) should form a free trade area. She pressed on with this idea and with Sweden, Norway, Denmark, Switzerland, Austria and Portugal formed the European Free Trade Association (EFTA) in 1960. But EFTA was relatively toothless and offered exporters a far smaller market than the European Economic Community.

By 1961 Britain's economy was no longer on the crest of a wave. Trade with EFTA countries was showing only moderate growth, trade with the Commonwealth no growth at all. But trade with EEC countries was showing a marked increase. In these circumstances Macmillan announced that Britain would seek membership of the EEC. This was not favoured by Commonwealth countries, who feared for their privileged markets in Britain. And many people in Britain – including Attlee and Eden – were opposed to entry. But the decisive factor was the opposition of de Gaulle who twice, in 1963 and 1967, flatly rejected Britain's admission to the EEC (see p. 284).

Edward Heath, July 1971. Under Macmillan, Heath, a convinced and forceful European, had tried to negotiate Britain's entry into the EEC. In 1971, when he was prime minister, Britain's entry was approved. In the same year he led Britain to victory in the Admiral's Cup – he had only taken up sailing in 1966

In 1970 Britain, under her new Conservative government, again applied for entry into the EEC. She eventually signed the Treaty of Rome in January 1972 and was admitted to the European Community on 1 January 1973, together with another EFTA member, Denmark.

The Labour Party, more conservative than the Conservatives over Britain's independence, over the undesirability of getting too involved with 'foreigners', and over commitments to the Commonwealth, was not pleased. Moreover, Wilson argued that the terms under which Britain entered should be renegotiated and submitted to the people in a referendum. After Labour came to office in 1974 Callaghan, then foreign secretary, was able to get some concessions. In 1975 a referendum was held and the British, by a two to one majority, decided to 'stay in Europe'.

Britain has had disputes, some of them long and bitter, with her fellow members of the EEC. She has had to abide by rules not always to her liking. Along with West Germany she has perhaps been liable for a disproportionate share of expenses. However, her trade in Europe has increased considerably. And it may be that membership of the EEC cannot be evaluated simply in pounds and pence. In 1981 the Labour Party at its annual conference voted for withdrawal from the EEC. In 1982 the members of the EEC supported Britain by imposing economic sanctions against Argentina.

29 Western Europe in the post-war years

Economic and political co-operation

In 1953 Adenauer, chancellor of West Germany, said:

'West European countries are no longer in a position to protect themselves individually [or] ... to salvage European culture. These objectives ... can only be attained if the west European nations form a political, economic and cultural union and, above all, if they render impossible any military conflicts among themselves.'

By 1953 the states of western Europe had already begun moving closer together. Britain, though eager to see them draw together, was somewhat uncertain in her attitude (see p. 279).

After the Treaty of Dunkirk (1947) came the Treaty of Brussels (1948) and the formation of the Western Union (see p. 243), which provided not only for mutual defence but for economic, cultural and social co-operation. After 1950 its military objectives were taken over by NATO (see p. 243). In 1955 the Western Union, expanded to include West Germany and Italy, became the Western European Union, with its own administrative organisation and arrangements for regular meetings.

In September 1944, while the Germans still occupied their homelands, representatives of Belgium, the Netherlands and Luxembourg (the Benelux countries) agreed to abolish all customs duties between their countries. There was also to be free movement of capital and labour. By 1960 the Benelux countries had achieved full economic union.

In 1948 the Organisation for European Economic Co-operation (OEEC) was formed by all the states that had accepted Marshall Aid (see p. 241). OEEC's initial task was to co-ordinate requests for aid and to ensure its effective use. When Marshall Aid ended in 1952 the OEEC took on the encouragement of tariff reduction, promotion of research and technical assistance and co-ordination of economic and financial policies among its members. The European Payments Unions, designed to make trading payments easier, was an offshoot of the OEEC. Another offshoot was the European Nuclear Energy Agency. In 1961 the OEEC became the OECD (Organisation for Economic Co-operation and Development), with a membership that included such non-European industrial states as the USA, Japan, Canada and Australia.

In 1948 members of the United Europe Movement and similar associations that had sprung up after the war met at The Hague. Churchill, Adenauer, Schuman and Monnet from France, de Gasperi from Italy, Paul-Henri Spaak from Belgium, and other leading figures, agreed to set up a Council of Europe to which all European states that protected human rights and freedom (all 'democratic' states) might belong. The Council of Europe came into formal existence in 1949. Initially it had ten members but by 1980 the number had risen to twenty-one. In 1969 Greece, then under brutally authoritarian military rule, withdrew from the council but later rejoined it. The headquarters of the council are in Strasbourg. A committee of ministers represents member governments. There is also a consultative assembly of delegates from the parliaments of the member states. The assembly cannot make laws but can make recommendations on matters other than defence. Its discussions on health and education, labour conditions and travel and other matters of European interest have proved useful. In 1950 the assembly recommended that its members accept a European convention for the protection of human rights and this they did. Problems concerning human rights were then referred to the council's court, whose decisions the member states promised to obey. Corporal punishment in schools in the Isle of Man and Scotland was one matter brought before this court.

Jean Monnet, a former League of Nations official, and Robert Schuman, the French foreign minister, were responsible for the formation of the European Coal and Steel Community (ECSC). Schuman, an officer in the German army in the First World War, became a French citizen with the return of Alsace-Lorraine to France. Both men were strongly European in outlook. By the Treaty of Paris (1951) France, West Germany, Italy and the Benelux countries formed the ECSC, thus establishing 'the foundation of a broad and independent community among peoples long divided by bloody conflicts'. The development and regulation of two great industries thus came under a supra-national body. The

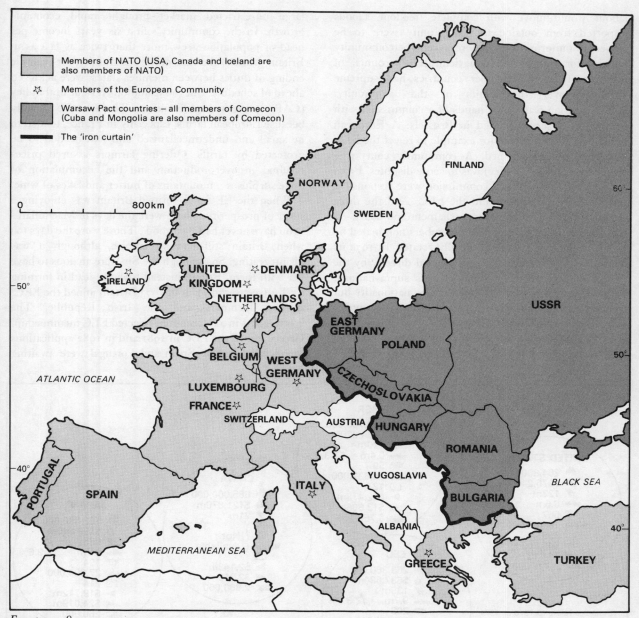

Europe, 1983

ECSC had its own assembly, council of ministers and court of justice (but see below). The first president of the high authority directing the ECSC was Monnet. Coal and steel began to move freely throughout the community. Housing was provided for workers and new industries were established for men thrown out of work by the closure of unprofitable mines.

In 1955 the Dutch proposed a customs union between the members of the ECSC. After a conference in Sicily

Monnet and Spaak, 'Mr Europe', set to work to prepare the details of such a scheme. Early in 1957 the six members of the ECSC signed the Treaty of Rome which set up the European Economic Community (the Common Market). Another treaty set up the European Atomic Energy Community (Euratom), for the peaceful use of atomic energy (see p. 286).

The object of the EEC was to create within fifteen years a free trade area within which goods, money and labour would move with complete freedom. Goods imported from outside the community were to be subject to uniform duties. There were to be community policies for transport and agriculture. A council of ministers from the member countries had supreme authority over the affairs of the community. Administration was in the hands of a commission with its own civil service, based in Brussels. A European parliament – with power for example to reject the EEC budget – was established. A community court (the European Court of Justice) was to settle disputes. From 1967 a single council and commission were responsible for the ECSC, Euratom and the EEC. And the three organisations have a common parliament and court. At first the parliament consisted of members nominated by the main political parties in the EEC states. In 1979 its members were for the first time elected directly by the people of each member state. In this supra-national parliament members are grouped not by nationality but by their parties. Thus liberals from different countries sit together and so on.

With a population at its formation of 170 million the EEC was comparable in size to the USA or the USSR. A large unrestricted market brought rapid economic growth. In the community's first six years income per head of population grew more than twice as fast as in Britain. Most of the aims of the community, for example ending of duties between member states, were achieved ahead of schedule. But the Common Agricultural Policy (CAP) presented difficulties. These arose mainly because European farms, especially in France, tended to be small and undermechanised and had needed to be protected by tariffs. Offering farmers assured prices resulted in overproduction and the accumulation of huge surpluses – mountains of butter and lakes of wine.

When the EEC was formed Britain was enjoying a surge of prosperity. Those were the days of Macmillan's 'You have never had it so good'. Those were the days too when Britain still had an empire, although it was disintegrating. So although the Six were anxious to have her with them, Britain instead took the lead in forming EFTA (see p. 279). But in 1973 Britain joined the EEC, as did Denmark and the Irish Republic. The Norwegians in a referendum rejected EEC membership. Greece joined the EEC in 1981 and in 1982 applications for membership by Spain and Portugal were awaiting

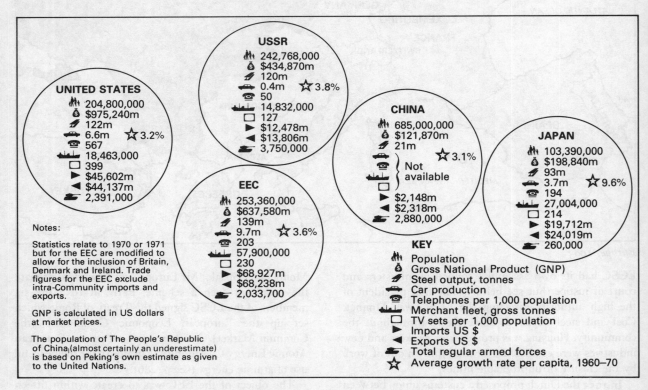

A comparison of major economies at the time of Britain's entry into the EEC (1973)

acceptance. In 1979 all members of the European Community except Britain formed the European Monetary System for adjusting the value of their currencies.

A complete list of institutions established for co-operation in Europe since the Second World War would be long indeed. There is for example the Nordic Council of Denmark, Norway, Sweden, Finland and Iceland. In these countries there is a common Scandinavian citizenship, complete mobility of labour and freedom of residence. There is also a European Space Research Organisation, there is the European Broadcasting Union which manages Eurovision and so on.

France

The Fourth Republic

After liberation France remained under a provisional government. In January 1946 de Gaulle, the head of this government, resigned. In October 1946, in a referendum, a narrow majority accepted a constitution setting up the Fourth Republic. This constitution differed little from that of the Third Republic except that women were given the right to vote. And a French Union consisting of France and her overseas territories was set up. All people in the union became French citizens with the right to elect representatives to the National Assembly (see p. 322).

There were still deep divisions within French society. On the extreme left were the communists. They had been very active in the war of resistance and de Gaulle in 1945 included communists in his cabinet. Until 1958 they were the largest party in parliament though after 1947 no communist held ministerial office. On the right was the Rally of the French People, followers of de Gaulle, discontented with the instability of government (there were eleven ministries in four and a half years) and afraid of communism.

In spite of frequent changes of ministries, in spite too of rising prices and strikes, shifting alliances of socialists, radicals and liberal Catholics brought about considerable economic recovery. The governments of the third force, as these alliances were called, nationalised the coal mines, gas and electricity companies, major banks and insurance companies, the aircraft construction and petroleum industries, and the Renault company, which had collaborated with the Germans. In 1947 Monnet's four-year plan to modernise and re-equip industry and agriculture was introduced and with the assistance of Marshall Aid progress was made.

Agriculture remained predominant but there was marked growth in industry and urbanisation. Between 1950 and 1975 France's population, which had been declining before the war, increased by 25 per cent. Economic recovery was accompanied by a drift towards the right in government. The war in Indo-China (see p. 312) and then the struggle for independence in Algeria (see p. 321) caused new divisions and instability. These wars involved vast expenditure and were a great drain on manpower. The crisis over Algeria was so acute that in May 1958 the prime minister warned the National Assembly that France was 'threatened by civil war'. In June 1958 de Gaulle was summoned from retirement and given emergency powers to restore stability.

The Fifth Republic: de Gaulle

In September 1958 de Gaulle presented to the nation a new constitution. This gave greatly increased powers to the president, who was to be popularly elected and to hold office for seven years. The authority of the National Assembly was correspondingly reduced. In a referendum 85 per cent of the people voted; 79 per cent approved the new constitution. In the elections that followed parties of the right won 70 per cent of the seats. The communists were reduced to ten seats. In December 1958 de Gaulle was elected president of the Fifth Republic. He was re-elected in 1965.

Under de Gaulle's authoritarian rule France enjoyed a stability unknown for almost a hundred years. The president, using his powers to the full, manipulated press and radio and the institutions of government, but in more than one referendum the electorate showed that they preferred this to the uncertainties of the earlier régime. One of de Gaulle's first achievements was the introduction of a new franc that greatly strengthened the economy. The franc remained stable until shortly after his resignation in 1969, when further devaluation was necessary. Among de Gaulle's achievements was the decolonisation of Africa including the settlement in 1962 of the crisis in Algeria.

Under the Fourth Republic Monnet, Schuman and Pleven had worked for the closer integration of western Europe. Though in 1954 the National Assembly rejected Pleven's plan for the European Defence Community (see p. 247) France took a leading part in creating the Western Union, NATO, the Council of Europe, the

"I suspect you of driving under the influence of America."

This Punch *cartoon of 1967 suggests de Gaulle's refusal to allow Britain to enter the EEC was due chiefly to his dislike of her 'special relationship' with the USA*

ECSC and the EEC. During this period her attitude towards Britain and the USA was friendly.

Though in war and peace France had had good reason to be grateful to her western allies, under the Fifth Republic de Gaulle adopted a nationalist and sometimes hostile attitude. In Europe he did not favour closer integration but rather a loose association in which France would be predominant. Unwilling to have France sheltering under the American umbrella, he decided that she must have her own nuclear weapons. In 1960 the French exploded an atomic bomb and in 1968 a hydrogen bomb. They built up a *Force de Frappe* (Striking Force) of supersonic bombers armed with nuclear bombs, missile-carrying nuclear submarines and land-based missiles. De Gaulle refused to assign such weapons to NATO – they were to form France's independent nuclear deterrent. It was not for France to entrust her existence to an unreliable foreign protector. 'Non', said de Gaulle in 1963, 'we are worthy of better than this.' Three times again in 1963 he issued his resounding 'Non'. He withdrew the French Atlantic fleet (and later other forces) from NATO command. He refused to join the Nuclear Test Ban Treaty (see

p. 252). And he refused to allow Britain, with her American and Commonwealth ties, to enter the EEC – as he did again in 1967.

In 1963 France made a treaty of friendship with West Germany (see p. 285). By visiting Moscow and by sending a representative to Peking, de Gaulle broke the ice in relations between the West and both the USSR and China. In 1966, in furtherance of France's independent stand, de Gaulle had all NATO troops withdrawn from French soil. However, France remained a member of the North Atlantic Alliance.

The Fifth Republic: after de Gaulle

In 1968 violent student disturbances and industrial unrest threatened the stability of France. De Gaulle appealed to the nation and won its full support. Order was restored but it was soon apparent that Gaullism had lost some of its charm. In 1969, when constitutional changes desired by de Gaulle were rejected in a referendum, he resigned. (He died the following year.) Georges Pompidou, prime minister from 1962 – 68, was elected president. On his death in 1974 Giscard d'Estaing, an Independent Republican, became president.

Under Pompidou and d'Estaing there was a further drift away from Gaullism. Thus Pompidou showed no objection to Britain's entry to the EEC. Relations with the USA became easier, though France maintained her independent line. She had by then less reason to fear being swamped by the USA – or for that matter by Britain. Her industries prospered. In 1981 she was the third largest arms exporter – after the USA and the USSR – in the world. However, agriculture lagged behind; its inefficiency was a burden to other members of the EEC.

In 1981 Francois Mitterand, who had been narrowly defeated by d'Estaing in 1974, became president. With the election of Mitterand, a socialist, the drift from the right seemed complete. Mitterand was the first socialist to hold real power in France since the days of Léon Blum and the Popular Front (see p. 175). But with his wide authority as president Mitterand had far more power than Blum had ever had.

The Federal Republic of Germany

Constitution

While the Soviet Union blockaded West Berlin (see

p. 242), in Bonn a constituent assembly was preparing a basic law or constitution for the Federal Republic of Germany (West Germany). The basic law was proclaimed in May 1949, coinciding with the end of the Berlin airlift. The basic law provided for a lower chamber (the Bundestag) elected by universal franchise and an upper chamber (the Bundesrat) of delegates from the parliaments of the ten *länder* (states). The president, elected for five years by the Bundestag and Bundesrat meeting together, was to have little power. The chancellor was to be elected by a clear majority of the Bundestag, to which he was responsible – though it could not dismiss him until it had agreed upon a successor. These arrangements were intended to provide a strong central government, whilst restoring the states whose rights Hitler had destroyed. (West Berlin, 'the eleventh state of the Federal Republic', is governed under the terms of the Four Power Agreement of 1971 (see p. 253).)

West Germany under Adenauer

In August 1949 80 per cent of the people came out to vote for their first freely elected parliament since 1933. In September Adenauer, leader of the Christian Democrats, a right-centre party descended from the Catholic Centre, was elected chancellor. The Social Democrats provided a strong opposition. With the election of the chancellor the Allied military government ended. The USA, Britain and France appointed high commissioners responsible for foreign affairs, security, refugees and other matters. The western allies continued to station large forces in West Germany.

From 1917 until dismissed by the Nazis in 1933 Adenauer had been the progressive mayor of Cologne. He was for a time in a concentration camp and was lucky not to be killed during the American advance across the Rhine. Since the French occupation of the Ruhr in 1923 (see p. 181) he had been convinced of the need for a community of economic interests between France and Germany, a community that would later attract to it other states. His policy therefore was to work in close co-operation with the western allies and to seek reconciliation with France.

In 1950, at the time of the Korean War, the western powers guaranteed the Federal Republic against attack and increased their forces there. They also relaxed controls on economic development, including limitations on steel production and shipbuilding. West Germany was allowed to become a member of the Council of Europe, to appoint its own delegate to the OEEC and to establish consular relations with other countries. She was also permitted to create security forces corresponding to the people's police which the USSR had allowed East Germany to form.

In 1951 West Germany signed the Treaty of Paris which set up the ECSC. When early in 1952 the USSR proposed 'a united democratic Germany with forces only for her own defence' Adenauer preferred to look to the west. In May 1952 he agreed to participate in the European Defence Community. When France rejected the EDC the western powers decided to strengthen NATO by admitting West Germany (see p. 247). Though West Germany was thus allowed to rearm, all her forces were to be under NATO command and other NATO states were to continue to station forces in the Federal Republic. On 5–5–55 (5 May 1955) the Federal Republic of Germany became fully independent. She was admitted to NATO and became a member of the Western European Union (see p. 243).

In September 1955, when Adenauer visited Moscow, the Russians consented to recognise the Federal Republic. And they agreed to release some 10,000 German prisoners – the sad remnant of more than a million missing servicemen and civilian deportees. According to the Germans 130,000 of these people were still alive.

Before he left Moscow Adenauer wrote to Nikolai Bulganin, the Soviet prime minister, stating that his government represented the whole of Germany and disputing the transfer of German territory to Poland and the USSR. Bulganin replied that there were two German governments and two German states and that their frontiers had been settled at Potsdam. A few days later the German Democratic Republic (East Germany) became fully independent – or as independent as a Soviet satellite could be.

By his pro-western policy Adenauer made West Germany 'a partner no longer dictated to but wooed'. In 1956, following a referendum, it was agreed that the Saar (see p. 203) should be re-incorporated in West Germany from 1957. In 1957 West Germany was a founder member of the EEC. In January 1963 she signed a treaty of friendship and collaboration in military, economic, political and cultural matters with France. The signing of the treaty was marked by a solemn *Te Deum* in Rheims cathedral. In the same year Adenauer, at the remarkable age of eighty-seven, resigned. Under him a truly civilian government had for the first time achieved control in Germany. He was singularly free of that 'corrosive nationalism' which in the past had twisted Germany's outlook.

Meanwhile the economics minister, the wizard Dr Ludwig Erhard, had led West Germany to prosperity. By the end of 1949, by an astonishing display of enterprise, organisation and hard work, and with some assistance from Marshall Aid, the level of production was 93 per cent of the 1936 level. In the 1950s West Germany underwent her 'economic miracle'. Erhard's policy was one of free enterprise to which the Germans responded with enthusiasm. A revived trade union movement was built around a small number of unions which did not compete with one another. Provision was made for worker participation in management. While other countries were nationalising industries, West Germany was denationalising. The Volkswagen company for example was turned over to private ownership. Medical and educational services and housing – paid for out of the wealth brought by the economic miracle –

were probably the best in Europe. By 1957 industrial output was double that of 1936. Although the population grew by 24 per cent between 1950 and 1975, there was a labour shortage which resulted in considerable migration from southern Europe and Turkey.

Meanwhile about a million West Germans migrated to other countries. Economic progress was assisted by the absence of such industrial strife as beset France, Italy and later Britain, and by political stability. In contrast with Italy and France communists won little support.

West Germany after Adenauer

Erhard succeeded Adenauer as chancellor. He was followed in 1966 by Kurt Kiesinger who led 'a grand coalition' of Christian Democrats, Christian Socialists and Social Democrats. In 1969 the Social Democrats in

O brave new world? One of Euratom's (see p. 281) projects is JET (Joint European Torus) in Oxfordshire. A huge complex houses a symphony in metal, the Torus shown here, which scientists hope will enable them to discover whether it is feasible to use nuclear fusion (instead of fission) as a source of power

coalition with the Liberals came to power, thus ending twenty years of Christian Democratic rule. Brandt (see p. 253) became chancellor. Brandt's *ostpolitik* regarded West Germany as a bridge between eastern and western Europe rather than a bulwark against communism. Brandt was also a strong supporter of Britain's admission to the EEC. He continued Adenauer's policy of alignment with France. In 1973, on the tenth anniversary of the Franco-German friendship treaty, he placed a wreath on the tomb of the Unknown Soldier at the Arc de Triomphe in Paris. At a ceremony at the Elysée Palace President Pompidou said: 'The understanding between France and Germany ... largely determines the stability of our continent and the development of co-operation between all countries from one end of Europe to the other.'

In 1974, following a spy scandal in which an associate of his was involved, Brandt resigned and Helmuth Schmidt became the new Social Democrat chancellor. Schmidt was another good European. So, though faces and parties changed over the years, policies did not appreciably change from Adenauer's time. Political stability, a strong economy and a European outlook continued to characterise West Germany. The Communist Party, banned from 1955 to 1968, won little support. A neo-Nazi movement made some headlines but did not appear to be a serious contender for power. Outbreaks of terrorism by the Baader-Meinhof gang did not seriously disturb the country. But by 1981 opposition – often expressed in mass demonstrations – to the government's policy of adherence to the North Atlantic Alliance and support for American nuclear strategy perhaps indicated a shift in outlook.

Italy

The last two years of the Second World War were embittered by what amounted to civil war as Mussolini's supporters continued to fight for the Germans while Badoglio's government had joined the Allied side (see p. 221). As the war ended left-wing partisans seized power in many areas and often remained in control. Abandoned weapons littered the countryside and there was much banditry. Though destruction was less severe than in some countries there was serious inflation and famine was widespread. UNRRA (see p. 230) helped with relief supplies, in restoring communications and so on. The use of DDT (a wartime discovery) against malarial mosquitoes had a dramatic effect. By her peace treaty (see p. 236) Italy lost territory and had to pay reparations.

In May 1946 Victor Emmanuel III abdicated. His son, Humbert II, ruled for only a few weeks. The monarchy had been too closely associated with Mussolini's regime and at a referendum after Victor Emmanuel's abdication 54 per cent of voters favoured establishment of a republic. The agricultural south was strongly in favour of the monarchy, the industrial north was republican. In January 1948 a new constitution came into force. The Senate and Chamber of Deputies were to be elected by the people. The president was to have little power. The country was divided into 24 regions, each with local powers. Sicily, Sardinia, Trentino and Aosta were given considerable autonomy.

From December 1945 until June 1953 the Christian Democrat, Alcide de Gasperi, 'the ablest Italian politician [in a century]' was prime minister. Although it received little help from the USSR the Italian Communist Party was the largest in Europe outside the iron curtain. For a short time Communists were included in de Gasperi's government. Under the direction of Moscow the Italian Communist Party from 1947 concentrated on promoting popular unrest, but in elections in 1948 it suffered heavy losses. De Gasperi's Christian Democrats, clerical but liberal, obtained a clear majority – larger than any party had held before in Italy. There were widespread strikes but de Gasperi persisted with a programme of reform, including redistribution of land in the south.

In 1948 Italy began receiving Marshall Aid. In 1950 she was a founder member of NATO. In 1951 she signed the Treaty of Paris setting up the ECSC. De Gasperi is said to have died of a heart attack when he learned that France had rejected a plan for a European Defence Community. Italy then accepted the scheme by which the Western Union was extended to include her and West Germany. In 1957 Italy was a founder member of the EEC.

After 1945 a state corporation originally set up by Mussolini was given control of various industries that were in effect nationalised. These included steel, shipping and shipbuilding, radio and television, the state airline, banks and a network of toll-paying motorways. Other state organisations were placed in control of the petroleum and electricity industries. Education, medicine and housing were improved. The discovery of oil and quantities of natural gas in several areas stimulated development. During the 1950s and 1960s Italy had one of the highest growth rates in the world.

Large-scale investment by the European Investment Bank helped to develop the backward south. During the 1960s an agreement with the USSR allowed Italy to make Fiat cars in the Soviet Union and to build a pipeline to carry natural gas from the Ukraine to Trieste.

Prosperity was accompanied by a rapid growth in population (a 20 per cent increase between 1950 and 1975). During the 1950s nearly a million migrants left Italy for Latin America, Australia, the USA and parts of Europe where there were labour shortages.

In spite of economic prosperity government became increasingly unstable. For long periods Italy was without a government as different parties negotiated to form coalitions. The individualism of her people has perhaps frustrated the growth of a strong national structure. This may account for Italy's relatively low profile in international affairs.

After 1953 both communists and right-wing parties (monarchists and neo-fascists) increased their representation in parliament, though the Christian Democrats remained the strongest party. Communists who wanted to show their independence of Moscow called themselves Euro-Communists. In 1981 a socialist became prime minister – Italy's first non-Christian Democrat prime minister since 1945.

From the 1970s society was troubled by political terrorists. The Red Brigade engaged in kidnappings of political figures and industrialists. Rightist terrorism resulted for example in an explosion which killed eighty-five people at Bologna station. In 1981 Pope John Paul II survived an assassination attempt by foreign terrorists. He continued to urge peaceful settlement of quarrels, whether in his homeland (Poland) or elsewhere.

Spain and Portugal

Spain remained under the dictatorship of Franco for thirty-six years. So repressive was his régime that for a time Spain was more or less ostracised. Not until 1955 was she admitted to UNO.

From 1953 Spain received American military and economic aid in return for allowing the USA to build naval and air bases. After 1960 Spain was associated with the OEEC (see p. 280). By west European standards she remained backward. Tourists brought some wealth whilst a million migrants, many of them in western Europe, remitted at least part of their earnings to Spain. In 1970 income per head was about half that in the United Kingdom. After that economic progress was more rapid and by the 1980s income per head was approaching that of Britain. In 1981 Spain became a member of NATO and her admission to the EEC seemed likely.

Franco had promised that the monarchy would eventually be restored. When in 1975 he died the young Don Juan Carlos was welcomed as king. Censorship was relaxed, political parties were formed, a constitution was drawn up and in 1976 free elections were held. The intervention of the king twice prevented army officers from recovering power. Regional movements, particularly among the Basques, who backed up demands for autonomy by terrorism, were more difficult to control. Withdrawal from colonies in Africa was accomplished without difficulty.

Salazar, who had ruled Portugal in an authoritarian though somewhat enlightened manner since 1932, was compelled by illness to give up power in 1969. Another dictator, Professor Caetano, took his place.

Portugal was a recipient of Marshall Aid and a founder member of NATO. She remained economically backward. Her problems increased when Britain withdrew from EFTA (see p. 279).

Under Salazar and Caetano Portugal clung to her African colonies. Large numbers of Portuguese continued to emigrate to the colonies. Black nationalist guerilla movements were ruthlessly resisted at immense cost to the Portuguese economy. Colonies that were claimed to be a market for Portugal's products and to provide her with food supplies in fact drained away her resources.

In 1974 army officers who opposed Caetano's costly colonial wars seized power in Portugal. Later that year Portuguese Guinea (Guinea-Bissau) and in 1975 Angola and Mozambique became independent (see p. 323). The flight of some 800,000 Portuguese settlers from Africa added to difficulties in their homeland.

Following a contest for control between groups of army officers and newly formed political parties a constitution was agreed upon in 1976. Left-wing parties were initially strong but by 1980 had lost much of their influence. Meanwhile, Portugal had applied for admission to the EEC. At frontier posts in western Europe one may see the slogan: 'Another frontier, but still Europe.' With the likely admission of Spain and Portugal to the EEC it seemed 'Europe' with its open frontiers might extend from the North Sea to Gibraltar and from the Irish Sea to the Aegean.

30 The USSR and her satellites in the post-war years

The USSR

The last years of Stalin's rule

After the Second World War Stalin had consolidated the Soviet Union's power. He had subjected much of eastern Europe to his authority. The explosion of an atomic bomb and, shortly after his death, of a hydrogen bomb put the Soviet Union in the same super-power class as the USA. And the economy was sufficiently restored for the USSR to be offering aid to client states. By taking reparations from Germany and her allies the USSR had acquired valuable resources for reconstruction. By keeping wages and consequently the standard of living low the state was able through such forced savings to accumulate capital to build up the economy.

The heavy loss of life during the war did not stop Stalin sending his fellow Russians to prisons and labour camps, where death was a common fate. During the war

whole national groups whose loyalty he mistrusted had been shifted from southern and western parts of the USSR (including the Baltic states) to camps in the east. When the war ended thousands of Russian prisoners of war and slave labourers, accused of 'allowing' themselves to be captured by the Germans, were immediately despatched to Russian camps. Russian prisoners who fell into British and American hands begged to be allowed to stay in the west – but this did not seem permissible or practicable. And in the following years the MGB, Stalin's instrument for silencing the very breath of dissent, kept the camps full to overflowing. (In 1946 the NKVD (see p. 133) became the MGB, Ministry of State Security.) Alexander Solzhenitsyn, exiled from the USSR in 1974, explained the working of the security system in *Gulag Archipelago*. Gulag comes

Russians queue to see Stalin lying in state in the House of the Unions, Moscow, 10 March 1953

from the initials of words meaning chief administration of labour camps. When Stalin died (1953) there were perhaps ten million people in corrective labour camps, half of them in Siberia. No tsar had been more ruthlessly despotic than Joseph Stalin, the originator of the planned economy, the architect of victory and the establisher of the USSR's hegemony.

A new order?

As their forbears had venerated the tsars so millions of Russians appeared to venerate Stalin as their Little Father. But when he died the Russians heaved a sigh of relief. The succession to power caused less upheaval than might have been expected. Rather than engaging in a Stalinist-type power struggle Stalin's survivors decided in favour of collective leadership. For a time Georgi Malenkov, an opponent of the old-style Stalinists, was prime minister. After two years Bulganin took Malenkov's place. But real power was by then falling into the hands of Khrushchev, first secretary of the Communist Party. Khrushchev was prime minister from 1958 to 1964.

The collective leadership began to dismantle the system of terror. When Stalin died Beria, head of the 500,000-strong MGB, was preparing to carry out a purge. Soon afterwards he admitted that the reason for the purge, the 'Doctors' Plot' to murder Stalin and other leaders, was his own invention. Beria was executed. Some prisoners were released and the MGB was replaced by the KGB (State Security Committee), which had somewhat more limited powers.

Under Malenkov light industries were encouraged so there were more consumer goods and some improvement in living standards. There was some relaxation in the Soviet Union's foreign relations. The taking of reparations from East Germany and the use of German prisoners as slave labourers ceased. Soviet leaders visited satellite capitals to advise on the adoption of more liberal policies.

In February 1956, at a secret meeting of the Communist Party, in a speech lasting three hours Khrushchev denounced Stalin and all he had stood for. He denounced his failure to be ready for Hitler's attack in 1941. He denounced his harsh economic policies. He denounced his persecutions, his concentration of power in his own hands and his self-glorification – the personality cult. Before long the contents of Khrushchev's speech were widely known in the Soviet Union, by communist parties abroad and eventually throughout the world. The blind adherence to Moscow's instructions of communist parties in other countries was seriously disturbed. In Peking hostility towards the Moscow leadership was soon apparent. And the satellite states became restless.

In 1953 Soviet agricultural production was less than in 1913. Centralised planning had resulted in much inefficiency and waste. In 1957 regional economic councils took over much of the responsibility for planning. Under Khrushchev an attempt was made to make agriculture meet the needs of an expanding urban population by opening up the Virgin Lands of south-west Siberia. Neither scheme met with much success. The Virgin Lands proved quite unsuitable for growing wheat and the regional planners were no more successful than the planners in Moscow. Though between 1950 and 1960 real wages in the USSR rose by about 80 per cent, the standard of living remained the lowest in Europe. However, during the Khrushchev period Soviet scientists and engineers achieved the brilliant but expensive success of putting the first man in space.

In 1964 Khrushchev was voted out of office by the central committee of the Communist Party. The reason given was ill-health. The real reasons were probably several – the victory of Tito (see p. 247), the dispute with China (see p. 251), the unsuccessful agricultural policy and Khrushchev's apparent desire for popularity. Alexei Kosygin succeeded as premier. The relatively peaceful manner in which Khrushchev acquired power and his undramatic dismissal indicated a new quality in Soviet politics.

The USSR under Brezhnev

Brezhnev was the dominant figure after 1964 – first as party secretary and later as president. Under Brezhnev the USSR moved gradually into the period of détente. At home the economic problems of a socialist society were not easily resolved. In 1965 planning was again centralised though factory managers were given greater freedom to organise their own affairs. After 1968 peasants received regular wages instead of a share in their collectives' profits. But agriculture remained relatively inefficient. With a 40 per cent increase in population since 1950 the USSR by the 1970s was obliged to import large quantities of wheat – mainly from the USA. A 1976 agreement with the USA for the purchase of wheat was interrupted by a partial embargo following the Soviet invasion of Afghanistan in December 1979. In 1981, after the United States lifted the embargo, the USSR was seeking some 40 million tonnes of wheat from America.

During the 1970s there was a shortage of labour in industry, though by then there were fewer workers on the land and a very high proportion of women were in employment, many of them in heavy manual work. Individuals had little opportunity to change their jobs. Heavy industry forged ahead (see table below). By 1964 steel production was 80 per cent of that of the USA and greater than that of West Germany, Britain and France combined. Defence consumed enormous resources, which was one reason why the USSR wanted to make disarmament agreements. However, there was an increase in consumer goods, though demand continued to outstrip supply and in general the range and quality of goods were poor. Housing improved (see table below) but remained inadequate, with the average unit occupying only 34 square metres.

Oil and steel production in the USSR (in million tonnes)

	1940	1945	1952	1958	1964	1977
Crude oil	31	19	119	113	225	545
Steel	18	12	34	54	84	147

New housing built in the USSR

	1946	1950	1955	1960	1976
Millions of square metres of floor space built	17.4	24.2	33.4	86.0	70.6

An outstanding achievement in recent years has been the development of eastern Siberia. Novosibirsk became a great research centre, with a population by 1968 of over a million – five times the total urban population of western Siberia in 1900. Farther east huge hydro-electric stations on the Angara and Yenisei rivers produced electricity for industry.

During the 1970s the USSR became less of a closed economy. Her dependence on grain imports has been noted. She has wanted to obtain western capital and has been especially interested in getting high technology equipment from abroad. To an increasing extent she has been affected by changes in the world economy.

The USSR remains a police state. Power is concentrated in the hands of the Communist Party and continuation of this power seems to depend on denying Soviet citizens the rights that the USSR proclaims abroad. *Samizdats*, the writings of dissidents, printed and circulated secretly, are read by a small minority. But

most Russians hear what the party wants them to hear. There have been cultural exchanges with the west and tourism is a flourishing industry. But few Russians are permitted to travel abroad and passports are required even for internal travel.

Some Jews and dissidents have been allowed to emigrate but they are exceptions. An unknown number of people still languishes in prison camps, though the number is much smaller than under Stalin. Writers, scientists and others who dare to criticise the régime are nowadays as likely to be sent to a psychiatric ward as to a prison camp.

The USSR has a minority problem in the fifty million Muslims of the Caucasus and central Asia – whose birth rate is twice as high as in the rest of the Soviet Union. The number of mosques has fallen to a few hundred since 1917 but many people cling to their Islamic faith. And the Muslims of the Soviet Union, who are virtually all Sunni (Orthodox) Muslims, do not suffer from the sectarian rivalries that plague Islam, particularly in the Middle East. Though they are better off in the USSR than their Muslim neighbours in Iran and Afghanistan, this has not appeased the national feeling that has been strengthened by the post-war resurgence of Islam. In Samarkand, close to the mosques and madrassehs (Islamic colleges) being restored for the benefit of tourists, Uzbek teenagers in 1980 were dancing to the disco hit 'Ra, Ra, Rasputin'. But the Uzbeks sang, 'Geng, Geng, Genghis Khan' – doubtless remembering that in that mighty ruler's day his central Asian hordes were the masters of the Russians.

The USSR and her satellites

Though after the Second World War the Russians showed little inclination to organise free elections in eastern Europe, initially they proceeded cautiously. This they did by making use of socialist and agrarian groups in coalition governments. However, local communists were in effective control by having for example charge of police and radio communications. In Yugoslavia communist partisans wasted no time – but shed much blood – in driving out non-communist partisans and establishing their own control.

Moscow was able to manipulate the local communist parties to suit its own purposes. This is what happened in 1947–48 when the façade of coalitions was demolished and communists took complete control (see p. 239). Finland, which was not strategically important, remained independent and neutral. And it was at this stage that Tito refused to accept Stalin's orders (see p. 239).

After 1947 Stalin through Cominform (see p. 240) kept a tighter hold over the governments of the satellite states. His supporters in eastern Europe were almost as unscrupulous as their master and for a time made the region 'virtually a complex of concentration camps'. However, the economic upheaval that accompanied these political changes, whilst causing hardship to many, undid the injustices of centuries – though it did not always lead to efficiency. Property was nationalised and land brought under collective cultivation.

In 1949, the year of the Molotov Plan, the Russians established a Council for Mutual Economic Assistance (Comecon) to co-ordinate the economies of the satellites with that of the USSR. The satellites were to provide the Soviet Union with food and raw materials whilst industrial development was to be concentrated in the USSR. There was strong resistance to the intentions of Comecon, which were only partially achieved. After Stalin died the satellites were given greater economic freedom. There was greater production of consumer goods and the severities of the police state were relaxed. However, it was made clear that there were limits beyond which the USSR would not allow her satellites to go. This was most clearly expressed by Brezhnev in 1968 in his doctrine of limited sovereignty in socialist states (see p. 253). The Soviet Union, he said, had the right to intervene at any time and anywhere if it felt that 'socialist acquisitions were threatened'.

From 1945 Russian armies were stationed in the satellite states and Russian secret police operated in them. The conclusion of the Warsaw pact in May 1955 (see p. 247) gave the satellites a degree of independence. Their military forces came under their own control. On the other hand the Soviet Union was formally permitted to station troops in their territories. This gave her a powerful means of exerting pressure when Warsaw pact members stepped out of line. The forces of the satellite states received Russian arms but the more sophisticated weapons remained in Soviet hands.

The monolithic unity of the communist bloc was not as impressive later as it was in the 1950s. National interests have rated more highly in some countries than the advancement of communism. Yugoslavia and China have gone their own ways. Albania withdrew from Comecon and from the Warsaw pact. On the other hand the Mongolian People's Republic (Outer Mongolia) joined Comecon in 1962. Cuba joined in 1972.

The standard of living in the satellite states has risen considerably since 1945. Apart from a few areas in Poland, Hungary and western Czechoslovakia there was little industry in the satellites before the Second World War. Manufacturing is now much more widespread. And the monopoly of land ownership by a small class is a thing of the past. The price paid in individual hardship and in political freedom – which in fact (except in Czechoslovakia) scarcely existed before the war – may not have been unduly high.

East Germany

In 1953, the year the German Democratic Republic became independent (see p. 248), Russian tanks crushed disturbances led by workers who were resisting demands to work harder on the construction of Stalin Allée (now Karl Marx Allée) in East Berlin. East Germany, then economically weak and politically dependent on the USSR in its relations with western Europe, was in no position to be difficult. She continued strict in her adherence to the Soviet system. After 1961 economic conditions greatly improved. By 1980 East Germany held a leading position not only in athletics. She was also one of the leading industrial nations in Europe.

Poland

The Poles have suffered much at the hands of the Russians in the past, and have strong links with the west. They are also devoted Catholics. In 1956, following Khrushchev's denunciation of Stalinism, economic grievances, the suppression of the church, opposition to police state methods and to over hasty collectivisation resulted in disturbances. In Poznan 50,000 workers went on strike demanding bread, free elections and the departure of the Russians. Order was restored by the use of Russian tanks – 53 people were killed.

In October 1956 Gomulka, who had been imprisoned for Titoism during the Stalinist period, was elected first secretary of the Polish Communist Party. His aim was to make Poland 'an equal and independent state', no longer a mere satellite. But the USSR was determined not to allow this. A few days after Gomulka's election Khrushchev and other Russian leaders arrived and Soviet troops began moving towards Warsaw. But when workers and students persisted in demonstrating in favour of Gomulka Khrushchev reluctantly agreed to

MAMY DEMOKRACJE....
MAMY DEMOKRACJE.....
MAMY DEMOKRACJE...
MAMY...

JULIAN BOHDANOWICZ

*A Polish cartoon of April 1981 mocks a party official
who tries by dulling repetition to convince the people,
and perhaps himself, that 'we [the Poles] have democracy'*

Gomulka's leadership. And the unpopular Marshal Rokossovsky, a Polish-born Russian who had been minister of defence and commander in chief since 1949, was dismissed. Gomulka decollectivised much of agriculture and lifted restrictions on the church. However, Poland, who feared for the security of her new western frontier, continued her close alignment with the Soviet Union. This frontier became more secure after Brandt's *ostpolitik* and acceptance of the frontier at Helsinki in 1975 (see p. 254).

During the 1960s there was renewed discontent. In 1968 fifty people were killed during food riots. Disturbances in 1970 led to the replacement of Gomulka by Edward Gierek. In 1971 price increases led to strikes. In 1976 there were meat riots in Warsaw and elsewhere. Though Gierek tolerated opposition groups he failed to produce the open society that the Poles wanted. National pride increased with the election of a Polish cardinal as Pope John Paul II.

In 1980 bad planning, management 'hedged around by a thicket of directions and instructions', excessive foreign borrowing, inefficient agriculture, all compounded by the rise in oil prices, resulted in a new crisis. A sharp increase in the price of meat and demands for increased production led to strikes. Economic demands merged into demands for sweeping political reforms. Gdansk shipyard workers demanded free trade unions, the right to strike, revision of censorship laws, the release of political prisoners, the opening of the media to the church. In August the creation of an inter-factory strike committee resulted in the formation of the trade union Solidarity. With its ten million members, under the leadership of Lech Walesa, Solidarity confronted the authority of the Communist Party. In September 1980 Gierek fell from power. His successor conceded free trade unions and other reforms. But the Poles, made wary by past experiences of broken promises, and united in their support of Solidarity, maintained their pressure on the government – while the USSR remained on the touchline. In December 1981 martial law was imposed in Poland under General Jaruzelski. Unrest and economic difficulties continued.

Hungary

Following the denunciation of Stalin in 1956 Hungary too tried to escape from the Soviet straitjacket. De-Stalinisation, as conducted by the Communist Party, failed to satisfy the people. They wanted free elections, the restoration of farm lands to private ownership and the withdrawal of Russian forces from Hungary. A movement which began with writers quickly spread among students and then throughout the whole nation. 'It seemed that dismay, hatred and bitterness had broken through after years of repression.' Rebels, joined by most of the Hungarian army, occupied public buildings and centres of production. Secret police were attacked. Mindszenty (see p. 239) and other political prisoners were released.

The man around whom this movement centred was Imre Nagy. In April 1956 he had been expelled from the Communist Party but on 24 October with Russian consent he was called back to power as prime minister. His new government included two non-communists. At this stage the Russian army intervened to assist the security police battling with strikers and rebels. Even with their tanks the Russians were unable to get control of Budapest and after five days of street fighting withdrew from the city. But when Nagy proposed that Hungary should withdraw from the Warsaw pact and Comecon the Russians resumed their attacks. The Soviet Union could not tolerate Hungary following

Yugoslavia into the neutralist camp. The rebels could hold out for only a few days against forces by then supported by 6,000 tanks. Some 30,000 Hungarians and 7,000 Russians were killed. When the fighting stopped there was a general strike.

On 4 November 1956 a Russian-supported government with Janos Kadar at its head took control of Hungary. Nagy was denounced as a traitor and executed. Thousands of Hungarians were deported on the 'black train' to the USSR. More than 150,000 others fled to the west. Mindszenty was granted asylum in the American embassy in Budapest. He was pardoned by the Hungarian authorities in 1970.

From these experiences it seems that several things were learnt. First it was apparent to all that the USA, despite its fine words, could not come to the rescue of a community in rebellion against the Soviet system. Second, the Hungarians learned that there was a point beyond which opposition to the system could not be carried. And the Russians learned that it was necessary to give way in some matters. Under Kadar Hungary was able to develop the most liberal economy in the Soviet bloc. As a result the Hungarians have a relatively high standard of living. If members of former privileged classes remain somewhat ill at ease, life for the masses has its rewards and society is relatively relaxed.

Czechoslovakia

Soon after the death of Stalin disturbances in Czechoslovakia resulted in some relaxation of police activity and an increase in consumer goods. But by the mid-1960s the standard of living was falling. In 1967 a mood of restlessness spread through Czechoslovakia. Early in 1968 the central committee of the Communist Party voted out of office its Stalinist first secretary and appointed Alexander Dubček in his place. Greater freedom of speech and of the press led to lively discussion. Supporters of Dubček were appointed to important posts. Dubček announced an action programme, 'The Czechoslovak Road to Socialism'. This programme criticised the excessive power of the party and the centralised control of industry. It also proposed freedom of speech, judicial reforms, the right to travel abroad and control of the secret police. All this, especially the attack on the Communist Party itself, created alarm in Moscow as well as in other Warsaw pact states. Soviet–Polish military exercises took place near

August 1968: another Czech woman weeps. She holds a photograph of Dubček and the president

the Czech frontier and Soviet leaders held discussions in Prague.

In June the formation of a National Front coalition of the Communist and non-communist parties was announced, though Czechoslovakia's loyalty to the alliance with the Soviet Union was stressed. By July there were signs that Czech revisionism might find followers in Poland and East Germany. A stern letter warned the Czechs: 'We cannot agree to have hostile forces push your country off the road to socialism.' Military 'exercises' continued around the Czech frontiers. On 20 August 1968 these exercises suddenly became real. Half a million Soviet, Hungarian, East German and Polish troops and 500 tanks moved in on Prague. The invasion met with the united but passive hostility of the people. Dubček's reforms were reversed though he and other leaders who had been arrested were released. China, Yugoslavia, Romania – and Albania – as well as the west condemned the invasion. Brezhnev, when he proclaimed the doctrine of limited sovereignty, showed that he too believed in domino logic (see p. 312). Yet changes went on in Czechoslovakia, although she remained part of the Soviet bloc. Czech films of the 1970s reflected a curiously bourgeois society.

Bulgaria

Bulgaria needed the support of the USSR in her longstanding dispute with Yugoslavia over territory in Macedonia. Her economic ties with the USSR have been beneficial to her. So Bulgaria has kept out of the limelight and has made reasonable progress. She exports wine and welcomes western holiday makers to the sunshine of her beaches.

Romania

Like Bulgaria, because of her geographic position Romania is not in the front line of the Soviet defence system. In 1958 Soviet troops stationed there under the Warsaw pact were withdrawn. In the 1960s a Comecon plan that would have made Romania merely a supplier of raw materials for the USSR was rejected. The Romanians have since built up an economy based on trade with both eastern and western Europe.

In 1963 Romania announced support of non-interference in the affairs of other states and refused to take part in Warsaw pact exercises or to allow such exercises in her territory. Other Warsaw pact members put pressure on her but she had the support of neighbouring Yugoslavia in resisting them.

In 1965 Ceausescu became first secretary of the Communist Party. In 1966 he called for the withdrawal of foreign troops from other countries and while the Soviet Union was having a war of words with China he welcomed Chou En-lai, the Chinese premier, to Bucharest. The next year Romania established diplomatic relations with West Germany and in 1968 condemned the Soviet bloc invasion of Czechoslovakia. Since 1968 there have been state visits to Romania by Presidents Nixon and Ford. Trade with the west has increased. And Romania has maintained good relations with Israel and China, despite Moscow's hostility to both countries. But there has been no room for dangerous thoughts of liberalism in domestic affairs. In that respect Romania has been 'one of the most orthodox communist countries in eastern Europe'.

Yugoslavia: not a satellite

After her expulsion from Cominform in 1948 Yugoslavia's economic and political development showed marked differences from the pattern prescribed in Moscow. Land was restored to the peasants. There was less centralised planning, more private enterprise, greater freedom of expression than in other communist states. From an early stage Yugoslavia traded with and even accepted aid from the USA and western Europe. A federal system of government checked the separatist tendencies of Croat and Slovene nationalists. Tito, himself a Croat, was a powerful unifying force.

In foreign relations Tito adopted a policy of non-alignment. He disapproved equally of Chinese intervention in Korea and of Soviet intervention in Czechoslovakia – and of American intervention in Vietnam. He supported the Bandung conference and thereafter tried to keep the non-alignment movement genuinely non-aligned – and not pro-Soviet (see p. 248). The months after Tito's death in 1980 saw no marked change in Yugoslavia's international position or in her individual style of socialism.

31 China, Japan and Korea: the post-war years

China

The victory of the communists

When in August 1945 the Japanese surrendered to the Allies the Nationalist (Kuomintang) government of Chiang Kai-shek was the recognised government of China. But it was a 'steadily decaying régime', dependent on American assistance for its survival. The Chinese had little time for a régime whose war effort had for years been minimal. And China's peasant masses had little time for a régime that had made no attempt to tackle land reform. Meanwhile the communists already controlled substantial areas.

After the USSR declared war on Japan (see p. 225) Soviet troops quickly occupied Manchuria. When the war ended the Nationalists, with whom the USSR had just made a treaty, asked the Russians to stay on until Chiang's troops could take control. In March 1946 the Russians, having removed most of the industrial equipment left by the Japanese, withdrew from Manchuria. Meanwhile the communists infiltrated the rural areas. Soon the nominal truce between the communists and Nationalists was replaced by open conflict in Manchuria. In January 1947 General Marshall, soon to be American secretary of state, who had sought to bring the Nationalists and communists to agreement, left China, convinced there was no hope of compromise. From about the time he left there was full-scale civil war.

The communists had superiority in command, in tactics and in morale. In 1947 the People's Liberation Army (PLA) was formally constituted under Lin Piao (see p. 164). By avoiding major defeats and taking small gains, the PLA moved closer to the Nationalists in numbers and equipment. By the end of 1947 the communists controlled all Manchuria except the largest cities. In these cities Kuomintang forces, avoiding the bitter winter, claimed to be 'sitting the enemy to death'. But in November 1948 the key city of Shenyang (Mukden), 'grim, desolate and hungry', fell after a long siege.

Other communist armies had begun a drive to the south. 'Wars are won not by gadgets but by dedicated men', said Mao Tsetung. The disciplined communist troops won over people weary of the corruption and extortions, the inefficiency, the colossal inflation and frequent brutality of Chiang Kai-shek's régime. Throughout November and December 1948 over a million men fought the battle of Huaihai, between the Huai River and *hai* (the sea), until a communist victory opened the way to central and south China. The Nationalists, lacking both dedication and popular support, crumbled away. Negotiations between the communists, whose terms by then amounted to virtual surrender, and the Kuomintang proved fruitless if not farcical and in April 1949 the PLA was ordered to cross the Yangtse. Nanking, which had again become Chiang's capital, fell. By the end of 1949 the communists controlled all mainland China.

The Nationalist armies melted away. Most of those who remained loyal to Chiang fled with him to Taiwan, taking with them China's gold reserves. During 1949 two million Nationalists entered Taiwan, where they made up about a fifth of the population. Other remnants of the Nationalist armies fled to the Golden Triangle where the borders of Burma, Thailand and Laos touch (see map p. 297).

The establishment of the People's Republic of China

In September 1949 a council was set up representing various organisations, but wholly controlled by the Chinese Communist Party (CCP). By authority of this council the establishment of the People's Republic of China (PRC) was proclaimed in Peking on 1 October 1949. 'Our nation will never again be an insulted nation. We have stood up', said Mao Tsetung looking down from T'ien An Men (Tian An Men – Heavenly Peace Gateway) upon the crowds below. 'With him we shall build a new China', the crowds shouted back. Meanwhile, the Republic of China (ROC), ruling only Taiwan and a few offshore islands, was recognised by virtually the entire world as the government of China.

In theory the National People's Congress is the supreme authority in China. It exercises its power through a standing committee and at its head has been

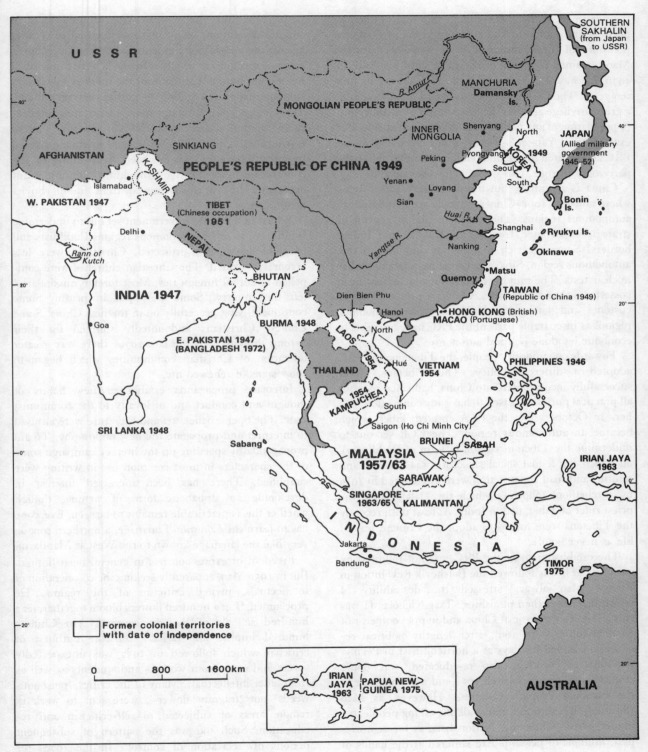

Post-war Asia

the chairman of the PRC. But in fact real power has been in the hands of the standing committee of the politburo of the Communist Party and its chairman. Mao remained chairman of the party until his death in 1976. He was also chairman of the PRC during its first ten years. The CCP continues to regard membership as a great privilege and has the lowest ratio of membership to population of any country under communist rule. For example Sun Yat-sen's widow, a vice-president of the PRC and revered throughout China, was admitted to the party only in 1981, two weeks before her death.

China is a 'unitary but multi-national' state. Areas where non-Han (non-Chinese) people are numerous are autonomous regions. These regions are in general of strategic importance, fronting the Russian and Indian borders. Some are rich in minerals and oil. In one autonomous region, Sinkiang, China has carried out her nuclear tests. The minorities have to some extent been cossetted by the communists, who have protected native customs and languages. However, the autonomous regions as inseparable parts of the PRC have no rights to economic let alone political autonomy.

Towards one minority people, the Tibetans, the PRC adopted a different policy. The Tibetans, never successfully incorporated into China, had since 1911 for all practical purposes ceased to have any connection with her. In October 1950 the PLA entered Tibet, which became an autonomous region. The CCP set out to undermine the Tibetan religion (a form of Buddhism), on which the feudal social structure was based. Land reforms and road construction were interrupted in 1959 by a rebellion, following which the Dalai Lama, the priest ruler of Tibet, fled to India. At least until recently the Tibetans were forced to adopt the Chinese way of life as never before.

The establishment of the PRC was not followed by such loss of life as followed the Bolshevik Revolution in Russia. Mao always stressed the desirability of reforming rather than punishing. Tsar Nicholas II was shot. The last emperor of China and puppet emperor of Manchukuo (see p. 169), after lengthy political re-education, ended his days as a horticulturist in Peking. In 1981 his brother, also re-educated, was doing research on the imperial archives – and was a member of the National People's Congress. However, as Mao admitted, 'Revolution is not at all like asking people to a dinner party.' Under the Nationalists, as for centuries past, millions of peasants had suffered at the hands of their landlords. The communists had suffered atrocities at the hands of the Nationalists. In 1950 and 1951, partly

perhaps because the Korean War aroused fears of counter-revolution, many of those accused of 'crimes against the people' were executed after trials in people's courts – meetings at which individuals were condemned by popular outcry. Estimates of the number killed vary from 'perhaps half a million' to 'perhaps several million'. Many more – Kuomintang spies, prostitutes, intellectuals, opium addicts and the ex-emperor – were re-educated. Those whom prolonged instruction failed to reform have in general been 'sent down to the country' for more effective remoulding – an unpleasant experience but worlds removed from life in Soviet prison camps.

Whilst in Tibet the government set out to undermine Buddhism, in other autonomous regions Buddhists and Muslims have been protected. Christians were less favourably treated. The Christian churches were compelled to cut all foreign ties. Most foreign missionaries left the country. Some were put in prison. Some continued living peacefully on in the new China. Some Chinese Christians undoubtedly suffered for their 'wrong thinking'. In the late 1970s there was greater toleration of Christian communities which began to show signs of renewed life.

Intensive propaganda established new habits of thought and conduct and of loyalty to the communist state. The opera, ballet, art and literature were all used to interpret and propagate the new philosophy. To aid propaganda by speeding up the literacy campaign some of the characters in most common use in writing were simplified. There has been increased interest in developing an alphabetic form of writing, though whether this is practicable remains to be seen. Everyone has to learn the Common Language, a northern tongue very like the language known to the West as Mandarin.

Freedom of expression has in general been limited. But in 1956 Mao, apparently seeking the co-operation of intellectuals, invited criticism of the régime. He proclaimed: 'Let a hundred flowers bloom together, let a hundred schools of thought contend.' (In Chinese hundred implies all, varied.) But the outburst of criticism which followed in 1957 was unexpectedly severe and came from workers and students as well as from older intellectuals. Many of the critics, 'poisonous weeds' not 'fragrant flowers', were sent to work in remote areas or subjected to self-criticism and re-education. Such too was the pattern of subsequent periods of 'relaxation of control'. In the 1970s for example the right to express one's thoughts on Democracy Wall in Peking was relatively short-lived.

The communes and the Great Leap Forward

After the sharing out of land that followed the 'liquid-ation' of the landlords, enterprising peasants began buying up land and the growth of a class of 'kulak' peasant proprietors (see p. 44) seemed likely. In 1953 agricultural producers' co-operatives concentrated fields into larger units, permitting mechanised farming and more effective irrigation. In 1956–57 higher co-operatives were introduced. Private ownership of land then ended, for in the higher co-operatives land was collectively owned, members being paid only for their labour.

In 1958 Mao saw in Honan (Henan) an experiment in setting up a 'people's commune'. In August 1958 a party directive ordered the general adoption of the commune system. Much larger than the co-operatives, the communes seemed to offer greater party control over all aspects of life. Their size seemed to make co-operative activity practicable not only in agriculture but in industry and commerce, in militia organisation and in the provision of hospitals, schools and so on. The communes were also able to undertake major irrigation and construction works.

Mao also called for a Great Leap Forward in industry. The nation, he said, must make itself self-sufficient by relying on native skills to establish new industries. It should learn 'to walk on two legs', to combine modern methods with ancient Chinese practices, large-scale industry with small factories, rural with urban industry. The Great Leap of 1958 produced a tremendous burst of activity. Steel manufacture became a nationwide cottage industry for amateurs, even for children. Farmers neglected their fields to make pig iron in their backyards. Soon excessive enthusiasm and misdirected effort caused difficulties. 'Overloaded communications jammed, overloaded machines broke down, and overloaded men broke down with them.'

Peasant hostility to the regimented life in the communes led to food shortages. Enthusiastic cadres exaggerated 'achievements' and for a time misled China's leaders as to the seriousness of the situation. Mao's radical policies were criticised by Marshal P'eng Te-huai (Peng Dehuai), the defence minister, who was more interested in getting modern arms from the USSR than in the swift achievement of economic self-sufficiency, and by Liu Shao-ch'i (Liu Shaoqi), a leading communist thinker. Liu displaced Mao as chairman of the PRC though not of the CCP. But P'eng was dismissed.

The party's central committee resolved there must be a return to incentives. Peasants were permitted to cultivate private plots and to keep a few animals. There was less emphasis on communal living. The communes were to engage chiefly in industries related to agriculture, for example fertiliser production. The size of the communes was reduced. Control operated at three levels: the commune, the production brigade which became the owning and accounting unit, and the production team. Radicals favoured wider powers for the communes whilst moderates wanted to transfer land ownership from the brigade to the team.

From 1959 to 1961 floods and droughts added to the difficulties caused by the Great Leap Forward. In 1960 the Russians, who had been assisting China since the 1950 treaty (see p. 244), with dramatic suddenness withdrew all aid. Russian technicians engaged in constructing scientific and industrial plants returned home – taking with them their blueprints. The palatial apartments built to house the Russians stood empty until, their paint peeling, they welcomed the tourists whom China began admitting in the 1970s.

Threatened with economic collapse, Liu Shao-ch'i in 1961 managed to return China to a more traditional economic organisation – much as Lenin had adopted the New Economic Policy (see p. 131). Greater emphasis was placed on agriculture and light industry. Peasants were allowed to sell the vegetables from their private plots in local markets. In the next few years both agriculture and industry recovered. Peking and other old cities grew tremendously and great new cities sprang up. Industry is no longer concentrated in a few large cities in the north-east and east of China. Shanghai, a ghost port, sprang to new life and new ports developed with the growth of coastal and foreign trade.

The Cultural Revolution

In 1966 Mao launched the Great Proletarian Cultural Revolution. Disputes which came to the fore during this revolution first came into the open in the ministry of culture. But the word cultural signified an attack on a whole way of life, an attempt to create a nation of selfless people dedicated to the well-being of all. Attacking the revisionism of the 'renegade, traitor and scab' Liu Shao-ch'i and all 'those who tread the capitalist road', Mao tried to lead the people of China back to the purer and more disciplined communism of the Long March and Yenan (see p. 166). Daringly he attacked the party and its leaders. In August 1966 he hung up his big character poster: 'Bombard the party headquarters.' At a rally in

The Cultural Revolution: cheering red guards at a rally in Peking. They hold aloft their Little Red Books containing The Thoughts of Chairman Mao

T'ien An Men square he gave his blessing to the red guards. Soon millions of these young people were roaming through China, attacking the 'monsters and demons' of reaction. From cities north of the Great Wall to tropical villages in the far south, they plastered their big character posters on all the walls of China.

Between 1966 and the national party congress of 1969 almost every leading figure in the CCP came under attack – Liu Shao-Ch'i, Chu Teh, even Chou En-lai. Day after day party leaders and officials, generals and professors, humbler men and women too, were subjected to self-criticism and on occasion paraded through the streets with dunces' hats on their heads. 'To think we all ate out of the same bowl once', said Chu Teh sadly. Amid the hysteria xenophobia flourished.

The Cultural Revolution at best caused economic confusion; at worst it caused havoc, violence and loss of life. Schools and universities remained closed for as long as four years. In 1968 the storm began to subside. As it had done during the Great Leap Forward the PLA helped rescue China from chaos. Some twenty million rowdy students were sent down to the country. The formation of revolutionary committees at all levels throughout China gave an appearance of unity. In theory at least these management committees included representatives of extremist as well as moderate factions.

The 1969 party congress made Marxism–Leninism–Mao Tsetung Thought the 'theoretical basis guiding' the CCP and named Lin Piao 'close comrade in arms and successor' to Mao. In due course many who had been purged and humiliated were rehabilitated. In 1973 Teng Hsiao-P'ing (Deng Xiaoping) whose contempt for incompetence and empty talk had brought him many enemies was restored to high office. It was Teng who dared to say: 'It's not the colour of the cat that matters; it's whether the cat catches the mice.' Liu Shao-ch'i had to wait until 1981 for rehabilitation – by which time he was dead.

After the Cultural Revolution there was renewed emphasis on mixing study with labour. For a time it was more important to be red than expert. Students who handed in blank answer sheets became 'heroes'. But by 1977 there was renewed interest in serious study.

After the Cultural Revolution: the gang of four

Much of the conflict of the Cultural Revolution was meaningless. Heady with power, red guards seemed to fight for fighting's sake, to argue for arguing's sake. However, the revolution revealed deep divisions within the CCP. Not all the divisions ended with the ending of the Cultural Revolution. In 1971 Lin Piao, 'close comrade in arms and successor' to Mao, was accused of 'leftist deviationism' and disappeared from public life. With a party of companions he seems to have died in an aircraft crash in Outer Mongolia, while fleeing to the USSR. It was claimed he had been plotting to overthrow Chairman Mao.

After Lin's downfall Chiang Ch'ing, the small-time starlet who had married Mao, and three fellow Shang-hainese who had screamed their way to prominence during the Cultural Revolution, took increasing control of affairs with, it seems, the aim of eventually ruling China. This so-called gang of four became ever more powerful, ever more destructive. A campaign they mounted against Teng Hsiao-p'ing, who had been expected to succeed Chou En-lai as premier, resulted in his being purged again (April 1976).

Chou En-lai died in January 1976. It was his practical genius that for over twenty-five years kept China on course. When more than once chaos threatened, Chou, often behind the scenes, restored order. In July Chu Teh, Father of the Red army, died. He too had exercised a moderating influence. When in that July an earthquake caused untold loss of life the superstitious saw it as a portent of the death of Mao.

Children in a crèche at the Five Rams clock factory in Canton, 1977. Earlier this century Chinese mothers often had to leave their children close to dangerous machinery

A classroom in a brigade-run school, 1977. Children wearing red scarves are Little Red Soldiers

In a brigade clinic a technician makes false teeth for people for whom dental care was once unheard of (1977)

A street in Linhsien, Honan (1977). On many roads trees stand four deep on either side

On 9 September 1976, at the mid-autumn festival, forty-nine years after he had led the Autumn Harvest uprising (see p. 164), Mao died. Mao was the Great Helmsman – the man who dared to 'clasp the moon in the Ninth Heaven and seize turtles deep down in the Five Seas'. Under Mao China had shown 'a breadth of mass participation, a degree of social equality and a measure of popular fervour unknown in human history'.

After Teng Hsiao-p'ing's dismissal, while Mao was dying, the gang of four disrupted every aspect of life. The new premier, Hua Kuo-feng (Hua Guofeng), a relative newcomer to power, had a difficult path to follow. But armed with Mao's blessing Hua became chairman of the CCP. In October 1976 Chairman Hua ordered the arrest of Chiang Ch'ing and her allies. There followed a vigorous campaign condemning the gang of four. With the return to power of Teng Hsiao-

p'ing in August 1977 there was a further shift to moderate policies. By 1982 Hua was discredited and it seemed that real power was in the hands of Teng, by then aged seventy-seven, and of Chairman Hu Yaobang, who as a young man of nineteen had gone on the Long March. And there were rumblings of criticism against the Great Helmsman, lying strangely chalky in his mausoleum in T'ien An Men square. But whatever the immediate judgement may be, the judgement of history must surely be that Mao sought 'to serve the people'.

Meanwhile the gang of four had been brought to trial.

Economic progress

In 1949 the PRC was a country in ruins. By 1952 industry and agriculture had recovered almost to pre-war levels. Heavy industries and banks had been nationalised. By 1956 most smaller businesses had been taken over by the state, which gave generous compensation to former owners. In 1952 China prepared her first five-year plan which concentrated on heavy industry and communications. For various reasons, including America's support of Taiwan, perhaps a natural desire to take her place as a great power – and later fear of the USSR – there was heavy expenditure on the armed forces.

Despite the problems that followed the establishment of communes, the disasters of the Great Leap Forward and the havoc of the Cultural Revolution, China continued to make progress. Schools, hospitals and workers' flats were built. Road and railway construction reached out to the remotest areas. Oilfields were discovered and China was probably self-sufficient in oil by about 1966. Flood control projects were built by armies of people with a great capacity for hard work. Even the Yellow River (Huang He), China's Sorrow, seems to have been tamed. Immense conservation schemes provided water for irrigation and generation of electric power. Afforestation checked soil erosion: China's new 'wall' is her green wall of forest north of the Great Wall. The explosion of an atom bomb (1964), a hydrogen bomb (1967) and the launching of the space satellite, *The east is red* (1970), are evidence of China's great technical advance, but consumed a high proportion of her resources.

Even during the troubled 1960s interest in foreign trade survived. Riots in Hong Kong in 1967, an overspill from the Cultural Revolution, found little sympathy in Peking. China then preferred to see the British colony engaged in trade from which she in her turn would gain substantial benefits. In the 1970s China showed much interest in sophisticated western products. Meanwhile her own ships and products were seen virtually the world over.

Foreign relations: 1949 to the great thaw

For a time the PRC seemed almost as isolated from the world outside as China had been in the early nineteenth century. Most states recognised the ROC (Taiwan). No state could recognise both 'Chinas'. In 1949 the USA had made it clear that she would offer the ROC neither military aid nor advice. But after the Chinese intervention in the Korean War Truman announced that the USA would intervene anywhere in the Pacific area where 'Chinese communism' was a threat. The

more strict of the many Americans employed in Hong Kong, in obedience to their trade embargo (1949) against China, refused to eat prawns from 'the mainland'. Some refused to bath in water pumped into the colony from the PRC. With the USA committing itself by treaty to the defence of Taiwan (1954) and continuing to veto the PRC's admission to UNO, China remained violently hostile to the United States.

After renewed confrontation in 1958 over Quemoy and Matsu (see p. 246) there was no significant conflict between the two Chinas, though Taiwan continued to challenge the legality of 'the mainland régime'. On the other side of the Straits of Taiwan, where American warships patrolled, people sang: 'Sitting on the seashore I look towards our province of Taiwan.'

Meanwhile Taiwan flourished under Chiang Kai-shek's semi-dictatorial rule. The Kuomintang worked an economic miracle they had never tried to work on the mainland. A land reform programme became a model for other Asian states. In time Taiwan was able to offer aid to African and South American countries.

The USSR, allied by her 1945 treaty to the Nationalists (see p. 222), did not help the communists in the civil war. The Chinese communist leaders, said Stalin, would not be able to unify China. But in February 1950 Mao Tsetung signed the thirty-year treaty of friendship, alliance and mutual assistance with the USSR (see p. 244). In 1952 the Russians handed over control of the Chinese Eastern and South Manchurian railways. When Russian occupation of

Chinese stamps issued on the tenth anniversary of the Sino-Soviet Treaty of Friendship of 1950. A Chinese and Soviet worker (left) and a Soviet and Chinese soldier (right) fraternise. Soon their countries were to be engaged in a bitter dispute

Lushun (Port Arthur) ended in February 1955 high officials from Peking gave the Russian soldiers badges engraved: 'Sino-Soviet friendship'.

After 1955 disputes began to disturb China's 'unshakeable' friendship with the USSR. Following Khrushchev's attack on Stalin, with its implied attack on Mao's leadership, and his declaration that war with the capitalist world was not inevitable, the rift widened. Peaceful co-existence was then anathema in China. In 1959 the USSR denounced an agreement to supply China with an atom bomb. In 1960 Mao openly attacked Russian policy. It was in 1960 that all Soviet aid was withdrawn from China. In a propaganda war the 'social imperialism' of 'the new tsars' was as much abused as American imperialism.

In religion there are no more bitter foes than divided followers of a common faith. The Chinese claimed that Mao was the only exponent of Marxism–Leninism and that Russian 'revisionism' would inevitably restore a bourgeois society. Only Albania supported the PRC, though a few communist states wavered. In recent years the Chinese have attacked the USSR's 'hegemonism', her attempt to extend her power beyond her own frontiers.

There are 8,000 kilometres of common frontier between the two states. The Chinese argued that the Sino-Russian treaties of 1858, 1860 and 1881 (see p. 14) were unequal treaties that should be renegotiated. Chou En-lai, conciliatory and realistic, indicated that China wanted border adjustments rather than extensive transfers of territory. The Russians denied the inequality of the treaties and argued that 'historically formed boundaries' could not be arbitrarily altered. From 1962 there were border incidents along the Amur River and in Sinkiang. In 1969 these incidents flared up on Chenpao (Damansky) Island in the Ussuri River. The border disputes were largely symptoms of mutual fear – Russian fear of China with its huge population and Chinese fear of the imperialist USSR, studded with nuclear missiles, many of them directed at Chinese cities. When, after 1971, China's relations with the rest of the world improved, relations with the USSR remained tense. Meanwhile, the Mongolian People's Republic (Outer Mongolia) remained openly pro-Russian.

After Tibet became part of the PRC the Chinese built roads along their new Himalayan frontier. In 1957 China laid claim to frontier territory which India also claimed. Border clashes were followed in 1962 by a brief but sharply fought war in which India was defeated.

After a border agreement with Pakistan China tended to play off India and Pakistan against one another. China supported Pakistan in her war with India over Bangladesh in 1971 (see p. 311).

With Burma China made frontier agreements although Kuomintang sympathisers continued to find refuge there. To North Vietnam she offered cautious assistance in the struggle to overrun the south and drive out 'American imperialism'. When in 1970 anti-communists forced Norodom Sihanouk to leave Cambodia (see p. 315) he was warmly welcomed in Peking – but received more sympathy than aid.

The Philippines, Malaysia and Thailand, all with substantial Chinese minorities, all at times troubled by communist rebels, maintained an anti-Chinese attitude. Indonesia under President Sukarno developed friendly relations with China. But difficulties arose when Indonesia followed nationalist policies towards its three million Chinese. With the fall of Sukarno (see p. 316) Indonesia joined the anti-communist camp of Southeast Asia.

In the early 1960s China was establishing contacts with numerous emergent nations. For a time her policy of promoting revolution made her offers of aid less attractive. And the excesses of the Cultural Revolution lost her friends.

The great thaw

China's relations with the rest of the world underwent a dramatic change after October 1971 when, with the lifting of the American veto, she was admitted to membership of UNO. She then took the seat vacated by Taiwan on the security council. Chiang Kai-shek, growing old in Taiwan, found himself alone. The Nationalist Republic of China was left to await an uncertain future. When Chiang died in 1975 his son succeeded to much of his power.

In February 1972 President Nixon was welcomed in Peking where he accepted the five principles agreed upon in 1955 at Bandung (see p. 248). From then on the USA moved closer towards friendship with the PRC. In 1972 Britain, who had recognised the PRC in 1950, established full diplomatic relations with Peking. Many other states, among them Japan (see p. 308), did the same. A thaw with the non-communist states of Southeast Asia began with the establishment of diplomatic relations between the PRC and Malaysia in 1974. On the other hand relations with communist Vietnam were increasingly bad. Vietnam's close contacts with the

USSR were resented and when refugees flooded over the border into China in 1979 Chinese forces attacked Vietnam. The Vietnamese overthrow of a pro-Chinese régime in Kampuchea (Cambodia) (see p. 315) also aroused hostility.

After 1970 there were renewed contacts with the third world. In 1970 construction of the 2,000-kilometre Tanzam Railway linking Tanzania with Zambia began. Completed a year ahead of schedule it was built largely by 15,000 members of the PLA. Several other schemes were undertaken, for example roads and textile mills in South Yemen. How much influence such aid brings is debatable. 'Seventy years of living under colonial rule did not change us into capitalists, and five years [of railway construction] cannot change us into communists', said President Kaunda of Zambia.

In 1980 China's policy seemed to be firmly defensive of her boundaries, but opposed to 'hegemonism':

> Dig tunnels deep,
> Store grain everywhere,
> Never follow hegemonism.

Perhaps her chief aim was to align herself with the developed states of the West and with the third world against the threat of the Soviet bloc.

Diplomatic delegations, scientific, cultural and economic missions, journalists, schoolchildren 'studying China', and tourists have poured into China. By 1977 the huge entrance hall of the Peking Hotel was thronged with Egyptians, Romanians, Albanians, Frenchmen, Japanese, Australians, Chileans, Brazilians, Americans, Canadians, Ghanaians, Englishmen, Burmese and many others. It was almost like the days when foreign envoys came bearing tribute to the Son of Heaven. By 1980 it was only in the more remote parts of the PRC that 'foreign guests' attracted curious crowds. The great unknown, it seemed, had opened up.

A better life

Starvation, even in severe drought, has been unknown in China for some years. Infanticide and the selling of children are probably things of the past. By the late 1970s people were probably better off than they had ever been. The 'three rounds and one sound' – watch, bicycle, sewing machine and radio – were much in evidence. In a remarkably egalitarian society there were few cars but millions of bicycles. Women enjoy equal rights with men. Late marriages and contraceptives are limiting population growth. If the scholar has been

Chairman Mao with Marshal Lin Piao on his left and Premier Chou En-lai at Peking airport on the occasion of the arrival of President Kaunda of Zambia

taken down from his ivory tower the worker has achieved a new dignity. Medical penetration teams visit the remotest places. Workers on holiday in distant provinces visit the great tombs and palaces which their ancestors toiled to build. The aged in their homes of respect are proud to show that they can read.

Working almost entirely without outside support, by the 1980s the Chinese seemed to be coming to terms with the world of the twentieth century whilst preserving that special identity which has made China a civilisation rather than a nation.

Macao and Hong Kong

In 1983 Portugal, first to come, still held her 'overseas province' of Macao. But Portugal is perhaps 'in office not in power' in this first European foothold in China. British Hong Kong continued to be China's window on the West and her chief source of foreign currency. Peking was investing vast sums in the development of the colony's industries. Meanwhile, legally or illegally, numbers of Chinese continued to cross the border into Hong Kong. (By arrangement with the PRC a quota of Chinese was allowed to enter Hong Kong daily.) Whether their exit from China signified dissatisfaction with conditions there is hard to assess. Hong Kong's phenomenal material success may have been the main attraction. In 1997 the lease from China of the New Territories (see p. 18), where most of Hong Kong's water supplies and much of her industry are located, is due to expire.

Japan

The Allied occupation

For a few days after Japan's surrender (August 1945) kamikaze pilots made flights over Tokyo to show their desire for further resistance. A number of army officers committed *seppuku* (ceremonial suicide). But for the most part the Japanese accepted their emperor's decision. When the first airborne occupation forces arrived, workers at Atsugi airfield, where kamikaze pilots had trained, greeted them with smiles and bows.

On 2 September 1945 General MacArthur formally accepted Japan's surrender on board USS *Missouri* in Tokyo Bay. Mamoru Shigemitsu, a signatory of the instrument of surrender, wrote: 'Only if [Japan] turns over a new leaf will she prosper and life be worth living. Her journey through hell will have had a meaning if she emerges worthy of herself.' At MacArthur's insistence Japanese surrenders elsewhere had to await surrender in Tokyo. During this interval, when neither the Japanese nor their victors were in control, nationalists in the Netherlands East Indies and French Indo-China proclaimed their independence (see pp. 312, 315).

The USA, which had played a major part in Japan's defeat, played the chief part in her post-war occupation and government. Although Britons, Australians and others took part, American policies, American soldiers and above all American leadership in the person of MacArthur, 'the blue eyed shogun', were in effective control. MacArthur, as Supreme Commander Allied Powers (SCAP), issued policy directives which the Japanese government carried out.

SCAP's first task was to provide food. 'Give me bread or give me bullets', said MacArthur. The armed forces were demobilised. Shinto, the nationalist state religion, lost its special position. In a purge of militarists some

Vice-Admiral Fujita, under escort of a British soldier 16 September 1945, the day the Japanese formally surrendered Hong Kong to the British. The Union Jack was then hoisted over Government House. Churchill had earlier rejected Chiang Kai-shek's claim that the Japanese should surrender the colony to the (Nationalist) government of China. The surrender to the British was therefore of special significance

200,000 people were excluded from official positions, though some later returned to public life. War criminals were tried in Tokyo, and elsewhere by the French, Russians and others. General Tojo, when about to be arrested, shot himself but was saved by a transfusion of American blood. Like some 700 others he was later sentenced to death. MacArthur's refusal to bring the emperor to trial aroused much criticism in the USA.

MacArthur's next aim was the democratisation of Japan. He ordered the release of people, including communists, who had been imprisoned for having 'dangerous thoughts'. In general liberal ideas were widely accepted. For a time communists had a considerable following.

On 1 January 1946 Emperor Hirohito made a second broadcast to his people; in this he renounced the ancestral claim to divinity. In May 1947 a new constitution came into effect. The emperor was declared to be 'the symbol of the state and of the unity of the people . . . with whom resides sovereign power'. Effective power was in the hands of the Diet from which the prime minister and cabinet were to be chosen. Members of the armed forces were excluded from holding ministerial office. Greatest power in the Diet rested in the lower house, elected by universal suffrage. The constitution guaranteed various liberties, including the right of citizens to sue the state for improper arrest and for workers to act collectively. The constitution also renounced for ever 'war . . . and the threat and use of force as a means of settling international disputes'.

Post-war prime ministers have exercised a genuine parliamentary authority. Elections in 1947 led to a coalition of socialists taking office, but within a year they were defeated. Yoshida Shigeru, a moderate liberal, then took office.

In 1945 Japan's economy was at a standstill. There was no oil. There was so little iron that ships were built of wood. By the end of 1945 there were thirteen million unemployed. The Russians had helped themselves to 'reparations' by stripping Manchuria of all Japanese equipment. Plans for heavy reparations to be paid to the other allies were abandoned as being too dangerous to the Japanese economy. Instead reparations were limited to token payments of 'blood money', the amount of which was fixed by agreements with the countries Japan had occupied.

SCAP, by restricting the amount of land an owner might hold and by prohibiting absentee ownership, made land available for redistribution. With the growth of a class of peasant proprietors there was a rapid increase in productivity and rural prosperity. This was perhaps the most important of MacArthur's reforms. A decentralisation act of 1946 broke up a number of giant cartels, the *zaibatsu* – Mitsui and Mitsubishi for example were each divided into over a hundred smaller firms. But within a decade they had recovered their dominant positions. *Zaibatsu* influence in politics remained strong for all parties relied on funds supplied by these industrial and commercial giants. SCAP also introduced laws to protect labour and encouraged trade union membership, which grew rapidly. Communist activity in the unions was restrained after the calling of a general strike in 1947. In general unions were less disruptive than in most countries. Education was freed from excessive central control and was no longer to be used for state propaganda. Perhaps the most dramatic

social change in post-war Japan was in the status of women who received the vote, entered employment and even sat in the Diet. 'After the war women and women's stockings were stronger.'

Pre-war Japanese products were often shoddy. The Chinese, punning on two words meaning Japanese, called them 'day and a half goods'. After the war not only women's stockings were 'stronger'. When the Korean War began Japanese industry, which was slowly recovering, enjoyed such a demand for its products that the whole country was swept forward on a wave of prosperity.

The Treaty of San Francisco, 1951

After the outbreak of the Korean War the Americans became anxious to use Japan as a support against possible Russian or Chinese aggression. When some of the American forces were withdrawn from Japan for service in Korea (see p. 245), MacArthur persuaded the government to raise an armed 'national police reserve' of 75,000 men. Many Japanese opposed this as a first step in a return to militarism.

In 1950 Truman appointed Dulles as his adviser to make a peace treaty with Japan. Japan was not consulted but offered no opposition to the peace terms as she was eager to recover her independence. In September 1951 a formal peace treaty was signed in San Francisco. Japan gave up all claims to Korea and Taiwan and Manchuria. She agreed to the transfer of the Pacific islands, which she had held as mandates, to the trusteeship of the USA. The Bonin and Ryukyu islands (including Okinawa), over which Japan had certain claims, were placed for the time being under American control. And Japan gave up all claims to any special rights and interests in China. The Kuriles and southern Sakhalin had already been taken by the USSR, as agreed at Yalta. Full control of Japan's affairs was to be restored to her in April 1952, when the occupying forces were to be withdrawn.

Japan after the peace treaty

At the time peace was made a security pact provided for American forces to be stationed in Japan until she could assume responsibility for her own defence. In 1954 Yoshida made a mutual defence agreement with the USA. This gave the Americans naval, military and air bases in Japan. It also involved the raising of armed self-defence units. This caused an outcry by Japanese socialists and pacifists. Opposition to the self-defence

Old and new in Tokyo: an ancient Buddhist temple adjoins the modern shopping precinct in the Asakusa district – noted also for theatres, bars and storippu *(striptease shops). A girl in jeans strides out with her plastic bag; a woman in the traditional dress trips along on* geta *(clogs), carrying her shopping in a silk* furoshiki

units and economic difficulties following the ending of the Korean War led to Yoshida's overthrow.

MacArthur's land reforms removed a major source of discontent but in the early post-war years slow economic recovery offered opportunities for communist propaganda. But the economic prosperity which accompanied the Korean War left the communists without their best arguments. Between 1952 and 1958 they won four seats in the Diet – in four elections. Divisions within their ranks weakened further the left-wing extremists who by 1969 included communists, Trotskyites, Maoists and anarchists. The student organisation, *Zengakuren*, which took part in numerous violent agitations, was probably more anarchist than communist in its sympathies. Government remained largely in the hands of moderates of the centre. However, in 1958 socialist opposition prevented constitutional changes intended to check excessive political action.

The long struggle in Vietnam (see pp. 312–14) led to a further demand for Japanese goods and services. By 1969 Japan's was the third largest economy in the world. Rapid industrial development resulted in a shortage of labour and a drift of population to the cities. The birth rate fell whilst the falling death rate extended the average length of life from fifty (men) and fifty-four (women) in 1946 to sixty-nine and seventy-four in 1967.

Japan has provided substantial aid to developing nations. But problems remained especially with escalating oil prices. For Japan is dependent on outside sources for oil and indeed for most of the raw materials needed by a country which in places is one vast conurbation. Prosperity is heavily dependent on exports. But in recent years the flooding of foreign markets with Japanese goods – for example, cars in Britain – has led to friction.

Foreign relations

One reason for Japan's prosperity may be that she enjoyed security under the shelter of American forces at minimal cost to herself. After her admission to the UN (see below), as an unarmed state she did not even have the cost of providing peace-keeping forces. However, her relationship with the USA caused problems. When in 1960 the security pact of 1951 was replaced by a ten-year treaty of mutual co-operation and security, the reactions of socialists and the *Zengakuren* were violent. The prime minister had to resign. Under the 1960 treaty certain concessions were made to Japan, but America retained her bases there. In 1970 when the treaty was renewed there were violent demonstrations by extremists of both right and left.

American occupation of the Ryukyu and Bonin islands was a subject of dispute during the 1960s. The maintenance of a nuclear establishment on Okinawa and the visits of nuclear ships to Japanese ports provoked violent opposition. However, the Bonins were returned to Japan in 1968 and Okinawa in 1972.

The Treaty of San Francisco was not signed by Nationalist China, the People's Republic of China or the USSR. In 1952 Japan made a separate treaty with Taiwan. In 1956 the Soviet Union entered into diplomatic relations with Japan; later there were economic agreements especially concerning Japanese investment in eastern Siberia. In 1956 the USSR ceased to veto Japan's admission to UNO of which she became an active member, who showed strong opposition to nuclear arms. In 1982 a dispute over the control of two small islands off the coast of Hokkaido still held up negotiations for a peace treaty with the USSR.

Japan's close association with the USA and her treaty with Taiwan made it difficult to establish relations with the People's Republic of China, though there were trade agreements during the 1960s. In September 1972, after the PRC's admission to UNO and her improved relationship with the USA, Tanaka Kakuei, prime minister of Japan, met Chou En-lai in Peking. After almost a century of conflict, they agreed to negotiate a treaty of peace and friendship. China gave up claims for reparations and Japan expressed 'understanding and respect' for the PRC's claim to Taiwan as 'an inalienable part of her territory'. The two countries established diplomatic relations, whereupon Taiwan broke off relations with Japan.

In 1981 the USA was urging Japan to strengthen her defences, on which she was spending less than 1 per cent of her gross national product. The Russian threat also led the non-communist states of South-east Asia to urge Japan to build up her defences. (Her constitution precludes Japan only from using her forces outside the homeland.)

Korea

The division of Germany gradually won acceptance by the Germans. Not so the division of Korea. From time to time approaches have been made to enter into discussions but neither side has been willing to give way.

North Korea, lacking the resources of South Korea and with little capital assistance from other communist countries, has remained relatively poor and economically backward. South Korea, with massive aid from the United States and capital investment from Japan and South-east Asia, has become another of the economic miracles of East Asia. With the introduction of five-year plans in 1962, industries, from textiles to shipbuilding, grew rapidly. By 1969 South Korea had moved from being an aid receiving state to being able to offer aid to other countries. With an army of 600,000 and intensely anti-communist, South Korea sent 48,000 troops to help the Americans in Vietnam (see p. 313).

In 1960 what in effect was the dictatorship of Syngman Rhee in South Korea ended when popular demonstrations forced him to resign. A spell of democratic rule ended in a military coup – and that pattern has persisted. The land of the economic miracle and luxuriant valleys has not been a show piece of democracy. In 1982 Kim Il-sung still ruled in North Korea.

32 Withdrawal from empire and the post-colonial period: South and South-east Asia

India and Pakistan

Independence: 1947

Before the Second World War an approach had been made towards self-government for India (see p. 154). A new scheme put forward in 1942 was rejected by Gandhi as 'a post-dated cheque' – 'on a crashing bank'. There was renewed civil disobedience and rioting and Gandhi and Nehru found themselves for a time back in prison.

By 1945 the only question was when and how India should become independent. To Attlee's Labour government India was a moral, financial and military burden to be got rid of as soon as possible. As discussions dragged on with irreconcilable Hindus and Muslims and with the rulers of the more than 500 princely states (see p. 153), Attlee decided to cut the Gordian knot; early in 1947 he announced that Britain would withdraw from India not later than June 1948. Lord Louis Mountbatten was appointed viceroy of India with the task of detaching from the British crown 'its brightest jewel'.

Macmillan, who visited India early in 1947, said the Hindus 'seemed to hope that a way would be found to keep India both united and a loyal member of the Commonwealth'. But Mohammed Ali Jinnah of the Muslim League, he said, recognised that though 'at different times ... India had been brought into a temporary unity by force', the differences were 'too great and too deep' for there ever to be 'a real unity of the people'. Hindu-Muslim enmity admitted of only one solution – partition into two states. As for the princely states, there comes a time when even longstanding treaty obligations may have to be disowned – and for Britain that time had come in India.

As rioting between Hindus and Muslims continued, Mountbatten in June 1947 announced that independence would be granted on 15 August of that year. All that remained for Britain to do was to draw boundary lines through the Punjab and Bengal where communities of Hindus and Muslims overlapped. So on 15 August 1947 the independent states of India and Pakistan came into being. The princely states had to decide for themselves with which of the two states they would throw in their lot – though geography left them little choice. Nehru became prime minister of India. Jinnah became governor-general of Pakistan. Pakistan consisted of East Pakistan (virtually Bengal) and West Pakistan (virtually the Punjab), lying some 1,600 kilometres apart. India (1949) and Pakistan (1956) became republics within a Commonwealth that ceased to be called British.

Muslim refugees shelter in the Jamma Masjid (mosque) in Old Delhi, September 1947

In both Hindu India and Muslim Pakistan there were large religious minorities. Both states laid claim to Kashmir, which had a Hindu ruler but whose people were mostly Muslims. When its ruler decided to join India Muslim Pathans from West Pakistan invaded Kashmir. Indian troops came in from the other side. A clash was halted by a UN truce. Kashmir remained divided and a source of bitterness.

Britain's peaceful withdrawal from India was followed by an upsurge of hatred that killed half a million Hindus, Muslims and Sikhs. Over twelve million refugees fled from one state to the other. In Calcutta violence was checked by Gandhi, who threatened to fast unto death. In January 1948, on his return to Delhi where fresh violence threatened, he was assassinated by a Hindu extremist. His simple tomb in Delhi, garlanded with marigolds, symbolises the affection with which he is remembered. Gandhi, the thin old man with the *dhoti* round his loins, captured the imaginations of millions of people throughout the world.

The Republic of India

The Republic of India is a federal union. Whereas (apart from one interval) the Congress Party has retained control of central government, in some states, notably Kerala in the south-east, communists have won control. In some states central government, following disorders, has used its constitutional powers to take over.

Under Nehru full civil rights were given to women and to the untouchables; however, the position of the untouchables has remained a problem in a land where caste still controls much of life. Those princes who joined India were given pensions and their lands were absorbed into the union. A series of five-year plans resulted in considerable economic growth – but scarcely enough to keep ahead of population which increased from 360 million in 1951 to 590 million in 1975. In spite of a green revolution resulting from use of higher-yield strains of rice and wheat and greater use of fertilisers and insecticides, India's people remained among the poorest in the world as the table above suggests.

Under the leadership of Nehru (1947–64), Lal Bahadur Shastri (1964–66) and then Mrs Indira Gandhi (Nehru's daughter but no relation to Gandhi), India until 1975 retained its democratic government. This was despite an 80 per cent illiteracy rate, sixty languages and numerous religious and ethnic divisions, but aided by a relatively large educated middle class.

In 1975 Mrs Gandhi was found by a court to have

Life expectancy at birth in years

	Early 1930s		Early 1970s		Mid-1970s	
	Males	Females	Males	Females	Males	Females
Australia	63	67	69	75	70	76
Chile	40	42	61	66	61	68
France	56	62	69	76	69	77
India	32	31	42	40	54	53
Poland	48	51	67	74	67	74
UK	59	63	69	75	69	75
USA	58	61	68	76	69	77

Life expectancy is a fair indication of living standards. Thus in 1900 it was 14.6 years less for American blacks than for whites; by 1975 it was 5.3 years less. In developing countries, though it has risen greatly (early this century it was 23 in India) it is still relatively low

acted corruptly in the 1971 elections. She thereupon declared a state of emergency and imprisoned her critics. Undeterred by her smudged reputation, Mrs Gandhi then undertook a crash programme to try to overcome India's most intractable problem – pressure of people on land. Irrigation schemes, distribution of land, action against food hoarders, the founding of credit banks were put in hand. Proposals for bigger and more efficient farms threatened the independence of small landholders, whilst a programme of birth control and drastic steps towards male sterilisation provoked an outcry. In 1977 Mrs Gandhi agreed to return to constitutional government. In elections that year the conservative Janata (People's) Party was dramatically successful. But in 1980 Mrs Gandhi was back in office.

India: wars with China and Pakistan

Nehru had intended that India should follow a neutral policy in the Cold War. He was a leading figure at the Bandung conference of non-aligned states. But in time non-alignment itself became a battleground between the forces of the right and left. And uneasy relationships with the People's Republic of China and Pakistan dragged India into the arena of power politics. 'Neutralist' India's forcible occupation of Portuguese Goa in 1961 was condemned in the United Nations. In 1962 India engaged in the brief but inglorious war against China (see p. 303). In 1965 India was invaded by Pakistan, who claimed territory in the Rann of Kutch desert and continued to claim Kashmir. A brief war was ended by Russian mediation. The dispute over the Rann was submitted to arbitration but the matter of Kashmir remained unsettled. War between India and Pakistan broke out again in December 1971 (see below).

Both India and Pakistan used up resources desperately needed for economic development on armaments. India received military aid from the Soviet Union. Pakistan obtained aid from the USA. India's ties with the USSR inclined China towards Pakistan.

Pakistan and Bangladesh

Democracy was short-lived in Pakistan. Jinnah died in 1948. In 1954, when East Pakistan objected to the predominance of the Punjabi Muslim League, military rule was introduced there. In 1958 Field Marshal Ayub Khan, who had trained in Britain, at Sandhurst, claiming that democracy was unsuited to politically inexperienced people, staged a military coup in West Pakistan. Ayub Khan restored order and initiated economic development. The capital was shifted from Karachi, first to Rawalpindi and later to a new city, Islamabad.

In 1969 Ayub Khan was obliged to resign. In 1970 elections were held. The relative remoteness of East Pakistan and its acute poverty caused much discontent among the Bengalis. In West Pakistan Ali Bhutto's People's Party won a majority. In East Pakistan Sheikh Mujibur Rahman's Awami League, which wanted separation from West Pakistan, won strong support. The following year the arrest of Sheikh Mujibur Rahman resulted in civil war. Ten million refugees fled from East Pakistan to India. In December 1971 India intervened. Within two weeks the Pakistani forces in East Pakistan surrendered. With the setting up of independent Bangladesh (Bengal State) in place of East Pakistan, (West) Pakistan agreed to end hostilities. Bangladesh became a member of the Commonwealth whereupon Pakistan withdrew.

Independence did not end the problems of overpopulated Bangladesh. In 1975 Sheikh Mujibur Rahman was assassinated. A similar fate was suffered by his successor in 1981. In Pakistan an army coup in 1977 resulted in the restoration of military rule under General Zia. Bhutto was imprisoned and in 1979 was hanged.

Burma, Ceylon and Malaysia

After granting independence to India and Pakistan Britain promised independence to other peoples under her rule as soon as they had sufficient education and experience to conduct their affairs. It was essentially a matter of timing. Nationalist parties with young leaders who in most cases had been educated in Britain were eager for independence without delay. The British feared that undue haste might create unnecessary problems.

In 1948 the Labour government in Britain agreed to Burma's demand for independence forthwith. In the same year Ceylon became independent and took its old name, Sri Lanka. Burma withdrew from the Commonwealth.

In multi-racial Malaya independence was delayed by a rebellion of Chinese communist guerillas who, with British backing, had fought against the Japanese. In 1948 these Chinese communists, led by Chin Peng, OBE, rose against the British. For some years terrorist attacks threatened Malaya's security. Support for the guerillas came from some half million Chinese squatters who supplied them with food. Once the squatters were resettled in 'new villages', with facilities unknown to them before, the guerillas were like fish out of water. There was no support for them from the Malays, whose 'hearts had been won' by a promise of independence – and who had little liking for communism, especially 'Chinese' communism. By 1954 British forces, assisted by troops from other Commonwealth countries, had virtually suppressed the greatly outnumbered communists. In 1957 the Federation of Malaya achieved its *merdeka* (independence). The state of emergency formally ended in 1960.

In 1959 Singapore won internal self-government. In 1963 the Federation of Malaya, Singapore, and the Borneo territories of Sabah (North Borneo) and Sarawak fused to form the Federation of Malaysia. Until 1965 Malaysia was threatened by confrontation from Indonesia (see p. 315). The small Borneo sultanate of Brunei was independent under British protection (and was to become fully independent in January 1984).

Singapore, where Chinese outnumber the native Malays, somewhat reluctantly seceded from Malaysia in 1965. Despite its small size and exposed position it continued to thrive under the leadership of Lee Kwanyew, who, perhaps at some cost to personal liberty, gave its people many of the benefits of a welfare state.

The rich resources of Malaya were developed in large part by Chinese immigrants, whose descendants, with a considerable Indian minority, comprise a substantial proportion of the population. As in much of South-east Asia the predominance of Chinese business interests has been a problem.

Britain, who in 1963 had accepted responsibility for Malaysia's defence, in 1968 declared she would have to withdraw all her forces 'east of Suez' by 1971. In fact she helped with the defence of Malaysia until 1975. By then the only British forces in the Far East were those in Hong Kong, paid for by the colony itself, and in Brunei, paid for by the sultan.

Laos and Cambodia

The French had greater difficulty than the British in withdrawing from empire. Perhaps their humiliation in the Second World War made it harder for them to make a graceful departure. In 1954, the year of the French defeat at Dien Bien Phu (see below), Laos became independent but was troubled by the communist Pathet Lao. Cambodia, lower down the great Mekong River, also became independent in 1954. Until 1970, under the leadership of Prince Norodom Sihanouk, Cambodia maintained a precarious independence. Sihanouk denounced American, Russian and Chinese imperialism by turn, whilst frontier disputes with Laos, Thailand and both North and South Vietnam led him to thunder against them. Cultural ties with France remained strong. French archaeologists continued to care for the remarkable temples of Angkor, built by the Khmers (Cambodians) some thousand years ago, until in 1970 Cambodia was swept up in the struggle that had been going on for years in Vietnam.

Vietnam

The French retreat

In Vietnam (the former Cochin–China, Annam and Tonkin) nationalist feeling was strong. In 1930 Ho Chi Minh (an undercover name meaning Ho who enlightens), who had studied Marxism in Paris and Moscow, founded a Vietnamese communist party. In 1940 he returned to Vietnam. He founded the Vietminh (Vietnam Independence League), a nationalist party opposed to either French or Japanese rule. The Vietminh had the backing of the Allies in its struggle against the Japanese. In September 1945 Ho Chi Minh proclaimed a Democratic Republic of Vietnam in Hanoi.

In November 1946 the French ordered the Vietminh forces to leave Hanoi. When the Vietminh disobeyed, the French bombed Hanoi and Haiphong. For nearly

eight years the French fought the Vietminh in a war in which the latter adopted the guerilla tactics used by Mao in China. In 1947 France set up a puppet régime in Saigon under the 'emperor' Bao Dai. After the establishment of the communist régime in China the USA gave France financial assistance and military advice. In May 1954 the French garrison at Dien Bien Phu, established to prevent the Vietminh from infiltrating into Laos, surrendered after a fifty-five-day siege. Two months later an international conference in Geneva decided temporarily to partition Vietnam at the 17th parallel. Free national elections were to be held in 1956 with the object of uniting Vietnam. The northern zone under Ho Chi Minh was communist. South Vietnam, where French influence had been strong, was in theory democratic under the leadership of President Diem.

The French left Vietnam in 1956. Meanwhile President Eisenhower had already advanced the domino theory: 'You have a row of dominoes set up, you knock over the first one and what will happen to the last one is a certainty that it will go over very quickly.' In Saigon American advisers were assisting President Diem's government to save the South Vietnamese 'domino' from being knocked over by communism.

The Vietnam War

The Democratic Republic of Vietnam (North Vietnam) demanded national elections as envisaged at Geneva in 1954. Diem's régime, corrupt, divided, inefficient and afraid that union would result in a communist takeover – and confident of American support – rejected North Vietnam's demand. In 1960 communist partisans operating throughout the south set up the Vietcong (National Front for the Liberation of South Vietnam), which aimed to unite the country under the northern régime. Confident that national elections would prove a victory for Ho Chi Minh, the Vietcong supported the north's demand for elections. A bitter struggle between the government of South Vietnam and its Vietcong insurgents followed. The latter received increasing assistance from North Vietnam, who in turn obtained varying amounts of aid from the USSR and the People's Republic of China. However, neither Russians nor Chinese, even as volunteers, fought in the war.

South Vietnam turned for assistance to the USA who gave more and more aid and sent in more and more advisers. Attempts to settle Vietcong supporters in 'pacified hamlets' met with much less success than the settling of Chinese squatters in Malaya's 'new villages' –

'They won't get us to the conference table will they?' says Ho Chi Minh. Alive or dead Ho will not yield. Cartoon by an Australian working in the USA, May 1967

partly because the Vietnamese peasants were uprooted from ancestral villages whereas the squatters in Malaya were rootless.

In August 1964 North Vietnam engaged American warships in international waters. And it was claimed that forces from the north were crossing the 17th parallel. In President Johnson's view the Hanoi government was being egged on by Peking as 'part of a worldwide pattern of aggressive purpose'. In February 1965 the Americans began bombing North Vietnam and so the undeclared Vietnam War began.

American forces joined the struggle against the Vietcong in increasing numbers – and with little success. In an attempt to destroy the Vietcong's protective cover of jungle helicopters sprayed defoliants over large areas. The use of napalm bombs that caused horrifying burns appalled people everywhere. American intervention in Vietnam soon aroused passions around the world comparable to those provoked by the Spanish Civil War.

In the *Tet* (New Year) offensive of January 1968 the Vietcong attacked Hué and Saigon. Soon over 500,000 American servicemen, some 50,000 allies (including South Koreans, Australians and New Zealanders), as well as South Vietnamese regular forces, were engaged in the war. Peace talks in 1968 came to nothing though for a time the bombing of North Vietnam was halted. In 1969 Ho Chi Minh, Uncle Ho with the wispy beard, who had become the embodiment of Vietnamese national spirit, died.

In 1969 the new American president, Nixon, announced the 'Vietnamisation' of the war, whereby the United States, while continuing to give aid to South Vietnam, would withdraw her forces and leave the Vietnamese to fight their own battles. Gradually the Americans withdrew. Fighting went on until in January 1973 the terms of a cease-fire were agreed on in Paris. The cost in lives had been great. The cost in money too had been great – in 1966 the price of destroying a single Vietcong guerilla was estimated at about US$400,000. And the USA had dropped on Vietnam more than twice

A South Vietnamese soldier and an American soldier question a peasant whom they suspect of belonging to the Vietcong. The 'VC' guerillas of course did not wear uniform

the weight of bombs that the Allies had dropped on Germany during the Second World War.

The communist victory

Both sides violated the cease-fire agreement. More Vietnamese died, perhaps 100,000. The north built up its strength. The old Ho Chi Minh jungle trail leading down through Laos and Cambodia into South Vietnam became a concrete road. By early April 1975 North Vietnamese forces were close to Saigon. The USA took

no action beyond flying out its nationals and a number of children fathered by American servicemen.

On 30 April 1975 a North Vietnamese tank smashed its way into the presidential palace in Saigon. South Vietnam surrendered and came under communist control. In 1976 Vietnam was formally united as the Socialist Republic of Vietnam with its capital in Hanoi – and with the USSR as its friend and financier. Saigon was renamed Ho Chi Minh City. At about this time a Chinese sailor in a ship making her way through battle-scarred Suez was seen using a flag as a paint rag. 'South

Vietnam flag. Finish South Vietnam', he said. But there was trauma yet to come, when the harsh policies of the communists caused tens of thousands of Vietnamese, mostly of Chinese origin, to flee their country in unseaworthy boats. How many of these 'boat people' perished in the attempt is unknown. And the flight of refugees across the border into China provoked a brief war between the People's Republic and Vietnam (1979). China remained unfriendly to the Russian-subsidised Vietnamese régime and its puppet, Kampuchea.

Kampuchea (Cambodia)

About the time Saigon fell Laos came under communist control. Cambodia, under the anti-communist Lon Nol, who had driven Norodom Sihanouk out in 1970, had since 1974 been under attack from the communist Khmer Rouge, which then had the support of China and North Vietnam. In April 1975, just before Saigon fell, the Khmer Rouge captured Phnom Penh, capital of Cambodia. Kampuchea, as Cambodia then became, after suffering under Lon Nol, suffered appalling atrocities as Pol Pot, the brutal Khmer Rouge leader, set about establishing a communist society. Most of the inhabitants of Phnom Penh and other towns were driven into the countryside. More than a million died or were killed. Early in 1979 Vietnamese forces drove out the Khmer Rouge and a government subservient to Hanoi was set up. 'Thanks to the tenacity of its inhabitants and to massive international aid' Kampuchea made a remarkable recovery. The pollution and the number of traffic accidents in Phnom Penh in 1981 were proof, it was said, that Kampuchea had 'returned to civilisation'. Sihanouk, who in a genuine attempt to preserve independence and to better his people had played off the two power blocs against one another, remained in eclipse, in the People's Republic of China.

Independence for Indonesia

In general the Dutch had exploited the Netherlands East Indies until in the late nineteenth century, under the ethical policy, various concessions were made. Serious stirrings of nationalism were apparent early in this century. In 1927–28 a young engineer, Achmed Sukarno, founded an Indonesian Nationalist Party which won much support. The nationalists were severely repressed. To speak of *merdeka* (independence) or to use the name Indonesia was dangerous. Sukarno spent the years 1933 to 1942, when the Japanese invaded the Netherlands East Indies, in exile. National spirit was encouraged by the Dutch failure to resist Japan's onslaught and by Japanese propaganda stressing that Asians must rule Asia – and by the harshness of the Japanese.

'We have been here for three hundred years; we shall remain here for another three hundred years. After that we can talk with the nationalists', the Dutch governor-general had said before the war against Japan began. But two days after the war ended Sukarno proclaimed the establishment of the Republic of Indonesia. The Dutch fought fiercely to recover control. Various compromises they suggested were rejected by the nationalists. In 1949 the UN security council called on the Dutch to recognise Indonesia's independence. Later that year the Netherlands transferred sovereignty over the East Indies to Indonesia. Batavia, the capital, was renamed Jakarta. In 1950 the Republic of Indonesia was admitted to UNO. Indonesia's claim to Dutch New Guinea complicated relations with the Netherlands. In 1963 Holland yielded control of Irian Jaya (Great Irian, the former Dutch New Guinea) to Indonesia, whose rule was confirmed by popular vote.

Sukarno, first president of Indonesia, took control into his own hands and in 1957 introduced 'guided democracy'. To him parliamentary democracy was 'fifty per cent-plus democracy' and 'free fight liberalism'. On the other hand, he said, 'Since ancient times we have flatly rejected dictatorships.' Guided democracy was not unlike the democratorship of Latin America.

Resources were wasted on palaces, giant statues, a mosque that was to be the biggest in the world, armaments. Hopes of economic progress were dashed. The loss of Dutch technical skill and finance was a handicap. As the economy declined and disorder grew Sukarno turned to the communists for support. He stressed the need for the new emerging forces of the world to resist 'the old established order'. In 1955 he had convened the Bandung conference (see p. 248) with this in mind.

After the creation of Malaysia in 1963 Sukarno attempted to crush the new federation, many of whose people were akin to the Indonesians and some at least of whose territory he coveted. The humiliating failure of Indonesia's armed infiltration into Malaysia provoked further discontent. Indonesia temporarily withdrew from UNO.

Monument to six Indonesian generals slaughtered in the coup of 1965. Bloody reprisals against the communists followed. The feathers of the national eagle – breast 17, head 8, wings 45 – symbolise the date on which Indonesia's independence was declared, 17 August 1945

In 1965 a communist-supported coup, of which Sukarno was almost certainly aware, was frustrated by General Suharto. Sukarno was eased from power and in 1966 Suharto became president. Gradually order was restored and elections were held in 1971. Portuguese (East) Timor became independent in 1975 and after some struggle became part of Indonesia.

The Republic of Indonesia is the world's fifth most populous nation. Regional tendencies have been apparent, especially in the Moluccas (see p. 327). However, to a surprising degree this archipelago, with its ethnic, religious and linguistic diversity, has achieved the motto on the republic's coat of arms – 'Bhinneka Tunggal Ika' (Unity in Diversity). The spread of a national tongue, *Bahasa* (language) *Indonesia*, has done much to weld the people together. But consciousness of nationhood among these peoples is largely the result of unified rule under the Dutch.

The Philippines

On 4 July 1946 the USA gave the Philippines their promised independence. Military bases were retained

and a defensive alliance made. For a time communist Huks, who had fought an underground war against the Japanese, carried on a rebellion in northern Luzon. In 1955 Magsaysay, who had fought as a guerilla against the Japanese, became president. His land reforms to some extent cut the ground from under the Huks' feet. By about 1956 the Huks had been driven underground. In the 1970s the southern islands were troubled by revolts by the Moros (Muslims), a minority group among the Christian Filipinos. Continuing poverty and lawlessness gave Marcos, elected president in 1965, an excuse for imposing martial law (1972–81). It was in the Philippines, in the 1960s, that scientists developed a high-yield strain of rice, with important results for agriculture in Asia.

Thailand

During the Second World War Thailand had little choice but to fall in with the Japanese. After 1945 it remained a constitutional monarchy – with the generals from time to time taking an active part in affairs. It prospered but was troubled by a communist minority in the north and earlier by Chinese communist infiltrators from Malaya. And being the next domino but one from Vietnam it kept a watchful eye on its eastern frontier. In 1979, when Vietnam took control of Kampuchea, Thailand was invaded by hordes of refugees and by the remnant of the Khmer Rouge army. The Khmer Rouge, with Chinese backing, persisted in using Thailand as a base for operations against their homeland.

The Association of South-east Asian Nations (ASEAN)

The long struggle in Vietnam gave other states in South-east Asia a breathing space in which to develop politically and economically. When Vietnam (and Laos and Cambodia) did fall under communist control the other dominoes seemed less likely to be knocked over than they had been in the 1950s. Meanwhile the threat of communism had drawn them closer together. As the South-east Asian Treaty Organisation, the creation of Dulles, began to fall apart the formation of the Association of South-east Asian Nations (1967) reflected their awareness of common interests in political and economic affairs.

33 Africa: decolonisation

The dissolution of the British empire in Africa

New classes, new ideas

After the First World War educational opportunities for Africans, limited though they were, resulted in the growth of a middle class of lawyers, journalists, teachers and so on. A lower middle class of clerks and skilled workers also emerged. Newspapers and trade unions began introducing new ideas to such educated Africans. In 1923 elections were held in Nigeria and Sierra Leone and two years later in the Gold Coast. So middle-class Africans had an opportunity to look for positions of limited authority within the colonial framework. In 1929 the first act providing financial support for colonial development was passed at Westminster. But with the onset of the world depression there was little enthusiasm or money for such development.

The Second World War speeded change. Africans who served in the armed forces came back with new ideas. They no longer regarded Europeans with awe. A Nigerian volunteer wrote: 'We overseas soldiers are coming back home with new ideas. . . . We have been told what we fought for . . . "freedom". We want freedom nothing but freedom. . . . ' Industry grew rapidly and with it towns and an urban proletariat. Post-war Britain, dependent for reconstruction on American aid, could not ignore American opposition to the continuance of colonial empires. And the United Nations Organisation was a much stronger force against colonialism than the League of Nations; its members increasingly aimed at ending rather than reforming the colonial system. The British themselves wanted peace, social security and prosperity – not empire. And Britain no longer had the financial and military power needed to maintain an immense empire.

The Manchester Pan-African congress, 1945

In 1945 a Pan-African congress was held in Manchester. Organised by Kwame Nkrumah of the Gold Coast, it was attended by such leaders as Jomo (Burning Spear) Kenyatta from Kenya, as well as French Africans and English socialists. A mass movement of the people, not just of the middle class, against colonialism became the aim of the African leaders. There was also opposition to the authority of tribal chiefs. Nkrumah and others looked forward to a close association between African states after their independence.

Soon after the Manchester congress the British government gave new constitutions to the Gold Coast and to Nigeria. However, most of the representatives in the councils then set up were to be nominated, either by the British or by the chiefs. In Nigeria a general strike was called to oppose the constitution and in support of universal suffrage.

The Gold Coast (Ghana) paves the way

In the Gold Coast Nkrumah led a people's party which had trade union support. Constitutional reforms introduced by Britain's Labour government in 1949 were met by demands for full self-government and dominion status. There was also opposition to the chiefs who were to keep their privileged positions under the new scheme. In 1950 Nkrumah led a campaign of non-violent resistance or, as he called it, 'positive action'. He and other leaders were imprisoned. But in elections held in 1951, under the 1949 constitution, Nkrumah's party won 34 out of the 38 elected seats. (Another 37 members were elected indirectly through chieftainship councils.)

After these elections Nkrumah was released from prison. He and the British governor, Sir Charles Arden-Clarke, co-operated in establishing responsible government. In 1952 Nkrumah became prime minister, but Britain kept control of internal security, defence and foreign affairs. The next year Nkrumah asked for responsible government based on direct elections and universal suffrage, to be followed by full independence. The British government, by then under the control of the Conservatives, did not oppose this.

In 1954 Nkrumah's party won 72 out of 104 seats. Muslim and tribal groups won little support. However, as there was a strong movement among the Ashanti of the north to have their own government, a new constitution provided for regional assemblies to deal

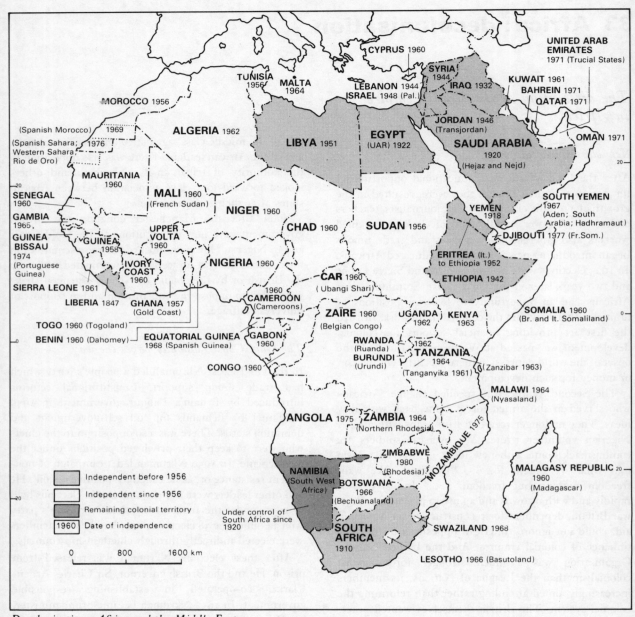

Decolonisation: Africa and the Middle East

with local affairs. In elections in 1956 Nkrumah's party again won 72 seats. When the new legislature called for full independence the British announced that on 6 March 1957 the new state of Ghana would come into existence. This was a victory for the whole of colonial Africa. 'The traditional mask of Africa was cracked.' Ghana became a republic within the Commonwealth of Nations.

Ghana's independence came soon after the Suez crisis (see p. 331) when many people in Britain and France showed active opposition to imperialist policies. Nationalist leaders in Africa were quick to realise that Britain would no longer seriously oppose their demands.

Nigeria

In the early post-war years only in the west of Nigeria was there a middle class pressing for reforms. But in

March 1957, the month Ghana became independent, a unanimous vote in the federal legislature demanded independence. Regional leaders, working out a new constitution, seemed willing to forget their rivalries. In October 1960 Nigeria, Britain's largest African colony with a population of well over fifty million, became independent. The constitution provided for universal suffrage, though for the time being women in the Islamic north were not to have the vote.

Regional influences remained strong. In 1967 civil war broke out between the central authority, dominated by the Hausa tribe, and the breakaway coastal state of Biafra, where the Ibo tribe were the majority. A long and bloody war brought bitter suffering, especially for the Biafrans. With the war came famine. There were times when thousands of people died of starvation in a single day. In 1970 the Biafrans yielded and Biafra remained part of Nigeria. However, General Gowon, president and leader of the federal army, acted with generosity towards the Ibo and restored a large degree of national unity.

East Africa

In East Africa, where there had been little higher education, the people were 'ignorant of events in the next village, more ignorant of the rest of the continent'. However, the granting of large areas of fertile land to Europeans, especially in Kenya, aroused hostility and a sense of nationalism among the Africans. (In the mandated (later trust) territory of Tanganyika the granting of land to Europeans was not allowed.) With better medical services the population was increasing; this led to growing pressure on land. The example of Ethiopia, who recovered her independence during the Second World War, was felt throughout East Africa. And many East Africans had served as soldiers during the war.

Tanganyika, where the UN trusteeship council pressed for more rapid political development, became independent in 1961 and in 1964 joined Zanzibar, independent from 1963, to form Tanzania. Uganda, despite a leadership which was afraid of power going to the people, became independent in 1962.

In Kenya, where the white settlers obstructed political advance, there were serious difficulties. Kenyatta, who had studied in London and Moscow and was principal of a teacher training college, became the popular leader. In 1950 members of the Mau Mau, a secret society, began making terrorist attacks on

Europeans and their property. Kenyatta, himself a Mau Mau leader, and other leaders were arrested. For several years there was civil war too. British troops were sent to Kenya. The Kikuyu tribe, from whom the Mau Mau came, suffered most severely. The cost in lives and material made the British increasingly determined not to support minority white rule in Kenya or anywhere else (for example in Rhodesia).

By 1956 the worst of the violence was over. Meanwhile, discussions about Kenya's future government had begun. By 1958 Africans and Europeans had an equal number of unofficial members in the legislative council. The following year Kenyatta was released from prison. The next year, at a conference in London, the principle of majority African rule was firmly established. In 1963 Kenya became independent with Kenyatta as president. Kenyatta was careful to reconcile the white settlers as well as the minority tribes that had often threatened to split national unity, but he treated the large Indian community harshly.

In February 1960, a few months before Nigeria became independent, Macmillan on a visit to Cape Town said: 'A wind of change is blowing through this continent.' The wind of change blew ever stronger, in Africa and throughout the world. One after another colonies advanced towards independence. On the whole there was little violence. The terrorism that preceded departure from Kenya – and from Cyprus and Aden (the Republic of South Yemen) – was exceptional. Acts passed at Westminster gave constitutional and democratic rule to the new states, most of which became republics. In every case a member of the British royal family took part in the ceremonies celebrating independence. Most of the new states remained members of the Commonwealth of Nations, which by October 1981 numbered forty-one members and included a quarter of the world's population. And as fast as the new nations came tumbling out of the British empire they were admitted to UNO.

Zimbabwe

The exception to speedy decolonisation among the British territories was Southern Rhodesia. In 1923 the 23,000 whites living there had been given virtual self-government, whilst the 1,500,000 Africans had no political rights. In 1964 Zambia (Northern Rhodesia), where only a few whites lived, became independent. But independence was not granted to Southern Rhodesia (later known simply as Rhodesia) because the substantial

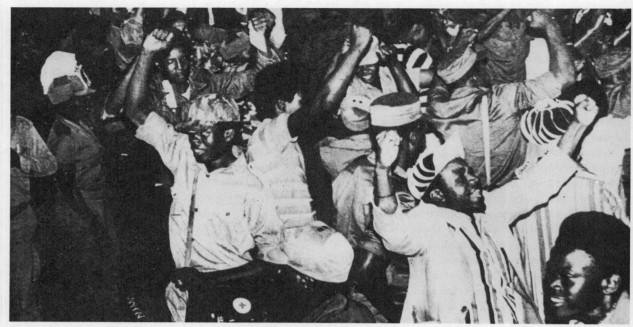

Zimbabwe, April 1980: jubilation in Harare (Salisbury) following the ceremony on Independence Day

white minority refused to accept terms which Britain regarded as essential to the interests of the African majority.

In 1965 Rhodesia made a unilateral and therefore illegal declaration of independence (UDI) and technically at least was in rebellion against Britain. The United Nations imposed economic sanctions against Rhodesia. With the help of South Africa Rhodesia carried on in spite of sanctions. In 1969 the white minority in a referendum voted to establish a republic outside the Commonwealth.

Successive British leaders unsuccessfully negotiated with the Rhodesian 'government' to establish an acceptable legal government. African nationalists began a guerilla campaign against the whites. Murders and massacres of white farmers and of missionaries in isolated areas led to retaliation and repression by the Rhodesian police and army.

In 1978, as the guerilla war intensified and international pressure increased and after African rule had been established in Mozambique and Angola (see p. 323), Ian Smith, the Rhodesian prime minister, came to an agreement with some of the nationalist leaders. By this agreement majority rule was to be established within a year.

Following elections held in 1979 Bishop Abel Muzorewa became Rhodesia's first African prime minister. But Robert Mugabe and Joshua Nkomo, who by then controlled large guerilla armies in Zambia and Angola, claimed the elections had been a fraud – as did the leaders of other African states. Nor were Britain and the USA satisfied and the United Nations economic sanctions remained in force. As the guerilla campaigns continued white settlers began leaving the country. In the autumn of 1979 Smith, Muzorewa, Mugabe and Nkomo were persuaded to attend a conference in London. Agreement was at last reached. For a few months British rule was restored in Rhodesia with Lord Soames as governor. Guerilla units emerged from the bush and entered camps controlled by British soldiers. In elections supervised by British officials Mugabe won a clear majority. In April 1980 the new state of Zimbabwe was formally declared independent, with Robert Mugabe as its first prime minister.

Withdrawal from the Belgian Congo

In 1945 the Belgians expected it would take thirty or forty years for the Congo to be ready for independence. They assisted economic development and provided social services but did not allow political activity. Meanwhile, across the Congo River political advance in French Equatorial Africa was rapid.

1962: an Indian of the Rajput Rifles, part of the ONU (UN) force in the Congo guards refugees at Elizabethville

In 1958, following a fall in copper prices, there was much unemployment. In 1959 there was rioting in Léopoldville (Kinshasa). Thereafter Belgium 'rushed headlong and panic stricken into abdication of all responsibility for the consequences of her previous policy'. However, she promised to give administrative, military and educational aid when the Congo became independent. Independence came in June 1960. In a population of about fifteen million there were fifteen graduates. However, 42 per cent of the population was literate, an unusually high proportion for Africa then.

Before long the territory administered by Belgium in 6 provinces broke up into 21 provinces, in which 224 parties fought for power. The copper-rich Katanga in the south, led by Moise Tshombe, attempted to secede almost as soon as independence was granted. The confused civil wars that followed were made worse by the entry of white mercenary adventurer soldiers and by the ambitions of tribal leaders. Thousands of warriors went into battle believing that the magic amulets they wore protected them against bullets. When charms proved of no avail, there were savage witch hunts – it was witches, people said, not bullets, that had 'eaten their men'. Brutality, chaos and threatened bankruptcy ended after the arrival of a UN peace-keeping force. By 1964 order had been sufficiently restored for this force to be withdrawn.

In 1965 Joseph Mobutu, 'The Saviour', came to power. As head of state, head of government, commander in chief, and head of the only political party allowed, Mobutu seemed able to check the divisive forces of tribalism. In 1971 the Congo was renamed Zaïre.

The dissolution of the French empire in Africa

North Africa

After an agreement made in 1954, at the time of their defeat in Indo-China, the French withdrew without serious conflict from Morocco and Tunisia in 1956. In 1957 Tunisia became a republic.

In Algeria – where more than 10 per cent of the population were French settlers, the *colons* – there was a bitter struggle. In 1954 Ahmed Ben Bella's National Liberation Front (NLF) revolted against French rule. Eventually 500,000 French troops were engaged in what became the Algerian War. Various concessions and compromises proved unacceptable to the NLF. On the other hand French interest in Algeria increased with the discovery of oil and natural gas in the Sahara. When de Gaulle came to power in 1958 he promised to settle the conflict on terms favourable to the French settlers. But though the French were strong enough not to be defeated by the Algerian nationalists they were not strong enough to win the war. Yet French generals, in part perhaps because of humiliating losses in the Second World War and Indo-China, were determined to support the *colons*. On three occasions generals tried to take over the government of Algeria in order to preserve French rule, but were frustrated by the loyalty of their troops to the government in Paris. The OAS (*Organisation de l'Armée Secrète*), formed by diehard *colons*, committed atrocities against the Muslims in Algeria – to which the latter responded with further atrocities.

Eventually the French had to agree that Algeria should be independent and in July 1962 Ben Bella, released from prison, became head of the republic. A quarter of a million lives – Algerian, French, civilians and soldiers – had been lost. Many settlers fled to the south of France, where they created serious social and economic problems.

West and Equatorial Africa

Each British colony, advancing at its own speed, obtained independence on its own. France treated her colonies in West and Equatorial Africa as a group.

The professed aim of French colonial policy had always been assimilation: all people in the colonies were to be French citizens. However, educational development was rather slow. In 1945, when the leaders of France's African colonies met in Paris, they asked only for a closer union with France. In 1946 these leaders helped to draw up the constitution of the Fourth Republic which gave 26 of the 622 seats in the French National Assembly to the African territories of the French Union. The constitution also set up local assemblies in the African colonies.

After 1946 France gave the colonies more money for education and economic development. Political parties were organised. Trade unions were active. But no French government was strong enough or lasted long enough to give much attention to colonial affairs. In these circumstances two Africans, Félix Houphouet-Boigny of the Ivory Coast and Léopold Senghor of Senegal, played a leading part in events. Houphouet-Boigny was a doctor and a descendant of a chieftain. Both he and Senghor had ties with the trade unions. Senghor set out to win tribal support and to include peasants in the unions.

Under the guidance of Houphouet-Boigny, who had become a member of the French cabinet, the local assemblies set up by the 1946 constitution became almost fully responsible governments. All citizens, even women in Muslim areas, had the right to vote for these assemblies. Meanwhile, the colonies continued to elect their quota of representatives to the French National Assembly.

After the establishment of the Fifth Republic in 1958 the formation of a French community in which the territories in Africa would be equal members with France was decided on. Each territory was to decide by referendum whether it would become independent or join the French community.

In 1958 French Guinea, led by Sékou Touré, was enjoying a mining boom and could afford to 'go it alone'. When she rejected the French community France abandoned her. There was a sudden end to economic aid and a mass withdrawal of French officials – who took with them their files, their office furniture and even their electric light bulbs. Ghana offered Guinea some assistance. Aid also came from China. Independent Guinea soon became a member of UNO.

The other colonies in 1958 voted to join the French community. But in 1960, influenced by the examples of Guinea and Ghana, they exercised their right, after referendums, to become independent states. France did not treat them as she had treated Guinea. She made agreements with them on defence, economic aid and cultural contacts.. Tribal influences remained strong, especially in Equatorial Africa where large French territories fragmented to form a number of new states. More than once French forces were called in to suppress tribal conflicts.

Spain and Portugal: first to come, last to go

In Africa Spain and Portugal, first to come, were the last to give independence to their territories. Spain gave up her zone of Morocco in 1969 and after Franco's death withdrew from Spanish (Western) Sahara (Rio de Oro), which in 1976 was divided between Morocco and Mauritania. Morocco and Mauritania then fought over the division of the spoils. When Mauritania gave up the struggle (1979) Libya and Algeria backed rebels trying to set up an independent Saharan republic.

For some years after independence had come to most of Africa Portugal continued to encourage large-scale immigration into Angola and Mozambique. In both territories she faced prolonged nationalist resistance – and as a result spent some 40 per cent of her budget on the armed forces in the 1960s. In April 1974 the new government of Portugal (see p. 288) announced plans to give independence to African possessions. Portuguese Guinea (Guinea-Bissau), where for some ten years there had been savage fighting against the Portuguese and among rival tribes, became independent in 1974. Angola and Mozambique became independent in 1975. In Angola fighting between the Popular Movement for the Liberation of Angola (MPLA) and the National Union for Complete Independence of Angola (UNITA) was halted only with the intervention of Cuban troops sent to support the former. An MPLA government was set up, but in 1982 the Cubans were still assisting the MPLA in a struggle with UNITA, which had South African backing. Cuban intervention, as elsewhere in Africa, was financed by the USSR.

South Africa

In 1983 only the Republic of South Africa (formerly the Union of South Africa) and Namibia (formerly South-west Africa) remained under white minority rule.

The Bantu, Africans who form some 80 per cent of the population of South Africa, from the outset had had only the most limited political and social freedom. Only in the Cape did any Africans have even the most limited voting rights and in time even these rights were withdrawn. Throughout South Africa the Africans were discriminated against. They were supposed to live only in the native reserves that comprised a small fraction of the country and in general were the least productive areas. In fact large numbers of blacks remained settled or squatted in areas reserved for whites. Africans were kept out of the better jobs. For example in the mines skilled work was not available to them. Their wages were low. They had limited educational opportunities.

By comparison with the Afrikaners (Boers), the English-speaking whites of South Africa were relatively liberal. After 1948, when their National Party came to power, hard-line Afrikaners outvoted less illiberal whites. The National Party set out to enforce a policy of strict racial separation, apartheid. At its best apartheid means separate development – living apart, being educated apart, even praying apart. Apartheid has its origins in the Afrikaners' conviction that the non-whites are an inferior race. There is the fear too of being swamped by the Bantu, a fear that has increased with the growth of a black proletariat, increased too as black majority rule has come to South Africa's neighbours. And in the view of the Afrikaners, as of their Boer ancestors, South Africa is their homeland, where their forefathers were settled before the Bantu moved in.

Under the National Party marriage or any sexual relationship between blacks and whites was made a crime. Blacks and whites were not permitted to attend the same schools and universities. The restriction of blacks to the reserves and 'separate locations' was rigidly enforced. From 1963 large numbers of Africans were forcibly transferred to their reserves. Pass (identity) cards, required to be carried at all times, enabled the police to enforce such restrictions. In recent years some of the reserves have become nominally independent Bantustans (Bantu states), with their own elected governments controlling domestic affairs. When in 1976 the Transkei became the first Bantustan, South African propaganda claimed that 'Westminster had come' to the Transkei capital. But the people of these poor and overcrowded Bantu 'states' rely on white South Africa to provide them with opportunities for a better living than they can scratch out from their 'homelands' So, despite the low wages offered, many blacks leave their Bantustans to work away from their families and are classified as migrants.

For a time black opposition to apartheid was a non-violent 'defiance'. In 1960 an outburst of anger by blacks at Sharpeville resulted in police opening fire. Sixty-seven Africans were killed and many were injured. Repression followed. The minister of justice, armed with special powers for suppressing opposition, whether by liberal whites or by blacks, armed too with the right to keep suspects in prison indefinitely, set out to crush all resistance, all protests, against apartheid. In 1963 nationalist leaders accused of treason were given heavy sentences.

In 1976 young people at Soweto demonstrated against a regulation that 50 per cent of their schooling should be in the Afrikaans language. Again the police opened fire. A number of children was killed. During disturbances in the following months some 500 blacks were killed. As before, other opponents of apartheid found themselves in prison, under house arrest, in exile or similarly silenced. In Cape Town harbour Robben Island hides away its political prisoners. No one has ever escaped from Robben Island.

Sporadic strikes, acts of violence, activities of various black organisations and expressions of indignation by white bishops, journalists, teachers and others failed to loosen to any great extent the bonds of apartheid. So too did international pressure. In 1961, when other Commonwealth members condemned apartheid, the Union of South Africa withdrew from the Commonwealth and became the Republic of South Africa. In 1963 UNO placed an arms embargo on South Africa but France, West Germany and later Britain and others ignored this. From its formation in 1963 the Organisation for African Unity exercised its influence against apartheid – without effect.

Some African states, for example Zambia which depends on South African railways for the export of much of its copper, have found it to their advantage to co-exist with the Republic of South Africa. Perhaps the most serious threat to the survival of apartheid has been the changed status of South Africa's neighbours. When black majority rule came to Angola, Mozambique and finally Zimbabwe, South Africa was left isolated.

In recent years there has been some inclination by the whites of South Africa to compromise. The 50 per cent rule has been abolished in schools and the enforcement of apartheid in sport and public amenities has been relaxed. While the black majority remain very poor they are better off than their fellows in many parts of Africa. Their lives are perhaps not as miserable as extreme propagandists make out. Under certain African rulers life for the blacks has been far harsher, far more insecure, than in South Africa.

Meanwhile the boom in the demand for gold has brought South Africa great riches. On the backs of cheap black labour and with abundant international investment she has become industrially highly developed and militarily well armed.

Namibia

Namibia is rich in uranium and other minerals. In 1950, in defiance of the United Nations, it was made virtually a part of the Union of South Africa, which had held it since 1920 as a mandate and later as a trust territory. After 1950 apartheid was extended to Namibia. In 1971 the International Court of Justice advised the UN security council that South Africa should end her illegal occupation of the territory. Under continued pressure from UNO, from the Organisation for African Unity, from the USA, Britain and the other west European powers, South Africa eventually agreed to give independence to Namibia when appropriate arrangements

could be made. In 1978, after elections held under South African supervision, Namibia gained partial independence. A moderate multi-racial party won most of the seats and set about dismantling apartheid. Progress towards independence was delayed by the attempts of the South-west African People's Organisation (SWAPO) to get control of the country. SWAPO's members mostly belong to the Ovambo tribe which makes up 45 per cent of Namibia's population and is much feared by smaller tribes. Recognised by UNO, financed by the Soviet Union and backed by Angola, from whose territory it operated, SWAPO had refused to take part in the 1978 elections and carried on a Rhodesian-style guerilla war. With the Cubans in effective control of Angola, South Africa in 1980 was, perhaps naturally, in no hurry to grant full independence to Namibia. Nor were Namibia's 100,000 whites eager to go beyond the halfway position arrived at in 1978.

The Organisation for African Unity

African nationalism was accompanied by a Pan-African movement. Nkrumah was the first to work for the linking of the African states into larger groups. Such leaders as Kenyatta, Senghor and Sékou Touré also supported unity. They wanted to strengthen Africa's voice in world affairs – and to prevent the super-powers from taking advantage of the weakness of their new states.

In 1958 nine states attended a Conference of Independent African States in Ghana. When the Conference of Independent African States met two years later there were five new members. At this meeting Nkrumah proposed the formation of a union with a central governing body. Nigerian leaders wanted a more gradual approach to a looser association. In 1963 more than thirty heads of state attended a Pan-African conference in Addis Ababa. There they agreed to form the Organisation for African Unity (OAU). Since 1963 the OAU has met yearly. In 1981 it had fifty members.

In 1963 the African leaders agreed that the OAU should settle all inter-African disputes. They also agreed to press for the ending of colonial rule. After most other African states had won independence the OAU took up the cause of Angola and Mozambique. White minority rule in Rhodesia was another target for the OAU. South Africa, and its control of Namibia, have for many years been attacked, with demands for sanctions and so on in

African leaders attend a 'little summit' at Nairobi, December 1966. Emperor Haile Selassie is third from the left. Fifth from the left stands Jomo Kenyatta of Kenya. In uniform is President Mobutu of Zaïre. On his left are Julius Nyerere of Tanzania, Dr Obote of Uganda and Kenneth Kaunda of Zambia.

NO. Whether the organisation will remain united if white minority rule in South Africa should cease to provide it with a target cannot be foreseen. The OAU has not been able to stop nationalist struggles in the Horn of Africa and in the western Sahara. Nor has it prevented Cuban intervention in Ethiopia and Angola, or Libyan intervention in Chad with its threat to the Sudan.

Africa after decolonisation

In Africa as in Asia and elsewhere independence did not bring with it an ideal society. Indeed it created new problems.

National spirit enabled leaders to win popular support in the struggle for independence. After independence nationalism sometimes provoked frontier conflicts as for example between Morocco and Mauritania. More often tribal spirit has created conflict within states where numerous hostile tribes found themselves part of a new 'national' state. Tribal loyalties sometimes emerged in the guise of political parties. There was a tendency towards one party, despotic or even brutal rule by the dominant tribe. In Ghana Nkrumah's one party rule did much harm. He was as ready to imprison his opponents without trial as the British had been to imprison him – but whereas he was released many of his critics died in prison. On the other hand the one party rule of Julius Nyerere in Tanzania was equitable. Leaders sometimes deliberately aroused tribal passions in an effort to win personal power or to settle old rivalries. Thus in Uganda Idi Amin in 1971 overthrew President Milton Obote, who was of another tribe. Amin maintained power by a barbaric despotism until 1979 when a Tanzanian army restored Obote.

In some cases power has remained with the representatives of traditional authority. Younger, more urban groups, often connected with the trade union movement, have tended to clash with such tribal or in some cases Islamic authorities. The leaders of the new professional armies have in many cases imposed their wills on their independent but divided states – to restore order or national unity or merely for the sake of power. Coups and assassinations have troubled many states. Benin (Dahomey) in its first twelve years of independence had five military coups, ten failed coups, twelve governments and six constitutions.

Ethiopia, March 1983: forced from their farms by drought these people wait for food provided by the UN-FAO World Food Programme. Without such help many Africans would starve. The drought affected over three million people

Racialism has not been confined to South Africa. The large Indian minority in Kenya, mostly traders and artisans, was harshly treated after independence. In 1972 Amin expelled most of the Indians settled in Uganda.

There has been much talk of democracy in Africa. A prime minister of Burma once described democracy as 'freedom to do as one pleases – subject to the legitimate rights and interests of others'. Democracy, he said, therefore requires 'self-restraint, tolerance and forbearance – three virtues with which unfortunately human nature is not richly endowed'. In the absence of these virtues, in Africa as elsewhere, the stronger have often allowed the weaker to go to the wall and have gravely abused personal freedom.

Nkrumah, before independence, said: '[We must] make the Gold Coast a paradise so that when the gates [of heaven] are opened by [Saint] Peter we shall sit in heaven and see our children driving their aeroplanes, commanding their own armies. . . . ' Aeroplanes are piloted by Africans, there are national armies – but large parts of Africa are far from paradise. If some Africans are healthier, freer and better off than before, for many life is no better than it was under foreign rule. Western medicine, bringing a falling death rate and a rapidly expanding population, seemed to add to problems.

Where popular parties were strong there was an inclination towards socialism. In general the states that wanted socialism wanted African socialism, Arab socialism, adjusted to their own ways and traditions – not Russian or Chinese communism. But foreign capital was essential to development. The communist states promised much but mostly did little and, especially in the case of the USSR, aid was tied to political and military concessions. Chinese aid, which in the 1960s seemed aimed at provoking revolution, in the 1970s seemed more disinterested. The newly independent states often had to look for aid to the capitalist states, as often as not to their former colonial rulers. Aid has also been given by the European Development Fund and by the European Bank. The United Nations Economic Commission for Africa has tried to encourage regional development, cutting across artificially formed frontiers that were a legacy of colonialism. Much of the aid has been wasted on party funds, even on such luxuries as ivory beds for party leaders, whilst others starved.

Price fluctuations on the world market for the cash crops and minerals on which much of Africa depends have left many economies dangerously vulnerable. For others heaven itself seems to have provided. The discovery of oil changed Nigeria's economy to a degree

hat generations of planning might not have done. In Libya oil seemed to arouse an aggressive nationalism under the despotic rule of Colonel Gadafi.

Despite many difficulties independence has seen some at least of the new states change from static, backward societies into progressive, modern states. For at least some people it has brought new opportunities in education, industry, cultural life and indeed in world affairs. If many others have suffered from authoritarian rule, sometimes of the most brutal kind, from tribal conflicts and frontier disputes, and from continuing poverty, independent Africa has a new dignity. Most Africans would perhaps agree with Nkrumah who said: 'We prefer self-government with danger to servitude in tranquillity.'

The effects of decolonisation on the western powers

Undoubtedly the stature of such states as Britain and France was reduced by the loss of their empires. In the power vacuum created by decolonisation in Africa, as in Asia and elsewhere, the USSR and the USA have competed for the support of newly established states. The USSR in particular has made use of former colonial territories for her own purposes. Some new states have tried to play off one super-power against the other. But a number of third-world states have stood aside from the Cold War.

It is doubtful whether the economies of the colonial powers suffered much on account of their loss of empires. International trade has perhaps flowed more freely since decolonisation. The great international companies – manufacturing cars or chemicals, soft drinks or soap powders – have their own empires that extend around the globe. Europe's century has ended but western Europe remains economically powerful. And if the citizens of the imperial powers had opportunities of employment in colonial territories, nowadays opportunities arise in business, engineering, teaching and other professions throughout the world. For 'westernisation' – modern education, medicine and transport, industrial growth, higher living standards – has become the goal of the entire developing world. 'The whole world aspires to European things – clothes and constitutions, cars and social services.' From the glittering shops of Rio de Janeiro to small stalls in Borneo the young and not-so-young buy their blue jeans and discs – and *Startrek* provides entertainment in places far removed from Britain and the USA.

There has been considerable migration from former colonies to western Europe. Britain today is a multi-cultural state. Much the same is true of France. To Holland there came many Indonesians. These migrants brought with them professional and other skills. On the other hand their arrival has strained the social services of the countries to which they have come. And immigration has resulted in serious racial tensions not only in Britain. In some cases immigrants have brought their social and political problems with them – and so disturbed their new homelands. For example, in Holland, South Moluccans aiming at the separation of the Moluccas from Indonesia held a school and a train full of passengers to ransom (1977) in an attempt to force the Dutch to take up their cause.

The former imperial powers have maintained connections of various kinds with the territories they ruled. Thus France's former colonies were given associate membership of the EEC. When Britain joined the EEC her former colonies had the opportunity to become associate members. In 1975 forty-six African, Caribbean and Pacific states signed the Lomé Convention which gave them a valuable connection with the EEC. The Commonwealth of Nations offers its members (including Britain herself) various benefits, especially in education and training.

Since decolonisation expensive commitments to the defence of overseas territories have been reduced to a minimum. In the case of Britain reduction of military forces elsewhere has enabled her to keep substantial forces in West Germany.

In some cases the language of the former colonial power has continued to be used, thus enabling people divided by different tongues to communicate with one another. And there has been a worldwide increase in the use of English. English language instruction is an export that earns considerable revenue for Britain, once the mother of empires.

An important result of decolonisation has been the rapid increase in membership of the United Nations Organisation. Once predominantly European and Latin American, UNO is now numerically dominated by the new nations created from colonial empires. The votes of, for example, Lesotho and Botswana, of Surinam and rich but small Singapore, are equal in value in the United Nations assembly to the votes of the USSR, Britain, France or any other power. The financial contributions which the new states make to the organisation are small but their voices are often loud in its debates.

International comparisons, 1977

	Population (millions)	Higher education[1] (thousands of students)	Passenger vehicles (millions)	TV sets or licences (millions)	Electricity produced (millions of kilowatt-hours)
Brazil	113	955	6.0	11.0	88.0
China	866[2]	1,000	0.05	0.35	125.0
Indonesia	138	278	0.4	0.3	4.0
Japan	114	2,094	19.0	26.0	512.0
Nigeria	79	33	0.15	0.45	3.4
Poland	35	306	1.3	7.0	109.0
Saudi Arabia	10	26	0.23	0.12	2.25
UK	56	678	14.0	18.0	283.0
USA	217	11,300	109.0	121.0	2,185.0
USSR	259	4,950	6.0	57.0	1,150.0
Zaïre	26	21	0.85	0.007	3.5

[1] Higher education is differently defined in different countries
[2] Probably an underestimate

Postscript

It is perhaps decolonisation which most clearly marks the ending of 'the European century'. When in 1981 Belize (British Honduras) became independent the process was virtually ended. In Africa, Asia, in Latin America and in islands scattered the oceans over the foreign flags had been hauled down (see maps pp. 297, 318). A few territories for one reason or another remained under foreign rule.

The British 'empire' was left with a few islands and territories – ranging from the British Antarctic Territory (with no population at all), St Helena (population 5,000) to Hong Kong (population over five million). Hong Kong with its large population was exceptional. It was exceptional in other ways too. It had become a financial and industrial centre of world stature, whose Chinese inhabitants, whilst in principle devoted to China and her culture, preferred to live in the capitalist world. Whether the People's Republic of China would remain content with that was uncertain. Spain and Argentina were far from content to allow Gibraltar (population 28,000) and the Falkland (Malvinas) Islands (population 1,800) to remain British, though their people showed a strong preference for the British connection. Portugal was left with Macao. France remained in New Caledonia and Tahiti. The Netherlands held Curaçao. With exceptions such as these the flags planted by the countries of western Europe were all hauled down.

But the flag of the Soviet Union still flies over vast non-Russian territories; the Uzbeks, the Tadjiks, the Buryat Mongols and many others who are subjects of the USSR are no more Russian than the Solomon Islanders or the Ashanti are British. Why is the USSR 'the only real empire left on earth'? Did the *Buenos Aires Herald* (9 August 1981) provide an answer? '[The Russian colonial empire] has survived because it is a land empire, held together by armies, whereas all the others were seaborne empires based mainly on trade and bluff.'

34 The Middle East

The inter-war years

In Syria, a French mandate, a rebellion (1925–27) of the Druze (a fanatical Muslim minority found in both Syria and Lebanon) resulted in the French having twice to abandon Damascus. Trouble smouldered on until in 1936 France agreed that Syria should be independent within three years. However, the Second World War intervened.

The British mandate in Palestine was troubled by conflict between Arabs and Jews, to whom near contradictory promises had been made by the McMahon Pledge (see p. 101) and the Balfour Declaration (see p. 108). Large British forces were required to garrison the country.

In 1921 the Emir Feisal, a son of Hussein of Mecca (of the Hashemite family, descendants of the Prophet Muhammad), became king of Iraq. In 1932 Britain gave up her mandate but retained the right to keep airfields and maintain forces in Iraq, already important on account of its oil.

Another son of Hussein was emir of Transjordan, also a British mandate (originally part of the Palestine mandate). Relations between Transjordan and its independent neighbour, Saudi Arabia, improved when in 1927 Transjordan was given the port of Aqaba which gave her access to the Red Sea. Transjordan was virtually independent from 1928.

Egypt had since 1914 been a British protectorate. In 1922 it became nominally independent under King Fuad. Britain, however, controlled its defence and garrisoned the Suez Canal. An ultra-nationalist party, the Wafd, continued to oppose all ties with Britain. In 1936 Britain agreed to a gradual withdrawal of her forces, though she continued to garrison the canal and in the event of war was to have the use of Egyptian airfields. In 1936 Fuad was succeeded by Farouk.

Cyprus

Disraeli's intention in acquiring Cyprus for Britain (see p. 12) was to provide a base for the protection of the Suez Canal. But after Britain got control of Egypt itself Cyprus was neglected. In 1960 Cyprus became independent under the leadership of the Greek Archbishop Makarios. The longstanding hostility between the Christian Greek Cypriots and the minority Muslim Turkish Cypriots then led to renewed conflict. This was checked for a time by the presence of a UN peacekeeping force. In 1974 a coup aimed at uniting Cyprus with Greece resulted in a Turkish invasion of the island. In Turkish areas (almost half the island) what amounted to an independent government was set up. The resulting dispute between Greece and Turkey led to the temporary withdrawal of Greece from NATO, of which Turkey was also a member. The dispute was later patched up but the island remained divided. Meanwhile, having lost control of Egypt (see p. 331), Britain took a renewed interest in Cyprus as a military base.

The Arab League

With the ending of the Second World War Syria, Lebanon and Transjordan became fully independent.

In 1945 Egypt, Syria, Lebanon, Iraq, Transjordan, Saudi Arabia and the Yemen formed the Arab League.

The Middle East, 1980

They were later joined by Libya and fourteen other Arab states. The real unifying factors in the Arab League have been hostility to the Jews and opposition to anything its members regard as colonialism. For although the Arab states are linked by Islam and the use of the Arabic language they have been torn by disputes – between conservatives and radicals, between republicans and monarchists, between ruling classes and minorities and between the followers of different Islamic sects. These divisions have diminished the new power that came to the Arab states with the discovery of immensely rich new oilfields (in particular in Saudi Arabia).

The West's dependence on its oil, the commercial and strategic importance of the Suez Canal, the competitive sale of arms by the outside world and the rivalries of the Cold War have complicated affairs in the Middle East.

Israel and her neighbours

The division of Palestine

During the 1930s the Jewish population of Palestine more than doubled as a result of immigration. The continued influx of Jews, which increased as Nazi persecution intensified, was opposed by the Palestinian Arabs. Both Arabs and Jews were opposed to the continuance of the British mandate. An Arab uprising against the British which began in 1936 continued for some three years. The Stern Gang and other Jewish nationalist organisations stepped up their terrorist activities in Palestine when the British, from 1939, tried to limit the entry of Jews.

Faced with the problem of a mandate inhabited by two peoples between whom there were apparently irreconcilable differences, Britain in 1947 referred the matter of Palestine to the United Nations. In November 1947 the UN assembly voted for the partition of Palestine into a Jewish and an Arab state. Both the USA and the USSR welcomed this 'solution' to the problem. The Jews, recognising that they would have a viable state which could continue to take in Jewish immigrants, if not favouring partition, accepted it. The Palestinian Arabs were determined that there should be one state, a Palestinian Arab state that would accept as citizens Jews already in Palestine. For them the creation of a Jewish state was totally unacceptable. In 1974 Yasser Arafat, chairman of the Palestine Liberation Organisation (see p. 335), said in an address to the UN assembly:

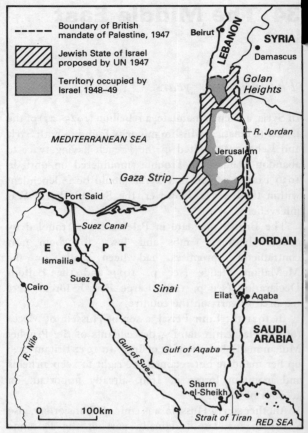

Israel and her neighbours, 1949

'The General Assembly partitioned what it had no right to divide – an indivisible homeland. When we rejected that decision, our position corresponded to that of the natural mother who refused to permit King Solomon to cut her son in two when the unnatural mother claimed the child for herself and agreed to his dismemberment.'

In May 1948 Britain withdrew from Palestine. The Jewish state of Israel was proclaimed forthwith. Chaim Weizmann, who in 1917 had persuaded Balfour to promise the Jews a home in Palestine, became president and David Ben Gurion prime minister. Arabs living within Israel were given political and other rights. In 1949 Israel was admitted to UNO.

Beleaguered Israel

From the outset the ring of Arab states surrounding Israel was bent on destroying her. The day after the establishment of Israel was proclaimed Egypt,

Transjordan, Syria, Lebanon and Iraq attacked her. In a war fought intermittently from May 1948 to July 1949 the beleaguered Israelis routed their Arab attackers and increased their territory. In September 1948 Count Bernadotte, a UN mediator who had negotiated a cease-fire, was murdered by the Stern Gang. He was succeeded by a Negro, Ralph Bunche, who by July 1949 had effected a series of armistices between Israel and her neighbours.

After the 1948–49 war Palestinian territory allotted to the Arabs west of the Jordan, the West Bank, became part of Transjordan. Transjordan became the Hashemite kingdom of Jordan. In 1952 Hussein, great grandson of the Hussein to whom the McMahon Pledge had been made in 1915, succeeded to the throne of Jordan while a cadet at Sandhurst. On Jordanian maps Israel appeared as Occupied Palestine. The Gaza Strip, also allotted by the UN to the Arabs, was administered after 1949 by Egypt. Jerusalem, holy to both Muslims and Jews, was to have been an international city. But the 1948–49 war left it divided, with the old eastern part under Jordanian rule and the newer western sector part of Israel. Places sacred to the Jews thus came under Arab rule.

There was little peace after the 1949 armistices. Desperately poor Palestinian refugees in Jordan and the Gaza Strip were a reservoir of hate; by the late 1950s they numbered more than a million. From Gaza and Egyptian territory east of Suez Arab guerillas made attacks on Israel, who in an all-out effort to secure her frontiers conscripted women for military service. Meanwhile the western powers tried to limit the sale of arms to both sides.

The Suez crisis, 1956

In 1952 a military coup led by the Free Officers overthrew King Farouk – whose chief interest was in belly dancers – and a strongly nationalist government was set up in Egypt. Among the Free Officers were Gamal Abdel Nasser and Anwar Sadat. In 1954 Colonel Nasser became prime minister and in June 1956 he was elected president. Britain in 1954 agreed to withdraw her forces from the canal zone and in June 1956 did so. She also withdrew from the Sudan which she had governed in partnership with Egypt since 1898.

Nasser's aim was to unite the Arab states under the leadership of Egypt in a holy war against Israel. When Iraq joined the 'neo-colonialist' Baghdad pact (see p. 247) Arab unity seemed to be threatened. The pact

seemed also to threaten the USSR's southern frontier. In these circumstances Egypt and the USSR began to establish ties with each other.

Arab raids into Israel and Israeli reprisals became more frequent. Egypt, who commanded the Strait of Tiran, was able to seal off the Israeli port, Eilat, at the head of the gulf of Aqaba. Meanwhile Israeli-bound vessels had been excluded from the Suez Canal, an international waterway. Though the USSR seems not to have intended to aggravate the situation the western powers were suspicious, especially as Czechoslovakia in September 1955 promised to supply Egypt with arms. Egypt also recognised the People's Republic of China and announced that the latter too would sell arms to her. Nasser said:

'I told the British and US ambassadors [in June 1955] that if their countries did not supply me with arms, I would have to obtain them from the USSR. I stated that it was not possible for me to remain silent while Israel imported weapons for her army from several sources and imposed a constant threat on us.'

Nasser undertook various social reforms. One of his projects was the extension of the Aswan dam, built in 1902 under the British administration. The USSR, the USA and Britain had offered financial help. But in July 1956 the USA and Britain, disturbed by Nasser's pro-Soviet policies, refused to grant loans. On 26 July Nasser announced that he would obtain the money for the dam by nationalising the Suez Canal Company. This was a British-French-Egyptian company whose rights were not due to expire until 1968. To Nasser the company was a relic of imperialism. However, he promised to compensate Britain and France.

For a time there was an outcry against Egypt. The outcry died down, but Britain and France were determined to stand up to Nasser. Britain no longer had an Indian empire but the canal was an important link with the Far East and with the oilfields of the Middle East. The French greatly resented the help given by Egypt to the Algerian nationalists (see p. 321). The USA tried to settle the dispute but by October 1956 French and British troops were assembled for action.

Meanwhile the guerilla attacks on Israel from Egyptian territory continued. On 29 October 1956 Israel invaded the Sinai peninsula. To what extent Britain and France had bound themselves to support an Israeli attack is not clear; what is clear is that the Israeli attack provided a welcome opportunity for them to send in troops to 'restore order' – and enforce their rights.

The Six Day War: advancing Israeli troops pass a truck carrying Egyptian prisoners of war

The Egyptians, though their army was much larger than the Israeli army, were sharply defeated. The Israelis occupied the Gaza Strip. They also captured Sharm el-Sheikh controlling the entrance to the Strait of Tiran. On 30 October Britain and France sent an ultimatum to both Egypt and Israel, ordering them to withdraw their forces to a line 16 kilometres from the canal; the French and British would then temporarily occupy ports along the canal to restore order. Israel, whose troops had not then reached the canal zone, accepted the ultimatum. Egypt rejected it. Within hours French and British forces bombed Egyptian air bases. Anglo-French forces also captured Port Said, at the northern end of the canal.

But France and Britain found themselves isolated in a hostile world. Their attack on Egypt was condemned on both sides of the iron curtain. The Americans expressed hostility. The Russians, whose tanks were at that very time smashing their way into Budapest (see p. 293), threatened to attack London and Paris with rockets. And in Britain and France many people were angered by the action of their governments.

Early in November an emergency meeting of the UN assembly, by an almost unanimous vote, demanded a cease-fire. Britain, France and later Israel withdrew their troops from Egyptian territory. A UN emergency force drawn from countries as far away as Iceland then occupied the Gaza Strip to protect Israel from raids. UN forces were also posted to Sharm el-Sheikh to protect shipping in the Strait of Tiran. In contrast to Aqaba, Jordan's port a few kilometres away, Israeli Eilat developed rapidly. Ships which the Egyptians had sunk to block the Suez Canal were raised. For another ten years the canal operated efficiently as a world waterway. It remained closed to Israeli shipping.

In the summer of 1958 the right-wing, pro-west government of Iraq, which three years before had joined the Baghdad pact, was overthrown in a coup. Meanwhile Syria was receiving considerable military aid from the USSR. Concerned for their own security, President Chamoun of Lebanon and King Hussein of Jordan asked the USA and Britain for support. American marines landed in Lebanon and British paratroopers arrived in Jordan. Though invited to intervene, the

Americans and British were also doubtless protecting their oil interests in Saudi Arabia and the Persian Gulf. After a few weeks they obeyed a UN order to withdraw their forces.

In 1958 Egypt and Syria united to form the United Arab Republic. This 'union' amounted to little and in 1961 Syria, fearful of Egyptian dominance, withdrew.

The Six Day War, 1967

In 1967 tension between Israel and the Arab states rose to fever pitch. Egypt, liberally supplied with arms by the Russians, in May demanded withdrawal of the UN forces that had been keeping the peace since the Suez crisis. U Thant, secretary general of UNO, agreed to this. Egypt then blocked the Strait of Tiran and massed troops in Sinai. Syria was shelling Israeli territory from the Golan Heights.

On 5 June 1967 Israel, convinced that Egypt was about to attack her, launched a massive attack on Egypt. In the Six Day War (5–10 June) that followed the entire Egyptian air force was destroyed. The Egyptian army was forced back with enormous losses of men and material to the west bank of the Suez Canal, leaving Israel in occupation of all Sinai. When Jordan began shelling the Israeli sector of Jerusalem the Israelis captured and occupied the old sector of the city and Jordan's West Bank, with its Palestinian Arab population. The Syrians were driven from the Golan Heights which were then occupied by Israel. (In 1981 Israel formally annexed the Golan Heights.) Fears that the conflict might spread were so acute that the hot line between Washington and Moscow was used for the first time. The swift Israeli victories were followed by a UN truce, though from time to time fighting flared up along the canal. With Israeli occupation of the West Bank, the number of Palestinian refugees across the river in Jordan increased significantly. The seizure of old Jerusalem aroused fresh bitternesss and was condemned by UNO.

During the Six Day War Egypt closed the canal by sinking block ships. Vessels which happened to be in the canal at the time were trapped and there they remained for eight years. Ships trading between Europe and Australia, the Persian Gulf, India and the Far East proceeded on the long haul round the Cape of Good Hope without undue delay or inconvenience. The Suez Canal, whose defence had for years seemed so important for Britain, proved less vital in the days of fast ships and huge tankers.

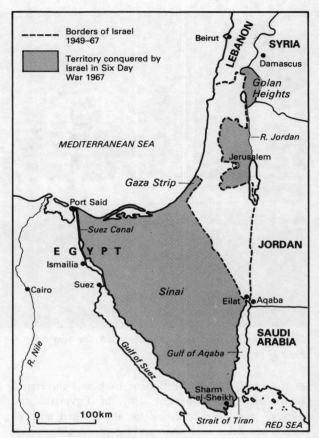

Israel after the Six Day War

The Yom Kippur War, 1973

In 1970, on the death of Nasser, Sadat, who proved to have considerable talent and courage, became president of Egypt. Soviet pressure in the Middle East had been increasing but in 1972 Sadat sent away some 17,000 Russian advisers brought in by Nasser, whilst continuing to get plentiful – and sophisticated – arms on his own terms.

In 1973, on Yom Kippur (6 October), the solemn Jewish Day of Atonement, Egypt and Syria made a sudden attack on Israel, Egypt from across the canal and Syria against the Golan Heights. The combined strength of the Arab armies was about one million men with over 5,000 tanks and more than 1,000 planes – about three times Arab strength in the Six Day War. The super-powers, caught like the Israelis by surprise, lifted supplies to their protégés by air. At first it seemed that the Israelis might be overwhelmed. However, they made an astonishing recovery, crossed to the west bank

Battle-scarred Suez, in September 1976, the year after the canal was re-opened. The ships in the background are in a bend of the canal

of the canal, forced the Syrians back and threatened both Cairo and Damascus. But the Egyptians and Syrians won much prestige for their initial success. Israeli casualties were heavy and Egypt was able to hold on to areas she had recaptured in Sinai. Moshe Dayan, Israel's dynamic one-eyed minister of defence, and a great hero to his people after the Six Day War, was blamed for being caught napping by the Egyptians.

So alarmed was the USA that on 24–25 October she ordered a worldwide nuclear alert. The oil-producing states of the Arab League, who in 1968 had formed the Organisation of Arab Petroleum Exporting Countries (OAPEC), took decisive action – they announced a 70 per cent increase in the price of oil and threatened an embargo against states offering aid to Israel. On 25 October the Israelis were obliged to accept a cease-fire under UN supervision.

Sadat had publicly stated that his aim in going to war was to bring peace to the Middle East by forcing Israel back to her pre-1967 borders and by winning recognition for Palestinian rights. In June 1974 the US secretary of state, Kissinger, brought about a disengagement of the opposing forces. In September 1975 Israel withdrew from part of Sinai whilst Egypt allowed Israeli-bound vessels through the Suez Canal, which was re-opened that year. Ironically, many ships were by

then too large to use it but it was later further widened and deepened.

The fact that the oil-producing countries could hold the world to ransom by raising prices or withholding supplies of oil was the great discovery of the Arabs at the time of the Yom Kippur War. Later, rapid price increases seriously affected the economies of countries rich and poor throughout the world. Fear of the oil weapon influenced international relations but the Organisation of Petroleum Exporting Countries (OPEC), formed in 1960, and indeed OAPEC, came to realise the need for caution in using this weapon. For example Saudi Arabia had to restrain Colonel Gadafi of Libya. For the western world reacted against price increases by reducing consumption, discovering new oilfields and developing alternative sources of energy.

Towards a Middle East détente?

After the Yom Kippur War Egypt turned increasingly to the USA for assistance in securing peace in the Middle East. Indeed the United States acted virtually as an agent between Egypt and Israel.

In 1977 Menachem Begin, once a member of a Jewish terrorist organisation, became prime minister of Israel.

Despite Begin's intransigence Sadat made headway. In November 1977 he visited Jerusalem, a 'trip of shame' according to his Arab neighbours. In a speech to the Knesset (Israeli parliament) Sadat defined the terms on which peace could be secured. Broadly these were those he had outlined during the Yom Kippur War. Shortly afterwards Begin visited Egypt.

In September 1978, at the invitation of President Carter, Sadat and Begin met in the USA, at Camp David, the president's holiday resort. Then, at the White House, they signed a 'framework for the conclusion of a peace between Egypt and Israel'. In March 1979 the peace treaty was signed and Egypt and Israel for the first time in over thirty years were not in a state of war. Israel was to withdraw her armed forces and civilians in three stages from Sinai, to the boundary that had existed between Egypt and mandated Palestine. Egypt bound herself to the continued passage of ships going to and from Israel through the Suez Canal and declared the Strait of Tiran and the gulf of Aqaba to be international waterways. By 1981 two stages of the withdrawal from Sinai had been completed. The remaining stage was to be completed in 1982.

In October 1981 Sadat was assassinated by Egyptian soldiers in Cairo. What effect this would have upon affairs in the Middle East remained to be seen. But his conciliatory attitude towards Israel had brought enmity from other Arab states, as did his giving asylum to the dying ex-shah of Iran (see below). While many world leaders were attending Sadat's funeral in Cairo, in Libya and Syria there was wild rejoicing at the death of a traitor to the Arab cause. In Egypt itself there was resentment over Sadat's attempted suppression of Muslim extremists and his unsuccessful economic policies. Meanwhile the problem of the Palestinians remained.

The Palestine Liberation Organisation

In 1964 the Palestinian refugees, thousands of whom had been settled in camps in Jordan, formed the Palestine Liberation Organisation (PLO). The PLO had as its aim the restoration of Palestine to the Palestinian Arabs. In 1974 the PLO was recognised at a summit meeting of Arab leaders as the legitimate representative of the Palestinians. A month later the United Nations recognised the right of the Palestinians to self-determination and national independence – how this was to be achieved was another matter.

Sadat and Begin after their Christmas day meeting (1977) at Ismailia on the canal. Hopes of peace were high then but in 1983 a question mark still hung over the Middle East

In September 1978, following their Camp David meetings, Sadat and Begin signed in Washington a 'framework for peace in the Middle East'. This second agreement seemed to envisage Israeli withdrawal from the West Bank and from the Gaza Strip and the eventual setting up in those areas of an autonomous Palestinian government. By the end of 1982 Israel had shown little inclination to grant autonomy to the Palestinians; indeed she had allowed Israelis to infiltrate into the West Bank and the Gaza Strip and to establish new settlements there.

Meanwhile Palestinian Arabs had been responsible for numerous acts of terrorism. At Munich in 1972 they murdered members of the Israeli Olympics team. They specialised in the hijacking of aircraft. In 1976, in a remarkably efficient exercise carried out with Egyptian connivance, Israel sent in airborne commandos to rescue a hijacked plane stranded on Entebbe airport in Uganda. And the PLO have complicated affairs in Lebanon, their main scene of operations since Hussein expelled them from Jordan (1970–71), by taking advantage of a civil war that broke out in 1975 between Muslims and

Revolution in reverse? Tehran, April 1982. What will be the fate of these children, not all of them in traditional Muslim dress, who accompanied their mothers to a demonstration in support of the Ayatollah Khomeini? The Ayatollah, upholder of the old Islamic order, was then supreme, but he was nearly 82. Two children hold their pictures of the Ayatollah upside down

Christians. From Lebanon the PLO continued to raid Israel, who retaliated by land, sea and air.

Resurgent Islam

The wealth that came with the discovery of oil in the Middle East brought changes so sudden that they presented problems in themselves – and sometimes provoked those who feared for the purity of Islamic ways to cling more tightly to old practices. In Saudi Arabia, where life had gone on unchanged for centuries, the rate of change was frenzied. Yet Islamic practices were rigidly adhered to and punishments prescribed in the Koran carried out – for example the cutting off of a hand.

The resurgence of Islam, in part due to the new power that has come to the 'Muslim oil world' – not only to the Middle East, but also to North Africa, Indonesia, Borneo, Nigeria – has sometimes taken a dangerous form. In Iran in 1979 a revolt – directed more against the modernising zeal of the shah than against his oppressive rule – occurred. The Muslims of Iran are predominantly Shi'ites, for whom the imams (priests) possess superhuman knowledge and power. Under the leadership of the Iranian imams pandemonium mounted. The shah was forced into exile. The Ayatollah Khomeini, a religious leader of extremist views, then returned from exile, whereupon Iran was plunged into 'a revolution in reverse'. Fanatical religious leaders became all powerful. While moderate leaders were being hounded out of the country and opposition was being silenced by firing squads, student followers of the Ayatollah Khomeini clamoured for the return of women to the veil. 'Freedom', whether from shah or tsar, may only bring subjection to a new authority.

Europe and the modern world

In 1983 there were strong protests against nuclear arms in the USA and western Europe – and more guardedly even in eastern Europe. At Madrid, after years of negotiation, the Helsinki agreement on human rights was extended. In November 1983, after the Americans began deploying Cruise and Pershing missiles in western Europe, the USSR withdrew from the nuclear arms reduction talks at Geneva. The Cold War was not over. In the USA Reagan followed a hardline policy against the Soviets – a policy understandable in view of, for example, the continued Soviet presence in Afghanistan. Meanwhile the USA was bolstering right-wing régimes in Honduras and El Salvador. In the USSR Brezhnev had been succeeded by the head of the KGB, Andropov. Though martial law ended in Poland, communist authoritarianism remained in control there – as elsewhere east of the curtain. All the Mediterranean states of Europe – France, Italy, Portugal, Spain and Greece – in 1983 had socialist governments. In West Germany the conservative Christian Democrats had replaced the Social Democrats. In Britain, in June 1983, despite three million unemployed but with Labour divided and inflation under 5 per cent, Thatcher was returned to power with an increased majority – though with fewer total votes than in 1979. The Alliance of Liberals and Social Democrats polled over eight million votes but won only a handful of seats. Labour, left licking its wounds, remained committed to unilateral nuclear disarmament – though it was Labour that had set Britain on the way to becoming a nuclear power. After spring-cleaning her cabinet Thatcher proceeded on a course of rather cautious privatisation of industry and union reform. In August 1983 yet another member of the Commonwealth – St Kitts and Nevis – was peacefully launched on the doubtful sea of independence, after over three centuries of British rule. But Thatcher faced grave problems – not only in the economy. Northern Ireland was much troubled. Remaining fragments of empire were cause for concern. The Falklands, by then Fortress Falklands, seemed likely to be a continuing problem. Following Thatcher's visit to Peking in 1982 negotiations over the future of Hong Kong proved difficult. China was in general following pragmatic policies – but would her attitude to Hong Kong prove pragmatic? Various factors favoured such an approach. But the people of Hong Kong, attached to their free society and relatively high standard of living, showed alarm. In foreign affairs, whilst urging the need for nuclear arms control, the Conservatives remained committed to NATO, the special American connection and Britain's independent nuclear deterrent. In Asia and Africa in 1983 ancient hatreds and quarrels of more recent origin continued to cause conflict. Past massacres provoked Armenians to murder Turks. The Vietnam War still took its toll as an assortment of refugees sought to overthrow the Vietnamese-maintained régime in Kampuchea. Africa's poorest state, Chad, Muslim in the north, Christian in the south, entered a third decade of conflict. Libya's Colonel Gadafi, seeking to pull chestnuts from the fire, supported the rebel north; the French, the former rulers, came to the rescue of the government in the south. In southern Africa the Republic of South Africa was still unwilling to give full independence to Namibia, whilst Angola harboured SWAPO guerillas within her borders. In Angola itself Cubans were helping government forces fend off UNITA rebels. In the Middle East Begin retired and Arafat, longtime leader of the PLO, perhaps at last inclined to seek a compromise, lost support. Little else changed. Israel remained entrenched on the West Bank of the Jordan. After fiercely fought battles in Beirut, Israeli forces had driven the forces of the PLO from the Lebanon. The Muslim Druze, with Syrian support, were then free to resume their quarrel with the majority Christians of the Lebanon. And before long the PLO were back in the mountains and on the coast of Lebanon. The USSR supplied arms to Syria. US warships bombarded the Druze positions. A UN force (American, British, French and Italian) seemed powerless to keep the peace in Lebanon. From 1980 two powerful Muslim states, Iran and Iraq, were at war; by mid-1983 a quarter of a million people had been killed.

In Europe itself, east and west of the curtain, the traveller in 1983 saw little to remind him of the bloody conflicts of the past hundred years. Journeying 'in the print of olden wars', in the vineyards of Alsace, in Flanders fields, crossing the Ardennes, on the road to Berlin, on the plains of Poland and Hungary, in Leningrad of the thousand day siege, 'all the land was green'. Would all the land remain green, the swords all sheathed? One thing seemed certain: for good or ill, the fortunes of Europe would be linked with the fortunes of the world beyond in ways and to an extent inconceivable in 1870.

Index